S0-BFF-111

$11.50

The American Film Institute

GUIDE TO COLLEGE COURSES IN FILM AND TELEVISION

Seventh Edition

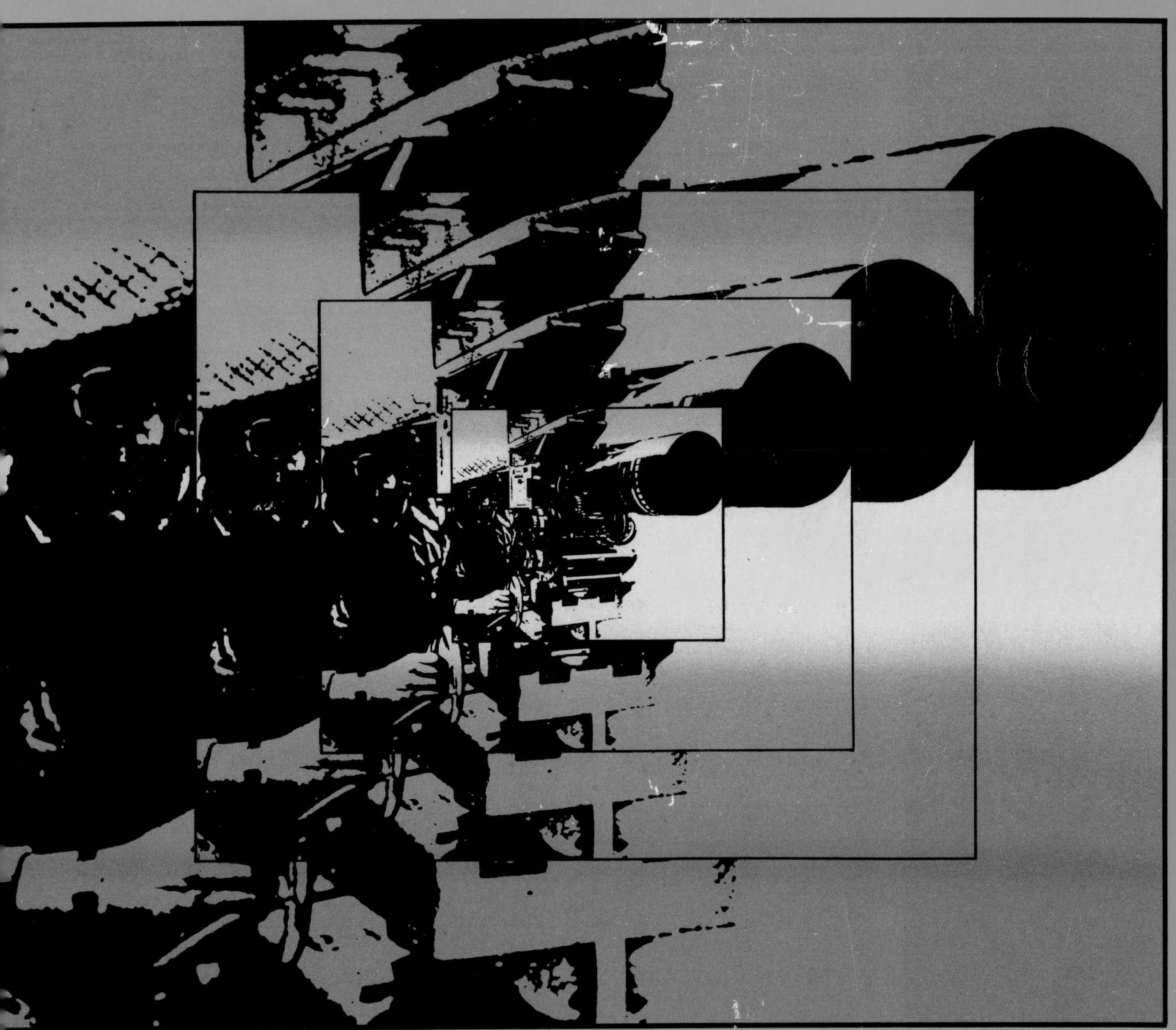

The official AFI listing of graduate and undergraduate courses

Peterson's Guides Princeton, New Jersey

EXPLORE THE BEST IN FILM AND TELEVISION

This is your invitation to participate in a unique, non-profit organization dedicated to the advancement of the film and video arts worldwide.

As a member, you'll benefit from a host of opportunities to learn about the art form and to understand how excellence comes to the screen. In particular, ten issues of the Institute's acclaimed magazine on film and television will bring you the insight of the most distinguished filmmakers, critics and authors.

American Film magazine is a marvelous exploration of cinematic creativity. Each issue discusses new film and television productions in progress, interviews major film and television artists, reports on the cultural impact of the screen arts, re-examines classic films and their creators and comments on the emerging home video scene.

But *American Film* is only one way AFI acts on your behalf to stimulate the kind of films that enrich the quality of our lives. Your membership helps support other worthwhile Institute activities, among them programs that preserve and exhibit classic films for study and appreciation; and that encourage new talent through grants and the AFI Center for Advanced Film Studies.

For an annual fee of just $16, you can join over 100,000 AFI members who share a special commitment to the art of the moving image. Use the attached order form to join today!

MEMBERSHIP BENEFITS

- ⋆ Access to information and research facilities
- ⋆ Ten issues annually of *American Film*
- ⋆ Discounts on worthwhile film books and merchandise
- ⋆ Film travel opportunities
- ⋆ Film courses, lectures, special events
- ⋆ Discount admissions to current and classic films
- ⋆ Your personal membership card signed by AFI Chairman Charlton Heston on behalf of the Board of Trustees

JOIN THE AMERICAN FILM INSTITUTE

Enjoy this fine magazine and many other benefits of membership!

The American Film Institute
GUIDE TO COLLEGE COURSES IN FILM AND TELEVISION

The American Film Institute
GUIDE TO COLLEGE COURSES IN FILM AND TELEVISION

Seventh Edition

Charles Granade Jr
editor

Margaret G Butt
associate editor

Peter J Bukalski, American Film Institute
consulting editor

Peterson's Guides
Princeton, New Jersey

The American Film Institute
The John F Kennedy Center for the Performing Arts
Washington, DC 20566
202-828-4000

Jean Firstenberg, Director
Robert F Blumofe, Director, AFI West

The American Film Institute Center for Advanced Film Studies
501 Doheny Road
Beverly Hills, CA 90210

Printed in the United States of America

Library of Congress Catalog Card Number 80-81121

ISBN 0-87866-158-1

Design, survey development, and data collection by Peterson's Guides, Inc.

Published by Peterson's Guides, Inc.
PO Box 2123, Princeton, NJ 08540

CONTENTS

THE AMERICAN FILM INSTITUTE

The American Film Institute, established in 1967 by the National Endowment for the Arts, is an independent, nonprofit, national organization dedicated to increasing the recognition and understanding of the moving image as an art form; to assuring the preservation of the art form; and to identifying, encouraging, and developing talent.

To these ends, the Institute serves as an advocate for, and a bridge between, individuals and organizations involved with the film and television and video arts. Within specific programs, as well, the AFI preserves films, operates an advanced conservatory for filmmakers, encourages new American filmmakers through grants and internships, provides information and guidance for students and educators, publishes *American Film: Magazine of the Film and Television Arts,* operates a repertory cinema in the Kennedy Center in Washington, D.C., and coordinates touring programs of film and video to exhibition sites around the country.

The American Film Institute Guide to College Courses in Film and Television is a project of the Education Services program of AFI. This program assists students and educators through the publication of informational materials; ongoing liaison with associations, schools, and colleges; and workshops for film and television educators.

YOU CAN BECOME A MEMBER OF THE AMERICAN FILM INSTITUTE

AFI members enjoy a number of fine benefits while helping to support the many significant programs and activities of the Institute.

A $16 one-year membership includes:

- 10 issues of *American Film* magazine—thoughtful coverage of the entire film, television, and home video scene
- Access to AFI information collections and research facilities
- Special discounts on AFI publications, merchandise, and significant film/TV books
- Discount admissions to the hundreds of films screened annually in Washington, D.C., Los Angeles, and other sites across the country

To become a member of AFI, write to: The American Film Institute, Membership Service Department, P.O. Box 966, Farmingdale, N.Y. 11737. Enclose $16, or ask to be billed after examining an issue of *American Film.*

ARE FILMS MORE IMPORTANT THAN LIFE?

by James Monaco

This is the seventh edition of *The American Film Institute Guide to College Courses in Film and Television.* The first appeared twelve years ago, and during that relatively short span of time this book has become an institution as it has documented in graphic form the veritable explosion that has taken place in academic film study.

Not so very long ago, courses in film and television available in the United States could be listed comfortably on a nice little mimeographed sheet. Now, you are confronted with a weighty directory. As late as 1965 film and television studies were limited, essentially, to a handful of programs, mainly at schools in Los Angeles and New York, and these film departments themselves were basically oriented toward the profession. They provided technical training and—perhaps—entrée into the tightly controlled industry.

Now, film courses can be found at almost every institution of higher learning in the country and at many secondary schools as well. And the programs aren't limited to technical expertise. On the contrary, many courses avoid practical filmmaking entirely to concentrate on what is known as film "appreciation," or criticism.

That's remarkable, and more than a little unnerving. How did it happen, and why? After all, the film industry itself has grown at a very moderate rate during this same period.

I think there are two basic factors that have been responsible for this extraordinary academic phenomenon, one of them practical, the other theoretical.

Let's examine the practice of film study first. During the late sixties, course requirements at schools across the country came tumbling down as students demonstrated against often archaic requirements. For better or worse (I think the latter), foreign language departments and history and humanities departments began to shrink as they were deprived of the steady flow of students that had existed under the strict course requirement system. The academic marketplace became subject to a sort of eighteenth-century system of laissez-faire, and film study immediately presented itself as a potential drawing card. Film courses sprang up in all sorts of unlikely departments as the academic establishment fought to maintain its turf.

This sounds like an inauspicious debut for film and TV courses, and often it was. After all, if you took a film course before the late seventies, it is highly unlikely that your instructor had ever taken a film course himself! There simply were none when he was in school. Yet that very lack of organization was often beneficial. There is something enormously attractive about an academic discipline that didn't have its first Ph.D. until the 1970s. The pioneers who taught film in the early seventies may not have had the depth of factual knowledge that the average well-trained film academic has now, but they had broad backgrounds that often were more valuable to their students.

Theoretically, at the same time that French and English and philosophy departments were attempting to hold their own in the competition for students by instituting film programs, academics in general, learning from their militant students, were coming around to an understanding of just how important film study could be to the sum total of a liberal education.

The audiovisual media—film and tape in all their forms—so thoroughly dominate our lives and inform them that not to spend some time during the course of a college education investigating how they do what they do, their history, and their technique borders on the irresponsible. We learn about literature, writing, and print in order to open up new possibilities; we must learn about film and tape in order to understand the pervasive cultural forces that have shaped us.

And, curiously, seen in this light, the study of film and television (we do need a new work to encompass the wide range of both) seems theoretically to belong in many academic departments—not just one. The situation that developed haphazardly in the seventies because of campus departmental politics, it turns out, is not illogical. Film and television should never be limited to "appreciation" courses—but then neither should English classes be limited to novels, poems, and plays.

Moreover, it seems to me important not to try to separate film from television. They are part of the same continuum. In fact, as the eighties continue we are likely to begin to regard film as simply a special case of television. One of the reasons film study did not become established on American campuses until recently may just be that television did not control our lives until twenty years ago. Theatrical movies before TV were, no doubt, a cultural force of enormous power, yet it took the box in the living room to realize the full force of this phenomenon. Eventually, academia understood this.

As an industry and a social force, theatrical film—the prestige product of the industry—is certainly an offshoot of TV. If theaters ceased to exist, we'd still see the same movies, just a few months later. The advent of videotape and videodisc will make this clear if it isn't already.

The conclusion to be drawn from all this is that film-and-television study has become a necessary and significant part of the academic curriculum.

Yet those of you who are about to make use of this book have a wide variety of aims. Many of you are looking at film and television as a future profession. Some think of it first as an art. Others may be interested in film and television *study* as a profession. But finally, everyone who gets a college degree these days in the United States should be familiar with the elements of film and the electronic media, for film is, like writing, a tool of language that we all experience and that we all should know how to use. In the eighties film is a fact of life, and it is not an exaggeration to state that any school that can't give its students a couple of courses in film and media ought not to be considered by anyone interested in a well-rounded liberal education.

But what about those of you who want to make film a profession? Paradoxically, you might be better off paying less attention to the information in this book and more attention to your own instincts about the suitability of a particular school. (Of course, this doesn't apply to graduate students who are—or should be—primarily interested in the practical value of courses offered and the prestige, and therefore clout, of the faculty.)

The one valuable trick that I learned in college—and that I would like to pass on to you—was *never* to choose a course because of its title, *always* to choose a course because of its instructor. We learn from people, not syllabi. The point I'm making is that often knowledge is not where we expect to find it. So that while this book can give you a good general idea of the programs that are offered, their extent, and the faculty who teach them, beware. Be sure to speak to people who know the faculty of a school. The fact is that the one valuable thing you can get from a college career that you can't get from books is to learn how to think. And you may just learn more that's useful to your future film career in an Italian class or in an economics class than in most courses ostensibly devoted to film.

This is practical advice as well as theoretical. Unless you are aiming for a narrowly defined profession (and even then, more than likely), it is going to be useful to generalize.

In the first place, let's face it, the film profession is not exactly underpopulated. Competition is tough. The wider your college experience, the better off you'll be in the job market—and you will certainly benefit more from a general education in the unfortunate case that your film career doesn't work out.

Secondly, filmmakers, like writers, who don't know anything else are thoroughly a waste of space. Film is a humanistic profession. You've got to have a passionate reason to make films—something you really want to say. And chances are you're going to find the reason for that passion somewhere else on campus—not necessarily at the cutting table, or behind the Arriflex.

Finally, with each passing year film becomes less separate from other areas of endeavor. The interconnections between and among film, television, publishing, records, and the other media are already too strong to be ignored. They will strengthen with each passing year. In order to be well prepared it's best to have a thorough grounding in a variety of specializations. Television courses already outnumber film courses in this book. By the time the tenth or eleventh edition rolls around, "media" departments should outnumber both.

Then, too, it's always possible that when you're twenty-five or thirty or even thirty-five you'll decide that there are more interesting things to do in the world than make movies. Don't lock yourself into the narrow path now. Keep your options open. Film is a tool; it shouldn't be thought of as anything more.

Remember what Alfred Hitchcock used to tell Ingrid Bergman. Write this down and hang it above your desk.

"Ingrid," he said, "it's only a movie."

François Truffaut put it this way: "Are films more important than life?" We shouldn't have any doubt how to answer that question.

TELEVISION EDUCATION, UNIVERSITIES, AND THE PUBLIC

by Horace M Newcomb

In 1977, writing in a *Wall Street Journal* television column, I suggested that anyone worried about the "effects" of television should support a massive program of public education in critical viewing skills. My analogy was to sex education, the only other area of "social problem" in which we had, as citizens, failed to respond in the traditional American manner of educating our children about potentially dangerous aspects of their experience. I also argued that public education in television viewing skills would do more than introduce children to the problematic aspects of the medium. It would, I said, carry back into the home a refined set of attitudes that might lead to a more critically aware audience at all levels. And an educated, critical audience, in my view, ultimately means better television. I am uneasy with pressures applied by "public interest" groups, and mass education is my favored, if old-fashioned, alternative.

By the summer of 1978 the United States Office of Education had prepared and distributed a Request for Proposals in the area of critical viewing skills. The RFP invited plans for curriculum development in the four practical areas: elementary, middle school, secondary, and postsecondary. By the fall of that year grants had been made to four groups, one for each target population. Each curriculum package was required to include not only in-class teaching materials but plans for teacher and parent education as well.

Those materials have now been developed and are in the first stage of distribution. Workshops are being conducted around the country, involving the curriculum developers, consultants, parents, teachers, administrators, and interested users of the materials. Additionally, during the distribution of information regarding the OE grants and their development, many other projects came to light. It seems that many people had moved, without knowledge of one another, in the same direction and had worked for some time on the development of critical skills applied to television. At least one national meeting has been held at which representatives from all these groups came together to share information and material, and to discuss problems of implementation, teacher training, curriculum modification, and public relations.

I cite all these developments here because the courses now being implemented in the public school systems will ultimately have a direct effect on the courses described in this guide to college and university offerings. Indeed, those of us who teach courses in the history, criticism, and analysis of television know already that our students bring to their classes an enormous amount of information and a degree of sophistication that might have been startling only a few years ago. While the sophistication is not always of the most articulate sort, one has the feeling that the students are often waiting only for an appropriate critical vocabulary, for a set of categories, some map or scheme to help them refine the knowledge they already possess.

Still, there is the nagging feeling, on our part sometimes, as well as on theirs, that they come with a heavy burden of social baggage. While it may be all right for them to study production, particularly in times when "skills" seem so necessary, the critical analysis of television is still somewhat suspect. It is as if one shouldn't take all this stuff too seriously. TV, after all, is not quite respectable.

The public school curriculum has the potential to correct this attitude, or to reinforce it. To the degree that the curricula are designed, or presented, or even perceived in the home, as inoculations against the disease of television, they will do us little good. To the degree that they are truly critical in nature, they can aid in changing our society's approach to its most public medium. To their credit, the materials I have examined are more critical than reactionary in tone. The nature of their presentation and acceptance remains to be seen.

And this presents us with another way in which these courses will affect our own. With their implementation, some more systematic approach to television will be abroad in the land, as is now the case with literature and film. Teachers in these other areas of university education now often feel that their duty is a grim one. Before they can "really teach" their subjects they often set out to "unteach" what has been offered to their students in the public schools. They have little respect for what is there and less interest in how it came to be there.

This brings us to the real center of our subject. For I am not merely concerned with the influence on our courses that flows *up* from a new approach to television. Indeed, I am more concerned with the effects *our* courses will have on the plans to teach television at all levels. I am concerned with the effects we might have on the acceptance and use of television in homes. Ultimately, perhaps in hopeless idealism, I am concerned with what effect we might have on television itself.

The courses described here, the courses that many of us teach, will have an effect on what is taught, how teachers are trained to teach it, and how families and individuals deal with that new knowledge in their lives. On one level this influence can be defined in terms of the relation of theory to practice. How do the sometimes too rarefied discussions that take place in university settings "trickle down" into the "trenches" of public education? On another, perhaps more important level, however, I think we must define the question in terms of the role of the scholar as citizen. How does our work relate—intellectually, politically, morally—to the public at large, the television viewing public, the public that supports us, in spite of our gripes about the nature and amount of that support, with money and with a general commitment to the idea of higher education?

This responsibility is comparable to our stated or implied faith in general education. The attitude that makes us want to "unteach" our students is counter to this commitment. To my thinking, most university educators have too little sense of the developmental nature of the learning process. If they have a sense of it, it is one that is grounded in the assumption that their students should be "finished," that is, be done with all their development by the time they reach the university. They should be "ready for university-level work" or they "should not be here at all." We are appalled at their inability or unwillingness to deal with *our* subjects on *our* terms. We too often take their genuine, naive interest as a mark of ignorance, and we set out to correct, to polish. The best, of course, catch on quickly. That is, they become like us.

I am not arguing for "lowering standards" or for simplifying the complexities of our subject matters. I am arguing for a point of view that believes in building, diffusing, *developing* a complex, theoretical overview rather than one that seeks to inject it. That, to my way of thinking, is merely another form of inoculation theory. Give that kid a shot of complexity. If it takes, he's in.

Even more forcefully I wish to argue that this model is the appropriate one for our role in the society at large. I believe that television is one of the most complex phenomena that can be studied. Certainly my own attempt has been to articulate a theoretical understanding of television that can counter the easy dismissal of the medium, the ideological attempts to "reform" it, or the foolish and ignorant calls to abolish it. It is diffusion that I am after, a general acknowledgment that there are few if any easy answers.

Whatever our own specialized, elaborate, historically informed view of our subject, we must, as citizen-scholars and citizen-teachers, be willing to translate that view into publicly available terms. We must be available, personally and in our writing and teaching, to our colleagues involved in teacher training, to public interest groups, to the public schools themselves. Talking to those who know our language is indeed a delight, particularly when we are called upon to match subtlety and precision. But it may only be when we are called upon to speak to those who do not know it that we find out whether or not we truly have anything to say.

We can, of course, assume a more cynical view. We can contribute to the attitude that television is an inherently inferior medium and that it has sought, found, and shaped its willing audience. But such a view contradicts our commitment to education. A more worthy goal is that we set out to aid in the creation of an enlightened audience, appreciative, yet critical, of television's illusions and delights. With such an audience, television will be as exciting and as ordinary as literature and film now are. A small part of the audience will choose to create or to study television. But our greatest achievements will be in contributing something to that larger part of the audience who will kick off shoes at the end of the day, watch an hour or so of TV, conclude that that was a good or bad show—and be able to tell their children why.

INTRODUCTION

The American Film Institute Guide to College Courses in Film and Television is a specialized reference resource for students, teachers, counselors, parents, and others interested or involved in film and television higher education. The book provides detailed listings of courses and programs offered at colleges, universities, and professional institutions in the United States and is based on firsthand information provided by college administrators and faculty members in response to a survey. The survey design and data collection were by Peterson's Guides. Phone contact was made with institutions not responding to the survey by Ann Martin and Ronal Mulligan of the Education Services staff of the American Film Institute. The three mailings of the AFI survey were organized by Janice Poinsett of Peterson's Guides, who also coordinated all incoming surveys for the editors.

The Guide can be used for a variety of purposes. Its primary aim is to help students and their parents determine which school and program best suits the particular interest and educational goals of the individual student. The Guide can also be of use to the administrator, counselor, teacher, and researcher who need to know various aspects of film and television education.

HOW TO USE THIS GUIDE

The main section of the Guide, US Colleges Offering Coursework in Film and Television, lists in alphabetical order by state all the institutions of higher education that responded to the American Film Institute survey by indicating that they offer opportunities for film or television study. The name of each institution is followed by a brief paragraph, which provides information about the type of institution, its accreditation, location, campus size, total enrollment, faculty size, calendar, and grading system. In some cases, this paragraph is followed by a note about special features such as a consortium membership or an unusual interdisciplinary arrangement.

An institution may be classified as one of six types:

- Two-year institution—primarily awards certificates or associate's degrees or offers two years of work applicable toward a bachelor's degree program
- Four-year institution—awards bachelor's degrees and may also award certificates and associate's degrees
- Upper-level institution—begins with the junior year, awards bachelor's degrees, and may also offer graduate work
- Comprehensive institution—awards bachelor's degrees (and sometimes certificates and associate's degrees) and offers graduate work at the master's degree or specialist level
- Professional institution—offers programs of study in one field only, leading to an undergraduate or graduate degree
- University—offers all four years of undergraduate work in addition to graduate work through the doctorate in more than two research-oriented and professional fields

Colleges use a growing variety of calendar systems. Among the most common are:

- Semesters—academic year divided into two periods of approximately 17-18 weeks each
- Trimesters—calendar year divided into three periods of approximately 15 weeks each, with students usually enrolling in two trimesters each year
- Quarters—calendar year divided into four periods of approximately 10-11 weeks each, with students usually enrolling in three quarters a year
- 4-1-4—a one-month winter term between four-month fall and spring terms
- 3-3—three courses taken during each of three terms

Within each institutional listing, program descriptions are provided for individual departments or other academic units that offer film or television study. The general address of each institution appears after the name of the first program being described.

Separate addresses for various programs within an institution are given only if they are different from the main address.

The length and scope of individual descriptions varies from school to school depending on the detail in which questionnaires were answered. The most complete listings include the following information:

- The number of majors in the department or program
- The name of the appropriate person to contact for further information about the department's offerings
- The type of degree or program offered
- Requirements and application deadlines for admission to the school as well as special requirements of the particular department or program (Deadlines may be indicated by a specific date, the term "rolling," or both. Under a policy of rolling admissions, applications are evaluated upon receipt and applicants are notified immediately.)
- Types of financial aid available through school-wide programs as well as special arrangements offered on a departmental basis; application deadlines
- Curricular emphasis of the program with respect to subject matter stressed in the areas of film and television study in general and in the specific areas of film and television production
- Special arrangements, including formal apprenticeship, internship, and independent study programs, as well as extracurricular offerings, such as on-campus film societies, film festivals, student publications, and student television production activities
- Equipment and facilities available to students
- Names of faculty members, both full and part time
- Courses offered

This information provides a profile of a school's film and/or television study and training activity. It must be remembered that college curricula change constantly; courses and programs are likely to begin changing before any volume can be committed to print. Furthermore, it should be noted that no attempt has been made to check the data provided for this volume by the schools listed here. Students should not hesitate to call or write the designated contact at the schools in which they are interested in order to obtain more detailed information.

Additional sections of the Guide provide helpful information about related aspects of the field. There are separate sections devoted to:

- Foreign Film and Television Schools—the names and addresses of schools in countries throughout the world offering courses in film or television
- Careers in Film and Television—information on where to find job listings and names and addresses of organizations helpful to the job seeker
- Grants and Scholarships for Students—organizations that offer grants and scholarships for students as well as bibliographic information
- Selected List of Film and Video Centers—regional centers that offer film and/or video facilities to the public
- Student Film/Video Festivals and Awards— names and addresses of competitions in which students may enter films or tapes
- National and International Organizations—names and addresses of organizations of interest to students, faculty, and departments of film and television

FILM AND TELEVISION ON CAMPUS: AN ANALYSIS OF THE CONTENTS OF THIS VOLUME

Courses

At the schools with entries in this volume, a total of 7,648 courses are offered in film, television, or media. This figure includes 3,991 film courses, 2,532 television courses, and 1,125 other media courses. In film, 2,770 courses are offered for undergraduates, 335 for graduates, and 886 for both undergraduates and graduates. In television, there are 2,018 undergraduate courses, 178 graduate courses, and 336 courses open to both graduates and undergraduates. In the area of interdisciplinary media courses there are 774 undergraduate courses, 205 graduate courses, and 176 courses open to both levels. These figures do not include courses with general titles such as independent study, dissertation, or thesis.

Faculty

At the responding institutions, there are 3,126 faculty members teaching in the areas of film, television, and media. Of these teachers, 2,034 are full-time faculty members, while 1,092 teach courses in film or television on a part-time basis.

Degrees

Many schools represented in the volume offer degrees in film or television. In film, 16 schools offer doctoral-level work, 76 offer programs at the master's level, and 227 offer bachelor's degrees. Twenty-eight schools offer associate's degrees in film. In television, 12 schools offer Ph.D. degrees, 71 grant master's degrees, 252 grant bachelor's degrees, and 60 grant associate's degrees. Many schools grant degrees in related or interdisciplinary areas, such as media, mass communication, communications, educational technology, etc., which involve the study of film and television. Among the schools that indicated that they offer related degrees, 17 award doctorates, 38 master's, 81 bachelor's, and 33 associate's degrees. Two hundred nine of the responding schools offer film and/or television courses but no degrees in either of these areas. At some of these schools, it is possible for students to major in a related area and minor in film or television.

Students

A total of 44,183 students are currently pursuing degrees in film or television, or in a closely related area. Television students account for 23,356 of these; film majors, 12,526; students majoring in related fields, 8,301. The number of students taking courses as nonmajors is, of course, much larger—approximately 200,000 each semester.

FILM AND TELEVISION STUDY: AN OVERVIEW

It should be remembered that film and television courses are taught in several different academic departments. While some colleges and universities have fully developed programs devoted specifically to film or television study and production, many offer these courses within more traditional areas such as English, art, history, or speech. The academic context that surrounds the teaching and study of film or television often determines the approach to the subject matter. For example, an English department teaching film appreciation may take a particularly literary approach to the study of film classics, drawing frequent comparisons between film and the novel or emphasizing structural development. A history department might treat film and television as historical documents relating to the times in which they were produced. Whether selecting a school or a course, the student should choose according to the overall context most likely to suit his or her interests and goals.

When choosing among schools that offer complete programs specifically in film or television, the student should investigate the particular interests and goals of each school's program in depth. For instance, some film programs are geared to the production and study of a single type of film such as documentary, experimental, or narrative film. Some television programs focus primarily on educational or public broadcasting. Others deal mainly with commercial television production and management. The Guide lists the curricular emphases of most of the programs in order of their priority; but here again, after selecting a number of possible choices, the student should contact each of the schools directly before making a final decision, to make sure that the program being considered provides the kind of training in which he or she is interested.

Film and television education are diverse and varied activities in our nation's colleges and universities. We hope that this book serves truly as a guide in helping students chart their courses of study.

US COLLEGES OFFERING COURSEWORK IN FILM AND TELEVISION

ALABAMA

Auburn University

State-supported coed university. Part of Auburn University System. Institutionally accredited by regional association, programs recognized by AACSB, NASA, ACPE. Small town location, 1871-acre campus. Total enrollment: 18,105. Undergraduate enrollment: 16,128. Total faculty: 1071 (1031 full-time, 40 part-time). Quarter calendar. Grading system: letters or numbers.

Speech Communication Department, Haley Center, Auburn, AL 36830 205-826-4682

CONTACT Bert E Bradley
DEGREES OFFERED BA, MA in speech communication with emphasis in film or television
ADMISSION Requirements — minimum grade point average, teachers' recommendations Undergraduate application deadline — 8/30, rolling
FINANCIAL AID Scholarships, student loans, work/study programs, teaching assistantships
CURRICULAR EMPHASIS Film study — (1) history; (2) criticism and aesthetics; (3) production Undergraduate filmmaking — (1) experimental; (2) documentary; (3) narrative Graduate filmmaking — (1) experimental; (2) narrative; (3) documentary Television study — (1) production; (2) history; (3) criticism and aesthetics Television production — (1) experimental/personal video; (2) news/documentary; (3) commercial
SPECIAL ACTIVITIES/OFFERINGS Film series, internships in film and television production, independent study
FACILITIES AND EQUIPMENT Film — 8mm and 16mm cameras, editing equipment, sound recording equipment, lighting equipment, projectors, editing room Television — complete black and white production equipment and complete color production equipment, black and white studio, color studio, audio studio, control room available on campus through cooperation with Alabama ETV Production Center
FACULTY Alan Ray, James Sanders, Barbara Sweeney, Ruth Ann Weaver

COURSE LIST

Undergraduate and Graduate
Modes of Film Communication
Cinema and Society
Television Production I, II
Film Production
Mass Communication Workshop I, II
Mass Communication Internship
TV-Radio-Film Writing
Studies in Mass Communication
Development of American Broadcasting
Broadcast Programming and Criticism
Broadcast Regulations

Spring Hill College

Independent Roman Catholic 4-year coed college. Institutionally accredited by regional association. Urban location. Undergraduate enrollment: 904. Total faculty: 69 (60 full-time, 9 part-time). Semester calendar. Grading system: letters or numbers.

Communication Arts Department, Mobile, AL 36608 205-460-2392

CONTACT Bettie W Hudgens
DEGREE OFFERED BA in communication arts
ADMISSION Application deadline — 8/15
CURRICULAR EMPHASIS Film study — (1) production; (2) history; (3) educational media/instructional technology Filmmaking — (1) narrative; (2) documentary; (3) experimental; (4) animated Television study — (1) production; (2) history; (3) educational Television production — commercial, news/documentary, experimental/personal video, educational treated equally
SPECIAL ACTIVITIES/OFFERINGS Program material produced for cable television, internships in film and television production, independent study
FACILITIES AND EQUIPMENT Film — complete 8mm and 16mm equipment Television — complete black and white studio and exterior production facilities, complete color exterior production facilities
FACULTY James Cherry, Bettie W Hudgens, Tom Loehr, Harris Ross

COURSE LIST

Undergraduate
Motion Picture Process
Filmmaking I, II
History and Criticism of Cinema
Writing for Media
TV Techniques
TV Production I, II
Broadcast Journalism
Theory of Film

Troy State University

State-supported comprehensive coed institution. Part of Troy State University System. Institutionally accredited by regional association. Small town location. Total enrollment: 10,728. Undergraduate enrollment: 8689. Total faculty: 579 (260 full-time, 319 part-time). Quarter calendar. Grading system: letters or numbers.

Troy State University (continued)

Radio and Television Department, University Avenue, Troy, AL 36081 205-566-3000

CONTACT Kenneth Croslin
DEGREES OFFERED AA, BA in radio/television
DEPARTMENTAL MAJORS Television — 49 students
ADMISSION Requirements — 1.0 minimum grade point average, ACT or SAT scores
FINANCIAL AID Scholarships, work/study programs, student loans Undergraduate application deadline — 5/1
CURRICULAR EMPHASIS Television study — criticism and aesthetics, educational, production treated equally Television production — news/documentary, experimental/personal video, educational treated equally
SPECIAL ACTIVITIES/OFFERINGS Program material produced for on-campus closed-circuit television and cable television, independent study, teacher training, vocational placement service
FACILITIES AND EQUIPMENT Television — color studio cameras, ½-inch VTR, ¾-inch cassette VTR, editing equipment, monitors, special effects generators, slide chain, portable color cameras, ¾-inch ENG, lighting equipment, sound recording equipment, audio mixers, film chain, time base corrector, TV sets, color studio, audio studio, control room

COURSE LIST

Undergraduate

Survey of Journalism
Introduction to Radio and Television
Reporting
Technology for Broadcasters
Television News Practicum
Internship
Independent Research
Seminar
Television Production Practicum

University of Alabama

State-supported coed university. Part of University of Alabama System. Institutionally accredited by regional association, programs recognized by NASM, AACSB, AOA. Small town location, 720-acre campus. Total enrollment: 15,861. Undergraduate enrollment: 12,859. Total faculty: 952 (808 full-time, 144 part-time). Semester calendar. Grading system: letters or numbers.

Department of Broadcast and Film Communication, PO Box D, University, AL 35486 205-348-6350

CONTACT W Knox Hagood
DEGREES OFFERED BA with emphasis in general, film, radio, television and news and public affairs; MA with emphasis in research and/or criticism
DEPARTMENTAL MAJORS Undergraduate film — 35 students Undergraduate television — 200 students Graduate film and television — 20 students
ADMISSION Undergraduate requirements — C average, ACT or SAT scores Graduate requirements — B average, GRE scores, interview, teachers' recommendations, written statement of purpose, professional recommendations Undergraduate application deadline — 8/1 for fall, 12/1 for spring
FINANCIAL AID Scholarships, work/study programs, student loans, fellowships, teaching assistantships, research assistantships Undergraduate application deadline — 3 months prior to registration
CURRICULAR EMPHASIS Undergraduate film study — (1) criticism and aesthetics; (2) history; (3) educational media/instructional technology Graduate film study — (1) research; (2) criticism and aesthetics; (3) history Undergraduate filmmaking — (1) experimental; (2) documentary; (3) narrative Graduate filmmaking — (1) documentary; (2) experimental; (3) educational Undergraduate television study — (1) production; (2) management; (3) criticism and aesthetics Graduate television study — (1) research; (2) criticism and aesthetics; (3) production Undergraduate television production — (1) commercial; (2) news/documentary; (3) educational Graduate television production — (1) news/documentary; (2) commercial; (3) research
SPECIAL ACTIVITIES/OFFERINGS University-wide Film Society; program material produced for cable television, local commercial television station, public television production center for state network; internships in television production; independent study; teacher training; vocational placement service
FACILITIES AND EQUIPMENT Film — 8mm cameras, editing equipment, lighting, projectors, 16mm cameras, editing equipment, sound recording equipment, lighting, projectors, screening room, editing room, sound mixing room, permanent film library of student films, video facilities for videotaping film Television — color studio cameras, ½-inch VTR, ¾-inch cassette VTR, editing equipment, monitors, special effects generators, slide chain, portable color cameras, ½-inch portapak recorders, lighting equipment, sound recording equipment, audio mixers, film chain, color studio, audio studio, control room
FACULTY Keith E Barze, Susan E Beckley, Jeremy G Butler, Raymond L Carroll, William Knox Hagood, Richard M Hartsook, George Katz, Christine M Miller, James M Rosene PART-TIME FACULTY Richard M Deason, Marian L Huttenstine, Yvonne Lamb, William H Melson, Charles C Self, James G Stovall

COURSE LIST

Undergraduate

TV Workshop
Telecommunication Fundamentals
Writing for the Mass Communication Arts
Motion Picture History and Criticism
Advanced Announcing
TV Production and Directing
Motion Picture Production and Directing
Modes of Film Communication
Public Affairs Programs
Introduction to Mass Media
Cable Television Proseminar
Broadcast and Film Practicum

Graduate

Cinema Seminar — Prior to 1946
Cinema Seminar — Contemporary Directors
Political Broadcast Seminar
Studies in Educational Media
Broadcast and Film Criticism
Seminar in Mass Media and the Public Interest
Special Problems in Communication

Undergraduate and Graduate

Mass Communication Research
Social Responsibility of the Mass Media
International Mass Communication
Instructional Video Publishing
International Cinema
The Documentary Form
Mass Media Law and Regulation
Theory of Mass Communication
Censorship and Freedom
Telecommunication Media Management
Survey of Educational Telecommunication
History of Mass Communication

University of Montevallo

State-supported comprehensive coed institution. Institutionally accredited by regional association. Small town location, 250-acre campus. Total enrollment: 2994. Undergraduate enrollment: 2526. Total faculty: 175 (135 full-time, 40 part-time). Semester calendar. Grading system: letters or numbers.

Instructional Television Department, Montevallo, AL 35115 205-665-2521

CONTACT Film — Karl A Perkins Television — Larry Smith
DEGREES OFFERED BA, BS in mass communications
DEPARTMENTAL MAJORS 60 students
CURRICULAR EMPHASIS Film study — production Television study — (1) production; (2) criticism and aesthetics Television production — (1) educational; (2) experimental/personal video
SPECIAL ACTIVITIES/OFFERINGS Film festivals, program material produced for local public television station
FACILITIES AND EQUIPMENT Film — 16mm cameras, editing equipment, projectors Television — complete color studio and exterior production facilities
PART-TIME FACULTY Jeff Payne, Karl Perkins, Larry Smith, Ray Sosa

COURSE LIST
Undergraduate
Introduction to Broadcasting
Introduction to Film I, II
Television Production I—III
ENG
Broadcasting Engineering I, II
Set Design
Broadcast Law
Announcing
Media Production Practicum
Media Seminar
Copywriting

Alabama

University of North Alabama

State-supported comprehensive coed institution. Institutionally accredited by regional association. Urban location. Total enrollment: 5146. Undergraduate enrollment: 4424. Total faculty: 223 (183 full-time, 40 part-time). Semester calendar. Grading system: letters or numbers.

Drama and Speech Department, Florence, AL 35630 205-766-4100

DEGREES OFFERED BS or BA in radio and television broadcasting
DEPARTMENTAL MAJORS Undergraduate television — 120 students
ADMISSION Requirements — ACT or SAT scores
FINANCIAL AID Scholarships, work/study programs, student loans
CURRICULAR EMPHASIS Television study — history, production, management treated equally Television production — commercial, news/documentary, experimental/personal video treated equally
SPECIAL ACTIVITIES/OFFERINGS Television — program material produced for on-campus closed-circuit television, cable television, local public television station, and local commercial television station; internships in television production, vocational placement service
FACILITIES AND EQUIPMENT Film — complete 8mm equipment Television — black and white studio cameras, color studio cameras, ½-inch VTR, 1-inch VTR, ¾-inch cassette VTR, portable black and white cameras, editing equipment, monitors, special effects generators, slide chain, portable color cameras, lighting equipment, sound recording equipment, audio mixers, film chain, time base corrector, black and white studio, color studio, control room

COURSE LIST
Undergraduate
Survey and History of Mass Media
Lighting
Directing
Television Production
Motion Picture Production
Radio and TV Practicum

University of South Alabama

State-supported coed university. Institutionally accredited by regional association, programs recognized by NASM, AACSB. Suburban location, 1527-acre campus. Total enrollment: 6971. Undergraduate enrollment: 5961. Total faculty: 307 (282 full-time, 25 part-time). Quarter calendar. Grading system: letters or numbers.

Educational Media Department, College of Education, Mobile, AL 36688 205-460-6201

CONTACT James J Thompson
DEGREES OFFERED MA, EdS in educational media with teacher certification
ADMISSION Application deadline — 9/10, rolling
FINANCIAL AID Assistantships
CURRICULAR EMPHASIS Television study — production
SPECIAL ACTIVITIES/OFFERINGS Program material produced for classroom use, teacher training
FACILITIES AND EQUIPMENT Television — complete black and white exterior production facilities
FACULTY Richard Daughenbaugh

COURSE LIST
Graduate
Closed-Circuit Television Production

ALASKA

Sheldon Jackson College

Independent Presbyterian 2-year coed college. Institutionally accredited by regional association. Small town location, 345-acre campus. Undergraduate enrollment: 170. 4-1-4 calendar. Grading system: letters or numbers.

Department of Educational Media/Television, Box 479, Sitka, AK 99835 907-747-3407

CONTACT Dan Etulain
ADMISSION Undergraduate requirements — ACT or SAT scores, teachers' recommendations
FINANCIAL AID Scholarships, work/study programs, student loans
CURRICULAR EMPHASIS Television study — (1) production Television production — (1) educational; (2) news/documentary; (3) religion
SPECIAL ACTIVITIES/OFFERINGS Program material produced for cable television and local public television station, apprenticeships, internships in television production, independent study, teacher training
FACILITIES AND EQUIPMENT Film — 8mm cameras, editing equipment, color film stock, projectors, 16mm projectors Television — ¾-inch cassette VTR, editing equipment, ¾-inch ENG, color studio, remote truck
FACULTY Dan Etulain

COURSE LIST
Undergraduate
Introduction to Television Production

University of Alaska

State-supported coed university. Part of University of Alaska System. Institutionally accredited by regional association. Small town location, 2250-acre campus. Total enrollment: 3267. Undergraduate enrollment: 2961. Total faculty: 395 (325 full-time, 70 part-time). Semester calendar. Grading system: letters or numbers.

Journalism and Broadcasting Department, Fairbanks, AK 99701 907-479-7761

CONTACT Jimmy Bedford or Gerald Weaver
DEGREE OFFERED BA in journalism with emphasis in broadcasting
ADMISSION Undergraduate requirements — 2.0 minimum grade point average, ACT scores Undergraduate application deadline — 8/1
FINANCIAL AID Work/study programs Undergraduate application deadline — 5/1
CURRICULAR EMPHASIS Film study — (1)production; (2) educational media/instructional technology; (3) history Filmmaking — (1) documentary; (2) educational; (3) experimental Television study — (1) production; (2) educational; (3) criticism and aesthetics Television production — (1) news/documentary; (2) educational; (3) commercial
SPECIAL ACTIVITIES/OFFERINGS Program material produced for on-campus public television station and state satellite, apprenticeships, internships in television production, independent study, teacher training
FACILITIES AND EQUIPMENT Film — complete 16mm equipment Television — color studio cameras, 1-inch VTR, 2-inch VTR, ¾-inch cassette VTR, editing equipment, monitors, special effects generators, slide chain, portable color cameras, lighting equipment, sound recording equipment, audio mixers, film chain, time base corrector, complete TV station (public) available to students for classes, color studio, audio studio, control room
FACULTY Gerald Weaver PART-TIME FACULTY Steve Smith, Juanita Tucker

COURSE LIST
Undergraduate
Television Production
Broadcast Journalism
Announcing
Advanced Broadcast Production
Cinematography
Audio Production
Instructional Television
Broadcast Management
Seminar in Media Problems
Media Practicum

ARIZONA

Arizona State University

State-supported coed university. Institutionally accredited by regional association, programs recognized by NASM, AACSB, NASA. Suburban location. Total enrollment: 37,122. Undergraduate enrollment: 26,798. Total faculty: 1269. Semester calendar. Grading system: letters or numbers.

Department of English, Tempe, AZ 85281 602-965-3704 or 602-965-3168

CONTACT Nicholas A Salerno
DEGREE OFFERED BA in English with a minor in film
CURRICULAR EMPHASIS Film study — (1) history; (2) criticism and aesthetics; (3) appreciation; (4) educational media/instructional technology
SPECIAL ACTIVITIES/OFFERINGS Film series, film festivals, film societies, student publications, independent study, teacher training, vocational placement service
FACILITIES AND EQUIPMENT Film — permanent film library of commercial or professional films
FACULTY Jay Boyer, Kenneth L Donelson, Nicholas A Salerno, Miles Hood Swarthout

COURSE LIST

Undergraduate

History and Art of the Film
The Silent Film
American Film Genres

Undergraduate and Graduate

Film Appreciation
Screenwriting

Journalism and Telecommunication Department 602-965-5011

CONTACT ElDean Bennett
DEGREES OFFERED BA, BS in broadcasting
DEPARTMENTAL MAJORS Television — 489 students
ADMISSION Requirements — 2.25 minimum grade point average, ACT or SAT scores, completion of 30 credit hours of general studies Application deadline — 8/1
FINANCIAL AID Scholarships, work/study programs, student loans
CURRICULAR EMPHASIS Film study — history, criticism and aesthetics, appreciation treated equally Television study — (1) broadcast news; (2) production; (3) management; (4) history Television production — commercial, news/documentary treated equally
SPECIAL ACTIVITIES/OFFERINGS Film festivals, film societies, program material produced for on-campus closed-circuit television and cable television, internships in television production, independent study, internships in promotion, industrial/business television, film promotion
FACILITIES AND EQUIPMENT Film — 8mm and 16mm cameras, editing equipment, projectors, 8mm lighting, screening room, editing room, library of video tapes Television — color studio cameras, ½-inch VTR, ¾-inch cassette VTR, portable black and white cameras, editing equipment (mostly for playback), monitors, slide chain, ½-inch portapak recorders, lighting equipment, sound recording equipment, audio mixers, film chain, time base corrector, color studio, audio studio, control room
FACULTY ElDean Bennett, John Craft, Frederic Leigh, Charles Moore, Benjamin Silver PART-TIME FACULTY Steve Feinberg, Larry Phillips, Mischa Axline Rice, Graham Robertson, Robert Wendt, J H Young

COURSE LIST

Undergraduate

Fundamentals of Radio-Television
Broadcast News Writing
Introduction to Mass Communications
Broadcast News
Broadcast Programming
Studio Techniques
Television Production
Broadcast Announcing
Communication Law
Public Affairs Broadcasting
International Communications
Broadcast Writing
Broadcast Station Operations: Sales/Promotion
Cable Television and Emerging Communication Systems
Television Directing
Broadcast Station Management
Broadcast Internship

Arizona

Arizona Western College

State and locally supported 2-year coed college. Part of State Board of Directors for Community Colleges, automatic transfer to main campus for baccalaureate. Institutionally accredited by regional association. Rural location, 640-acre campus. Undergraduate enrollment: 3872.Total faculty: 214 (69 full-time, 145 part-time). Semester calendar. Grading system: letters or numbers.

Communications Department, PO Box 929, Yuma, AZ 85364 602-726-1000

CONTACT Bob Davis
ADMISSION Application deadline — rolling
FINANCIAL AID Scholarships, student loans, work/study programs Application deadline — 3/15, rolling
CURRICULAR EMPHASIS Film study — (1) appreciation; (2) criticism and aesthetics; (3) history Filmmaking — (1) experimental; (2) documentary; (3) animated Television study — (1) educational; (2) appreciation; (3) criticism and aesthetics Television production — (1) educational; (2) experimental/personal video; (3) news/documentary
SPECIAL ACTIVITIES/OFFERINGS Film series, film festivals, program material produced for classroom use, independent study
FACILITIES AND EQUIPMENT Film — complete Super-8mm equipment, permanent film library Television — black and white studio cameras, ½-inch VTR, ¾-inch cassette VTR, portable black and white cameras, monitors, special effects generators, ½-inch portapak recorder, lighting equipment, sound recording equipment, audio mixers
FACULTY Bob Davis, Nick Graves

COURSE LIST

Undergraduate

Individual Studies — Film
Movies as Literature
History of Film

Cochise College

County-supported 2-year coed college. Institutionally accredited by regional association. Rural location. Undergraduate enrollment: 2947. Total faculty: 276 (68 full-time, 208 part-time). Semester calendar. Grading system: letters or numbers.

Communications, Humanities and Fine Arts Department, Douglas, AZ 85607 602-364-7943

CONTACT John Doty
FINANCIAL AID Scholarships, work/study programs, student loans
CURRICULAR EMPHASIS Film study — history, criticism and aesthetics, appreciation treated equally
SPECIAL ACTIVITIES/OFFERINGS Film series

Cochise College (continued)

FACILITIES AND EQUIPMENT Film — 16mm projectors, films on cassette, screening room, permanent film library of commercial or professional films Television — ¾-inch cassette VTR, monitors, special effects generators, sound recording equipment, black and white studio, color studio
FACULTY John Doty

COURSE LIST
Undergraduate
Introduction to Film

Mesa Community College

District-supported 2-year coed college. Part of Maricopa County Community College District System. Institutionally accredited by regional association. Urban location, 120-acre campus. Undergraduate enrollment: 11,027. Total faculty: 423 (173 full-time, 250 part-time). Semester calendar. Grading system: letters or numbers.

English/Humanities/Journalism/Speech Departments, 1833 W Southern Avenue, Mesa, AZ 85202 602-833-1261

CONTACT Film — Jerry Huffaker Television — Linda Larson
DEGREE OFFERED AA in journalism with emphasis in telecommunications
ADMISSION Application deadline — 8/15, rolling
FINANCIAL AID Scholarships, student loans, work/study programs
CURRICULAR EMPHASIS Film study — (1) history; (2) appreciation; (3) criticism and aesthetics Television study — (1) appreciation; (2) production; (3) educational; (4) news/documentary
FACILITIES AND EQUIPMENT Film — 8mm camera, editing equipment Television — complete black and white production facilities
FACULTY Doyle Burke, Mary Jeane Higbee, Jerry Huffaker, Linda Larson, Ron McIntyre, Mark Setlow

COURSE LIST
Undergraduate
Introduction to Cinema
Contemporary Cinema
Introduction to Television Arts
Television Techniques
Media and Society
Radio and Television Announcing
Fundamentals of Radio and Television

University of Arizona

State-supported coed university. Institutionally accredited by regional association, programs recognized by NASM, AACSB, ACPE. Urban location. Total enrollment: 30,826. Undergraduate enrollment: 23,231. Total faculty: 1762 (1525 full-time, 237 part-time). Semester calendar. Grading system: letters or numbers.

Department of Radio-Television, 221 Modern Languages Building, Tucson, AZ 85721 602-626-4731

CONTACT William T Slater, Head
DEGREES OFFERED BA in radio-television, BFA in general fine arts with a minor in television
DEPARTMENTAL MAJORS Film — 25 students Television — 465 students
ADMISSION Application deadline — 7/1, rolling
FINANCIAL AID Scholarships, work/study programs, student loans Application deadline — 5/1, rolling
CURRICULAR EMPHASIS Film study — (1) production for television; (2) criticism and aesthetics; (3) history Filmmaking — (1) documentary; (2) narrative; (3) educational Television study — criticism and aesthetics, production, management treated equally Television production — (1) news/documentary; (2) commercial; (3) educational
SPECIAL ACTIVITIES/OFFERINGS Filmmaking clubs; film series; film festivals; program material produced for cable television, local public television station, local commercial television station; apprenticeships; internships in film production; internships in television production; independent study; practicum
FACILITIES AND EQUIPMENT Film — 8mm and 16mm equipment, screening room, 35mm screening facilities, editing room, sound mixing room, permanent film library of student films, permanent film library of commercial or professional films Television — complete black and white and color studio production equipment, complete black and white and color exterior production equipment, black and white studio, color studio, mobile van/unit, remote truck, audio studio, control room
FACULTY Harry Atwood, Frank Barreca, George Bauer, Dennis Carr, Frances M Darnton, Eddie B Eiselein, Bruce Fowler, Gordon E Hamilton, Westley B Marshall, John McCleary, Brett E Miller, William T Slater, Marvin Smith, Michael Thomsen

COURSE LIST
Undergraduate
Introduction to Radio, Television, and Film
Aesthetics and Theory of Media Production
Survey of Law and Regulation of Electronic Media and Film
Electronic Media and Society
Development of the Motion Picture and Television
Fundamentals of Broadcast Production
Beginning Motion Picture Production
Broadcast Writing
Introduction to Broadcast Journalism
Creative Advertising
Beginning Graphic Design
Public Relations
Intermediate Broadcast Production
Advanced Broadcast Production
Intermediate Motion Picture Production
Writing for News and Documentary
Dramatic Writing for Radio and Television
Reporting for Radio and Television News
Producing Public Affairs and Documentary Programs
Introduction to Electronic Media Research

History of Broadcasting
Broadcast Criticism
Community Audio-Video Production
Minority Broadcasting
Broadcast Programming
Broadcast Management
Readings in Broadcasting and Film
Law, Policy and Regulation of Broadcasting and Cable
Audience Research
Instructional Media Design
Internship
Proseminar
Workshop
Independent Study
Practicum

ARKANSAS

Arkansas College

Independent Presbyterian 4-year coed college. Institutionally accredited by regional association. Small town location. Undergraduate enrollment: 534. Total faculty: 44 (32 full-time, 12 part-time). 4-1-4 calendar. Grading system: letters or numbers.

Media Arts Department, 2400 East College, Batesville, AR 72501 501-793-9813

CONTACT Gary Byrd
DEGREE OFFERED BA in media arts
DEPARTMENTAL MAJORS Film — 35 students Television — 35 students
ADMISSION Requirement — ACT or SAT scores
FINANCIAL AID Work/study programs, student loans
CURRICULAR EMPHASIS Film study — history, criticism and aesthetics, appreciation, educational media/instructional technology treated equally Filmmaking — documentary, narrative, experimental, animated, educational treated equally Television study — history, criticism and aesthetics, appreciation, educational, production, management treated equally Television production — commercial, news/documentary, experimental/personal video, educational treated equally
SPECIAL ACTIVITIES/OFFERINGS Filmmaking clubs; film series; film festivals; film societies; program material produced for on-campus closed-circuit television, cable television, local public television station; apprenticeships; internships in film production; internships in television production; independent study; teacher training
FACILITIES AND EQUIPMENT Film — complete 8mm equipment, 16mm cameras, editing equipment, lighting, black and white film stock, color film stock, projectors, sound stage, screening room, editing room, sound mixing room, permanent film library of student films, permanent film library of commercial or professional films Television — complete black and white and color studio production equipment, complete black and white and color exterior production equipment, black and white studio, color studio, mobile van/unit, audio studio, control room
FACULTY Gary W Byrd, Chris Jones, Jay Summers PART-TIME FACULTY Jan Browning, Nana Farris, George Langford, George Zilbergeld

COURSE LIST
Undergraduate
Introduction to Mass Communication
Fundamentals of Photography
Basic Documentary Technique
Planning and Script Writing for A/V Productions
Analysis of Contemporary Film
Theater Practicum
Underwater Photography
Fundamentals of Motion Picture Production
Basic Television Production
Basic Stagecraft
Broadcast Media Advertising I
Public Opinion in Mass Media
Principles of Scene Design and Lighting
Advanced Still Photography
Advanced Motion Picture Production
Advanced Television Production
Film History
Advertising Theory
A/V Productions for Education

Arkansas State University

State-supported comprehensive coed institution. Institutionally accredited by regional association, programs recognized by NASM, AACSB. Small town location, 800-acre campus. Total enrollment: 7300. Undergraduate enrollment: 6641. Total faculty: 339 (317 full-time, 22 part-time). Semester calendar. Grading system: letters or numbers.

Department of Radio-Television, Box 4B, State University, AR 72467 501-972-3070

CONTACT Charles L Rasberry
DEGREES OFFERED BS in radio-television; MSMC in radio-television
DEPARTMENTAL MAJORS Undergraduate — 275 students Graduate — 9 students
FINANCIAL AID Scholarships, student loans, work/study programs, part-time employment
CURRICULAR EMPHASIS Film study — production Filmmaking — news Television study — (1) production; (2) management; (3) educational Television production — (1) commercial; (2) news/documentary; (3) educational
SPECIAL ACTIVITIES/OFFERINGS Program material produced for on-campus closed-circuit television, cable television, local public television station, local commercial television station; independent study; practicum; vocational placement service
FACILITIES AND EQUIPMENT Film — 16mm cameras, editing equipment, lighting equipment, black and white and color film stock, projectors, editing room, animation board Television — complete black and white studio and exterior production equipment, complete color studio production equipment, black and white studio, color studio, mobile van/unit, remote truck, audio studio, control room
FACULTY Gene Cagle, Richard Carvell, Howard Coleman, John Cramer, George Inzer, Kenneth Lane, Michael McHush

COURSE LIST
Undergraduate
Development of the Motion Picture
Introduction to Broadcasting
Survey of Radio-TV
Survey of Cable TV
TV Production
TV Directing
TV Film Techniques
Radio-TV Announcing
Radio-TV Copywriting
Broadcast News I, II
Advanced TV Practices I, II
Special Problems in Radio-TV

Arkansas State University (continued)

Graduate
Advanced Television Directing and Producing
Advanced Studies in Broadcast Management
Broadcast News II
Broadcasting Seminar
Advanced Studies in Communications Law
Public Opinion, Propaganda and the Mass Media

Henderson State University

State-supported comprehensive coed institution. Institutionally accredited by regional association. Small town location. Undergraduate enrollment: 2611 Total faculty: 180. Semester calendar. Grading system: letters or numbers.

Oral Communication Department, Arkadelphia, AR 71923 501-246-5511

CONTACT Film — Kenneth Gilliam Television — Edwin Ryland
DEGREE OFFERED BA in oral communication
ADMISSION Application deadline — 8/29, rolling
FINANCIAL AID Work/study programs Application deadline — 7/30
CURRICULAR EMPHASIS Television study — production Television production — news/documentary
SPECIAL ACTIVITIES/OFFERINGS Program material produced for on-campus closed-circuit television, practicum, teacher training
FACILITIES AND EQUIPMENT Television — complete black and white studio and exterior production facilities
FACULTY Kenneth Gilliam

John Brown University

Independent 4-year coed college. Institutionally accredited by regional association. Rural location, 300-acre campus. Undergraduate enrollment: 717. Total faculty: 56 (46 full-time, 10 part-time). Semester calendar. Grading system: letters or numbers.

Broadcasting Department, PO Box 600, West University Street, Siloam Springs, AR 72761 501-524-3131

CONTACT Mike Flynn
DEGREES OFFERED AS, BS in broadcasting
DEPARTMENTAL MAJORS 40 students
ADMISSION Requirements — ACT scores, written statement of purpose Application deadline — rolling
FINANCIAL AID Scholarships, student loans, work/study programs Application deadline — 4/1
CURRICULAR EMPHASIS Television study — (1) production; (2) management; (3) criticism and aesthetics Television production — (1) religious; (2) commercial; (3) news/documentary
SPECIAL ACTIVITIES/OFFERINGS Program material produced for cable television, practicum
FACILITIES AND EQUIPMENT Television — complete color studio and exterior production equipment, color studio, audio studio
FACULTY Carl Windsor

COURSE LIST

Undergraduate
Television Broadcasting
Television Workshop

University of Arkansas at Little Rock

State-supported 4-year and professional coed institution. Part of University of Arkansas System. Institutionally accredited by regional association. Urban location, 145-acre campus. Total enrollment: 9652. Undergraduate enrollment: 8591. Total faculty: 400 (311 full-time, 89 part-time). Semester calendar. Grading system: letters or numbers.

Department of Radio, Television and Film, 33rd Street and University, Little Rock, AR 72204 501-569-3164

CONTACT David Guerra
DEGREE OFFERED BA in radio, TV, film
DEPARTMENTAL MAJORS 160 students
ADMISSION Requirements — 2.0 minimum grade point average, ACT or SAT scores
FINANCIAL AID Scholarships, work/study programs, student loans
CURRICULAR EMPHASIS Film study — history, criticism and aesthetics treated equally Filmmaking — documentary Television study — history, educational, production, management treated equally Television production — experimental/personal video
SPECIAL ACTIVITIES/OFFERINGS Program material produced for student participation, internships in film production, internships in television production, independent study
FACILITIES AND EQUIPMENT Film — 8mm cameras, projectors Television — color studio cameras, ½-inch VTR, ¾-inch cassette VTR, portable black and white cameras, editing equipment, monitors, slide chain, ½-inch portapak recorders, color studio, audio studio, control room
FACULTY David Guerra, Don Singleton, Lynn Wahl

COURSE LIST

Undergraduate
Introduction to Radio/TV
Elements of Broadcast Production
Introduction to Film
Broadcast Film in American Society
Writing for TV/Radio
Broadcast Film Performances
TV Program Production
Film Production I
Special Topics Cable TV

University of Arkansas, Fayetteville

State-supported coed university. Part of university of Arkansas System. Institutionally accredited by regional association, programs recognized by NASM, AACSB. Small town location. Total enrollment: 14,421. Undergraduate enrollment: 11,349. Total faculty: 719 (669 full-time, 50 part-time). Semester calendar. Grading system: letters or numbers.

The Film Program, 417 Communication Center, Fayetteville, AR 72701 501-575-2953

CONTACT Bill Harrison, Frank Scheide
DEGREES OFFERED BA in film, BA in speech with an emphasis in broadcasting, MA in speech with an emphasis in broadcasting or film
PROGRAM MAJORS Undergraduate film — 28 students Undergraduate television — 3 students Graduate film — 3 students
ADMISSION Undergraduate requirements — 2.0 minimum grade point average, ACT or SAT scores Graduate requirement — 2.5 minimum grade point average
FINANCIAL AID Scholarships, work/study programs, student loans, teaching assistantships
CURRICULAR EMPHASIS Undergraduate film study — (1) appreciation; (2) criticism and aesthetics; (3) history; (4) educational media/instructional technology Graduate film study — (1) appreciation; (2) criticism and aesthetics; (3) history; (4) educational media/instructional technology Undergraduate filmmaking — (1) narrative; (2) documentary; (3) experimental; (4) educational; (5) animated Graduate filmmaking — (1) documentary; (2) narrative; (3) experimental; (4) educational; (5) animated Undergraduate television study — (1) production; (2) appreciation; (3) criticism and aesthetics; (4) history; (5) educational Graduate television study — (1) production; (2) appreciation; (3) criticism and aesthetics; (4) history; (5) educational Undergraduate television production — (1) news/documentary; (2) commercial; (3) experimental/personal video; (4) educational Graduate television production — (1) news/documentary; (2) commercial; (3) experimental/personal video; (4) educational
SPECIAL ACTIVITIES/OFFERINGS Film series, film festivals, film societies, program material produced for cable television and local public television station, internships in film production, internships in television production, independent study, teacher training
FACILITIES AND EQUIPMENT Film — complete 8mm equipment, 16mm cameras, editing equipment, lighting, projectors, screening room, editing room, animation board, permanent film library of student films, permanent film library of commercial or professional films Television — complete black and white studio production equipment, black and white studio cameras, ½-inch VTR, monitors, lighting equipment, sound recording equipment, audio mixers, black and white studio, control room
FACULTY Frank Scheide PART-TIME FACULTY Kent Brown, James Cowan, Bill Harrison, Jon Hassel, John Clellon Holmes

COURSE LIST

Undergraduate
Film Lecture (Introductory Course)

Undergraduate and Graduate
Film Production I, II
Film History I: 1889-1939
Film History II: 1939 to Present
Documentary Film
Film Writing Workshop
Literature into Film
American Film Survey
Continental Film
TV Programming/Production
Television Writing
Seminar in Television
Special Problems
Seminar in Film Studies

University of Central Arkansas

State-supported comprehensive coed institution. Institutionally accredited by regional association, programs recognized by NASM. Small town location. Total enrollment: 5394. Undergraduate enrollment: 4600. Total faculty: 252 (212 full-time, 40 part-time). Semester calendar. Grading system: letters or numbers.

Speech and Theatre Arts Department, Box 1716, Conway, AR 72032 501-329-2931

CONTACT Film — Glenn Smith Television — John McCormack
DEGREES OFFERED BA, BS with an emphasis in broadcasting
DEPARTMENTAL MAJORS Television — 50 students
ADMISSION Requirements — 2.0 minimum grade point average, ACT or SAT scores, interview, teachers' recommendations
FINANCIAL AID Scholarships, work/study programs, student loans
CURRICULAR EMPHASIS Film study — history Television study — history, criticism and aesthetics, appreciation, educational, production, management treated equally Television production — commercial, news/documentary treated equally
SPECIAL ACTIVITIES/OFFERINGS Film festivals; program material produced for on-campus closed-circuit television, cable television, local public television station, local commercial television station; apprenticeships; internships in television production; independent study
FACILITIES AND EQUIPMENT Television — complete black and white and color studio production equipment, black and white studio, color studio
FACULTY John McCormack, Glenn Smith

COURSE LIST

Undergraduate
Broadcast Activities
Introduction to Broadcasting
Broadcast Announcing
Broadcast News Practices
Broadcast Management
History of Cinema
Television Production
Writing for Radio and TV
Broadcasting and the Law
Internship in Communications

CALIFORNIA

Allan Hancock College

State and locally supported 2-year coed college. Part of California State University and Colleges System. Institutionally accredited by regional association. Small town location. Semester calendar. Grading system: letters or numbers.

Fine Arts Department, 800 South College, Santa Maria, CA 93454 805-925-6966

CONTACT Casey Case
PROGRAM OFFERED Media major with emphasis in film, graphics, or photography
ADMISSION Application deadline — rolling
FINANCIAL AID Work/study programs Application deadline — 8/1, rolling
CURRICULAR EMPHASIS Film study — (1) production; (2) appreciation; (3) criticism and aesthetics Filmmaking — (1) narrative; (2) documentary; (3) experimental
SPECIAL ACTIVITIES/OFFERINGS Film series, film festivals, independent study, program material produced for on-campus closed-circuit television, cable television, local public television station
FACILITIES AND EQUIPMENT Film — complete Super 8mm equipment, screening room, editing room, sound mixing and recording studio, animation board, permanent film library Television — complete color studio production equipment, color studio
FACULTY Casey Case, Roger Kutz, Steven Lewis

COURSE LIST

Undergraduate

Introduction to Motion Picture Production
Intermediate Motion Picture Production
Topics in Film: Experimental Filmmaking
Introduction to Animation
Film as Art and Communication
The Varieties of Film Experience
Film Aesthetics and Criticism
Special Problems in Motion Picture Production
Sound Studio Recording I, II

American Film Institute Center for Advanced Film Studies

Independent 1-year coed institution. Suburban location. Total enrollment: 91. Total faculty: 16 (9 full-time, 7 part-time). Semester calendar. Grading system: pass/fail.

501 Doheny Road, Beverly Hills, CA 90210 213-278-8777

CONTACT Nancy Peter
PROGRAM MAJORS 75 students
ADMISSION Requirements — portfolio, professional work experience, production credits, professional recommendations, teachers' recommendations, written statement of purpose
FINANCIAL AID Tuition loans
CURRICULAR EMPHASIS Film study — production Filmmaking — narrative Television production — narrative
SPECIAL ACTIVITIES/OFFERINGS Independent projects, directing workshop, weekly seminars
FACILITIES AND EQUIPMENT Film — complete 16mm and ¾-inch video equipment, 35mm screening facilities, editing rooms, sound mixing room, Charles K Feldman film research library Television — complete black and white exterior production facilities
FACULTY John Bloch, Tony Brand, Gilbert Cates, Dolores Dorn, William Fadiman, George Folsey, Martin Hornstein, Robert Kaplan, Robert Ellis Miller, Daniel Petrie, Lois Peyser, James Powers, Joe Rave, Howard Schwartz, Gordon Stulberg, Antonio Vellani

COURSE LIST

Graduate

Directing Workshop
Directing the Actor
Screenwriting Workshops I, II
Cinematography Workshops I, II
ASC-AFI Cinematography Seminars
Film Analysis
Producing the Film
The Entertainment Industry: Its Structure and Its Economy
Seminars
Editing Workshop

Art Center College of Design

Independent professional coed institution. Institutionally accredited by regional association, programs recognized by NASA. Suburban location. Total enrollment: 1059. Undergraduate enrollment: 1057. Total faculty: 174 (35 full-time, 139 part-time). Trimester calendar. Grading system: letters or numbers.

Film Department, 1700 Lida Street, Pasadena, CA 91103 213-577-1700

CONTACT Jim Jordan, Chairman, or Hanna Roman, Associate Chairman
DEGREES OFFERED BFA in film, MFA in film
DEPARTMENTAL MAJORS Undergraduate film — 50 students Graduate film — 2 students
ADMISSION Undergraduate requirements — 2.5 minimum grade point average, ACT or SAT scores, interview, written statement of purpose, portfolio, prior college strongly recommended Graduate requirements — 3.0 minimum grade point average, interview, written statement of purpose, portfolio Undergraduate application deadline — rolling
FINANCIAL AID Scholarships, student loans, BEOG

CURRICULAR EMPHASIS Undergraduate film study — history, criticism and aesthetics, appreciation treated equally Graduate film study — history, criticism and aesthetics, appreciation treated equally Undergraduate filmmaking — documentary, narrative, educational, television commercials treated equally Graduate filmmaking — documentary, narrative, educational, television commercials treated equally
SPECIAL ACTIVITIES/OFFERINGS Film series, internships in film production, independent study, student film production of sponsored films for nonprofit organizations
FACILITIES AND EQUIPMENT Film — 8mm and 16mm cameras, editing equipment, sound recording equipment, lighting, projectors, animation stand and camera, stage, screening room, editing room, sound mixing room, animation board, permanent film library of student films, permanent film library of commercial or professional films, video recording and playback in ¾-inch and ½-inch
FACULTY Michael Ahnemann, Kirk Axtell, Paul Babb, Arnold Baker, Rudy Behlmer, Mitch Block, Larry Boelens, Richard Bohn, Sid Field, Gary Freund, Jean-Pierre Geuens, Robert Gips, Sterling Johnson, Jim Jordan, Bruce Kerner, Robert Leonard, Tony Miller, Bob Petersen, Jerry Robertson, Hanna Roman, Barry Sherman, Eric Sherman, Selwyn Touber, Robert Wollin, John Woodruff

COURSE LIST
Undergraduate
Basic Film Production
Lighting I, II
Advanced Lighting I, II
Analysis of Film I, II
Production and Personnel Management Seminar
Film Editing I, II
Advanced Film Editing I, II
Cinematography I, II
Advanced Cinematography I, II
Film Directing I, II
Film Directors Laboratory I, II
Film Sound Production I, II
Film Graphics Camera I, II
Film Production I, II
Advanced Film Production I, II
Film Writing I, II
Advanced Film Writing I, II
Film Production Design I, II
Film Vignettes I, II

Undergraduate and Graduate
Independent Film Projects I, II
Independent Film Studies I, II

California

Berkeley Film Institute

Independent professional coed institution. Urban location. Total enrollment: 600. Total faculty: 13. Quarter calendar. Grading system: written reports by faculty members.

2741 8th Street, Berkeley, CA 94710 415-843-9271

CONTACT Registrar
PROGRAM MAJORS Undergraduate film — 300 students
ADMISSION Open enrollment policy
FINANCIAL AID Work/study programs
FACILITIES AND EQUIPMENT Complete 16mm equipment, screening room, editing room, sound mixing room, permanent film library of student films, permanent film library of commercial or professional films, two Moviola M-77 flatbed editing consoles, optical printer
FACULTY Lauren Kusmider, Maurice J Solkov PART-TIME FACULTY Dorothy Desrosiers, Lisa Fruchtman, Nelson Morgan, Carole Roberts, Bob Schiappacasse, Jane Stubbs

COURSE LIST
16mm Production Workshop
Filmcraftsman
Summer Intensive Workshop
Lighting
Sound
Screenwriting
Film Business
Film Acting
Editing
Directing
Camera Operations

Brooks Institute

Independent professional coed institution. Institutionally accredited by regional association. Urban location, 25-acre campus. Total enrollment: 782. Undergraduate enrollment: 15. Total faculty: 32 (23 full-time, 9 part-time). Trimester calendar. Grading system: letters or numbers.

Cinema/TV Department, School of Photographic Art and Science, 2190 Alston Road, Santa Barbara, CA 93108 805-969-2291

CONTACT Film — Rex Fleming Television — Herb Boggie
DEGREE OFFERED BA in cinema/TV
DEPARTMENTAL MAJORS Undergraduate — 69 students
ADMISSION Requirements — 2.20 minimum grade point average, interview, written statement of purpose, 30 credit hours of general education
FINANCIAL AID Scholarships, work/study programs, student loans
CURRICULAR EMPHASIS Film study — criticism and aesthetics, appreciation, educational media/instructional technology treated equally Filmmaking — documentary, educational, full theatre production treated equally Television study — history, criticism and aesthetics, appreciation, educational, production, management treated equally Television production — commercial, news/documentary, educational treated equally
SPECIAL ACTIVITIES/OFFERINGS Film festivals, student publications, apprenticeships, internships in television production, independent study, vocational placement service
FACILITIES AND EQUIPMENT Film — 16mm cameras, editing equipment, sound recording equipment, lighting, color film stock, projectors, sound stage, screening room, editing room, sound mixing room, animation board, permanent film library of student films, permanent film library of commercial or professional films Television — ¾-inch cassette VTR, editing equipment, monitors, special effects generators, portable color cameras, ¾-inch ENG, lighting equipment, sound recording equipment, audio mixers, color studio, audio studio, control room

Brooks Institute (continued)

FACULTY William Behrenbrak, Herbert T A Boggie, Margaret Braiden, Rex Fleming, William Johnson, Rasheed Khan, Steve Nelson, Steve Semple, Nick Vincent

COURSE LIST

Undergraduate

Introduction to Broadcast TV
TV Commercials
Non-Broadcast Documentary and Training Tapes
Basic Photography
Basic Lighting
Basic Motion Picture
Sound
Optics/Animation
Visual Communications
Printing
Advanced Motion Picture

Butte College

District-supported 2-year coed college. Part of California Community Colleges System. Institutionally accredited by regional association. Rural location, 900-acre campus. Undergraduate enrollment: 7486. Total faculty: 330 (130 full-time, 200 part-time). Quarter calendar. Grading system: letters or numbers.

Telecommunications Department, Pentz Highway, Oroville, CA 95956 916-895-2361

CONTACT Mark Hall
DEGREES OFFERED AA in telecommunications production, AA in telecommunications management
DEPARTMENTAL MAJORS 50 students
ADMISSION Requirement — 2.0 minimum grade point average Application deadline — rolling
FINANCIAL AID Student loans, work/study programs Application deadline — 6/1, rolling
CURRICULAR EMPHASIS Television study — (1) production; (2) management; (3) educational; (4) history; (5) criticism and aesthetics; (6) appreciation Television production — (1) news/documentary; (2) commercial; (3) educational; (4) experimental/personal video
SPECIAL ACTIVITIES/OFFERINGS Program material produced for on-campus closed-circuit television, cable television, local public television station, local commercial television station; apprenticeships; internships in television production; independent study
FACILITIES AND EQUIPMENT Film — 8mm cameras, editing equipment, sound recording equipment, lighting equipment, projectors, permanent film library Television — complete black and white studio and exterior production equipment, complete color studio production equipment, black and white studio, color studio, audio studio, control room
FACULTY Mark Hall PART-TIME FACULTY Rolfe Auerbach, Jim Raglund, Joe Rich, Steve Robertson, Dick Shears

COURSE LIST

Undergraduate

Introduction to Telecommunications
Basic Audio Production
Basic Television Production
News Production
Film Appreciation
Documentary Films
Advanced Television Production
Advertising
Sales Management
Copywriting

California College of Arts and Crafts

Independent comprehensive coed institution. Institutionally accredited by regional association, programs recognized by NASA. Urban location, 4-acre campus. Total enrollment: 1136. Undergraduate enrollment: 930. Total faculty: 145 (25 full-time, 120 part-time). Trimester calendar. Grading system: letters or numbers.

Film/Video Department, 5212 Broadway, Oakland, CA 94618 415-653-8118

CONTACT David Heintz
DEGREES OFFERED BFA, MFA in film, video
DEPARTMENTAL MAJORS Undergraduate film — 20 students Undergraduate television — 10 students Graduate film — 2 students Graduate television — 2 students
ADMISSION Undergraduate requirement — C average Graduate requirements — B average, written statement of purpose, portfolio, interview recommended Undergraduate application deadline — 9/1
FINANCIAL AID Scholarships, work/study programs, student loans, teaching assistantships, lab technicianships
CURRICULAR EMPHASIS Undergraduate filmmaking — (1) experimental; (2) animated; (3) narrative Graduate filmmaking — (1) experimental; (2) animated; (3) narrative Undergraduate television production — (1) experimental/personal video; (2) news/documentary Graduate television production — (1) experimental/personal video; (2) news/documentary
SPECIAL ACTIVITIES/OFFERINGS Film series, visiting film artists, performance-media shows; program material produced for on-campus closed-circuit television and cable television, apprenticeships, internships in film production, internships in television production, independent study
FACILITIES AND EQUIPMENT Film — 8mm and 16mm cameras, editing equipment, sound recording equipment, lighting, projectors, optical printer and animation stand, screening room, editing room, animation board, permanent film library of commercial or professional films Television — black and white studio cameras, ¾-inch cassette VTR, portable black and white cameras, editing equipment, monitors, special effects generators, slide chain, portable color cameras, ½-inch portapak recorders, lighting equipment, sound recording equipment, audio mixers, film chain, image processor, sound synthesizer, black and white studio
PART-TIME FACULTY Rick Blanchard, Donald Day, Jody Gillerman, David Heintz, Marc Lesueur, Dennis Pies

COURSE LIST

Undergraduate and Graduate

Film I
Animation Workshop
Video I
Intermediate Film
Video Systems and Electronics
Advanced Film/Video
Film Production
Mixed Media and Performance
Drama for Film-TV
Film History and Theory

California Institute of the Arts

Independent professional comprehensive coed institution. Institutionally accredited by regional association, programs recognized by NASM, NASA. Suburban location, 60-acre campus. Total enrollment: 715. Undergraduate enrollment: 543. Total faculty: 139 (70 full-time, 69 part-time). Semester calendar. Grading system: pass/fail.

School of Film and Video, 24700 McBean Parkway, Valencia, CA 91355 805-255-1050

CONTACT Ed Emshwiller, Dean
DEGREES OFFERED BA in film/video, MA in film/video, certificate in film/video
DEPARTMENTAL MAJORS Undergraduate film — 100 students Undergraduate television — 25 students Graduate film — 30 students Graduate television — 15 students
ADMISSION Undergraduate requirements — written statement of purpose, portfolio Graduate requirements — written statement of purpose, portfolio
FINANCIAL AID Scholarships, work/study programs, student loans, teaching assistantships (grad only)
CURRICULAR EMPHASIS Undergraduate film study — (1) independent projects; (2) criticism and aesthetics; (3) history Graduate film study — (1) independent projects; (2) criticism and aesthetics; (3) history Undergraduate filmmaking — documentary, narrative, experimental, animated treated equally Graduate filmmaking — documentary, narrative, experimental, animated treated equally Undergraduate television study — (1) production; (2) criticism and aesthetics; (3) history Graduate television study — (1) production; (2) criticism and aesthetics; (3) history Undergraduate television production — (1) experimental/personal video; (2) news/documentary; (3) commercial Graduate television production — (1) experimental/personal video; (2) news/documentary; (3) commercial
SPECIAL ACTIVITIES/OFFERINGS Film series, independent study
FACILITIES AND EQUIPMENT Film — complete 8mm and 16mm equipment, sound stage, screening room, 35mm screening facilities, editing room, sound mixing room, animation board, permanent film library of student films, permanent film library of commercial or professional films Television — black and white studio cameras, color studio cameras, ½-inch VTR, ¾-inch cassette VTR, editing equipment, monitors, special effects generators, slide chain, portable color cameras, ¾-inch ENG, lighting equipment, sound recording equipment, audio mixers, film chain, time base corrector, video synthesizer, black and white studio, color studio, control room
FACULTY Myron Emery, Ed Emshwiller, Jules Engel, Jack Hannah, Bill Jackson, Don Levy, Alexander Mackendrick, John Mahin, Kris Malkiewicz, Robert McCrea, Terry Sanders, Don Worthen PART-TIME FACULTY Fred Crippen, Mark Harris, T Hee, David Lebrun, Bill Moore, Elmer Plummer, Michael Scroggins, Steve Socki, Mildren "Chick" Strand

COURSE LIST

Undergraduate
Caricature I, II
Advanced Caricature III, IV
Life Drawing I, II
Basic Character Animation I
Animation II, III
Senior Project Year Animation IV
Color and Design I, II
Sound Recording

Undergraduate and Graduate
Composition in Motion
Lighting Workshop
Optical Printer Operations
Film Production
Film/Video Sound Recording and Reproduction
Portapak Production Workshop
Feedback Screening Seminar
Dramatic Construction in Feature Film
Avant-Garde Cinema
Radical and Personal Cinema
Film Now
Conceptual History of the Cinema
Videographics
Paik/Abe Videosynthesizer
Docu-drama Production Workshop
Film History
Film Grammar
Super Eight
F/V Production, Cinematography, Editing
Editing Workshop
Screenwriting Workshop
Basic Video Studio Operation
Optical Effects Workshop
Documentary Explorations
Survival (Aesthetic and Economic)
Sound Recording: Special Projects
Color Video Production Workshop
Advanced Film Technique
Experimental Cross-Metier F/V Workshop
Independent Projects
Production Crew Credit
Interactive Arts Workshop
Structuring Strategies
Film and Theater Directing for the Screen
Oxberry Camera Operation
Film Graphics and Animation Analysis
Basic Film Graphics Workshop
Basic Film Animation
Basic Film Production for Animators
Direct Animation
Experimental Film Graphics Workshop
Independent Projects in Film Graphics

California Lutheran College

Independent Lutheran comprehensive coed institution. Accredited by regional association and AICS. Suburban location, 285-acre campus. Undergraduate enrollment: 1200. Total faculty: 256 (72 full-time, 184 part-time). 4-1-4 calendar. Grading system: letters or numbers.

Department of Drama, 60 West Olsen Road, Thousand Oaks, CA 91360 805-492-2411

CONTACT Film — Richard G Adams Television — Don W Haskell
DEGREES OFFERED BA in communication arts, BA in drama
ADMISSION Requirement — ACT or SAT scores
FINANCIAL AID Work/study programs, student loans
CURRICULAR EMPHASIS Filmmaking — (1) experimental; (2) documentary Television study — production, management treated equally Television production — (1) experimental/personal video; (2) educational
SPECIAL ACTIVITIES/OFFERINGS Program material produced for on-campus closed-circuit television, teacher training
FACILITIES AND EQUIPMENT Film — 8mm cameras, editing equipment, sound recording equipment, lighting, color film stock, projectors, screening room, editing room, permanent film library of student films Television — black and white studio cameras, ½-inch VTR, 1-inch VTR, 2-inch VTR, ¾-inch cassette VTR, portable black and white cameras, editing equipment, monitors, ½-inch portapak recorders, lighting equipment, sound recording equipment, black and white studio, audio studio, control room

California Lutheran College (continued)

FACULTY Richard G Adams, Don W Haskell, Tim Schultz

COURSE LIST

Undergraduate

Television Production I, II
Film Production
Cinema
TV Production Activity

California Polytechnic State University

State-supported comprehensive coed institution. Part of California State University and Colleges System. Institutionally accredited by regional association. Small town location, 5000-acre campus. Total enrollment: 15,592. Undergraduate enrollment: 14,669. Total faculty: 850 full-time. Quarter calendar. Grading system: letters or numbers.

English Department 805-546-2597

CONTACT Charles Strong
ADMISSION Application deadline — rolling
CURRICULAR EMPHASIS Film study — appreciation
SPECIAL ACTIVITIES/OFFERINGS Film series, film festivals, film societies
FACILITIES AND EQUIPMENT Film — 8mm cameras, editing equipment, lighting equipment, projectors, screening room
FACULTY John Harrington, Charles Strong

COURSE LIST

Undergraduate

Introduction to Cinema
Topics in Cinema

California State College, Stanislaus

State-supported 4-year coed college. Institutionally accredited by regional association. Small town location. Total enrollment: 3500. Total faculty: 170. Semester calendar. Grading system: letters.

Turlock, CA 95380 209-633-2361

CONTACT William H Phillips (English) or James Piskoti (Art)
FINANCIAL AID Scholarships, work/study programs, student loans Undergraduate application deadline — rolling
CURRICULAR EMPHASIS Film study — (1) criticism and aesthetics; (2) appreciation; (3) history Filmmaking — (1) animated; (2) experimental; (3) narrative
SPECIAL ACTIVITIES/OFFERINGS Film series, film societies, independent study
FACILITIES AND EQUIPMENT 16mm cameras, editing equipment, sound recording equipment, lighting, projectors, permanent film library of commercial or professional films
FACULTY William H Phillips, James Piskoti

COURSE LIST

Undergraduate

Contemporary Film
Classic Foreign Films
Hitchcock
Classic American Films
Scriptwriting
Film/Video: Sources and Analysis
Filmmaking
Film Animation

California State Polytechnic University

State-supported comprehensive coed institution. Part of California State University and Colleges System. Institutionally accredited by regional association. Suburban location, 1100-acre campus. Total enrollment: 14,448. Undergraduate enrollment: 12,879. Total faculty: 813. Quarter calendar. Grading system: letters or numbers.

Communication Arts Department, 3801 West Temple Avenue, Pomona, CA 91768 714-598-4639

CONTACT Gary D Keele, Chair
DEGREE OFFERED BS in communication arts with option in broadcast communication
DEPARTMENTAL MAJORS 100 students
ADMISSION Requirement — ACT or SAT scores
FINANCIAL AID Scholarships, work/study programs, student loans
CURRICULAR EMPHASIS Television study — history, criticism and aesthetics, production treated equally Television production — commercial, news/documentary treated equally
SPECIAL ACTIVITIES/OFFERINGS Program material produced for cable television, internships in television production, vocational placement service
FACILITIES AND EQUIPMENT Film — 8mm editing equipment, sound recording equipment, projectors Television — black and white studio cameras, color studio cameras, ¾-inch cassette VTR, monitors, lighting equipment, film chain, black and white studio, color studio, control room
FACULTY Ross Figgins, David Jones, Norman Stein

COURSE LIST

Undergraduate

History of Mass Communications
Broadcast History
Introduction to the Film
Introduction to Broadcast Techniques
Television Practices
The Constitution and the Media
Broadcast Regulation
Intermediate Broadcast Techniques
Advanced Radio Practices
Advanced Television Practices
TV and Radio News Analysis
The Documentary Film
Introduction to Film Production Techniques
Intermediate Film Production Techniques
Television Directing

Remote Broadcast Production
Writing/Producing for Broadcast Media
Broadcast Media Criticism
Managerial Radio Practices
Managerial Television Practices

California State University, Chico

State-supported comprehensive coed institution. Part of California State University and Colleges System. Institutionally accredited by regional association, programs recognized by NASM, AACSB, NASA. Small town location. Total enrollment: 13,134. Undergraduate enrollment: 11,440. Total faculty: 810 (630 full-time, 180 part-time). 4-1-4 calendar. Grading system: letters or numbers.

Center for Information and Communications Studies, Chico, CA 95929 916-895-5751

CONTACT Film — William White Television — George Benson
DEGREES OFFERED BA in information and communication studies, MA in information and communication studies
DEPARTMENTAL MAJORS Undergraduate — 430 students Graduate — 15 students
ADMISSION Undergraduate requirements — 2.0 minimum grade point average, ACT or SAT scores, EPT (English Placement Test)
FINANCIAL AID Scholarships, work/study programs, student loans
CURRICULAR EMPHASIS Undergraduate film study — (1) history; (2) criticism and aesthetics; (3) appreciation Undergraduate filmmaking — (1) narrative; (2) experimental; (3) documentary Undergraduate television study — (1) production; (2) management; (3) educational Undergraduate television production — (1) educational; (2) experimental/personal video; (3) news/documentary
SPECIAL ACTIVITIES/OFFERINGS Film series; student publications; program material produced for on-campus closed-circuit television, cable television, local public television station, local commercial television station; internships in television production; independent study
FACILITIES AND EQUIPMENT Film — 8mm cameras, editing equipment, sound recording equipment, lighting, projectors, editing room, sound mixing room, animation board, permanent film library of commercial or professional films Television — black and white studio cameras, color studio cameras, 1-inch VTR, 2-inch VTR, ¾-inch cassette VTR, portable black and white cameras, editing equipment, monitors, special effects generators, slide chain, portable color cameras, ¾-inch ENG, lighting equipment, sound recording equipment, audio mixers, film chain, time base corrector, video disk players, black and white studio, color studio, mobile van/unit, audio studio, control room
FACULTY George Benson, Myron Buzzini, John Ittleson, George Rogers, William White

COURSE LIST

Undergraduate
Information and Communications Systems
Principles and Practices of Writing for Media
Information Studies
History of Communications
Visual Communication Concepts
Public Relations
Principles of Broadcasting
Principles of Station Operation
Photo Communications
Theories of Information and Communication
Systems of Graphic Communications
Analysis of Applied Media Methods
Computer Graphic Media Application
Basics of Advertising Copywriting
Advanced Public Relations
Magazine Writing
School Journalism
News Editing and Copyreading
Directed Work Experience in Media
Laboratory Newspaper
Press Photography
Publication Design
The Film — Its Origins and Meanings
Film Production Techniques I, II
Kinegraphics
Packaging
The Documentary Film
The Film and Television
Content Analysis/Learner Needs
Developing Behavioral Objectives for Instructional Technology
Sequential Content and Learning Tasks
Media Selection Processes/Form Selection
Evaluation of Content/Product
Radio-Television News
Radio-Television Announcing
Public Affairs Programming
Broadcast Programming and Management
Theories and Regulation of Broadcasting
Television A and B
Writing for Media
Application for Photo Systems
Color Photography
Special Problems
Communication Research
Interpersonal Communication Theories
Communication and Society
Specialized Information and Media Centers
Institutional Design Systems
Visual Communications and Environment
Public Opinion and Propaganda
Creative Problem Solving
Organizational Communications Theories
Public Communications and the Law
Advanced Reporting
International Communications
Current Trends in the Motion Pictures
Advanced Film Production
Advanced Television Production
Educational Television
Computer-Assisted Instruction Courseware Systems
Design of Instructional Systems
Survey of Information and Communication Studies
Media Production/Design Team Approach
Media Production for Complex Media
Photographic Copying and Titling Techniques
Photographic Lighting and Studio Lighting
Advertising and Product Photography
Specialized Photographic Techniques

Graduate
Seminar in Communication Studies
Seminar in Communication Research Methods
Forum in Communication and Instructional Technology

California State University, Dominguez Hills

State-supported comprehensive coed institution. Part of California State University and Colleges System. Institutionally accredited by regional association, programs recognized by NASM. Urban location, 350-acre campus. Total enrollment: 6972. Undergraduate enrollment: 5117. Total faculty: 307 (257 full-time, 50 part-time). Quarter calendar. Grading system: letters or numbers.

California State University, Dominguez Hills (continued)

Communications Department, 1000 East Victoria Street, Carson, CA 90747 213-515-3313

CONTACT Film — Hal Marienthal Television — Steve Roye
DEGREE OFFERED AB in communications
ADMISSION Requirements — ACT or SAT scores, teachers' recommendations Undergraduate application deadline — 8/15
FINANCIAL AID Work/study programs, student loans, BEOG
CURRICULAR EMPHASIS Film study — (1) appreciation; (2) history; (3) criticism and aesthetics Filmmaking — (1) narrative; (2) documentary; (3) experimental Television study — (1) production; (2) history; (3) directing
SPECIAL ACTIVITIES/OFFERINGS Program material produced for cable television and local public television station, internships in television production, independent study
FACILITIES AND EQUIPMENT Film — complete 8mm equipment, 16mm projectors, screening room, editing room, permanent film library of commercial or professional films Television — black and white studio cameras, color studio cameras, portable black and white cameras, monitors, slide chain, ½-inch portapak recorders, lighting equipment, film chain, black and white studio, color studio, audio studio, control room
PART-TIME FACULTY Jerry Leshay, Hal Marienthal, Steve Roye

COURSE LIST
Undergraduate
Introduction to Film
Introduction to Television
History of Film I, II
Workshop in Film
Documentary in Film
Writing for TV and Film
TV Production
Advanced TV Production
TV Directing
Newswriting for Radio and TV
TV News and Documentary Production

California State University, Fresno

State-supported comprehensive coed institution. Part of California State University and Colleges System. Institutionally accredited by regional association, programs recognized by NASM, AACSB. Urban location, 1410-acre campus. Total enrollment: 14,717. Undergraduate enrollment: 11,858. Total faculty: 937 (731 full-time, 206 part-time). Semester calendar. Grading system: letters or numbers.

Department of Radio-TV-Cinema, Cedar and Shaw Avenues, Fresno, CA 93740 209-487-2627

CONTACT Philip J Lane
DEGREES OFFERED BA in radio-TV-film, MA in mass communications
DEPARTMENTAL MAJORS Undergraduate television — 130 students Graduate television — 25 students
ADMISSION Undergraduate requirement — 2.5 minimum grade point average Graduate requirements — 2.8 minimum grade point average, GRE scores, interviews Undergraduate application deadline — 7/29, rolling
FINANCIAL AID Student loans, work/study programs Undergraduate application deadline — 3/1, rolling
CURRICULAR EMPHASIS Undergraduate film study — (1) appreciation; (2) production; (3) criticism and aesthetics; (4) history; (5) educational media/instructional technology Graduate film study — (1) criticism and aesthetics; (2) appreciation; (3) production, educational media/instructional technology; (4) history Filmmaking — (1) narrative; (2) documentary Undergraduate television study — (1) production; (2) management; (3) educational Graduate television study — (1) educational; (2) management; (3) criticism and aesthetics Television production — (1) commercial; (2) educational; (3) news/documentary
SPECIAL ACTIVITIES/OFFERINGS Film series; student publications; program material produced for on-campus closed-circuit television, local public television station, local commercial television station; independent study; practicum
FACILITIES AND EQUIPMENT Film — complete Super 8mm and 16mm equipment, sound stage, editing room, sound mixing room Television — complete black and white studio and exterior production equipment, complete color studio production equipment, black and white studio, color studio, audio studio, control room
FACULTY R C Adams, Lee Alden, John Highlander, Philip Lane, William Monson

COURSE LIST
Undergraduate
Fundamentals of Broadcast Performance
Foundations of Broadcasting
Television Production
Radio Production
Advanced Broadcasting Laboratory

Graduate
Criticism of Broadcasting and Film
Comparative and International Broadcasting
Seminar in Theory and Research
Seminar in Literature of Mass Communications
Seminar in Radio-Television-Film

Undergraduate and Graduate
Broadcast Program Appreciation
Motion Picture Appreciation
Motion Picture Production
Broadcasting and the Public
Broadcast and Film Writing
Radio and Television News Broadcasting
Advanced Television Production
Producing the Educational Broadcast
Directing the Broadcast Program
Advanced Broadcast Performance
Broadcast Regulation
Cinematography
Proseminar in Station Management
Internship and Broadcasting and Film
Topics in Film Studies
Topics in Broadcasting
Projects in Production
Topics in Radio-Television-Cinema

California State University, Fullerton

State-supported comprehensive coed institution. Part of California State University and Colleges System. Institutionally accredited by regional association, programs recognized by NASM, AACSB, NASA. Suburban location. Total enrollment: 21,435. Undergraduate enrollment: 16,524. Total faculty: 1247 (747 full-time, 500 part-time). Semester calendar. Grading system: letters or numbers.

Communications Department, Fullerton, CA 92634 714-773-3517

CONTACT George A Mastroianni
DEGREES OFFERED BA, MA in communications with emphasis in film or television

ADMISSION Undergraduate application deadline — rolling
FINANCIAL AID Scholarships, teaching assistantships Undergraduate application deadline — rolling
CURRICULAR EMPHASIS Film study — (1) criticism and aesthetics; (2) production; (3) history Filmmaking — (1) documentary; (2) narrative; (3) animated; (4) experimental Undergraduate television study — (1) criticism and aesthetics; (2) production, management; (3) social responsibility Graduate television study — (1) criticism and aesthetics; (2) production; (3) research Undergraduate television production — (1) commercial; (2) news/documentary; (3) educational Graduate television production — (1) news/documentary; (2) commercial; (3) educational
SPECIAL ACTIVITIES/OFFERINGS Film series, film festivals, program material produced for on-campus closed-circuit television and cable television, internships in film and television production, independent study, practicum, vocational placement service
FACILITIES AND EQUIPMENT Film — 8mm and 16mm cameras, editing equipment, lighting equipment, projectors, 16mm sound recording equipment, sound stage, screening room, 35mm screening facilities, editing room, sound mixing room, permanent film library Television — complete black and white studio and exterior production equipment, black and white studio, audio studio, control room
FACULTY Ron Dyas, Harry So, Larry Ward PART-TIME FACULTY Steve Milner, Harry Rattner, Warren Wright

COURSE LIST

Undergraduate
History/Aesthetics of Film
Television/Film Writing
Beginning Film Production
Beginning Television Production
Audio Production (Radio-Television-Film)
Broadcasting in America

Undergraduate and Graduate
Advanced Film Production
Documentary Film Production
Advanced Television Production
Radio/Television News
Internship
Documentary Film
Film Theory
Film Directors and Genres
Telecommunication Regulations
Telecommunication Management
Telecommunication Programming

California

Department of Theater Arts 714-870-3626

CONTACT Alvin J Keller, Chairman
DEGREES OFFERED BA in film, BA in television/film, MA in radio/television
ADMISSION Requirements — 2.5 minimum grade point average, ACT or SAT scores, teachers' recommendations Undergraduate application deadline — rolling
FINANCIAL AID Scholarships, work/study programs, teaching assistantships, fellowships Undergraduate application deadline — rolling
CURRICULAR EMPHASIS Film study — (1) production; (2) criticism and aesthetics; (3) history; (4) educational media/instructional technology Filmmaking — (1) narrative; (2) documentary; (3) experimental; (4) animated; (5) educational Television study — (1) production; (2) educational; (3) management; (4) history; (5) criticism and aesthetics Television production — (1) news/documentary, educational; (2) commercial; (3) experimental/personal video

California State University, Humboldt

State-supported 4-year coed university. Institutionally accredited by regional association. Small town location. Total enrollment: 7500. Total faculty: 450 full-time. Quarter calendar. Grading system: letters.

Theatre Arts/Film Department, Arcata, CA 95521 707-826-3566

CONTACT John Heckel
DEGREES OFFERED BA in theatre/film production, MA in theatre/film production, MA in theatre/film directing
DEPARTMENTAL MAJORS Undergraduate film — 25 students Graduate film — 9 students
ADMISSION Undergraduate requirements — ACT or SAT scores, written statement of purpose Graduate requirements — teachers' recommendations, written statement of purpose, portfolio
FINANCIAL AID Scholarships, work/study programs, student loans, teaching assistantships (grad only)
CURRICULAR EMPHASIS Undergraduate film study — (1) appreciation; (2) history; (3) criticism and aesthetics Graduate film study — (1) criticism and aesthetics; (2) history; (3) appreciation Undergraduate filmmaking — (1) documentary; (2) narrative; (3) educational; (4) narrative/documentary Graduate filmmaking — (1) documentary; (2) narrative; (3) educational; (4) narrative/documentary
SPECIAL ACTIVITIES/OFFERINGS Filmmaking clubs, film festivals, film societies, apprenticeships, independent study, teacher training
FACILITIES AND EQUIPMENT Film — complete 8mm and 16mm equipment, sound stage, screening room, editing room, sound mixing room, animation board, permanent film library of student films, permanent film library of commercial or professional films Television — ½-inch VTR, portable black and white cameras, monitors, ½-inch portapak recorders, lighting equipment
FACULTY Douglass Cox, George Goodrich, John Heckel PART-TIME FACULTY Geoffrey De Valois, Winston Jonnes, Charlie Myers, Richard Rothrock

COURSE LIST

Undergraduate
Visual Communications
Super-8 Production
Undergraduate Film Workshop

Graduate
Graduate Film Workshop
Graduate Seminar in Motion Pictures
Graduate Film Project
Directory Theory

Undergraduate and Graduate
Intermediate Super-8 Production
Audio Production
16mm Sync Sound
Documentary Film
History of Silent Film
History of Sound Film
Seminar in Motion Picture
Experimental Film
Film Directing
Film Acting
Advanced Audio Production
Film Theory and Criticism
Script Analysis
Beginning 16mm Production
Film Studies

California State University, Long Beach

State-supported comprehensive coed institution. Part of California State University and Colleges System. Institutionally accredited by regional association. Urban location, 320-acre campus. Total enrollment: 31,769. Undergraduate enrollment: 24,556. Total faculty: 1500. Semester calendar. Grading system: letters or numbers.

Radio-Television Department, 1250 Bellflower Boulevard, Long Beach, CA 90840 213-498-5404

CONTACT Robert G Finney
DEGREE OFFERED BA in radio-television
DEPARTMENTAL MAJORS Undergraduate film — 50 students Undergraduate television — 300 students
ADMISSION Requirements — ACT or SAT scores, interview Application deadline — 8/15, rolling
FINANCIAL AID Scholarships, work/study programs, student loans
CURRICULAR EMPHASIS Film study — history, criticism and aesthetics, appreciation treated equally Filmmaking — documentary, narrative, experimental, animated, educational treated equally Television study — history, criticism and aesthetics, appreciation, educational, production, management, programming and telecommunications policy treated equally Television production — commercial, news/documentary, experimental/personal video, educational treated equally
SPECIAL ACTIVITIES/OFFERINGS Filmmaking clubs; film societies; symposium on latest theatrical films; program material produced for on-campus closed-circuit television, cable television, commercial and public stations outside area; apprenticeships; internships in film production; internships in television production; independent study; vocational placement service (informal)
FACILITIES AND EQUIPMENT Film — complete 8mm and 16mm equipment, screening room, 35mm screening facilities, editing room Television — color studio cameras, ¾-inch cassette VTR, portable black and white cameras, editing equipment, monitors, special effects generators, slide chain, portable color cameras, lighting equipment, sound recording equipment, audio mixers, film chain, color studio, audio studio, control room
FACULTY Dan Baker, Robert Balon, Robert Finney, Joe Langston, Howard Martin, Saundra McMillan, Hugh Morehead PART-TIME FACULTY Carl Glassford, Patrick Griffin, Stephen Hubbert, Jon Peterson, Gary Prebula, Victor Webb, Saundra Woodruff

COURSE LIST

Undergraduate

Introduction to Radio-Television
Writing and Production Planning
Broadcast Audio Operations
Television Studio Operations
Film Camera Operations
History of Radio-TV Programs
Television Production
Radio-Television-Film Activity
The Documentary: Critics and Persuaders
Writing for Broadcasting and Motion Pictures
Advertising and Electronic Media
Theatrical Film Symposium
Television Programming Symposium
Techniques of Motion Picture Production
Television, Film, Media Graphic Production
Broadcasting/Film Organizations
Electronic Media in Education and Industry
Mass Media and Society
Children's TV Programming
Documentary Program Production
Film History
Broadcast and Media Management
Broadcast/Cablecast Regulation
Media Criticism
Women in the Mass Media
Popular Culture and the Mass Media
Broadcasting and Religion
Radio-Television Sales and Research
Special Topics
Special Projects in TV, Radio and Film

California State University, Los Angeles

State-supported comprehensive coed institution. Part of California State University and Colleges System. Institutionally accredited by regional association, programs recognized by NASM, AACSB, NASA. Urban location. Total enrollment: 24,100. Total faculty: 1200 (900 full-time, 300 part-time). Quarter calendar. Grading system: letters or numbers.

Department of Broadcasting/Speech Communication, 5151 State University Drive, Los Angeles, CA 90032 213-224-3457

CONTACT Film — Suzanne Regan Television — Kathryn Montgomery
DEGREES OFFERED BA in radio and television broadcasting, BA in radio and television broadcasting with an emphasis in film
DEPARTMENTAL MAJORS Film — 50 students Television — 100 students
ADMISSION Requirement — ACT or SAT scores
FINANCIAL AID Scholarships, work/study programs, student loans, free tuition for California residents
CURRICULAR EMPHASIS Film study — history, criticism and aesthetics, industry management and economics treated equally Filmmaking — documentary, educational treated equally Television study — history, criticism and aesthetics, management, radio history, theory treated equally Television production — commercial, news/documentary, educational, radio production treated equally
SPECIAL ACTIVITIES/OFFERINGS Film series, program material produced for cable television, internships in film production, internships in television production, independent study, vocational placement service, radio internships
FACILITIES AND EQUIPMENT Film — complete 16mm equipment, 8 mm cameras, editing equipment, sound recording equipment, lighting, color film stock, projectors, sound stage, screening room, editing room, animation board, permanent film library of commercial or professional films Television — black and white studio cameras, color studio cameras, ½-inch VTR, ¾-inch cassette VTR, portable black and white cameras, editing equipment, monitors, special effects generators, slide chain, portable color cameras, ½-inch portapak recorders, lighting equipment, sound recording equipment, audio mixers, film chain, time base corrector, black and white studio, color studio, audio studio, control room
FACULTY Kathryn Montgomery, Suzanne Regan PART-TIME FACULTY Beverly Biber, Mark Blinoff, William Bollinger, Angelina Chen, Garrett Hart, Jean-Ives Pitoun, Duane Ratliff, Sharon Rubin, George Vinovich

COURSE LIST

Undergraduate

Introduction to Broadcast Production
Introduction to Broadcasting
Survey of Film
Advanced Broadcast Production
History of Broadcasting and Film
Broadcast and Film Writing
Broadcast Responsibility and Regulation

Cross-cultural Broadcasting and Film
The Documentary in Broadcasting and Film
Factual Film for Television
Educational and Instructional Uses of Broadcasting and Film
Noncommercial Broadcasting and Film
Broadcasting and Film Aesthetics
Criticism of Broadcasting and Film
Broadcasting and Film as Shapers of the Public Mind
Administration and Studio Operation
Selected Studies in Broadcasting and Film (Revolving Topics)
Independent Study in Broadcasting and Film
Cooperative Education (Internship)

California State University, Northridge

State-supported comprehensive coed institution. Part of California State University and Colleges System. Institutionally accredited by regional association. Suburban location, 350-acre campus. Total enrollment: 27,976. Undergraduate enrollment: 21,883. Total faculty: 1500 (915 full-time, 585 part-time). Semester calendar. Grading system: letters or numbers.

Radio-TV-Film Department, 18111 Nordhoff Street, Northridge, CA 91330 213-885-3192

CONTACT Film — John Allyn Television — Don Wood
DEGREES OFFERED BA in film production, BA in television production, BA in instructional media
DEPARTMENTAL MAJORS 800 students
ADMISSION Application deadline — 6/1, rolling
FINANCIAL AID Student loans, work/study programs Application deadline — 4/15, rolling
CURRICULAR EMPHASIS Film study — (1) production; (2) history; (3) criticism and aesthetics Filmmaking — (1) narrative; (2) documentary; (3) educational; (4) experimental; (5) animated Undergraduate television study — (1) production; (2) management; (3) educational; (4) history; (5) criticism and aesthetics Graduate television study — (1) management; (2) criticism and aesthetics; (3) educational; (4) production Television production — (1) commercial; (2) educational; (3) news/documentary
SPECIAL ACTIVITIES/OFFERINGS Film societies, internships in film and television production, independent study
FACILITIES AND EQUIPMENT Film — 8mm and 16mm cameras, editing equipment, sound recording equipment, lighting equipment, projectors, screening room, editing room, permanent film library Television — complete black and white studio and exterior production equipment, complete color studio production equipment, black and white studio, color studio, audio studio, control room
FACULTY John Allyn, Doris Brewer, Tom Burrows, Fred Kuretski, Sid Salkow, John Schultheiss, Don Wood PART-TIME FACULTY Anthony Allegro, Jim Briley, Peter Leu

COURSE LIST

Undergraduate

Radio-Television-Film Performance
Radio Workshop
Introduction to Writing for Television and Film
Radio-Television-Film Activities
Television Production
Television Operations/Controls
Fundamentals of Film Production
Mass Communication Arts
Design of the Mass Media Message
History of Broadcasting
Film as Literature
History of American Cinema
Writing for Broadcasting and Film
Program Production
Advanced Dramatic and Documentary Radio Production
Television Techniques
Cinematography and Editing
Radio-Television Advertising
Process and Effects of the Mass Media
Mass Communication Research
International Broadcasting
Advanced Film Theory: Studies in Film Style
Analysis of Classic Film Makers
Criticism in Broadcast Media
Advanced Writing for Broadcasting and Film
Television Directing
Directing the Television Documentary
Directing the Television Drama and Variety Program
Television Film Production
Advanced Television Film Production
Film Directing
Public Broadcasting
Instructional Television
Principles of Mediated Programmed Instruction
Administration of Educational Media Programs
Audience Analysis
Radio-Television Programming
Network Practices
Government Regulation of Broadcasting
Field Study
Selected Topics in Radio-Television-Film
Internships

Graduate

Seminar in Research Methods
Seminar in Film Theory
Seminar in Analysis of Media Performance I, II
Seminar in the Future of Mass Communication
Research Practicum
Department Colloquium
Studies in Mass Communication
Television-Film Aesthetics

Undergraduate and Graduate

Introduction to Mass Communication Arts
Introduction to Radio and Television

California State University, Sacramento

State-supported comprehensive coed institution. Part of California State University and Colleges System. Institutionally accredited by regional association, programs recognized by NASM, AACSB, NASA. Urban location, 288-acre campus. Total enrollment: 20,563. Undergraduate enrollment: 15,572. Total faculty: 1000. Semester calendar. Grading system: letters or numbers.

Art Department, 6000 J Street, Sacramento, CA 95819 916-454-6166

CONTACT Jim Kallett or Philip Hitchcock, Chairman
PROGRAMS OFFERED Interdepartmental film minor; BA, special major, arts and sciences, with emphasis in film (by petition)
DEPARTMENTAL MAJORS Film — 4 students
FINANCIAL AID Work/study programs
CURRICULAR EMPHASIS Film study — criticism and aesthetics Filmmaking — (1) experimental; (2) animated

California State University, Sacramento (continued)

SPECIAL ACTIVITIES/OFFERINGS Filmmaking clubs, film series, film symposium, guest film-related artists, independent study
FACILITIES AND EQUIPMENT Film — 8mm cameras, 16mm cameras, editing equipment, sound recording equipment, lighting, projectors, sound mixing room, animation board, permanent film library of commercial or professional films, optical printer
FACULTY Jim Kallett, Roger Vail

COURSE LIST

Undergraduate
Cinematography
Special Effects: Optical Printing for Filmmaking
The Moving Image
Photo/Cinema Studio

Cañada College

District-supported 2-year coed college. Part of San Mateo County Community College District System. Institutionally accredited by regional association. Suburban location, 131-acre campus. Undergraduate enrollment: 7613. Total faculty: 253 (116 full-time, 137 part-time). Semester calendar. Grading system: letters or numbers.

English Department, Humanities Division, 4200 Farmhill Boulevard, Redwood City, CA 94061 415-364-1212

CONTACT William C Kenney
CURRICULAR EMPHASIS Undergraduate film study — history, criticism and aesthetics, appreciation treated equally Undergraduate filmmaking — (1) narrative; (2) educational
SPECIAL ACTIVITIES/OFFERINGS Film series
FACILITIES AND EQUIPMENT Film — 8mm cameras, editing equipment, sound recording equipment, black and white film stock, color film stock, projectors, 16mm editing equipment, projectors, editing room, permanent film library of student films Television — ½-inch VTR
FACULTY William C Kenney

COURSE LIST

Undergraduate
Film Study

Cerritos College

State and locally supported 2-year coed college. Institutionally accredited by regional association. Suburban location. Undergraduate enrollment: 21,426. Total faculty: 700 (265 full-time, 435 part-time). Semester calendar. Grading system: letters or numbers.

Theatre Department, 11110 East Alondra Boulevard, Norwalk, CA 90650 213-860-2451

CONTACT Frank G Bock
DEPARTMENTAL MAJORS Undergraduate film — 4 students Undergraduate television — 3 students
FINANCIAL AID Work/study programs, student loans
CURRICULAR EMPHASIS Undergraduate film study — history, appreciation treated equally Undergraduate television study — history, production treated equally Undergraduate television production — experimental/personal video, educational treated equally
FACILITIES AND EQUIPMENT Film — 8mm cameras, editing equipment, lighting, projectors, 16mm projectors Television — black and white studio cameras, ½-inch VTR, ¾-inch cassette VTR, portable black and white cameras, editing equipment, monitors, special effects generators, ½-inch portapak recorders, lighting equipment, sound recording equipment

COURSE LIST

Undergraduate
Motion Picture, Radio, TV
Introduction to Broadcasting
Television Production
Appreciation and History of the Motion Picture
Motion Picture Production

Chapman College

Independent comprehensive coed institution affiliated with Disciples of Christ Church. Institutionally accredited by regional association. Suburban location, 33-acre campus. Total enrollment: 1707. Undergraduate enrollment: 1252. Total faculty: 167 (97 full-time, 70 part-time). 4-1-4 calendar. Grading system: letters or numbers.

Communications Department, 333 North Glassell, Orange, CA 92666 714-997-6856

CONTACT Ron Thronson, Chairman
DEGREE OFFERED BA in communications with emphasis in drama, mass media, or public relations
DEPARTMENTAL MAJORS Film — 10–12 students Television — 25–35 students
ADMISSION Requirements — ACT or SAT scores
FINANCIAL AID Scholarships, work/study programs, student loans Application deadline — 7/15
CURRICULAR EMPHASIS Film study — history, criticism and aesthetics, appreciation, educational media/instructional technology treated equally Filmmaking — documentary, narrative, experimental, features treated equally Television study — production, history, criticism and aesthetics, management treated equally Television production — commercial, news/documentary, experimental/personal video, educational, features and special events treated equally
SPECIAL ACTIVITIES/OFFERINGS Filmmaking clubs; film series; film festivals; film societies; program material produced for on-campus closed-circuit television, cable television, local public television station; apprenticeships; internships in film production; internships in television production; independent study

FACILITIES AND EQUIPMENT Film — complete 16mm equipment, sound stage, screening room, 35mm screening facilities, editing room, sound mixing room, permanent film library of student films, permanent film library of commercial or professional films Television — black and white studio cameras, color studio cameras, ½-inch VTR, ¾-inch cassette VTR, portable black and white cameras, editing equipment, monitors, special effects generators, slide chain, portable color cameras, ½-inch portapak recorders, ¾-inch ENG, lighting equipment, sound recording equipment, audio mixers, film chain, black and white studio, color studio, mobile van/unit

COURSE LIST
Undergraduate
TV Production
TV Field Production
TV Project
TV Documentary Production
History of Film
Film Aesthetics
International Film
Film Genre Studies
Film Production
Film Workshops I, II

City College of San Francisco

State and locally supported 2-year coed college. Institutionally accredited by regional association. Urban location. Total enrollment: 25,498. Total faculty: 800. Semester calendar. Grading system: letters or numbers.

Photography and Film Production Department, 50 Phelan Avenue, San Francisco, CA 94112 415-239-3651 or 415-239-3422

CONTACT Dick Ham
DEGREES OFFERED AS in film production, AA in film production
DEPARTMENTAL MAJORS 159 students
FINANCIAL AID Scholarships, work/study programs, student loans
CURRICULAR EMPHASIS Film study — (1) appreciation; (2) educational media/instructional technology; (3) history, criticism and aesthetics Filmmaking — (1) educational; (2) documentary, narrative (sound), industrial; (3) experimental, animated
SPECIAL ACTIVITIES/OFFERINGS Filmmaking clubs, film series, film festivals, student publications, independent study, vocational placement service
FACILITIES AND EQUIPMENT Film — 8mm cameras, editing equipment, lighting, projectors, 16mm cameras, editing equipment, sound recording equipment, lighting, black and white film stock, color film stock, projectors, screening room, editing room, sound mixing room, animation board, permanent film library of student films, permanent film library of commercial or professional films Television — ½-inch VTR, portable black and white cameras, monitors, ½-inch portapak recorders, lighting equipment, sound recording equipment, audio mixers
FACULTY Dick Ham PART-TIME FACULTY Todd Flinchbaugh, Este Gardener, Celia Lighthill, Brian Szabo

COURSE LIST
Undergraduate
Basic Cinematography
Film History: Evolution of Film Expression
Film History: Contemporary Film Expression
Pre-Production Planning
Editing of Motion Pictures
Cinematography
Lighting
Sound for Motion Pictures
Directing Motion Pictures
Film Production Workshop
Cinematography Laboratory
Special Effects

Broadcasting Department 415-239-3525

CONTACT Henry Leff
DEGREES OFFERED AA, AS in communication arts
DEPARTMENTAL MAJORS 50 students
CURRICULAR EMPHASIS Television study — (1) production; (2) history; (3) criticism and aesthetics Television production — (1) commercial; (2) news/documentary; (3) educational
SPECIAL ACTIVITIES/OFFERINGS Program material produced for on-campus closed-circuit television and cable television, internships in television production
FACILITIES AND EQUIPMENT Television — complete black and white and exterior production equipment, complete color studio and exterior production equipment, black and white studio, color studio, audio studio, control rooms
FACULTY Robert Berke, Phillip Brown, Henry Leff PART-TIME FACULTY Sidney Diamond, David Grieve, George Heuga, David Martin, Francine Podenski

COURSE LIST
Undergraduate
Introduction to Broadcasting
Broadcast Audio Operations
Broadcast Audio Production
Broadcast Field Experience
Announcing
Black Communications
Television Studio Operations
Television Studio Techniques
Television Production
Mass Media

Claremont Men's College

Independent 4-year college, coed as of 1976. Part of The Claremont Colleges. Institutionally accredited by regional association. Suburban location, 40-acre campus. Undergraduate enrollment: 865. Total faculty: 99. Semester calendar. Grading system: letters or numbers.

Claremont, CA 91711 714-621-8088

CONTACT Michael Riley

College of Alameda

District-supported 2-year coed college. Part of Peralta Community College System. Institutionally accredited by regional association. Urban location, 64-acre campus. Undergraduate enrollment: 7219. Total faculty: 220 (95 full-time, 125 part-time). Quarter calendar. Grading system: letters or numbers.

College of Alameda (continued)

Fine, Applied, and Language Arts Division, 555 Atlantic Avenue, Alameda, CA 94501 415-522-7221

CONTACT Barbara Cannon
ADMISSION Application deadline — rolling
CURRICULAR EMPHASIS Film study — criticism and aesthetics, production treated equally Filmmaking — (1) narrative; (2) documentary Television study — (1) production; (2) criticism and aesthetics; (3) history
FACILITIES AND EQUIPMENT Film — 8mm cameras, editing equipment, screening room, editing space
FACULTY Stanley Shaff

COURSE LIST
Undergraduate
Theory of Film
Filmmaking

College of Marin

State-supported 2-year coed college. Institutionally accredited by regional association. Undergraduate enrollment: 6100. Semester calendar. Grading system: letters or numbers.

Communications Department, Kentfield, CA 94704 415-485-9363

CONTACT Film — David Newby Television — Wendy Blair
DEGREE OFFERED AA in film or television
DEPARTMENTAL MAJORS Film — 25 students Television — 40 students
ADMISSION Requirement — interviews
FINANCIAL AID Work/study programs
CURRICULAR EMPHASIS Film study — (1) production; (2) appreciation; (3) criticism and aesthetics Filmmaking — (1) experimental; (2) narrative; (3) animated Television study — (1) production; (2) educational; (3) appreciation Television production — (1) experimental/personal video; (2) educational; (3) news/documentary
SPECIAL ACTIVITIES/OFFERINGS Filmmaking clubs; film series; film festivals; film societies; program material produced for on-campus closed-circuit television, cable television, local public television station; independent study

College of Notre Dame

Independent Roman Catholic comprehensive coed institution. Institutionally accredited by regional association, programs recognized by NASM. Suburban location, 100-acre campus. Total enrollment: 1232. Undergraduate enrollment: 910. Total faculty: 114 (60 full-time, 54 part-time). 4-1-4 calendar. Grading system: letters or numbers.

English Department, Belmont, CA 94002 415-593-1601

CONTACT Terry Andrews
PROGRAM OFFERED Only course offered — Language of Film — may be taken to satisfy requirements for general education (humanities) or for the English or art major
FINANCIAL AID Scholarships, work/study programs, student loans
CURRICULAR EMPHASIS Film study — (1) appreciation; (2) criticism and aesthetics; (3) history
SPECIAL ACTIVITIES/OFFERINGS Film series
FACILITIES AND EQUIPMENT Film — screening room
FACULTY Terry Andrews

COURSE LIST
Undergraduate
Language of Film

College of San Mateo

State and locally supported 2-year coed college. Institutionally accredited by regional association. Suburban location. Undergraduate enrollment: 3942. Total faculty: 750. Semester calendar. Grading system: letters or numbers.

Film Department, 1700 West Hillsdale Boulevard, San Mateo, CA 94402 415-574-6349

CONTACT Richard Williamson
DEGREE OFFERED AA in film
DEPARTMENTAL MAJORS 25 students
ADMISSION Requirement — written statement of purpose Application deadline — rolling
FINANCIAL AID Work/study programs
CURRICULAR EMPHASIS Film study — (1) production; (2) criticism and aesthetics; (3) appreciation Filmmaking — (1) experimental; (2) narrative; (3) animated; (4) documentary
SPECIAL ACTIVITIES/OFFERINGS Filmmaking clubs, film series, independent study, practicum, teacher training (in cooperation with San Francisco State University)
FACILITIES AND EQUIPMENT Film — complete 8mm equipment, 16mm cameras, editing equipment, sound recording equipment, lighting equipment, projectors, sound stage, screening room, editing room, sound mixing room, animation board, access to privately owned library of over 4000 films
FACULTY John Cafferata, Joe Price, Larry Steward, Richard Williamson

COURSE LIST
Undergraduate
Special Projects in Filmmaking
Film Production I–IV
Film History and Aesthetics I, II

Telecommunications Department

CONTACT Doug Montgomery
DEGREES OFFERED AA in television broadcasting, AA in broadcast engineering
FINANCIAL AID Work/study programs
CURRICULAR EMPHASIS Television study — (1) production; (2) educational; (3) technical Television production — (1) commercial; (2) educational; (3) news/documentary
SPECIAL ACTIVITIES/OFFERINGS Program material produced for on-campus closed-circuit television, local public television station, local commercial television station; vocational placement service
FACILITIES AND EQUIPMENT Film — 16mm editing equipment, lighting equipment, black and white film stock, projectors, editing room, sound mixing room Television — complete black and white studio and exterior production equipment, black and white studio, mobile van unit, audio studio, control room
PART-TIME FACULTY Don Beaty, Sue Blumenberg, Ed Cosci, Jim Monroe, Doug Montgomery, Dan Odum, Flip Prindle, Bernie Rausch, Bob Vainowski

COURSE LIST
Undergraduate
Introduction to Broadcasting
Technical Operations and Maintenance
News Writing
Motion Picture Production
Broadcast Announcing
Commercial Licenses
Projects in Television
Television Studio Techniques
Selected Topics
Cooperative Education

College of the Desert

State and locally supported 2-year coed college. Part of California Community Colleges System. Institutionally accredited by regional association. Small town location. Undergraduate enrollment: 9300. Total faculty: 270 (110 full-time, 160 part-time). Semester calendar. Grading system: letters or numbers.

Communications Department, 43-500 Monterey Avenue, Palm Desert, CA 92260 714-346-8041

CONTACT Roy Wilson
DEGREES OFFERED AA in television
DEPARTMENTAL MAJORS 5 students
ADMISSION Application deadline — 8/15, rolling
CURRICULAR EMPHASIS Film study — production Filmmaking — depends upon current student interest Television study — production Television production — depends upon current student interest
SPECIAL ACTIVITIES/OFFERINGS Film series, film festivals, program material produced for on-campus closed-circuit television, apprenticeships, internships in film and television production, independent study, vocational placement service
FACILITIES AND EQUIPMENT Film — 8mm cameras, lighting equipment, projectors, screening room Television — complete black and white studio and exterior production facilities, complete color exterior production facilities
FACULTY Roy Wilson PART-TIME FACULTY Mike Klasey, Joyce Wade-Maltais

COURSE LIST
Undergraduate
The Motion Picture: History and Criticism
Introduction to Broadcasting
Television Production
Radio and Television Writing
Advanced Television Production
Television Production Workshop
Radio and Television Announcing

College of the Redwoods

State and locally supported 2-year coed college. Part of California Community Colleges System. Institutionally accredited by regional association. Rural location. Undergraduate enrollment: 8160. Total faculty: 120 full-time. Quarter calendar. Grading system: letters or numbers.

Creative Arts Department, Tompkins Hill Road, Eureka, CA 95501 707-448-8411

CONTACT Film — Geoffrey de Valois Television — St Clair B Adams
DEGREES OFFERED AA in telecommunications
DEPARTMENTAL MAJORS 5 students
ADMISSION Requirement — minimum grade point average
FINANCIAL AID Student loans, work/study programs
CURRICULAR EMPHASIS Film study — criticism and aesthetics, production treated equally Filmmaking — (1) experimental; (2) narrative; (3) documentary Television study — (1) production; (2) appreciation; (3) criticism and aesthetics Television production — (1) educational; (2) news/documentary; (3) experimental/personal video
SPECIAL ACTIVITIES/OFFERINGS Program material produced for on-campus closed-circuit television, local public television station, local commercial television station
FACILITIES AND EQUIPMENT Film — complete 8mm equipment Television — complete black and white studio production equipment, complete color studio production equipment, black and white studio, color studio, control room
PART-TIME FACULTY St Clair B Adams, Geoffrey de Valois, Fred Endert

COURSE LIST
Undergraduate
Television Production I, II
Television Directing
Cinema Production I, II
Film Appreciation
Film Literature

College of the Sequoias

State and locally supported 2-year coed college. Part of California Community Colleges System. Institutionally accredited by regional association. Small town location. Undergraduate enrollment: 7068. Total faculty: 160. Semester calendar. Grading system: letters or numbers.

College of the Sequoias (continued)

Drama Department, Mooney Boulevard, Visalia, CA 93277 209-733-2050

CONTACT George C Pappas
CURRICULAR EMPHASIS Film study — (1) appreciation; (2) criticism and aesthetics; (3) history
FACULTY Noble Johnson, Paul Jones

COURSE LIST
Undergraduate
Cinema I, II: Film Appreciation

Columbia College–Hollywood

Independent 4-year coed college. Accredited, National Association of Trade and Technical Schools. Urban location. Total enrollment: 300. Total faculty: 35. Quarter calendar. Grading system: letters.

Department of Cinema, 925 North LaBrea Avenue, Hollywood, CA 90038 213-851-0550

CONTACT Director of Admissions
DEGREE OFFERED BA in cinema
DEPARTMENTAL MAJORS Undergraduate — 125 students
ADMISSION Undergraduate requirements — 2.0 minimum grade point average, interviews, professional recommendations, teachers' recommendations
FINANCIAL AID Scholarships, loans, grants
CURRICULAR EMPHASIS Film study — (1) production; (2) technology; (3) criticism and aesthetics Filmmaking — (1) narrative; (2) documentary; (3) industrial/sales
SPECIAL ACTIVITIES/OFFERINGS Practicum, professional seminars
FACILITIES AND EQUIPMENT Film — complete 8mm and 16mm equipment, sound recording equipment, lighting equipment, projectors, sound stage, screening room, 35mm screening facilities, editing room, sound mixing room, permanent film library, script library
PART-TIME FACULTY Bruce Block, Charles Dugger, Norman Jacob, William Mayhew, William Navarro, Ernest Nukanin, Edmund Penney, Ron Peterson, Charles Sladen, Donald Sylvester, Harry Thomas, Leland Thomas, Donald Thompson, Ross Wylie

COURSE LIST
Undergraduate
Cinematography I—III
Film and Laboratory Science
Motion Picture Sound I, II
Motion Picture Editing I, II
Sound Effects and Music Editing
Motion Picture Directing
Studio Production
Motion Picture Design
Screenwriting
Videotape Editing
Stagecraft
Introduction to Videotape Recording
Videotape Production
Motion Picture Makeup
Motion Picture Production Workshop
Entertainment Law
Entertainment Packaging
Production Budgeting
Motion Picture Analysis
Motion Picture History
Practicum in Motion Picture Production
The Documentary Motion Picture

Department of Broadcasting

CONTACT Director of Admissions
DEGREES OFFERED AA, BA in broadcasting
DEPARTMENTAL MAJORS Undergraduate — 150 students
ADMISSION Undergraduate requirements — 2.0 minimum grade point average, interviews, professional recommendations, teachers' recommendations
FINANCIAL AID Scholarships, loans, grants
CURRICULAR EMPHASIS Undergraduate television study — (1) production; (2) engineering; (3) journalism
SPECIAL ACTIVITIES/OFFERINGS Internships in television production, practicum
FACILITIES AND EQUIPMENT Television — complete color studio production equipment, color studio, audio studio, control room, news room
PART-TIME FACULTY David Boston, Larry Boxert, Joseph Cala, Richard Clayton, Anthony Georgilas, Willis Hawkins, Boris Isaacson, Rob Keif, Joan Lence, William Mayhew, Ellen Miller, Robert Miller, William Navarro, Luther Newby, Jeff O'Den, Lawrence Punter, Christopher Roth, Petar Sardelich, Andrew Trentacosta

COURSE LIST
Undergraduate
News Department Structure and Operation
Photojournalism
Journalistic Ethics and Practices
Reporting
Public Relations
Newswriting Laboratory
Investigative Reporting
Editorial Writing
Radio and Television Sports Reporting
Feature Assignment
Television Station Operation
Television Production I–III
Television Directing
Broadcasting: Structure and Economy
Principles of Broadcast Technology
Pictorial Composition and Graphics
Television Studio Facility Operation
Television Announcing
Television Copywriting
Broadcast Law
Television Studio Lighting
Television Program Budgeting
Television Filmcraft
Television Makeup
Production Design and Stagecraft
Advertising and Sales
Station Programming and Operations
Promotion
FCC Test Preparation
Fundamentals of Video
Studio Operation
Broadcast Audio
Control Room Operation
Videotape Recording
Station Operation
Station Financing and Construction
Station Organization and Management
Community Relations
Principles of Business Management
Censorship and the Broadcaster
Videotape Editing
Videotape Production

Cosumnes River College

District-supported 2-year coed college. Part of Los Rios Community College District System. Institutionally accredited by regional association. Suburban location, 50-acre campus. Undergraduate enrollment: 4872. Total faculty: 194 (76 full-time, 118 part-time). Semester calendar. Grading system: letters or numbers.

Communications Department, 8401 Center Parkway, Sacramento, CA 95823 916-421-1000

CONTACT Film — Harry Wood Television — Doree Steinmann
DEGREE OFFERED AA in communications media
DEPARTMENTAL MAJORS 160 students
ADMISSION Application deadline — 8/6
FINANCIAL AID Scholarships, work/study programs, student loans
CURRICULAR EMPHASIS Film study — (1) appreciation; (2) history; (3) production Television study — production Television production — (1) educational; (2) experimental/personal video; (3) news/documentary; (4) commercial
SPECIAL ACTIVITIES/OFFERINGS Film series; program material produced for on-campus closed-circuit television, local public television station, local commercial television station; internships in television production; independent study; vocational placement service
FACILITIES AND EQUIPMENT Film — complete 8mm equipment, editing room, sound mixing room, permanent film library Television — complete color exterior production facilities, complete color studio production equipment, color studio, audio studio, control room
FACULTY Richard Baldwin, Mauvra Osborn, Doree Steinmann, Harry Wood PART-TIME FACULTY Alan Hinderstein, Howard Lowe

COURSE LIST
Undergraduate
Mass Media Theory and Technology
Television Studio Operations
Introduction to Broadcasting
Broadcast Announcing and Writing
Television Production
Advanced Television Production
Broadcast Journalism
Filmmaking
Art of the Cinema
Multi-Media Graphics
Multi-Media Production
Work Experience
Photography Appreciation

Cypress College

State-supported 2-year coed college. Institutionally accredited by regional association. Urban location. Undergraduate enrollment: 12,750. Total faculty: 430. Semester calendar. Grading system: letters or numbers.

Photography Department, 9200 Valley View, Cypress, CA 90630 714-826-2220

CONTACT John Wycoff
ADMISSION Requirement — completion of basic and intermediate photography courses Application deadline — rolling
CURRICULAR EMPHASIS Film study — production Filmmaking — (1) educational; (2) animated; (3) experimental Television study — (1) production; (2) criticism and aesthetics; (3) educational Television production — (1) commercial; (2) news/documentary; (3) experimental/personal video
SPECIAL ACTIVITIES/OFFERINGS Student productions
FACILITIES AND EQUIPMENT Film — 8mm and 16mm cameras, editing equipment, lighting equipment, black and white film stock, color film stock, projectors Television — complete black and white studio production equipment, complete color studio production equipment, black and white studio, color studio, audio studio
FACULTY John Wycoff

COURSE LIST
Undergraduate
Basic Cinema
Television Production

De Anza College

State and locally supported 2-year coed college. Part of California Community Colleges System. Institutionally accredited by regional association. Urban location. Undergraduate enrollment: 13,553. Total faculty: 855 (285 full-time, 570 part-time). Quarter calendar. Grading system: letters or numbers.

Film-TV Department, 21250 Stevens Creek Boulevard, Cupertino, CA 95014 408-996-4708

CONTACT Zaki Lisha
DEGREE OFFERED AA in film-TV
DEPARTMENTAL MAJORS Undergraduate film — 30 students Undergraduate television — 10 students
ADMISSION Requirement — 2.0 minimum grade point average
FINANCIAL AID Work/study programs, student loans
CURRICULAR EMPHASIS Film study — history, criticism and aesthetics treated equally Filmmaking — documentary, narrative, animated treated equally Television production — commercial, educational treated equally
SPECIAL ACTIVITIES/OFFERINGS Film series, film festivals, independent study
FACILITIES AND EQUIPMENT Film — 8mm cameras, editing equipment, sound recording equipment, lighting, projectors, flatbeds, 16mm cameras, editing equipment, lighting, projectors, screening room, editing room, sound mixing room, animation board Television — ½-inch VTR, ¾-inch cassette VTR, portable black and white cameras, editing equipment, special effects generators, sound recording equipment, audio mixers, black and white studio
FACULTY Zaki Lisha PART-TIME FACULTY Mary Dermody, Todd Flinchbaugh, Dennis Irwin, Susan Tavernetti, Wah Ho Young

De Anza College (continued)

COURSE LIST

Undergraduate

Basic Super-8 Production
Super-8 Sound Production I, II
Filmmakers Workshop
Film Animation
Optical Printing
16mm Production
History of Film (1895-1950)
History of Film (1950-Present)
History of Film Animation
Television Workshop
Black and White Television
Color Television
Audio Production

Diablo Valley College

State and locally supported 2-year coed college. Institutionally accredited by regional association. Suburban location. Undergraduate enrollment: 20,300. Total faculty: 625. Semester calendar. Grading system: letters or numbers.

Film Department, 321 Golf Club Road, Pleasant Hill, CA 94523 415-685-1230

CONTACT Film — Gerard T Hurley Television — Gene Hambleton
DEGREE OFFERED AA in film
FINANCIAL AID Scholarships, work/study programs, student loans
CURRICULAR EMPHASIS Film study — (1) history; (2) production; (3) appreciation; (4) criticism and aesthetics; (5) educational media/instructional technology Filmmaking — (1) documentary; (2) narrative; (3) experimental; (4) educational; (5) animated Television study — (1) production; (2) management; (3) educational; (4) history Television production — (1) news/documentary; (2) commercial; (3) educational; (4) experimental/personal video
SPECIAL ACTIVITIES/OFFERINGS Film series, film festivals, program material produced for on-campus closed-circuit television and cable television, internships in television production, independent study, teacher training
FACILITIES AND EQUIPMENT Film — 8mm and 16mm cameras, editing equipment, sound recording equipment, lighting, projectors, screening room, editing room, sound mixing room, animation board, permanent film library of student films, permanent film library of commercial or professional films Television — complete black and white and color studio production equipment, complete black and white and color exterior production equipment, black and white studio, color studio, audio studio, control room
FACULTY Gene Hambleton, Gerard T Hurley, Sherry MacGregor, Ann Stewart, Clark Sturgis

COURSE LIST

Undergraduate

Introduction to Film I, II
The Short Film
16mm Workshop
Film/TV Script Writing
Writing About Film
Film Experience
TV Production Techniques
Acting on Camera
Women Through Film

Feather River College

District-supported 2-year coed college. Institutionally accredited by regional association. Rural location. Undergraduate enrollment: 871. Total faculty: 56 (21 full-time, 35 part-time). Semester calendar. Grading system: letters or numbers.

English Department, PO Box 1110, Quincy, CA 95971 916-283-0202

CONTACT Louiz Gutierrez
FACULTY Louiz Gutierrez

COURSE LIST

Undergraduate

Film Appreciation

Foothill Community College

District-supported 2-year coed college. Part of Foothill/DeAnza Community College District System. Institutionally accredited by regional association. Suburban location, 122-acre campus. Undergraduate enrollment: 16,347. Total faculty: 545 (195 full-time, 350 part-time). Quarter calendar. Grading system: letters or numbers.

Film and Television Department, 12345 El Monte Road, Los Altos, CA 94022 415-948-8590

CONTACT Stuart Roe
DEGREES OFFERED AA in television, AA in film
DEPARTMENTAL MAJORS Film — 20 students Television — 30 students
ADMISSION Application deadline — rolling
FINANCIAL AID Scholarships, student loans, work/study programs, teaching assistantships
CURRICULAR EMPHASIS Film study — (1) production; (2) appreciation; (3) history Filmmaking — (1) narrative; (2) documentary; (3) experimental; (4) animated Television study — (1) production; (2) appreciation; (3) educational Television production — (1) news/documentary; (2) educational; (3) commercial
SPECIAL ACTIVITIES/OFFERINGS Film series, film festivals, film societies, program material produced for on-campus closed-circuit television, apprenticeships, independent study
FACILITIES AND EQUIPMENT Film — complete 8mm and 16mm equipment, sound stage, screening room, editing room, sound mixing room, animation board, permanent film library Television — complete black and white studio and exterior production equipment, complete color studio and exterior production facilities, black and white studio, mobile van/unit, audio studio, control room
FACULTY Zaki Lisha, Stuart Roe PART-TIME FACULTY Douglas Droese, Todd Flinchbaugh, Jack Hasling, Brian Szabo

COURSE LIST
Undergraduate
Film Analysis
Film Production
Television Production
Film Animation
Introduction to Broadcasting
Broadcast Journalism
Television-Film Writing

Grossmont College

State and locally supported 2-year coed college. Part of California Community Colleges System. Institutionally accredited by regional association, programs recognized by AACSB. Suburban location, 135-acre campus. Undergraduate enrollment: 14,928. Total faculty: 659 (299 full-time, 360 part-time). Semester calendar. Grading system: letters or numbers.

Telecommunications Department, El Cajon, CA 92020 714-465-1700

CONTACT J D Scouller
DEGREES OFFERED AA, AS in telecommunications
DEPARTMENTAL MAJORS Film — 35 students Television — 145 students
FINANCIAL AID Work/study programs, student loans
CURRICULAR EMPHASIS Film study — (1) appreciation; (2) criticism and aesthetics; (3) history Filmmaking — (1) documentary; (2) narrative; (3) educational Television study — (1) production; (2) management; (3) educational Television production — (1) commercial; (2) educational; (3) industrial/business
SPECIAL ACTIVITIES/OFFERINGS Program material produced for on-campus closed-circuit television and cable television, internships in television production
FACILITIES AND EQUIPMENT Film — complete 8mm and 16mm equipment, screening room, editing room, permanent film library of commercial or professional films Television — black and white studio cameras, color studio cameras, ½-inch VTR, ¾-inch cassette VTR, portable black and white cameras, editing equipment, monitors, special effects generators, slide chain, portable color cameras, ½-inch portapak recorders, lighting equipment, sound recording equipment, audio mixers, film chain, time base corrector, character generators, black and white studio, mobile van/unit, remote truck, audio studio, control room
FACULTY Keith Bryden, Gay Russell, J D Scouller PART-TIME FACULTY Anthony Kretovicz, Francis Seeley, D Settel

COURSE LIST
Undergraduate
Introduction to Broadcasting
Audio Studio Operations
Television Studio Operations
Announcing Skills
Beginning Television Production
Advanced Television Production
Filmmaking for Television
Advanced Filmmaking for Television
Educational Television Workshop
Script Writing for Radio-Television-Film
Broadcast Management
Broadcast Internship

Laney College

District-supported 2-year coed college. Part of Peralta Community College System. Institutionally accredited by regional association. Urban location. Semester calendar. Grading system: letters or numbers

Media Communications–Photography Department, 900 Fallon Street, Oakland, CA 94606 415-834-5740, ext 955 or ext 315

CONTACT Film — Billy Nall Television — Roger Ferragallo
DEGREES OFFERED AA in TV production, TV broadcasting, and TV engineering
DEPARTMENTAL MAJORS Television — 150 students
FINANCIAL AID Work/study programs, student loans, instructional aids, Channel S student managers
CURRICULAR EMPHASIS Film study — (1) educational media/instructional technology; (2) criticism and aesthetics Filmmaking — (1) documentary; (2) commercial; (3) narrative Television study — appreciation, educational, production, management, engineering treated equally Television production — commercial, news/documentary, experimental/personal video, educational, local origination TV programming treated equally
SPECIAL ACTIVITIES/OFFERINGS Film series; program material produced for on-campus closed-circuit television, cable television, local public television station; apprenticeships; internships in television production; independent study; vocational placement service; work experience on Channel S
FACILITIES AND EQUIPMENT Film — 8mm cameras, editing equipment, sound recording equipment, lighting, projectors, 16mm cameras, editing equipment, lighting, projectors, sound stage, editing room, sound mixing room, animation board Television — complete black and white and color studio production equipment, complete black and white and color exterior production equipment, black and white studio, color studio, audio studio, control room, cable channel
FACULTY Roger Ferragallo, Billy Nall, Earl Robinson, Bernie Scharlach PART-TIME FACULTY Dean Freeman, Robert Fuller

COURSE LIST
Undergraduate
Cinematography: Basic Techniques
Cinematography: Advanced Production
TV Production
TV Advanced Production
TV Broadcasting
TV Drama Directing and Acting
TV Systems Operation
TV Systems Operation Advanced
TV Electronics
TV/Radio Broadcasting

Loma Linda University, La Sierra Campus

Independent Seventh-Day Adventist comprehensive coed institution. Administratively affiliated with Loma Linda University. Institutionally accredited by regional association. Suburban location, 40-acre campus. Total enrollment: 2560.Undergraduate enrollment: 2212. Total faculty: 174 (140 full-time, 34 part-time). Quarter calendar. Grading system: letters or numbers.

Loma Linda University, La Sierra Campus (continued)

Department of Communication, 4700 Pierce, Riverside, CA 92515 714-785-2159 or 714-785-2169

CONTACT Larry Arany
DEGREE OFFERED BA in mass media
ADMISSION Requirements — 2.0 minimum grade point average, ACT or SAT scores, interview, teachers' recommendations
FINANCIAL AID Scholarships, work/study programs, student loans
CURRICULAR EMPHASIS Filmmaking — (1) documentary; (2) narrative; (3) experimental and animated treated equally Television study — (1) management; (2) production Television production — news/documentary, educational treated equally
SPECIAL ACTIVITIES/OFFERINGS Film series, student publications, internships in film production, internships in television production, independent study, vocational placement service
FACILITIES AND EQUIPMENT Film — 8mm cameras, editing equipment, sound recording equipment, lighting, projectors, double system sound—Super-8, screening room, editing room, sound mixing room Television — ¾-inch ENG, lighting equipment, sound recording equipment, audio mixers, audio studio

COURSE LIST

Undergraduate

Fundamentals of Cinemotography
Advanced Film Production
Documentary Film Production I, II
Television Production I, II
Script Writing
Internship
Practicum

Long Beach City College

State and locally supported 2-year coed college. Institutionally accredited by regional agency. Suburban location. Total enrollment: 29,000. Total faculty: 1211. Semester calendar. Grading system: letters or numbers.

Film Department, 4901 East Carson Street, Long Beach, CA 90808 213-420-4279

CONTACT Shashin Desai
DEGREE OFFERED AA
DEPARTMENTAL MAJORS Film — 125 students
ADMISSION Requirements — teachers' recommendations, written statement of purpose
FINANCIAL AID Scholarships, work/study programs, student loans
CURRICULAR EMPHASIS Film study — history, appreciation treated equally Filmmaking — narrative, experimental, animated treated equally
SPECIAL ACTIVITIES/OFFERINGS Filmmaking clubs, film festivals, internships in film production
FACILITIES AND EQUIPMENT Film — 8mm and 16mm cameras, editing equipment, sound recording equipment, lighting, projectors, screening room, editing room, sound mixing room, permanent film library of commercial or professional films

COURSE LIST

Undergraduate

Introduction to Film
Film Comedy
Women in Film
Science Fiction Film
Gangster Film
American Classics
Musicals
Film Production
Advanced Film Production
Stage and Screen Writing
Special Projects

Los Angeles City College

District-supported 2-year coed college. Part of Los Angeles Community College District System. Institutionally accredited by regional association. Urban location. Undergraduate enrollment: 20,058. Total faculty: 905 (300 full-time, 605 part-time). Semester calendar. Grading system: letters or numbers.

Radio-TV-Film Department, 855 North Vermont Avenue, Los Angeles, CA 90029 213-663-9141

CONTACT James Bentley, Chairman
DEGREES OFFERED AA in television, AA in cinema, AA in radio broadcasting
DEPARTMENTAL MAJORS Film — 110 students Television — 180 students
ADMISSION Application deadline 9/1
FINANCIAL AID Work/study programs, student loans, teaching assistantships Application deadline — 5/15
CURRICULAR EMPHASIS Film study — history, criticism and aesthetics, appreciation treated equally Filmmaking — documentary, narrative, animated treated equally Television study — history, criticism and aesthetics, appreciation, educational, production, management treated equally Television production — commercial, news/documentary, educational treated equally
SPECIAL ACTIVITIES/OFFERINGS Filmmaking clubs; film series; film festivals; program material produced for on-campus closed-circuit television, local public television station, local commercial television station; internships in film production; internships in television production; independent study
FACILITIES AND EQUIPMENT Film — complete 8mm and 16mm equipment, 35mm cameras, editing equipment, sound recording equipment, screening rooms, sound stage, screening room, 35mm screening facilities, editing room, sound mixing room, animation boards, permanent film library of commercial or professional films Television — complete color studio and exterior production equipment, color studio, audio studio, control room, ENG and EFP facilities
FACULTY John Acken, James Bentley, George Bowden, Charles Edwards, Jean-Pierre Geuens, Jerry Hendrix, Robert Smith, Robert Stahley, Richard Stanton, Tom Stempel PART-TIME FACULTY Tom Avery, Norman Cobb, Bruce Cook, Shelly Katz, Joe Nixon, Vaughn Obern, Petar Sardelich, David Schmoeller, James Ursini, Anthony Zaza

COURSE LIST

Undergraduate

Introduction to Motion Picture Production Techniques
Beginning Motion Picture Workshop
History of the Motion Picture
History of the Documentary Film
Introduction to Screenwriting
Motion Picture Photography
Advanced Motion Picture Photography
Current Practices in the Motion Picture Industry
Motion Picture and Television Sound
Introduction to Film Directing
Motion Picture Editing
Workshop in the Animation Film
Workshop in the Short Fiction Film
Workshop in the Documentary Film
Contemporary Film Trends
Business Aspects of Motion Picture Production
Contemporary French Cinema
Introduction to Multi-Media Production
Advanced Multi-Media Production
Television Program Orientation
Current Practices in the Television Industry
Television Camera Lighting and Sound
Studio and Remote Production
Television Announcing
Introduction to Television and Film Equipment Procedures
Television and Film Continuity Writing
Television and Film Dramatic Writing
Television News Writing
Television Production
Television Programming Production and Videotape Workshop
Television Production Workshop
Television-Film Actor-Director Workshop
Television Sales and Advertising
The Use of Film in Television
Color Television, Theory and Practice
Advanced Videotape, Film Project Laboratory

Los Angeles Harbor College

State and locally supported 2-year coed college. Part of Los Angeles Community College District System. Institutionally accredited by regional association. Suburban location, 80-acre campus. Undergraduate enrollment: 12,500. Semester calendar. Grading system: letters or numbers.

Communications Department, 1111 Figueroa Avenue, Wilmington CA 90744 213-518-1000

CONTACT Claudia Fonda-Bonardi
ADMISSION Application deadline — 9/12
CURRICULAR EMPHASIS Film study — (1) criticism and aesthetics; (2) history; (3) appreciation Filmmaking — (1) narrative; (2) experimental; (3) documentary; (4) animated Television study — (1) criticism and aesthetics; (2) history; (3) appreciation Television production — (1) news/documentary; (2) commercial; (3) experimental/personal video; (4) educational
SPECIAL ACTIVITIES/OFFERINGS Film series, program material produced for on-campus closed-circuit television
FACULTY Claudia Fonda-Bonardi, Nancy Webber

COURSE LIST

Undergraduate

Film and Literature
Images of Women in Film
Film Media

Los Angeles Pierce College

State-supported 2-year coed college. Institutionally accredited by regional association. Suburban location. Total enrollment: 21,500. Total faculty: 571 (344 full-time, 227 part-time). Semester calendar. Grading system: letters or numbers.

English Department, 6201 Winnetka, Woodland Hills, CA 91371 213-347-0551, ext 322/331

CONTACT Richard FitzGerald
DEGREE OFFERED AA in English
DEPARTMENTAL MAJORS Film — 125 students
FINANCIAL AID Scholarships, work/study programs, student loans Application deadline 9/7
CURRICULAR EMPHASIS Film study — criticism and aesthetics
SPECIAL ACTIVITIES/OFFERINGS Film series, film festivals, student publications
FACILITIES AND EQUIPMENT Film — screening room, permanent film library of commercial or professional films Television — black and white studio cameras, 1-inch VTR, portable black and white cameras, monitors, lighting equipment, sound recording equipment
FACULTY Richard FitzGerald

COURSE LIST

Undergraduate

Literature and the Motion Picture I, II

Los Angeles Southwest College

District-supported 2-year coed college. Urban location. Total enrollment: 8000. Semester calendar. Grading system: numbers.

Visual Arts Program, 1600 West Imperial Highway, Los Angeles, CA 90047 213-777-2225

CONTACT Jonathan Kuntz
DEGREES OFFERED AA in visual arts, certificate in visual arts
PROGRAM MAJORS Undergraduate film — 25 students Undergraduate television — 25 students
FINANCIAL AID Scholarships, work/study programs, student loans
CURRICULAR EMPHASIS Film study — (1) criticism and aesthetics; (2) history; (3) Black cinema Filmmaking — (1) educational; (2) documentary; (3) narrative Television study — (1) production; (2) history; (3) criticism and aesthetics Television production — (1) educational; (2) commercial; (3) news/documentary

Los Angeles Southwest College (continued)

SPECIAL ACTIVITIES/OFFERINGS Program material produced for on-campus closed-circuit television, internships in television production

FACILITIES AND EQUIPMENT Film — 8mm and 16mm cameras, editing equipment, lighting, projectors, sound stage, screening room, editing room Television — complete color studio production facilities equipment, complete color exterior production equipment, color studio, control room

FACULTY Jonathan Kuntz PART-TIME FACULTY James Desmarais

COURSE LIST

Undergraduate

Fundamentals of Film
Film Production
History of Film
Film and TV Writing
Introduction to Broadcasting
Television Production
Advanced Television Production
Black Cinema

Los Angeles Valley College

State and locally supported 2-year coed college. Part of Los Angeles Community College District System. Institutionally accredited by regional association. Urban location. Undergraduate enrollment: 22,870. Total faculty: 650 (350 full-time, 300 part-time). Semester calendar. Grading system: letters or numbers.

California

Department of Theater Arts (Film) and Department of Speech (TV), 5800 Fulton Avenue, Van Nuys, CA 91401 213-781-1200

CONTACT Film — Milton Timmons Television — Jim Eskilson

DEGREES OFFERED AA in film, AA in broadcasting; occupational certificate in film, occupational certificate in broadcasting

DEPARTMENTAL MAJORS Film — 150 students Television — 150 students

ADMISSION Application deadline — 9/15 and 2/1

FINANCIAL AID Scholarships, work/study programs, student loans

CURRICULAR EMPHASIS Film study — (1) history; (2) criticism and aesthetics Filmmaking — (1) educational; (2) narrative; (3) documentary Television study — (1) production; (2) criticism and aesthetics Television production — (1) commercial; (2) news/documentary

SPECIAL ACTIVITIES/OFFERINGS Program material produced for on-campus closed-circuit television, apprenticeships, internships in film production, internships in television production, independent study, vocational placement service

FACILITIES AND EQUIPMENT Film — complete 8mm and 16mm equipment, sound stage, screening room, editing room, sound mixing room, permanent film library of student films, permanent film library of commercial or professional films Television — complete color studio production facilities

FACULTY Milt Timmons PART-TIME FACULTY Elliott Bliss, Joe Daccurso, Hans Stern

COURSE LIST

Undergraduate

Fundamentals of Radio and Television
Voice and Diction for Radio and Television
Radio and Television Acting
Radio and Television Production
Industrial and Commercial Voice-Over Techniques
Radio and Television Activities
Radio/TV/Film Writing
TV-Film Aesthetics
Film Documentary
Television Announcing
Fundamentals of Television Production
Broadcast Fieldwork
Fundamentals of Motion Picture Production
Main Currents in Motion Pictures
Introduction to Cinema
History of Film
Beginning Camera
Motion Picture Editing
Motion Picture Workshop I, II
Advanced Cinematography
Motion Picture Sound

Loyola Marymount University

Independent Roman Catholic coed university. Institutionally accredited by regional association. Suburban location, 100-acre campus. Total enrollment: 5879. Undergraduate enrollment: 3629. Total faculty: 325 (221 full-time, 104 part-time). Semester calendar. Grading system: letters or numbers.

Communication Arts Department, 7101 West 80th Street, Los Angeles, CA 90045 213-642-3033

CONTACT Film — Michael A Callahan SJ Television — Lamar Caselli

DEGREES OFFERED BA, MA in communication arts with an emphasis in writing for film and television

DEPARTMENTAL MAJORS Undergraduate film — 120 students Undergraduate television — 120 students Undergraduate writing — 120 students Graduate film — 20 students Graduate television — 20 students Graduate writing — 30 students

ADMISSION Undergraduate requirement — ACT or SAT scores Graduate requirements — GRE scores, written statement of purpose, TOEFL for foreign students Undergraduate application deadline — rolling but limited to first 112

CURRICULAR EMPHASIS Undergraduate film study — (1) production; (2) writing; (3) history Graduate film study — (1) writing; (2) production; (3) criticism and aesthetics Filmmaking — depends upon current student interest Undergraduate television study — (1) production; (2) writing; (3) management Graduate television study — (1) writing; (2) production Television production — depends upon current student interest

SPECIAL ACTIVITIES/OFFERINGS Film series, film festivals, film societies, television productions, apprenticeships, internships in film and television production, special study, independent study, practicum, vocational placement service

FACILITIES AND EQUIPMENT Film — complete 8mm, 16mm, and 35mm equipment, sound stage, screening room, 35mm screening facilities, editing room, sound mixing room, animation board, permanent film library of student films, permanent film library of commercial or professional films Television — complete color studio production and color exterior production equipment, color studio cameras, ½-inch VTR, 2-inch VTR, ¾-inch cassette VTR, portable black and white cameras, editing equipment, monitors, special effects generators, slide chain, portable color cameras, ½-inch portapak recorders, ¾-inch ENG, lighting equipment, sound recording equipment, audio mixers, film chain, time base corrector, color studio, audio studio, control room

FACULTY Bernard V Abbene, Michael A Callahan SJ, Lamar Caselli, Patrick J Connolly SJ, Milton S Gelman, Lynne S Gross, Thomas Kelly, Warren C Sherlock, Donald Zirpola PART-TIME FACULTY Edward Anhalt, Michael Bloebaum, Charles Champlin, Ian Conner, Michael Gonzales, Boris Kaplan, Elodie Keene, Peter Krikes, Robert Merrill, Kemp Niver, Thomas Reynolds, James Thompson, Gary Zacuto, Robert Zalk, Anthony Zaza

COURSE LIST

Undergraduate

Introduction to the Communication Arts
Stagecraft for Film and Television
Survey of Mass Communications
Art of the Cinema
Beginning Film and Television Writing
Beginning Television
Beginning Radio Broadcasting
Beginning Film
Advanced Super-8 Film Production
Process and Theory of Communication
Visual Comedy
Film: The First Twenty Years
Cinema History I, II
Advanced Writing for Film and Television
Comedy Writing
Writing for Radio Broadcasting
Television Production Techniques
Remote Television Production
Television Lighting
Radio Production Techniques
Broadcast Announcing
Motion Picture Production Techniques
Motion Picture Lighting
Motion Picture Editing
Motion Picture Sound
Motion Picture Production Planning
Directing for Film and/or Television
Mass Media and Society
Politics and Mass Media
Motion Picture Analysis
Film Genres
The Art of the Cinematographer
The Films of Alfred Hitchcock
History and Criticism of Radio and Television
Advanced Writing Project
Writing for the Stage
Writing the Documentary
Adaptation: One Medium to Another
Writer's Workshop
Advanced Television Production I, II
Advanced Radio Production
Radio Management Practicum
Advanced Film Production I, II
Animation
Advanced Animation
The Documentary
Art Direction
The American Musical
Communication Practicum I, II
Senior Thesis Project

Graduate

Film: The Creative Process
Seminar in Critical Writings
Advanced Writing for Film and Television
Graduate Television Project
Graduate Film Project
Graduate Writing Project: Story Outline and First Draft
Graduate Writing Project: Second and Final Draft

Undergraduate and Graduate

Media Planning and Operations
Radio and Television Management
Effects of Mass Media
Aesthetics of Mass Media
Theories of Film Criticism
Motion Picture Lighting
Motion Picture Editing
Producing Educational Media
Directing for Film and/or Television

New College of California

Independent 4-year and professional coed institution. Institutionally accredited by regional association. Urban location. Total enrollment: 300. Undergraduate enrollment: 140. Total faculty: 20 (8 full-time, 12 part-time). Trimester calendar. Grading system: pass/fail.

777 Valencia Street, San Francisco, CA 94110 415-626-1694

CONTACT Film — Robert Edgar Television — John Luck
DEGREES OFFERED BA in film, BA in TV (video production)
PROGRAM MAJORS Film — 5 students Television — 5 students
ADMISSION Requirements — interview, written statement of purpose
FINANCIAL AID Scholarships, work/study programs, student loans, BEOG, SEOG, NDSL, FISL, CW-S, Cal Application deadline — 2/1 Cal grant, 4/15 school aid
CURRICULAR EMPHASIS Film study — history, criticism and aesthetics, appreciation, educational media/instructional technology, production, documentary production treated equally Filmmaking — documentary, narrative, experimental, educational treated equally Television study — history, criticism and aesthetics, appreciation, educational, production, management, documentary production treated equally Television production — commercial, news/documentary, experimental/personal video, educational treated equally
SPECIAL ACTIVITIES/OFFERINGS Film series, student publications, program material produced for cable television, apprenticeships, internships in film production, internships in television production, independent study
FACILITIES AND EQUIPMENT Film — 8mm cameras, sound recording equipment, projectors, 16mm projectors, 35mm editing equipment, black and white film stock Television — black and white studio cameras, color studio cameras, ¾-inch cassette VTR, portable black and white cameras, monitors, portable color cameras, ½-inch portapak recorders, sound recording equipment, color studio
FACULTY Robert Edgar, Tom Ferentz, John Luck, Joseph M Yates

COURSE LIST

Undergraduate

Film and Video Production
Video Synthesis
The Art of Seeing
Four-Week Photo Workshop

Occidental College

Independent 4-year coed college. Accredited by regional association and AICS. Urban location, 120-acre campus. Total enrollment: 1636. Undergraduate enrollment: 1602. Total faculty: 154 (114 full-time, 40 part-time). 3-3 calendar. Grading system: letters or numbers.

Theater Arts and Rhetoric Department, 1600 Campus Road, Los Angeles, CA 91042 213-259-2771

CONTACT Film — Chick Strand Television — Pier Marton
DEGREES OFFERED BA in theater arts with an emphasis in film, independent major in film or video, MA in film

Occidental College (continued)

DEPARTMENTAL MAJORS Undergraduate film — 13 students Graduate film — 1 student
ADMISSION Undergraduate requirements — 3.0 minimum grade point average, ACT or SAT scores, interview, teachers' recommendations, written statement of purpose, portfolio Graduate requirements — 3.0 minimum grade point average, GRE scores, interview, teachers' recommendations, written statement of purpose, portfolio, professional recommendations Undergraduate application deadline — 2/1
FINANCIAL AID Scholarships, work/study programs, student loans
CURRICULAR EMPHASIS Undergraduate film study — (1) criticism and aesthetics; (2) history; (3) writing Graduate film study — (1) criticism and aesthetics; (2) history; (3) writing Undergraduate filmmaking — (1) experimental; (2) documentary; (3) narrative; (4) animated Graduate filmmaking — (1) experimental; (2) documentary; (3) narrative; (4) animated Undergraduate television study — (1) production; (2) criticism and aesthetics Graduate television study — (1) production; (2) criticism and aesthetics Undergraduate television production — (1) experimental/personal video; (2) news/documentary; (3) commercial Graduate television production — (1) experimental/personal video; (2) news/documentary; (3) commercial
SPECIAL ACTIVITIES/OFFERINGS Film series, film festivals, program material produced for on-campus closed-circuit television, apprenticeships, internships in film production, internships in television production, independent study
FACILITIES AND EQUIPMENT Film — 8mm and 16mm cameras, sound recording equipment, lighting, projectors, 8mm editing equipment, screening room, editing room, sound mixing room, animation board Television — black and white studio cameras, color studio cameras, ½-inch VTR, ¾-inch cassette VTR, portable black and white cameras, editing equipment, monitors, portable color cameras, ½-inch portapak recorders, ¾-inch ENG, lighting equipment, sound recording equipment, audio mixers, black and white studio, color studio, audio studio, control room
FACULTY Marsha Kinder, Pier Marton, Chick Strand

COURSE LIST
Undergraduate and Graduate
Beginning Film Production
Advanced Production Seminar (Film)
Third World Films
Documentary Film Workshop
Ethnographic/Documentary Films
Independent Studies: Film/Video/Photography
Film Aesthetics
Personal Video
Video Diary
Creative Writing for the Screen
Beginning Photography

Orange Coast College

State and locally supported 2-year coed college. Part of Coast Community College District System. Institutionally accredited by regional association. Urban location. Undergraduate enrollment: 26,691. Total faculty: 877 (331 full-time, 546 part-time). Semester plus summer session calendar. Grading system: pass/fail.

**Film Department/Television Department, 2701 Fairview Road, Costa Mesa, CA 92626
714-556-5637**

CONTACT Film — Brian Lewis Television — Peter Scarpello
DEGREES OFFERED AA in photography–motion picture; certificate in photography–motion picture
DEPARTMENTAL MAJORS Film — 50 students Television — 160 students
ADMISSION Undergraduate application deadline — rolling
FINANCIAL AID Scholarships, work/study programs
CURRICULAR EMPHASIS Film study — (1) criticism and aesthetics; (2) appreciation; (3) history Filmmaking — (1) experimental; (2) educational; (3) documentary Television study — (1) management; (2) criticism and aesthetics; (3) history Television production — (1) commercial; (2) experimental/personal video; (3) news/documentary
SPECIAL ACTIVITIES/OFFERINGS Filmmaking clubs, film series, film festivals, independent study
FACILITIES AND EQUIPMENT Film — complete 8mm and 16mm equipment, screening room, editing room, sound mixing room, animation board Television — color studio cameras, ¾-inch cassette VTR, portable black and white cameras, editing equipment, monitors, special effects generators, slide chain, portable color cameras, ¾-inch ENG, lighting equipment, sound recording equipment, audio mixers, film chain, color studio, audio studio, control room, portapak
FACULTY Brian Lewis, Peter Scarpello PART-TIME FACULTY Jerry Lenington, R Martin, Chris McCabe, Salvatore Romeo, Olney Stewart

COURSE LIST
Undergraduate
History and Appreciation of the Cinema
Great Directors of the Cinema
Motion Picture Workshop
Basic Motion Picture Production
Advanced Film Production
Workshop in Script Writing
Theatre and TV Lighting
Preparation for TV Production
Introduction to Broadcasting
TV for Film and Art
TV Acting
Television for the Classroom
Television: The First 25 Years
Regional/International Field Studies—Broadcast Arts
Television Studio Production
Television Lab

Pasadena City College

State and locally supported 2-year coed college. Institutionally accredited by regional association. Urban location. Semester calendar. Grading system: letters or numbers.

**Communications Department, 1570 East Colorado Boulevard, Pasadena, CA 91106
213-578-7216**

CONTACT Chrystal Watson, Chairperson
DEGREES OFFERED AA in television production and direction, AA in television controls
DEPARTMENTAL MAJORS 160 students
ADMISSION Application deadline — rolling
SPECIAL ACTIVITIES/OFFERINGS Program material produced for on-campus closed-circuit television and cable television, internships in television production, independent study, practicum, vocational placement service
FACILITIES AND EQUIPMENT Television — complete color studio and exterior production equipment, color studio, mobile van/unit, remote truck, audio studio, control room
FACULTY Gerald R Finn, Anthony Georgilas, Jay Hern, Harvey Hetland, Joseph Keane, Robert Wright

COURSE LIST

Undergraduate

Television Controls Laboratory
Radio and Television Performance
Radio and Television Continuity Writing
Television Production and Direction
Radio and Television News Writing
Television and Society
Broadcast Management
Television Studio Controls
Television Script Writing
Broadcasting Rules and Regulations

Pepperdine University

Independent 4-year and professional coed institution affiliated with Church of Christ. Institutionally accredited by regional association. Suburban location, 650-acre campus. Total enrollment: 2231. Undergraduate enrollment: 2049. Total faculty: 169 (75 full-time, 94 part-time). Trimester calendar. Grading system: letters or numbers.

Communication Department, Malibu, CA 90265 213-456-4211

CONTACT Ron Whittaker, Director of Broadcasting
DEGREES OFFERED BA in broadcasting with emphases in radio production and presentation, television production and presentation, broadcast news, and broadcast sales and management; MA in Broadcast Management
DEPARTMENTAL MAJORS Undergraduate film — 30 students Undergraduate television — 175 students Graduate television — 15 students
ADMISSION Undergraduate requirements — ACT or SAT scores, writing competency test Graduate requirements — 3.0 minimum grade point average, GRE scores Undergraduate application deadline — 7/7
FINANCIAL AID Scholarships, work/study programs, student loans, fellowships, research assistantships Undergraduate application deadline — 7/1
CURRICULAR EMPHASIS Undergraduate film study — (1) production; (2) criticism and aesthetics; (3) appreciation Undergraduate filmmaking — (1) narrative; (2) documentary; (3) experimental Undergraduate television study — (1) production; (2) management; (3) criticism and aesthetics Graduate television study — (1) management; (2) production; (3) criticism and aesthetics Undergraduate television production — (1) commercial; (2) news/documentary; (3) educational
SPECIAL ACTIVITIES/OFFERINGS Program material produced for on-campus closed-circuit television and cable television, apprenticeships, internships in film production, internships in television production, independent study, vocational placement service
FACILITIES AND EQUIPMENT Film — 8 mm cameras, editing equipment, sound recording equipment, lighting, projectors, sound stage, screening room, editing room, sound mixing room Television — black and white studio cameras, color studio cameras, ½-inch VTR, ¾-inch cassette VTR, editing equipment, monitors, special effects generators, portable color cameras, ½-inch portapak recorders, lighting equipment, sound recording equipment, audio mixers, time base corrector, color studio, mobile van/unit, remote truck, audio studio, control room
FACULTY Ron Whittaker

COURSE LIST

Undergraduate

Introduction to Broadcasting
Audio Production and Announcing
Beginning Cinematography
Radio Production I, II
Television Production I, II
Advanced Cinematography
Advanced Radio Production
Broadcast Writing
Broadcast Journalism
Broadcast Issues and Programming
Advanced Broadcast News Reporting
Law of Mass Communication
Advanced Radio Production and Programming

Graduate

Seminar in Ethics Values and Legal Foundations
Graduate Practicum
Broadcast Directed Study
Communication Theory
Media Worldwide
Advanced Communication Theory

Undergraduate and Graduate

Telecommunication Production Seminar
Broadcast Management
Broadcast Internship
Media Sales
Communication Research Methods
Psychology of Communication
History and Philosophy of American Mass Media

Pitzer College

Independent 4-year coed college. Part of The Claremont Colleges. Institutionally accredited by regional association. Suburban location, 25-acre campus. Undergraduate enrollment: 740. Total faculty: 103 (55 full-time, 48 part-time). Semester calendar. Grading system: letters or numbers.

Pitzer College is one of the Claremont Colleges, a consortium of schools that participate in an intercollegiate film studies program. (See listings for Claremont Men's College and Scripps College.)

Communications Department, Milla Avenue, Claremont, CA 91711 714-626-8511

CONTACT Linda Malm
DEGREES OFFERED BA in film studies, BA in communications
DEPARTMENTAL MAJORS Film — 10 students Television — 10 students
ADMISSION Requirements — 2.0 minimum grade point average, interviews, portfolio, professional work experience, production credits Application deadline — 2/1, rolling
FINANCIAL AID Scholarships, student loans, work/study programs Application deadline — 2/1
CURRICULAR EMPHASIS Film study — (1) history, criticism and aesthetics; (2) production; (3) appreciation Filmmaking — (1) documentary, narrative; (2) experimental Television study — (1) production; (2) educational; (3) criticism and aesthetics Television production — (1) news/documentary; (2) experimental/personal video; (3) educational
SPECIAL ACTIVITIES/OFFERINGS Film series, film festivals, internships in film and television production, independent study
FACILITIES AND EQUIPMENT Film — complete 8mm and 16mm equipment, sync sound Television — complete black and white studio and exterior production equipment, black and white studio, mobile van/unit, control room
PART-TIME FACULTY Beverle Houston, Linda Malm

Pitzer College (continued)

COURSE LIST

Graduate

Film, an Introduction
Introduction to Religion and Film: Language of Film
History and Aesthetics of Film
Images of Women in Film
The Grammar of Film
Advanced Filmmaking
Seminar: Women in Novel and Film
Filmmaking in the Black Community
Special Studies in Film
Film and the Novel
History of European Film
Film Arts
Documentary and Experimental Film
Workshop in Film: Robert and Frances Flaherty
Seminar in Religion and Film: Film and Social Problems
History of American Film
Seminar in Religion and Film: Walt Disney
Seminar in Religion and Film: Robert Flaherty
Seminar in Religion and Film: D W Griffith
Television Studio Production
Remote Television Production
Independent Studies: Screenplay Writing
Independent Studies: Criticism
Independent Studies: Documentary

Rio Hondo Community College

State and locally supported 2-year coed college. Part of California Community Colleges System. Institutionally accredited by regional association. Suburban location. Undergraduate enrollment: 12,993. Total faculty: 347 (219 full-time, 128 part-time). Semester calendar. Grading system: letters or numbers.

Communications Department, Whittier, CA 90608 213-692-0921

CONTACT Dave Hopkins
FACULTY Jay Loughrin

COURSE LIST

Undergraduate

Television Production

Department of Fine Arts, Theater Division

CONTACT John Jacobs

COURSE LIST

Undergraduate

Creative Filmmaking
Survey of Motion Picture and TV

Sacramento City College

State and locally supported 2-year coed college. Institutionally accredited by regional association. Urban location. Semester calendar. Grading system: letters or numbers.

Theater Arts/Art Department, Sacramento, CA 95822 916-449-7537

CONTACT George Anastasiou
ADMISSION Application deadline — 8/5
FACULTY George Anastasiou, Darrell Forney

COURSE LIST

Undergraduate

History of the Film
Filmmaking

San Bernardino Valley College

District-supported 2-year coed college. Institutionally accredited by regional association. Suburban location. Total enrollment: 15,763. Semester calendar.

Telecommunications Department, 701 South Mount Vernon Avenue, San Bernardino, CA 92403 714-888-6511

CONTACT Robert Burningham
DEGREE OFFERED AS in telecommunications (radio/television)
ADMISSION Requirements — professional recommendations, teachers' recommendations
FINANCIAL AID Student loans, work/study programs
CURRICULAR EMPHASIS Filmmaking — (1) documentary; (2) narrative Television study — production Television production — (1) commercial; (2) news/documentary; (3) educational
SPECIAL ACTIVITIES/OFFERINGS Program material produced for on-campus closed-circuit television and local public television station, internships in television production
FACILITIES AND EQUIPMENT Film — 16mm cameras, editing equipment, lighting equipment, black and white film stock, color film stock, projectors, editing room Television — complete color studio and exterior production equipment, color studio, remote truck, audio studio, control room
FACULTY Dale Brix, Robert Burningham, Thomas Little PART-TIME FACULTY Lew Warren

COURSE LIST

Undergraduate

Introduction to Broadcasting	News for Radio/Television	Television Broadcast Operations
Introduction to Television Production	Speech for Radio/Television	Advanced Television Directing
Introduction to Television Materials	Television Production Laboratory	Cinematography
	Beginning Television Production	

San Diego State University

State-supported coed university. Part of California State University and Colleges System. Institutionally accredited by regional association, programs recognized by NASM, AACSB, NASA. Urban location, 300-acre campus. Total enrollment: 30,313. Undergraduate enrollment: 23,512. Total faculty: 1702 (908 full-time, 794 part-time). Semester calendar. Grading system: letters or numbers.

Telecommunications and Film Department, College Avenue, San Diego, CA 92182 714-286-6575

CONTACT Chairperson
DEGREES OFFERED BA, BS, MA in broadcast/film
ADMISSION Undergraduate requirements — minimum grade point average, ACT or SAT scores, written statement of purpose, writing competence Graduate requirements — minimum grade point average, GRE scores, written statement of purpose, writing competence Undergraduate application deadline — rolling
FINANCIAL AID Scholarships, work/study programs, teaching assistantships Undergraduate application deadline — 2/1
CURRICULAR EMPHASIS Undergraduate film study — (1) production; (2) appreciation; (3) relationship to other media Graduate film study — (1) criticism and aesthetics; (2) appreciation; (3) production planning and writing Undergraduate filmmaking — (1) narrative; (2) documentary; (3) animated Graduate filmmaking — (1) narrative; (2) informational; (3) documentary Undergraduate television study — (1) production; (2) management; (3) advertising Graduate television study — (1) sociological aspects; (2) educational; (3) management Undergraduate television production — (1) drama/sitcom; (2) news/documentary; (3) commercial Graduate television production — (1) educational; (2) drama; (3) news/documentary
SPECIAL ACTIVITIES/OFFERINGS Film series; film festivals; program material produced for on-campus closed-circuit television, cable television, local public television station; independent study; practicum; nonproduction internships
FACILITIES AND EQUIPMENT Film — complete 8mm and 16mm equipment; screening room, editing room, sound mixing room, animation board, permanent film library Television — complete black and white studio and exterior production equipment, complete color studio production equipment, black and white studio, color studio, audio studio, control room

California

San Francisco Art Institute

Independent professional coed institution. Institutionally accredited by regional association, programs recognized by NASA. Urban location, 3-acre campus. Total enrollment: 870. Undergraduate enrollment: 750. Total faculty: 63. Semester calendar. Grading system: pass/fail.

Filmmaking Department, 800 Chestnut Street, San Francisco, CA 94133 415-771-7020

CONTACT Don Lloyd, Chairman
DEGREES OFFERED BFA, MFA in filmmaking, also nondegree studio courses
DEPARTMENTAL MAJORS Undergraduate film — 100 students Graduate film — 25 students
ADMISSION Undergraduate requirement — written statement of purpose Graduate requirements — written statement of purpose, portfolio Undergraduate application deadline — 4/1
FINANCIAL AID Scholarships, work/study programs, student loans, teaching assistantships, film production assistance Undergraduate application deadline — 4/1
CURRICULAR EMPHASIS Undergraduate film study — history Graduate film study — criticism and aesthetics Undergraduate filmmaking — documentary, narrative, experimental, animated, educational treated equally Graduate filmmaking — experimental, personal, independent treated equally
SPECIAL ACTIVITIES/OFFERINGS Film series, film festivals, film societies, student publications, apprenticeships, independent study, teacher training
FACILITIES AND EQUIPMENT Film — 8mm and 16mm equipment, screening room, editing room, sound mixing room, animation board, permanent film library of student films, Super 8 and 16 flatbeds, sound editing, animation stands, optical printers
FACULTY James Broughton, Simon Edery, Phil Greene, Larry Jordan, George Kuchar, Janis Lipzin, Don Lloyd, Gunvor Nelson, Dennis Pies, Roy Ramsing, Al Wong, Kathy Zheutlin

COURSE LIST

Graduate
Seminar
Review

Undergraduate and Graduate

Beginning	Cinematography/Lighting	Film Writing
Film Equipment	Sound Mix Seminar	Film Directing
Film History	Sound and Electronics	Contemporary History (Critique and Analysis)
Tutorial (Individual Adviser)	Film Performance	Independent Study
Animation	Documentary	
Optical Printing	Dramatic Narrative	

San Francisco State University

State-supported comprehensive coed institution. Part of California State University and Colleges System. Institutionally accredited by regional association, programs recognized by NASM, AACSB, NASA. Urban location, 90-acre campus. Total enrollment: 36,377. Undergraduate enrollment: 11,161. Total faculty: 1728 (719 full-time, 1009 part-time). Semester calendar. Grading system: letters or numbers.

San Francisco State University (continued)

Film and Creative Arts Interdisciplinary Department, 1600 Holloway Avenue, San Francisco, CA 94132 415-469-1629

CONTACT Chairperson
DEGREES OFFERED BA, MA in film, BA, MA in creative arts (interdisciplinary)
ADMISSION Undergraduate requirements — portfolio, teachers' recommendations, written statement of purpose, 8mm or 16mm film evaluation Graduate requirements — portfolio, teachers' recommendations, written statement of purpose
FINANCIAL AID Student loans, work/study programs, teaching assistantships
CURRICULAR EMPHASIS Undergraduate film study — criticism and anesthetics, production, writing treated equally Graduate film study — (1) criticism and aesthetics; (2) history; (3) production Filmmaking — documentary, narrative, experimental, animated, educational treated equally
SPECIAL ACTIVITIES/OFFERINGS Film series, film societies, annual student film screening, internships in film production, independent study, cinematheque, academic year abroad program offered through affiliation with the Inter-University Center for Film Studies in Paris
FACILITIES AND EQUIPMENT Film — complete 8mm and 16mm equipment, editing room, sound mixing room, animation board, permanent film library

Broadcast Communication Arts Department 415-469-1787

CONTACT Chairperson
DEGREES OFFERED BA, MA in broadcast communication arts
DEPARTMENTAL MAJORS 590
CURRICULAR EMPHASIS Television production — commercial, news/documentary, experimental/personal video, educational treated equally
SPECIAL ACTIVITIES/OFFERINGS Program material produced for on-campus closed-circuit television and cable television, apprenticeships, internships in television production, independent study, vocational placement service
FACILITIES AND EQUIPMENT Television — complete black and white studio and exterior production facilities, complete color studio and exterior production facilities

San Jose City College

District-supported 2-year coed college. Part of San Jose Community College District System. Institutionally accredited by regional association. Urban location. Undergraduate enrollment: 13,197. Total faculty: 541 (157 full-time, 384 part-time). Semester calendar. Grading system: letters or numbers.

Drama Department, Moorpark, San Jose, CA 95114

CONTACT Ray Collins
DEGREE OFFERED AA in broadcast (drama)
DEPARTMENTAL MAJORS Television — 20 students
FINANCIAL AID Work/study programs, student loans
CURRICULAR EMPHASIS Television study — (1) production; (2) history and appreciation Television production — commercial, news/documentary treated equally
SPECIAL ACTIVITIES/OFFERINGS Internships in television production
FACILITIES AND EQUIPMENT Television — 1-inch VTR, 2-inch VTR, special effects generators, slide chain, film chain, time base corrector, black and white studio, color studio, control room
FACULTY Ray Collins

COURSE LIST

Undergraduate
Introduction to Broadcasting
Broadcast Announcing
Broadcast Production
Acting for Television

San Jose State University

State-supported comprehensive coed institution. Part of California State University and Colleges System. Institutionally accredited by regional association, programs recognized by NASM, AACSB, NASA. Urban location, 104-acre campus. Total enrollment: 26,951. Undergraduate enrollment: 21,426. Total faculty: 1685 (1026 full-time, 659 part-time). Semester calendar. Grading system: letters or numbers.

Theatre Arts Department, School of Humanities and the Arts, Seventh and San Fernando, San Jose, CA 95192 408-277-2763

CONTACT Film — Charles Chess Television — Clarence Flick
DEGREES OFFERED BA in radio-television, BA in radio-television with emphasis in film, MA in theatre arts
DEPARTMENTAL MAJORS Undergraduate film — 30 students Undergraduate television — 200 students Graduate film — 3 students Graduate television— 15 students
ADMISSION Undergraduate requirements — 2.0 minimum grade point average, ACT or SAT scores Graduate requirement — 3.0 minimum grade point average Undergraduate application deadline — rolling
FINANCIAL AID Student loans, work/study programs Undergraduate application deadline — 3/1
CURRICULAR EMPHASIS Film study — (1) criticism and aesthetics; (2) production; (3) history; (4) appreciation; (5) educational media/instructional technology Filmmaking — depends upon current student interest Television study — (1) criticism and aesthetics; (2) production; (3) history; (4) educational; (5) appreciation; (6) management
SPECIAL ACTIVITIES/OFFERINGS Film series; film festivals; program material produced for on-campus closed-circuit television, cable television, local public television station, local commercial television station; independent study; vocational placement service
FACILITIES AND EQUIPMENT Film — complete 8mm and 16mm equipment, sound stage, screening room, editing room, sound mixing room, animation board, permanent film library Television — complete black and white studio and exterior production equipment, complete color studio and exterior production equipment, black and white studio, color studio, remote truck, audio studio, control room
FACULTY Charles Chess, Clarence Flick, Gordon Greb, Richard McCafferty, Frank McCann, Wayne Whitaker PART-TIME FACULTY Roland Buckman, Robert Hasfeldt, Noreen Mitchell

COURSE LIST

Undergraduate

Broadcast Communications
Film
Sound Production
Radio-Television Acting

Undergraduate and Graduate

Television Production
Broadcast Management
Advanced Radio-Television Production
Television Film Writing
Television in Education
Modern Film
Advanced Acting—Film/Television
Film Production Technique
Television Criticism

Santa Monica College

State and locally supported 2-year coed college. Institutionally accredited by regional association. Urban location. Undergraduate enrollment: 17,817. Total faculty: 781 (204 full-time, 577 part-time). Semester calendar. Grading system: letters or numbers.

Communications Department, 1900 Pico Boulevard, Santa Monica, CA 90405 213-450-5150

CONTACT H Wendell Smith
DEGREE OFFERED AA in communication with a major in radio-television
FINANCIAL AID Student loans, work/study programs Application deadline — 9/9, rolling
FACULTY Alan Casty, Ray Cooper, H J Crane, James Hanlon

COURSE LIST

Undergraduate

Introduction to Communication
Radio/Television Announcing
Broadcasting Newswriting
Radio/Television Writing
Radio-Dramatic Production
Work Experience

Santa Rosa Junior College

District-supported 2-year coed college. Part of California Community Colleges System, automatic transfer to main campus for baccalaureate. Institutionally accredited by regional association. Small town location. Semester calendar. Grading system: letters or numbers.

Speech Department, 1501 Mendocino Avenue, Santa Rosa, CA 95401 707-527-4398

CONTACT John Whitman Bigby
FINANCIAL AID Scholarships, student loans, work/study programs, film production grants
CURRICULAR EMPHASIS Film study — (1) criticism and aesthetics; (2) history; (3) production Filmmaking — (1) documentary; (2) experimental; (3) narrative Television study — (1) criticism and aesthetics; (2) history; (3) appreciation Television production — (1) experimental/personal video; (2) news/documentary; (3) commercial
SPECIAL ACTIVITIES/OFFERINGS Film series, student publications, program material produced for on-campus closed-circuit television and cable television, independent study
FACILITIES AND EQUIPMENT Film — complete 8mm equipment, sound stage, screening room, editing room, sound mixing room, animation board, permanent film library Television — complete black and white studio and exterior production equipment, black and white studio, audio studio, control room
FACULTY John Whitman Bigby PART-TIME FACULTY Ed LaFrance, Walter F McCallum

COURSE LIST

Undergraduate

Introduction to Mass Communications
Introduction to Film (History)
Introduction to Film (Form)
Film Production
Broadcasting
Radio Production
Radio Station Operation
Radio-TV News
Video Production
Special Studies

Scripps College

Independent 4-year women's college. Part of the Claremont Colleges. All course work, in certain fields, must be taken at other Claremont Colleges, through cross-registration. Institutionally accredited by regional association. Suburban location, 26-acre campus. Undergraduate enrollment: 576. Total faculty: 63 (48 full-time, 15 part-time). Semester calendar. Grading system: letters or numbers.

Scripps College is one of the Claremont Colleges, a consortium of colleges that participate in an intercollegiate film studies program. (See listings for Claremont Men's College and Pitzer College.)

Film Arts Department, Claremont, CA 91711 714-626-8511

CONTACT Paul Darrow
DEGREE OFFERED BA in film
DEPARTMENTAL MAJORS Undergraduate — 5 students Graduate — 3 students
ADMISSION Requirement — minimum grade point average
FINANCIAL AID Student loans, teaching assistantships
CURRICULAR EMPHASIS Filmmaking — animated, educational treated equally
SPECIAL ACTIVITIES/OFFERINGS Film series, film festivals, film societies, student publications, independent study
FACILITIES AND EQUIPMENT Film — 8mm and 16mm cameras, editing equipment, projectors, screening room, animation board
FACULTY Paul Darrow

COURSE LIST

Undergraduate and Graduate

Film Arts

Shasta College

District-supported 2-year coed college. Institutionally accredited by regional agency. Small town location. Total enrollment: 12,500. Total faculty: 393 (143 full-time, 250 part-time). Semester calendar. Grading system: letters or numbers.

Fine Arts Division, Redding, CA 96099 916-241-3523

CONTACT Film — Dan Ralston Television — Jean Carpenter
SPECIAL ACTIVITIES/OFFERINGS Program material produced for on-campus closed-circuit televison and local public television station, independent study
FACILITIES AND EQUIPMENT Television — complete black and white studio production facilities, complete color exterior production facilities
FACULTY Jean Carpenter, Dan Ralston

COURSE LIST
Undergraduate
Introduction to Television Production I, II
Introduction to Broadcasting
Experimental Filmmaking
Exploring Contemporary Television
Portable Television

Sherwood Oaks Experimental College

Independent coed institution. Urban location. Total enrollment: 700. Total faculty: 20. Quarter calendar.

1445 North Las Palmas, Hollywood, CA 90028 213-462-0669

CONTACT Gary Shusett
FINANCIAL AID Scholarships, work/study programs, teaching assistantships
SPECIAL ACTIVITIES/OFFERINGS Film festivals, independent study
FACILITIES AND EQUIPMENT Film — 8mm and 16mm editing equipment, lighting, projectors, 35mm cameras, lighting, projectors, screening room, 35mm screening facilities, editing room, permanent film library of student films, permanent film library of commercial or professional films

Sierra College

State and locally supported 2-year coed college. Part of California Community Colleges System. Institutionally accredited by regional association. Rural location. Undergraduate enrollment: 6890. Total faculty: 321 (133 full-time, 188 part-time). Semester calendar. Grading system: letters or numbers.

Department of Media Arts, 5000 Rocklin Road, Rocklin, CA 95677 916-624-3333

CONTACT Film — Raymond D Oliva Television — Keith Bing
CURRICULAR EMPHASIS Undergraduate film study — history, criticism and aesthetics, appreciation, educational media/instructional technology treated equally Undergraduate filmmaking — documentary, narrative, experimental treated equally Undergraduate television study — production Undergraduate television production — experimental/personal video, educational treated equally
SPECIAL ACTIVITIES/OFFERINGS Film series, program material produced for on-campus closed-circuit television
FACILITIES AND EQUIPMENT Film — complete 8mm equipment, screening room, editing room, sound mixing room, permanent film library of commercial or professional films Television — black and white studio cameras, ½-inch VTR, 1-inch VTR, ¾-inch cassette VTR, portable black and white cameras, editing equipment, monitors, slide chain, ½-inch portapak recorders, lighting equipment, sound recording equipment
FACULTY Keith Bing, Mike Hunter, Raymond D Oliva

COURSE LIST
Undergraduate
Introduction to Film
American and British Film Masterpieces
International Film Masterpieces
History of Film
Film Production
TV Production
Audio-Visual Production

Solano Community College

County-supported 2-year coed college. Institutionally accredited by regional association. Suburban location, 192-acre campus. Undergraduate enrollment: 10,275. Total faculty: 152. Semester calendar. Grading system: letters or numbers.

Department of Telecommunications, PO Box 246, Suisun City, CA 94585 707-864-7000

CONTACT Maile Ornellas
DEGREE OFFERED AA in telecommunications
DEPARTMENTAL MAJORS Film — 35 students Television — 35 students
ADMISSION Requirement — 2.0 minimum grade point average Application deadline — 8/7 and 1/7
FINANCIAL AID 3 student assistant positions
CURRICULAR EMPHASIS Film study — history, appreciation, production treated equally Filmmaking — (1) documentary, narrative; (2) animated; (3) educational Television study — history, production treated equally Television production — commercial, public affairs treated equally
SPECIAL ACTIVITIES/OFFERINGS Film series, film festivals, program material produced for on-campus closed-circuit television, internships in television production
FACILITIES AND EQUIPMENT Film — complete 8mm equipment, 16mm cameras, editing equipment, lighting, sound stage, screening room, editing room, animation board, permanent film library of commercial or professional films Television — black and white studio cameras, color studio cameras, ½-inch VTR, 1-inch VTR, ¾-inch cassette VTR, portable black and white cameras, editing equipment, monitors, special effects generators, slide chain, portable color cameras, ½-inch portapak recorders, ¾-inch ENG, lighting equipment, sound recording equipment, audio mixers, film chain, time base corrector, black and white studio, color studio

FACULTY Maile Louise Ornellas PART-TIME FACULTY Richard Colman, Michael Meagher

COURSE LIST

Undergraduate

The Art of Cinema
Film Production I, II
Introduction to Broadcasting
Beginning TV Production
Advanced TV Production
Writing for Film and TV

Southern California College

Independent 4-year coed college affiliated with Assemblies of God. Institutionally accredited by regional association. Suburban location. Undergraduate enrollment: 580. Total faculty: 58 (34-full-time, 24 part-time). 4-1-4 calendar. Grading system: letters or numbers.

55 Fair Drive, Costa Mesa, CA 92626 714-556-3610, ext 256

CONTACT Harry Sova
DEGREE OFFERED BA in communication with emphasis in television
DEPARTMENTAL MAJORS Undergraduate television — 45 students
ADMISSION Requirements — 2.25 minimum grade point average, ACT or SAT scores, interview, written statement of purpose
FINANCIAL AID Scholarships, work/study programs, student loans
CURRICULAR EMPHASIS Television study — (1) production; (2) management; (3) broadcast sales Television production — (1) commercial; (2) educational; (3) corporate video
SPECIAL ACTIVITIES/OFFERINGS Program material produced for on-campus closed-circuit television, cable television, local public television station, local commercial television; loan and sale of cassettes of student-produced series; apprenticeships; internships in television production; independent study
FACILITIES AND EQUIPMENT Film — sound mixing room Television — complete color studio and exterior production equipment, black and white studio, color studio, audio studio
FACULTY Harry Sova, Steve Taylor PART-TIME FACULTY Dave Harlan, Terry Hickey, Tammy Montgomery

COURSE LIST

Undergraduate

Introduction to Broadcasting
Journalism
Introduction to Audio Production
Introduction to TV Production
Advanced Audio Production
Advanced TV Production
Directing and Producing Television
Broadcast Station Management and Sales
Broadcast Advertising
SIMTEL, a computer simulation for broadcast management, programming and sales

Stanford University

Independent coed university. Institutionally accredited by regional association. Suburban location. Total enrollment: 11,727. Undergraduate enrollment: 6559. Total faculty: 1103 (1103 full-time, 0 part-time). Quarter calendar. Grading system: letters or numbers.

Communication Department, Cypress Hall, Stanford, CA 94305 415-497-4621

CONTACT Henry Breitrose
DEGREES OFFERED BA, MA in film production; BA, MA in broadcast management and news
DEPARTMENTAL MAJORS Undergraduate film — 30 students Graduate film — 15 students
ADMISSION Undergraduate requirements — ACT or SAT scores, teachers' recommendations Graduate requirements — GRE scores, teachers' recommendations, written statement of purpose, work sample Undergraduate application deadline — 1/1
FINANCIAL AID Scholarships, fellowships, teaching assistantships Undergraduate application deadline — 1/1
CURRICULAR EMPHASIS Undergraduate film study — (1) history; (2) criticism and aesthetics; (3) production Graduate film study — (1) production; (2) criticism and aesthetics; (3) history Filmmaking — (1) documentary; (2) narrative; (3) educational Television study — (1) management; (2) history; (3) criticism and aesthetics Television production — (1) news/documentary; (2) educational; (3) commercial
SPECIAL ACTIVITIES/OFFERINGS Film series, film societies, visiting speakers and filmmakers, internships in television production, independent study
FACILITIES AND EQUIPMENT Film — complete 8mm and 16mm equipment, screening room, 35mm screening facilities, editing rooms, sound mixing room, permanent film library Television — black and white studio cameras, ¾-inch cassette VTR, portable black and white cameras, monitors, special effects generators, ¾-inch color portapak recorder, lighting equipment, sound recording equipment, audio mixers
FACULTY Ron Alexander, Julian Blaustein, Henry Breitrose, Irv Drasnin, Jules Dundes PART-TIME FACULTY Jon Else, Celia Lighthill, Arthur Mayer, Kristine Samuelson, Stephen Stept

COURSE LIST

Undergraduate

Introduction to Film and Video
Visual and Aural Communication Techniques
Writing for the Visual Media
Broadcast News

Graduate

Film Production I–III
Seminar in Film and Broadcasting I–III
Writing for Film I–III
Fiction Writing I, II
Script Analysis I, II

Undergraduate and Graduate

Broadcast News Techniques and Production
Documentary Film
Topics in Film Study
Seminar in Broadcast Management
Film Aesthetics
History of Film
Broadcast Communications
Broadcasting and Film Criticism
Television Production
Seminar in Government, Industry, and Consumer Relations in Broadcasting

University of California, Berkeley

State-supported coed university. Part of University of California System. Institutionally accredited by regional association. Urban location. Total enrollment: 28,820. Undergraduate enrollment: 19,850. Total faculty: 3163. Quarter calendar. Grading system: letters or numbers.

Graduate School of Journalism, Berkeley, CA 94720 415-642-3383

CONTACT Andrew A Stern
DEGREE OFFERED MA in journalism with emphasis in broadcast journalism
PROGRAM MAJORS Graduate television — 20 students
ADMISSION Graduate requirements — GRE scores, teachers' recommendations, written statement of purpose
FINANCIAL AID Scholarships, work/study programs, student loans, fellowships, research assistantships
CURRICULAR EMPHASIS Filmmaking (video) — documentary, narrative treated equally Television study — history, production treated equally Television production — news/documentary
SPECIAL ACTIVITIES/OFFERINGS Program material produced for on-campus closed-circuit television, cable television, local public television station, and local commercial television station; internships in television production; independent study
FACILITIES AND EQUIPMENT Film — complete 16mm equipment, sound stage, screening room, 35mm screening facilities, editing room, sound mixing room, permanent film library of student films, permanent film library of commercial or professional films Television — complete black and white studio production equipment, complete color studio production equipment, complete black and white exterior production equipment, complete color exterior production equipment, black and white studio, color studio, mobile van/unit, remote truck, audio studio, control room
FACULTY Samuel R Shore, Andrew A Stern

COURSE LIST

Graduate
Reporting for Television
Documentary
Thesis Documentary

University of California, Irvine

State-supported coed university. Part of University of California System. Institutionally accredited by regional association. Suburban location. Total enrollment: 9954. Undergraduate enrollment: 7668. Total faculty: 685 (573 full-time, 112 part-time). Quarter calendar. Grading system: letters or numbers.

Film Studies, School of Humanities, Irvine, CA 92717 714-833-5386 or 714-833-6279

CONTACT Franco Tonelli, Director
DEGREE OFFERED BA in humanities with a concentration in film studies
PROGRAM MAJORS Film — 10 students
FINANCIAL AID Work/study programs, student loans
CURRICULAR EMPHASIS Film study — history, criticism and aesthetics, appreciation treated equally Filmmaking — documentary, narrative, experimental, animated treated equally
SPECIAL ACTIVITIES/OFFERINGS Filmmaking clubs, film series, film societies, Film Theatrical Symposium: dialogue with the industry
FACILITIES AND EQUIPMENT Film — 8mm cameras, editing equipment, sound recording equipment, lighting, projectors, miscellaneous camera accessories (tripods, filters, etc), permanent film library of commercial or professional films
FACULTY David Carroll, Eugenio Donato, Renee R Hubert, Anton Kaes, Alejandro Morales, Franco Tonelli PART-TIME FACULTY Susan Barber, Thomas Girvin

COURSE LIST

Undergraduate
Study in Film Technique
Theatrical Film Symposium
History of Film
Theory of Film
Study in Film Genres
Author Theory
French Film
Italian Film
German Film
Russian Film
Spanish Film
Classical Mythology
Individual Study
Group Study
Directed Research

University of California, Los Angeles

State-supported coed university. Part of University of California System. Institutionally accredited by regional association. Urban location, 411-acre campus. Total enrollment: 31,743. Undergraduate enrollment: 20,189. Total faculty: 2700. Quarter calendar. Grading system: letters or numbers.

Theater Arts Department, 405 Hilgard Avenue, Los Angeles, CA 90024 213-825-7891

CONTACT John W Young, Chairman
DEGREES OFFERED BA, MFA in production and writing; BA, MA, PhD in critical studies
DEPARTMENTAL MAJORS Undergraduate — 150 students Graduate — 250 students
ADMISSION Undergraduate requirements — 3.0 minimum grade point average, portfolio, teachers' recommendations, written statement of purpose, original writing Graduate requirements — 3.0 minimum grade point average, GRE scores, portfolio, teachers' recommendations, written statement of purpose, original writing Undergraduate application deadline — rolling
FINANCIAL AID Scholarships, student loans, work/study programs, teaching assistantships, research assistantships, fellowships Undergraduate application deadline — 11/30
CURRICULAR EMPHASIS Undergraduate film study — (1) history; (2) production; (3) writing Graduate film study — (1) production; (2) writing; (3) criticism and aesthetics Filmmaking — (1) personal; (2) narrative; (3) animated, documentary; (4) experimental Television study — production Television production — (1) experimental/personal video; (2) news/documentary

SPECIAL ACTIVITIES/OFFERINGS Student publications; program material produced for on-campus closed-circuit television, cable television, local public television station; internships in film and television production; independent study; UCLA Film-Television Archives; Harold Leonard Scholarships for International Research

FACILITIES AND EQUIPMENT Film — complete 16mm equipment, 8mm editing equipment, lighting equipment, projectors, 35mm screening facilities, editing rooms, sound mixing room, animation board, permanent film library, scoring stage, animation crane, motion picture stages, re-recording rooms, projection facilities Television — complete black and white studio and exterior production equipment, complete color studio and exterior production equipment, black and white studio, color studio, mobile van/unit, audio studio, control room, computer tape editing facility

FACULTY William Adams, John Boehm, Edgar Brokaw, Nick Browne, Shirley Clarke, Arthur Friedman, William Froug, Teshome Gabriel, Hugh Grauel, Peter Guber, Richard Hawkins, Walter Kingson, Frank LaTourette, Mark McCarty, Dan McLaughlin, Stephen Mamber, William Menger, Bob Nakamura, Jorge Preloran, Robert Rosen, Delia Salvi, Ruth Schwartz, Louis Stoumen, Howard Suber, Robert Trachinger, Lyne Trimble, Frank Valert, Richard Walter, Abe Wollock, John W Young

COURSE LIST

Undergraduate

History of the American Motion Picture
History of the European Motion Picture
History of African, Asian, and Latin American Film
The Development of Film in Europe and the United States: From World War I through the Depression
The Development of Film in Europe and the United States: From World War II to the Present
Experimental Film
History of Documentary Film
History of Television and Radio
Film Distribution and Exhibition
Film and Social Change
Film Authors
Film Genres
Producers and Their Films
Criticism
Advanced Acting for Television and Motion Pictures
Broadcast Speech
The Film Image
Nontheatrical Motion Picture/Television Writing
Motion Picture/Television Writing
Advanced Motion Picture/Television Writing
Basic Motion Picture/Television Photography
Advanced Motion Picture/Television Photography
Design for Motion Pictures and Television
Motion Picture/Television Sound Recording
Color Cinematography
Motion Picture/Television Editing
Direction of Actors for Motion Pictures/Television
Direction for Motion Pictures
Direction for Television
Television and Radio News Writing
Motion Picture Production
Motion Picture/Television Production
Workshop in Broadcast News and Documentary
Animation Design in Theater Arts
Writing for Animation
Animation Workshop
Television Portapak Production
Production for Community Cable Television
Community Television Programming and Management
Television Production
Television Laboratory
Remote Television Broadcasting
The Aesthetics of Visual Communication
Film Curatorship
Television Curatorship

Graduate

Bibliography and Methods of Research in Theater Arts
Seminar in Film and the Fine Arts
Seminar in Film and the Performing Arts
Seminar in European Motion Picture History
Seminar in American Motion Picture History
Seminar in Realism, Naturalism, and the Film
Seminar in Expressionism and Film
Seminar in Social Realism and Film
Seminar in Surrealism and Film
Seminar in Neo-Realism and Film
Seminar in Film Structure
Film Aesthetics
Advanced Aesthetics
Seminar in Documentary Film
Seminar in Fictional Film
Seminar in Ethnographic Film
Seminar in Contemporary Broadcast Media
Historiography
Seminar in Critical Methods
Film, Television, and Society
Seminar in Film Authors
Seminar in Film Genres
Seminar in Visual Perception
The Expanding Visual Media
Production Planning in Television
Advanced Design for Motion Pictures
Seminar in Film and Television Direction
Ethnographic Film Direction
Seminar in Film and Television Criticism
Seminar in Television Drama
Seminar in Television Documentary
Seminar in Educational Television
Special Studies in Theater Arts
Advanced Directing of the Actor for Motion Pictures and Television
Manuscript Evaluation
Advanced Motion Picture/Television Writing
Nontheatrical Writing for Motion Picture/Television
Production Planning in Motion Pictures
Advanced Motion Picture/Television Sound
Music Recording Workshop
Advanced Motion Picture/Television Sound Re-Recording
Design for Television
Motion Picture Direction
Advanced Television Direction
Film Project 3
Workshop in Radio and Television News
Advanced Animation Workshop
Advanced Television Production
Educational Television Workshop
Problems in the Teaching of Theater Arts
Professional Internship in Theater Arts
Directed Individual Studies: Research
Directed Individual Studies: Writing
Directed Individual Studies: Directing
Directed Individual Studies: Design
Directed Individual Studies: Acting
Directed Individual Studies: Production

University of California, Riverside

State-supported coed university. Part of University of California System. Institutionally accredited by regional association. Suburban location. Total enrollment: 4575. Undergraduate enrollment: 3277. Total faculty: 458 (408 full-time, 50 part-time). Quarter calendar. Grading system: letters or numbers.

History Department, Riverside, CA 92521 714-787-5401

CONTACT Carlos E Cortés

DEGREES OFFERED BA, MA, PhD in history

ADMISSION Undergraduate requirement — 3.3 minimum grade point average Graduate requirements — 3.2 minimum grade point average, GRE scores, teachers' recommendations, written statement of purpose

FINANCIAL AID Scholarships, work/study programs, student loans, teaching assistantships

University of California, Riverside (continued)

CURRICULAR EMPHASIS Undergraduate film study — film as historical document
FACULTY Leon Campbell, Carlos E Cortés

COURSE LIST

Undergraduate

Filmic Approach to Race and Ethnicity in the Americas
Filmic Approach to the History of the 1960's
Frontiers in the Americas Through Film
Film as Revolutionary Weapon
Latin American Experience Through Film
Historical Dilemmas in Film

University of California, Santa Barbara

State-supported coed university. Part of University of California System. Institutionally accredited by regional association. Suburban location. Total enrollment: 14,473. Undergraduate enrollment: 12,623. Total faculty: 890 (624 full-time, 266 part-time). Quarter calendar. Grading system: letters or numbers.

Film Studies Program, Santa Barbara, CA 93106 805-961-2347

CONTACT Patrizio Rossi, Chairman
DEGREE OFFERED BA in film studies
PROGRAM MAJORS Film — 80 students
ADMISSION Requirements — 2.78 minimum grade point average, ACT or SAT scores
FINANCIAL AID Scholarships, work/study programs, student loans Undergraduate application deadline — 4/15
CURRICULAR EMPHASIS Film study — (1) criticism and aesthetics; (2) history; (3) appreciation Filmmaking — narrative
SPECIAL ACTIVITIES/OFFERINGS Film series, film societies, student publications, independent study
FACILITIES AND EQUIPMENT Film — 8mm cameras, editing equipment, sound recording equipment, lighting, projectors, 16mm cameras, editing equipment, projectors, screening room, 35mm screening facilities, editing room, sound mixing room, permanent film library of commercial or professional films
FACULTY Charles Wolfe PART-TIME FACULTY Naomi Greene, Harry Lawton, Paul Lazarus, Torborg Lundell, Patrizio Rossi, Alexander Sesonske, Garrett Stewart

COURSE LIST

Undergraduate

Introduction to Motion Pictures
History of Cinema
Film Production
Hollywood Studio
Contemporary Film Theory and Style
Japanese Cinema
Documentary Film
Silent Comedy Tradition
Comedy Tradition
Soviet Cinema, 1917-1945
British Cinema
Westerns Since 1950
Science Fiction, Science Fantasy
American Film: 1930s
American Film: 1940s
The American Left in Hollywood
Directors
Hitchcock-Hawks
Theatre and Film
Heroes, Heroines, and Sex Roles
Film and Social Reality
Musical Film
Film Noir
Renoir and Lang
Basic Screenwriting
Semiology
Film Criticism
Theory of Film
Film Narrative
French Film Directors
French Novel Into Film
Contemporary French Drama and Film
French Surrealist Film
Personal Documentary: From Vertov to Cinema Vérité
French Film: Theory and Practice
Key Works of the French Cinema
French Cinema of the 1930s
French Cinema Since World War II
Italian Novel Into Film
Introduction to Italian Cinema
World Cinema
Expressionism in the Film, in Art, and the Theater
Swedish Film
Spanish Cinema
Latin-American Cinema
Luso-Brazilian Cinema

University of California, Santa Cruz

State-supported coed university. Part of University of California System. Institutionally accredited by regional association. Small town location, 2000-acre campus. Total enrollment: 5880. Undergraduate enrollment: 5534. Total faculty: 526 (328 full-time, 198 part-time). Quarter calendar. Grading system: faculty reports.

Theater Arts Board, Santa Cruz, CA 95064 408-429-2974

CONTACT Eli Hollander, Janey Place
DEGREE OFFERED BA in film/theater arts
DEPARTMENTAL MAJORS 30 students
ADMISSION Requirements — interviews, portfolio, production credits, written statement of purpose Application deadline — rolling
FINANCIAL AID Scholarships, student loans, work/study programs Application deadline — 1/15, rolling
CURRICULAR EMPHASIS Film study — (1) production; (2) criticism and aesthetics; (3) history Filmmaking — (1) narrative; (2) documentary; (3) experimental
SPECIAL ACTIVITIES/OFFERINGS Film series, film festivals, film societies, student publications, apprenticeships, internships in film production, independent study
FACILITIES AND EQUIPMENT Film — complete 8mm and 16mm equipment, sound stage, screening room, editing rooms, sound mixing room, animation camera
FACULTY Eli Hollander, Janey Place

COURSE LIST

Undergraduate

Filmmaking Studio I, II
Film Directing
Film Writing
Film Genres
National Cinemas
Seminar in Theory and Criticism
Nonfiction Film
The Film Experience
American Fictions: Film and Novels
Documentary Filmmaking
Independent Projects
Screenwriting

University of San Diego

Independent Roman Catholic coed university. Institutionally accredited by regional association. Urban location, 170-acre campus. Total enrollment: 3772. Undergraduate enrollment: 2326. Total faculty: 230 (152 full-time, 78 part-time). 4-1-4 calendar. Grading system: letters or numbers.

Communication Arts Department, San Diego, CA 92110 714-291-6480

CONTACT Benjamin Nyce
ADMISSION Application deadline — 5/1
FACULTY Benjamin Nyce

COURSE LIST
Undergraduate
Film Analysis
Development of Film

University of Santa Clara

Independent Roman Catholic coed university. Institutionally accredited by regional association. Suburban location, 63-acre campus. Total enrollment: 7160. Undergraduate enrollment: 3600. Total faculty: 387 (237 full-time, 150 part-time). Quarter calendar. Grading system: letters or numbers.

Television Facility, Department of Theater Arts, Santa Clara, CA 95053 408-984-4520

CONTACT John Privett, SJ
DEGREES OFFERED BA in theater arts with emphasis in television, BA in general humanities with emphasis in public communication, BS in political science with emphasis in television and public affairs
DEPARTMENTAL MAJORS Television — 15 students
ADMISSION Requirements — 3.0 minimum grade point average, ACT or SAT scores, teachers' recommendations, written statement of purpose, competitive college preparatory high school record Application deadline 3/1
FINANCIAL AID Scholarships, work/study programs, student loans Application deadline — 5/1
CURRICULAR EMPHASIS Television study — (1) criticism and aesthetics; (2) production; (3) history Television production — (1) commercial; (2) news/documentary; (3) educational
SPECIAL ACTIVITIES/OFFERINGS Film series; film festivals; film societies; student publications; program material produced for on-campus closed-circuit television, cable television, local public television station; internships in television production; independent study
FACILITIES AND EQUIPMENT Film — complete 8mm equipment, screening room, editing room, sound mixing room, permanent film library of student films, permanent film library of commercial or professional films Television — black and white studio cameras, color studio cameras, ½-inch VTR, ¾-inch cassette VTR, portable black and white cameras, editing equipment, monitors, special effects generators, slide chain, portable color cameras, ½-inch portapak recorders, lighting equipment, sound recording equipment, audio mixers, film chain, black and white studio, color studio, audio studio, control room, portable/remote carts
FACULTY John Privett, SJ, Thomas Shanks PART-TIME FACULTY James Risinger

COURSE LIST
Undergraduate
Introduction to Mass Communication
Introduction to Television Production
Television Production Planning
Television Directing I, II
Advanced Producing and Directing
Broadcast Journalism
Television Dramatic Writing
Creative Project or Independent Study

University of Southern California

Independent coed university. Institutionally accredited by regional association, programs recognized by NASM, AACSB, ACPE. Urban location, 162-acre campus. Total enrollment: 25,299. Undergraduate enrollment: 15,319. Total faculty: 2695 (1570 full-time, 1125 part-time). Semester calendar. Grading system: letters or numbers.

Division of Cinema/Television, School of Performing Arts, University Park, Los Angeles, CA 90007 213-743-2235

CONTACT Film — E Russell McGregor, Co-chairman Television — Morton Zarcoff, Co-chairman
DEGREES OFFERED BA, MA, MFA, MS in cinema; PhD in communication-cinema; MFA in professional writing; MS in film education; BA in television
PROGRAM MAJORS Undergraduate — 150 students Graduate — 250 students
ADMISSION Undergraduate requirements — SAT scores, interviews, portfolio Graduate requirements — GRE scores, interviews, portfolio Undergraduate application deadline — rolling
FINANCIAL AID Work/study programs, teaching assistantships, fellowships Undergraduate application deadline — 1/31
CURRICULAR EMPHASIS Film study — (1) production; (2) history, criticism and aesthetics; (3) educational media/instructional technology Filmmaking — documentary, narrative, experimental, animated, educational treated equally Television study — production
SPECIAL ACTIVITIES/OFFERINGS Film series, film festivals, film societies, independent study, teacher training, foreign study
FACILITIES AND EQUIPMENT Film — complete 8mm and 16mm equipment, animation cranes, optical printers, sound stage, screening room, 35mm and 70mm screening facilities, editing room, sound mixing room, animation board, permanent film library, film processing laboratory, three-camera television studio, extensive print library
FACULTY Allan Casebier, Joseph Casper, Gene Coe, Herbert E Farmer, Trevor Greenwood, Richard Harber, Richard Jewell, David W Johnson, Edward Kaufman, Marsha Kinder, Arthur Knight, E Russell McGregor, Margaret Mehring, Kenneth Miura, Melvin Sloan, Wolfram von Hanwehr, Daniel Wiegand, Frank Withop, Morton Zarcoff

University of Southern California (continued)

PART-TIME FACULTY Morris Abrams, Bruce Block, Mitchell W Block, Jim Boyle, Jae Carmichael, Jim Castle, Kenneth Evans, Peter Gibbons, Bernard Gruver, Mark Harris, Robert Knutson, Max Lamb, Howard Lavick, Marc Mancini, Betsy A McLane, Eric Morris, Edward Mosk, Art Murphy, Ernie Neukanen, Marty Roberts, Kenneth Robinson, Leon Roth, Ben Shedd, Sidney P Solow, Norman Taurog, William Tuttle, Duke Underwood, Charles Walters, Max Weinberg, Bernard Weitzman

COURSE LIST

Undergraduate

Techniques in Motion Picture Production
Fundamentals of Film
Visual Communication
History of the American Film
Language of Film
Introduction to Film
Filmwriting
Image of the Film
Motion Picture Camera
Motion Picture Editing
Motion Picture Sound Recording
Film Directing
Colloquium: Motion Picture Production Techniques
Art and Industry of the Theatrical Film
History of the American Sound Film
History of Entertainment Television
Practicum in Development of Dramatic Program Materials
Beginning Dramatic Television Production
Television Drama Writing I, II
Directing for Television
Television Drama Production
Television Editing
Entertainment Program Development
Seminar in Preproduction
Senior Television Drama Production II
Senior Television Seminar

Graduate

Seminar in Cinema History and Criticism
Seminar in the Film
History of Motion Pictures
History of the Sound Film in America
Creative Cinema
Film and the Classroom Teacher
The New Language in Film
Censorship in Cinema
Studies in Film
Seminar in the Documentary Film
Writing the Short Script II
Practicum in Screenwriting
Advanced Motion Picture Script Analysis
Practicum in Writing the Nonfiction Film
Practicum in Makeup
Seminar in Production Planning
Seminar in Camera
Special Effects in Cinema
Development of Prototype Materials
Seminar in Film Editing
Practicum in Sound
Seminar in Motion Picture Engineering
Animation Camera Workshop
Studies in Film Graphics-Animation
Advanced Studies in Film Graphics
Seminar in Film Graphics
History of Film Graphics
Production Design
Seminar in Motion Picture Distribution, Budgeting, and Management
Publicity in the Performing Arts
Seminar in Motion Picture Business
Seminar in Film Genres
Seminar in Film Analysis
Seminar in the Theatrical Film
Adaptation: Stage to Screen II
Film Style Analysis II
Seminar in Film Direction
Practicum in Film Directing
Critical Film Theories
Research and Theory in Instructional Technology
Direction of Instruction Materials Centers
Graduate Production Workshop
Evaluation of Instructional Media
Educational Film Workshop
Designing Large Group and Multimedia Presentations
Historiography and Methodology in Film Studies
Graduate Film Seminar
Directed Research
Historical and Critical Research Methods in Communication
Seminar in Film Research and Testing
Learning, Perception, and Mass Communication Theory Applied to Mediated Instruction
Advanced Programming for Individual Instruction
Seminar in Instructional Technology
Special Problems

Undergraduate and Graduate

Documentary Film
Film History and Criticism
Literature of the Film
Filmic Expression
Censorship in Cinema
Analysis of Contemporary Cinema
Studies in Film—National Cinemas
Writing the Short Script I
Introduction to Dramatic Writing
Advanced Writing
Motion Picture Script Analysis
Makeup for Motion Pictures
Production Planning
Composition for Films and Television
Motion Picture Processing
Animation Camera
Introduction to Film Graphics-Animation
Advanced Production in Film Graphics
Animation Theory and Techniques
Art Direction
Film Business Procedures and Distribution
Film Genres
Informational Film Symposium
Theatrical Film Symposium
Adaptation: Stage to Screen I
Film Style Analysis I
Directing of Informational Motion Pictures
Basic Film Theories
Music in Motion Pictures
Ethnographic Film Analysis
Ethnographic Film Production
Use of Instructional Media in the Elementary School
Practicum in Pre-Production
Production Workshop I, II
Cinema Workshop
Special Problems
Senior Film Seminar
Advanced Camera and Lighting
Process and Theories of Communication

School of Journalism/Broadcasting 213-741-2391

CONTACT Joe Saltzman, Coordinator of Broadcasting
DEGREES OFFERED BA in broadcast journalism, BA in broadcast management, MA in broadcasting
PROGRAM MAJORS Undergraduate television — 250 students Graduate television — 35 students
ADMISSION Undergraduate requirements — 3.25 minimum grade point average, ACT or SAT scores, teachers' recommendations, written statement of purpose, portfolio, professional recommendations, written work Graduate requirements — 3.25 minimum grade point average, GRE scores, teachers' recommendations, written statement of purpose, portfolio, written work Undergraduate application deadline — 5/1
FINANCIAL AID Scholarships, work/study programs, student loans, fellowships, teaching assistantships, research assistantships, laboratory assistantships-technical expertise-TV Undergraduate application deadline — 5/1
CURRICULAR EMPHASIS Undergraduate television study — (1) management; (2) production; (3) history Undergraduate television production — (1) news/documentary; (2) public affairs; (3) commercial Graduate television production — (1) news/documentary; (2) public affairs; (3) commercial
SPECIAL ACTIVITIES/OFFERINGS Program material produced for cable television, local public television station, local commercial television station, industry, and education; internships in television production; independent study; vocational placement service
FACILITIES AND EQUIPMENT Film — 8mm cameras, editing equipment, sound recording equipment, screening

room Television — black and white studio cameras, ½-VTR, 1-inch VTR, ¾-inch cassette VTR, portable black and white cameras, editing equipment, monitors, special effects generators, slide chain, portable color cameras, ½-inch portapak recorders, ¾-inch ENG, lighting equipment, sound recording equipment, audio mixers, film chain, time base corrector, black and white studio, mobile van/unit, remote truck, audio studio, control room
FACULTY James Brown, Norman Corwin, Joe Saltzman PART-TIME FACULTY Peter Andrews, Eli Bregman, Stuart Brower, Mike Daniels, Pat Dunavan, Bob Flick, Mike Gavin, Nate Kaplan, Rick Marks, Peter Noyes, Warren Olney, Jack Petri, Joe Sullivan

COURSE LIST

Undergraduate

Principles of TV Production
History of Broadcasting
Radio and Television News
Media Advertising
Advertising Copywriting
Media and Marketing
Advertising and Media Production
Radio and Television Programming
Critical Writing

Graduate

Advanced Broadcast Documentary Production
Advanced Broadcast Reporting
Non-Fiction Color Television Production Practicum
Advanced Broadcast News Production
Broadcast Criticism
Public-Interest Broadcast Programming
Directed Research (Special Projects)

Undergraduate and Graduate

Broadcast Reporting
Television News Production
Broadcast Documentary Production
Advanced Broadcast Production
Videotape Editing for Non-Fiction TV
Broadcast Management
Social Responsibility of the News Media
Introduction to Journalism: Broadcasting, Print, Public Relations
Law of Mass Communication

California

University of the Pacific

Independent coed university. Institutionally accredited by regional association, programs recognized by NASM. Suburban location, 150-acre campus. Total enrollment: 4228. Undergraduate enrollment: 3719. Total faculty: 344 (275 full-time, 69 part-time). 4-1-4 calendar. Grading system: letters or numbers.

English Department, Stockton, CA 95211 209-946-2121

CONTACT Louis Leiter
DEGREES OFFERED BA, MA in English with emphasis in film
ADMISSION Undergraduate application deadline — rolling
FINANCIAL AID Scholarships, student loans, work/study programs, teaching assistantships, research assistantships, fellowships Undergraduate application deadline — 2/15
CURRICULAR EMPHASIS Undergraduate film study — (1) criticism and aesthetics; (2) appreciation; (3) history Graduate film study — (1) criticism and aesthetics; (2) appreciation
FACULTY Diane Borden, Arlen Hansen, Louis Leiter

COURSE LIST

Undergraduate and Graduate

Aesthetics of Film
Comparative Aesthetics
Special Topics in Film
Major Filmmakers
Filmmaking

Ventura College

District-supported 2-year coed college. Institutionally accredited by regional association. Urban location. Semester calendar. Grading system: letters or numbers.

Humanities Division, 4667 Telegraph Road, Ventura, CA 93003 805-648-7688

CONTACT Film — George Wymer or Tom Roe Television — Stu Condron
FINANCIAL AID Scholarships, work/study programs, student loans Undergraduate application deadline — through first two weeks of any semester
CURRICULAR EMPHASIS Undergraduate film study — appreciation Undergraduate filmmaking — documentary, narrative, experimental, animated, educational treated equally Undergraduate television study — criticism and aesthetics
SPECIAL ACTIVITIES/OFFERINGS Film series; film festivals; program material produced for on-campus closed-circuit television, cable television, local public television station; independent study
FACILITIES AND EQUIPMENT Film — 8mm cameras, editing equipment, sound recording equipment, projectors, 16mm cameras, projectors, screening room, permanent film library of student films, permanent film library of commercial or professional films Television — black and white studio cameras, monitors, black and white studio
FACULTY Bruce Collins, Stu Condron, Rita Goldman, Tom Roe, George Wymer

COURSE LIST

Undergraduate

Aesthetics of Film
Focus on Film
Principles of Filmmaking
Mass Communication: TV and Radio

West Los Angeles College

District-supported 2-year coed college. Part of Los Angeles Community College District System. Institutionally accredited by regional association. Urban location, 80-acre campus. Undergraduate enrollment: 10,050. Total faculty: 375 (120 full-time, 255 part-time). Semester calendar. Grading system: letters or numbers.

West Los Angeles College (continued)

Theatre/Cinema/Television Department, 4800 Frehman Drive, Culver City, CA 90230 213-836-7110

CONTACT Film — Marc L Mancini Television — Glen King
DEGREE OFFERED AA with emphasis in film, television, or theatre arts
DEPARTMENTAL MAJORS Film — 20 students Television — 20 students
ADMISSION Undergraduate application deadline — rolling
FINANCIAL AID Work/study programs, student loans
CURRICULAR EMPHASIS Film study — history, criticism and aesthetics, appreciation treated equally Filmmaking — (1) narrative; (2) documentary Television study — history, criticism and aesthetics, appreciation, production treated equally Television production — commercial, news/documentary, educational treated equally
SPECIAL ACTIVITIES/OFFERINGS Film series, film festivals, program material produced for on-campus closed-circuit television
FACILITIES AND EQUIPMENT Film — 8mm cameras, editing equipment, sound recording equipment, lighting, projectors, 16mm cameras, lighting, projectors, screening room, permanent film library of commercial or professional films Television — complete color studio production equipment, color studio
FACULTY Glen King, Marc L Mancini PART-TIME FACULTY David Einstein, Robert Perry

COURSE LIST
Undergraduate
Introduction to Motion Picture Production
History of Motion Pictures and Television
Motion Picture Workshop I, II
Main Currents in Motion Pictures
The Film as an Art Form
Fundamentals of Radio and Television Broadcasting
Advanced Cinematography and Creative Techniques
Radio and Television Production
Fundamentals of Television Production

Yuba College

State and locally supported 2-year coed college. Institutionally accredited by regional association. Rural location. Undergraduate enrollment: 8500. Total faculty: 270. Semester calendar. Grading system: letters or numbers.

Mass Communications Department, Beale Road at Linda, Marysville, CA 95901 916-742-7351

CONTACT Ernest Sandoval
DEGREE OFFERED Undergraduate degree in mass communication with emphasis in television
ADMISSION Application deadline — 9/12, rolling
FINANCIAL AID Student loans, work/study programs Application deadline — 5/31, rolling
CURRICULAR EMPHASIS Film study — (1) production; (2) educational media/instructional technology; (3) criticism and aesthetics Filmmaking — (1) experimental; (2) animated; (3) documentary Television study — (1) production; (2) educational; (3) criticism and aesthetics Television production — (1) experimental/personal video; (2) news/documentary; (3) commercial
SPECIAL ACTIVITIES/OFFERINGS Film festivals, student publications, program material produced for on-campus closed-circuit television and cable television, independent study
FACILITIES AND EQUIPMENT Film — complete 8mm equipment, 16mm editing equipment, sound recording equipment, lighting equipment, projectors, screening room, editing room, sound mixing room, permanent film library Television — complete black and white studio and exterior production equipment, complete color studio and exterior production equipment, color studio, audio studio, control room
FACULTY Ernest Sandoval

COURSE LIST
Undergraduate
Cinematography
Studio Operations
Television Production

COLORADO

Colorado Mountain College, West Campus

State and locally supported 2-year coed college. Institutionally accredited by regional association. Rural location, 680-acre campus. Undergraduate enrollment: 702. Total faculty: 43 (32 full-time, 11 part-time). Quarter calendar. Grading system: letters or numbers.

Communication/Humanities Department, 3000 County Road 114, Glenwood Springs, CO 81601 303-945-7481

CONTACT Clay Boland
DEGREE OFFERED AA in communication/humanities
ADMISSION Application deadline — 9/1, rolling
FACULTY Clay Boland

COURSE LIST
Undergraduate
Elements of Film
Fiction into Film
Film as a Reflector and Shaper of Values
Experiencing the Arts: Film

Colorado State University

State-supported coed university. Institutionally accredited by regional association, programs recognized by NASM, AACSB. Small town location, 400-acre campus. Total enrollment: 18,223. Undergraduate enrollment: 15,346. Total faculty: 1158 (905 full-time, 253 part-time). Semester calendar. Grading system: letters or numbers.

Speech and Theatre Arts Department, 302 Liberal Arts Building, Fort Collins, CO 80523 303-491-6140

CONTACT Film — J A Stitzel Television — R L MacLauchlin
DEGREES OFFERED BA, MA in speech and theatre arts with emphasis on television-radio
DEPARTMENTAL MAJORS Graduate film — 3 students Undergraduate television — 60 students Graduate television — 8 students
ADMISSION Undergraduate requirements — 2.0 minimum grade point average, ACT or SAT scores, interviews, professional recommendations, written statement of purpose Graduate requirements — 3.0 minimum grade point average, GRE scores, interviews, professional recommendations, written statement of purpose Undergraduate application deadline — rolling
FINANCIAL AID Teaching assistantships
CURRICULAR EMPHASIS Film study — (1) history; (2) appreciation; (3) criticism and aesthetics Filmmaking — (1) documentary; (2) narrative; (3) educational; (4) experimental Undergraduate television study — (1) history; (2) criticism and aesthetics; (3) appreciation; (4) production; (5) management; (6) educational Graduate television study — (1) criticism and aesthetics; (2) management; (3) educational; (4) history Undergraduate television production — (1) commercial; (2) experimental/personal video; (3) educational Graduate television production — (1) commercial; (2) news/documentary; (3) educational
SPECIAL ACTIVITIES/OFFERINGS Film series; film festivals; film societies; program material produced for on-campus closed-circuit television, local public television station, local commercial television station; apprenticeships; internships in television production; independent study; practicum; teacher training; vocational placement service
FACILITIES AND EQUIPMENT Film — 16mm projectors, permanent film library Television — complete black and white studio production equipment, complete color studio production equipment, black and white studio, color studio, audio studio, control room
FACULTY G Jack Gravlee, Robert MacLauchlin, Dennis Phillips, James Stitzel

COURSE LIST

Undergraduate
Television-Radio in Society
Television-Radio Speaking
History and Appreciation of Film
Evaluating Contemporary Television
Television-Radio Writing and Production I, II
Evaluating Contemporary Film
Television-Radio Programming/Management
Television-Radio-Film Individual Study
History of Documentary Film

Graduate
Broadcasting in the Public Interest
Broadcast Audience Analysis
International Broadcasting
Independent Study in Television-Radio-Film
Film Seminar
Television Seminar
Television Internship

Undergraduate and Graduate
Film Theory and Criticism
Television-Radio Internship

Journalism Department, C-225 Social Science Building, Fort Collins, CO 80521 303-491-6310

CONTACT Fred Shook
DEGREE OFFERED Undergraduate degree in broadcast news and television production
ADMISSION Requirement — 2.2 minimum grade point average Application deadline — rolling
FINANCIAL AID Scholarships, student loans, work/study programs Application deadline — 4/1
CURRICULAR EMPHASIS Film study — (1) production; (2) criticism and aesthetics; (3) history; (4) appreciation; (5) educational media/instructional technology Filmmaking — (1) personal; (2) documentary; (3) narrative; (4) educational; (5) experimental; (6) animated Television production — (1) experimental/personal video; (2) educational; (3) news/documentary
SPECIAL ACTIVITIES/OFFERINGS Film series; film festivals; program material produced for on-campus closed-circuit television, local public television station, local commercial television station; internships in film and television production; independent study; practicum; teacher training
FACILITIES AND EQUIPMENT Film — complete 16mm equipment, sound stage, screening room, editing room, sound mixing room, animation board, permanent film library Television — complete black and white studio and color exterior production equipment, black and white studio, color studio, audio studio, control room, ENG facilities, audio studio
FACULTY Dan Hilleman, Fred Shook

COURSE LIST

Graduate
Broadcast News
Cinematography
Documentary Film
Special Studies in Film/Television
Film and Videotape Editing
CATV News

Community College of Denver, Auraria Campus

State-supported 2-year coed college. Part of Community College of Denver System. Institutionally accredited by regional association. Urban location. Undergraduate enrollment: 3785. Total faculty: 221 (87 full-time, 134 part-time). Semester calendar. Grading system: letters or numbers.

Arts and Humanities Department, 1111 West Colfax, Denver, CO 80204 303-629-2474

CONTACT Film — Maria Siddeck Television — David Knauber
DEGREE OFFERED AA in speech/communication
DEPARTMENTAL MAJORS 10 students

Community College of Denver, Auraria Campus (continued)

CURRICULAR EMPHASIS Film study — (1) appreciation; (2) history; (3) criticism and aesthetics Filmmaking — (1) narrative; (2) documentary; (3) experimental Television study — (1) history; (2) criticism; (3) production Television production — commercial, news, educational treated equally
SPECIAL ACTIVITIES/OFFERINGS Apprenticeships
FACILITIES AND EQUIPMENT Television — complete black and white studio and exterior production equipment, complete color studio and exterior production equipment, black and white studio, color studio, audio studio, control room available in Tri-Campus Media Center
FACULTY David Knauber, Maria Siddeck

COURSE LIST
Undergraduate
The Movies (Introduction)
The Movies (Genres)
Radio and Television
Introduction to Mass Media

Regis College

Independent Jesuit 4-year coed college. Institutionally accredited by regional association. Suburban location, 50-acre campus. Undergraduate enrollment: 1150. Total faculty: 95 (72 full-time, 23 part-time). Semester calendar. Grading system: letters or numbers.

Communication Arts Department, West 50th and Lowell Boulevard, Denver, CO 80221 303-458-4100, ext 4969

CONTACT John Griess
DEGREE OFFERED BA in communication arts with an emphasis in film or broadcast media; minor in communication arts
DEPARTMENTAL MAJORS Undergraduate film — 10 students Undergraduate television — 32 students
ADMISSION Undergraduate requirements — 2.00 minimum grade point average, interview, teachers' recommendations, written statement of purpose
FINANCIAL AID Scholarships, work/study programs, student loans
CURRICULAR EMPHASIS Film study — (1) history; (2) criticism and aesthetics; (3) film genres Filmmaking — (1) narrative; (2) documentary Television study — (1) criticism and aesthetics; (2) history; (3) production Television production — (1) news/documentary; (2) commercial; (3) educational
SPECIAL ACTIVITIES/OFFERINGS Film series, internships in film production, internships in television production, independent study
FACILITIES AND EQUIPMENT Film — 8mm cameras, editing equipment, sound recording equipment, lighting, projectors, screening room, editing room, permanent film library of student films Television — black and white studio cameras, portable black and white cameras, editing equipment, lighting equipment, sound recording equipment
FACULTY Dennis Gallagher, John L Griess

COURSE LIST
Undergraduate
Mass Media
The American Film
Film Art
Mass Communications Law
Mass Media and Mass Society
Broadcast Announcing
Filmmaking Practice
Film Review Writing
Themes and Genres in Film
Women and Minorities in Film
Film Comedy
Perspectives on Television
Broadcast Media Writing
Television Production
Internship in Mass Media and Film
Independent Study in Mass Media and Film

University of Colorado, Boulder

State-supported coed university. Part of University of Colorado System. Institutionally accredited by regional association. Suburban location, 590-acre campus. Total enrollment: 20,153. Undergraduate enrollment: 17,000. Total faculty: 1200 (964 full-time, 236 part-time). Semester calendar. Grading system: letters or numbers.

Department of Communication, 1165 Broadway, Boulder, CO 80302 303-492-7306

CONTACT Film — Stephen Hinerman Television — Dan Niemeyer
DEGREE OFFERED Undergraduate degree in communications with emphasis in radio-television-film
DEPARTMENTAL MAJORS 250 students
ADMISSION Requirement — minimum grade point average Application deadline — rolling
FINANCIAL AID Scholarships, work/study programs, student loans, fellowships, teaching assistantships Application deadline — 2/15
CURRICULAR EMPHASIS Film study — (1) history; (2) criticism and aesthetics; (3) educational media/instructional technology Filmmaking — documentary, narrative, animated treated equally Television study — (1) production; (2) history; (3) management Television production — (1) commercial; (2) news/documentary; (3) educational
SPECIAL ACTIVITIES/OFFERINGS Film series, film festivals, film societies, program material produced for on-campus closed-circuit television, internships in television production, independent study
FACILITIES AND EQUIPMENT Film — complete 8mm and 16mm equipment, screening room, editing room, permanent film library of commercial or professional films Television — complete black and white and color studio production equipment, complete black and white exterior production equipment, black and white studio, color studio
FACULTY Harold Hill, Stephen Hinerman, Stephen Jones, Dan Niemeyer

COURSE LIST
Undergraduate
Introduction to Broadcasting and Film
Introduction to Filmmaking
Introduction to Television Production
Introduction to Radio Production
Television II, III
Advanced Radio
Advanced Television Theory
Rhetorical and Aesthetic Dimension of Communication

Undergraduate and Graduate

Mass Media and Society
Internship in Radio-TV-Film
Station Organization and Operation
Seminar in Broadcasting: Controls
TV in Education

Film Studies Program, Hunter 102, Boulder, CO 80309 303-492-7903

CONTACT Virgil Grillo
DEGREES OFFERED BA, MA in communications with an emphasis in film or TV, BFA in fine arts with an emphasis in film, BA, PhD in English or humanities with an emphasis in film
ADMISSION Undergraduate application deadline — one semester before enrollment
FINANCIAL AID Work/study programs, student loans
CURRICULAR EMPHASIS Undergraduate film study — history, criticism and aesthetics, appreciation treated equally Undergraduate filmmaking — documentary, narrative, experimental, animated treated equally Undergraduate television study — history, criticism and aesthetics, appreciation, educational treated equally Undergraduate television production — (1) news/documentary; (2) commercial; (3) educational; (4) experimental/personal video
SPECIAL ACTIVITIES/OFFERINGS Filmmaking clubs, film series, film festivals, avant-garde film series with visiting filmmakers, program material produced for on-campus closed-circuit television, independent study
FACILITIES AND EQUIPMENT Film — 8mm and 16mm cameras, editing equipment, sound recording equipment, lighting, projectors, screening room, editing room, animation board, permanent film library of student films, permanent film library of commercial or professional films Television — black and white studio cameras, color studio cameras, ½-inch VTR, 1-inch VTR, 2-inch VTR, ¾-inch cassette VTR, portable black and white cameras, editing equipment, monitors, slide chain, ½-inch portapak recorders, lighting equipment, sound recording equipment, audio mixers, time base corrector, black and white studio, audio studio, control room
PART-TIME FACULTY Jerry Aronson, Leslie Brill, Virgil Grillo, Steve Hinerman, Bruce Kawin, Joyce Lebra, James Otis, James Palmer, Sue Robinson, Fred Worden, Donald Yannacito

COURSE LIST

Undergraduate

Beginning Filmmaking
Film History I, II
Major Film Directors
Study in Documentary Film
Japanese History Through Film
Film and Fiction
Film Narrative
Intermediate Filmmaking
Film Theory

School of Journalism, Campus Box 287, Boulder, CO 80309

CONTACT Sam Kuczun
DEGREES OFFERED BS in journalism (radio-TV), MA in journalism
PROGRAM MAJORS Undergraduate television — 45 students Graduate television — 2 students
ADMISSION Undergraduate requirement — written statement of purpose Graduate requirements — teachers' recommendations, written statement of purpose
FINANCIAL AID Scholarships, work/study programs, teaching assistantships
CURRICULAR EMPHASIS Undergraduate television study — (1) criticism and aesthetics; (2) production; (3) management Graduate television study — (1) criticism and aesthetics; (2) appreciation Undergraduate television production — (1) news/documentary; (2) experimental/personal video; (3) commercial
SPECIAL ACTIVITIES/OFFERINGS Program material produced for on-campus closed-circuit television, internships in television production, independent study, vocational placement service
FACILITIES AND EQUIPMENT Television — black and white studio cameras, color studio cameras, ½-inch VTR, 1-inch VTR, ¾-inch cassette VTR, portable black and white cameras, editing equipment, monitors, special effects generators, slide chain, ½-inch portapak recorders, ¾-inch ENG, lighting equipment, sound recording equipment, audio mixers, film chain, time base corrector, black and white studio, color studio, audio studio, control room
FACULTY Sam Archibald, Harold Hill, Stephen Jones, Sam Kuczun, Don Somerville PART-TIME FACULTY Daniel Niemeyer

COURSE LIST

Undergraduate

Radio-TV News
Principles of Broadcast Production
Advanced Radio Programming and Production
TV Production II, III
Advanced TV Programming
Journalism and the Law
Contemporary Mass Media

Undergraduate and Graduate

Radio-TV Station Organization and Operation
Advanced Radio-TV News
Broadcast News Projects

University of Colorado, Colorado Springs

State-supported comprehensive coed institution. Part of University of Colorado. Institutionally accredited by regional association, programs recognized by AACSB. Suburban location, 400-acre campus. Total enrollment: 4390. Undergraduate enrollment: 3212. Total faculty: 215 (125 full-time, 90 part-time). Semester calendar. Grading system: letters or numbers.

Media Studies, Austin Bluffs Parkway, Colorado Springs, CO 80907 303-593-3000

CONTACT Film — Jane Stanbrough Television — Pam Shockley
DEGREE OFFERED BA in communication (distributed studies degree)
ADMISSION Requirement — ACT or SAT scores Application deadline — 7/1 for fall, 12/1 for spring
FINANCIAL AID Work/study programs, student loans
CURRICULAR EMPHASIS Film study — history, appreciation treated equally Filmmaking — documentary, experimental treated equally Television study — production Television production — commercial, news/documentary, educational treated equally
SPECIAL ACTIVITIES/OFFERINGS Film series, internships in film production, internships in television production

University of Colorado, Colorado Springs (continued)

FACILITIES AND EQUIPMENT Film — 8mm cameras, editing equipment, sound recording equipment, lighting, projectors, fullcoat recording and mixing, editing room, sound mixing room Television — color studio cameras, ¾-inch cassette VTR, portable black and white cameras, monitors, special effects generators, slide chain, ½-inch portapak recorders, lighting equipment, sound recording equipment, audio mixers, time base corrector, Super-8 videoplayer, color studio, control room

COURSE LIST

Undergraduate

TV Production
Advanced TV Production
TV Programming
Filmmaking
Advanced Filmmaking
Film Study
History of Cinema

University of Denver

Independent coed university. Institutionally accredited by regional association, programs recognized by NASM, AACSB, NASA. Suburban location, 125-acre campus. Total enrollment: 7727. Undergraduate enrollment: 4262. Total faculty: 600 (475 full-time, 125 part-time). Quarter calendar. Grading system: letters or numbers.

Mass Communications Department, 2490 South Gaylord, Denver, CO 80210 303-753-2166

CONTACT Phillip Stephens
PROGRAM OFFERED Major in mass communications with emphasis in film or television
ADMISSION Undergraduate requirements — 3.0 minimum grade point average, SAT scores, interviews Graduate requirements — 3.0 minimum grade point average, GRE scores, interviews Undergraduate application deadline — 7/1, rolling
FINANCIAL AID Scholarships, student loans, work/study programs, teaching assistantships, research assistantships Undergraduate application deadline — 4/1
CURRICULAR EMPHASIS Film study — (1) criticism and aesthetics; (2) audience study; (3) production Filmmaking — (1) fundamental skills; (2) documentary; (3) experimental Television study — (1) production; (2) management; (3) criticism and aesthetics Television production — (1) commercial; (2) news/documentary; (3) educational
SPECIAL ACTIVITIES/OFFERINGS Independent study, practicum
FACILITIES AND EQUIPMENT Film — complete 8mm and 16mm equipment, screening room, editing room, permanent film library Television — complete black and white studio and exterior production equipment, black and white studio, audio studio, control room
FACULTY Harold Mendelsohn, Garret O'Keefe, Robert Snyder, H T Spetnagel, Phillip Stephens, Lawrence Thompson, Diane Waldman, Donna Wilson, Michael Wirth

COURSE LIST

Undergraduate

Economics of Mass Communication
Television and Film as Art Forms
Broadcast News and Documentary
Writing for Motion Pictures

Undergraduate and Graduate

Producing Films
Television Writing and Production
Advanced Television Writing and Production
Broadcast Journalism
Workshop in Teaching by Television
Television News and Documentary
Motion Picture Production I, II
Film Arts
Cable Television
Creative Writing for Film
Television Documentary and Teleplay
Experiment—Television Production

CONNECTICUT

Asnuntuck Community College

State-supported 2-year coed college. Part of Connecticut Community College System. Institutionally accredited by regional association. Suburban location. Undergraduate enrollment: 1560. Total faculty: 37 (16 full-time, 21 part-time). Semester calendar. Grading system: letters or numbers.

Media–Mass Communications Department, 111 Phoenix Avenue, Enfield, CT 06082 203-745-1603

CONTACT Robert Bergquist
DEGREE OFFERED AA in mass communications
DEGREES OFFERED Film — 25 students Television — 25 students
ADMISSION Requirement — minimum grade point average Application deadline — rolling
FINANCIAL AID Student loans, work/study programs Application deadline — rolling
CURRICULAR EMPHASIS Film study — (1) production; (2) history; (3) criticism and aesthetics Filmmaking — (1) documentary; (2) narrative; (3) animated Television study — (1) production; (2) educational Television production — (1) news/documentary; (2) experimental/personal video; (3) educational
SPECIAL ACTIVITIES/OFFERINGS Film series, film festivals, film societies, program material produced for on-campus closed-circuit television and local public television station, independent study, practicum, teacher training
FACILITIES AND EQUIPMENT Film — complete 8mm equipment, screening room, editing room, sound mixing room, animation board, permanent film library Television — complete black and white studio and exterior production facilities, complete color studio and exterior production equipment, color studio, mobile van unit, control room
FACULTY Robert Bergquist

COURSE LIST

Undergraduate

Filmmaking I, II
Television Production I, II
Film History
Introduction to Mass Communications

Central Connecticut State College

State-supported comprehensive coed institution. Part of Connecticut State Colleges System. Institutionally accredited by regional association. Suburban location, 135-acre campus. Total enrollment: 11,433. Undergraduate enrollment: 9337. Total faculty: 658 (420 full-time, 238 part-time). Semester calendar. Grading system: letters or numbers.

English Department, 1615 Stanley Street, New Britain, CT 06050 203-827-7247

CONTACT Allan Hirsh
PROGRAM OFFERED Major in English with emphasis in film or television
ADMISSION Requirement — interviews Undergraduate application deadline — rolling
CURRICULAR EMPHASIS Film study — history, criticism and aesthetics, appreciation treated equally Filmmaking — documentary, narrative treated equally
SPECIAL ACTIVITIES/OFFERINGS Film series, film festivals, film societies
FACILITIES AND EQUIPMENT Film — 8mm and 16mm cameras, editing equipment, lighting equipment, black and white stock, color film stock, projectors, editing room, sound mixing room, animation board
FACULTY Allan Hirsh, Roy Temple

COURSE LIST

Undergraduate

Language of Film

Undergraduate and Graduate

Film and Literature
Studies in Major American Directors

Fairfield University

Independent Roman Catholic comprehensive coed institution. Institutionally accredited by regional association. Suburban location, 200-acre campus. Total enrollment: 4704. Undergraduate enrollment: 2788. Total faculty: 326 (171 full-time, 155 part-time). Semester calendar. Grading system: letters or numbers.

Graduate School of Corporate and Political Communication, Fairfield, CT 06430 203-255-5411

CONTACT T A Cheney
DEGREES OFFERED MA in communication, graduate certificate in video programming
SPECIAL ACTIVITIES/OFFERINGS Program material produced for local public television station, independent study
FACILITIES AND EQUIPMENT Television — complete black and white studio and exterior production equipment, black and white studio, control room
PART-TIME FACULTY Ray Abel, Guy Fraumeni, Meg Gottemoeller, Bruce Harding

COURSE LIST

Graduate

Film Making
Video Production Techniques
Advanced Video Production Techniques
Video Workshop
Professional Portfolio Productions
Writing for Private Network Video
Writing for the Visual Media
Independent Productions

Holy Apostles College

Independent Roman Catholic 4-year college primarily for men. Candidate for institutional accreditation. Suburban location, 15-acre campus. Undergraduate enrollment: 72. Total faculty: 16 (11 full-time, 5 part-time). Semester calendar. Grading system: letters or numbers.

Art Department, 33 Prospect Hill Road, Cromwell, CT 06416 203-635-5311

DEGREES OFFERED BA in humanities, BA in religious studies, BA in philosophy, BA in social sciences
FINANCIAL AID Scholarships, work/study programs
CURRICULAR EMPHASIS Film study — (1) philosophy, religion; (2) social sciences, history
SPECIAL ACTIVITIES/OFFERINGS Film festivals, masses televised occasionally for local public television station
FACILITIES AND EQUIPMENT Film — sound mixing room Television — 1-inch VTR, sound recording equipment, audio mixers, audio studio

Manchester Community College

State-supported 2-year coed college. Part of Connecticut Community College System. Institutionally accredited by regional association. Suburban location. Undergraduate enrollment: 5000. Total faculty: 200 (125 full-time, 75 part-time). Semester calendar. Grading system: letters or numbers.

Manchester Community College (continued)

Media Program, Manchester, CT 06040 203-646-4900

CONTACT Richard Dana, Coordinator
ADMISSION Application deadline — rolling

COURSE LIST
Undergraduate
Film Study and Appreciation
Filmmaking
Television Production
Broadcast Writing
Broadcast Production
Introduction to Media Careers
Television Writing
Broadcast Announcing

Middlesex Community College

State-supported 2-year coed college. Part of Connecticut Community College System. Institutionally accredited by regional association. Small town location, 38-acre campus. Undergraduate enrollment: 2000. Total faculty: 75 (60 full-time, 15 part-time). Semester calendar. Grading system: letters or numbers.

Cable Telecommunications Department, 100 Training Hill Road, Middletown, CT 06457 203-347-7411

CONTACT Virginia Pettiross
DEGREE OFFERED AS in cable telecommunications
DEPARTMENTAL MAJORS 40 students
ADMISSION Requirement — interviews Application deadline — rolling
FINANCIAL AID Scholarships, student loans, work/study programs Application deadline — rolling
CURRICULAR EMPHASIS Television study — (1) current problems and regulatory matters; (2) production; (3) management Television production — (1) news/documentary; (2) experimental/personal video; (3) local access
SPECIAL ACTIVITIES/OFFERINGS Student publication; program material produced for on-campus closed-circuit television, cable television. local public television station; apprenticeships; internships in television production; practicum
FACILITIES AND EQUIPMENT Television — complete color remote production facilities, complete color studio and exterior production equipment, color studio, audio studio, control room
FACULTY Kathy Gunst, Virginia Pettiross PART-TIME FACULTY Anthony Agnes, Thomas Hricko, Earl Roberts

COURSE LIST
Undergraduate
Introduction to CATV I, II
Engineering Graphics
CATV Graphics
Fundamentals of Electronics
Operation and Maintenance of Supplementary CATV Equipment
Technical Practice
Nontechnical Practice
Basic TV
Advanced TV
Advanced Electronics
Repairs and Maintenance
Internship
Management

Norwalk Community College

State-supported 2-year coed college. Part of Connecticut Community College System. Institutionally accredited by regional association. Urban location. Undergraduate enrollment: 3207. Total faculty: 99 (67 full-time, 32 part-time). Semester calendar. Grading system: letters or numbers.

English and Film Department, 333 Wilson Avenue, Norwalk, CT 06854 203-853-2040

CONTACT Ada Lambert
ADMISSION Application deadline — 8/15, rolling
CURRICULAR EMPHASIS Film study — (1) appreciation; (2) history; (3) criticism and aesthetics Filmmaking — (1) narrative; (2) documentary; (3) experimental
SPECIAL ACTIVITIES/OFFERINGS Film series, film societies, independent study
FACILITIES AND EQUIPMENT Film — 8mm cameras, editing equipment, sound recording equipment, lighting equipment, black and white film stock, projectors, screening room, analyzing projector, animation board, permanent film library
FACULTY Ada Lambert

COURSE LIST
Undergraduate
Communications
Film Appreciation
American Film

Sacred Heart University

Independent Roman Catholic comprehensive coed institution. Institutionally accredited by regional association. Suburban location. Total enrollment: 2912. Undergraduate enrollment: 1180. Total faculty: 168 (65 full-time, 103 part-time). Semester calendar. Grading system: letters or numbers.

Media Studies Department, 5229 Park Avenue, Bridgeport, CT 06606 203-374-9441

CONTACT Donald Coonley or Steven Ross
PROGRAM OFFERED Major in media studies with emphasis in film or television
ADMISSION Requirement — grade of C or better in basic media course Application deadline — 9/1, rolling

Connecticut

CURRICULAR EMPHASIS Film study — (1) appreciation; (2) production; (3) history, (4) criticism and aesthetics Filmmaking — (1) documentary; (2) experimental; (3) animated; (4) narrative; (5) educational Television study — (1) production; (2) appreciation; (3) criticism and aesthetics Television production — (1) news/documentary; (2) commercial; (3) experimental/personal video
SPECIAL ACTIVITIES/OFFERINGS Film series, program material produced for community organizations, independent study, practicum, vocational placement service
FACILITIES AND EQUIPMENT Film — complete 8mm equipment, 16mm projectors, sound stage, screening room, editing room Television — black and white studio cameras, ¾-inch color recording and editing equipment, ½-inch VTR, portable black and white cameras, editing equipment, monitors, special effects generators, ½-inch portapak recorder, lighting equipment, sound recording equipment, audio mixers, black and white studio, audio studio, control room
FACULTY Donald Coonley, Steven Ross PART-TIME FACULTY Chris Campbell, Dennis Kearns, Ada Lambert, Paul Morton, Steve Winters

COURSE LIST

Undergraduate

Media: The Extensions of Man
Video Skills I, II
Filmmaking Workshop I, II
Development of Motion Pictures I, II
Film Seminar
Kinetics: Studies in the Moving Image
World War II: A Filmic Image
Internships in Film and TV Industry
The Roaring Twenties: A Filmic Image
Media Practicum
Images of Women in Film

Southern Connecticut State College

State-supported comprehensive coed institution. Part of Connecticut State Colleges System. Institutionally accredited by regional association. Urban location. Total enrollment: 8502. Undergraduate enrollment: 6620. Total faculty: 639 (382 full-time, 257 part-time). Semester calendar. Grading system: letters or numbers.

Theater Department, 501 Crescent, New Haven, CT 06515 203-397-4554

CONTACT Daniel Ort
CURRICULAR EMPHASIS Undergraduate film study — history, criticism and aesthetics, appreciation treated equally Undergraduate filmmaking — documentary, narrative, experimental treated equally
SPECIAL ACTIVITIES/OFFERINGS Film festivals
FACILITIES AND EQUIPMENT Film — 8mm and 16mm cameras, editing equipment, lighting, projectors, 8mm sound recording equipment, screening room, editing room

COURSE LIST

Undergraduate

Introduction to Film
Westerns
American Film Directors
Filmmaking I, II
Video Drama
Film and Tape Journalism

Department of Communications 203-397-4575

CONTACT B P McCabe
DEGREE OFFERED BS in corporate video/communication
DEPARTMENTAL MAJORS Television — 350 students
ADMISSION Requirement — interview Application deadline — 8/31
FINANCIAL AID Work/study programs
CURRICULAR EMPHASIS Television study — production Television production — industrial television
SPECIAL ACTIVITIES/OFFERINGS Program material produced for on-campus closed-circuit television, cable television, local public television station, Corporate Video Productions by Owl Video Productions (nonprofit); apprenticeships; internships in television production; independent study; vocational placement service; assignment to Owl Video Productions, nonprofit company of department
FACILITIES AND EQUIPMENT Television — color studio and exterior production equipment, color studio, mobile van/unit, control room, ENG/EFP professional facilities with Owl Video Productions

COURSE LIST

Undergraduate

Communication for Management and Business
Industrial and Technical Communication
Organizational Communication
ENG/EFP
Field Experience in Corporate Communication
Principles of Electronics in Communications
Persuasion in Mass Media
Video Technology
Broadcast Management
TV/Radio Advertising and Sales
Communicating on TV
Electronic Editing for ENG/EFP
Scripting for Corporate Productions
Producing for Corporate Video

University of Bridgeport

Independent comprehensive coed institution. Institutionally accredited by regional association. Urban location, 87-acre campus. Total enrollment: 6956. Undergraduate enrollment: 4800. Total faculty: 437. Semester calendar. Grading system: letters.

Cinema Department, 84 Iranistan Avenue, Bridgeport, CT 06602 203-576-4430

CONTACT Gerald Wenner, Chairman
DEGREES OFFERED BA, BFA in cinema
DEPARTMENTAL MAJORS Film — 75 students
ADMISSION Requirements — SAT scores, interviews, portfolio (when possible), professional recommendations, teachers' recommendations, written statement of purpose Application deadline — rolling
FINANCIAL AID Scholarships, student loans, work/study programs, teaching assistantships Application deadline — 4/1

University of Bridgeport (continued)

CURRICULAR EMPHASIS Film study — (1) production; (2) criticism and aesthetics, appreciation; (3) history Filmmaking — documentary, narrative, experimental, animated treated equally
SPECIAL ACTIVITIES/OFFERINGS Film series, film festivals, film societies, student publications, apprenticeships, internships in film production, independent study, practicum, teacher training, vocational placement service
FACILITIES AND EQUIPMENT Film — complete 16mm equipment, sound stage, screening room, editing room, sound mixing room, animation room, permanent film library Television — complete color studio and exterior production equipment
FACULTY Yuri Denysenko, Michael Kerbel, Gerald Wenner PART-TIME FACULTY Susan Granger, John McCally, George Morris, Richard Sanca, Jon Sonneborn

COURSE LIST
Undergraduate
Film Technique I, II
Film Sound and Editing
Cinematography I–III
Directing
Screenwriting I, II
Film Production Seminar
Independent Studies in Film
TV Production and Direction
Animation
Documentary Film
Special Effects
Experimental Film Workshop
Lighting Seminar
Audio Experimentation
Video Art
Film Theory
Silent Film
Sound Film I, II
American Film I, II
Film History Seminars
Orson Welles Seminar
Foreign Film Seminar
Alfred Hitchcock Seminar
Film Criticism Seminar
French New Wave
Western Seminar
Comedy Seminar
Horror Film Seminar
Science Fiction Seminar

Journalism/Communications Department, North Hall, Bridgeport, CT 06602 203-576-4178

CONTACT Gene Lichtenstein
DEGREES OFFERED BA, BS in broadcast journalism
DEPARTMENTAL MAJORS Television — 30 students
ADMISSION Requirements — ACT or SAT scores, teachers' recommendations, written statement of purpose, high school record
FINANCIAL AID Scholarships, work/study programs, student loans
CURRICULAR EMPHASIS Television study — history, production, broadcast newsreporting, documentary treated equally Television production — commercial, news/documentary, educational, community treated equally
SPECIAL ACTIVITIES/OFFERINGS Program material produced for cable television and local public television station, apprenticeships, internships in television production, independent study, broadcast internship
FACILITIES AND EQUIPMENT Television — color studio cameras, ½-inch VTR, ¾-inch cassette VTR, portable black and white cameras, editing equipment, monitors, portable color cameras, ½-inch portapak recorders, sound recording equipment, color studio, audio studio, control room
FACULTY Margot Hardenbergh, Gene Lichtenstein, David Smith

COURSE LIST
Undergraduate
Broadcast Newswriting
TV Production and Direction
History of Broadcasting
TV Cable Production
Advanced Audio Experimentation
TV Documentary
Portable Video Workshop
TV Commercials: Workshop
Introduction to Broadcasting

University of Connecticut

State-supported 4-year coed college. Institutionally accredited by regional association. Rural location. Total enrollment: 200. Total faculty: 19 (9 full-time, 10 part-time). Semester calendar. Grading system: letters or numbers.

Dramatic Arts Department, RFD University Drive, Torrington, CT 06790 203-482-7635

CONTACT Dan Calabrese
ADMISSION Undergraduate requirements — ACT or SAT scores, portfolio Graduate requirements — GRE scores Undergraduate application deadline — 7/1
FINANCIAL AID Scholarships, work/study programs, student loans Undergraduate application deadline — 7/1
CURRICULAR EMPHASIS Graduate film study — history, appreciation treated equally
SPECIAL ACTIVITIES/OFFERINGS Film series, film festivals, film societies, program material produced for on-campus closed-circuit television
FACILITIES AND EQUIPMENT Film — 16mm projectors
FACULTY Dan Calabrese

COURSE LIST
Undergraduate
Dramatic Arts

University of Hartford

Independent coed university. Institutionally accredited by regional association, programs recognized by NASM, NASA. Suburban location. Total enrollment: 9274. Undergraduate enrollment: 6646. Total faculty: 618 (288 full-time, 330 part-time). Semester calendar. Grading system: letters or numbers.

English Department, Bloomfield Avenue, West Hartford, CT 06117 203-243-4415

CONTACT Paul H Stacy
ADMISSION Application deadline — 6/1, rolling
FINANCIAL AID Scholarships, student loans, work/study programs, teaching assistantships, fellowships Application deadline — 3/1, rolling
CURRICULAR EMPHASIS Film study — (1) appreciation; (2) criticism and aesthetics; (3) history Filmmaking — (1) narrative; (2) documentary; (3) experimental

SPECIAL ACTIVITIES/OFFERINGS Film series
FACILITIES AND EQUIPMENT Film — 8mm and 16mm projectors, permanent film library
FACULTY Gary Hogan, James Keener, Paul H Stacy PART-TIME FACULTY Regina Cornwall

COURSE LIST

Undergraduate
Cinema and Literature
Film History
Film and Novel

University of New Haven

Independent comprehensive coed institution. Institutionally accredited by regional association. Urban location, 53-acre campus. Total enrollment: 7254. Undergraduate enrollment: 2399. Total faculty: 475 (135 full-time, 340 part-time). 4-1-4 calendar. Grading system: letters or numbers.

Communication Department, 300 Orange Avenue, West Haven, CT 06516 203-934-6321

CONTACT M L McLaughlin
PROGRAM OFFERED Major in communication with emphasis in film, television, or radio
ADMISSION Requirement — SAT scores Application deadline — 8/15, rolling
FINANCIAL AID Scholarships, student loans, work/study programs
CURRICULAR EMPHASIS Film study — (1) production; (2) criticism and aesthetics; (3) appreciation Filmmaking — (1) industrial; (2) educational; (3) documentary Television study — (1) production; (2) management; (3) criticism and aesthetics Television production — (1) commercial; (2) educational; (3) news/documentary
SPECIAL ACTIVITIES/OFFERINGS Film series, program material produced for cable television, apprenticeships, independent study, Fall Forum '78 (a special one-day workshop on Children's Television); Annual Summer Institute (runs three weeks on special topics)
FACILITIES AND EQUIPMENT Film — complete 16mm equipment, Super-8mm film, sound stage, screening room, editing room, sound mixing room Television — black and white and color studio and exterior production equipment, audio studio, control room
FACULTY James Dull, Lawrence Londino, M L McLaughlin, Stephen Raucher

COURSE LIST

Undergraduate
Film Production Theory
Film Production I, II
Television Production I, II
Advanced Television Production
Radio Production
Writing for Television and Radio
Broadcast Journalism
Television/Radio Management
Problems of Mass Communication
Dramatic Scriptwriting for Film and Television

Graduate
Basics of Business Media Production Techniques
Planning Audio Visual Systems for Business
Scripting the Media Presentations
Media Presentations for Business

Wesleyan University

Independent coed university. Institutionally accredited by regional association. Small town location, 100-acre campus. Total enrollment: 2550. Undergraduate enrollment: 2400. Total faculty: 269 (239 full-time, 30 part-time). Semester calendar. Grading system: letters or numbers.

Art Department, Middletown, CT 06457 203-347-9411

CONTACT John Frazer
DEGREE OFFERED BA in art with emphasis in film
DEPARTMENTAL MAJORS 20 students
ADMISSION Requirement — minimum grade point average Application deadline — 1/15
FINANCIAL AID Scholarships, student loans, work/study programs Application deadline — 1/15
CURRICULAR EMPHASIS Film study — (1) history; (2) criticism and aesthetics; (3) production Filmmaking — (1) narrative; (2) documentary; (3) experimental Television production — (1) experimental/personal video; (2) news/documentary
SPECIAL ACTIVITIES/OFFERINGS Film series, internships in television production
FACILITIES AND EQUIPMENT Film — complete 16mm equipment, screening room, 35mm screening facilities, editing room, sound mixing room, animation board Television — ½-inch VTR, portable black and white cameras, editing equipment, monitors, special effects generators, ½-inch portapak recorder, black and white studio
FACULTY Jeanine Basinger, John Frazer, Joseph W Reed, Richard Slotkin

COURSE LIST

Undergraduate
The Language of Film
The Studio System
The Musical Film
The Western
Film Noir
The French Film
British Film
Japanese Film
Directorial Style
Film Workshop

Graduate Liberal Studies

CONTACT John Frazer
DEGREE OFFERED MA in liberal studies with an emphasis in film
ADMISSION Requirements — minimum grade point average, interviews (when possible), written statement of purpose
FINANCIAL AID Scholarships, student loans, work/study programs
CURRICULAR EMPHASIS Film study — (1) criticism and aesthetics; (2) production; (3) history Filmmaking — (1) narrative; (2) documentary; (3) experimental Television production — (1) experimental/personal video; (2) news/documentary

Wesleyan University (continued)

SPECIAL ACTIVITIES/OFFERINGS Film series, independent study, teacher training
FACILITIES AND EQUIPMENT Film — complete 16mm equipment, sound recording equipment, lighting equipment, screening room, 35mm screening facilities, editing room, sound mixing room, animation board, Saudek-Omnibus Collection
PART-TIME FACULTY Jeanine Basinger, Gary Collins, John Frazer, Joseph Reed, Michael Stern

COURSE LIST

Graduate

Film Narrative
The American Film
Focus on Directors
Film Production
Genre and Authorship
French Film
Fantasy Film
Video Production

Western Connecticut State College

State-supported comprehensive coed institution. Part of Connecticut State Colleges System. Institutionally accredited by regional association. Urban location, 278-acre campus. Total enrollment: 5496. Undergraduate enrollment: 2706. Total faculty: 220 (165 full-time, 55 part-time). Semester calendar. Grading system: letters or numbers.

Photography, Film and TV Department, 181 White Street, Danbury, CT 06001 203-797-4047

CONTACT Joan Fleckenstein
DEGREE OFFERED BS in film and television
DEPARTMENTAL MAJORS Film — 10 students Television — 10 students
ADMISSION Undergraduate requirements — 2.5 minimum grade point average, interview Undergraduate application deadline — rolling
FINANCIAL AID Work/study programs, student loans
CURRICULAR EMPHASIS Filmmaking — documentary, narrative, educational treated equally Television study — production Television production — (1) news/documentary; (2) educational; (3) commercial
SPECIAL ACTIVITIES/OFFERINGS Film series; film festivals; film societies; student publications; program material produced for on-campus closed-circuit television, cable television, and local public television station; internships in film production, internships in television production, vocational placement service
FACILITIES AND EQUIPMENT Film — complete 8mm equipment, 16mm cameras, editing equipment, projectors, editing room, animation board Television — black and white studio cameras, color studio cameras, ½-inch VTR, ¾-inch cassette VTR, portable black and white cameras, editing equipment, monitors, special effects generators, slide chain, portable color cameras, ½-inch portapak recorders, ¾-inch ENG, lighting equipment, sound recording equipment, film chain, black and white studio, color studio
FACULTY Joan Fleckenstein, Richard Procopio PART-TIME FACULTY Benjamin Goldstein, Guy Luster, Yvonne Rabdau, George Theisen

COURSE LIST

Undergraduate

Sight, Sound, Motion
Design for Media
Advanced Media Graphics
Current Concepts in Media
Introduction to Filmmaking
Intermediate Filmmaking
Advanced Filmmaking
Basic Video Production
TV Studio Production Systems
TV Workshop
Seminar
Script Writing

Yale University

Independent coed university. Institutionally accredited by regional association. Urban location, 175-acre campus. Total enrollment: 9611. Undergraduate enrollment: 5231. Total faculty: 1468 (1438 full-time, 30 part-time). Semester calendar. Grading system: letters or numbers.

French Department, 316 WLH, New Haven, CT 06520 203-436-0873

CONTACT Annette Insdorf
ADMISSION Application deadline — 1/1
CURRICULAR EMPHASIS Film study — (1) criticism and aesthetics; (2) history; (3) appreciation Filmmaking — (1) narrative; (2) experimental; (3) documentary
SPECIAL ACTIVITIES/OFFERINGS Film series, film festivals, film societies
FACILITIES AND EQUIPMENT Film — 16mm projectors, screening room, 35mm screening facilities, permanent film library

DELAWARE

University of Delaware

State-related coed university. Institutionally accredited by regional association. Small town location, 1300-acre campus. Total enrollment: 16,928. Undergraduate enrollment: 13,352. Total faculty: 935 (792 full-time, 143 part-time). 4-1-4 calendar. Grading system: letters or numbers.

Communications Department, 301 Kirkbride Hall, Newark, DE 19711 302-738-2777

PROGRAM OFFERED Major in communications with emphasis in television
ADMISSION Application deadline — 5/1, rolling
FINANCIAL AID Teaching assistantships, fellowships Application deadline — 5/1, rolling

CURRICULAR EMPHASIS Film study — (1) appreciation; (2) criticism and aesthetics Undergraduate television study — (1) criticism and aesthetics; (2) production; (3) appreciation; (4) history; (5) management Graduate television study — (1) criticism and aesthetics; (2) appreciation; (3) production; (4) history; (5) management Television production — (1) commercial; (2) news/documentary; (3) experimental/personal video
SPECIAL ACTIVITIES/OFFERINGS Film series, program material produced for on-campus closed-circuit television and cable television, internships in film and television production, independent study
FACILITIES AND EQUIPMENT Film — 8mm and 16mm editing equipment and projectors, 35mm cameras and projectors, sound stage, editing room, permanent film library Television — complete black and white studio production equipment, complete color studio production equipment, black and white studio, color studio, audio studio, control room
FACULTY Douglas Boyd, Elliot Schreiber PART-TIME FACULTY Charles Althoff

COURSE LIST

Undergraduate
Introduction to Mass Communications

Undergraduate and Graduate
Beginning TV Production
Advanced TV Production
Rhetoric of Film and TV
Broadcast Programming
International Mass Communications
Mass Communications Effects
Mass Communications and Culture
Mass Communications Seminar
Broadcast Journalism

English Department, 204 Memorial Hall, Newark, DE 19711 302-738-2361

CONTACT Vance Kepley Jr, Director of Film Studies
PROGRAM OFFERED Major in English with emphasis in film
ADMISSION Application deadline — 5/1, rolling
FINANCIAL AID Student loans Application deadline — 5/1, rolling
CURRICULAR EMPHASIS Film study — (1) appreciation; (2) criticism and aesthetics; (3) history
SPECIAL ACTIVITIES/OFFERINGS Film series, film festivals, independent study
FACILITIES AND EQUIPMENT Film — 8mm and 16mm cameras, editing equipment, lighting equipment, projectors, 16mm sound recording equipment, screening room, editing room, sound mixing room, animation board, permanent film library, film studies center
FACULTY Vance Kepley Jr, Thomas Pauly

COURSE LIST

Undergraduate
Introduction to Film
Film History
Movies in America
Film Genres
Film and American Society
Film Theory and Criticism

DISTRICT OF COLUMBIA

American University

Independent Methodist coed university. Institutionally accredited by regional association, programs recognized by NASM. Suburban location. Total enrollment: 8275. Undergraduate enrollment: 5567. Total faculty: 912 (358 full-time, 554 part-time). Semester calendar. Grading system: letters or numbers.

School of Communication, Washington, DC 20016 202-686-2055

CONTACT Film — Glenn Harnden Television — Larry Kirkman
DEGREES OFFERED BA in film/television/photography, MA in film, BA in cinema studies offered in Literature Department
DEPARTMENTAL MAJORS Undergraduate film and television — 100 students Graduate film — 20 students
ADMISSION Undergraduate requirements — 2.0 minimum grade point average, teachers' recommendations, written statement of purpose, professional recommendations Graduate requirements — 3.0 minimum grade point average, teachers' recommendations, written statement of purpose, professional recommendations
FINANCIAL AID Scholarships, work/study programs, student loans, fellowships, part-time employment, federal aid Undergraduate application deadline — 3/1
CURRICULAR EMPHASIS Undergraduate film study — history, criticism and aesthetics, appreciation treated equally Graduate film study — history, criticism and aesthetics, appreciation treated equally Undergraduate filmmaking — documentary, narrative, educational treated equally Graduate filmmaking — documentary, narrative, educational treated equally Undergraduate television study — (1) production; (2) criticism and aesthetics; (3) history Undergraduate television production — commercial, news/documentary, educational treated equally
SPECIAL ACTIVITIES/OFFERINGS Filmmaking clubs, film series, film festivals, program material produced for on-campus closed-circuit television, internships in film production, internships in television production, independent study
FACILITIES AND EQUIPMENT Film — complete 8mm and 16mm equipment, screening room, 35mm screening facilities, editing room, sound mixing room, permanent film library of student films, permanent film library of commercial or professional films Television — black and white studio cameras, ½-inch VTR, ¾-inch cassette VTR, portable black and white cameras, editing equipment, monitors, special effects generators, slide chain, portable color cameras, ½-inch portapak recorders, ¾-inch ENG, lighting equipment, sound recording equipment, audio mixers, film chain, time base corrector, black and white studio, audio studio, control room
FACULTY John Douglass, Glenn Harnden, Jack Jorgens, Larry Kirkman, Arnost Lastig, Steven Schoenbaum, Ronald Sutton, Skip Winitsky PART-TIME FACULTY Larry Behrens, William Blackwell, Stephen Szabo, Sidney Tabak, Bonnie Willette, Ann Zelk

COURSE LIST

Undergraduate
Introduction to Moving Image

American University (continued)

Undergraduate and Graduate
Film Production I, II
Business of Film
Writing for TV/Film I, II
Film Study: Special Topics
TV Documentary
Individual Filmmakers
TV Production I, II
Fundamentals TV/VTR
Film Production Techniques
TV Studio Operations
History of Motion Pictures I, II
Documentary Film
Visual Anthropology
Developmental Communications (Third World Countries)

Department of Literature: Cinema Studies, College of Arts and Sciences, Nebraska and Massachusetts Avenues, Washington, DC 20760 202-686-2450

CONTACT Jack J Jorgens
DEGREE OFFERED BA in cinema studies
DEPARTMENTAL MAJORS 10 students
ADMISSION Requirements — SAT scores, interviews, teachers' recommendations, written statement of purpose Application deadline — 8/1
CURRICULAR EMPHASIS Film study — (1) criticism and aesthetics; (2) appreciation; (3) history Filmmaking — (1) narrative; (2) documentary; (3) experimental
SPECIAL ACTIVITIES/OFFERINGS Film series, film festivals, film societies, apprenticeships, independent study, internships with the American Film Institute
FACILITIES AND EQUIPMENT Film — complete 8mm equipment, screening room, editing room, animation board, permanent film library
FACULTY Jack J Jorgens, Arnost Lustig, Ronald Sutton PART-TIME FACULTY Laurence Behrens, Frank Turaj

COURSE LIST
Graduate
History of Film I, II
Introduction to Moving Image
Documentary Film
Nonfiction Film

Undergraduate and Graduate
Critical Approach to Cinema
National Cinemas
Film Genres
Scriptwriting
Major Filmmakers
Selected Topics

District of Columbia

Corcoran School of Art

Independent 4-year coed institution. Institutionally accredited by the National Association of Schools of Art. Urban location. Total enrollment: 800. Total faculty: 60. Semester calendar. Grading system: letters.

Open Program, Washington, DC 20006 202-628-9484
FACULTY Michael Day, John Simmons, Sheldon Tromberg

COURSE LIST
Beginning Filmmaking
Intermediate Filmmaking
Making Money Making Movies

Gallaudet College

Independent comprehensive coed institution. Institutionally accredited by regional association. Urban location. Total enrollment: 1435. Undergraduate enrollment: 1135. Total faculty: 197. Semester calendar. Grading system: letters or numbers.

Communication Arts Department, Kendall Green, Washington, DC 20002 202-651-5328

CONTACT Herbert Woofter, Chairman
ADMISSION Requirement — teachers' recommendations Application deadline — 1/1
CURRICULAR EMPHASIS Television study — (1) production; (2) appreciation; (3) criticism and aesthetics Television production — (1) experimental/personal video; (2) commercial; (3) educational
SPECIAL ACTIVITIES/OFFERINGS Program material produced for on-campus closed-circuit television, local public television station, local commercial television station; internships in television production; independent study
FACILITIES AND EQUIPMENT Film — 8mm cameras, editing equipment, lighting equipment, color film stock, projectors, screening room, sound mixing room Television — complete color studio and exterior production equipment, black and white studio, audio studio, control room
FACULTY Jayne Lytle

COURSE LIST
Undergraduate
Introduction to Mass Communication
Introduction to Television Broadcasting
Workshops in Television and Film

Georgetown University

Independent Roman Catholic coed university. Institutionally accredited by regional association. Suburban location, 110-acre campus. Total enrollment: 11,615. Undergraduate enrollment: 5664. Total faculty: 1434 (895 full-time, 539 part-time). Semester calendar. Grading system: letters or numbers.

Fine Arts Department, Maguire Building, Washington, DC 20057 202-625-4085

CONTACT Joel E Siegel
ADMISSION Application deadline — 1/15
FINANCIAL AID Student loans, work/study programs Application deadline — 1/15
CURRICULAR EMPHASIS Film study — (1) criticism and aesthetics; (2) appreciation; (3) history Filmmaking — (1) narrative; (2) experimental; (3) documentary
SPECIAL ACTIVITIES/OFFERINGS Film series, film societies, independent study, cooperative arrangements with the American Film Institute and the Smithsonian Institution

FACULTY Joel E Siegel

COURSE LIST

Undergraduate and Graduate
Cinematic Style
Style as Emotion

George Washington University

Independent coed university. Institutionally accredited by regional association, programs recognized by AACSB. Urban location, 30-acre campus. Total enrollment: 16,669. Undergraduate enrollment: 6100. Total faculty: 1512 (1019 full-time, 493 part-time). Semester calendar. Grading system: letters or numbers.

American Studies Program, 2108 G Street NW, Washington, DC 20052 202-676-6070

CONTACT Bernard Mergen
DEGREE OFFERED Degree in American studies with emphasis in film or television
ADMISSION Undergraduate application deadline — 3/1, rolling
CURRICULAR EMPHASIS Undergraduate film study — (1) history; (2) criticism and aesthetics; (3) appreciation Graduate film study — history
SPECIAL ACTIVITIES/OFFERINGS Film societies, independent study
FACILITIES AND EQUIPMENT Film — 16mm projectors
FACULTY Bernard Mergen PART-TIME FACULTY Margot Kernan

COURSE LIST

Undergraduate
American Cinema

Undergraduate and Graduate
Reading and Research at the Library of Congress

Howard University

Independent coed university. Institutionally accredited by regional association, programs recognized by NASM, AACSB, NASA, ACPE. Urban location, 75-acre campus. Total enrollment: 10,150. Undergraduate enrollment: 6703. Total faculty: 1856 (1085 full-time, 771 part-time). Semester calendar. Grading system: letters or numbers.

Department of Radio, TV and Film, 2600 Fourth Street NW, Washington, DC 20059 202-636-7927

CONTACT Arthur L France, Chairman
DEGREE OFFERED BA in communications with specializations in broadcast production (radio and TV), broadcast management, and film directing
ADMISSION Requirements — 2.5 minimum grade point average, SAT scores, interview Application deadline — 4/1
FINANCIAL AID Scholarships, work/study programs, student loans Application deadline — 4/1
CURRICULAR EMPHASIS Film study — history, criticism and aesthetics, film and society treated equally Filmmaking — documentary, narrative, experimental treated equally Television study — criticism and aesthetics, production, management treated equally Television production — news/documentary, experimental/personal video, educational treated equally
SPECIAL ACTIVITIES/OFFERINGS Filmmaking clubs, film series, film festivals, film societies, student publications, program material produced for local public television station, apprenticeships, internships in film production, internships in television production, vocational placement service
FACILITIES AND EQUIPMENT Film — complete 8mm and 16mm equipment, sound stage, screening room, editing room, sound mixing room, animation board, permanent film library of student films, permanent film library of commercial or professional films Television — complete color studio and exterior production equipment, color studio, mobile van/unit, remote truck, audio studio, control room
FACULTY Taquiena Boston, Angela Burnett, Bernard Carver, Alonzo Crawford, Abiyi Ford, Arthur France, Oscar Gandy, Haile Gerima, Thomas Hardy, David Honig, Marion Hull, Russell Johnson, Robert Jones, Paula Matabane, Beryl Miller, Leroy Miller, Howard Myrick, Bill Pratt, Ted Roberts, Abdulai Vandi

COURSE LIST

Undergraduate
Broadcast Advertising and Sales
Introduction to Mass Communications
Basic Research Methods
Broadcast Programming
Advanced Cinematography
Film Analysis
Documentary Film Critique
Practicum Film
History of Film
Introduction to Communications Technology
Fundamentals of Broadcasting
Blacks in Film
Creative Writing/Film
Film Production Arts
Film Criticism
Practicum Management
Broadcast Management
Broadcast Marketing and Finance
Alternate Systems
Contemporary Topics in Mass Communications
Radio Production I
Producing Film and TV
Television Practicum
Scriptwriting
Broadcast Criticism
Broadcast and Government
Broadcast Research
Broadcast Announcing and Interviewing
Practicum Radio
Still Photography
TV Directing and Lab
Advance TV Production

Mount Vernon College

Independent 4-year women's college. Institutionally accredited by regional association. Urban location, 26-acre campus. Undergraduate enrollment: 461. Total faculty: 60 (24 full-time, 36 part-time). Modular calendar. Grading system: letters or numbers.

Mount Vernon College (continued)

Communication Department, 2100 Foxhall Road, Washington, DC 20007 202-331-3416

CONTACT Mark Johnson
DEGREE OFFERED BA in communication with sequences in radio-TV, film
DEPARTMENTAL MAJORS Film — 15 students Television — 85 students
ADMISSION Requirements — C + minimum grade average, ACT or SAT scores, teachers' recommendations
FINANCIAL AID Scholarships, work/study programs, student loans
CURRICULAR EMPHASIS Film study — (1) history; (2) appreciation; (3) educational media/instructional technology Filmmaking — (1) narrative; (2) documentary; (3) experimental Television study — (1) production; (2) management; (3) history Television production — (1) commercial; (2) news/documentary; (3) educational
SPECIAL ACTIVITIES/OFFERINGS Filmmaking clubs, film series, film festivals, student publications, program material produced for local public television station and local commercial television station, apprenticeships, internships in film production, internships in television production, independent study, vocational placement service
FACILITIES AND EQUIPMENT Film — complete 8mm and 16mm equipment, screening room, editing room, sound mixing room, permanent film library of student films, permanent film library of commercial or professional films Television — complete black and white studio production equipment, complete black and white exterior production equipment, black and white studio, audio studio, control room
FACULTY William Barlow, Lydia Blanchard, Richard Howard, Mark Johnson PART-TIME FACULTY Robert L Mann, Phillip Morgan, Andrew Pyne, Judi Strobel, Marion Weiss

COURSE LIST
Undergraduate
Cinematography
TV Studio Operations
Mass Media Production
Radio-TV-Film Writing
Audio Production
Cinema Theory and Practice
Advanced Problems in Production
History of Communications
History of the Motion Picture
Radio-TV News

University of the District of Columbia, Mount Vernon Square Campus

District-supported comprehensive coed institution. Institutionally accredited by regional association. Urban location, 28-acre campus. Total enrollment: 13,290. Undergraduate enrollment: 12,790. Total faculty: 1022 (669 full-time, 353 part-time). Semester calendar. Grading system: letters or numbers.

Communicative Arts Department, 916 G Street NW, Building T-10, Washington, DC 20001 202-727-2717

CONTACT J G Gathings
DEGREES OFFERED BA in film production, BA in television production
DEPARTMENTAL MAJORS Film — 40 students Television — 40 students
ADMISSION Requirement — 2.5 minimum grade point average Application deadline — 7/25, rolling
FINANCIAL AID Student loans, work/study programs Application deadline — 4/15
CURRICULAR EMPHASIS Film study — (1) production; (2) educational media/instructional technology Filmmaking — (1) documentary; (2) narrative; (3) educational; (4) experimental Television study — (1) production (2) educational Television production — (1) commercial; (2) news/documentary; (3) educational; (4) experimental/personal video
SPECIAL ACTIVITIES/OFFERINGS Filmmaking clubs, film festivals, student publications, program material produced for on-campus closed-circuit television, apprenticeships, internships in television production, independent study, vocational placement service.
FACILITIES AND EQUIPMENT Film — 8mm and 16mm cameras, editing equipment, black and white film stock, projectors, sound recording equipment, lighting equipment, editing room, animation board Television — complete black and white studio production equipment, black and white studio, color studio, control room
FACULTY J G Gathings, Peter J Koper

COURSE LIST
Undergraduate
Processes of Communications
Principles of Speech
Audio-Visual Foundations
Introduction to Mass Media
Lighting I, II
Fundamentals of Television
Fundamentals of Film Production
Communicative Arts Seminar
Film Production and Cinematography I, II
Sound Film Editing
Special-Purpose Film
Directed Study — Film
Independent Study — Film Media I, II
Television Production I, II
Advanced Television Production and Direction
Directed Study — Film Television Production I, II
Independent Study — Media I, II
Directing I, II
Stagecraft I
Feature Writing
Sound Film Editing
Writing for Media

FLORIDA

Broward Community College

State-supported 2-year coed college. Part of Florida Community Colleges System. Institutionally accredited by regional association. Urban location. Undergraduate enrollment: 16,000 Total faculty: 1239 (789 full-time, 450 part-time). Trimester calendar. Grading system: letters or numbers.

English and Speech Departments, Communications Division, 3501 Southwest Davie Road, Fort Lauderdale, FL 33314 305-475-6865
FINANCIAL AID Scholarships, work/study programs, student loans

CURRICULAR EMPHASIS Undergraduate film study — history, criticism and aesthetics, appreciation treated equally
SPECIAL ACTIVITIES/OFFERINGS Film series, program material produced for on-campus closed-circuit television
FACILITIES AND EQUIPMENT Film — 8mm cameras Television — black and white studio cameras, color studio cameras, ½-inch VTR, ¾-inch cassette VTR, portable black and white cameras, editing equipment, monitors, special effects generators, slide chain, portable color cameras, ½-inch portapak recorders, ¾-inch ENG, lighting equipment, sound recording equipment, audio mixers, film chain, color studio, audio studio, control room
FACULTY Luke Grande, Mary Ellen Grasso, Robert Meeker, Robert Pedrazas, Eric Reno, Debbie Rosen

COURSE LIST
Undergraduate
Film as Literature
Introduction to Radio and Television
Television Production I

Art Department, Fort Lauderdale, FL 33314 305-475-6517

CONTACT Steve Eliot
ADMISSION Application deadline — 8/2, rolling
FACULTY Steve Eliot, Russell Green

COURSE LIST
Undergraduate
Motion Picture Production I, II
Video-Art

Florida Atlantic University

State-supported upper-level coed institution. Part of State University System of Florida. Institutionally accredited by regional association, programs recognized by NASM, AACSB, ECPD. Suburban location. Total enrollment: 7142. Undergraduate enrollment: 4951. Total faculty: 317 (307 full-time, 10 part-time). Quarter calendar. Grading system: letters or numbers.

Department of Communication, Boca Raton, FL 33431 305-395-5100 ext 2874

CONTACT Film — Mike Budd or Clay Steinman Television — Steve Craig
DEGREE OFFERED BA in communication with emphasis in film or TV
DEPARTMENTAL MAJORS Film — 25 students Television — 50 students
ADMISSION Requirements — 2.0 minimum grade point average, completion of two years' college work
FINANCIAL AID Scholarships, work/study programs, student loans
CURRICULAR EMPHASIS Film study — history, criticism and aesthetics, theory treated equally Filmmaking — documentary, narrative, experimental treated equally Television study — (1) criticism and aesthetics; (2) production; (3) management Television production — commercial, news/documentary, experimental/personal video treated equally
SPECIAL ACTIVITIES/OFFERINGS Film series, program material produced for on-campus closed-circuit television and local public television station, internships in film production, internships in television production, independent study, vocational placement service
FACILITIES AND EQUIPMENT Film — 8mm cameras, editing equipment, sound recording equipment, lighting, color film stock, projectors, 16mm cameras, editing equipment, lighting, projectors, screening room, editing room, permanent film library of commercial or professional films Television — complete color studio and exterior production equipment, black and white studio, color studio, audio studio, control room
FACULTY Mike Budd, Steve Craig, Clay Steinman

COURSE LIST
Undergraduate
Audio Production
TV Program Production
Advanced TV Production
Broadcasting and Society
Station Practices
Broadcast Laboratory
Communication Practicum
Special Topics in Communication
Mass Communication Law and Regulation
Criticism and Communication
The Motion Picture I, II
Film Theory
Documentary Film
Film Appreciation
Film Production
Hollywood in the Forties
The Films of Hitchcock
The Politics of Film
Structuralism and Film

Florida State University

State-supported coed university. Part of State University System of Florida. Institutionally accredited by regional association. Urban location, 343-acre campus. Total enrollment: 21,379. Undergraduate enrollment: 15,387. Total faculty: 976 (943 full-time, 33 part-time). Quarter calendar. Grading system: letters or numbers.

Department of Communication, Diffenbaugh Building, Room 356, Tallahassee, FL 32306 904-644-5034

CONTACT Film — Barry S Sapolsky Television — Norman Medoff
DEGREES OFFERED BS in Media Production, BS in Media Communication
DEPARTMENTAL MAJORS Undergraduate film — 20 students Undergraduate television — 60 students
ADMISSION Requirements — 2.8 minimum grade point average, special application form (available upon request) Undergraduate application deadline — 4/1
FINANCIAL AID Scholarships, work/study programs
CURRICULAR EMPHASIS Film study — (1) criticism and aesthetics; (2) history; (3) appreciation Filmmaking — (1) narrative; (2) experimental; (3) documentary Television study — production, management, social effects treated equally Television production — (1) commercial; (2) experimental/personal video; (3) news/documentary
SPECIAL ACTIVITIES/OFFERINGS Film series, program material produced for on-campus closed-circuit television and cable television, internships in film production, internships in television production, independent study

Florida State University (continued)

FACILITIES AND EQUIPMENT Film — complete 8mm and 16mm equipment, screening room, editing room, permanent film library of student films Television — complete black and white studio production equipment, black and white studio cameras, ½-inch VTR, ¾-inch cassette VTR, portable black and white cameras, editing equipment, monitors, portable color cameras, ¾-inch ENG, lighting equipment, sound recording equipment, black and white studio, audio studio, control room

FACULTY Theodore Clevenger, Edward Forrest, Thomas Hoffer, Norman Medoff, Barry Sapolsky, Donald Ungurait

COURSE LIST

Undergraduate

Film Communication (Super 8)
16mm Film Production
Media Techniques
Television Production
Audio Production
Writing for the Electronic Media
TV Workshop
Radio Workshop
Film Workshop
Elements of Film
Elements of Broadcasting
Mass Media and Society
Cinema as a Social Force
History of Film
Speech for Radio-TV
Seminar on Entertainment
Communication Activities
Internship

Jacksonville University

Independent comprehensive coed institution. Institutionally accredited by regional association, programs recognized by NASM. Suburban location, 273-acre campus. Total enrollment: 2104. Undergraduate enrollment: 1988. Total faculty: 128 (97 full-time, 31 part-time). Modified trimester calendar. Grading system: letters or numbers.

Department of Theatre Arts, Jacksonville, FL 32211 904-744-3950, ext 276

CONTACT Davis Sikes
DEGREES OFFERED BFA, BA in theater arts with work available in TV and Film
ADMISSION Requirements — 2.0 minimum grade point average, ACT or SAT scores
FINANCIAL AID Scholarships, work/study programs, student loans
CURRICULAR EMPHASIS Film study — appreciation Filmmaking — experimental Television study — production Television production — experimental/personal video
SPECIAL ACTIVITIES/OFFERINGS Film series; program material produced for cable television, local public television station, local commercial television station; apprenticeships; internships in television production; independent study
FACILITIES AND EQUIPMENT Television — local cable TV studio, equipment, and personnel
PART-TIME FACULTY R Wayne Kight

COURSE LIST

Undergraduate

Introduction to TV and Motion Pictures
Fine Arts Practicum
Literature and Film

Manatee Junior College

State-supported 2-year coed college. Institutionally accredited by regional association. Small town location. Total enrollment: 4200. Total faculty: 150 (102 full-time, 48 part-time). Semester calendar. Grading system: letters.

Film Division, Department of Fine Arts, 5840 26th Street W, Bradenton, FL 33507 813-755-1511, ext 249

CONTACT Walter J Engel or John W James
DEGREE OFFERED AA with an emphasis in theater and film
DEPARTMENTAL MAJORS Film — 12 students
ADMISSION Requirements — 2.0 minimum grade point average, ACT or SAT scores, interview Application deadline — 8/1
FINANCIAL AID Scholarships, work/study programs, student loans Application deadline — 7/1
CURRICULAR EMPHASIS Film study — (1) history; (2) appreciation; (3) educational media/instructional technology Filmmaking — (1) educational; (2) commercial ads; (3) documentary
SPECIAL ACTIVITIES/OFFERINGS Film series
FACILITIES AND EQUIPMENT Film — 8mm cameras, editing equipment, color film stock, projectors, sound stage, permanent film library of student films, permanent film library of commercial or professional films Television — color studio cameras, ¾-inch cassette VTR, slide chain, portable color cameras, audio mixers, film chain, color studio, control room
FACULTY Walter J Engel, John W James

COURSE LIST

Undergraduate

Film Production Workshop
Intermediate Film Workshop
History and Appreciation of Cinema

Nova University

Independent comprehensive coed institution. Institutionally accredited by regional agency. Urban location. Total enrollment: 3000. Undergraduate enrollment: 900. Total faculty: 100. Trimester calendar. Grading system: letters or numbers.

Nova College, 3301 College Avenue, Fort Lauderdale, FL 33314 305-475-8300

CONTACT David F Barone
PROGRAM OFFERED Major in communication
FINANCIAL AID Student loans, work/study programs
CURRICULAR EMPHASIS Undergraduate film study — (1) production; (2) appreciation; (3) criticism and aesthetics
SPECIAL ACTIVITIES/OFFERINGS Film societies; program material produced for on-campus closed-circuit television, cable television, local public television station; internships in film and television production; independent study; practicum

FACILITIES AND EQUIPMENT Film — complete 8mm and 16mm equipment, sound stage, screening room, 35mm screening facilities, editing room, sound mixing room, permanent film library Television — complete black and white studio and exterior production facilities, complete color studio production equipment, color studio, audio studio, control room

COURSE LIST

Undergraduate

The Telecommunications Industry
Television-Radio Script and Copy Writing
Visual Communication

Seminole Community College

State and locally supported 2-year coed college. Institutionally accredited by regional association. Rural location. Undergraduate enrollment: 3882. Total faculty: 102 (100 full-time, 2 part-time). Trimester calendar. Grading system: letters or numbers.

Humanities Division, Sanford, FL 32771 305-323-1450

CONTACT Film — G C Minor Television — Pat Thomas
ADMISSION Application deadline — 8/13, rolling
CURRICULAR EMPHASIS Film study — (1) appreciation; (2) criticism and aesthetics Television study — (1) production; (2) educational Television production — (1) news/documentary; (2) educational
SPECIAL ACTIVITIES/OFFERINGS Program material produced for on-campus closed-circuit television, independent study
FACILITIES AND EQUIPMENT Film — editing equipment, projectors, screening room Television — ½-inch VTR, portable black and white cameras, editing equipment, ½-inch portapak recorder
FACULTY G C Minor, Pat Thomas

COURSE LIST

Undergraduate

Art of Film
Film Practicum
Television Programming
Survey of Mass Media

Florida

University of Florida

State-supported coed university. Part of State University System of Florida. Institutionally accredited by regional association, programs recognized by NASM, AACSB, ACPE. Suburban location, 2000-acre campus. Total enrollment: 31,133. Undergraduate enrollment: 25,393. Total faculty: 2802 (2674 full-time, 128 part-time). Quarter calendar. Grading system: letters or numbers.

English Department (Film Studies Program), 4008 GPA Building, Gainesville, FL 32601 904-392-0777

CONTACT William C Childers
DEGREES OFFERED BA, MA, PhD in English with emphasis in film studies; BA in film studies (interdisciplinary degree offered through College of Liberal Arts and Sciences and College of Journalism and Communications)
PROGRAM MAJORS Undergraduate film — 25 students Graduate film — 10 students
ADMISSION Undergraduate requirements — 2.0 minimum grade point average, ACT or SAT scores Graduate requirements — 3.0 minimum grade point average, GRE scores Undergraduate application deadline — 3/1
FINANCIAL AID Scholarships, work/study programs, student loans, fellowships, teaching assistantships, research assistantships
CURRICULAR EMPHASIS Undergraduate film study — history, criticism and aesthetics, appreciation treated equally
SPECIAL ACTIVITIES/OFFERINGS Filmmaking clubs, film series, film festivals, film societies, Kipnis Film Library (includes large collection of Russian films both 16 and 35mm), internships in film production, independent study, vocational placement service
FACILITIES AND EQUIPMENT Film — screening room, 35mm screening facilities, permanent film library of commercial or professional films
FACULTY William Childers, Ben Pickard, William Robinson, Julian Smith PART-TIME FACULTY Ray Beirne, Kent Beyette, Corbin Carnell, Andy Gordon, Robert Ray, Frank Sciadini

COURSE LIST

Undergraduate

Understanding Film
Movies as a Narrative Art
History of Film I, II
Film Studies (variable topics in film)

Graduate

Film Theory and Criticism
Studies in the Movies (variable topics)
Seminar in Movies (variable topics)

University of Miami

Independent coed university. Institutionally accredited by regional association. Urban location, 260-acre campus. Total enrollment: 13,845. Undergraduate enrollment: 9458. Total faculty: 1612 (1264 full-time, 348 part-time). Semester calendar. Grading system: letters or numbers.

Communications Department, PO Box 248127, Coral Gables, FL 33124 305-284-2265

CONTACT Chairperson
DEGREES OFFERED BA, BFA in communications with a major in film or television; BFA in cinema

University of Miami (continued)

ADMISSION Requirements — 3.0 minimum grade point average, interviews, teachers' recommendations, written statement of purpose (for BFA candidates only)
FINANCIAL AID Scholarships, student loans, work/study programs, teaching assistantships
CURRICULAR EMPHASIS Film study — (1) production; (2) criticism and aesthetics; (3) history, writing; (4) appreciation; (5) educational media/instructional technology Filmmaking — (1) narrative; (2) documentary; (3) experimental; (4) educational; (5) animated Television study — (1) production; (2) management; (3) history; (4) educational; (5) criticism and aesthetics; (6) appreciation Television production — (1) commercial; (2) news/documentary; (3) educational; (4) experimental/personal video
SPECIAL ACTIVITIES/OFFERINGS Film series, film festivals, film societies, student publications, internships in film and television production, independent study, practicum
FACILITIES AND EQUIPMENT Film — complete 8mm and 16mm equipment, sound stage, screening room, editing room, sound mixing room, permanent film library Television — complete black and white studio production equipment, complete color exterior production facilities, black and white studio, audio studio, control room

University of South Florida

State-supported coed university. Part of State University System of Florida. Institutionally accredited by regional association. Urban location, 1695-acre campus. Total enrollment: 19,673. Undergraduate enrollment: 17,041. Total faculty: 1059 (941 full-time, 118 part-time). Quarter calendar. Grading system: letters or numbers.

Department of Mass Communications, LET 418, Tampa, FL 33620 813-974-2591

CONTACT Film — Emery L Sasser or Carl Storr Television — Emery L Sasser or Manny Lucoff
DEGREES OFFERED BA in mass communications with an emphasis in film or TV, MA in mass communications with an emphasis in TV
DEPARTMENTAL MAJORS Undergraduate film — 20 students Undergraduate television — 180 students
ADMISSION Undergraduate requirement — 2.5 minimum grade point average Graduate requirements — 3.0 minimum grade point average, GRE score of 1000, interview, teachers' recommendations, written statement of purpose, professional work experience, portfolio, professional recommendations Undergraduate application deadline — 8/15
FINANCIAL AID Scholarships, work/study programs, student loans, fellowships, teaching assistantships
CURRICULAR EMPHASIS Undergraduate film study — (1) educational media/instructional technology; (2) history; (3) writing Undergraduate filmmaking — (1) documentary; (2) educational; (3) commercial Undergraduate television study — (1) writing; (2) management; (3) production Undergraduate television production — (1) news/documentary; (2) commercial
SPECIAL ACTIVITIES/OFFERINGS Program material produced for on-campus closed-circuit television, cable television, local public television station, local commercial television station; internships in film production; internships in television production; independent study
FACILITIES AND EQUIPMENT Film — complete 16mm equipment, editing room, sound mixing room Television — complete color studio production equipment and color exterior production equipment, color studio, audio studio, control room
FACULTY George Daugherty, Manny Lucoff, Carl Storr, David Togie, Denis Vogel

COURSE LIST

Undergraduate

Introduction to Broadcasting
Writing for Radio and TV
Radio Production and Direction
Broadcasting Announcing
Broadcast News
Radio Practicum
Advanced TV Production and Direction
TV Production and Direction
TV News Film
Media Criticism: Broadcasting
The Broadcast Program
Broadcast Law
TV Practicum
The Film as Mass Communication I–III
Introduction to Film Writing
Classics of the Silent Film
Classics of the Sound Film
Philosophy and the Film
Advanced Camera Techniques
Advanced Film Lighting
Sensitometry and Photometrics
Film Directing
Cinema Dynamics
The Documentary Film
Social History of the Film to 1945
Social History of the Film 1945 to the Present
Film Criticism

University of West Florida

State-supported upper-level coed institution. Part of State University System of Florida. Institutionally accredited by regional association, programs recognized by NASM. Suburban location, 1000-acre campus. Total enrollment: 5173. Undergraduate enrollment: 4318. Total faculty: 308 (218 full-time, 90 part-time). Quarter calendar. Grading system: letters or numbers.

Communication Arts Department, Pensacola, FL 32504 904-476-9500

CONTACT Film — Amir M Karimi Television — Churchill L Roberts
DEGREES OFFERED BA, MA in communications arts with emphasis in film and television
DEPARTMENTAL MAJORS 75 students
ADMISSION Application deadline — 8/5
SPECIAL ACTIVITIES/OFFERINGS Program material produced for on-campus closed-circuit television, local public television, cable television; internships in television production; news program
FACILITIES AND EQUIPMENT Film — complete 16mm equipment Television — complete color studio production facilities, complete color exterior production facilities
FACULTY Amir M Karimi, Churchill L Roberts

COURSE LIST

Undergraduate

The Documentary Film
American Film History
Film Criticism
Broadcast Production
International Communication
Advanced Broadcast Production
Regulation of Broadcasting
Seminar in Political Broadcasting
Directed Studies in Broadcasting and Film
Social Impact of Media

Undergraduate and Graduate
Film Production
Current Trends in Media
Broadcast Journalism

Valencia Community College

State-supported 2-year coed college. Part of Florida Community Colleges System, automatic transfer to main campus for baccalaureate. Institutionally accredited by regional association. Urban location. Undergraduate enrollment: 8957. Total faculty: 430 (146 full-time, 284 part-time). Semester calendar. Grading system: letters or numbers.

Communications Department, PO Box 3028, Orlando, FL 32802 305-299-5000, ext 313

CONTACT Film — Don Tighe Television — Audrey Williams
FINANCIAL AID Scholarships, work/study programs, student loans
CURRICULAR EMPHASIS Undergraduate film study — history, appreciation treated equally Undergraduate television study — history, criticism and aesthetics, appreciation treated equally
SPECIAL ACTIVITIES/OFFERINGS Film series

COURSE LIST
Undergraduate
Introduction to Film
Introduction to Television

GEORGIA

Abraham Baldwin Agricultural College

State-supported 2-year coed college. Part of University System of Georgia, automatic transfer to main campus for baccalaureate. Institutionally accredited by regional association. Rural location, 450-acre campus. Undergraduate enrollment: 2430. Total faculty: 140 (138 full-time, 2 part-time). Quarter calendar. Grading system: letters or numbers.

Communications — Media Department, Tifton, GA 31794 912-386-3250

CONTACT Lew S Akin or James M Burt
SPECIAL ACTIVITIES/OFFERINGS Film series, film festivals, program material produced for on-campus closed-circuit television
FACILITIES AND EQUIPMENT Film — screening room Television — black and white studio cameras, ½-inch VTR, 1-inch VTR, monitors, sound recording equipment, black and white studio, audio studio, control room

COURSE LIST
Undergraduate
Speech
Broadcast Journalism
Radio-TV Announcing

Atlanta College of Art

Independent professional 4-year coed college. Institutionally accredited by regional association, programs recognized by NASA. Urban location. Undergraduate enrollment: 260. Total faculty: 30 (18 full-time, 12 part-time). Semester calendar. Grading system: letters or numbers.

Video Imagery Department, 1280 Peachtree Street NE, Atlanta, GA 30309 404-892-3600

CONTACT Ben Davis
DEGREE OFFERED BFA with emphasis in television
ADMISSION Application deadline — 8/1
CURRICULAR EMPHASIS Television study — (1) criticism and aesthetics; (2) production Television production — experimental/personal video
SPECIAL ACTIVITIES/OFFERINGS Program material produced for local public television station
FACILITIES AND EQUIPMENT Television — complete black and white studio and exterior production facilities
FACULTY Ben Davis

COURSE LIST
Undergraduate
Television and Video Techniques
Video Production
Independent Study
Audio Visual Imagery

Augusta College

State-supported comprehensive coed institution. Part of University System of Georgia. Institutionally accredited by regional association, programs recognized by NASM. Urban location, 72-acre campus. Total enrollment: 3685. Undergraduate enrollment: 3378. Total faculty: 173 (152 full-time, 21 part-time). Quarter calendar. Grading system: letters or numbers.

English Department, 2500 Walton Way, Augusta, GA 30904 404-828-3706

CONTACT Charles L Willig
ADMISSION Application deadline — 8/15, rolling

Augusta College (continued)

FINANCIAL AID Scholarships, student loans, work/study programs, teaching assistantships Application deadline — 3/15, rolling
CURRICULAR EMPHASIS Film study — (1) appreciation; (2) history; (3) production Filmmaking — (1) documentary; (2) narrative; (3) experimental Television study — (1) production; (2) criticism and aesthetics; (3) appreciation Television production — (1) news/documentary; (2) experimental/personal video; (3) educational
SPECIAL ACTIVITIES/OFFERINGS Film series, film festivals, student publications, program material produced for cable television
FACILITIES AND EQUIPMENT Film — complete 8mm equipment, editing room, permanent film library Television — black and white studio cameras, color studio cameras, 2-inch VTR, ¾-inch cassette VTR, portable black and white cameras, monitors
FACULTY Norman Prinsky, Charles Willig

COURSE LIST
Undergraduate
Advanced Filmmaking
Introduction to Film
Television Production
Literature into Film
Special Topics
Filmmaking

Berry College

Independent comprehensive coed institution. Institutionally accredited by regional association, programs recognized by NASM. Suburban location, 30,000-acre campus. Total enrollment: 1562. Undergraduate enrollment: 1385. Total faculty: 98 (82 full-time, 16 part-time). Quarter calendar. Grading system: letters or numbers.

English and Speech Department, Box J, Mount Berry, GA 30149 404-232-5374

CONTACT Barbara Destefano
ADMISSION Application deadline — 8/1, rolling
CURRICULAR EMPHASIS Film study — appreciation
SPECIAL ACTIVITIES/OFFERINGS Film festivals, film societies, independent study
FACILITIES AND EQUIPMENT Film — 35mm screening facilities, permanent film library
PART-TIME FACULTY Michael Boyd, D Dean Cantrell, Barbara Destefano

COURSE LIST
Undergraduate
The Motion Picture
Novel, Drama, Cinema

Clark College

Independent 4-year coed college affiliated with United Methodist Church. Institutionally accredited by regional association. Urban location, 27-acre campus. Undergraduate enrollment: 1876. Total faculty: 136 (117 full-time, 19 part-time). Semester calendar. Grading system: letters or numbers.

Department of Mass Communications, 240 Chestnut Street SW, Atlanta, GA 30314 404-688-5069

CONTACT Film — Herb Eichelberger Television — Sidney Simmons or Bill Ronsam
DEGREES OFFERED BA in mass communications, BA in film, BA in TV, BA in journalism
DEPARTMENTAL MAJORS Film — 18 students Television — 25 students
ADMISSION Requirements — C minimum grade average, ACT or SAT scores, interview, teachers' recommendations, portfolio, production credits
FINANCIAL AID Scholarships, work/study programs, student loans
CURRICULAR EMPHASIS Film study — (1) educational media/instructional technology; (2) criticism and aesthetics; (3) history; (4) appreciation Filmmaking — (1) documentary; (2) educational; (3) narrative; (4) experimental; (5) animated Television study — (1) production; (2) educational; (3) management; (4) criticism and aesthetics; (5) history; (6) appreciation Television production — (1) news/documentary; (2) commercial; (3) experimental/personal video; (4) educational
SPECIAL ACTIVITIES/OFFERINGS Filmmaking clubs, film series, film festivals, student publications, program material produced for on-campus closed-circuit television, apprenticeships, internships in film production, internships in television production, independent study, teacher training, vocational placement service
FACILITIES AND EQUIPMENT Film — 8mm cameras, editing equipment, sound recording equipment, lighting, color film stock, projectors, complete 16mm equipment, screening room, editing room, sound mixing room, permanent film library of student films Television — black and white studio cameras, color studio cameras, ½-inch VTR, ¾-inch cassette VTR, portable black and white cameras, editing equipment, monitors, portable color cameras, ½-inch portapak recorders, lighting equipment, sound recording equipment, audio mixers, black and white studio, color studio, audio studio, control room

COURSE LIST
Undergraduate
Cinematography I, II
Advanced Cinematography
TV Production
Advanced TV Production

Emory University

Independent Methodist coed university. Institutionally accredited by regional association. Suburban location, 550-acre campus. Total enrollment: 7683. Undergraduate enrollment: 2900. Total faculty: 250. Quarter calendar. Grading system: letters or numbers.

English Department, North Decatur Road, Atlanta, GA 30322 404-329-7991

CONTACT David A Cook
PROGRAM OFFERED Major in English with emphasis in film
ADMISSION Undergraduate requirement — 2.0 minimum grade point average Graduate requirements — 3.0 minimum grade point average, GRE scores Undergraduate application deadline — rolling
FINANCIAL AID Work/study programs, teaching assistantships Undergraduate application deadline — 4/15, rolling
CURRICULAR EMPHASIS Undergraduate film study — (1) history; (2) criticism and aesthetics; (3) appreciation Graduate film study — (1) criticism and aesthetics; (2) history; (3) comparative literature Filmmaking — (1) narrative; (2) documentary; (3) experimental
SPECIAL ACTIVITIES/OFFERINGS Filmmaking clubs, multiple film series, film festivals, film societies, independent study
FACILITIES AND EQUIPMENT Film — 8mm editing equipment, sound recording equipment, lighting equipment, projectors, 16mm projectors, screening room, editing room, permanent film library of over 250 features
FACULTY Jerome Beaty, David A Cook, Judy Kinney, Harry Rusche

COURSE LIST

Undergraduate
Film History, Origins to 1938
Film History, 1938 to the Present
Film Theory
Introduction to Film
Genre Studies
Shakespeare and Film
Nineteenth-Century Fiction and Film
Independent Study in Film
History of Electronic Media

Undergraduate and Graduate
Narrative Structures in Film and Literature
Film Studies Methodology and Research
Film History and Historiography

Georgia Southern College

State-supported comprehensive coed institution. Part of University System of Georgia. Institutionally accredited by regional association, programs recognized by NASM, AACSB. Small town location, 457-acre campus. Total enrollment: 6525. Undergraduate enrollment: 5478. Total faculty: 355 (300 full-time, 55 part-time). Quarter calendar. Grading system: letters or numbers.

Speech-Drama Department, LB 8091, Statesboro, GA 30460 912-681-5138

CONTACT Clarence McCord
DEGREE OFFERED BS in speech with an emphasis in broadcasting
DEPARTMENTAL MAJORS Television broadcasting — 25 students
ADMISSION Requirement 2.0 minimum grade point average
FINANCIAL AID Work/study programs, student loans
CURRICULAR EMPHASIS Film study — appreciation Television study — (1) production; (2) history; (3) management Television production — (1) commercial; (2) news/documentary; (3) educational
SPECIAL ACTIVITIES/OFFERINGS Program material produced for cable television, internships in television production, independent study
FACILITIES AND EQUIPMENT Television — complete black and white studio production equipment, black and white studio, audio studio, control room
FACULTY Douglas Sims, Maryland Wilson

COURSE LIST

Undergraduate
Introduction to the Cinema
Broadcast Media
Broadcast Law and Regulation
Broadcast Management
TV Internship

Undergraduate and Graduate
Stage and Studio Lighting
Television Production I, II
Radio/TV News and Interview
Radio/TV Script Writing

Georgia State University

State-supported coed university. Part of University System of Georgia. Institutionally accredited by regional association, programs recognized by NASM, AACSB, NASA. Urban location. Total enrollment: 20,021. Undergraduate enrollment: 13,098. Total faculty: 843 (728 full-time, 115 part-time). Quarter calendar. Grading system: letters or numbers.

Department of Journalism, University Plaza, Atlanta, GA 30303 404-658-3200

CONTACT Edward G Luck
DEGREE OFFERED BA in journalism with an emphasis in broadcasting
FINANCIAL AID Work/study programs
CURRICULAR EMPHASIS Undergraduate television study — production Graduate television study — production Undergraduate television production — commercial, news/documentary, educational, industrial and corporate treated equally Graduate television production — commercial, educational, industrial and corporate treated equally
SPECIAL ACTIVITIES/OFFERINGS Film series, program material produced for on-campus closed-circuit television, internships in television production, independent study, teacher training, vocational placement service

Georgia State University (continued)

FACILITIES AND EQUIPMENT Television — black and white studio cameras, ½-inch VTR, ¾-inch cassette VTR, portable black and white cameras, monitors, special effects generators, ½-inch portapak recorders, lighting equipment, sound recording equipment, black and white studio

FACULTY Edward G Luck, William B Steis

COURSE LIST

Undergraduate and Graduate

Development of Materials for Television
Television Script Writing
Special Projects in Television

University of Georgia

State-supported coed university. Part of University System of Georgia. Institutionally accredited by regional association, programs recognized by NASM, AACSB, NASA, ACPE. Small town location, 1435-acre campus. Total enrollment: 23,286. Undergraduate enrollment: 16,611. Total faculty: 1901 (1823 full-time, 78 part-time). Quarter calendar. Grading system: letters or numbers.

Radio-TV-Film Department, School of Journalism, Athens, GA 30602 404-542-3785

CONTACT Worth McDougald

DEGREES OFFERED BA, MA in radio-television-film

DEPARTMENTAL MAJORS Undergraduate film — 40 students Undergraduate television — 195 students Graduate film — 7 students Graduate television — 15 students

ADMISSION Undergraduate requirements — minimum grade point average, SAT scores, English usage examination, typing examination Graduate requirements — minimum grade point average, GRE scores Undergraduate application deadline — 3/1, rolling

FINANCIAL AID Scholarships, student loans, work/study programs, teaching assistantships Undergraduate application deadline — 3/1

CURRICULAR EMPHASIS Undergraduate film study — (1) production; (2) criticism and aesthetics; (3) history Graduate film study — (1) production; (2) appreciation; (3) history Undergraduate filmmaking — (1) educational; (2) narrative; (3) documentary Graduate filmmaking — (1) educational; (2) documentary; (3) narrative Television study — (1) production; (2) management; (3) educational Television production — (1) commercial; (2) news/documentary; (3) educational

SPECIAL ACTIVITIES/OFFERINGS Film series; film societies; program material produced for on-campus closed-circuit television, local public television station, local commercial television station; internships in film and television production; independent study; vocational placement service; George Foster Peabody Broadcasting Awards collection

FACILITIES AND EQUIPMENT Film — complete 8mm and 16mm equipment, sound stage, screening room, editing room, sound mixing room, animation board, permanent film library Television — complete black and white studio and exterior production equipment, complete color studio and exterior production equipment, black and white studio, color studio, mobile van/unit, audio studio, control room, 16mm flatbed editor

FACULTY Marcus Bartlett, Graeme Bond, Joseph Dominick, James Fletcher, Edward Foote, William Lee, Ed Lynch, Worth McDougald, Barbara McKenzie, Roger Wimmer, Al Wise

COURSE LIST

Undergraduate

Production Techniques
Introduction to Broadcasting

Undergraduate and Graduate

Advanced Radio-Television News
The Documentary
Motion Picture History
Theories of Film
Educational Television Utilization
Educational Television Production
Fundamentals of Television Directing
Television Acting and Performing
Advanced Television Directing
Advanced Program in Television
Television Staging
Television Lighting
Television Station Management
Television Production
Cinematography
Screen Writing
Motion Picture Production
Programming on Radio and Television

Valdosta State College

State-supported comprehensive coed institution. Part of University System of Georgia. Institutionally accredited by regional association. Suburban location. Total enrollment: 5050. Undergraduate enrollment: 3972. Total faculty: 257 (226 full-time, 31 part-time). Quarter calendar. Grading system: letters or numbers.

Speech and Drama Department, Valdosta, GA 31601 912-247-3306

CONTACT A Anthony Oseguera

DEGREE OFFERED BFA in theater arts: radio-TV-film

DEPARTMENTAL MAJORS 75 students

ADMISSION Application deadline — 9/1, rolling

CURRICULAR EMPHASIS Broadcasting study — production Film study — production

SPECIAL ACTIVITIES/OFFERINGS Program material produced for cable television, filmmaking clubs, independent study

FACILITIES AND EQUIPMENT Film — 8mm cameras, editing equipment, lighting equipment, projectors, sound stage, screening room, editing room, sound mixing room, animation board, permanent film library Television — complete black and white studio and exterior production facilities

FACULTY A A Oseguera, John H Rudy

COURSE LIST

Undergraduate

Introduction to Radio and Television
Television Performing and Production
Television Laboratory
Cinematography
Television Writing
Documentary Film
Television Directing
History of Broadcasting
Theory of Broadcasting
Video Editing
Film Theory
Television Practicum

IDAHO

Idaho State University

State-supported coed university. Institutionally accredited by regional association, programs recognized by NASM, AASCB, ACPE. Small town location. Total enrollment: 6287. Undergraduate enrollment: 5569. Total faculty: 505 (415 full-time, 90 part-time). Semester calendar. Grading system: letters or numbers.

Speech-Drama/English Departments, PO Box 8169, Pocatello, ID 83201 208-236-3695

CONTACT A Blomquist
ADMISSION Application deadline — 8/15, rolling
FACULTY A Blomquist, W Huck

Lewis-Clark State College

State-supported 4-year coed college. Institutionally accredited by regional association. Urban location, 40-acre campus. Undergraduate enrollment: 1256. Total faculty: 100 (85 full-time, 15 part-time). Semester calendar. Grading system: letters or numbers.

Media Center, Eighth Avenue and Sixth Street, Lewiston, ID 83501 208-746-2341

CONTACT Robert G Knipe
FINANCIAL AID Work/study programs
CURRICULAR EMPHASIS Television study — (1) production; (2) educational Television production — (1) educational; (2) experimental/personal video
SPECIAL ACTIVITIES/OFFERINGS Student publication, program material produced for on-campus closed-circuit television, student work experience in television production
FACILITIES AND EQUIPMENT Film — 8mm cameras, sound recording equipment, lighting equipment, projectors, sound stage, screening room, sound mixing room Television — complete black and white studio and exterior production equipment, black and white studio, audio studio, control room, color studio, video U-matic editing
PART-TIME FACULTY Robert G Knipe

COURSE LIST

Undergraduate

Television Production Workshop

University of Idaho

State-supported coed university. Institutionally accredited by regional association, programs recognized by NASM. Small town location, 450-acre campus. Total enrollment: 7636. Undergraduate enrollment: 6034. Total faculty: 535 (496 full-time, 39 part-time). Semester calendar. Grading system: letters or numbers.

School of Communication, Moscow, ID 83843 208-885-6458

CONTACT Film — Peter Haggart Television — Art Hook
DEGREES OFFERED BA, BS in telecommunications; BA, BS in journalism (radio-TV news); BA, BS with photo/film option of communication degree
DEPARTMENTAL MAJORS Film — 10 students Television — 70 students
ADMISSION Requirement — 2.5 minimum grade point average Application deadline — 8/1, 12/15
FINANCIAL AID Scholarships, work/study programs, student loans
CURRICULAR EMPHASIS Film study — history, criticism and aesthetics, appreciation treated equally Filmmaking — (1) news; (2) documentary; (3) experimental Television study — criticism and aesthetics, production, management treated equally Television production — commercial, news/documentary, educational treated equally
SPECIAL ACTIVITIES/OFFERINGS Film series, film societies, program material produced for local public television station, apprenticeships, internships in film production, internships in television production, independent study
FACILITIES AND EQUIPMENT Film — 8mm cameras, editing equipment, lighting, black and white film stock, color film stock, projectors, complete 16mm equipment, screening room, editing room Television — complete color studio and exterior production equipment, color studio, audio studio, control room
FACULTY Peter Haggart PART-TIME FACULTY Bill Berg, Cecil Bondurant, Art Hook, C Parker Van Hecke

University of Idaho (continued)

COURSE LIST

Undergraduate

Introduction to Telecommunication Equipment
Mass Communication in a Free Society
R-TV Newswriting
Radio Production
Television Production
Broadcast Advertising/Sales
Telecommunication Programming
Law of Mass Communication
Telecommunication Law and Regulation
Senior Seminar
Radio News Production
Television News Production
Cinematography
History of American Film
Documentary Film
Workshop
Internship
Directed Study

ILLINOIS

Augustana College

Independent comprehensive coed institution affiliated with Lutheran Church. Institutionally accredited by regional association, programs recognized by NASM. Urban location. Undergraduate enrollment: 2220. Total faculty: 179 (140 full-time, 39 part-time). Quarter calendar. Grading system: letters or numbers.

Speech Department, Rock Island, IL 61201 309-794-7000

CONTACT Chad Meyer
DEGREE OFFERED BA in speech
ADMISSION Application deadline — rolling
CURRICULAR EMPHASIS Television study — (1) criticism and aesthetics; (2) production Television production — commercial, news/documentary, experimental/personal video, educational treated equally
SPECIAL ACTIVITIES/OFFERINGS Program material produced for local commercial television station, internships in television production, independent study, vocational placement service
FACILITIES AND EQUIPMENT Television — facilities available through local commercial television station
FACULTY Chad Meyer

COURSE LIST

Undergraduate

Television Broadcasting
Essentials of Television

English Department, Rock Island, IL 61201 309-794-7280

CONTACT Dale S Huse
ADMISSION Application deadline — rolling
CURRICULAR EMPHASIS Film study — (1) history; (2) appreciation; (3) criticism and aesthetics
SPECIAL ACTIVITIES/OFFERINGS Film series, film societies, internships in television production, independent study, teacher training, vocational placement service
FACULTY Dale S Huse, Clarence Meyer, Harry Stelling

COURSE LIST

Undergraduate

History and Technology of Film
Novel in Film

Belleville Area College

District-supported 2-year coed college. Part of Illinois Community College System. Institutionally accredited by regional association. Suburban location. Undergraduate enrollment: 11,582. Total faculty: 467 (119 full-time, 348 part-time). Semester calendar. Grading system: letters or numbers.

English Department, 2500 Carlyle Road, Belleville, IL 62221 618-235-2700

CONTACT Wayne Lanter
ADMISSION Application deadline — 8/1, rolling
CURRICULAR EMPHASIS Film study — (1) appreciation; (2) criticism and aesthetics
SPECIAL ACTIVITIES/OFFERINGS Film series, film festival
FACILITIES AND EQUIPMENT Film — complete 8mm equipment, screening room, editing room Television — complete black and white studio production equipment, complete color studio production equipment, black and white studio, color studio
FACULTY Byron Davidson, Wayne Lanter

COURSE LIST

Undergraduate

Contemporary Film

Bethany Seminary

Independent Church of the Brethren upper-level coed institution. Institutionally accredited by regional association. Suburban location. Total enrollment: 128. Total faculty: 18 (12 full-time, 6 part-time). Quarter calendar. Grading system: pass/fail.

Communication Department, Oak Brook, IL 60521 312-620-2200

CONTACT LeRoy Kennel

ADMISSION Requirement — minimum grade point average
FINANCIAL AID Work/study programs
CURRICULAR EMPHASIS Film study — educational media/instructional technology Filmmaking — educational Television study — (1) educational; (2) production; (3) appreciation Television production — (1) educational; (2) experimental/personal video; (3) news/documentary
SPECIAL ACTIVITIES/OFFERINGS Film series, film festivals, independent study, practicum
FACILITIES AND EQUIPMENT Film — 8mm cameras, editing equipment, sound recording equipment, lighting equipment, 8mm, 16mm, and 35mm projectors, sound stage, screening room, 35mm screening facilities, editing room, sound mixing room Television — 1-inch VTR, editing equipment, monitors, special effects generators, ½-inch portapak recorder, black and white studio, audio studio, control room
FACULTY LeRoy Kennel

COURSE LIST

Graduate
Mass Media, Society, and Church
Celebrative Arts
Audio-Visual Communication
Mass Mediated Culture
Film and Literature

Blackburn College

Independent United Presbyterian 4-year coed college. Institutionally accredited by regional association. Small town location, 80-acre campus. Undergraduate enrollment: 550. Total faculty: 48 (40 full-time, 8 part-time). Semester calendar. Grading system: letters or numbers.

Illinois

Speech Communication and Theatre Arts Department, Carlinville, IL 62626 217-854-3231

CONTACT Thomas D Anderson
DEGREES OFFERED BA in communication, BA in theatre arts
ADMISSION Requirements — 2.5 minimum grade point average, ACT or SAT scores, written statement of purpose
FINANCIAL AID Work/study programs, student loans
CURRICULAR EMPHASIS Film study — appreciation, production treated equally Television study — appreciation, educational, production treated equally Television production — experimental/personal video
SPECIAL ACTIVITIES/OFFERINGS Program material produced for cable television, internships in television production, independent study
FACILITIES AND EQUIPMENT Television — ½-inch VTR, ¾-inch VTR, portable black and white cameras, sound recording equipment

COURSE LIST

Undergraduate
Media and Mass Communication

Black Hawk College, Quad Cities Campus

State-supported 2-year coed college. Part of Black Hawk College District System. Institutionally accredited by regional association. Rural location. Undergraduate enrollment: 720. Total faculty: 101 (26 full-time, 75 part-time). Semester calendar. Grading system: letters or numbers.

Communication Arts Department, 6600 34th Avenue, Moline, IL 61265 309-796-1311

CONTACT Ralph D Drexler
DEGREES OFFERED AA, AAS with an emphasis in broadcasting
DEPARTMENTAL MAJORS Television — 14 students
ADMISSION Requirement — interview Application deadline — 8/25
FINANCIAL AID Scholarships, work/study programs, student loans, achievement awards Application deadline — 7/15
CURRICULAR EMPHASIS Film study — history, appreciation treated equally Filmmaking — (1) narrative; (2) experimental; (3) documentary Television study — history, appreciation, production treated equally Television production — (1) commercial; (2) experimental/personal video; (3) news/documentary
SPECIAL ACTIVITIES/OFFERINGS Program material produced for on-campus closed-circuit television and cable television, internships in television production, independent study
FACILITIES AND EQUIPMENT Film — 16mm cameras, editing equipment, black and white film stock, color film stock, projectors, tripods, light meters, editing room, sound mixing room Television — color studio cameras, 2-inch VTR, ¾-inch cassette VTR, portable black and white cameras, editing equipment, monitors, special effects generators, slide chain, ½-inch portapak recorders, ¾-inch ENG, lighting equipment, sound recording equipment, audio mixers, film chain, time base corrector, computer graphics, character generator, cable distribution, color studio, audio studio, control room
FACULTY Ralph D Drexler, William Hannan

COURSE LIST

Undergraduate
Introduction to Film Production
TV Graphics
Introduction to Radio
Broadcast Internship
History and Appreciation of the Motion Picture
Introduction to Television
TV Production & Direction
Broadcast Perspectives
Broadcast Announcing

Bradley University

Independent comprehensive coed institution. Institutionally accredited by regional association, programs recognized by NASM, AACSB. Suburban location, 55-acre campus. Total enrollment: 5238. Undergraduate enrollment: 4554. Total faculty: 377 (280 full-time, 97 part-time). Semester calendar. Grading system: letters or numbers.

Art Department, 1501 West Bradley Avenue, Peoria, IL 61625 309-676-7611

CONTACT Gerald Fromberg

Bradley University (continued)

DEGREES OFFERED BA, BFA, BS in art with emphasis in film; BA, BFA, BS in art/mass communications; BA, BS in radio and television
ADMISSION Requirement — 2.0 minimum grade point average Application deadline — rolling
CURRICULAR EMPHASIS Film study — (1) production; (2) criticism and aesthetics Filmmaking — (1) narrative; (2) experimental; (3) animated Television study — (1) production; (2) management Television production — (1) commercial; (2) news/documentary; (3) educational
SPECIAL ACTIVITIES/OFFERINGS Film series, internships in film and television production, independent study, practicum
FACILITIES AND EQUIPMENT Film — complete 8mm and 16mm equipment, 16mm animation stand, contact printer, optical printer, editing room, sound mixing room, animation board, permanent film library Television — complete black and white studio production facilities, complete color studio production facilities
FACULTY Gerald Fromberg, Henry Vander Heyden PART-TIME FACULTY Joel Hartman

COURSE LIST
Undergraduate
Introduction to Radio and Television
Television Production and Directing
Filmmaking Studio
Animated Film
Film Aesthetics
Advanced Television Production and Directing
Mass Media Practicum

City Colleges of Chicago, Richard J Daley College

State and locally supported 2-year coed college. Part of City Colleges of Chicago System. Institutionally accredited by regional association. Urban location. Semester calendar. Grading system: letters or numbers.

Human and Public Services Department, 7500 South Pulaski, Chicago, IL 60652 312-735-3000

CONTACT Tom Palozzolo
FACILITIES AND EQUIPMENT Film — 8mm and 16mm cameras, lighting equipment, projectors, 8mm editing equipment Television — complete black and white studio and exterior production facilities
FACULTY Rich Jeske, Tom Palozzolo

COURSE LIST
Undergraduate
Beginning Television Techniques
Advanced Television Techniques
Cinematography I, II
Communications Design

Humanities Department

CONTACT Nancy LaPaglia
DEGREE OFFERED AA in liberal arts with an emphasis in film/television
ADMISSION 7/25, rolling
FACILITIES AND EQUIPMENT Film — 8mm and 16mm production and editing equipment Television — video production and editing equipment (¾-inch)
SPECIAL ACTIVITIES/OFFERINGS Film library
FACULTY Joan Kalk, Nancy LaPaglia

COURSE LIST
Undergraduate
Production in Film and Video
Film Appreciation

City Colleges of Chicago, Wilbur Wright College

State and locally supported 2-year coed college. Part of City Colleges of Chicago System. Institutionally accredited by regional association. Urban location. Undergraduate enrollment: 7126. Total faculty: 213 (205 full-time, 8 part-time). Early semester calendar. Grading system: letters or numbers.

Humanities Department, Chicago, IL 60634 312-777-7900

CONTACT John J Gardzie
FACULTY John J Gardzie

COURSE LIST
Undergraduate
The World of the Cinema

College of DuPage

State and locally supported 2-year coed college. Institutionally accredited by regional association. Suburban location, 273-acre campus. Undergraduate enrollment: 16,654. Total faculty: 201. Quarter calendar. Grading system: letters or numbers.

Media Technology Department, 22nd Street and Lambert Road, Glen Ellyn, IL 60137 312-858-2800

CONTACT Robert W Johnson
DEGREE OFFERED AAS in media
DEPARTMENTAL MAJORS Film — 47 students Television — 54 students
ADMISSION Requirement — interview
FINANCIAL AID Student loans

CURRICULAR EMPHASIS Film study — (1) educational media/instructional technology; (2) criticism and aesthetics; (3) history Filmmaking — (1) educational; (2) documentary; (3) narrative Television study — (1) production; (2) educational; (3) criticism and aesthetics Television production — (1) educational; (2) news/documenatry; (3) experimental/personal video
SPECIAL ACTIVITIES/OFFERINGS Independent study
FACILITIES AND EQUIPMENT Film — complete 8mm and 16mm equipment, sound stage, screening room, editing room, sound mixing room, animation board Television — black and white studio cameras, ¾-inch cassette VTR, portable black and white cameras, editing equipment, monitors, special effects generators, portable color cameras, lighting equipment, sound recording equipment, audio mixers, black and white studio, audio studio, control room, portapak remote black and white units
FACULTY Robert W Johnson, Thomas Klodin PART-TIME FACULTY James Gustafson, William Hight, Mike Murschell, Ted Sodergren

COURSE LIST

Undergraduate

Film I, II
TV I, II
Media Aesthetics
Creating and Writing for Media
Media Workshop

Columbia College

Independent 4-year coed college. Institutionally accredited by regional association. Urban location. Undergraduate enrollment: 2916. Total faculty: 295 (51 full-time, 244 part-time). Semester calendar. Grading system: letters or numbers.

Illinois

Television Department, 600 South Michigan Avenue, Chicago, IL 60605 312-663-1600

CONTACT Film — Anthony Loeb Television — H Thaine Lyman
DEGREES OFFERED BA in television production, broadcast management, broadcast journalism, television performance, industrial television
DEPARTMENTAL MAJORS Television — 650 students
ADMISSION Open admissions Application deadline — rolling
FINANCIAL AID Scholarships, work/study programs, student loans Application deadline — state scholarship 2/15, BEOG 3/15, work/study CSS form 3/16
CURRICULAR EMPHASIS Television study — (1) production; (2) management; (3) criticism and aesthetics Television production — (1) commercial; (2) news/documentary; (3) experimental/personal video
SPECIAL ACTIVITIES/OFFERINGS Film festivals; student publications; program material produced for on-campus closed-circuit television, local public television station, local commercial television station; internships in television production; independent study; vocational placement service
FACILITIES AND EQUIPMENT Television — black and white studio cameras, color studio cameras, ½-inch VTR, ¾-inch cassette VTR, portable black and white cameras, editing equipment, monitors, special effects generators, slide chain, portable color cameras, ½-inch portapak recorders, ¾-inch ENG, lighting equipment, sound recording equipment, audio mixers, film chain, time base corrector, black and white studio, color studio, audio studio, control room, editing room
FACULTY Will Horton, Thaine Lyman, Al Parker PART-TIME FACULTY Richard Bernal, Peter Bordwell, Mike Bozidarevic, Tom Carlson, Douglas Challos, Malcolm Chisholm, Jim Disch, Brian Dolan, Robert Edmonds, Robert Elliott, David Erdman, George Friedman, Rivka Green, Don Howell, Sandra Iannone, Morris Jones, Bonnie Kopisch, Ouida Lindsey, Hugh Martin, Orrin McDaniels, James McPharlin, Ray Meinke, Bill Nigut, Virginia Paddock, Jim Passin, Gil Peters, Dick Petrash, Robert Petty, Hershell Reiter, Naurice Roberts, Sid Roberts, Joe Rodger, Tom Rossi, Morry Roth, Gary Rowe, Roger Schatz, Jim Seemiller, Robert Seid, Jack Sell, Howard Shapiro, Jim Shaw, Bruce Shuster, Cheryl Stutzke, Don Tait, Joe Turner, Ron Vasser, Ron Weiner

COURSE LIST

Undergraduate

Fundamentals of TV
Television I: Facilities
Television II: Studio
Telvision III: Production
TV Directing I, II
TV Production Workshop I, II
TV Production: News
The TV Producer
Television Production: Children's Programming
Television Production: Commercials
Television Production: Drama Workshop
Television Production: Acting Workshop
Television Workshop: Scene Design
The Television Commercial: Is It Art?
Television and Radio: The Golden Age
Television Operations Procedures
Television: A Third View
Television Announcing I, II
Television Documentary
The Documentary Concept: Planning and Organization
Radio and Television Continuity Management
Sound Engineering I–III
Introduction to Video Tape
Video Tape Editing Technique I, II
Television: Star Series
Black Culture and the Media
Freedom of the News Media
The Law and the Electronic Journalist
Communications and the Law
Radio and Television Traffic Management
Broadcast Management
Broadcast Responsibility
Broadcast Research
Broadcast Sales
Television and Radio Commercial Writing
Network Television
Audio-Visuals for Business Communication
Writing for the Marketplace
Broadcast Labor Relations
Television Basics
Corporate Video
Career Development in Communications
The Tube: American Change of Life
Television and Professional Growth
Visual Production Seminar I, II
Investigative Broadcast News
Commercial Announcing
Writing Television News I, II
Speech Techniques in Broadcasting
Television Writing: Beginning
Television Writing: Advanced
Speech for Non-Theater Students
Screenwriting I, II: Film and Television
Marketing Foundations: Advertising
Stage Lighting I, II
Accounting Fundamentals for the Business of the Arts
Television Independent Projects
Television Internship
Entrepreneurship: Basic Business Principles
Survey of the Recording Industry
Talent Booking and Management
Basics in Journalism
Film for Television
Fundamentals in Journalism
Broadcast Sports
Advertising Design for Print and TV

Columbia College (continued)

Film Department 312-663-1600

CONTACT Anthony Loeb, Chairman
DEGREES OFFERED BA in film; Certificate of Advanced Film Study
DEPARTMENTAL MAJORS Undergraduate film — 350 students Graduate film — 65 students
FINANCIAL AID Scholarships, work/study programs, teaching assistantships Undergraduate application deadline — rolling
CURRICULAR EMPHASIS Undergraduate film study — screenwriting, history, criticism and aesthetics, production technique treated equally Graduate film study — Screenwriting, history, criticism and aesthetics, production technique treated equally Undergraduate filmmaking — documentary, narrative, animated treated equally Graduate filmmaking — documentary, narrative, animated treated equally
SPECIAL ACTIVITIES/OFFERINGS Film series, film festivals, student publications, apprenticeships, internships in film production, independent study, vocational placement service
FACILITIES AND EQUIPMENT Film — complete 16mm equipment, mix, sound stage, screening room, editing room, sound mixing room, animation board, permanent film library of student films, permanent film library of commercial or professional films
FACULTY Dan Dinello, Chappelle Freeman Jr, Anthony Loeb, James Martin, Michael Rabiger PART-TIME FACULTY Gary Adkins, Joseph Calomino, Richard Coken, Chris Cuttance, Michael Danko, George Eastman, Robert Edmonds, Richard Girvin, Gary Houston, John Lafferty, David Morenz, Robert Neches, Paul Rubenstein, Howard Sandroff, Gordon Sheehan, Alan Spencer, Carol White, Jack Whitehead, Barry Young

COURSE LIST

Undergraduate

Film Techniques I–III
Acting for Film
Adaptation from Book to Movie
Aesthetics of Visual Composition
Animation I–IV
Drawing for Animation I, II
Animation: Studio Production
Optical Printing I, II
Animation: Special Projects
Budgeting for Film
Camera Seminar I, II
Cinematography
Comedy on Film
Developing the Documentary
Directing the Dramatic Film
Experimental Filmmaking
Film Editing I, II
The Film Producer
Form and Structure: Analysis of Classic Film Scripts
French New Wave Cinema
History of the Cinema I–III
Improvisation and the Filmmaker
Lighting: Basics
Lighting: Advanced
Negative Cutting
Production Seminar: Intermediate
Production Seminar: Advanced
Professional Apprenticeship
Screenwriting I, II: Dramatic for Film and TV
Feature Screenwriting
The Short Film
Introduction to Sound Technique
Sound Studio: Introduction
Special Seminar: The Mix
Music and Sound Effects Editing
Music for Film
Strategies in Film Criticism
Visual Analysis: "Bonnie & Clyde" and "Citizen Kane"
Women in Film
Working in Chicago

Eastern Illinois University

State-supported comprehensive coed institution. Institutionally accredited by regional association, programs recognized by NASM. Small town location, 312-acre campus. Total enrollment: 9585. Undergraduate enrollment: 8745. Total faculty: 539 (473 full-time, 66 part-time). Semester calendar. Grading system: letters or numbers.

Speech Communication Department, 114 Coleman, Charleston, IL 61920 217-581-3819

CONTACT Joe Heumann
PROGRAM OFFERED Major in speech communication with emphasis in film or television
ADMISSION Application deadline — 8/15, rolling
FINANCIAL AID Scholarships, student loans, work/study programs, teaching assistantships Application deadline — 3/1, rolling
SPECIAL ACTIVITIES/OFFERINGS Film series, film festivals, film societies, apprenticeships, internships in television production, independent study
FACILITIES AND EQUIPMENT Film — complete 8mm equipment, screening room, editing room, sound mixing room Television — complete black and white studio production equipment, black and white studio, audio studio, control room
FACULTY Joe Heumann, Earl McSwain

COURSE LIST

Undergraduate

Understanding Media
Introduction to Mass Communications

Undergraduate and Graduate

Film and Communication
Film Production
News and Special Events
Television Production
TV Criticism
Film History
News Writing
TV Economics

Eureka College

Independent 4-year coed college affiliated with Disciples of Christ Church. Institutionally accredited by regional association. Small town location, 120-acre campus. Undergraduate enrollment: 450. Total enrollment: 37 (31 full-time, 6 part-time). Four 8-week term calendar. Grading system: letters or numbers.

Speech and Theatre Department, Humanities Division, 300 East College Avenue, Eureka, IL 61530 309-467-3721

CONTACT William Davis
PROGRAM OFFERED Major in speech and theatre with emphasis in television
ADMISSION Requirement —admission to the college Application deadline — rolling

CURRICULAR EMPHASIS Television study — (1) educational; (2) criticism and aesthetics; (3) management Television production — (1) educational; (2) experimental/personal video; (3) news/documentary
SPECIAL ACTIVITIES/OFFERINGS Internships in television production, independent study, practicum, teacher training, vocational placement service
FACILITIES AND EQUIPMENT Television — black and white studio cameras, ½-inch VTR, VHS cassette VTRs, portable black and white cameras, monitors, lighting equipment, sound recording equipment, audio mixers
FACULTY William Davis, Donald Littlejohn, Tella Metzel

COURSE LIST
Undergraduate
Introduction to Broadcasting
Mass Media

Governors State University

State-supported upper-level coed institution. Institutionally accredited by regional association. Suburban location, 200-acre campus. Total enrollment: 3901. Undergraduate enrollment: 1537. Total faculty: 288 (153 full-time, 135 part-time). Trimester calendar. Grading sytem: pass/fail.

Media Communications Program, Park Forest South, IL 60466 312-534-5000

CONTACT Film — Marian Marzynski Television — Mel Muchnik
DEGREES OFFERED BA, MA in media communications; BA, MA in educational technology
PROGRAM MAJORS Undergraduate film — 10 students Undergraduate television — 25 students Graduate film — 15 students Graduate television — 40 students
ADMISSION Undergraduate requirement — minimum C average Graduate requirements — interview, minimum B average Undergraduate application deadline — rolling
FINANCIAL AID Scholarships, work/study programs, student loans, research assistantships
CURRICULAR EMPHASIS Undergraduate film study — criticism and aesthetics, educational media/instructional technology treated equally Graduate film study — criticism and aesthetics, educational media/instructional technology treated equally Undergraduate filmmaking — documentary, educational treated equally Graduate filmmaking — documentary, educational treated equally Undergraduate television study — history, criticism and aesthetics, educational, production treated equally Graduate television study — history, criticism and aesthetics, educational, production treated equally Undergraduate television production — news/documentary, experimental/personal video, educational treated equally Graduate television production — news/documentary, experimental/personal video, educational treated equally
SPECIAL ACTIVITIES/OFFERINGS Film — Filmmaking clubs, film series, film societies, program material produced for on-campus closed-circuit televison and cable televison, internships in television production, independent study
FACILITIES AND EQUIPMENT Film — complete 8mm equipment, 16mm editing equipment, lighting, projectors, editing room, animation board, permanent film library of commercial or professional films Television — color studio cameras, 1-inch VTR, ¾-inch cassette VTR, portable black and white cameras, special effects generators, slide chain, portable color cameras, ¾-inch ENG, lighting equipment, sound recording equipment, audio mixers, film chain, time base corrector, color studio, control room
FACULTY Marian M Marzynski, Melvyn M Muchnik, Linda Gail Phillips, Paul R Schranz, Linda C Steiner PART-TIME FACULTY Richard Burd, Frank Jackson, Ralph Kruse, Lamarr Scott, Linda Willard

COURSE LIST
Undergraduate
Film Project I, II

Graduate
Contemporary Issues: Broadcast Responsibility
Graduate Film Production I, II

Undergraduate and Graduate
Media and Society
Mass Communications Law
Television Directing
Television: Remote Color Techniques
Film and Television Documentary
Film Seminar
Chicago Media Laboratory
Broadcasting in America
Children and Television
Media Animation
Television Production
Television: Advanced Color Production
Women in the Media
Multi-Media Production I, II
Media Team Field Project
Media Symposium
Television Production (Workshop)
Film and Filmmakers I, II
Media: Broadcast Journalism
Media: Urban Journalism

Highland Community College

District-supported 2-year coed college. Institutionally accredited by regional association. Rural location. Undergraduate enrollment: 1729. Total faculty: 103 (45 full-time, 58 part-time). Semester calendar. Grading system: letters or numbers.

Humanities/Speech Departments, Pearl City Road, Freeport, IL 61032 815-235-6121

CONTACT Sid Fryer
PROGRAM OFFERED Major in humanities/speech with emphasis in television
ADMISSION Application deadline — 8/25, rolling
FINANCIAL AID Student loans, work/study programs Application deadline — 7/1, rolling
CURRICULAR EMPHASIS Television study — (1) production; (2) management; (3) history Television production — (1) commercial; (2) news/documentary; (3) experimental/personal video
SPECIAL ACTIVITIES/OFFERINGS Program material produced for on-campus closed-circuit television and cable television, independent study
FACILITIES AND EQUIPMENT Film — 8mm and 16mm projectors Television — complete black and white studio and exterior production equipment, complete color studio production equipment, black and white studio, audio studio, control room

Highland Community College (continued)

FACULTY Alan Wenzel PART-TIME FACULTY Sid Fryer

COURSE LIST

Undergraduate

Introduction to Broadcasting
Television Production

Illinois State University

State-supported coed university. Institutionally accredited by regional association, programs recognized by NASM, NASA. Small town location, 711-acre campus. Total enrollment: 19,250. Undergraduate enrollment: 17,191. Total faculty: 1089 (949 full-time, 140 part-time). Semester calendar. Grading system: letters or numbers.

Information Sciences Department, Normal, IL 61761 309-438-3671

CONTACT Film — Ray Wiman Television — Jeffrey Szmulewicz
DEGREE OFFERED BS in mass communications with emphasis in broadcast journalism
ADMISSION Requirements — ACT or SAT scores, written statement of purpose Application deadline — rolling
FINANCIAL AID Teaching assistantships Application deadline — 3/1, rolling
CURRICULAR EMPHASIS Film study — (1) educational media/instructional technology; (2) production Undergraduate filmmaking — (1) news film; (2) educational; (3) documentary Graduate filmmaking — educational Television study — (1) history, criticism and aesthetics; (2) production; (3) management Television production — (1) news/documentary; (2) commercial; (3) educational
SPECIAL ACTIVITIES/OFFERINGS Film festivals, film societies, program material produced for on campus closed-circuit television and cable television, internships in television production, independent study, teacher training
FACILITIES AND EQUIPMENT Film — complete 8mm equipment Television — complete black and white studio and exterior production equipment, black and white studio, mobile van/unit, audio studio, control room
FACULTY William Jesse, Ralph Smith, Jeffrey Szmulewicz, Lee Thornton, Wenmouth Williams, Raymond Wiman, Forrest Wisely PART-TIME FACULTY Lenore L Hutton

COURSE LIST

Undergraduate

Workshop in Small System Television
Television Production
Broadcast News I, II
Mass Communications: Cultural Criticism
Advanced Television Production
Broadcast Programming
Documentary in Film and Broadcasting

Graduate

Seminar in Mass Communication
Independent Study

Undergraduate and Graduate

Mass Communications: Theory and Effects
Instructional Television
Broadcast Management
Motion Picture Production
Regulation of Communications Industry
Directed Projects
Workshop in the Consumer and Mass Media

Knox College

Independent 4-year coed college. Institutionally accredited by regional association. Small town location, 60-acre campus. Undergraduate enrollment: 1042. Total faculty: 86 (80 full-time, 6 part-time). 3-3-1 calendar. Grading system: letters or numbers.

English Department, Galesburg, IL 61401 309-343-0112

CONTACT Edward Niehus
ADMISSION Application deadline — rolling
FACULTY Edward Niehus

COURSE LIST

Undergraduate

Introduction to Film

Lincoln Land Community College

State and locally supported 2-year coed college. Institutionally accredited by regional association. Suburban location. Undergraduate enrollment: 5790. Total faculty: 292 (132 full-time, 160 part-time). Semester calendar. Grading system: letters or numbers.

Performing Arts Division, Shepherd Road, Springfield, IL 62708 217-786-2200

CONTACT Anthony P J Cerniglia
ADMISSION Application deadline — rolling
CURRICULAR EMPHASIS Film study — (1) appreciation; (2) criticism and aesthetics; (3) history Filmmaking — (1) experimental; (2) educational; (3) narrative
FACILITIES AND EQUIPMENT Film — 8mm cameras, editing equipment, projectors, screening room, permanent film library Television — black and white studio cameras, 1-inch VTR, ¾-inch cassette VTR, sound recording equipment
FACULTY Anthony P J Cerniglia

COURSE LIST

Undergraduate

Introduction to Film Art

Loyola University of Chicago

Independent Roman Catholic coed university. Institutionally accredited by regional association, programs recognized by AACSB. Urban location. Total enrollment: 13,279. Undergraduate enrollment: 8445. Total faculty: 1370. Semester calendar. Grading system: letters or numbers.

**Communication Arts Department, 820 North Michigan Avenue, Chicago, IL 60611
312-670-3116**

CONTACT Don J Norwood
DEGREE OFFERED BA in communication arts
DEPARTMENTAL MAJORS Film — 75 students Television — 100 students
ADMISSION Requirement — 2.0 minimum grade point average Application deadline — 8/19
FINANCIAL AID Scholarships, student loans, work/study programs Application deadline — 6/1
CURRICULAR EMPHASIS Film study — (1) criticism and aesthetics; (2) production; (3) educational media/instructional technology; (4) history; (5) appreciation Filmmaking — documentary, narrative, experimental treated equally Television study — (1) production; (2) criticism and aesthetics; (3) educational; (4) management; (5) appreciation Television production — commercial, news/documentary, educational treated equally
SPECIAL ACTIVITIES/OFFERINGS Filmmaking clubs, film series, film festivals, film societies, program material produced for on-campus closed-circuit television, apprenticeships, internships in film and television production, independent study, practicum, teacher training, vocational placement service
FACILITIES AND EQUIPMENT Film — complete Super-8 equipment, editing equipment, projectors, sound stage, screening room, editing room, sound mixing room, animation board, permanent film library Television — complete black and white and color studio and exterior production equipment, audio studio, control room
FACULTY Bert Akers, Sammy Danna, Don J Norwood PART-TIME FACULTY Robert Perkowski

COURSE LIST
Undergraduate
Mass Media Communication
Propaganda and Mass Media
Advanced Television Production
Teleplay Production
Film Communication
Film Production
Communications Consulting
History/Criticism of American Broadcasting
Mass Communication Law
International Mass Communications
Media Management
Instructional Television
Film and Television Practicum
Film Genre

Millikin University

Independent 4-year coed college affiliated with United Presbyterian Church. Institutionally accredited by regional association, programs recognized by NASM. Suburban location, 60-acre campus. Undergraduate enrollment: 1648. Total faculty: 121 (96 full-time, 25 part-time). 4-1-4 calendar. Grading system: letters or numbers.

English Department, 1184 West Main Street, Decatur, IL 62522 217-424-6250

CONTACT R Pacholski
ADMISSION Application deadline — rolling
PART-TIME FACULTY P Gregory Springer

COURSE LIST
Undergraduate
Literature of the Film

Monmouth College

Independent 4-year coed college affiliated with Presbyterian Church. Institutionally accredited by regional association. small town location, 30-acre campus. Undergraduate enrollment: 675. Total faculty: 76 (54 full-time, 22 part-time). 3-3 calendar. Grading system: letters or numbers.

Speech/Communication Arts Department, Monmouth, IL 61462 309-457-2398

CONTACT James De Young
ADMISSION Application deadline — rolling
FINANCIAL AID Scholarships, student loans Application deadline — rolling
CURRICULAR EMPHASIS Filmmaking — (1) experimental; (2) narrative; (3) documentary Television study — (1) production; (2) criticism and aesthetics; (3) educational; (4) management; (5) appreciation; (6) history Television production — (1) educational; (2) experimental/personal video; (3) news/documentary; (4) commercial
SPECIAL ACTIVITIES/OFFERINGS Film series, program material produced for cable television, independent study
FACILITIES AND EQUIPMENT Film — complete 8mm equipment, screening room, editing room Television — complete black and white studio production equipment, black and white studio, control room, portapak
FACULTY James De Young, Martin Feeney, George Waltershausen

COURSE LIST
Undergraduate
Introduction to Theater and Film Appreciation
Seminar in Film Criticism
Mass Media and Modern Society
Television Production
Filmmaking
Photography

North Central College

Independent United Methodist 4-year coed college. Institutionally accredited by regional association. Suburban location. Undergraduate enrollment: 1036. Total faculty: 77 (54 full-time, 23 part-time). 3-3 calendar. Grading system: letters or numbers.

North Central College (continued)

Speech Communications Department, 30 North Brainard Street, Naperville, IL 60540 312-420-3464

CONTACT Jonathan L Yoder
DEGREE OFFERED BA in speech communications
ADMISSION Application deadline — rolling
FINANCIAL AID Scholarships, student loans Application deadline — rolling
CURRICULAR EMPHASIS Film study — history, criticism and aesthetics, appreciation, educational media/instructional technology treated equally Filmmaking — documentary, narrative treated equally Television study — criticism and aesthetics, appreciation, production treated equally Television production — commercial, news/documentary, educational treated equally
SPECIAL ACTIVITIES/OFFERINGS Film festivals, program material produced for on-campus closed-circuit television, independent study
FACILITIES AND EQUIPMENT Television — black and white studio cameras, 1-inch VTR, monitors, portable color cameras, lighting equipment, sound recording equipment, audio mixers, black and white studio, 4000-watt FM station
FACULTY John Cerovski, Jonathan L Yoder

COURSE LIST
Undergraduate
Mass Media and Society
Radio Production
Television Production
Writing for Radio, Television, and Film
Station Programming

Northern Illinois University

State-supported coed university. Institutionally accredited by regional association, programs recognized by NASA. Small town location, 589-acre campus. Total enrollment: 21,669. Undergraduate enrollment: 17,079. Total faculty: 1233 (1072 full-time, 161 part-time). Semester calendar. Grading system: letters or numbers.

English Department, DeKalb, IL 60115 815-753-0611

CONTACT Robert T Self
DEGREE OFFERED MA in English with emphasis in literature and film
ADMISSION Requirements — 3.0 minimum grade point average, GRE scores, teachers' recommendations
FINANCIAL AID Teaching assistantships, research assistantships
CURRICULAR EMPHASIS Undergraduate film study — (1) criticism and aesthetics; (2) history Graduate film study — (1) criticism and aesthetics; (2) history; (3) educational media/instructional technology
SPECIAL ACTIVITIES/OFFERINGS Film series, film societies
FACULTY Robert T Self, Lynne M Waldeland PART-TIME FACULTY Gerald Berkowitz, Rose Marie Burwell, Charles Pennel

COURSE LIST
Undergraduate
Drama into Film
Literature and Film
Narrative Film
Shakespeare and Film
Composition and the Media
Graduate
The Teaching of Film
Literature & Film

Speech Communication Department 815-753-1563

CONTACT Jon T Powell, Chair
DEGREES OFFERED BA, MA in speech communication with emphasis in film/television
DEPARTMENTAL MAJORS Undergraduate film — 300 students Undergraduate television — 300 students Graduate film — 25 students Graduate television — 25 students
ADMISSION Undergraduate requirements — 2.0 minimum grade point average, ACT or SAT scores Graduate requirements — 3.0 minimum grade point average, GRE scores, teachers' recommendations Undergraduate application deadline — 8/1, rolling
FINANCIAL AID Work/study programs, student loans, fellowships, teaching assistantships Undergraduate application deadline — rolling
CURRICULAR EMPHASIS Undergraduate film study — history, criticism and aesthetics, educational media/instructional technology treated equally Graduate film study — history, criticism and aesthetics, educational media/instructional technology treated equally Undergraduate filmmaking — documentary, narrative, experimental, animated, educational treated equally Graduate filmmaking — documentary, narrative, experimental, animated, educational treated equally Undergraduate television study — history, educational, production, management treated equally Graduate television study — educational, production, management treated equally Undergraduate television production — commercial, news/documentary, experimental/personal video, educational treated equally Graduate television production — commercial, news/documentary, experimental/personal video, educational treated equally
SPECIAL ACTIVITIES/OFFERINGS Filmmaking clubs; film series; film festivals; film societies; student publications; program material produced for on-campus closed-circuit television, cable television, local commercial television station; internships in film production; internships in television production; independent study; teacher training
FACILITIES AND EQUIPMENT Film — complete 8mm equipment, 16mm cameras, editing equipment, sound recording equipment, lighting, projectors, editing room, sound mixing room, animation board, permanent film library of commercial or professional films Television — complete black and white and color studio and exterior production equipment
FACULTY Steward W Blakley, Myles P Breen, Roderrick Deihl, John Wellman PART-TIME FACULTY Arthur Doederlein, Philip Gray

COURSE LIST
Undergraduate
Introduction to Broadcasting
Impact of Film
Production for Nonmajors
Television Production
Continuity Writing

Graduate
Seminar in Broadcasting
Broadcast Research
Problems of Broadcast Production
Topics in Broadcast Management

Undergraduate and Graduate
Basic Filmmaking
Advanced Filmmaking
Comparative Systems of Broadcasting
International Broadcasting
Broadcast Law and Regulations
History of Film
Television Film Documentary
Film Theory and Criticism
Advanced Television Production
Instructional Television
Broadcasting and Society

Northwestern University

Independent coed university. Institutionally accredited by regional association. Suburban location, 185-acre campus. Total enrollment: 15,725. Undergraduate enrollment: 9300. Total faculty: 1673 (1292 full-time, 381 part-time). Quarter calendar. Grading system: letters or numbers.

Radio, Television, and Film Department, School of Speech, Evanston, IL 60201 312-492-7315

CONTACT Film — Paddy Whannel Television — John Gartley
DEGREES OFFERED BS, MA, MFA, PhD in film; BS, MA, MFA, PhD in television
DEPARTMENTAL MAJORS Undergraduate film — 150 students Undergraduate television — 150 students Graduate film — 25 students Graduate television — 25 students
ADMISSION Undergraduate requirements — minimum grade point average, SAT scores, teachers' recommendations, written statement of purpose Graduate requirements — minimum grade point average, GRE scores, teachers' recommendations, written statement of purpose Undergraduate application deadline — 2/15
FINANCIAL AID Scholarships, student loans, teaching assistantships, fellowships
CURRICULAR EMPHASIS Undergraduate film study — (1) criticism and aesthetics; (2) production; (3) history Graduate film study — (1) criticism and theory; (2) history; (3) production Filmmaking — depends upon current student interest Television study — history, criticism and aesthetics, production, management treated equally Television production — (1) commercial; (2) news/documentary
SPECIAL ACTIVITIES/OFFERINGS Film series, film festivals, film societies, student publications, internships in film and television production, independent study, academic year abroad program of film analysis offered through affiliation with the Inter-University Center for Film Studies in Paris
FACILITIES AND EQUIPMENT Film — complete 8mm and 16mm equipment, screening rooms, editing rooms, sound mixing room, animation board, permanent film library Television — complete black and white studio and exterior production facilities, complete color studio and exterior production facilities
FACULTY Louis Castelli, Michelle Citron, Jack Ellis, John Gartley, Lynn Gartley, Dana Hodgdon, Stuart Kaminsky, Chuck Kleinhans, Martin Maloney, Stephen May, Robert Pekurny, Paddy Whannel

COURSE LIST

Undergraduate
Introduction to Television Production
Introduction to Radio Production
Radio and Television Announcing
Introduction to Popular Culture in Mass Media
Creative Processes in Sight and Sound
Introduction to Film Production
Introduction to Film History and Criticism

Graduate
Problems in Film Scholarship
Problems in Film Aesthetics
Film Theory and Practice
Comparative Broadcast Systems
Cultural Analysis of Mass Media
Mass Communication and National Development
Studies in Popular Culture in the Mass Media Film

Undergraduate and Graduate
Television in Education
Radio, Television, and Film Dramatic Writing
Radio Production Procedures
Problems in Continuity Writing
Program Planning and Building
Materials and Backgrounds of Mass Media Criticism
Television Station Management
Dramatic Television Studio Directing
Non-Dramatic Television Studio Directing
Television Production
Internship in Television Production
Studies in the History of Broadcasting
Studies in Psychological and Sociological Aspects of the Mass Media
Studies in Writing for Broadcast
International Mass Communication
Studies in Film Theory
Studies in National Cinema
Studies in Film Authorship
Studies in Film Genre
Film Production
Basic 16mm Film Production
The Experimental Film
The History of Film
Modes of Film Communication
Internship in Film Production
The Documentary Film
Studies in Filmmaking
Studies in Film Criticism
Regulation of Broadcasting
Innovations: Mass Media and Technology
Mass Media: The Program Production Process
History of the Television Program
History of Radio Programming
Cable Broadcasting
Television Field Production Practices
Symposium on Issues in Mass Media
Independent Study

Rock Valley College

District-supported 2-year coed college. Institutionally accredited by regional association. Suburban location, 217-acre campus. Undergraduate enrollment: 5499. Total faculty: 390 (130 full-time, 260 part-time). Semester calendar. Grading system: letters or numbers.

Communications Department, 3301 North Mulford Road, Rockford, IL 61101 815-226-2600

CONTACT Robert Branda
ADMISSION Application deadline — 8/29

Rock Valley College (continued)

COURSE LIST

Undergraduate

Film as Literature

Rosary College

Independent Roman Catholic comprehensive coed institution. Institutionally accredited by regional association. Suburban location, 30-acre campus. Total enrollment: 1641. Undergraduate enrollment: 948. Total faculty: 132 (75 full-time, 57 part-time). Semester calendar. Grading system: letters or numbers.

Communications Department, 7900 West Division Street, River Forest, IL 60305 312-366-2490

CONTACT Patricia Erens
DEGREE OFFERED BA in communications with an emphasis in film
ADMISSION Requirements — upper half of class, B average, score of 18 on ACT Application deadline — rolling
FINANCIAL AID Scholarships, work/study programs, student loans
CURRICULAR EMPHASIS Film study — history, criticism and aesthetics, appreciation treated equally Filmmaking — documentary, narrative, experimental treated equally Television study — history, critcism and aesthetics, production treated equally Television production — news/documentary, experimental/personal video treated equally
SPECIAL ACTIVITIES/OFFERINGS Film series, student publications, program material produced for on-campus closed-circuit television, independent study, teacher training, vocational placement service, study abroad: London
FACILITIES AND EQUIPMENT Film — complete 8mm equipment, editing room, permanent film library of commercial or professional films on video tape Television — ½-inch VTR, ¾-inch cassette VTR, portable black and white cameras, monitors, portable color cameras, ½-inch portapak recorders, sound recording equipment, audio mixers
FACULTY Joe Bell, Patricia Erens

COURSE LIST

Undergraduate

Introduction to Film History and Theory
Contemporary American Film
Film Authorship
Film Genre
Film Comedy
National Cinema
Documentary Film
Feminism and Film
Super-8 Film Production
Radio and Television Survey

Saint Xavier College

Independent Roman Catholic comprehensive coed institution. Institutionally accredited by regional association. Urban location, 40-acre campus. Total enrollment: 1910. Undergraduate enrollment: 1726. Total faculty: 150. 4-1-4 calendar. Grading system: letters or numbers.

Program in Mass Communications, 3700 West 103rd Street, Chicago, IL 60655 312-779-3300

CONTACT Joel Sternberg, Coordinator
DEGREE OFFERED BA in mass communications with an emphasis in film and broadcasting
DEPARTMENTAL MAJORS Television — 35 students
FINANCIAL AID Scholarships, work/study programs, student loans
CURRICULAR EMPHASIS Film study — (1) history; (2) criticism and aesthetics; (3) appreciation; (4) educational media/instructional technology Filmmaking — (1) documentary; (2) experimental; (3) educational Television study — (1) management; (2) educational; (3) production; (4) criticism and aesthetics; (5) history Television production — (1) educational; (2) experimental/personal video; (3) news/documentary; (4) commercial
SPECIAL ACTIVITIES/OFFERINGS Film series, program material produced for on-campus closed-circuit television and Chicago-based medical and industrial concerns, internships in television production, independent study
FACILITIES AND EQUIPMENT Film — complete 8mm and 16mm equipment, editing room, sound mixing room Television — ½-inch VTR, ¾-inch cassette VTR, portable black and white cameras, editing equipment, monitors, portable color cameras, ½-inch portapak recorders, lighting equipment, sound recording equipment, audio mixers, audio studio
FACULTY Donald Lash, Joel Sternberg PART-TIME FACULTY Mary Ann Bergfeld, Tom Deegan, Don Pukala

COURSE LIST

Undergraduate

Visual Communications
Writing for Media
Photography
Film Theory and Criticism
Introduction to Mass Communications
Mass Communications II
History of Film
Survey of Contemporary Broadcasting
Law of Communications
Instructional Applications of TV
Media Programming
Radio Production
Radio, Television and Film
Dramatic Writing
Filmmaking I
Introduction to Television Production
Television Directing
Media Producer
Symposium in Mass Communications
Internship/Practicum

Department of Art 312-779-3300

CONTACT Brent Wall, Chairperson
PROGRAM OFFERED Minor in film-photography
FINANCIAL AID Scholarships, work/study program, student loans

CURRICULAR EMPHASIS Film study — (1) history; (2) criticism and aesthetics; (3) appreciation Filmmaking — (1) documentary; (2) experimental Television study — production Television production — (1) experimental/personal video; (2) news/documentary
SPECIAL ACTIVITIES/OFFERINGS Film series, program material produced for on-campus closed-circuit television, independent study
FACILITIES AND EQUIPMENT Film — complete 8mm and 16mm equipment, editing room, sound mixing room Television — ½-inch VTR, ¾-inch cassette VTR, portable black and white cameras, editing equipment, monitors, portable color cameras, ½-inch portapak recorders, lighting equipment, sound recording equipment, audio mixers, audio studio
PART-TIME FACULTY Mary Ann Bergfeld, Tom Deegan, Gretchen Garner, Don Pukala

COURSE LIST
Undergraduate
Visual Communication
Introduction to Film
Film Theory and Criticism
History of Film
Selected Topics in Film
Contemporary Cinema
Filmmaking
Introduction to Video Production

Sauk Valley College

State and locally supported 2-year coed college. Institutionally accredited by regional association. Rural location, 150-acre campus. Undergraduate enrollment: 3063. Total faculty: 171 (56 full-time, 115 part-time). Semester calendar.

Humanities – Communication Arts Department, RR No 1, Dixon, IL 61021 815-288-5511

CONTACT Deborah H Urhei
DEGREES OFFERED AA, AS in speech – communication arts
DEPARTMENTAL MAJORS Television — 5 students
ADMISSION Requirements — interview, teachers' recommendations, professional recommendations
FINANCIAL AID Scholarships, work/study programs, student loans
CURRICULAR EMPHASIS Film study — (1) history; (2) educational media/instructional technology; (3) appreciation Filmmaking — (1) experimental; (2) educational; (3) narrative Television study — (1) production; (2) history; (3) appreciation Television production — (1) experimental/personal video; (2) educational; (3) news/documentary
SPECIAL ACTIVITIES/OFFERINGS Film series, student publications, program material produced for on-campus closed-circuit television, independent study
FACILITIES AND EQUIPMENT Film — 8mm projectors, screening room, 35mm screening facilities, permanent film library of student films, permanent film library of commercial or professional films Television — complete black and white studio production equipment, black and white studio, audio studio, control room
FACULTY Deborah H Urhei

COURSE LIST
Undergraduate
History of Broadcasting
Introduction to Radio and TV Production
Independent Study

School of the Art Institute of Chicago

Independent professional comprehensive coed institution. Institutionally accredited by regional association, programs recognized by NASA. Urban location. Total enrollment: 1179. Undergraduate enrollment: 934. Total faculty: 110 (65 full-time, 45 part-time). 4-1-4 calendar. Grading system: pass/fall.

Filmmaking Department, Columbus Drive and Jackson Boulevard, Chicago, IL 60603 312-443-3700

CONTACT Fred Camper
DEGREES OFFERED BFA, MFA with emphasis in filmmaking
DEPARTMENTAL MAJORS Undergraduate film — 25 students Graduate film — 20 students
ADMISSION Undergraduate requirements — teachers' recommendations, written statement of purpose, portfolio Graduate requirements — teachers' recommendations, written statement of purpose, portfolio Undergraduate application deadline — rolling
FINANCIAL AID Scholarships, work/study programs, student loans, fellowships (grad only) teaching assistantships (grad only), research assistantships (grad only) Undergraduate application deadline — 3/1
CURRICULAR EMPHASIS Undergraduate film study — (1) appreciation; (2) criticism and aesthetics; (3) history Graduate film study — (1) appreciation; (2) criticism and aesthetics; (3) history Undergraduate filmmaking — (1) experimental; (2) animated; (3) documentary Graduate filmmaking — (1) experimental; (2) animated; (3) documentary
SPECIAL ACTIVITIES/OFFERINGS Film series, film societies, seminars and informal meetings of students and faculty, visiting filmmakers, independent study, teacher training
FACILITIES AND EQUIPMENT Film — 8mm and 16mm cameras, editing equipment, lighting, projectors, optical printers, animation stands, rotoscope, 16mm sound recording equipment, screening room, 35mm screening facilities, editing room, sound mixing room, animation board, permanent film library of student films, permanent film library of commercial or professional films, extensive film library of independent films
FACULTY Fred Camper, Sharon Couzin, Owen Land (née George Landow), John Luther PART-TIME FACULTY Stan Brakhage, Byron Grush, Tom Palazzolo, P Adams Sitney

School of the Art Institute of Chicago (continued)

COURSE LIST

Undergraduate

Basic Filmmaking
Documentary Filmmaking
Animation I
Drawing for Animation I
Advanced Cinema Projects

Graduate

Graduate Projects

Undergraduate and Graduate

Animation II
Drawing for Animation II
Technical Introduction to Filmmaking I, II
Film Aesthetics
Theory of Cinema
Filmmaking Group Project
Theory and Practice of Sound Cinema
Optical Printing
Film Editing
Sound for Film
Experimental Theater Workshop
Acting for Film
Introduction to Film History
History of the Avant-Garde Cinema
Modern European Cinema
The Abstract Film
Dream and Film
Personal Filmmaking: Visiting Artists

Southern Illinois University at Carbondale

State-supported coed university. Institutionally accredited by regional association, programs recognized by NASM, AACSB. Rural location. Total enrollment: 22,537. Undergraduate enrollment: 18,836. Total faculty: 3304 (1668 full-time, 1636 part-time). Semester calendar. Grading system: letters or numbers.

Department of Cinema and Photography, Carbondale, IL 62901 618-453-2365 (cinema) or 618-453-4343 (television)

CONTACT Film — C W Horrell Television — Eugene Dybvig
DEGREES OFFERED BS, MFA in film production; BS in film history/theory; MA in public visual communications with emphasis in film or television
DEPARTMENTAL MAJORS Undergraduate — 400 students Graduate — 30 students
ADMISSION Undergraduate requirements — 2.0 minimum grade point average, ACT scores Graduate requirements — 2.4 minimum grade point average; interviews; portfolio; film, videotape, or research paper; teachers' recommendations; written statement of purpose Undergraduate application deadline — rolling
FINANCIAL AID Student loans, work/study programs, teaching assistantships, fellowships Undergraduate application deadline — rolling
CURRICULAR EMPHASIS Film study — (1) production; (2) history; (3) theory and aesthetics Filmmaking — (1) documentary; (2) experimental; (3) narrative; (4) animated; (5) educational
SPECIAL ACTIVITIES/OFFERINGS Film series, film festivals, film societies, apprenticeships, internships, internships in film production, independent study, practicum, academic year abroad program offered through affiliation with the Inter-University Center for Film Studies in Paris
FACILITIES AND EQUIPMENT Film — complete 8mm and 16mm equipment, sound stage, screening room, black and white and color processing, screening facilities, editing room, sound mixing room, animation board, permanent film library
FACULTY Richard M Blumenberg, Loren D Cocking, Michael D Covell, Charles H Harpole, John Mercer, Frank R Paine

COURSE LIST

Undergraduate

Introduction to Motion Picture History/Theory
Film Production I, II
Film Analysis and Criticism

Graduate

Introduction to Public Visual Communications
Researching and Developing Public Telecommunications Programming
International Telecommunications
Seminar: Photographic Communications
Audience Communications Research
Seminar in Film History
Public Telecommunications Program Analysis and Criticism
Regulation and Control of Public Communications
Management of the Photographic Unit
Public Telecommunications Management
Contemporary Film Theory
Seminar: Current Trends in Public Telecommunications
Seminar: Public Communications in a Dynamic Society
Individual Study in Public Visual Communications
Production Seminar: Cinema, Photography, Television

Undergraduate and Graduate

Advanced Film Theory
Film Planning and Scripting
History of Animated Film
Graphic/Animated Film Production
Film Production III, IV
History of Sound Narrative Film
History of Silent Film
History of Experimental Film
Contemporary Film
Advanced Topics in Cinema
Individual Study in Cinema or Photography
Internship in Cinema or Photography

Radio-Television Department, Communications Building, Carbondale, IL 62901 618-453-4343

CONTACT Eugene Dybvig
DEGREE OFFERED BS in radio-television
DEPARTMENTAL MAJORS Undergraduate — 600 students Graduate — 25 students
ADMISSION Requirements — graduation in upper half of high school class, ACT scores Application deadline — rolling
CURRICULAR EMPHASIS Television study — (1) management; (2) production; (3) news Television production — (1) commercial; (2) news/documentary; (3) educational
SPECIAL ACTIVITIES/OFFERINGS Program material produced for on-campus closed-circuit television and local public television station, independent study, practicum, vocational placement service, television station operated by the Southern Illinois University Broadcasting Service
FACILITIES AND EQUIPMENT Film — complete 16mm equipment Television — complete black and white studio and exterior production facilities, complete color studio, audio studio, control room

FACULTY Eugene Dybvig, John Kurtz, Nien-sheng Lin, Alan Richardson, Charles W Shipley, K S Sitaram PART-TIME FACULTY Juanita Anderson, Edward Brown, William Criswell, Kenneth Garry, Robert Hartnett, Diane Havinga, Richard Hildreth, Alan Pizzato, Thomas Schwartz, Myers Walker, Charles Warner

COURSE LIST

Undergraduate

Radio-Television: Writing, Performance, Production
Radio-Television Foundation and Programs
Basic Communications Research
Broadcast Laws and Policies
Broadcast News Writing
Survey of Cable Communications
CATV Programming-Production
Production Analysis and Media Criticism
Programs and Audiences
Radio and Television Performance
Television Studio Operations
Basic Television Directing
Television Newsfilm Production
Graphics for Television
Basic Radio-Television Writing
Radio-Television Practicum
Operations and Management

Undergraduate and Graduate

Public Affairs
Public Broadcasting
Documentary Film Production
Radio-Television Production Survey
ITV Administration, Production, Utilization
Advanced Radio-Television Writing
Radio-Television Workshop
Independent Study

Master's Program in Public Visual Communication, Carbondale, IL 62901
(supported by the Departments of Cinema and Photography and Radio-Television)

CONTACT John Mercer
DEGREES OFFERED MA in history/theory, film production, television production, television studies
PROGRAM MAJORS Film — 15 students Television — 25 students
ADMISSION Requirements — 2.4 minimum grade point average, portfolio, film, videotape, research paper, creative writing, written statement of purpose
FINANCIAL AID Scholarships, teaching assistantships, fellowships
CURRICULAR EMPHASIS Film study — (1) theory and aesthetics; (2) production; (3) history Filmmaking — (1) documentary; (2) experimental; (3) narrative Television study — (1) educational; (2) management; (3) production Television production — (1) experimental/personal video; (2) educational; (3) news/documentary; (4) writing
SPECIAL ACTIVITIES/OFFERINGS Filmmaking clubs, film series, film festivals, film societies, program material produced for on-campus closed-circuit television and local public television station, internships in film and television production, independent study, practicum, teacher training, vocational placement service
FACILITIES AND EQUIPMENT Film — complete 8mm and 16mm equipment, sound stage, screening room, editing room, sound mixing room, animation board Television — complete black and white studio and exterior production equipment, complete color studio production equipment, black and white studio, color studio, audio studio, control room
FACULTY Lorin Cocking, Mike Covel, Eugene Dybvig, David Gilmore, Bill Horrell, John Kurtz, John Mercer, Frank Paine, Bill Shipley, Charles Swedlund, John Yoder PART-TIME FACULTY Richard Blumenberg, Richard Hildreth

COURSE LIST

Graduate

Advanced Film Theory
Film Planning and Scripting
History and Techniques of Animated Film
Graphic/Animated Film Production
Film Production III, IV
History of the Silent Narrative Film
History of the Sound Narrative Film
History of the Documentary Film
History of the Experimental Film
History of the Sound Narrative Film: Contemporary
Individual Study in Cinema or Photography
Internship in Cinema or Photography
Projects in Cinema or Photography
Public Affairs and the Radio-Television Establishment
Public Broadcasting
Radio-Television Production Survey
Documentary Film Production
ITV Administration, Production, Utilization
Advanced Radio-Television Writing
Radio-Television Workshop
Introduction to Public Visual Communications
Researching and Developing Public Telecommunications Programming
International Telecommunications
Seminar in Photographic Communications
Audience Communications Research
Seminar in Film History
Public Telecommunications Program Analysis and Criticism
Regulation and Control of Public Communications
Public Telecommunications Management
Contemporary Film Theory
Seminar in Current Trends in Public Telecommunications
Seminar in Public Communications in a Dynamic Society
Individual Study in Public Communications
Production Seminar in Cinema, Photography, and Television

Curriculum, Instruction, and Media Department, Pulliam 323, Carbondale, IL 62901 618-453-5764

CONTACT Film — Dan Sutter Television — Marc Rosenburg
ADMISSION Requirements — 2.4 minimum grade point average, GRE and MAT scores, professional recommendations, teachers' recommendations, written statement of purpose
FINANCIAL AID Teaching assistantships, research assistantships, fellowships, work/study programs
CURRICULAR EMPHASIS Film study — educational media/instructional technology Filmmaking — educational Television study — (1) educational; (2) management Television production — (1) educational; (2) commercial
SPECIAL ACTIVITIES/OFFERINGS Program material produced for classroom use, practicum, teacher training
FACILITIES AND EQUIPMENT Television — black and white studio cameras, ½-inch VTR, 1-inch VTR, ¾-inch cassette VTR, portable black and white cameras, monitors, special effects generators, ½-inch portapak recorder, audio mixers
FACULTY Pierre Barrette, Doris Dale, Marc Rosenburg, Dan Sutter

COURSE LIST

Graduate

Classroom Use of Television
Seminar in Educational Television
Seminar in Educational Media

Trinity Christian College

Independent Christian Reformed 4-year coed college. Institutionally accredited by regional association. Suburban location. Undergraduate enrollment: 390. Total faculty: 47 (30 full-time, 17 part-time). 4-1-4 calendar. Grading system: letters or numbers.

6601 College Drive, Palos Heights, IL 60463 312-597-3000

CONTACT Dan Diephouse
ADMISSION Application deadline — 8/15, rolling
CURRICULAR EMPHASIS Film study — introductory
FACILITIES AND EQUIPMENT Film — 8mm cameras, 8mm and 16mm projectors
FACULTY Dan Diephouse

COURSE LIST
Undergraduate
Aesthetics of Cinema

University of Chicago

Independent coed university. Founded 1890. Institutionally accredited by regional association. Urban location, 165-acre campus. Total enrollment: 7781. Undergraduate enrollment: 2670. Total faculty: 1040 (1040 full-time, 0 part-time). Quarter calendar. Grading system: letters or numbers.

Department of English and General Studies in the Humanities, 5811 South Ellis Avenue, Chicago, IL 60637 312-753-2913

CONTACT Gerald Mast
DEGREES OFFERED BA, MA, Ph.D. in English, general studies, humanities, history, philosophy with an emphasis in film
DEPARTMENTAL MAJORS Undergraduate film — 10 students Graduate film — 6 students
ADMISSION Graduate requirements — GRE scores, teachers' recommendations Undergraduate application deadline — 1/15
FINANCIAL AID Scholarships, work/study programs, student loans, fellowships, teaching assistantships, research assistantships (grad only) Undergraduate application deadline — 1/15
CURRICULAR EMPHASIS Undergraduate film study — (1) criticism and aesthetics; (2) appreciation; (3) history Graduate film study — (1) criticism and aesthetics; (2) history
SPECIAL ACTIVITIES/OFFERINGS Film series, film societies
FACILITIES AND EQUIPMENT Film — 16mm cameras, editing equipment, projectors, screening room, editing room, permanent film library of commercial or professional films
FACULTY John G Cawelti, Tom Mapp, Gerald Mast, Joel Snyder

COURSE LIST
Graduate
Seminar: Howard Hawks
Seminar: D W Griffith
Seminar: Charles Chaplin

Undergraduate and Graduate
Introduction to Cinema I, II
Silent Film Comedy
The Western
The American Musical
Film Theory
Film and Theater
Film and Narrative
The Detective Story: Film and Fiction
History of Photography
Experimental Film
Theories of Film and Photography

University of Illinois, Chicago Circle

State-supported coed university. Part of University of Illinois System. Institutionally accredited by regional association. Urban location. Total enrollment: 20,663. Undergraduate enrollment: 17,998. Total faculty: 1171. Quarter calendar. Grading system: letters or numbers.

Department of Communications and Theatre, Box 4840, Chicago, IL 60680 414-962-6119

CONTACT Anthony Graham-White
DEGREES OFFERED BA, MA in mass communications
DEPARTMENTAL MAJORS Undergraduate television — 50 students Graduate television — 20 students
ADMISSION Graduate requirements — 4.0 minimum grade point average on 5-point scale, teachers' recommendations, written state of purpose
FINANCIAL AID Work/study programs, student loans, teaching assistantships, tuition waivers Undergraduate application deadline — rolling
CURRICULAR EMPHASIS Undergraduate television study — history, criticism and aesthetics, production treated equally Graduate television study — history, behavioral research on various aspects of mass media treated equally Undergraduate television production — news/documentary, experimental/personal video treated equally
SPECIAL ACTIVITIES/OFFERINGS Internships in television production, independent study
FACILITIES AND EQUIPMENT Television — complete color studio production equipment, complete color exterior production equipment, color studio, audio studio, control room, editing facility
FACULTY Marsha F Cassidy, Fred Fejes, Jin Keon Kim

COURSE LIST
Undergraduate
Mass Media and Society
Visual Aesthetics in Theatre and Television
Survey of Contemporary Broadcasting
Mass Media and the Popular Arts
Audio Production
Television Directing

Graduate
Issues in the Mass Media
Special Topics in Media Criticism
International Mass Communication
Television and Society

Undergraduate and Graduate
TV Programming
Radio Programming
Special Topics in Mass Communications
Global Mass Communications
Continuity Writing
Media and the Law
Instructional Applications of Television and Radio
Media Internship

English Department, Box 4348, Chicago, IL 60680 312-996-3260

CONTACT Virginia Wexman
FINANCIAL AID Student loans, work/study programs, teaching assistantships
CURRICULAR EMPHASIS Film study — (1) appreciation; (2) criticism and aesthetics; (3) educational media/instructional technology Television study — (1) appreciation; (2) criticism and aesthetics Television production — (1) news/documentary; (2) experimental/personal video; (3) commercial
SPECIAL ACTIVITIES/OFFERINGS Film series, student publications, independent study, practicum, teacher training
FACILITIES AND EQUIPMENT Film — screening room Television — editing equipment, ½-inch portapak recorder, video cassette playback
FACULTY Virginia Wexman, Linda Williams

COURSE LIST
Undergraduate
Introduction to Film and Literary Narrative
Topics in Film Literature

Illinois

University of Illinois, Urbana-Champaign

State-supported coed university. Part of University of Illinois System. Institutionally accredited by regional association, programs recognized by NASM, AACSB, NASA. Small town location. Total enrollment: 33,684. Undergraduate enrollment: 25,413. Total faculty: 2762 (2504 full-time, 258 part-time). Semester calendar. Grading system: letters or numbers.

Unit for Cinema Studies, 2111 Foreign Languages Building, Urbana, IL 61801 217-333-3356

CONTACT Edwin Jahiel, Director
DEGREES OFFERED BA in cinema studies; BA in teacher education with minor in cinema studies; MA, PhD in expanded French studies, English, comparative literature with concentration in cinema studies
PROGRAM MAJORS Undergraduate film — 20 students Graduate film — 6 students
ADMISSION Undergraduate requirements — 3.0 minimum grade point average, ACT or SAT scores Graduate requirements — 4.0 minimum grade point average, GRE scores Undergraduate application deadline — 11/15
FINANCIAL AID Scholarships, work/study programs, student loans, teaching assistantships, research assistantships Undergraduate application deadline — 1/1
CURRICULAR EMPHASIS Undergraduate film study — (1) history; (2) national cinemas; (3) criticism and aesthetics Graduate film study — (1) history; (2) national cinemas; (3) criticism and aesthetics
SPECIAL ACTIVITIES/OFFERINGS Film series, film festivals, film societies, student publications, personal appearances by filmmakers, critics, and scholars
FACILITIES AND EQUIPMENT Film — screening room, 35mm screening facilities, permanent film library of student films, permanent film library of commercial or professional films, large library holding of film scripts Television — permanent library of videotapes with individual access
FACULTY Robert L Carringer, Steven P Hill, Edwin Jahiel, Henry L Mueller, Klaus Phillips, Barry Sabath, John Stubbs PART-TIME FACULTY Bernard Benstock, John P Frayne, Rocco Fumento, Richard J Leskosky, Daniel Majdiak, William Schroeder, Rochelle Wright

COURSE LIST
Undergraduate
Introduction to Film
Film as Literature
Art of the Screen: Humor
History of European Cinema as Visual Art
History of American Films as Visual Art
French and Comparative Cinema I, II
Survey of World Cinema I, II
Studies in Cinema: Sound and Image
Film in Depression America
Horror Classics: Fiction and Film
Philosophy and Film
Novels into Film

Graduate
Proseminar in the Teaching of Film
Seminar in French and Comparative Cinema
The Hollywood Studio System

Undergraduate and Graduate
Hollywood Comedy from Chaplin to Kubrick
Hollywood in the Thirties and Forties
Three Writer-Directors: Fellini, Hitchcock, Kubrick
Art of the Screen: Narration
Studies in the History of Film as a Visual Art
Film Theory and Criticism
Russian and East European Cinema
The Films of Ingmar Bergman
The German Cinema

Cinematography Program, Department of Art and Design, 129 Fine Arts Building, Champaign, IL 61820 217-333-0855

CONTACT Julius Rascheff, Chairman
DEGREES OFFERED BA in film through independent plans of study (cinematography), MFA in cinematography

University of Illinois, Urbana-Champaign (continued)

PROGRAM MAJORS Undergraduate film — 6 students Graduate film — 2 students
ADMISSION Undergraduate requirements — 4.0 minimum grade point average, interview, written statement of purpose Graduate requirements — 4.0 minimum grade point average, interview, teachers' recommendations, written statement of purpose, professional work experience, portfolio, professional recommendations Undergraduate application deadline — 11/15
FINANCIAL AID Scholarships, work/study programs, student loans, fellowships, teaching assistantships, research assistantships Undergraduate application deadline — 11/15
CURRICULAR EMPHASIS Undergraduate filmmaking — (1) documentary; (2) experimental; (3) animated Graduate filmmaking — (1) narrative; (2) documentary; (3) animated Undergraduate television production — experimental/personal video Graduate television production — experimental/personal video
SPECIAL ACTIVITIES/OFFERINGS Filmmaking clubs, film series, film festivals, film societies, student publications, internships in film production, independent study, teacher training
FACILITIES AND EQUIPMENT Film — 8mm and 16mm cameras, editing equipment, sound recording equipment, lighting, projectors, mixing, optical printing, workprinting, sound stage, screening room, 35mm screening facilities, editing room, sound mixing room, animation board, permanent film library of student films, permanent film library of commercial or professional films, microfiche cinematographic analysis
FACULTY Michael Cook, Norman Gambill, Julius Rascheff

COURSE LIST

Undergraduate and Graduate

History of European Cinema as Visual Art
Studies in the History of Cinema as Visual Art — Contemporary Hollywood Set Design, 1940 to Present
Cinematography I – III
Screenwriting
Lighting — Studio and Location
Camera Placement
Camera Movements
Documentary Cinematography
Creative Editing
Technical Editing
Feature Films Cinematography
Educational Films Cinematography
Cinematography for TV Commercials
Sound Recording
Mixing
Music Composition in Film
Propaganda Films Cinematography
Color in Film
Cinematic Styles: Image
Cinematic Styles: Genres
Cinematographic Analysis
Pixillation, Claymation
Printing, Grading, and Color Correction
Hi-Fi Cinematography
Introduction to Holography
Sensitometry and Processing for Cinema
Optical Printing
Slit-Scan Cinematography
Film Budgeting
Continuity
Make-up: Color and Black and White
Distribution
Drawing and Painting on Film
Flowpix Process
Sublipix Process
Experimental Film Cinematography
Titling for Film
Censorship in Film
Film Graphics
Production Management and Planning
Laboratory Practices

Illinois

Wabash Valley College

State and locally supported 2-year coed college. Institutionally accredited by regional association. Rural location. Total enrollment: 3000. Total faculty (approx.): 80 full-time and 50 part-time. Quarter calendar. Grading system: Pass/fail and letters.

Radio-TV Broadcasting Department, 2200 College Drive, Mt. Carmel, IL 62863 618-262-8641

CONTACT Frank E Parcells
DEGREES OFFERED AAS in radio-TV Broadcasting with a major in radio or TV, AA, AS in mass communications, AA, AS in speech communication
DEPARTMENTAL MAJORS Television — 15 students
ADMISSION Requirements — ACT or SAT scores, interview
FINANCIAL AID Scholarships, work/study programs, student loans
CURRICULAR EMPHASIS Film study — history, criticism and aesthetics, appreciation treated equally Filmmaking — documentary, narrative, experimental treated equally Television study — history, appreciation, educational, production, management treated equally Television production — commercial, practicum required at commercial station for graduation
SPECIAL ACTIVITIES/OFFERINGS Student publications, program material produced for on-campus closed-circuit television and cable television, apprenticeships, internships in television production, independent study, vocational placement service
FACILITIES AND EQUIPMENT Film — 8mm and 16mm cameras, editing equipment, projectors, 16mm sound recording equipment Television — color studio cameras, ½-inch VTR, editing equipment, monitors, special effects generators, portable color cameras, ½-inch portapak recorders, lighting equipment, sound recording equipment, audio mixers, film chain, color studio, mobile van/unit, audio studio, control room
FACULTY Frank Parcells, Don Swift, Len Wells

COURSE LIST

Undergraduate

Television Production
Advanced TV Production
Cinema History and Appreciation
Film Practice and Production
Special Problems in Broadcasting
Practicum in Broadcasting
Broadcast Speech
Broadcast Advertising and Copywriting

Western Illinois University

State-supported comprehensive coed institution. Institutionally accredited by regional association, programs recognized by AACSB. Small town location, 1056-acre campus. Total enrollment: 11,293. Undergraduate enrollment: 10,328. Total faculty: 741 (683 full-time, 58 part-time). Semester calendar. Grading system: letters or numbers.

English Department, Macomb, IL 61455 309-298-1103 or 309-298-1422

CONTACT Janice R Welsch

PROGRAMS OFFERED Minor in film (liberal arts), minor in film (teacher education)
ADMISSION Undergraduate requirement — ACT or SAT scores
FINANCIAL AID Work/study programs, student loans
CURRICULAR EMPHASIS Undergraduate film study — (1) criticism and aesthetics; (2) history; (3) appreciation
SPECIAL ACTIVITIES/OFFERINGS Film series, film societies, program material produced for on-campus closed-circuit television and cable television, internships in television production, independent study, teacher training, vocational placement service
FACULTY George Kurman, John R Orlandello, Janice R Welsch

COURSE LIST

Undergraduate
Introduction to Film
Film History I (beginning to 1945)
Film History II (1945 to present)
Film and Literature
Film Criticism
Basic Motion Picture Photography
Motion Picture Production
Film and Television Documentary
Film and the Public Interest
Politics and the Cinema

Graduate
Film Style Analysis

Learning Resources Department 309-298-1952

CONTACT Don L Crawford
ADMISSION Undergraduate requirement — ACT or SAT scores Undergraduate application deadline — 8/1, rolling
FINANCIAL AID Work/study programs, student loans
CURRICULAR EMPHASIS Undergraduate filmmaking — (1) educational; (2) documentary; (3) narrative Undergraduate television production — (1) educational; (2) commercial; (3) news/documentary
SPECIAL ACTIVITIES/OFFERINGS Program material produced for on-campus closed-circuit television and cable television, independent study, teacher training, vocational placement service
FACILITIES AND EQUIPMENT Film — complete 8mm equipment, 16mm cameras, editing equipment, lighting, black and white film stock, color film stock, projectors, sound stage Television — black and white studio cameras, color studio cameras, ½-inch VTR, 2-inch VTR, ¾-inch cassette VTR, editing equipment, monitors, special effects generators, slide chain, lighting equipment, audio mixers, film chain, color studio, control room.
FACULTY Don L Crawford, Norman L L'hommedieu, James W Prange

COURSE LIST

Undergraduate
Instructional Television Production
Basic Motion Picture Production
Visual Production
Motion Picture Production II
Independent Study Seminar

Wheaton College

Independent Protestant comprehensive coed institution. Institutionally accredited by regional association, programs recognized by NASM. Suburban location, 70-acre campus. Total enrollment: 2385. Undergraduate enrollment: 1970. Total faculty: 184. Quarter calendar. Grading system: letters or numbers.

Speech Communication Department, Wheaton, IL 60187 312-682-5093

CONTACT E A Hollatz
PROGRAM OFFERED Major in speech communication with emphasis in film or television
ADMISSION Application deadline — 1/1
CURRICULAR EMPHASIS Film study — (1) appreciation; (2) production; (3) criticism and aesthetics Filmmaking — (1) documentary; (2) experimental; (3) educational Television study — (1) production; (2) appreciation; (3) criticism and aesthetics Television production — (1) news/documentary; (2) educational; (3) experimental/personal video
SPECIAL ACTIVITIES/OFFERINGS Film series, film societies, apprenticeships, internships in film and television production, independent study, teacher training
FACILITIES AND EQUIPMENT Film — complete 8mm equipment, sound mixing room, permanent film library Television — complete black and white studio and exterior production equipment, black and white studio
FACULTY Douglas Gilbert, Edwin A Hollatz, Stuart Johnson

COURSE LIST

Undergraduate
Introduction to Radio-Television and Film
Radio-Television and Film Writing
Radio-Television Announcing
Television Production
Advanced Television Production
Film Theory and Technique

INDIANA

Ball State University

State-supported coed university. Institutionally accredited by regional association, programs recognized by NASM, AACSB. Suburban location. Total enrollment: 17,012. Undergraduate enrollment: 14,725. Total faculty: 982 (882 full-time, 100 part-time). Quarter calendar. Grading system: letters or numbers.

Department of Telecommunication, 2000 University Avenue, Muncie, IN 47306 317-285-4485

CONTACT Film — Wes D Gehring Television — John Kurtz
DEGREES OFFERED BS, MA in telecommunication, with majors in radio and television, as well as a minor in film
DEPARTMENTAL MAJORS Undergraduate television — 650 students Graduate television — 12 students

Ball State University (continued)

ADMISSION Undergraduate requirement — ACT or SAT scores Graduate requirement — B average
FINANCIAL AID Scholarships, work/study programs, student loans, teaching assistantships
CURRICULAR EMPHASIS Undergraduate film study — history, criticism and aesthetics, appreciation treated equally Graduate film study — history, criticism and aesthetics, appreciation treated equally Undergraduate filmmaking — documentary, narrative, experimental treated equally Graduate filmmaking — documentary, narrative, experimental treated equally Undergraduate television study — history, criticism and aesthetics, educational, production, management treated equally Graduate television study — history, criticism and aesthetics, educational, production, management treated equally Undergraduate television production — commercial, news/documentary, experimental/personal video, educational treated equally Graduate television production — commercial, news/documentary, experimental/personal video, educational treated equally
SPECIAL ACTIVITIES/OFFERINGS Filmmaking clubs; film societies; film discussion group for students; program material produced for on-campus closed-circuit television, local public television station, state educational television network; internships in film production; internships in television production; independent study; vocational placement service
FACILITIES AND EQUIPMENT Film — 8mm and 16mm cameras, editing equipment, lighting, projectors, screening room, permanent film library of commercial or professional films Television — complete color studio and exterior production equipment, ¾-inch cassette VTR, color studio, audio studio, control room

COURSE LIST

Undergraduate

Trends — Genre Study in Film
World Film History Until World War II
World Film History Since World War II
Introduction to Film
Censorship in Film
Film Production I, II

Undergraduate and Graduate

Seminar in Film History
Seminar in Film Theory
Film Practicum

Butler University

Independent comprehensive coed institution. Institutionally accredited by regional association. Suburban location, 300-acre campus. Total enrollment: 3852. Undergraduate enrollment: 2449. Total faculty: 249 (151 full-time, 98 part-time). Semester calendar. Grading system: letters or numbers.

Radio-Television Department, 46th and Sunset, Indianapolis, IN 46208 317-283-9241

CONTACT James R. Phillippe, Chairman
DEGREES OFFERED BS, MS in radio-television
DEPARTMENTAL MAJORS 110 students
ADMISSION Requirement — interviews Undergraduate application deadline — 8/19
CURRICULAR EMPHASIS Television study — (1) production; (2) criticism and aesthetics Television production — commercial, news/documentary, experimental/personal video, educational treated equally
SPECIAL ACTIVITIES/OFFERINGS Internships in television production, independent study, teacher training, vocational placement service
FACILITIES AND EQUIPMENT Television — access to off-campus studio facilities
FACULTY Hal Barron, Ann Harper, James R. Phillippe PART-TIME FACULTY Howard Cauldwell, John Krom, Jim Mathis

COURSE LIST

Undergraduate and Graduate

Broadcasting in America
Principles and Techniques of Cinematography
Television Production and Operation I, II
Music in Broadcasting
Use of Radio-Television in the Classroom
Station Orientation
Sportscasting
Technical Foundations of Broadcasting
Television Production and Operation
Writing for Broadcasting
Station Management
Radio and Television Newscasting
Broadcast Law

Department of Speech 317-283-9314

CONTACT Nicholas M Cripe
FACULTY Nicholas M Cripe

COURSE LIST

Undergraduate

The American Motion Picture: 1905-1929
The American Motion Picture: 1930-Present
Appreciation and Criticism of Film

Calumet College

Independent Roman Catholic 4-year coed college. Institutionally accredited by regional association. Urban location. Undergraduate enrollment: 1500. Total faculty: 75 (38 full-time, 37 part-time). Semester calendar. Grading system: letters or numbers.

Communication Arts Department, 2400 New York Avenue, Whiting, IN 46394 219-473-4386

CONTACT Film — Brother Edward Lampa Television — Reverend Joseph Rodak
DEGREE OFFERED BA in communication arts with sequences in journalism and radio/television/film
DEPARTMENTAL MAJORS Television — 15 students
ADMISSION Requirements — C minimum average, ACT or SAT scores, interview, teachers' recommendations
FINANCIAL AID Scholarships, work/study programs, student loans
CURRICULAR EMPHASIS Film study — history, criticism and aesthetics, educational media/instructional technology treated equally Filmmaking — documentary, narrative, educational treated equally Television study — criticism and aesthetics, production, management treated equally Television production — commercial, news/documentary, educational treated equally

SPECIAL ACTIVITIES/OFFERINGS Student publications, program material produced for local public television station and industry, apprenticeships, internships in television production, independent study
FACILITIES AND EQUIPMENT Film — complete 8mm and 16mm equipment Television — complete black and white studio and exterior production equipment, complete color studio and exterior production equipment
FACULTY Robert W Andersen, Robert D Donnelly, Brother Edward Lampa, Roger Myers, Reverend Joseph Rodak PART-TIME FACULTY Joe Dejanovic, Jim Holly

COURSE LIST

Undergraduate

Introduction to Mass Communications
Appreciation of Theater Arts: Stage, Screen, and Television
Writing for Radio and Television
Cinematography I, II
TV Production I, II
Photojournalism
Radio Production I, II
Critical Analysis of Photography
TV Broadcasting Practicum
Cinematography Practicum
Broadcast Legislation
Ethics and Laws of Mass Communications
Survey of Broadcasting
Black and White Photography
Color Photography
Honors Seminar

DePauw University

Independent United Methodist comprehensive coed institution. AICS accredited, programs recognized by NASM. Small town location, 116-acre campus. Total enrollment: 2373. Undergraduate enrollment: 2251. Total faculty: 185 (138 full-time, 47 part-time). 4-1-4 calendar. Grading system: letters or numbers.

Communication Arts and Sciences Department, Greencastle, IN 46135 317-653-9721

CONTACT Larry Sutton
DEGREE OFFERED BA in communication arts and sciences with coursework in television
DEPARTMENTAL MAJORS 100 students
ADMISSION Application deadline — rolling
CURRICULAR EMPHASIS Television study — production Television production — commercial, news/documentary, experimental/personal video, educational treated equally
SPECIAL ACTIVITIES/OFFERINGS Teacher training
FACILITIES AND EQUIPMENT Television — access to local commercial television studio facilities
FACULTY James Elrod

COURSE LIST

Undergraduate

Broadcast Journalism
TV Programming and Production

Hanover College

Independent United Presbyterian 4-year coed college. Institutionally accredited by regional association. Rural location, 550-acre campus. Undergraduate enrollment: 1000. Total faculty: 73 (70 full-time, 3 part-time). 4-1-4 calendar. Grading system: letters or numbers.

Theatre and Communication Department, Hanover, IN 47243 814-866-2151

CONTACT Film — Tom Evans Television — Jon Shorr
DEGREE OFFERED BA in communication with an emphasis in mass media
DEPARTMENTAL MAJORS Television — 10 students
FINANCIAL AID Scholarships, work/study programs, student loans
CURRICULAR EMPHASIS Film study — (1) appreciation; (2) criticism and aesthetics Filmmaking — narrative Television study — (1) criticism and aesthetics; (2) appreciation; (3) production Television production — (1) experimental/personal video; (2) commercial, news/documentary, educational
SPECIAL ACTIVITIES/OFFERINGS Film series, program material produced for cable television, independent study, teacher training
FACILITIES AND EQUIPMENT Film — 8mm cameras, editing equipment, sound recording equipment, projectors Television — color studio cameras, ¾-inch cassette VTR, monitors, special effects generators, portable color cameras, ¾-inch ENG, lighting equipment, sound recording equipment, audio mixers, color studio, audio studio, control room, capability to move cameras and mixer for remote productions
FACULTY Tom Evans, Jon Shorr

COURSE LIST

Undergraduate

Filmmaking
TV/Radio Production
Broadcast Writing
Film as Literature
News and Documentary
Societal Effects of TV/Film
Independent study in TV/Film

Huntington College

Independent comprehensive coed institution affiliated with Church of the United Brethren in Christ. Institutionally accredited by regional association. Small town location, 50-acre campus. Total enrollment: 581. Undergraduate enrollment: 544. Total faculty: 60 (33 full-time, 27 part-time). 4-1-4 calendar. Grading system: letters or numbers.

Speech Department, 2303 College Avenue, Huntington, IN 46750 219-356-6000

CONTACT Carl D Zurcher, Chairman
DEGREES OFFERED BA in speech, BA in communications (print journalism and broadcasting), BS in education with major in speech communication and theater (secondary school certification)

Huntington College (continued)

ADMISSION Requirements — 2.0 minimum grade point average, ACT or SAT scores, teachers' recommendations, written statement of purpose
FINANCIAL AID Scholarships, work/study programs, student loans
CURRICULAR EMPHASIS Television study — history, production treated equally Television production — commercial, news/documentary treated equally
SPECIAL ACTIVITIES/OFFERINGS Program material produced for on-campus closed-circuit television and cable television, internships in television production, independent study
FACILITIES AND EQUIPMENT Television — black and white studio cameras, 1-inch VTR, ¾-inch cassette VTR, portable black and white cameras, monitors, special effects generators, portable color cameras, ½-inch portapak recorders, lighting equipment, sound recording equipment, audio mixers, black and white studio, control room
PART-TIME FACULTY Grant Hoatson

COURSE LIST
Undergraduate
Principles of Broadcasting
Radio and Television Production
Advanced Television Production
Writing and Editing for Radio and Television

Indiana Central University

Independent United Methodist comprehensive coed institution. Accredited by regional association and AICS, programs recognized by NASM. Suburban location, 60-acre campus. Total enrollment: 1520. Undergraduate enrollment: 1322. Total faculty: 190 (80 full-time, 110 part-time). 4-1-4 calendar. Grading system: letters or numbers.

Speech and Theatre Department, 1400 East Hanna Avenue, Indianapolis, IN 46227 317-788-3226

CONTACT Don Cushman
DEGREE OFFERED BA in speech and theatre
FINANCIAL AID Scholarships, work/study programs, student loans Application deadline — 8/15
CURRICULAR EMPHASIS Television study — (1) history; (2) production; (3) appreciation Television production — (1) experimental/personal video; (2) news/documentary; (3) educational
SPECIAL ACTIVITIES/OFFERINGS Student publications, program material produced for on-campus closed-circuit television, independent study
FACILITIES AND EQUIPMENT Film — 8mm editing equipment, sound recording equipment, lighting, projectors,16mm cameras, editing equipment, projectors, sound mixing room Television — color studio cameras, ¾-inch cassette VTR, portable black and white cameras, editing equipment, monitors, special effects generators, portable color cameras, ½-inch portapak recorders, ¾-inch ENG, lighting equipment, sound recording equipment, audio mixers, time base corrector, color studio, audio studio, control room
FACULTY James W Ream

COURSE LIST
Undergraduate
Introduction to Radio and Television

Indiana State University at Evansville

State-supported 4-year coed college. Part of Indiana State University System. Institutionally accredited by regional association. Suburban location, 300-acre campus. Undergraduate enrollment: 2863. Total faculty: 161 (102 full-time, 59 part-time). Semester calendar. Grading system: letters or numbers.

Communications Department, 8600 University Boulevard, Evansville, IN 47712 812-464-8600

CONTACT Chairman
ADMISSION Application deadline — 8/15, rolling

Indiana State University, Terre Haute

State-supported coed university. Institutionally accredited by regional association, programs recognized by NASM. Urban location, 91-acre campus. Total enrollment: 11,474. Undergraduate enrollment: 9738. Total faculty: 728 (661 full-time, 67 part-time). Semester calendar. Grading system: letters or numbers.

Speech Department, Terre Haute, IN 47802 812-232-6311

CONTACT Film — S Russell Television — J Duncan
PROGRAM OFFERED Major in speech with emphasis in film or television
ADMISSION Undergraduate requirements — 2.0 minimum grade point average, professional recommendations, teachers' recommendations Graduate requirements — 3.0 minimum grade point average, GRE scores, professional recommendations, teachers' recommendations Undergraduate application deadline — 8/15, rolling
FINANCIAL AID Work/study programs, teaching assistantships Undergraduate application deadline — 3/1
CURRICULAR EMPHASIS Undergraduate film study — (1) production; (2) appreciation; (3) history Graduate film study — (1) educational media/instructional technology; (2) production Filmmaking — (1) experimental; (2) narrative; (3) management Television study — (1) history; (2) production; (3) management Television production — (1) news/documentary; (2) commercial; (3) experimental/personal video
SPECIAL ACTIVITIES/OFFERINGS Film festivals; film societies; program material produced for on-campus closed-circuit television, cable television, local public television station, local commercial television station; independent study; practicum

FACILITIES AND EQUIPMENT Film — complete 8mm and 16mm equipment, screening room, editing room Television — complete black and white studio and exterior production equipment, complete color studio and exterior production equipment, black and white studio, color studio, audio studio, control room
FACULTY G Adkins, J Boyle

Indiana University at South Bend

State-supported comprehensive coed institution. Institutionally accredited by regional association. Urban location. Total enrollment: 5846. Undergraduate enrollment: 4370. Total faculty: 388. Semester calendar. Grading system: letters or numbers.

History Department, Northside and Greenlawn, South Bend, IN 46615 219-237-4231

CONTACT Dean R Garrett
PROGRAM OFFERED Minor in film
ADMISSION Undergraduate application deadline — 7/15, rolling
FINANCIAL AID Scholarships, student loans, work/study programs, fellowships Undergraduate application deadline — 2/15, rolling
CURRICULAR EMPHASIS Film study — (1) history; (2) appreciation; (3) criticism and aesthetics Filmmaking — (1) narrative; (2) documentary; (3) animated; (4) experimental Television study — history
SPECIAL ACTIVITIES/OFFERINGS Film series, film societies, student publications, independent study, vocational placement service
FACILITIES AND EQUIPMENT Film — 8mm and 16mm cameras, editing equipment, projectors, sound stage, screening room, permanent film library Television — black and white studio camera, color studio camera, ½-inch VTR, portable black and white cameras, editing equipment, lighting equipment, sound recording equipment
FACULTY Paul Scherer

COURSE LIST

Undergraduate
History of the Motion Picture

Undergraduate and Graduate
The History of European and American Films, I, II

Indiana University, Bloomington

State-supported coed university. Part of Indiana University System. Institutionally accredited by regional association, programs recognized by NASM, AACSB, AOA. Small town location. Total enrollment: 31,840. Undergraduate enrollment: 21,611. Total faculty: 1453. Semester calendar. Grading system: letters or numbers.

Film Studies, Comparative Literature Program, Indiana University, Bloomington, IN 47401 812-337-1072

CONTACT H M Geduld, Program Director
PROGRAM OFFERED Film is studied as a component of the Comparative Literature Program; graduate theses/dissertations can have film orientation
ADMISSION Undergraduate requirements — minimum grade point average, teachers' recommendations, Introduction to Film course Graduate requirements — minimum grade point average, written statement of purpose
FINANCIAL AID Scholarships, work/study programs, student loans, fellowships, teaching assistantships, research assistantships
CURRICULAR EMPHASIS Undergraduate film study — history, criticism and aesthetics, appreciation treated equally Graduate film study — history, criticism and aesthetics, appreciation treated equally
SPECIAL ACTIVITIES/OFFERINGS Film series, film festivals, conventions and guest lecturers, independent study
FACILITIES AND EQUIPMENT Television — ½-inch VTR, editing equipment, monitors
FACULTY Peter Bondanella, Harry M. Geduld, Claudia Gorbman, Robert Heinich, Phyllis Klotman, William Kroll, Howard Levie, James Naremore PART-TIME FACULTY Carolyn Geduld, Yoshio Iwamoto, Sumie Jones, Dodona Kiziria-Smith, Jerome Mintz, Murray Sperber

COURSE LIST

Undergraduate
An Introduction to Film
Contemporary Black Film
Images of Blacks in Films 1903–1960
American Film Culture
German Film Culture
Individual Studies in Film and Literature

Graduate
Readings in the Italian Cinema
Projects in Radio-TV/Film
Studies in Film and Literature
Readings in Film and Literature
Educational Motion Picture Production
Filmic Expression
Special Topic: Film and Narrative
Film Production for Television
Special Projects

Undergraduate and Graduate
Anthropological and Documentary Film
Asian Film and Literature
The Film and Society
History of European and American Film
British and American Film Studies
Studies in the Italian Film
The Soviet Film
The Film: Theory and Aesthetics
Genre Study in Film
Authorship in the Cinema
Comedy in Film and Literature
Film Criticism: Theory/Practice
Film Production

Telecommunications Department, Radio and Television Center, Bloomington, IN 47405 812-337-6895

CONTACT Dolf Zillmann, Acting Chairperson
DEGREES OFFERED BA, MA, MS in telecommunications; PhD in mass communications
DEPARTMENTAL MAJORS Undergraduate — 448 students Graduate — 30 students

Indiana University, Bloomington (continued)

ADMISSION Undergraduate requirements — 2.0 minimum grade point average, SAT scores, grade of C or better in Foundations and Law Graduate requirements — 3.0 minimum grade point average, GRE scores, professional recommendations, teachers' recommendations, written statement of purpose Undergraduate application deadline — 7/1, rolling
FINANCIAL AID Student loans, work/study programs, teaching assistantships, research assistantships, fellowships Undergraduate application deadline — 2/15, rolling
CURRICULAR EMPHASIS Undergraduate television study — (1) management; (2) audience and behavioral effects; (3) law and public policy; (4) broadcast journalism Graduate television study — (1) management; (2) economics; (3) law; (4) effects Television production — (1) commercial; (2) news/documentary; (3) experimental/personal video
SPECIAL ACTIVITIES/OFFERINGS Film series, film societies, student publications, program material produced for local public television station, internships in television production, independent study, career symposia
FACILITIES AND EQUIPMENT Television — complete color studio and exterior production equipment, color studio, audio studio, control room
FACULTY Donald Agostino, Leroy Bannerman, Fredric Brewer, Richard Burke, Walter Gantz, Rolland Johnson, William Kroll, James Perry, Herbert Seltz, Herbert Terry, Jacob Wakshlag, Brien Williams, Richard Yoakam, Jayne Zehaty, Dolf Zillmann

COURSE LIST
Undergraduate
Introduction to Mass Communications
Foundations of Broadcasting
Broadcast Performance
The Broadcast Program
Processes and Effects of Mass Communications
Audio Production
Film Production
Television Production
Radio and Television Advertising
Broadcast Writing
Television Writing
Program and Audience Analysis
Telecommunication Field Experience
Topical Seminar in Telecommunications
Projects in Radio-Television-Film
Foreign Study in Telecommunications
Independent Study for Honors
Principles of Broadcast News
Broadcast News Editing
Television News
Broadcast Media Analysis

Graduate
Research Methods in Telecommunications
Television Production-Direction
Problems of Broadcast News
World and International Broadcasting
Survey of Contemporary Telecommunications
Communications Theory and Effects
Cable/Broadband Communications
Special Projects in Telecommunications
Instructional Television Program Design
Instructional Television System Design
Radio-Television Workshop
Topical Seminar in Telecommunications Law and Public Policy
Topical Seminar in Telecommunications Theory and Effects
Topical Seminar in Telecommunications Management
Topical Seminar in Mass Communications
Topical Seminar in Audience and Program Evaluation
Topical Seminar in Advanced Research Methods in Telecommunications
Topical Seminar in International Telecommunications

Undergraduate and Graduate
Social Action via Mass Media
Law and Ethics in Telecommunications
Broadcast Station Management
Film Production for Television
Television Direction
The Broadcast Documentary
Television Aesthetics and Criticism
Comparative Broadcasting Systems
Entertainment in Broadcasting

Indiana University—Purdue University at Fort Wayne

State-supported comprehensive coed institution. Part of Indiana and Purdue Universities. Institutionally accredited by regional association. Urban location, 412-acre campus. Total enrollment: 9015. Undergraduate enrollment: 7781. Total faculty: 495 (277 full-time, 218 part-time). Semester calendar. Grading system: letters or numbers.

Communication Department, 2101 Coliseum Boulevard E, Fort Wayne, IN 46805 219-482-5348

CONTACT Timothy Singleton
DEGREE OFFERED BA in radio-tv-film
DEPARTMENTAL MAJORS 50 students
ADMISSION Requirements — ACT or SAT scores, upper half of high school class Application deadline — rolling
FINANCIAL AID Scholarships, work/study programs, student loans, teaching assistantships, BEOG, SEOG, institutional grants Application deadline — 3/1, rolling
CURRICULAR EMPHASIS Film study — criticism and aesthetics, appreciation, educational media/instructional technology treated equally Filmmaking — documentary, narrative, educational treated equally Television study — (1) production; (2) criticism and aesthetics; (3) appreciation Television production — commercial, news/documentary, educational treated equally
SPECIAL ACTIVITIES/OFFERINGS Program material produced for on-campus closed-circuit television, cable television, local public television station, local commercial television station, industry and private institutions; internships in film production; internships in television production; independent study
FACILITIES AND EQUIPMENT Film — 8mm cameras, editing equipment, lighting, color film stock, projectors, 16mm cameras, editing equipment, lighting, projectors, editing room Television — color studio cameras, ¾-inch cassette VTR, editing equipment, special effects generators, slide chain, portable color cameras, ¾-inch ENG, lighting equipment, sound recording equipment, audio mixers, film chain, time base corrector, color studio, audio studio, control room
FACULTY Anthony Ferri, Timothy Singleton PART-TIME FACULTY Mike Barnard

COURSE LIST

Undergraduate

Mass Communication and Society
Introduction to Electronic Media
Theories of Mass Communication
Radio Production
TV Production
Film Production
Practicum in Radio
Practicum in TV
Practicum in Film

Undergraduate and Graduate

Broadcast Journalism
Problems in Contemporary Broadcasting
Broadcast Management
Radio and Television Writing
Radio and Television in Education

Indiana University—Purdue University at Indianapolis

State-supported coed university. Part of Indiana University System. Institutionally accredited by regional association, programs recognized by NASA. Urban location, 300-acre campus. Total enrollment: 20,654. Undergraduate enrollment: 14,098. Total faculty: 2000. Semester calendar. Grading system: letters or numbers.

English Department, 925 West Michigan Street, Indianapolis, IN 46202 317-264-3824

CONTACT John Barlow or Norman Mikesell
PROGRAM OFFERED Major in English with emphasis in television
ADMISSION Application deadline — rolling
CURRICULAR EMPHASIS Film study — (1) educational media/instructional technology; (2) appreciation; (3) history Television study — (1) educational; (2) production Television production — educational
SPECIAL ACTIVITIES/OFFERINGS Film series, program material produced for on-campus closed-circuit television
FACILITIES AND EQUIPMENT Television — complete black and white studio production equipment, black and white studio
FACULTY John Barlow, Warren French, Alinda Levinson, Norman Mikesell

COURSE LIST

Undergraduate

Introduction to Film Study
Film and Society
Popular Culture

Indiana

Manchester College

Independent comprehensive coed institution affiliated with Church of the Brethren. Institutionally accredited by regional association, programs recognized by NASM. Small town location, 100-acre campus. Total enrollment: 1152. Undergraduate enrollment: 1128. Total faculty: 105 (85 full-time, 20 part-time). 4-1-4 calendar. Grading system: letters or numbers.

Department of Speech, College Avenue, North Manchester, IN 46962 219-982-2141

CONTACT Samuel M Davis
ADMISSION Application deadline — rolling
CURRICULAR EMPHASIS Film study — educational media/instructional technology Filmmaking — narrative, experimental, animated treated equally Television study — production, educational, management treated equally Television production — commercial, news/documentary, experimental/personal video treated equally
SPECIAL ACTIVITIES/OFFERINGS Program material produced for on-campus closed-circuit television, internships in television production, practicum, teacher training
FACILITIES AND EQUIPMENT Film — complete 8mm equipment, editing room, sound mixing room, animation board Television — complete black and white studio production equipment, portable black and white cameras, portable color cameras, black and white studio, audio studio, control room
FACULTY Samuel M Davis

COURSE LIST

Undergraduate

Introduction to Film
Film Animation

Purdue University—Calumet

State-supported comprehensive coed institution. Part of Purdue University. Institutionally accredited by regional association. Urban location. Total enrollment: 6658. Undergraduate enrollment: 5622. Total faculty: 377 (208 full-time, 169 part-time). Semester calendar. Grading system: letters or numbers.

Communication and Creative Arts Department, Hammond, IN 46323 219-844-0520

CONTACT Film — Richard Caplan Television — Lee Goodman
DEGREE OFFERED BA in radio-television
DEPARTMENTAL MAJORS 40 students
ADMISSION Requirement — 2.0 minimum grade point average
FINANCIAL AID Scholarships, student loans, work/study programs
CURRICULAR EMPHASIS Film study — (1) appreciation; (2) criticism and aesthetics; (3) production Filmmaking — (1) narrative; (2) documentary; (3) experimental Television study — (1) production; (2) management; (3) criticism and aesthetics Television production — (1) commercial; (2) news/documentary; (3) educational
SPECIAL ACTIVITIES/OFFERINGS Film series, program material produced for on-campus closed-circuit television and local public television station, independent study, practicum, teacher training
FACILITIES AND EQUIPMENT Film — complete 8mm equipment, 16mm editing equipment, lighting equipment, projectors, permanent film library Television — complete black and white studio and exterior production equipment, complete color exterior production equipment, black and white studio, audio studio, control room

Purdue University—Calumet (continued)

FACULTY Richard Caplan, Lee Goodman

COURSE LIST

Undergraduate

Mass Communications in Society
Radio and Television Performance
Film Production
Theories of Mass Communications
Radio Production
Television Broadcasting
Practicum in Film
Practicum in Radio
Practicum in Television
Broadcast Journalism

Undergraduate and Graduate

Problems in Contemporary Broadcasting
Broadcast Management
Radio and Television Writing
Radio and Television in Education
Comparative Broadcast Systems

Purdue University, West Lafayette

State-supported coed university. Part of Purdue University System. Institutionally accredited by regional association, programs recognized by AACSB, ACPE. Small town location. Total enrollment: 30,445. Undergraduate enrollment: 25,146. Total faculty: 3748 (1809 full-time, 1939 part-time). Semester calendar. Grading system: letters or numbers.

Department of Communication, Heavilon Hall, West Lafayette, IN 47907 317-749-2692

Indiana

CONTACT Film — W K Schwienher Television — M N Diskin
DEGREES OFFERED BS, MA, PhD in mass communications
DEPARTMENTAL MAJORS Undergraduate — 75 students Graduate — 10 students
ADMISSION Requirements — minimum grade point average, interviews, teachers' recommendations, written statement of purpose Undergraduate application deadline — rolling
FINANCIAL AID Student loans, work/study programs, teaching assistantships, research assistantships, fellowships Undergraduate application deadline — 2/1
CURRICULAR EMPHASIS Film study — (1) appreciation, (2) production; (3) criticism and aesthetics Filmmaking — (1) documentary; (2) narrative; (3) educational Television study — (1) appreciation; (2) production; (3) criticism and aesthetics Television production — (1) news/documentary; (2) educational; (3) commercial
SPECIAL ACTIVITIES/OFFERINGS Film series, film societies, program material produced for on-campus closed-circuit television and cable television, internships in television production, independent study, practicum
FACILITIES AND EQUIPMENT Film — complete 16mm equipment, sound stage, screening room, 35mm screening facilities, editing room, sound mixing room, animation board, permanent film library Television — complete black and white studio production equipment, black and white studio, audio studio, control room
FACULTY M N Diskin, M P Pierce, L Rado, W K Schwienher, J Turow PART-TIME FACULTY R E Wolf

COURSE LIST

Undergraduate

Mass Communication
Introduction to Electronic Media
Television Production
Film Production
Television Practicum
Film Practicum
Radio, Television, and Film Writing
News Reporting
Theories of Mass Communication
Mass Communication Law

Undergraduate and Graduate

Documentary Film
Radio and Television in Education
Broadcast Journalism
Problems in Contemporary Broadcast
Broadcast Management
Comparative Broadcast Systems
Seminar

Saint Mary's College

Independent Roman Catholic 4-year college primarily for women. Institutionally accredited by regional association, programs recognized by NASM, NASA. Suburban location, 275-acre campus. Undergraduate enrollment: 1839. Total faculty: 156 (115 full-time, 41 part-time). Semester calendar. Grading system: letters or numbers.

Saint Mary's College participates in a cooperative arrangement with the University of Notre Dame. (See also listing for the University of Notre Dame.)

Department of Communication and Theatre, Notre Dame, IN 46556 219-284-4935

CONTACT Mitchell Lifton
DEGREE OFFERED BA in communication with concentration in film and video
DEPARTMENTAL MAJORS Film — 36 students Television — 45 students
ADMISSION Requirements — 3.2 minimum grade point average, ACT or SAT scores, teachers' recommendations, written statement of purpose Application deadline — 3/1
FINANCIAL AID Scholarships, work/study programs, student loans
CURRICULAR EMPHASIS Film study — history, criticism and aesthetics treated equally Filmmaking — documentary, narrative, experimental treated equally Television study — history, criticism and aesthetics treated equally Television production — commercial, experimental/personal video treated equally
SPECIAL ACTIVITIES/OFFERINGS Filmmaking clubs; film series; film societies; program material produced for on-campus closed-circuit television, cable television, local public television station; independent study
FACILITIES AND EQUIPMENT Film — 8mm and 16mm cameras, editing equipment, sound recording equipment, lighting, projectors, 35mm projectors, 35mm screening facilities, editing room, permanent film library of student films, permanent film library of commercial or professional films Television — black and white studio cameras, ½-inch VTR cassette, editing equipment, monitors, portable color cameras, ½-inch portapak recorders, lighting equipment, sound recording equipment

COURSE LIST
Undergraduate
Basics of Film Studies
Basics of Mass Communication
Film and Video Production: (Super 8)
History of Film
History of Mass Media
Aspects of Film: Film Cultures
Generic Studies in Film
Telecommunications
Film Theory and Criticism
Advanced Film and Video Production (16mm)
Senior Topics in Film Studies

University of Evansville

Independent United Methodist comprehensive coed institution. Institutionally accredited by regional association, programs recognized by NASM. Suburban location, 75-acre campus. Total enrollment: 4817. Undergraduate enrollment: 4206. Total faculty: 278 (197 full-time, 81 part-time). Quarter calendar. Grading system: letters or numbers.

Department of Communications, PO Box 329, Evansville, IN 47702 812-479-2377

CONTACT Chairperson
DEGREE OFFERED BS in communication with a major in film or television
ADMISSION Requirement — 2.0 minimum grade point average Application deadline — 9/1, rolling
FINANCIAL AID Student loans, work/study programs Application deadline — 3/1, rolling
CURRICULAR EMPHASIS Film study — (1) criticism and aesthetics; (2) history; (3) production Filmmaking — (1) documentary; (2) narrative; (3) experimental Television study — (1) production; (2) criticism and aesthetics; (3) appreciation Television production — (1) news/documentary; (2) commercial; (3) educational
SPECIAL ACTIVITIES/OFFERINGS Film series, film festivals, program material produced for on-campus closed-circuit television, internships in film and television production, independent study, practicum, Summer Media Institute
FACILITIES AND EQUIPMENT Film — Complete 8mm equipment, screening room, editing room, permanent film library Television — complete black and white studio and exterior production equipment, complete color studio production equipment, black and white studio, color studio, audio studio, control room

Indiana

University of Notre Dame

Independent Roman Catholic coed university. Institutionally accredited by regional association. Urban location, 1250-acre campus. Total enrollment: 8200. Undergraduate enrollment: 6800. Total faculty: 798 (798 full-time). Semester calendar. Grading system: letters or numbers.

The University of Notre Dame participates in a cooperative arrangement with Saint Mary's College. (See also listing for Saint Mary's College.)

Department of Communication and Theatre, Notre Dame, IN 46556 219-284-4935

CONTACT Mitchell Lifton
DEGREE OFFERED BA in communication with concentration in film and video
DEPARTMENTAL MAJORS Film — 36 students Television — 45 students
ADMISSION Requirements — 3.2 minmum grade point average, ACT or SAT scores, teachers' recommendations, written statement of purpose Undergraduate application deadline — 3/1
FINANCIAL AID Scholarships, work/study programs, student loans
CURRICULAR EMPHASIS Film study — history, criticism and aesthetics treated equally Filmmaking — documentary, narrative, experimental treated equally Television study — history, criticism and aesthetics treated equally Television production — commercial, experimental/personal video treated equally
SPECIAL ACTIVITIES/OFFERINGS Filmmaking clubs; film series; film societies; program material produced for on-campus closed-circuit television, cable television, local public television station; independent study
FACILITIES AND EQUIPMENT Film — 8mm and 16mm cameras, editing equipment, sound recording equipment, lighting, projectors, 35mm projectors, 35mm screening facilities, editing room, permanent film library of student films, permanent film library of commercial or professional films Television — black and white studio cameras, ½-inch VTR cassette, editing equipment, monitors, portable color cameras, ½-inch portapak recorders, lighting equipment, sound recording equipment

COURSE LIST
Undergraduate
Basics of Film Studies
Basics of Mass Communication
Film and Video Production: (Super 8)
History of Film
History of Mass Media
Aspects of Film: Film Cultures
Generic Studies in Film
Telecommunications
Film Theory and Criticism
Advanced Film and Video Production (16mm)
Senior Topics in Film Studies

Valparaiso University

Independent Lutheran comprehensive coed institution. Institutionally accredited by regional association, programs recognized by NASM, ECPD. Small town location, 300-acre campus. Total enrollment: 4019. Undergraduate enrollment: 3503. Total faculty: 360 (302 full-time, 58 part-time). Semester and early semester with optional miniterm calendar. Grading system: letters or numbers.

Interdisciplinary Film Studies Program, Valparaiso, IN 46383 219-464-5022

CONTACT Richard Maxwell
DEGREE OFFERED BA with special concentration in film studies

Valparaiso University (continued)

CURRICULAR EMPHASIS Film study — (1) criticism and aesthetics; (2) history; (3) appreciation
SPECIAL ACTIVITIES/OFFERINGS Film series, film festivals, film societies
FACULTY Richard Lee, Richard Maxwell, Ronald Sommer

COURSE LIST
Undergraduate
Film History
Film Aesthetics
Literature and Film
Seminar

IOWA

Drake University

Independent coed university. Institutionally accredited by regional association, programs recognized by NASM, AACSB, NASA, AOA, ACPE. Suburban location, 75-acre campus. Total enrollment: 6568. Undergraduate enrollment: 4871. Total faculty: 340 (275 full-time, 65 part-time). Semester calendar. Grading system: letters or numbers.

Broadcast Journalism, School of Journalism, 25th and University, Des Moines, IA 50311 515-271-3194

CONTACT Film — John Lytle Television — James Duncan
DEGREES OFFERED BA in journalism, MA in mass communication with varied emphasis
PROGRAM MAJORS Undergraduate television — 25 students Graduate television — 2 students
ADMISSION Undergraduate application deadline — rolling
FINANCIAL AID Scholarships, work/study programs, student loans, teaching assistantships (grad only)
CURRICULAR EMPHASIS Undergraduate film study — (1) educational media/instructional technology; (2) appreciation; (3) criticism and aesthetics Undergraduate filmmaking — (1) news; (2) documentary; (3) educational Undergraduate television study — criticism and aesthetics, production, management treated equally Undergraduate television production — news/documentary
SPECIAL ACTIVITIES/OFFERINGS Program material produced for cable television, internships in television production, independent study, teacher training, vocational placement service
FACILITIES AND EQUIPMENT Film — 8mm and 16mm cameras, editing equipment, sound recording equipment, lighting, projectors, light meters, screening room, editing room Television — black and white studio cameras, ½-inch VTR, ¾-inch cassette VTR, portable black and white cameras, editing equipment, monitors, slide chain, portable color cameras, ¾-inch ENG, lighting equipment, sound recording equipment, audio mixers, film chain, black and white studio, audio studio, control room
FACULTY James Duncan, Michael Havice, John Lytle PART-TIME FACULTY John Carl

COURSE LIST
Undergraduate
Television Newsfilm
Newsfilm Practicum
Broadcast News Reporting and Editing

Undergraduate and Graduate
TV News Reporting
Broadcasting Public Affairs

Iowa State University

State-supported coed university. Institutionally accredited by regional association, programs recognized by NASM. Small town location, 1700-acre campus. Total enrollment: 23,052. Undergraduate enrollment: 19,746. Total faculty: 1866 (1713 full-time, 153 part-time). Quarter calendar. Grading system: letters or numbers.

Speech–Telecommunicative Arts Department, College of Sciences and Humanities, 21 Exhibit Hall, Ames, IA 50011 515-294-5000

CONTACT Linda Busby
DEGREE OFFERED BA in speech–telecommunicative arts with emphasis in film or television
ADMISSION Requirement — graduation in upper half of high school class Application deadline — rolling
FINANCIAL AID Student loans, work/study programs Application deadline — 3/1
CURRICULAR EMPHASIS Undergraduate film study — (1) production; (2) history/theory; (3) criticism and aesthetics Graduate film study — (1) production; (2) educational media/instructional technology Filmmaking — (1) educational; (2) documentary; (3) experimental Television study — (1) production; (2) educational; (3) criticism and aesthetics Television production — (1) educational; (2) commerial; (3) experimental/personal video
SPECIAL ACTIVITIES/OFFERINGS American Archives of the Factual Film (AAFF); over 5,000 business (industrial) educational films; film series; film festivals; program material produced for on-campus closed-circuit television, cable television, local public television station, local commercial television station; apprenticeships; internships in film production; independent study; practicum; Focus Grants for Films
FACILITIES AND EQUIPMENT Film — complete 16mm equipment, sound stage, screening room, editing room, sound mixing room, animation board, cinemicrography equipment, time lapse and high speed cameras, permanent film library Television — complete black and white studio and exterior production equipment, complete color studio and exterior production equipment, black and white studio, color studio, audio studio, control room
FACULTY Charles P Connolly Jr, Daniel J Perkins, George P Wilson Jr PART-TIME FACULTY Jeffrey M Gibson, Richard H Kraemer

COURSE LIST

Undergraduate

Telecommunicative Arts Seminar
Television Workshop — Beginning
Television Workshop — Intermediate
Television Workshop — Directing
Development of the Motion Picture I–III
Motion Picture Techniques
Television and Radio Broadcasting
Television and Radio Speech
Television Performance
Film Theory
Film/Television Criticism
Costuming for Stage, Television, and Film
Television Production-Lecture-Discussion
Television Direction Laboratory
Documentary Film
Film Animation
Special Problems
Introduction to Mass Communication

Graduate

Special Topics
Seminar in Broadcasting-Film
Special Problems in Broadcasting

Undergraduate and Graduate

Telecommunicative Arts/Television Production — Advanced
Telecommunicative Arts/Film Production — Advanced
Intermediate Film Production
Film Practicum I, II

English Department, 203 Ross Hall, Ames, IA 50011 515-294-2180

CONTACT Charles L P Silet
PROGRAM OFFERED Major in English with emphasis in film
ADMISSION Application deadline — rolling
CURRICULAR EMPHASIS Film study — history, criticism and aesthetics
SPECIAL ACTIVITIES/OFFERINGS Film series, film festivals
FACULTY Gretchen Bataille, Donald Dunlop, Joseph Geha, Leland Poague, Charles L P Silet

COURSE LIST

Undergraduate

Introduction to Film and Theater
Film
Script Writing
Propaganda Analysis
Seminars in Film
Film Theory

Kirkwood Community College

District-supported 2-year coed college. Institutionally accredited by regional association. Urban location, 315-acre campus. Undergraduate enrollment: 4528. Total faculty: 250. Quarter calendar. Grading system: letters or numbers.

Communication Arts Department, 6301 Kirkwood Boulevard, Cedar Rapids, IA 52406 319-398-5538

CONTACT Doreen Maronde
ADMISSION Application deadline — rolling
FACULTY Robert Aldridge

Luther College

Independent 4-year coed college affiliated with American Lutheran Church. Institutionally accredited by regional association, programs recognized by NASM. Small town location, 175-acre campus. Undergraduate enrollment: 1999. Total faculty: 148 (124 full-time, 24 part-time). 4-1-4 calendar. Grading system: letters or numbers.

English Department, Decorah, IA 52101 319-387-2000

CONTACT Harland Nelson
ADMISSION Application deadline — 8/1, rolling
FINANCIAL AID Scholarships, student loans, work/study programs Application deadline — rolling
CURRICULAR EMPHASIS Film study — criticism and aesthetics, appreciation treated equally Filmmaking — (1) narrative; (2) documentary; (3) experimental
FACULTY Harland Nelson

COURSE LIST

Undergraduate

Film

University of Iowa

State-supported coed university. Institutionally accredited by regional association, programs recognized by NASM, AACSB, NASA, ACPE. Small town location. Total enrollment: 23,000. Undergraduate enrollment: 15,200. Total faculty: 1600 (1475 full-time, 125 part-time). Semester calendar. Grading system: letters or numbers.

Division of Broadcasting and Film, Department of Speech and Dramatic Art, Iowa City, IA 52242 319-353-4403

CONTACT J Dudley Andrew or Robert Pepper
DEGREES OFFERED BA, MA, PhD in broadcasting and film
ADMISSION Undergraduate requirements — ACT scores, teachers' recommendations, written statement of purpose Graduate requirements — GRE scores, teachers' recommendations, written statement of purpose Undergraduate application deadline — rolling

University of Iowa (continued)

FINANCIAL AID Student loans, work/study programs, teaching assistantships, research assistantships, fellowships Undergraduate application deadline — 2/1

CURRICULAR EMPHASIS Film study — (1) criticism and aesthetics; (2) production; (3) history Undergraduate television study — (1) production; (2) criticism and aesthetics; (3) history Graduate television study — (1) process and effects/social impact; (2) criticism and aesthetics; (3) control systems/policy/regulation Television production — (1) dramatic; (2) news/documentary; (3) experimental/personal video

SPECIAL ACTIVITIES/OFFERINGS Filmmaking clubs; film series; film festivals; film societies; student publications; program material produced for on-campus closed-circuit television, cable television, local public television station, local commercial television station; apprenticeships; internships in television production; independent study; vocational placement service

FACILITIES AND EQUIPMENT Film — complete 8mm equipment, complete 16mm equipment, sound stage, screening room, editing room, sound mixing room, permanent film library of student films, permanent film library of commercial or professional films Television — complete color studio production equipment, portable black and white cameras, portable color cameras, color studio, audio studio, control room, electronic editing facility

FACULTY J Dudley Andrew, Samuel Becker, Richard Dyer MacCann, Franklin Miller, Robert Pepper, John Winnie PART-TIME FACULTY Hugh Cordier, George Klinger

COURSE LIST

Undergraduate and Graduate

Introduction to Broadcasting and Film Production
Mass Media and Mass Society
American Broadcasting
Survey of Film
Selected Films
New Directions in Video
Technology of Film Production
Television in Society
Broadcasting and Film Writing
The Criticism of Broadcasting
Teaching Broadcasting and Mass Communication
History of Broadcasting
Regulation of Broadcasting
Contemporary Issues in Broadcasting
Social Impact of Mass Communication
Mass Communication Process and Effects
Film and Public Policy
Broadband Communications
Documentary and Public Issues Broadcasting
Broadcasting and Education
Comparative Systems of Broadcasting
International Broadcasting
Public Broadcasting
Broadcast Management
Documentary Film
Film and Ideology
The American Film
European Film History
French Cinema
National Cinema (England, Italy, Japan, Germany, or Russia)
Film Criticism
Film Theory
Film Script Analysis
Literature and the Film
Film and Art Movements
Narrative and Related Art Forms
Film Styles and Genres
Influences on Film Production
American Film and American Culture
Research Methods in Mass Communication
Seminar: National Cinema
Seminar: Film Aesthetics and Criticism
Seminar: Film Theory
Seminar: Film History
Seminar: Broadcasting
Seminar: Mass Communication Research
Film for Television
Television Production I, II
Television Workshop
Film Production I, II
Film Workshop
Producing Drama for the Screen

KANSAS

Benedictine College

Independent Roman Catholic 4-year coed college. Institutionally accredited by regional association. Small town location, 225-acre campus. Undergraduate enrollment: 1006. Total faculty: 75. 4-1-4 calendar. Grading system: letters or numbers.

Theatre Arts Department, South Campus, Atchison, KS 66002 913-367-6110, ext 283

CONTACT Film — Doug McKenzie Television — Rick Cumings

DEGREES OFFERED BA in communications, BA in theatre arts

ADMISSION Requirements — C+ average, ACT or SAT scores Application deadline — 8/15, rolling

FINANCIAL AID Scholarships, work/study programs, student loans Undergraduate application deadline — 8/15, rolling

CURRICULAR EMPHASIS Film study — (1) appreciation; (2) history; (3) criticism and aesthetics; (4) production; (5) educational media/instructional technology Filmmaking — experimental Television study — (1) production; (2) educational; (3) criticism and aesthetics; (4) appreciation Television production — (1) educational; (2) news/documentary

SPECIAL ACTIVITIES/OFFERINGS Film series, film festivals, program material produced for on-campus closed-circuit television and cable television, independent study, practicum

FACILITIES AND EQUIPMENT Film — complete 8mm equipment, sound stage, screening room, 35mm screening facilities, editing room, permanent film library of commercial or professional films Television — complete black and white studio production equipment, black and white studio, control room

FACULTY Rick Allen Cumings, Anne Marie LaLonde, Douglas C McKenzie

COURSE LIST

Undergraduate

Introduction to Cinema
Introduction to Mass Media
Radio and Television Script
Survey of Motion Picture History
Television Workshop
Independent Study
Special Topics

Bethany College

Independent Lutheran 4-year coed college. Institutionally accredited by regional association, programs recognized by NASM. Small town location, 48-acre campus. Undergraduate enrollment: 827. Total faculty: 67 (51 full-time, 16 part-time). 4-1-4 calendar. Grading system: letters or numbers.

English, Speech, and Drama Department, Lindsborg, KS 67456 913-227-3311

CONTACT Delmar C Homan, Head
ADMISSION Application deadline — rolling
CURRICULAR EMPHASIS Film study — (1) appreciation; (2) criticism and aesthetics; (3) history Television study — (1) appreciation; (2) educational
SPECIAL ACTIVITIES/OFFERINGS Film series
FACULTY William Berenson, Elston Flohr, Delmar Homan

COURSE LIST

Undergraduate
Writing and the Mass Media
The Art of Film

Fort Hays State University

State-supported comprehensive coed institution. Institutionally accredited by regional association, programs recognized by NASM. Small town location, 200-acre campus. Total enrollment: 5453. Undergraduate enrollment: 3947. Total faculty: 308 (288 full-time, 20 part-time). Semester calendar. Grading system: letters or numbers.

Radio-Television-Film Department, Hays, KS 67601 913-628-5373

CONTACT Director of Radio-Television & Film
PROGRAM OFFERED Major in Communication with emphasis in radio-television-film
ADMISSION Undergraduate application deadline — rolling
FINANCIAL AID Scholarships, student loans, work/study programs, fellowships Undergraduate application deadline — rolling
CURRICULAR EMPHASIS Film study — (1) production; (2) criticism and aesthetics; (3) educational media/instructional technology Filmmaking — (1) documentary; (2) educational; (3) narrative Television study — (1) production; (2) management; (3) educational Television production — (1) commercial; (2) educational; (3) news/documentary
SPECIAL ACTIVITIES/OFFERINGS Program material produced for on-campus closed-circuit television, cable television, local commerical television station; apprenticeships; internships in television production
FACILITIES AND EQUIPMENT Film — complete 8mm and 16mm equipment, sound stage, screening room, 35mm screening facilities, editing room Television — complete color studio and exterior production equipment, color studio, mobile van/unit, audio studio, control room
FACULTY Jack R Heather, Dave Lefurgey

COURSE LIST

Undergraduate
Introduction to Broadcasting
Radio-Television Announcing
Advanced Radio-Television Announcing
Campus Station Operation
Cinematography I

Undergraduate and Graduate
Radio-Television News Writing
Radio-Television Continuity Writing
Radio-Television Production
Advanced Television Production
Cinematography II
Broadcast Management/Sales
Electronic News Production and Documentary Films
Social Issues and Broadcasting
Closed-Circuit Television Operation
Internship in Broadcasting

Kansas City Kansas Community College

County-supported 2-year coed college. Institutionally accredited by regional association. Suburban location. Undergraduate enrollment: 3300. Total faculty: 222 (97 full-time, 125 part-time). Semester calendar. Grading system: letters or numbers.

English Department, Kansas City, KS 66112 913-334-1100

CONTACT Charles Cowdrick
FACULTY Charles Cowdrick

COURSE LIST

Undergraduate
Film Appreciation

Kansas State University

State-supported coed university. Institutionally accredited by regional association, programs recognized by AACSB, NASA. Small town location, 340-acre campus. Total enrollment: 18,293. Undergraduate enrollment: 14,525. Total faculty: 3000 (2500 full-time, 500 part-time). Semester calendar. Grading system: letters or numbers.

Department of Journalism and Mass Communications—Radio/TV, 104 Kedzie Hall, Manhattan, KS 66506 913-532-6890

CONTACT Robert Fidler
DEGREES OFFERED BA, BS in radio-TV, MA in radio-TV
DEPARTMENTAL MAJORS Undergraduate television — 135 students Graduate television — 5 students
ADMISSION Undergraduate requirement — ACT or SAT scores Graduate requirements — B minimum grade average in junior and senior years, written statement of purpose, letters of recommendation Undergraduate application deadline — rolling
FINANCIAL AID Scholarships, work/study programs, student loans, teaching assistantships Undergraduate application deadline — rolling

Kansas State University (continued)

CURRICULAR EMPHASIS Undergraduate television study — criticism and aesthetics, production, management treated equally Graduate television study — criticism and aesthetics, production, management treated equally Undergraduate television production — commercial, news/documentary, industrial video treated equally Graduate television production — commercial, news/documentary, industrial video treated equally

SPECIAL ACTIVITIES/OFFERINGS Program material produced for on-campus closed-circuit television, cable television, local public television station, local commercial television station; internships in television production; independent study; vocational placement service

FACILITIES AND EQUIPMENT Television — complete black and white and color studio production equipment, complete color exterior production equipment, black and white studio, color studio, mobile van/unit, audio studio, control room, video editing laboratory, character generator, 3 complete color ENG units

FACULTY Robert Fidler, Lionel Grady, David MacFarland, Paul Prince

COURSE LIST

Undergraduate

Radio-Television and Society
Fundamentals of Radio-TV Production
Radio-TV Continuity
Public Broadcasting
Fundamentals of Radio-TV Performance
Reporting for Radio-TV
Intermediate Radio Production
Intermediate Television Production
XSPB-FM Participation
Television Participation

Undergraduate and Graduate

Entertainment Script Writing
Documentary Script Writing
Radio-TV Advertising
Radio-TV Programming
History of Broadcasting
Radio-TV Regulation and Responsibility
Radio-TV Criticism
Radio-TV Management
Radio-TV Research

McPherson College

Independent 4-year coed college affiliated with Church of the Brethren. Institutionally accredited by regional association. Rural location, 24-acre campus. Undergraduate enrollment: 493. Total faculty: 42 (35 full-time, 7 part-time). 4-1-4 calendar. Grading system: letters or numbers.

Audio-Visual Communication Department, McPherson, KS 67460 316-241-0731

CONTACT Herbert Johnson

DEGREE OFFERED BA in audiovisual communications

DEPARTMENTAL MAJORS 10 students

ADMISSION Application deadline — 8/1, rolling

SPECIAL ACTIVITIES/OFFERINGS Program material produced for cable television

FACILITIES AND EQUIPMENT Television — complete black and white studio and exterior production facilities, complete color studio production facilities

FACULTY Herbert Johnson, Joan Johnson

COURSE LIST

Undergraduate

Practicum: Audio-Visual Communication
Stage Makeup
Television in Instruction
Stage Lighting
Media Production Practice

University of Kansas

State-supported coed university. Institutionally accredited by regional association, programs recognized by NASM, AACSB, NASA, ACPE. Small town location, 960-acre campus. Total enrollment: 23,564. Undergraduate enrollment: 16,898. Total faculty: 1027. Semester calendar. Grading system: letters or numbers.

Radio-Television-Film Department, 217 Flint Hall, Lawrence, KS 66045 913-864-3991

CONTACT Bruce Linton

DEGREES OFFERED BA, BS, BSJ, MA, MS in radio-television-film

DEPARTMENTAL MAJORS Undergraduate film — 50 students Undergraduate television — 173 students Graduate film — 10 students Graduate television — 25 students

ADMISSION Undergraduate requirements — professional recommendations, teachers' recommendations, written statement of purpose Graduate requirements — 3.0 minimum grade point average, GRE scores, professional recommendations, teachers' recommendations, written statement of purpose Undergraduate application deadline — 8/1, rolling

FINANCIAL AID Student loans, work/study programs, teaching assistantships Undergraduate application deadline — 2/15, rolling

CURRICULAR EMPHASIS Film study — (1) production; (2) criticism and aesthetics; (3) history; (4) educational media/instructional technology Filmmaking — (1) documentary; (2) experimental; (3) educational Television study — (1) management; (2) criticism and aesthetics; (3) history; (4) educational Television production — (1) news/documentary; (2) educational; (3) commercial

SPECIAL ACTIVITIES/OFFERINGS Film series; film festivals; film societies; program material produced for on-campus closed-circuit television, cable television, local public television station, local commercial television station; internships in film and television production; independent study; practicum

FACILITIES AND EQUIPMENT Film — complete 16mm equipment, sound stage, screening room, editing rooms, sound mixing room, permanent film library Television — broadcast quality color television cameras, switcher, TBC, color ENG, ¾-inch tape editing, audio, broadcast journalism newsroom, studios

FACULTY Charles Berg, Richard Colyer, Francis Ellis, Dale Gadd, Bruce Linton, George Rasmussen, Mae Sunada PART-TIME FACULTY Greg Black, Glen Price

Wichita State University

State-supported coed university. Institutionally accredited by regional association, programs recognized by NASM, AACSB, ECPD. Urban location, 325-acre campus. Total enrollment: 16,000. Undergraduate enrollment: 12,400. Total faculty: 800. Semester calendar. Grading system: letters or numbers.

Radio-TV-Film Division, Box 31, Wichita, KS 67208 316-689-3390

CONTACT Frank Chorba
DEGREES OFFERED BA in radio-TV-film, BA in broadcast journalism, MA in mass communication
DEPARTMENTAL MAJORS Undergraduate television — 75 students Graduate television — 35 students
ADMISSION Undergraduate requirements — 2.0 minimum grade point average, ACT or SAT scores Graduate requirements — 2.75 minimum grade point average, GRE scores Undergraduate application deadline — 8/1
FINANCIAL AID Scholarships, work/study programs, student loans, teaching assistantships (grad only)
CURRICULAR EMPHASIS Undergraduate film study — (1) educational media/instructional technology; (2) history; (3) production Undergraduate filmmaking — (1) documentary; (2) animated; (3) educational Undergraduate television study — (1) production; (2) management; (3) educational Undergraduate television production — (1) commercial; (2) news/documentary; (3) educational
SPECIAL ACTIVITIES/OFFERINGS Filmmaking clubs; film series, film festivals; program material produced for cable television, local public television station, local commercial television station; internships in film production; internships in television production; independent study; vocational placement service
FACILITIES AND EQUIPMENT Film — 8mm cameras, editing equipment, sound recording equipment, lighting, projectors, 16mm cameras, editing equipment, projectors, screening room, editing room, permanent film library of commercial or professional films Television — black and white studio cameras, color studio cameras, ½-inch VTR, ¾-inch cassette VTR, editing equipment, monitors, special effects generators, slide chain, portable color cameras, ¾-inch ENG, lighting equipment, sound recording equipment, audio mixers, film chain, time base corrector, black and white studio, color studio, audio studio, control room

COURSE LIST

Undergraduate

Introduction to Film Studies
Cinematography
Radio-TV Writing
Television Production and Directing (black and white)

Undergraduate and Graduate

Propaganda-Documentary Films
Advanced TV Production (color)
Educational Television
Advanced TV News
TV Management
Audience Measurement

KENTUCKY

Eastern Kentucky University

State-supported comprehensive coed institution. Institutionally accredited by regional association, programs recognized by NASM. Small town location, 1076-acre campus. Total enrollment: 13,871. Undergraduate enrollment: 11,509. Total faculty: 798 (701 full-time, 97 part-time). Semester calendar. Grading system: letters or numbers.

Department of Mass Communications, Wallace 302, Richmond, KY 40475 606-622-3435

CONTACT James S Harris, Chairman
DEGREES OFFERED BA in broadcasting, BA in journalism, BA in public relations, minor in film
DEPARTMENTAL MAJORS Undergraduate television — 206 students
ADMISSION In-state: no requirements Out-of-state: Upper 1/3 graduating class
FINANCIAL AID Scholarships, work/study programs, student loans
CURRICULAR EMPHASIS Film study — (1) history; (2) appreciation; (3) criticism and aesthetics Filmmaking — (1) documentary; (2) educational; (3) narrative Television study — (1) production; (2) management; (3) criticism and aesthetics Television production — (1) commercial; (2) news/documentary; (3) educational
SPECIAL ACTIVITIES/OFFERINGS Film series; film festivals; program material produced for on-campus closed-circuit television, cable television, local public television station, local commercial television station; internships in film production; internships in television production; independent study; vocational placement service
FACILITIES AND EQUIPMENT Film — complete 8mm and 16mm equipment, screening room, editing room, sound mixing room, permanent film library of student films, permanent film library of commercial or professional films Television — complete black and white and color studio production facilities, complete black and white and color exterior production facilities, black and white studio, color studio, mobile van/unit, audio studio, control room
FACULTY Dean C Cannon, James S Harris, Mark Lloyd, Jerry P Perry, Donna Williams, Carol Wright PART-TIME FACULTY Fred Kolloff, Barry W Peel, Tony Warren

COURSE LIST

Undergraduate

Cinema History I, II
Literature and Film
Special Problems in Communications: Film
Special Problems in Communications: Television
Introduction to Radio and Television
Broadcast Performance
Broadcast News
Broadcast Writing
Film Production
Film Practicum
Television Production
Television Practicum
Advanced Broadcast News
Broadcast Law
Broadcast Station Management
Advanced Film Production
Broadcast Sales
Broadcasting in the Public Interest
Advanced Television Production
Cooperative Study: Broadcasting

Henderson Community College, University of Kentucky

State-supported 2-year coed college. Part of University of Kentucky Community College System, automatic transfer to main campus for baccalaureate. Institutionally accredited by regional association. Small town location. Semester calendar. Grading system: letters or numbers.

Communications Department, Henderson, KY 42420 502-827-1867, ext 55

CONTACT Tony Strawn
CURRICULAR EMPHASIS Film study — (1) production; (2) educational media/instructional technology Filmmaking — (1) news; (2) documentary; (3) educational Television study — production Television production — news/documentary
SPECIAL ACTIVITIES/OFFERINGS Program material produced for cable television, internships in television production, vocational placement service
FACILITIES AND EQUIPMENT Film — 8mm cameras, editing equipment, sound recording equipment, projectors, sound mixing room Television — complete black and white studio and ENG production equipment
FACULTY Tony Strawn

COURSE LIST
Undergraduate
Introduction to Mass Communications
Broadcast Productions
Communications Practicum
Broadcast Internship
Graphics of Communications
Art of the Motion Picture
Writing for the Mass Media

Northern Kentucky University

State-supported comprehensive coed institution. Institutionally accredited by regional association. Suburban location. Total enrollment: 6803. Undergraduate enrollment: 5899. Total faculty: 375 (236 full-time, 139 part-time). Semester calendar. Grading system: letters or numbers.

Department of Communications, Highland Heights, KY 41076 606-292-5435

CONTACT Byron B Renz
DEGREE OFFERED BA in radio/television/film
DEPARTMENTAL MAJORS Television — 78 students
ADMISSION Requirement — ACT scores
FINANCIAL AID Scholarships, work/study programs, student loans Application deadline — 3/1
CURRICULAR EMPHASIS Film study — (1) criticism and aesthetics; (2) history; (3) appreciation Filmmaking — (1) narrative; (2) documentary; (3) experimental Television study — (1) production; (2) management; (3) criticism and aesthetics Television production — (1) commercial; (2) news/documentary; (3) educational
SPECIAL ACTIVITIES/OFFERINGS Program material produced for on-campus closed-circuit television and cable television, internships in film production, internships in television production, independent study
FACILITIES AND EQUIPMENT Film — 8mm cameras, editing equipment, lighting, projectors, editing room Television — color studio cameras, 1-inch VTR, ¾-inch cassette VTR, portable black and white cameras, monitors, special effects generators, ½-inch portapak recorders, lighting equipment, sound recording equipment, audio mixers, color studio, audio studio, control room
FACULTY William Burns, Byron B Renz

COURSE LIST
Undergraduate
Contemporary Mass Media
Introduction to Broadcasting
Broadcast Announcing
Introduction to Cinematography
Television Performance
Television Production I: Basic Production
Television Production II: Directing
Basic Film Production
Current Issues in Broadcasting
Broadcast Writing
Broadcast News Writing
Broadcast Programming
Broadcast Sales and Advertising
Broadcast Promotion
Advanced Television Performance
Television Production III: Producing
Special Projects in Broadcasting: Studio Operations, Television
Sports Announcing, Television
Sports Production, Independent Project in Television/Radio
Intermediate Film Production
Radio and Television Practicum
Law of Broadcasting
National Systems of Broadcasting
Radio and Television Internship
Broadcasting Criticism
History of Broadcasting
Communication Theories
Filmmaking for the Cinema and/or Television
Advanced Broadcast Writing
Broadcast Management
Broadcast Engineering Principles and Regulations: FCC First Class License
Independent Study

Pikeville College

Independent United Presbyterian 4-year coed college. Institutionally accredited by regional association. Small town location, 25-acre campus. Undergraduate enrollment: 615. Total faculty: 52 (40 full-time, 12 part-time). 4-1-4 calendar. Grading system: letters or numbers.

Department of Speech, Pikeville, KY 41501 606-432-9200

CONTACT Sandy Branam
FACILITIES AND EQUIPMENT Television — black and white studio cameras, VTR cassettes and recorders

Western Kentucky University

State-supported comprehensive coed institution. Institutionally accredited by regional association. Small town location. Total enrollment: 13,305. Undergraduate enrollment: 10,253. Total faculty: 606 (579 full-time, 27 part-time). Semester calendar. Grading system: letters or numbers.

Communication and Theater Department, IWCFA 190, Bowling Green, KY 42101 502-745-3296

CONTACT J Regis O'Connor, Chairman
DEGREES OFFERED BS in broadcasting, BS in mass communications, minor in film
DEPARTMENTAL MAJORS 450 students
ADMISSION Requirement — 2.0 minimum grade point average Resident application deadline — 8/1, rolling Nonresident application deadline — 6/1, rolling
FINANCIAL AID Work/study programs Application deadline — 3/15
CURRICULAR EMPHASIS Film study — (1) appreciation; (2) history; (3) criticism and aesthetics; (4) production Filmmaking — (1) narrative; (2) documentary; (3) educational; (4) animated; (5) experimental Television study — criticism and aesthetics, production treated equally Television production — (1) commercial; (2) educational; (3) news/documentary
SPECIAL ACTIVITIES/OFFERINGS Film series, film festivals, program material produced for on-campus closed-circuit television, internships in television production, independent study, practicum
FACILITIES AND EQUIPMENT Film — complete 8mm and 16mm equipment, editing room, permanent film library Television — complete black and white studio and exterior production facilities, complete color studio and exterior production facilities
FACULTY Charles Anderson, Joseph Boggs, Chuck Morse, James A Pearse, James Wesolowski, Dale Wicklander, J Barry Williams PART-TIME FACULTY Thayton Traughber

COURSE LIST

Undergraduate

Introduction to Cinema
Cinema History
Basic Cinematography
News Cinematography
Theory and Criticism of Cinema
Basic Television Production
Advanced Television Production
Television Producing and Directing
Broadcast News Reporting
Advanced Broadcast News Reporting
Advocacy in the Mass Media
History of Mass Communications
Problems in Mass Communications
Evaluation of Mass Communications Media
Current Issues in Mass Communications
Comparative Mass Communications
Mass Communications: Law and Ethics
Survey of Mass Media
Process and Effects of Mass Communications

LOUISIANA

Grambling State University

State-supported comprehensive coed institution. Institutionally accredited by regional association. Small town location, 340-acre campus. Total enrollment: 3639. Undergraduate enrollment: 3442. Total faculty: 200 (182 full-time, 18 part-time). Semester calendar. Grading system: letters or numbers.

Speech and Drama Department, Main Street, Grambling, LA 71245 318-247-6941

CONTACT Film — Roy B Moss Television — Roy B Moss, Allen Williams
DEGREE OFFERED BA in radio and television
DEPARTMENTAL MAJORS 57 students
ADMISSION Requirements — 2.3 minimum grade point average, SAT scores, interviews Application deadline — 7/15
FINANCIAL AID Scholarships, student loans, work/study programs Application deadline — rolling
CURRICULAR EMPHASIS Television study — (1) educational; (2) history; (3) production; (4) management; (5) appreciation; (6) criticism and aesthetics Television production — (1) experimental/personal video; (2) news/documentary; (3) commercial; (4) educational
SPECIAL ACTIVITIES/OFFERINGS Program material produced for on-campus closed-circuit television, apprenticeships, internships in television production, independent study, practicum, vocational placement service
FACILITIES AND EQUIPMENT Television — complete black and white studio and exterior production equipment, black and white studio, audio studio, control room
FACULTY Roy B Moss, Allen Williams

COURSE LIST

Undergraduate

Cinematography

Louisiana State University and A&M College

State-supported coed university. Part of Louisiana State University System. Institutionally accredited by regional association, programs recognized by NASM, AACSB. Suburban location, 1944-acre campus. Total enrollment: 24,952. Undergraduate enrollment: 20,638. Total faculty: 1078 (975 full-time, 103 part-time). Semester calendar. Grading system: letters or numbers.

Speech Department, Baton Rouge, LA 70803 504-388-4172

CONTACT Film — J Donald Ragsdale Television — John H Pennybacker
DEGREES OFFERED BA, MA, PhD in speech with a major in television
DEPARTMENTAL MAJORS Undergraduate — 12 students Graduate — 3 students
ADMISSION Undergraduate application deadline — rolling
FINANCIAL AID Teaching assistantships
CURRICULAR EMPHASIS Undergraduate film study — (1) appreciation; (2) criticism and aesthetics; (3) history Graduate film study — history Filmmaking — (1) narrative; (2) documentary; (3) experimental Television study — (1) production; (2) history; (3) management Television production — (1) educational; (2) news/documentary; (3) commercial

Louisiana State University and A&M College (continued)

SPECIAL ACTIVITIES/OFFERINGS Film series, film festivals, program material produced for on-campus closed-circuit television, independent study

FACILITIES AND EQUIPMENT Film — 8mm and 16mm sound recording equipment, lighting equipment, projectors, screening room Television — complete black and white studio production facilities, black and white studio, audio studio, control room

FACULTY John H Pennybacker, J Donald Ragsdale

COURSE LIST

Undergraduate

Introduction to Film

Undergraduate and Graduate

History of Film

Television Production I, II

Radio and Television in Society

Northwestern State University of Louisiana

State-supported coed university. Institutionally accredited by regional association, programs recognized by NASM. Small town location. Total enrollment: 5894. Undergraduate enrollment: 4653. Total faculty: 225. Semester calendar. Grading system: letters or numbers.

Speech Department, Natchitoches, LA 71457 318-357-5213

CONTACT Tom Whitehead

PROGRAM OFFERED Major in speech with emphasis in television

ADMISSION Requirement — ACT scores Application deadline — rolling

SPECIAL ACTIVITIES/OFFERINGS Program material produced for on-campus closed-circuit television and state agencies, internships in television production, independent study, teacher training

FACILITIES AND EQUIPMENT Television — complete black and white studio production equipment, complete color studio and exterior production equipment, black and white studio, color studio, mobile van/unit, control room

FACULTY Tom Hennigan, Thomas N Whitehead

COURSE LIST

Undergraduate

Basic Television Production Techniques

Advanced Television Production

Scriptwriting

Undergraduate and Graduate

Television Directing

Southeastern Louisiana University

State-supported comprehensive coed institution. Part of Louisiana State Educational System. Institutionally accredited by regional association. Small town location, 365-acre campus. Total enrollment: 7200. Undergraduate enrollment: 6346. Total faculty: 294 (254 full-time, 40 part-time). Semester calendar. Grading system: letters or numbers.

Teacher Education Department, PO Box 754, University Station, Hammond, LA 70401 504-549-2230

CONTACT John Magee

ADMISSION Requirement — basic audiovisual course Application deadline — rolling

CURRICULAR EMPHASIS Television study — (1) educational; (2) production; (3) management Television production — educational

SPECIAL ACTIVITIES/OFFERINGS Film series, teacher training

FACILITIES AND EQUIPMENT Film — 8mm cameras, editing equipment, lighting equipment, projectors, editing room Television — complete black and white studio production equipment, portable black and white cameras, black and white studio

FACULTY John L Magee

COURSE LIST

Undergraduate and Graduate

Television Production

University of New Orleans

State-supported coed university. Part of Louisiana State University System. Institutionally accredited by regional association, programs recognized by AACSB. Urban location, 195-acre campus. Total enrollment: 13,909. Undergraduate enrollment: 12,033. Total faculty: 534 (461 full-time, 73 part-time). Semester calendar. Grading system: letters or numbers.

Drama and Communications Department, Lakefront, New Orleans, LA 70122 504-283-0317

CONTACT Film — H Wayne Schuth Television — George A Wood

DEGREES OFFERED BA, MA, MFA in drama and communications with a major in film or television

DEPARTMENTAL MAJORS Undergraduate film — 140 students Undergraduate television — 140 students Graduate film — 10 students Graduate television — 10 students

ADMISSION Undergraduate requirement — 2.0 minimum grade point average Graduate requirements — 2.5 minimum grade point average, GRE scores Undergraduate application deadline — 7/1, rolling

FINANCIAL AID Scholarships, student loans, work/study programs, teaching assistantships Undergraduate application deadline — 7/1, rolling

CURRICULAR EMPHASIS Film study — (1) criticism and aesthetics; (2) history; (3) production Filmmaking — (1) narrative; (2) documentary; (3) experimental Undergraduate television study — (1) production; (2) criticism and aesthetics; (3) management Graduate television study — (1) criticism and aesthetics; (2) production; (3) management Undergraduate television production — (1) commercial; (2) news/documentary; (3) experimental/personal video Graduate television production — (1) experimental/personal video; (2) educational; (3) commercial
SPECIAL ACTIVITIES/OFFERINGS Film series, film festivals, student publications, program material produced for on-campus closed-circuit television and cable television, internships in film and television production, independent study, practicum, teacher training
FACILITIES AND EQUIPMENT Film — complete Super-8mm and 16mm equipment, sound stage, screening room, editing room, sound mixing room, animation board, permanent film library Television — complete black and white studio and exterior production equipment, black and white studio, mobile van/unit, audio studio, control room
FACULTY Barbara Alkofer, Mona Brooks, Barbara Coleman, Louis J Dezseran, Stephen Hank, May Jones, H Wayne Schuth, Harlan Shaw, George A Wood PART-TIME FACULTY Patricia Clements

COURSE LIST
Undergraduate
Introduction to Mass Communications
Introduction to Cinema Techniques
Introduction to Television Techniques
Broadcast News
Promotion, Publicity, and Propaganda in Mass Media
Media Graphics and Visuals
Introduction to Theatrical Arts
Lighting for Stage and Screen
Visual Design for Stage, Screen, and Television
Introduction to Acting
Introduction to Journalism in the Mass Media
Advanced Journalism in the Mass Media
The Black Experience on Stage and Screen
Introduction to Directing for Stage and Screen
Media Studio

Graduate
Seminar in Contemporary Cinema
Seminar in the Documentary
Problems in Theatre History and Media
Seminar in Mass Communications
Seminar in the Experimental Film
Seminar in Film Structure
Directing for the Media
Seminar in International Broadcasting

Undergraduate and Graduate
Intermediate Film Production
Scriptwriting
Film Production Management
Advanced Cinema Production
Development of Cinema
Film Theory and Criticism
Advanced Television Production
Mass Media and the Law
Mass Media and Society
Scene Design for Stage and Screen
Costume Design for Stage and Screen
Advanced Acting

University of Southwestern Louisiana

State-supported coed university. Institutionally accredited by regional association, programs recognized by NASM. Urban location, 735-acre campus. Total enrollment: 13,010. Undergraduate enrollment: 11,896. Total faculty: 600 (555 full-time, 45 part-time). Semester calendar. Grading system: letters or numbers.

Speech (Radio/TV) Department, Box 42091, Lafayette, LA 70504 318-264-6140

CONTACT B W Crocker
DEGREES OFFERED BA, MS in mass communications with an emphasis in radio/TV
DEPARTMENTAL MAJORS Undergraduate television — 155 students Graduate television — 3 students
ADMISSION Undergraduate requirement — ACT or SAT scores Graduate requirements — GRE scores, interview, professional work experience, portfolio, production credits Undergraduate application deadline — 5/30
FINANCIAL AID Scholarships, student loans, teaching assistantships (grad only)
CURRICULAR EMPHASIS Undergraduate film study — educational media/instructional technology Graduate film study — educational media/instructional technology Undergraduate filmmaking — documentary, educational treated equally Graduate filmmaking — educational Undergraduate television study — history, educational, production, management treated equally Graduate television study — history, educational, production, management treated equally Undergraduate television production — news/documentary, educational, cultural and enrichment programs treated equally Graduate television production — news/documentary, educational, cultural and enrichment programs treated equally
SPECIAL ACTIVITIES/OFFERINGS Program material produced for on-campus closed-circuit television, cable television, local public television station, local commercial television station; internships in television production
FACILITIES AND EQUIPMENT Film — 16mm cameras, editing equipment, sound recording equipment, lighting, projectors, 35mm cameras, editing room, sound mixing room Television — black and white studio cameras, color studio cameras, 2-inch VTR, ¾-inch cassette VTR, editing equipment, monitors, special effects generators, slide chains, portable color cameras, ¾-inch ENG, lighting equipment, sound recording equipment, audio mixers, film chain, time base corrector, black and white and color studio, audio studio, control room
FACULTY Bernard W Crocker, Gerald Flannery, William Hagerman

COURSE LIST
Undergraduate
Media Writing
Introduction to Mass Media
Media Graphics
Advertising Copywriting
Media Strategy and Planning
Scriptwriting for TV, Radio and Film
Senior Seminar in Mass Communications
Audience Measurement and Sampling
Practicum in Mass Communications
Mass Communications Workshops
Sound Production and Recording
Radio Workshop
Survey of Broadcasting
Broadcast Station Operation
Basic TV Production
Television Workshop
Continuity Writing
Broadcast News Writing
Advanced Sound Production
Television Producing and Directing
Film Production for Television
Broadcast Management
Television News Production
Documentary Production
International Broadcasting
Televised Instruction

MAINE

Bowdoin College

Independent professional coed institution. Accredited by regional association and AICS, programs recognized by NASM. Urban location. Total enrollment: 539. Undergraduate enrollment: 481. Total faculty: 108. Semester calendar. Grading system: letters or numbers.

English Department, Division of Communication, Sills Hall, Brunswick, ME 04011 207-725-8731

CONTACT Barbara Kaster
ADMISSION Application deadline — 2/1
FINANCIAL AID Scholarships, student loans, work/study programs Application deadline — 2/1
CURRICULAR EMPHASIS Film study — (1) history; (2) production Filmmaking — (1) narrative; (2) documentary; (3) experimental Television study — (1) production; (2) educational Television production — (1) news/documentary; (2) commercial; (3) experimental/personal video
SPECIAL ACTIVITIES/OFFERINGS Filmmaking clubs, film series, film festivals, film societies, program material produced for on-campus closed-circuit television and cable television, independent study, practicum
FACILITIES AND EQUIPMENT Film — complete 8mm and 16mm equipment, screening room, editing room, sound mixing room, animation board, permanent film library Television — complete black and white studio and exterior production equipment, black and white studio, audio studio, control room
FACULTY Barbara Kaster PART-TIME FACULTY Ruth Abraham, John McKee

COURSE LIST
Undergraduate
Television Production
Film Production
History, Theory, Criticism of Film

University of Maine at Orono

State-supported coed university. Part of University of Maine System. Institutionally accredited by regional association, programs recognized by NASM, AACSB, NASA. Small town location, 3292-acre campus. Total enrollment: 11,091. Undergraduate enrollment: 10,083. Total faculty: 664 (610 full-time, 54 part-time). Semester calendar. Grading system: letters or numbers.

Art Department, Carnegie Hall, Orono, ME 04469 207-581-7691

CONTACT Michael H Lewis
SPECIAL ACTIVITIES/OFFERINGS Film series
FACILITIES AND EQUIPMENT Film — 8mm cameras, editing equipment, lighting, projectors, tripods
FACULTY Michael H Lewis

COURSE LIST
Undergraduate
Introduction to Filmmaking

Broadcasting/Film Division, School of Performing Arts, Orono, ME 04473 207-581-1110

CONTACT Gregory L Bowler
DEGREE OFFERED BA in broadcasting
PROGRAM MAJORS 40 students
CURRICULAR EMPHASIS Film study — production Filmmaking — documentary Television study — production Television production — commercial, news/documentary, experimental/personal video, educational treated equally
SPECIAL ACTIVITIES/OFFERINGS Program material produced for classroom use, internships in television production, independent study
FACILITIES AND EQUIPMENT Film — 16mm cameras, editing equipment, lighting equipment, projectors, editing room Television — complete black and white studio and exterior production facilities
FACULTY Gregory L Bowler, Robert White

COURSE LIST
Undergraduate
Introduction to Broadcasting
Problems in Broadcasting
Problems in Film
History of Film
Introduction to Filmmaking

Undergraduate and Graduate
Writing for Broadcasting I, II
Basic Television Production
Basic Film Production
Advanced Television Production
Television Laboratory
Broadcasting and Government
Independent Study in Film

English Department, E-M Building 207-581-7307

CONTACT Ulrich Wicks
FACULTY Ulrich Wicks

COURSE LIST
Undergraduate and Graduate
Fiction on Film (offered on demand)

University of New England

Independent comprehensive coed institution. Institutionally accredited by regional association. Small town location, 122-acre campus. Total enrollment: 442. Undergraduate enrollment: 406. Total faculty: 45 (34 full-time, 11 part-time). 4-1-4 calendar. Grading system: letters or numbers.

Media Center, 605 Pool Road, Biddeford, ME 04005 207-283-0172

CONTACT H J Poissant
FINANCIAL AID Scholarships, work/study programs, student loans
CURRICULAR EMPHASIS Undergraduate television study — educational, production treated equally Undergraduate television production — experimental/personal video, educational treated equally
FACILITIES AND EQUIPMENT Film — 8mm cameras, editing equipment, lighting, projectors, 16mm projectors, 35mm cameras, lighting, permanent film library of commercial or professional films Television — black and white studio cameras, ½-inch VTR, ¾-inch cassette VTR, portable black and white cameras, monitors, ½-inch portapak recorders, lighting equipment, audio mixers, black and white studio

University of Southern Maine

State-supported comprehensive coed institution. Institutionally accredited by regional association. Small town location. Total enrollment: 8000. Total faculty: 300. Semester calendar. Grading system: letters or numbers.

Department of Art, College Avenue, Gorham, ME 04038 207-780-5460

CONTACT Juris Ubans
FINANCIAL AID Scholarships, work/study programs, student loans
CURRICULAR EMPHASIS Undergraduate film study — history, criticism and aesthetics, appreciation treated equally
SPECIAL ACTIVITIES/OFFERINGS Filmmaking clubs, film series, film festivals, program material produced for cable television, independent study
FACULTY Juris Ubans

COURSE LIST
Undergraduate
Film as Image and Idea
Topics in Film

MARYLAND

Allegany Community College

State-supported 2-year coed college. Institutionally accredited by regional association. Suburban location, 370-acre campus. Undergraduate enrollment: 1791. Total faculty: 98 (80 full-time, 18 part-time). Semester calendar. Grading system: letters or numbers.

Media Technology Department, Willowbrook Road, Cumberland, MD 21502 301-724-7700, ext 330

CONTACT Film — Sam Parsons Television — Ken White
DEGREE OFFERED AA in media technology
DEPARTMENTAL MAJORS Film — 22 students Television — 22 students
ADMISSION Requirement — interview Application deadline — 8/22
FINANCIAL AID Scholarships, work/study programs, student loans Application deadline — midsummer
CURRICULAR EMPHASIS Film study — (1) educational media/instructional technology; (2) appreciation; (3) criticism and aesthetics Filmmaking — (1) experimental; (2) narrative; (3) animated Television study — (1) production; (2) management; (3) criticism and aesthetics Television production — (1) news/documentary; (2) experimental/personal video; (3) commercial
SPECIAL ACTIVITIES/OFFERINGS Film festivals, TV news show, program material produced for on-campus closed-circuit television and cable television, independent study
FACILITIES AND EQUIPMENT Film — complete 8mm and 35mm equipment, editing room, sound mixing room, animation board, permanent film library of student films Television — black and white studio cameras, color studio cameras, ½-inch VTR, 1-inch VTR, ¾-inch cassette VTR, portable black and white cameras, editing equipment, monitors, special effects generators, slide chain, portable color cameras, ½-inch portapak recorders, lighting equipment, sound recording equipment, audio mixers, film chain, black and white studio, color studio, audio studio, control room
FACULTY Sam Parsons, Ken White

COURSE LIST
Undergraduate
Film Production
Television I, II

Anne Arundel Community College

County-supported 2-year coed college. Institutionally accredited by regional association. Suburban location. Undergraduate enrollment: 6502. Total faculty: 355 (167 full-time, 188 part-time). Semester calendar. Grading system: letters or numbers.

Anne Arundel Community College (continued)

Communications Arts Technology Department, 101 College Parkway, Arnold, MD 21012 301-647-7100

CONTACT Ernest Berger Jr
DEGREE OFFERED AA in communications arts technology
ADMISSION Requirement — minimum grade point average
FINANCIAL AID Student loans, work/study programs
CURRICULAR EMPHASIS Film study — (1) educational media/instructional technology; (2) production; (3) criticism and aesthetics Filmmaking — documentary, narrative, experimental, animated, educational treated equally Television study — (1) production; (2) criticism and aesthetics; (3) educational Television production — (1) educational; (2) commercial; (3) experimental/personal video
SPECIAL ACTIVITIES/OFFERINGS Film series, film festivals, program material produced for cable television, internships in television production, independent study, practicum, teacher training, vocational placement service
FACILITIES AND EQUIPMENT Film — complete 8mm equipment, sound stage, screening room, editing room, sound mixing room, animation board, permanent film library Television — complete black and white studio and exterior production equipment, complete color studio production equipment, electronic editing equipment, black and white studio, color studio, audio studio, control room
FACULTY Ernest A Berger, Joyce E Drenanz, H Scott McCann, James M Privitera, Richard Weinberg PART-TIME FACULTY Timothy Gaither

COURSE LIST
Undergraduate
Landmarks of the American Film
Landmarks of World Cinema
Basic Television Utilization
Studio Television Methods
Basic Film Making
Advanced Film Making
Radio Station Operations and Orientation
Studio Lighting Methods
Photography I, II

Bowie State College

State-supported comprehensive coed institution. Institutionally accredited by regional association. Suburban location. Total enrollment: 2722. Undergraduate enrollment: 1877. Total faculty: 159 (102 full-time, 57 part-time). Semester calendar. Grading system: letters or numbers.

Department of Communication, Bowie, MD 20715 301-464-3000

CONTACT Elaine Bournie Heath
DEGREES OFFERED BA, BS in communications
ADMISSION Undergraduate application deadline — rolling

Capitol Institute of Technology

Independent professional 4-year coed college. Institutionally accredited by regional association. Suburban location, 3-acre campus. Undergraduate enrollment: 525. Total faculty: 26 (10 full-time, 16 part-time). Quarter calendar. Grading system: letters or numbers.

Humanities Department, Kensington, MD 20795 301-933-3300

CONTACT Chairman
ADMISSION Application deadline — rolling

Charles County Community College

State and locally supported 2-year coed college. Institutionally accredited by regional association. Rural location. Undergraduate enrollment: 3462. Total faculty: 218 (44 full-time, 174 part-time). Semester calendar. Grading system: letters or numbers.

English Department, PO Box 910, La Plata, MD 20646 301-934-2251

CONTACT Roger Horn
ADMISSION Application deadline — rolling
FINANCIAL AID Scholarships, student loans, work/study programs Application deadline — rolling
CURRICULAR EMPHASIS Film study — (1) criticism and aesthetics; (2) history; (3) appreciation Filmmaking — (1) narrative; (2) documentary; (3) experimental
SPECIAL ACTIVITIES/OFFERINGS Film series
FACILITIES AND EQUIPMENT Film — 8mm and 16mm projectors
FACULTY Roger Horn

COURSE LIST
Undergraduate
Film as an Art Form

College of Notre Dame of Maryland

Independent Roman Catholic 4-year college primarily for women. Institutionally accredited by regional association. Suburban location. Undergraduate enrollment: 653. Total faculty: 75 (55 full-time, 20 part-time). 4-1-4 calendar. Grading system: letters or numbers.

Communications Department, 4701 North Charles Street, Baltimore, MD 21210 301-435-0100

CONTACT Film — Sister M Elena McCormack Television — Sister Patricia Ostdick

DEGREE OFFERED BA in communication arts with an emphasis in broadcasting
DEPARTMENTAL MAJORS 55 students
ADMISSION Requirements — ACT or SAT scores, interview
FINANCIAL AID Scholarships, work/study programs, student loans
CURRICULAR EMPHASIS Film study — appreciation Television study — production, theoretical treated equally Television production — commercial, news/documentary treated equally
SPECIAL ACTIVITIES/OFFERINGS Internships in television production, independent study
FACILITIES AND EQUIPMENT Film — 8mm cameras, editing equipment, lighting, color film stock, projectors, screening room, editing room Television — black and white studio cameras, ½-inch VTR, ¾-inch cassette VTR, portable black and white cameras, monitors, special effects generators, slide chain, lighting equipment, sound recording equipment, audio mixers, black and white studio, audio studio, control room
FACULTY Sister M Elena McCormack, Sister Patricia Ostdick PART-TIME FACULTY Sister Sharon Dei

Dundalk Community College

County-supported 2-year coed college. Part of Baltimore County Community Colleges System. Institutionally accredited by regional association. Suburban location. 4-1-4 calendar. Grading system: letters or numbers.

Media Technology Department, 7200 Sollers Point Road, Dundalk, MD 21222 301-282-6700, ext 312

CONTACT Penny Alexander
DEGREE OFFERED AA in media technology
DEPARTMENTAL MAJORS 5 students
ADMISSION Application deadline — 9/1
FINANCIAL AID Scholarships, work/study programs, student loans
CURRICULAR EMPHASIS Film study — production Filmmaking — production Television study — production Television production — basics
SPECIAL ACTIVITIES/OFFERINGS Film series; film festivals; program material produced for on-campus closed-circuit television, cable television, local public television station, local commercial television station; internships in film production; internships in television production; independent study; vocational placement assistance
FACILITIES AND EQUIPMENT Film — complete 8mm equipment, editing room, sound mixing room, permanent film library of commercial or professional films Television — color studio cameras, ½-inch VTR, ¾-inch cassette VTR, portable black and white cameras, editing equipment, monitors, slide chain, portable color cameras, ½-inch portapak recorders, lighting equipment, sound recording equipment, audio mixers, film chain, time base corrector, color studio, mobile unit, audio studio, control room
PART-TIME FACULTY Penny Alexander, Tom Burton, Alan Lifton, Mary Jo Tarello, Robert Tracey

COURSE LIST

Undergraduate
Filmmaking
Television I, II

Essex Community College

State and locally supported 2-year coed college. Part of Baltimore County Community Colleges System. Institutionally accredited by regional association. Suburban location, 150-acre campus. Undergraduate enrollment: 9785. Total faculty: 392 (204 full-time, 188 part-time). Semester calendar. Grading system: letters or numbers.

Department of Speech Communication and Theatre, Humanities and Arts Division, 2701 Rossville Boulevard, Baltimore County, MD 21237 301-682-6000

CONTACT John R Lyston
ADMISSION Requirement — minimum grade point average
CURRICULAR EMPHASIS Film study — (1) history; (2) appreciation; (3) criticism and aesthetics Filmmaking — (1) narrative; (2) documentary; (3) educational
SPECIAL ACTIVITIES/OFFERINGS Film series
FACULTY John R Lyston

COURSE LIST

Undergraduate
The Movies: Historical and Aesthetic Perspectives

Frostburg State College

State-supported comprehensive coed institution. Institutionally accredited by regional association. Small town location, 220-acre campus. Total enrollment: 3600. Undergraduate enrollment: 3200. Total faculty: 185 (150 full-time, 35 part-time). Semester calendar. Grading system: letters or numbers.

Communication Media Department, Frostburg, MD 21532 301-689-4353

CONTACT Howard Parnes
PROGRAM OFFERED Minor in film
ADMISSION Requirement — interviews Application deadline — rolling
FINANCIAL AID Student loans, work/study programs Application deadline — 1/5
CURRICULAR EMPHASIS Film study — (1) production; (2) educational media/instructional technology; (3) criticism and aesthetics Filmmaking — (1) narrative; (2) documentary; (3) educational Television study — (1) production; (2) educational; (3) appreciation Television production — (1) experimental/personal video; (2) educational; (3) news/documentary

Frostburg State College (continued)

SPECIAL ACTIVITIES/OFFERINGS Film series, independent study
FACILITIES AND EQUIPMENT Film — complete 8mm and 16mm equipment, screening room, editing room, sound mixing room, animation board Television — complete black and white exterior production equipment, audio studio
FACULTY Howard Parnes PART-TIME FACULTY David Press

COURSE LIST
Undergraduate
Introduction to Film Studies
Film Production Workshops
Screenwriting
Production of Communication Materials
Independent Studies

Goucher College

Independent comprehensive women's institution. Accredited by regional association and AICS. Suburban location, 330-acre campus. Total enrollment: 1053. Undergraduate enrollment: 1039. Total faculty: 122. Semester calendar. Grading system: letters or numbers.

Communication Department, Towson, MD 21204 301-825-3300

CONTACT Brownlee Sands Corrin
DEGREE OFFERED BA in communication
DEPARTMENTAL MAJORS Undergraduate television — 6 students
ADMISSION Requirement — normal college admission Undergraduate application deadline — 3/1
FINANCIAL AID Scholarships, work/study programs, student loans Undergraduate application deadline — rolling
CURRICULAR EMPHASIS Television study — production, management, content and effects analyses treated equally Television production — commercial, news/documentary, entertainment treated equally
SPECIAL ACTIVITIES/OFFERINGS Program material produced for academic courses, college archives, faculty lecture/presentations; internships in television production; independent study in television
FACILITIES AND EQUIPMENT Television — complete black and white and color studio production equipment available through local production studio, ½-inch VTR, ¾-inch cassette VTR, editing equipment, monitors, lighting equipment, sound recording equipment, audio mixers, ½ VHS (VCR) recorder, playback, color camera, black and white studio, color studio, audio studio, control room
FACULTY Brownlee Sands Corrin

COURSE LIST
Undergraduate
Technique and Performance in Broadcast Media
Broadcast Media Production
Recording and Broadcast Engineering
Video Production
Media: Management and Content
Communication and Emotion
Wit, Humor and Satire in Mass Communication
Persuasive Communication
Human Communication
Internships and Independent Work in Communication

Hagerstown Junior College

County-supported 2-year coed college. Institutionally accredited by regional association. Suburban location, 187-acre campus. Undergraduate enrollment: 2244. Total faculty: 107 (61 full-time, 46 part-time). Semester calendar. Grading system: letters or numbers.

Communications, Humanities Department, 751 Robinwood Drive, Hagerstown, MD 21740 301-790-2800

CONTACT Ralph Chapin
DEGREE OFFERED AA
FINANCIAL AID Work/study programs
CURRICULAR EMPHASIS Television study — production
FACILITIES AND EQUIPMENT Television — complete black and white and color studio production equipment, black and white studio, color studio, audio studio, control room
FACULTY Ralph Chapin, Dixie LeHardy, Robert Mitchell, Larry Sharpe

COURSE LIST
Undergraduate
Fundamentals of Radio and Television
Radio and Television Continuity Writing
Television Production
Communication Internship

Hood College

Independent comprehensive institution primarily for women. Institutionally accredited by regional association. Suburban location, 100-acre campus. Total enrollment: 1783. Undergraduate enrollment: 1190. Total faculty: 140 (83 full-time, 57 part-time). Semester calendar. Grading system: letters or numbers.

English and Communications, Rosemont Avenue, Frederick, MD 21701 301-663-3131

CONTACT Stephen Hu
DEGREE OFFERED BA in communications
ADMISSION Application deadline — rolling
FINANCIAL AID Scholarships, work/study programs, student loans
CURRICULAR EMPHASIS Film study — (1) appreciation; (2) history; (3) criticism and aesthetics Filmmaking — (1) documentary; (2) narrative Television production — (1) news/documentary; (2) educational
SPECIAL ACTIVITIES/OFFERINGS Film series, film societies, internships in film production, independent study, teacher training, vocational placement service

FACILITIES AND EQUIPMENT Film — complete 8mm equipment, screening room, editing room, permanent film library of commercial or professional films Television — ¾-inch cassette VTR, portable black and white cameras, editing equipment, monitors, lighting equipment, sound recording equipment, automatic editing equipment

Johns Hopkins University

Independent coed university. Institutionally accredited by regional association. Suburban location, 140-acre campus. Total enrollment: 2963. Undergraduate enrollment: 2156. Total faculty: 382 (307 full-time, 75 part-time). 4-1-4 calendar. Grading system: letters or numbers.

The Humanities Center, Baltimore, MD 21218 301-338-7616 or 301-338-7619

CONTACT Film — Richard Macksey Television — Bruce Jaffe
DEGREES OFFERED BA with film and video concentrations within humanistic studies area major, MA/PhD with critical and historical work in film as part of comparative literature program
PROGRAM MAJORS Undergraduate film — 10 students Undergraduate television — 12 students Graduate film — 3 students
ADMISSION Graduate requirements — GRE scores, interview, teachers' recommendations, written statement of purpose
FINANCIAL AID Work/study programs, student loans, fellowships, teaching assistantships
CURRICULAR EMPHASIS Undergraduate film study — history, criticism and aesthetics, appreciation treated equally Graduate film study — history, criticism and aesthetics, appreciation treated equally Undergraduate filmmaking — (1) documentary; (2) narrative; (3) experimental Undergraduate television study — (1) production; (2) criticism and aesthetics; (3) educational Undergraduate television production — (1) news/documentary; (2) experimental/personal video; (3) educational
SPECIAL ACTIVITIES/OFFERINGS Filmmaking clubs, film series, film festivals, film societies, program material produced for on-campus closed-circuit television and local public television station, apprenticeships, internships in film production, internships in television production, independent study
FACILITIES AND EQUIPMENT Film — complete 8mm and 16mm equipment, 35mm projectors, screening room, 35mm screening facilities, editing room, animation board, permanent film library of student films, permanent film library of commercial or professional films Television — complete black and white and color studio production equipment, complete black and white and color exterior production equipment
FACULTY Leo Braudy, Stanley E Fish, John Irwin, Bruce Jaffe, Hugh Kenner, Richard Macksey, Mark C Miller, Bonita Perry, Stuart Rome, Carl Schultz, Ronald Walter, George Wilson, Sam Zappas

COURSE LIST

Undergraduate

Novels into Film: An Introduction to Visual and Verbal Literacy
The American Cinema
History of the Silent Film
Film: Theory and Practice
Video Production Workshop
Film Aesthetics
Media Center Internship
Film Production Workshop
Reading Toward Performance
Lighting Workshop (Intersession)

Graduate

Signs and Society: C S Peirce
Dissertation Research
Eye and Mind

Undergraduate and Graduate

The Films of Ingmar Bergman
Directed Readings in History of Film
Verbal and Visual Representation
The French Cinema
The Films and Fictions of Robert Bresson
Evolution of the Genre Film
The Director's Cinema (courses have been devoted to Kubrick, Renoir, Antonioni, Hitchcock)
Criticism and the Audio-Visual Media
Photography Seminar

Loyola College

Independent Roman Catholic comprehensive coed institution. Institutionally accredited by regional association. Suburban location. Total enrollment: 4136. Undergraduate enrollment: 1946. Total faculty: 302 (114 full-time, 188 part-time). 4-1-4 calendar. Grading system: letters or numbers.

English/Fine Arts Department, 4501 North Charles Street, Baltimore, MD 21210 301-323-1010, ext 335

CONTACT Ed Ross
DEGREE OFFERED BA in fine arts with an emphasis in film, photography, or media
DEPARTMENTAL MAJORS Film — 3 students Television — 2 students
ADMISSION Requirement — ACT or SAT scores Undergraduate application deadline — 7/31
FINANCIAL AID Scholarships, work/study programs, student loans
CURRICULAR EMPHASIS Film study — history, criticism and aesthetics, appreciation treated equally
SPECIAL ACTIVITIES/OFFERINGS Film series, internships in television production, independent study
FACILITIES AND EQUIPMENT Film — 8mm cameras, editing equipment, lighting, projectors

COURSE LIST

Undergraduate

History of Film I, II
Contemporary Cinema
Internships

Montgomery College—Rockville Campus

State and locally supported 2-year coed college. Institutionally accredited by regional association. Suburban location. Undergraduate enrollment: 11,208. Total faculty: 542 (263 full-time, 279 part-time). Semester calendar. Grading system: letters or numbers.

Montgomery College—Rockville Campus (continued)

51 Mannakee Street, Rockville, MD 20850 301-279-5256

CONTACT Philip B Martin
DEGREE OFFERED AA with a television or radio option
PROGRAM MAJORS Television — 125 students
ADMISSION Open door policy
FINANCIAL AID Scholarships, work/study programs, student loans
CURRICULAR EMPHASIS Film study — (1) production; (2) appreciation; (3) educational media/instructional technology Filmmaking — (1) documentary; (2) educational; (3) narrative Television study — (1) production; (2) educational; (3) appreciation Television production — (1) news/documentary; (2) educational; (3) experimental/personal video
SPECIAL ACTIVITIES/OFFERINGS Program material produced for on-campus closed-circuit television, internships in film production, internships in television production, independent study, Alpha Epsilon Rho broadcast fraternity chapter
FACILITIES AND EQUIPMENT Film — complete 16mm equipment, 8mm cameras, editing equipment, lighting, color film stock, projectors, 16mm audio transfer, sound stage, screening room, editing room, sound mixing room Television — black and white studio cameras, color studio cameras, ½-inch VTR, 1-inch VTR, ¾-inch cassette VTR, portable black and white cameras, editing equipment, monitors, special effects generators, slide chain, portable color cameras, ½-inch portapak recorders, ¾-inch ENG, lighting equipment, sound recording equipment, audio mixers, film chain, character generator, chroma-keyer, mini-cam units, color studio, audio studio, control room, separate editing room (¾-inch)
FACULTY Philip B Martin, Christianne H Schafer, William Torrey PART-TIME FACULTY Robert Priseler, William Shade, Steve Siegel, Harry A Swope

COURSE LIST

Undergraduate

Audiovisual Technology
Media Appreciation
Introduction to Broadcasting
Television Production
Audio Production Techniques
Radio Production
Broadcast Journalism
Television Directing
Writing for TV, Radio, and Film
Advanced Television Production
Basic Photography
Cinematography
Broadcast Management and Engineering
Advanced Broadcast Journalism
Radio Station Operation
TV Station Operation
Electronic News Gathering
Film Production
TV/Radio Internship Program

Maryland

Mount Saint Mary's College

Independent Roman Catholic comprehensive coed institution. Institutionally accredited by regional association. Rural location, 1500-acre campus. Total enrollment: 1555. Undergraduate enrollment: 1405. Total faculty: 83 (68 full-time, 15 part-time). Semester and optional January term calendar. Grading system: letters or numbers.

Communication Arts Department, Emmitsburg, MD 21727 301-447-6122

CONTACT Robert Ducharme
PROGRAM OFFERED — Minor in communication of which film study is a part
CURRICULAR EMPHASIS Film study — history, criticism and aesthetics, appreciation treated equally
SPECIAL ACTIVITIES/OFFERINGS Film series
PART-TIME FACULTY Robert Ducharme

COURSE LIST

Undergraduate

American Film History
Film Comedy
The Western
Major Directors

Prince George's Community College

County-supported 2-year coed college. Institutionally accredited by regional association. Suburban location. Undergraduate enrollment: 13,828. Total faculty: 645 (238 full-time, 407 part-time). Semester plus 2 summer sessions calendar. Grading system: letters or numbers.

Department of Speech Communication and Theatre, Largo, MD 20870 301-366-6000

CONTACT Martin Burke
ADMISSION Application deadline — 7/1, rolling
FINANCIAL AID Work/study programs Application deadline — 5/15
CURRICULAR EMPHASIS Film study — (1) history; (2) appreciation; (3) criticism and aesthetics Television study — (1) production; (2) criticism and aesthetics; (3) history Television production — (1) news/documentary; (2) experimental/personal video; (3) commercial
SPECIAL ACTIVITIES/OFFERINGS Filmmaking clubs, film series, program material produced for on-campus closed-circuit television
FACILITIES AND EQUIPMENT Film — 8mm cameras, editing equipment, lighting equipment, color film stock, projectors, 16mm screening room, permanent film library Television — complete black and white studio and exterior production equipment, black and white studio, audio studio, control room
FACULTY Martin Burke, Mary Stevenson

COURSE LIST

Undergraduate

Introduction to Film
Television Production

Salisbury State College

State-supported comprehensive coed institution. Part of Maryland State Colleges and Universities System. Institutionally accredited by regional association. Small town location. Total enrollment: 4361. Undergraduate enrollment: 3644. Total faculty: 238 (183 full-time, 55 part-time). Semester calendar. Grading system: letters or numbers.

Film Concentration, English Department, Salisbury, MD 21801 301-546-3261

CONTACT Film — Jim Welsh Television — John Balas
DEGREES OFFERED BA in English/film, BA in communications/media
DEPARTMENTAL MAJORS Film — 10 students Television — 10 students
ADMISSION Requirements — ACT or SAT scores, professional work experience
FINANCIAL AID Work/study programs, student loans
CURRICULAR EMPHASIS Film study — history, criticism and aesthetics, appreciation, educational media/instructional technology treated equally Filmmaking — narrative, educational treated equally Television study — production Television production — commercial, educational treated equally
SPECIAL ACTIVITIES/OFFERINGS Film series, film festivals, literature/film quarterly publication, program material produced for on-campus closed-circuit television, apprenticeships, internships in television production, independent study, teacher training
FACILITIES AND EQUIPMENT Film — 8mm cameras, editing equipment, sound recording equipment, projectors, 16mm projectors, screening room, permanent film library of commercial or professional films Television — complete black and white studio production equipment, black and white studio
FACULTY John Balas, Thomas L Erskine, Leland Starnes, James M Welsh, Art Wilby, Kenneth Wilkerson

COURSE LIST

Undergraduate
Introduction to Film
Film History
Literature and Film
Film Genre
Elements of Filmmaking
Television Production
Radio and TV Announcing
Mass Media and Society

Undergraduate and Graduate
Major Directors
Workshop in Critical Reviewing

Towson State University

State-supported comprehensive coed institution. Institutionally accredited by regional association. Urban location. Total enrollment: 15,340. Undergraduate enrollment: 13,499. Total faculty: 811 (449 full-time, 362 part-time). 4-1-4 calendar. Grading system: letters or numbers.

Speech and Mass Communication Department, 8000 York Road, Baltimore, MD 21204 301-321-2891

CONTACT Film — Barry Moore Television — William Poulos
DEGREES OFFERED BA, BS in mass communication
ADMISSION Requirements — 2.0 minimum grade point average, SAT scores Application deadline — 3/1, rolling
FINANCIAL AID Scholarships, student loans, work/study programs Application deadline — 4/1
CURRICULAR EMPHASIS Film study — (1) production; (2) criticism and aesthetics; (3) history Filmmaking — (1) documentary, narrative; (2) experimental; (3) animated Television study — (1) production; (2) appreciation; (3) criticism and aesthetics Television production — (1) experimental/personal video; (2) news/documentary; (3) commercial
SPECIAL ACTIVITIES/OFFERINGS Filmmaking clubs, film series, film festivals, film societies, student publications, apprenticeships, internships in film and television production, independent study
FACILITIES AND EQUIPMENT Film — complete 8mm and 16mm equipment, editing room, sound mixing room, animation board Television — complete black and white studio and exterior production equipment, complete color studio production equipment, black and white studio, color studio, audio studio, control room
FACULTY Barry Moore, William Poulos

COURSE LIST

Undergraduate
Basic Television Techniques
Advanced Television Techniques
Television Writing
Independent Study in Television
Internship in Television
Introduction to Film
Film Communication (Production)
Practica
Aesthetics of Film
History of Film
Independent Study in Film

University of Maryland at College Park

State-supported coed university. Part of University of Maryland System. Institutionally accredited by regional association, programs recognized by NASM, AACSB, ACPE. Suburban location, 1300-acre campus. Total enrollment: 36,905. Undergraduate enrollment: 29,422. Total faculty: 2018 (1614 full-time, 404 part-time). Semester calendar. Grading system: letters or numbers.

Radio-Television-Film Division, College Park, MD 20742 301-454-2541

CONTACT Robert F McCleary
DEGREES OFFERED BA, MA in cinema study; BA, MA in film production; BA, MA in history and criticism; BA, MA in television production; BA, MA in television studies; PhD in public communications
PROGRAM MAJORS Undergraduate film — 150 students Undergraduate television — 500 students Graduate film — 30 students Graduate television — 30 students

University of Maryland at College Park (continued)

ADMISSION Undergraduate requirements — 2.0 minimum grade point average, professional recommendations, teachers' recommendations, written statement of purpose Graduate requirements — 3.0 minimum grade point average, GRE scores, portfolio, professional recommendations, teachers' recommendations, written statement of purpose
FINANCIAL AID Scholarships, student loans, work/study programs, teaching assistantships, research assistantships, fellowships
CURRICULAR EMPHASIS Film study — history, criticism and aesthetics, production treated equally Filmmaking — depends upon current student interest Television study — history, criticism and aesthetics, appreciation, production, educational, management treated equally Television production — commercial, news/documentary, experimental/personal video, educational treated equally
SPECIAL ACTIVITIES/OFFERINGS Filmmaking clubs, film series, film festivals, film societies, student publications, apprenticeships, internships in film and television production, independent study, practicum, teacher training
FACILITIES AND EQUIPMENT Film — 8mm cameras, editing equipment, lighting, color film stock, projectors, 16mm cameras, editing equipment, sound recording equipment, lighting, color film stock, projectors, screening room, editing room, sound mixing room, permanent film library of student films Television — complete black and white and color studio production equipment, complete color exterior production equipment, black and white studio, color studio, audio production studios, audio editing studio, control room
FACULTY Thomas Aylward, James Baldwin, Michael DuMonceau, Terry Hinch, Donald Kirkley, Robert Kolker, Robert McCleary, Grover Niemeyer, Gene Robinson, Judith Saxton, Harvey Thompson, Gene Weiss PART-TIME FACULTY Larry Lichty, David Parker, Joseph Philport

COURSE LIST

Undergraduate

Mass Communications in 20th Century Society (for nonmajors)
Introduction to Radio
The Television Program Planning and Management
Sound Production
Introduction to Film
Radio and Television Continuity Writing
Public Broadcasting
Television Production
Television News and Public Affairs
Television Programming
Film Production I: Introduction
Film Production II: Cinematography
Field Work Experience
Field Work Analysis
Advanced Sound Production
The History of Film
Contemporary America Cinema
Contemporary European Cinema
Dramatic Writing for Broadcasting and Film
The Film Auteur (Hitchcock, Griffith, Kurosawa, Godard, etc.)
Film Genres (Black Image, the Comedy Film, the Political Film, the War Film, etc.)
The Documentary Film
Film Criticism and Theory
Television and Politics
Television Direction I, II
Television Workshop
Radio and Television Station Management
Broadcast Criticism
International and Comparative Broadcasting Systems
Broadcasting and Government
Cable Television
Film Production III: Synchronous Sound Film Systems
Film Production IV: Advanced
Seminar (Cable TV, Children in Television, Perspectives in Management, TV Commercial: Selling of America, Plug in Drug)

Graduate

Visual Communication
Formal Film Analysis
Seminar in Film
Special Problems in Film
History of Broadcasting
Introduction to Graduate Study
Seminar in Broadcasting and Film
Special Problems in Broadcasting and Film
Advanced Television Direction

Undergraduate and Graduate

Contemporary American Cinema
Contemporary European Cinema
The Documentary Film
Dramatic Writing for Broadcasting and Film
Television and Politics
Television Direction
Television Workshop
Radio and Television Station Management
Broadcasting and Government
Advanced Film Production
Broadcast Criticism
Film as an Art Form
International and Comparative Broadcast Systems
History of the Film
The Film Genre
Elements of the Film
Criticism and Theory

American Studies Department

CONTACT Myron Lounsbury
CURRICULAR EMPHASIS Film study — cultural history Television study — cultural
FACULTY Myron Lounsbury, Lawrence Mintz

COURSE LIST

Undergraduate and Graduate

Popular Film in America
Film in American Culture
Popular Culture in America

University of Maryland, Baltimore County

State-supported coed university. Part of University of Maryland System. Institutionally accredited by regional association, programs recognized by NASM, NASA. Suburban location. Total enrollment: 5396. Undergraduate enrollment: 5000. Total faculty: 330. 4-1-4 calendar. Grading system: letters or numbers.

Visual Arts Department, 5401 Wilkens Avenue, Catonsville, MD 21228 301-455-2150 or 301-455-2959

CONTACT LeRoy Morais
DEGREE OFFERED BA in visual and performing arts with an emphasis in visual arts and a concentration in film or video
DEPARTMENTAL MAJORS Film — 65 students Television — 10 students
ADMISSION Requirements — ACT or SAT scores, interview, written statement of purpose
FINANCIAL AID Scholarships, work/study programs, student loans Application deadline — 3/31

CURRICULAR EMPHASIS Film study — (1) criticism and aesthetics; (2) history; (3) appreciation Filmmaking — documentary, narrative, experimental, animated treated equally Television study — (1) video art; (2) production; (3) criticism and aesthetics Television production — (1) experimental/personal video; (2) news/documentary; (3) educational
SPECIAL ACTIVITIES/OFFERINGS Film series, film festivals, program material produced for cable television and as independent work for festivals and competition, internships in film production, internships in television production, independent study
FACILITIES AND EQUIPMENT Film — complete 8mm and 16mm equipment, sound stage, screening room, editing room, sound mixing room, animation board, permanent film library of commercial or professional films, optical printer, computer graphics terminal, video colorizer, 16mm and Super-8 to video transfer Television — complete black and white and color studio production equipment, black and white studio, color studio, postproduction image reprocessing/synthesis
FACULTY James A Fasanelli, LeRoy Morais, Fred Stern, Stan Vanderbeek

COURSE LIST

Undergraduate

Basic Filmmaking
Basic Video
Documentary Film
Animation
Experimental Film
Narrative Form
Intermediate/Advanced Video
Screenwriting
Advanced Film or Video
Independent Studies

Western Maryland College

Independent comprehensive coed institution. Institutionally accredited by regional association, programs recognized by NASM. Small town location, 160-acre campus. Total enrollment: 2104. Undergraduate enrollment: 1359. Total faculty: 119 (85 full-time, 34 part-time). 4-1-4 calendar. Grading system: letters or numbers.

Theatre Arts Department, Westminster, MD 21157 301-848-7000, ext 590

CONTACT Ken Gargaro, Chairperson
ADMISSION Application deadline — rolling

COURSE LIST

Undergraduate

Introduction to the Film
Special Studies in Dramatic Art
Screenwriting

MASSACHUSETTS

Amherst College

Independent 4-year college, coed as of 1975. Institutionally accredited by regional association. Small town location, 950-acre campus. Undergraduate enrollment: 1463. Total faculty: 175 (155 full-time, 20 part-time). 4-0-4 calendar. Grading system: letters or numbers.

Dramatic Arts Department, Amherst, MA 01002 413-542-2000

CONTACT Helene Keyssar
ADMISSION Application deadline — 2/1
FACULTY Helene Keyssar

COURSE LIST

Undergraduate

Problems in Film Criticism
The Art of the Film

Assumption College

Independent Roman Catholic comprehensive coed institution. Institutionally accredited by regional association. Suburban location, 140-acre campus. Total enrollment: 2400. Undergraduate enrollment: 1400. Total faculty: 100 (70 full-time, 30 part-time). 4-1-4 calendar. Grading system: letters or numbers.

500 Salisbury Street, Worcester, MA 01609 617-752-5615

CONTACT Film — Richard Oehling Television — Roger Trahan
ADMISSION Application deadline — 3/1, rolling
FINANCIAL AID Scholarships, student loans, work/study programs Application deadline — 2/1, rolling
CURRICULAR EMPHASIS Film study — (1) criticism and aesthetics; (2) history; (3) educational media/instructional technology Filmmaking — (1) narrative; (2) educational Television study — (1) management; (2) production Television production — educational
SPECIAL ACTIVITIES/OFFERINGS Film series, film festivals, program material produced for on-campus closed-circuit television, internships in television production, independent study
FACILITIES AND EQUIPMENT Film — film production facilities available through the consortium arrangement Television — complete color studio production equipment, color studio, control room
FACULTY John Burke, Richard Oehling, Roger Trahan

Assumption College (continued)

COURSE LIST

Undergraduate

History and Film
The American Film Since 1940
Radio and Television Writing
Television Production

Graduate

The Historian and Film

Boston College

Independent Roman Catholic coed university. Accredited by regional association and AICS, programs recognized by AACSB. Suburban location, 200-acre campus. Total enrollment: 13,313. Undergraduate enrollment: 10,185. Total faculty: 674 (542 full-time, 132 part-time). Semester calendar. Grading system: letters or numbers.

Fine Arts Department, 855 Centre Street, Newton Centre, MA 02159

CONTACT Film — Fine Arts Department (Newton campus) Television — Speech and Communications Department (main campus)
PROGRAM OFFERED Major in communication: radio, television, journalism
PROGRAM MAJORS Undergraduate television — 10 students
ADMISSION Requirements — ACT or SAT scores, interview, teachers' recommendations, written statement of purpose
FINANCIAL AID Scholarships, work/study programs, student loans
CURRICULAR EMPHASIS Film study — (1) history (especially European); (2) criticism and aesthetics; (3) educational media/instructional technology Filmmaking — (1) animated; (2) narrative; (3) documentary Television study — criticism and aesthetics, appreciation, production, management treated equally Television production — commercial, news/documentary, experimental/personal video treated equally
SPECIAL ACTIVITIES/OFFERINGS Film series, film festivals, program material produced for local commercial television station, internships in television production, independent study
FACILITIES AND EQUIPMENT Television — black and white studio cameras, ½-inch VTR, ¾-inch cassette VTR, portable black and white cameras, editing equipment, monitors, special effects generators, ½-inch portapak recorders, lighting equipment, sound recording equipment, audio mixers, black and white studio, audio studio, control room

COURSE LIST

Undergraduate

Propaganda Film
The American Film
History of European Film
Animated Film
Elementary and Intermediate Filmmaking
Pleiade of French Literary Filmmakers
The Documentary Film
Eastern European Film

Massachusetts

Boston State College

State-supported 4-year and professional coed institution. Urban location. Undergraduate enrollment: 5000. Total faculty: 354. Semester calendar. Grading system: letters.

Art Department, 625 Huntington Avenue, Boston, MA 02115 617-731-3300, ext 405

CONTACT R Polito
PROGRAM OFFERED Minor in film and photography
ADMISSION Undergraduate requirement — admission to the college Graduate requirement — admission to the college
FINANCIAL AID Work/study programs
CURRICULAR EMPHASIS Undergraduate film study — history, criticism and aesthetics, appreciation treated equally Graduate film study — history, criticism and aesthetics, appreciation treated equally Undergraduate filmmaking — (1) documentary, narrative; (2) experimental; (3) animated Graduate filmmaking — (1) documentary, narrative; (2) experimental; (3) animated Undergraduate television study — criticism and aesthetics, production treated equally Undergraduate television production — experimental/personal video
SPECIAL ACTIVITIES/OFFERINGS Independent study
FACILITIES AND EQUIPMENT Film — complete 8mm equipment, screening room, editing room, sound mixing room, animation board, permanent film library of commercial or professional films Television — complete black and white and color exterior production equipment, black and white and color mini-studio configurations
FACULTY R Polito

COURSE LIST

Undergraduate

Introduction to the Art of Film
Survey of Film
Television: Theory and Practice I
Art and Film Technology

Graduate

Film Analysis

Undergraduate and Graduate

Photography: Theory and Practice I, II
Basic Film Production
Screen Education/Visual Literacy I, II
Animated Film Workshop

Boston University

Independent coed university. Institutionally accredited by regional association, programs recognized by NASM, AACSB. Urban location, 60-acre campus. Total enrollment: 19,452. Undergraduate enrollment: 11,279. Total faculty: 2449 (1514 full-time, 935 part-time). Semester calendar. Grading system: letters or numbers.

Department of Broadcasting and Film, School of Public Communication, 640 Commonwealth Avenue, Boston, MA 02215 617-353-3483

CONTACT Robert R Smith
DEGREES OFFERED BS, MS in broadcasting/film
DEPARTMENTAL MAJORS Undergraduate film — 150 students Undergraduate television — 140 students Graduate film — 40 students Graduate television — 60 students
ADMISSION Undergraduate requirements — 2.5 minimum grade point average, SAT scores, interviews, portfolio, professional work experience, production credits, professional recommendations, teachers' recommendations, written statement of purpose Graduate requirements — 3.0 minimum grade point average, GRE and MAT scores, interviews, portfolio, professional work experience, production credits, professional recommendations, teachers' recommendations, written statement of purpose Undergraduate application deadline — 2/1, rolling
FINANCIAL AID Student loans, work/study programs, teaching assistantships Undergraduate application deadline — 1/15
CURRICULAR EMPHASIS Film study — (1) production; (2) criticism and aesthetics; (3) history Filmmaking — depends upon current study interest Television study — (1) production; (2) educational; (3) management Television production — depends upon current student interest
SPECIAL ACTIVITIES/OFFERINGS Film series; film festivals; film societies; visiting professionals; program material produced for on-campus closed-circuit television, cable television, local public television station, local commercial television station; apprenticeships; internships in film and television production; independent study; practicum; vocational placement service
FACILITIES AND EQUIPMENT Film — complete 8mm and 16mm equipment, screening room, editing room, sound mixing room, animation board, permanent film library Television — complete black and white studio and exterior production equipment, black and white studio, color studio, audio studio, control room, broadcast journalism news room
FACULTY Arnold Baskin, Iran Berlow, George Bluestone, Hyman Goldin, Robert Jones, John Lord, Roger Manvell, Richard Nielsen, Robert R Smith, Murray R Yeager

COURSE LIST

Undergraduate

Broadcast Writing
Newswriting and Reporting
Broadcast Programming
Myth, Symbol, and Mass Communication
Film Industry in the United States
Commercial Broadcasting
Social Aspects of Broadcasting and Film
Broadcasting and Government
American Film
European Film
Television Documentary
Functional Film
Experimental Film
Film Design
Aspects of Film History and Criticism
Television Workshop
Film Workshop I

Graduate

Graduate Television Production
Structure and Regulation of Broadcasting
Social Aspects of Broadcasting
Advanced Television Production
Film for Television
Rhetoric and Communication
Broadcast Programming and Criticism
Teaching of Communication
Management
International Broadcasting
Alternative Broadcast Systems
Creative Project
Analytic Project
International Communication
Broadcasting Seminars
Film Studies I–IV

Bridgewater State College

State-supported comprehensive coed institution. Part of Massachusetts State College System. Institutionally accredited by regional association. Suburban location, 120-acre campus. Total enrollment: 5955. Undergraduate enrollment: 4250. Total faculty: 272 (218 full-time, 54 part-time). Semester calendar. Grading system: letters or numbers.

Department of Media and Librarianship, Bridgewater, MA 02324 617-697-8321

CONTACT Alan Lander, Chairman
PROGRAM OFFERED Undergraduate minor in radio and television operation and production
FINANCIAL AID Work/study programs, student loans
CURRICULAR EMPHASIS Undergraduate film study — educational media/instructional technology Graduate film study — educational media/instructional technology Undergraduate filmmaking — experimental, educational treated equally Graduate filmmaking — experimental, educational treated equally Undergraduate television study — educational, production treated equally Graduate television study — educational, production treated equally Undergraduate television production — experimental/personal video, educational treated equally Graduate television production — experimental/personal video, educational treated equally
SPECIAL ACTIVITIES/OFFERINGS Film series, program material produced for on-campus closed-circuit television
FACILITIES AND EQUIPMENT Film — 8mm cameras, editing equipment, lighting, projectors Television — black and white studio cameras, color studio cameras, ½-inch VTR, 1-inch VTR, ¾-inch cassette VTR, portable black and white cameras, editing equipment, monitors, special effects generators, slide chain, portable color cameras, ½-inch portapak recorders, lighting equipment, sound recording equipment, audio mixers, film chain, black and white studio, color studio, control room

COURSE LIST

Undergraduate and Graduate

Scriptwriting for Radio and Television
Radio and TV Production I, II
Cinematography I

English Department

CONTACT J Liggera

COURSE LIST

Undergraduate

Film Study: Introduction to the Art
The Director's Art
Genres
Literature into Film

Clark University

Independent coed university. Institutionally accredited by regional association. Urban location, 40-acre campus. Total enrollment: 2350. Undergraduate enrollment: 1850. Total faculty: 150. 4-1-4 calendar. Grading system: letters or numbers.

Screen Studies Department, Worcester, MA 01610 617-793-7330

CONTACT Anthony W Hodgkinson
DEGREE OFFERED BA with emphasis in screen studies
ADMISSION Application deadline — 2/1
FINANCIAL AID Work/study programs, teaching assistantships Application deadline — 2/15
CURRICULAR EMPHASIS Film study — (1) appreciation; (2) history; (3) criticism and aesthetics; (4) future of media
SPECIAL ACTIVITIES/OFFERINGS 35mm repertory cinema, film societies, program material produced for cable television, internships, independent study, teacher training
FACILITIES AND EQUIPMENT Film — complete 8mm equipment, screening room, editing room, sound mixing room, animation board, permanent film library Television — black and white exterior production facilities, black and white studio cameras
FACULTY Anthony W Hodgkinson PART-TIME FACULTY Charles H Slatkin

COURSE LIST
Undergraduate
Introduction to Screen Studies I, II
Screen Literacy
The Film Studio Team
Aspects of Screen History
Screen and Society
Screen Literature
Screen Analysis
Screen Auteurs
Internships
Directed Readings
Special Projects
Elementary Screen Production
Literature and the Screen

College of the Holy Cross

Independent Roman Catholic comprehensive coed institution. Institutionally accredited by regional association. Suburban location, 174-acre campus. Undergraduate enrollment: 2570. Total faculty: 207 (169 full-time, 38 part-time). Semester calendar. Grading system: letters or numbers.

Department of Modern Languages and Literatures, College Street, Worcester, MA 01610 617-793-2608

CONTACT Charles A Baker
ADMISSION Application deadline — 2/1, rolling
CURRICULAR EMPHASIS Film study — criticism and aesthetics
SPECIAL ACTIVITIES/OFFERINGS Film series
FACULTY Charles A Baker

COURSE LIST
Undergraduate
Contemporary Cinema and Humanism

Emerson College

Independent Roman Catholic comprehensive women's institution. Institutionally accredited by regional association. Urban location, 19-acre campus. Total enrollment: 584. Undergraduate enrollment: 522. Total faculty: 92 (53 full-time, 39 part-time). Semester calendar. Grading system: letters or numbers.

Department of Mass Communication, 148 Beacon Street, Boston, MA 02116 617-262-2010

CONTACT Film — Ann-Carol Grossman, Section Head Television — George Quenzel, Section Head; George Douglas, Chairman
DEGREES OFFERED BFA in film, BA in mass communication with emphases in film and television, BS in mass communication with emphases in film and television, MA in mass communication with emphases in film and television, MS in mass communication with emphases in film and television
DEPARTMENTAL MAJORS Undergraduate film — 100 students Undergraduate television — 225 students Graduate film — 3 students Graduate television — 25 students
ADMISSION Undergraduate requirements — ACT or SAT scores, teachers' recommendations Graduate requirements — 2.5 minimum grade point average, teachers' recommendations, written statement of purpose
FINANCIAL AID Scholarships, work/study programs, student loans, fellowships, teaching assistantships Undergraduate application deadline — 2/15
CURRICULAR EMPHASIS Undergraduate film study — history, criticism and aesthetics treated equally Undergraduate filmmaking — documentary, narrative, animated treated equally Graduate filmmaking — (1) documentary; (2) narrative; (3) animated Undergraduate television study — production, management treated equally Graduate television study — educational, production, management treated equally Undergraduate television production — commercial, news/documentary treated equally Graduate television production — commercial, news/documentary treated equally
SPECIAL ACTIVITIES/OFFERINGS Filmmaking clubs; film series; film festivals; film societies; student publications; program material produced for on-campus closed-circuit television, cable television, local commercial television station; internships in film production; internships in television production; independent study; vocational placement service
FACILITIES AND EQUIPMENT Film — complete 16mm equipment, 8mm cameras, editing equipment, projectors, screening room, editing room, animation board, permanent film library of student films Television — color studio cameras, ¾-inch cassette VTR, editing equipment, monitors, special effects generators, slide chain, portable color cameras, ¾-inch ENG, lighting equipment, sound recording equipment, audio mixers, film chain, time base corrector, color studio, control room
FACULTY Tobe Berkovitz, Ann-Carol Grossman, William Jackson, Linda Podheiser, George Quenzel, Paul Rabin PART-TIME FACULTY Randel Cole, Michelle Dickoff, Daniel Jones, Steven Tringale

COURSE LIST

Undergraduate

Studio Operations
Film Basics
Film Analysis
Standards of Criticism
Seminar in Mass Communication
Introduction to Management
Sales in Broadcasting
Directed Study

Graduate

Graduate Directed Readings
Film in Education
Educational Uses of TV
Audience Analysis

Undergraduate and Graduate

Television Production
Film Production I, II
Film Composition I, II
Film Animation I, II
Ethics in the Mass Media
Critical Writing
Communications Law
Film Methods
Film Practicum
Advanced TV
Television Practicum
Film Business
Film Studies: American Film
Film Studies: Documentary Film
Film Studies: Genres
Film Studies: National Cinemas
Film Studies: Personal Film
Film Studies: Directors
Film Studies: Blacks in Film

Greenfield Community College

State-supported 2-year coed college. Part of Massachusetts Community College System. Institutionally accredited by regional association. Small town location, 80-acre campus. Undergraduate enrollment: 1379. Total faculty: 72 (55 full-time, 17 part-time). Semester calendar. Grading system: letters or numbers.

Media Communication Program, One College Drive, Greenfield, MA 01301 413-774-3131

CONTACT Tom Boisvert or Robert Tracy
DEGREE OFFERED AS in media communication
ADMISSION Application deadline — rolling
FINANCIAL AID Scholarships, student loans, work/study programs, assistantships Application deadline — rolling
CURRICULAR EMPHASIS Film study — (1) educational media/instructional technology; (2) production Filmmaking — educational Television study — (1) educational; (2) production; (3) appreciation Television production — (1) educational; (2) news/documentary
SPECIAL ACTIVITIES/OFFERINGS Program material produced for on-campus closed-circuit television and cable television, internships in television production, independent study
FACILITIES AND EQUIPMENT Film — complete 8mm equipment, sound stage, sound mixing room, animation board Television — complete black and white studio and exterior production equipment, complete color studio production equipment, black and white studio, color studio, audio studio, control room
PART-TIME FACULTY Tom Boisvert, Robert Tracy

COURSE LIST

Undergraduate

Production of Audiovisual Material
Television Production
Photography and Graphics

Hampshire College

Independent 4-year coed college. Institutionally accredited by regional association. Small town location, 550-acre campus. Undergraduate enrollment: 1200. Total faculty: 105 (78 full-time, 27 part-time). 4-1-4 calendar. Grading system: faculty reports.

Film and Photography Department, Route 116, Amherst, MA 01002 413-549-4600, ext 575

CONTACT Jerome Liebling
DEGREES OFFERED BA in film or photography, MFA with University of Massachusetts in photography
DEPARTMENTAL MAJORS Undergraduate film — 50 students
ADMISSION Undergraduate requirements — interview, teachers' recommendations, written statement of purpose, portfolio
FINANCIAL AID Scholarships, work/study programs, student loans
CURRICULAR EMPHASIS Undergraduate film study — (1) history, criticism and aesthetics, appreciation; (2) educational media/instructional technology Undergraduate filmmaking — (1) documentary, narrative, experimental, animated; (2) educational Undergraduate television study — (1) educational, production; (2) history, criticism and aesthetics, appreciation; (3) management Undergraduate television production — (1) news/documentary, experimental/personal video, educational; (2) commercial
SPECIAL ACTIVITIES/OFFERINGS Filmmaking clubs, film series, film societies, student publications, program material produced for on-campus closed-circuit television, internships in film production, independent study
FACILITIES AND EQUIPMENT Film — 8mm and 16mm cameras, editing equipment, sound recording equipment, lighting, projectors, screening room, editing room, sound mixing room, animation board, permanent film library of student films, permanent film library of commercial or professional films Television — complete black and white and color studio production equipment, complete black and white and color exterior production equipment, black and white studio, color studio, audio studio, control room
FACULTY Thomas Joslin, Jerome Liebling, Elaine Mayes, Richard Mueller, Abraham Ravett PART-TIME FACULTY Tim Holt

COURSE LIST

Undergraduate

Film Workshop I, II
60's Through Film
Film History and Criticism
Film/Photo Concentrators' Seminar

Television Department, School of Language and Communication

CONTACT Richard Muller
DEGREE OFFERED BA in television production

Hampshire College (continued)

DEPARTMENTAL MAJORS 10 students
ADMISSION Requirements — interviews, portfolio, teachers' recommendations Application deadline — 2/15 (fall), 12/1 (spring)
CURRICULAR EMPHASIS Television study — (1) media theory; (2) history; (3) production; (4) criticism and aesthetics
SPECIAL ACTIVITIES/OFFERINGS Program material produced for on-campus closed-circuit television, cable television, local public television station; apprenticeships; internships in television production; independent study; practicum
FACILITIES AND EQUIPMENT Television — complete black and white studio production equipment, black and white and color exterior production equipment, black and white studio, audio studio, control room
FACULTY David Kerr, Jim Miller, Richard Muller

COURSE LIST

Undergraduate

Structure and Control of American Media
Mass Communications Theory
Television Production Process
Public Communication
Documentary Television
Public Access Television

Harvard University

Independent coed university. Institutionally accredited by regional association. Urban location. Total enrollment: 15,559. Undergraduate enrollment: 6491. Total faculty: 5832 (2915 full-time, 2917 part-time). Semester calendar. Grading system: letters or numbers.

Department of Visual and Environmental Studies, 19 Prescott Street, Cambridge, MA 02138 617-495-3251

CONTACT Chairperson
PROGRAM OFFERED Major in visual and environmental studies with emphasis in film
FINANCIAL AID Scholarships, student loans, teaching assistantships
CURRICULAR EMPHASIS Film study — (1) criticism and aesthetics; (2) history; (3) appreciation Filmmaking — (1) documentary; (2) animated; (3) experimental Television study — (1) criticism and aesthetics; (2) history; (3) production Television production — (1) news/documentary; (2) experimental/personal video; (3) educational
SPECIAL ACTIVITIES/OFFERINGS Filmmaking clubs, film series, film festivals, film societies, independent study
FACILITIES AND EQUIPMENT Film — complete 16mm equipment, 35mm projectors, optical printer, screening room, 35mm screening facilities, editing room, sound mixing room, animation board, permanent film library Television — black and white studio camera, ½-inch VTR, portable black and white cameras, editing equipment, monitors, special effects generators, ½-inch portapak recorder, lighting equipment, sound recording equipment, audio mixers, black and white studio, control room

Massachusetts

Lesley College

Independent comprehensive women's institution. Institutionally accredited by regional association. Urban location. Total enrollment: 1190. Undergraduate enrollment: 790. Total faculty: 60 (40 full-time, 20 part-time). 4-1-4 calendar. Grading system: letters or numbers.

Drama Department, Cambridge, MA 02138 617-868-9600

CONTACT Albert Brower
ADMISSION Application deadline — rolling
FACULTY Albert Brower

COURSE LIST

Undergraduate

The Film as Dramatic Art

Massachusetts Institute of Technology

Independent coed university. Institutionally accredited by regional association. Urban location, 125-acre campus. Total enrollment: 8148. Undergraduate enrollment: 4291. Total faculty: 1700 (925 full-time, 775 part-time). 4-1-4 calendar. Grading system: letters or numbers (for freshmen).

Film/Video Section, Department of Architecture, Building N51, 77 Massachusetts Avenue, Cambridge, MA 02139 617-253-1606

CONTACT Film — Richard Leacock Television — Benjamin Bergery
DEGREES OFFERED BS in architecture with a concentration in film/video, MS in visual studies with a concentration in film/video
PROGRAM MAJORS Graduate film — 3 students Graduate television — 3 students
ADMISSION Graduate requirements — teachers' recommendations, written statement of purpose, portfolio, professional recommendations
FINANCIAL AID Work/study programs, student loans
CURRICULAR EMPHASIS Undergraduate film study — (1) production; (2) criticism and aesthetics; (3) history Graduate film study — (1) production; (2) criticism and aesthetics; (3) history Undergraduate filmmaking — (1) documentary; (2) experimental Graduate filmmaking — (1) documentary; (2) experimental Undergraduate television study — (1) production; (2) criticism and aesthetics; (3) history Graduate television study — (1) production; (2) criticism and aesthetics; (3) history Undergraduate television production — (1) experimental/personal video; (2) news/documentary Graduate television production — (1) experimental/personal video; (2) news/documentary
SPECIAL ACTIVITIES/OFFERINGS Film series; film societies; visiting filmmakers; program material produced for on-campus closed-circuit television, cable television, local public television station, local commercial television station; independent study, academic year abroad through affiliation with the Inter-University Center for Film Studies in Paris

FACILITIES AND EQUIPMENT Film — complete 8mm and 16mm equipment, screening room, editing room, sound mixing room, permanent film library of student films, permanent film library of commercial or professional films Television — black and white studio cameras, color studio cameras, ½-inch VTR, 2-inch VTR, ¾-inch cassette VTR, portable black and white cameras, editing equipment, monitors, special effects generators, slide chain, portable color cameras, lighting equipment, sound recording equipment, audio mixers, film chain, time base corrector, color studio, control room
FACULTY Richard Leacock

Mount Wachusett Community College

State-supported 2-year coed college. Rural location. Total enrollment: 1450. Total faculty: 87 full-time. Semester calendar. Grading system: numbers.

Public Communications Curriculum, 444 Green Street, Gardner, MA 01440 617-632-6600

CONTACT Vincent S Ialenti
DEGREE OFFERED AS in public communications
PROGRAM MAJORS Television — 120 students
ADMISSION Requirement — written statement of purpose Application deadline — 6/30
FINANCIAL AID Scholarships, work/study programs, student loans
CURRICULAR EMPHASIS Film study — history, criticism and aesthetics, appreciation treated equally Filmmaking — documentary, narrative, experimental treated equally Television study — (1) production; (2) management; (3) criticism and aesthetics Television production — (1) commercial; (2) news/documentary; (3) industrial
SPECIAL ACTIVITIES/OFFERINGS Film festivals; student publications; program material produced for on-campus closed-circuit television, cable television, local commercial television station; internships in television production; independent study; vocational placement service
FACILITIES AND EQUIPMENT Film — 8mm and 16mm cameras, editing equipment, sound recording equipment, lighting, projectors, sound stage, screening room, editing room, sound mixing room, permanent film library of commercial or professional films Television — color studio cameras, ½-inch VTR, 1 inch VTR, ¾-inch cassette VTR, portable black and white cameras, editing equipment, monitors, special effects generators, slide chain, portable color cameras, ½-inch portapak recorders, ¾-inch ENG, lighting equipment, sound recording equipment, audio mixers, film chain, time base corrector, image enhancer, ¾-inch, ½-inch, and 1-inch editing systems, color studios, mobile van/unit, audio studios, control room
FACULTY Joel W Anderson, Vincent S Ialenti PART-TIME FACULTY Frank K Hirons, John Kellogg, Thomas Milligan, Francis Wironen, Norman Wironen

COURSE LIST

Undergraduate
Introduction to Broadcasting
Audio Production
TV Production I, II
Film Production
Photography
Broadcast Station Management
Broadcast Journalism
Field Work Experience/Internships
Advanced Independent Video/Audio Production

North Adams State College

State-supported comprehensive coed institution. Part of Massachusetts State College System. Institutionally accredited by regional association. Small town location, 95-acre campus. Total enrollment: 2900. Undergraduate enrollment: 2200. Total faculty: 190 (110 full-time, 80 part-time). 4-1-4 calendar. Grading system: letters or numbers.

English Department, Church Street, North Adams, MA 01247 413-664-4511

CONTACT Film — Robert Bishoff Television — Joseph Mansfield
DEGREE OFFERED BA in English with emphasis in electronic media
ADMISSION Requirement — ACT or SAT scores Undergraduate application deadline — 4/1, rolling
FINANCIAL AID Work/study programs, BEOG grants Undergraduate application deadline — 5/30, rolling
CURRICULAR EMPHASIS Film study — (1) appreciation; (2) history; (3) criticism and aesthetics Television study — (1) production; (2) appreciation; (3) history Television production — educational
SPECIAL ACTIVITIES/OFFERINGS Film series, program material produced for cable television, internships in television production, independent study
FACILITIES AND EQUIPMENT Film — 8mm and 16mm cameras, editing equipment, lighting, projectors, film inspection equipment, screening room, sound mixing room, animation board, permanent film library of commercial or professional films, 2 auditoriums for film showings Television — black and white studio cameras, color studio cameras, ¾-inch cassette VTR, monitors, special effects generators, slide chain, portable color cameras, ½-inch portapak recorders, lighting equipment, sound recording equipment, audio mixers, film chain, black and white studio, color studio, control room
FACULTY Robert Bishoff, Harris Elder, Joseph Mansfield

COURSE LIST

Undergraduate
Radio and TV: Art as Business
Television Production I, II
History of Film
Art of Film
Literary Genre: Film and Literature

Northeastern University

Independent coed university. Institutionally accredited by regional association. Urban location, 50-acre campus. Total enrollment: 49,384. Undergraduate enrollment: 16,405. Total faculty: 2183 (737 full-time, 1446 part-time). Quarter calendar. Grading system: letters or numbers.

Boston, MA 02115 617-437-2660

CONTACT Gerald Herman

Northeastern University (continued)

PROGRAMS OFFERED Media studies (interdisciplinary) minor; Historical Agencies Program (MA); the College of Education offers Educational/Instructional Technology master's degree and CAGS through the Department of Curriculum and Instruction and the Office of Learning Resources
FINANCIAL AID Scholarships, work/study programs, student loans, fellowships, teaching assistantships, cooperative education placements
CURRICULAR EMPHASIS Undergraduate film study — history, film as a primary source for the study of social values Graduate film study — film as a primary source for the study of social values Graduate filmmaking — (1) film compilation as part of TV production; (2) documentary; (3) educational Undergraduate television study — history Graduate television study — (1) history; (2) production; (3) educational Graduate television production — (1) news/documentary; (2) educational
SPECIAL ACTIVITIES/OFFERINGS Film series, program material produced for on-campus closed-circuit television, internships in television production, independent study, teacher training, cooperative education placements
FACILITIES AND EQUIPMENT Film — 8mm and 35mm cameras, editing equipment, sound recording equipment, lighting, black and white film stock, projectors, screening room, permanent film library of commercial or professional films Television — black and white studio cameras, ½-inch VTR, 1-inch VTR, ¾-inch cassette VTR, portable black and white cameras, editing equipment, monitors, special effects generators, slide chain, ½-inch portapak recorders, ¾-inch ENG, lighting equipment, sound recording equipment, audio mixers, film chain, time base corrector, media lab, graphics and photographic services, black and white studio, audio studio, control room

COURSE LIST
Undergraduate
History and Film
History of Media
Graduate
Media and History (Production Course)

North Shore Community College

State-supported 2-year coed college. Part of Massachusetts Community College System. Institutionally accredited by regional association. Urban location. Undergraduate enrollment: 2080. Total faculty: 120. Semester calendar. Grading system: letters or numbers.

Media Communications Department, 3 Essex Street, Beverly, MA 01966 617-927-4850, ext 224

DEGREE OFFERED AA
ADMISSION Requirement — written statement of purpose Application deadline — 6/30
FINANCIAL AID Work/study programs Application deadline — 6/1
CURRICULAR EMPHASIS Film study — history, criticism and aesthetics, appreciation treated equally Television study — history, appreciation treated equally
FACILITIES AND EQUIPMENT Film — 16mm projectors, videotape Television — ½-inch VTR, 1-inch VTR, 2 inch VTR, ½-inch portapak recorders
FACULTY Peter Foss, Robert Froese

COURSE LIST
Undergraduate
Film Studies
Mass Media

Simmons College

Independent comprehensive women's institution. Institutionally accredited by regional association. Urban location, 12-acre campus. Total enrollment: 2644. Undergraduate enrollment: 1728. Total faculty: 289 (180 full-time, 109 part-time). Semester calendar. Grading system: letters or numbers.

Department of Communications, 300 The Fenway, Boston, MA 02115 617-738-2216

CONTACT Lynda Beltz, Chairperson
PROGRAM OFFERED Major in communications with emphasis in film or television
ADMISSION Application deadline — 3/15, rolling
FINANCIAL AID Work/study programs Application deadline — 2/1, rolling
CURRICULAR EMPHASIS Film study — (1) communications tool; (2) production; (3) criticism and aesthetics Filmmaking — (1) documentary; (2) animated; (3) experimental Television study — (1) communications tool; (2) production; (3) criticism and aesthetics Television production — (1) news/documentary; (2) experimental/personal video; (3) educational
SPECIAL ACTIVITIES/OFFERINGS Film series, internships in film and television production, student publications, independent study, vocational placement service
FACILITIES AND EQUIPMENT Film — complete 8mm equipment, sound mixing room, animation board, permanent film library Television — black and white studio cameras, ½-inch VTR, 1-inch VTR, ¾-inch cassette VTR, portable black and white cameras, editing equipment, monitors, special effects generators, ½-inch portapak recorder, lighting equipment, sound recording equipment, audio mixers, VHS and BETA ½-inch VTRs, color studio
FACULTY Robert F White PART-TIME FACULTY Stacy Greenspan, Gail Harris

COURSE LIST
Undergraduate
Communications Media
Video Production
Broadcast Journalism
Individual Study: Advanced Video
Individual Study: Filmmaking
Individual Study: Animation
Senior Project: Slide Show
Senior Project: Video
Senior Project: Animation
Simmons Review: Videomagazine Article
Cinematography

Suffolk University

Independent comprehensive coed institution. Institutionally accredited by regional association. Urban location. Total enrollment: 6123. Undergraduate enrollment: 2780. Total faculty: 277 (134 full-time, 143 part-time). Semester calendar. Grading system: letters or numbers.

Journalism Department, Beacon Hill, Boston, MA 02114 617-723-4700

CONTACT Malcolm J Barach
DEGREE OFFERED BS in journalism with tracks in film communication and mass communication (broadcast)
DEPARTMENTAL MAJORS Film — 20 students Mass communications (broadcast) — 35 students
ADMISSION Requirements — ACT or SAT scores, teachers' recommendations Application deadline — 5/31
FINANCIAL AID Scholarships, work/study programs, student loans Undergraduate application deadline — 5/31
CURRICULAR EMPHASIS Film study — (1) appreciation and writing documentaries; (2) history and criticism/aesthetics; (3) educational media/instructional technology Television study — (1) writing; (2) history and appreciation
SPECIAL ACTIVITIES/OFFERINGS Film series, student publications, program material produced for on-campus closed-circuit television, internships in film production, internships in television production, independent study
FACILITIES AND EQUIPMENT Film — screening room, affiliated with Emerson College, where students have the opportunity to take film production courses and film equipment is available Television — black and white studio, color studio, control room
FACULTY M J Barach PART-TIME FACULTY Arch MacDonald, Sharon Rivo

COURSE LIST

Undergraduate
Documentary Film
American Cinema
Broadcast Journalism-TV
The Television Documentary
Seminar in TV News and Public Affairs

Tufts University

Independent coed university. Accredited by regional association and AICS. Suburban location. Total enrollment: 6593. Undergraduate enrollment: 4350. Total faculty: 419 (277 full-time, 142 part-time). Semester calendar. Grading system: letters or numbers.

English Department, East Hall, Medford, MA 02155 617-628-5000

CONTACT Sarah Smith
PROGRAM OFFERED Major or minor in film by special arrangement only
PROGRAM MAJORS Undergraduate film — 3 students
ADMISSION Undergraduate requirements — ACT or SAT scores, interview, written statement of purpose, normal admission to college Undergraduate application deadline — 2/1
FINANCIAL AID Scholarships, work/study programs, student loans Undergraduate application deadline — 2/1
CURRICULAR EMPHASIS Undergraduate film study — (1) appreciation; (2) history; (3) criticism and aesthetics Undergraduate television study — (1) appreciation; (2) history; (3) production Undergraduate television production — (1) news/documentary; (2) commercial; (3) educational
SPECIAL ACTIVITIES/OFFERINGS Filmmaking clubs, film series, film festivals, film societies, program material produced for on-campus closed-circuit television and cable television, apprenticeships, internships in film production, internships in television production, independent study
FACILITIES AND EQUIPMENT Film — 8mm cameras, editing equipment, sound recording equipment, projectors, 16mm projectors, screening room, permanent film library of commercial or professional films, film library Television — color studio production facilities, color exterior production facilities, ¾-inch cassette VTR, editing equipment, monitors, special effects generators, portable color cameras, lighting equipment, sound recording equipment, audio mixers, color studio
FACULTY Linda Bamber, Martin Green, Sarah Smith PART-TIME FACULTY Elizabeth Hewitt, Kathryn Huffhines, Nancy Scholar

COURSE LIST

Undergraduate
Film in Language Study

Undergraduate and Graduate
Film History
Film Theory
Film as Rhetoric

Romance Languages Department

CONTACT Martine Loutfi
ADMISSION Application deadline — 2/1
FACULTY Jeanne Dillon, Martine Loutfi

COURSE LIST

Undergraduate and Graduate
French Cinema
Italian Cinema

University of Massachusetts, Amherst

State-supported coed university. Part of University of Massachusetts. Institutionally accredited by regional association. Small town location. Total enrollment: 24,018. Undergraduate enrollment: 19,041. Total faculty: 1465 (1230 full-time, 235 part-time). Semester calendar. Grading system: letters or numbers.

Communication Studies Department, Amherst, MA 01003 413-545-2260

University of Massachusetts, Amherst (continued)

CONTACT Film — Richard Stromgren Television — Leslie Davis
PROGRAM OFFERED Major in communications with emphasis in film or television
ADMISSION Undergraduate requirements — 2.75 minimum grade point average, teachers' recommendations, written statement of purpose Graduate requirements — 2.75 minimum grade point average, GRE scores, teachers' recommendations, written statement of purpose Resident undergraduate application deadline — 3/1, rolling Nonresident undergraduate application deadline — 2/1
FINANCIAL AID Student loans, work/study programs, teaching assistantships Undergraduate application deadline — 3/1, rolling
CURRICULAR EMPHASIS Undergraduate film study — (1) criticism and aesthetics; (2) history; (3) production Graduate film study — (1) criticism and aesthetics; (2) history; (3) behavioral research Filmmaking — (1) documentary; (2) experimental; (3) narrative Undergraduate television study — (1) effective communication; (2) criticism and aesthetics; (3) production Graduate television study — (1) effective communication; (2) criticism and aesthetics; (3) management Television production — (1) technique manipulation; (2) experimental/personal video; (3) news/documentary
SPECIAL ACTIVITIES/OFFERINGS Film series, film festivals, program material produced for cable television and local commercial television station, internships in film and television production, independent study, practicum, teacher training, vocational placement service
FACILITIES AND EQUIPMENT Film — complete 16mm equipment, 8mm cameras, editing equipment, lighting equipment, color film stock, projectors, screening room, editing room, sound mixing room, permanent film library Television — complete black and white studio and exterior production equipment, black and white studio, audio studio, control room
FACULTY Alison Alexander, Jennings Bryant, Leslie Davis, Kim Elliott, Richard Harper, Martin Norden, Maurice Shelby, Richard Stromgren

COURSE LIST
Undergraduate
Introduction to Media Production
Program Process in Television
Creative Television Production
History of Film
Modes of Film Communication
History of Broadcasting
Film Production
Film Styles and Genres
Pro-Seminar in Film

Graduate
Graduate Film Seminar

Undergraduate and Graduate
Film Theory and Criticism

Worcester State College

State-supported comprehensive coed institution. Part of Massachusetts State College System. Institutionally accredited by regional association. Urban location, 55-acre campus. Total enrollment: 3394. Total faculty: 207 (184 full-time, 23 part-time). Semester calendar. Grading system: letters or numbers.

Department of Media, 486 Chandler Street, Worcester, MA 01602 617-752-7700, ext 153

CONTACT William D Joyce
DEGREES OFFERED BA/BS in media, MS in Education with a concentration in AV media
DEPARTMENTAL MAJORS Undergraduate television — 55 students Graduate film — 20 students
ADMISSION Undergraduate requirement — ACT or SAT scores Graduate requirements — 2.75 minimum grade point average, GRE or MAT scores, teachers' recommendations, written statement of purpose
FINANCIAL AID Scholarships, work/study programs, student loans
CURRICULAR EMPHASIS Undergraduate film study — (1) educational media/instructional technology; (2) appreciation; (3) criticism and aesthetics; (4) history Graduate film study — educational media/instructional technology Undergraduate filmmaking — (1) narrative; (2) animated; (3) experimental; (4) documentary Graduate filmmaking — (1) educational; (2) animated Undergraduate television study — (1) production; (2) educational; (3) history; (4) appreciation Graduate television study — (1) production; (2) educational Undergraduate television production — (1) educational; (2) commercial; (3) news/documentary; (4) experimental/personal video Graduate television production — (1) educational; (2) commercial; (3) news/documentary; (4) experimental/personal video
SPECIAL ACTIVITIES/OFFERINGS Film series, program material produced for on-campus closed-circuit television, internships in television production, independent study, vocational placement service
FACILITIES AND EQUIPMENT Film — 8mm cameras, editing equipment, sound recording equipment, lighting, projectors, sound stage, screening room, editing room, sound mixing room, permanent film library of commercial or professional films Television — black and white studio cameras, color studio cameras, ½-inch VTR, ¾-inch cassette VTR, portable black and white cameras, editing equipment, monitors, special effects generators, slide chain, portable color cameras, ½-inch portapak recorders, ¾-inch ENG, lighting equipment, sound recording equipment, audio mixers, film chain, time base corrector, Super-8 videoplayer, black and white studio, color studio, audio studio, control room
FACULTY William D Joyce, Garrett Mitchell Jr, Jeffrey Roberts, David Seiffer, Anne Marie Shea PART-TIME FACULTY Donald Bullens, Robert Jones

COURSE LIST
Undergraduate
Film and Literature
Art of the Motion Picture
Elements of Closed-Circuit Television
Classroom Use of Radio and Television
Producing and Directing the TV Program I, II
Videotape Production
Writing for Screen and Stage
Speech for the Professional

Graduate
Television Production I, II

Undergraduate and Graduate
Basic 8mm Film Production

MICHIGAN

Andrews University

Independent Seventh-Day Adventist coed university. Institutionally accredited by regional association, programs recognized by NASM. Small town location. Total enrollment: 2924. Undergraduate enrollment: 2026. Total faculty: 248 (218 full-time, 30 part-time). Quarter calendar. Grading system: letters or numbers.

Communication Department, Berrien Springs, MI 49104 616-471-3126

CONTACT Film — Paul Denton Television — Colleen S Garber
DEGREES OFFERED BA, BS communication, BA, BS mass communication
ADMISSION Requirements — 2.0 minimum grade point average, ACT or SAT scores, teachers' recommendations
FINANCIAL AID Scholarships, work/study programs, student loans
CURRICULAR EMPHASIS Film study — educational media/instructional technology Filmmaking — documentary, narrative, educational treated equally Television study — history, educational, production treated equally Television production — commercial, educational treated equally
SPECIAL ACTIVITIES/OFFERINGS Program material produced for on-campus closed circuit television, independent study
FACILITIES AND EQUIPMENT Film — 8mm and 16mm cameras, editing equipment, lighting, projectors, editing room Television — black and white studio cameras, ½-inch VTR, ¾-inch cassette VTR, portable black and white cameras, monitors, ½-inch portapak recorders, lighting equipment, audio mixers, black and white studio
FACULTY Paul Denton, Colleen C Garber

COURSE LIST

Undergraduate
Introduction to Film

Undergraduate and Graduate
Film Production
Introduction to Videotape Production

Center for Creative Studies–College of Art and Design

Independent 4-year coed college. Institutionally accredited by regional association, programs recognized by NASA. Urban location, 6-acre campus. Undergraduate enrollment: 1098. Total faculty: 99 (34 full-time, 65 part-time). Semester calendar. Grading system: letters or numbers.

Photography Department, 245 East Kirby, Detroit, MI 48202 313-872-3118

CONTACT Film — Robert Vigiletti Television — Valley Boyd
DEGREE OFFERED BFA in photography with emphasis in film or audiovisual
DEPARTMENTAL MAJORS Undergraduate film — 2 students Undergraduate television — 1 student
ADMISSION Requirements — 2.5 minimum grade point average, ACT or SAT scores, interview, teachers' recommendations, portfolio Undergraduate application deadline — 4/15
FINANCIAL AID Scholarships, work/study programs, student loans, Basic Educational Opportunity Grants, Michigan tuition grants, Michigan differential grants
CURRICULAR EMPHASIS Film study — (1) educational media/instructional technology; (2) criticism and aesthetics; (3) history Filmmaking — documentary, experimental, animated treated equally Television study — (1) criticism and aesthetics; (2) production Television production — experimental/personal video
SPECIAL ACTIVITIES/OFFERINGS Film series
FACILITIES AND EQUIPMENT Film — complete 8mm and 16mm equipment, screening room, editing room, sound mixing room, animation board Television — color studio cameras, ½-inch VTR, ¾-inch cassette VTR, portable black and white cameras, monitors, portable color cameras, ½-inch portapak recorders, lighting equipment, black and white studio, color studio
PART-TIME FACULTY Valley Boyd, Terry Kelley, William Rauhauser, Robert Vigiletti

COURSE LIST

Undergraduate
History of World Cinema I, II
Filmmaking and Video Production Workshop, I, II
Animation I, II
Independent Studies in Film and Video
Photographic Thesis Project I, II

Central Michigan University

State-supported coed university. Institutionally accredited by regional association. Small town location. Total enrollment: 16,203. Undergraduate enrollment: 14,353. Total faculty: 830 (715 full-time, 115 part-time). Semester calendar. Grading system: letters or numbers.

Broadcast and Cinematic Arts Department, 340 Moore Hall, Mount Pleasant, MI 48858 517-774-3852

CONTACT Joe Misiewicz, Chairperson
DEGREES OFFERED BA, BFA, BS, BAA in broadcast and cinematic arts, MA in speech, MS in administration of broadcasting with a minor in film and television
PROGRAM MAJORS Undergraduate — 475 students Graduate — 10 students

Central Michigan University (continued)

ADMISSION Undergraduate requirement — 2.7 minimum grade point average Graduate requirements — 2.7 minimum grade point average, 15 hours in speech Undergraduate application deadline — rolling
FINANCIAL AID Scholarships, student loans, work/study programs, assistantships Undergraduate application deadline — 4/1
CURRICULAR EMPHASIS Film study — (1) production; (2) history, criticism and aesthetics Filmmaking — (1) documentary; (2) news film/instructional; (3) narrative Television study — (1) production; (2) criticism and aesthetics Television production — (1) news/documentary; (2) commercial
SPECIAL ACTIVITIES/OFFERINGS Film series; film festivals; program material produced for cable television, local public television station, community service, classroom use; internships in film and television production; independent study; practicum; vocational placement service
FACILITIES AND EQUIPMENT Film — complete 8mm and 16mm equipment, screening room, editing room Television — complete black and white studio and exterior production equipment, complete color studio production equipment, black and white studio, color studio, control room
FACULTY Robert Braunlich, John Robert Craig, Jerome Henderson, H Greydon Hyde, W M Keiser, Joe Misiewicz, Peter B Orlik, Randall Stith, Dwight Wilhelm PART-TIME FACULTY Thomas Endres, William Grigilunais, Thomas Hunt

COURSE LIST

Undergraduate

Survey of the Mass Media
Broadcast Production
History and Appreciation of the Cinema
Basic Broadcast Writing
Broadcasting Critique
Radio-Television Announcing
Radio-Television Newswriting
Broadcast Electronics I
Cinematography
Practicum in Radio-Television-Film
History and Analysis of the Documentary Film

Graduate

Telecommunications Media Policy
Music in Broadcasting
Special Topics in Broadcast and Cinematic Arts

Undergraduate and Graduate

Broadcast Law
Broadcast Sales
Broadcast Promotion
Broadcast Management
Newscasting
Broadcast Programming
Special Topics in Broadcast Content
Advanced Television Production
Staging and Lighting
Advanced Film Production
Music in Cinematic Arts
Internship in Radio-Television-Film
Broadcast Drama and Documentary Writing
Broadcast Electronics II
Producing Broadcast News

Delta College

State-supported 2-year coed college. Institutionally accredited by regional association, programs recognized by ECPD. Rural location, 640-acre campus. Undergraduate enrollment: 9317. Total faculty: 337 (199 full-time, 138 part-time). Trimester calendar. Grading system: letters or numbers and pass/fail.

Television Department, Delta Road, University Center, MI 48710 517-686-9346

CONTACT William J Ballard
DEGREE OFFERED Associate in R/TV
DEPARTMENTAL MAJORS Undergraduate television — 80 students
FINANCIAL AID Work/study programs, student loans
CURRICULAR EMPHASIS Television study — history, production treated equally Television production — commercial, news/documentary, educational treated equally
SPECIAL ACTIVITIES/OFFERINGS Program material produced for on-campus closed-circuit television and local public television station, independent study, vocational placement service
FACILITIES AND EQUIPMENT Film — 16mm editing equipment, sound recording equipment, lighting, black and white film stock, projectors, screening room, editing room Television — complete black and white and color studio production equipment, complete black and white and color exterior production equipment, black and white studio, color studio, audio studio, control room, public television station and closed-circuit television facilities available
FACULTY William J Ballard, Thomas E Haskell, Leonard Marsico, M Andersen Rapp, Guy E Serumgard PART-TIME FACULTY Helen Branyan, Rick Sykes

COURSE LIST

Undergraduate

Studio Operations I, II
Broadcast Writing
Broadcast Performance
Radio Broadcasting
Television Field Production
Communications History, Law and Responsibilities
Broadcast Sales
Television Producing and Directing
Advanced Radio-Broadcasting
Advanced TV Field Production
Assistant Director
Current Practices and Issues
Special Projects in Radio/Television

Eastern Michigan University

State-supported comprehensive coed institution. Institutionally accredited by regional association. Small town location. Total enrollment: 18,500. Undergraduate enrollment: 13,500. Total faculty: 746. Semester calendar. Grading system: letters or numbers.

Speech and Dramatic Arts Department, 129 Quirk, Ypsilanti, MI 48197 313-487-0064

CONTACT Henry B Aldridge
DEGREES OFFERED BA, BS in speech with emphasis in film or television
DEPARTMENTAL MAJORS 160 students
ADMISSION Requirement — 2.0 minimum grade point average
FINANCIAL AID Student loans, work/study programs, teaching assistantships

CURRICULAR EMPHASIS Film study — (1) history, appreciation; (2) production; (3) criticism and aesthetics Filmmaking — (1) experimental; (2) documentary; (3) animated Television study — (1) production; (2) management; (3) history, criticism and aesthetics Television production — (1) commercial; (2) news/documentary; (3) experimental/personal video
SPECIAL ACTIVITIES/OFFERINGS Film series, film festivals, film societies, student publications, program material produced for on-campus closed-circuit television, apprenticeships, internships in film and television production, independent study, practicum
FACILITIES AND EQUIPMENT Film — complete 16mm equipment, screening room, editing room, sound mixing room, animation board Television — complete black and white studio production equipment, portable black and white cameras, ½-inch portapak recorder, color studio, audio studio, control room
FACULTY Henry B Aldridge, Ray Lukasavitz, William V Swisher PART-TIME FACULTY Lewis Saalbach

COURSE LIST
Undergraduate
Introduction to Mass Communication
Radio Production I, II
Introduction to Broadcasting/Film
Introduction to Broadcasting/Film Production
Broadcast Announcing
Broadcast Acting
Film History
Cinematography
Special Topics in Film
TV Production I
Broadcasting/Filmwriting
Internship Activities

Undergraduate and Graduate
Film Theory
TV Production II
Broadcast Management
Broadcasting in Society

Ferris State College

State-supported 4-year coed college. Institutionally accredited by regional association. Small town location. Total enrollment: 10,500. Total faculty: 480. Quarter calendar. Grading system: letters or numbers.

Learning Resources Department, School of Education and Learning Resources, Big Rapids, MI 49307 616-796-9971

CONTACT C F Ritchie, Associate Dean
DEGREES OFFERED AAS in audiovisual technology, BS in television production
DEPARTMENTAL MAJORS Audiovisual technology — 50 students Television — 60 students
ADMISSION Application deadline — rolling
FINANCIAL AID Scholarships, student loans, work/study programs, basic federal grants Application deadline — 7/1
CURRICULAR EMPHASIS Film study — (1) educational media/instructional technology; (2) production; (3) criticism and aesthetics Filmmaking — (1) educational; (2) documentary Television study — (1) educational; (2) production; (3) criticism and aesthetics Television production — (1) educational; (2) corporate; (3) broadcast; (4) experimental/personal video
SPECIAL ACTIVITIES/OFFERINGS Internship in television production, client-centered communications projects, part-time work assignments
FACILITIES AND EQUIPMENT Film — complete 16mm equipment Television — color studio cameras, ¾-inch VTR, portable color cameras, editing equipment, audio studio, telecine
FACULTY James Breault, Frank Brister, Al Harrott PART-TIME FACULTY Robert Hunter, Jerry Sholl

COURSE LIST
Undergraduate
Audio Production
Cinematography I, II
Video Production
Instructional and Training Development
Broadcast Writing
Stagecraft
Broadcast Communication
Elements of Television Production I, II
Advanced Television Production/Direction
Seminar in Television Production
Television Production Internship

Grand Valley State Colleges

State-supported comprehensive coed institution. Institutionally accredited by regional association. Suburban location, 900-acre campus. Total enrollment: 7066. Undergraduate enrollment: 6200. Total faculty: 375 (275 full-time, 100 part-time). Quarter calendar. Grading system: letters or numbers.

Arts and Media Department, College Landing, Allendale, MI 49401 616-895-6611

CONTACT John Jellema, Assistant Dean
PROGRAM OFFERED Major in arts and media with emphasis in film and television
DEPARTMENTAL MAJORS Film — 40 students Television — 35 students
ADMISSION Application deadline — rolling
CURRICULAR EMPHASIS Film study — production Filmmaking — (1) documentary; (2) experimental; (3) animated Television study — production Television production — (1) news/documentary; (2) experimental/personal video
SPECIAL ACTIVITIES/OFFERINGS Program material produced for cable and broadcast television, internships in film and television production, independent study
FACILITIES AND EQUIPMENT Film — complete 8mm and 16mm equipment, optical printer, sound stage, screening room, editing room, animation board, permanent film library Television — complete black and white studio and exterior production facilities, complete color studio and exterior production facilities
FACULTY Jim Jerkaitis, Deanna Morse, Roz Moscovitz, Barbara Roos, Walter Wright

Grand Valley State Colleges (continued)

COURSE LIST

Undergraduate

Media Production
Directing Talent Before the Camera
Advanced Media Production: Television Studio Production
Advanced Media Production: 16mm Film Production
Advanced Media Production: Photojournalism and Documentary
Advanced Media Production: Radio and Television Electronics
Personal Expression in Media
Media as Performance
Portfolio
Senior Project
Field Study
Audience
Media and Society
Media and Society: News
Broadcasting
Film and TV Interpretation
Film Theories
Psychology of Media
Media in Industry
Language and Communications Theory
Topics in Arts and Media
Animation I, II
Computer Graphics
Writing in the Professions (including Grantwriting)
Scriptwriting I, II
Broadcast Newswriting
Dance for Cameras
Media in Education

Henry Ford Community College

State and locally supported 2-year coed college. Institutionally accredited by regional association. Urban location. Undergraduate enrollment: 17,105. Total faculty: 860 (210 full-time, 650 part-time). Semester calendar. Grading system: letters or numbers.

Mass Communication Department, 5101 Evergreen, Dearborn, MI 48128 313-271-2750

CONTACT Film — Jay B Korinek Television — Erik Fitzpatrick
DEGREE OFFERED Associate of Arts with an emphasis in mass communication
DEPARTMENTAL MAJORS Film — 25 students Television — 40 students
ADMISSION Requirement — 2.0 minimum grade point average
FINANCIAL AID Scholarships, work/study programs, student loans
CURRICULAR EMPHASIS Film study — history, criticism and aesthetics, business of filmmaking treated equally Filmmaking — documentary, narrative, educational treated equally Television study — history, criticism and aesthetics, management treated equally Television production — commercial, news/documentary, educational treated equally
SPECIAL ACTIVITIES/OFFERINGS Film series, student publications, program material produced for on-campus closed-circuit television and cable television, internships in film production, internships in television production, independent study
FACILITIES AND EQUIPMENT Film — complete 8mm production equipment, permanent film library of commercial or professional films Television — complete color studio and exterior production equipment, color studio, audio studio, control room
FACULTY Erik Fitzpatrick, Jay Korinek

COURSE LIST

Undergraduate

Introduction to Mass Communication
History and Criticism of the Motion Picture
Film Production
Television Production
Documentary Film
Films of Buster Keaton
Science Fiction in Film
Films of Alfred Hitchcock

Hope College

Independent 4-year coed college affiliated with Reformed Church in America. Institutionally accredited by regional association, programs recognized by NASM, NASA. Suburban location, 45-acre campus. Undergraduate enrollment: 2371. Total faculty: 168 (142 full-time, 26 part-time). Semester calendar. Grading system: letters or numbers.

Communication Department, Holland, MI 49423 616-392-5111

CONTACT Ted Nielsen
DEGREE OFFERED BA in communication with an emphasis in mass media
DEPARTMENTAL MAJORS 52 students
ADMISSION Application deadline — rolling
FINANCIAL AID Scholarships, work/study programs, student loans
CURRICULAR EMPHASIS Film study — history, appreciation treated equally Filmmaking — (1) documentary; (2) educational; (3) narrative Television study — (1) production; (2) history; (3) criticism and aesthetics Television production — (1) news/documentary; (2) educational; (3) commercial
SPECIAL ACTIVITIES/OFFERINGS Film series, program material produced for on-campus closed-circuit television and cable television, apprenticeships, internships in film production, internships in television production, independent study
FACILITIES AND EQUIPMENT Film — 8mm cameras, editing equipment, sound recording equipment, lighting, color film stock, projectors, sound stage, editing room, sound mixing room Television — black and white studio cameras, color studio cameras, ½-inch VTR, ¾-inch cassette VTR, portable black and white cameras, editing equipment, monitors, ½-inch portapak recorders, lighting equipment, sound recording equipment, audio mixers, black and white and color studio, audio studio, control room
FACULTY Ted Nielsen

COURSE LIST

Undergraduate

Introduction to Mass Media
Issues in the Mass Media
Beginning Media Production
Advanced Production I: Studio Dramatic
Advanced Production II: Studio Documentary
Television On-Location Documentary
Community Television Production
Beginning Film Production
Radio, Television, Film Internships

Lansing Community College

State and locally supported 2-year coed college. Institutionally accredited by regional association. Urban location, 120-acre campus. Quarter calendar. Grading system: letters or numbers.

Instructional Media Department, PO Box 40010, Lansing, MI 48901 517-373-7056

CONTACT Film — Glenn Rand Television — Lee Thornton
DEGREE OFFERED AA in photography–motion picture production
DEPARTMENTAL MAJORS Film — 30 students Television — 200 students
ADMISSION Open enrollment policy
FINANCIAL AID Scholarships, work/study programs, student loans
CURRICULAR EMPHASIS Filmmaking — (1) production; (2) business practices; (3) criticism and aesthetics; (4) documentary, narrative, experimental, animated, educational Television study — history, appreciation, educational, production (studio and remote), management, news, cable treated equally Television production — news/documentary, educational treated equally
SPECIAL ACTIVITIES/OFFERINGS Filmmaking clubs; film series; film festivals; film societies; student publications; program material produced for on-campus closed-circuit television, cable television, local public television station, local commercial television station; internships in film production; independent study
FACILITIES AND EQUIPMENT Film — complete 16mm equipment, still photography labs and studios, sound stage, screening room, editing room, sound mixing room, animation board, permanent film library of student films, permanent film library of commercial or professional films Television — complete black and white and color studio production equipment, complete black and white and color exterior production equipment
FACULTY William Blanchard, James Greene, Al LaGuire, Glenn Rand PART-TIME FACULTY Susan Bellingham, Dick Brundle, Douglas Collar, Robert Crawford, R Bradley Cummings, Dave Downing, James Ellis, Dick Estelle, Dave Machtel, Martha Parisian, Gene Parker, James Sumbler, Lee Thornton

COURSE LIST
Undergraduate
Basic Motion Picture Production
Fundamentals of Cinematography
Fundamentals of Lighting
Fundamentals of Film Sound
Fundamentals of Film Editing
Fundamentals of Film Directing
Workshop in 8mm Film Production
Workshop in Documentary Film Production
Workshop in Educational Film Production
Workshop in Dramatic Film Production
Workshop in Advertising Film Production
Workshop in Public Service Film Production
Workshop in TV News Film Production
Workshop in Animation
Workshop in Medical Film Production
Portfolio
Media Materials I, II
Multimedia Workshop
Introduction to Broadcasting
Third Class License
Cable Television Operations
Fundamentals of Telecommunications
TV Production I, II
TV Producer-Director
Media and/or the Future
TV-Film Script
TV-Film Graphics
TV-Film Graphic Workshop
Graphic Arts for Reproduction
Film for Television News
Broadcast Promotion and Sales
Cable Television Workshop
Current Issues Seminar
Broadcast Engineering
Experimental Video
Special Seminar — Production Problems
Program for Public Access
Media in Education
Directed Independent Study — Media
Directed Independent Study — TV

Michigan

Macomb County Community College

County-supported 2-year coed college. Institutionally accredited by regional association. Suburban location. Undergraduate enrollment: 25,314. Total faculty: 734 (344 full-time, 390 part-time). Semester calendar. Grading system: letters or numbers.

Humanities Department, Mt Clemens, MI 48043 313-286-2000

CONTACT Glenn Lahti
ADMISSION Application deadline — 8/31
FACULTY Glenn Lahti

COURSE LIST
Undergraduate
Film as Art

Madonna College

Independent 4-year coed college. Institutionally accredited by regional association. Suburban location, 49-acre campus. Undergraduate enrollment: 3011. Total faculty: 132 (70 full-time, 62 part-time). Semester calendar. Grading system: letters or numbers.

Communication Arts Department, 36600 Schoolcraft, Livonia, MI 48150

CONTACT Ernest Nolan
DEGREE OFFERED BA in communication arts with an emphasis in TV production
ADMISSION Requirements — 2.0 minimum grade point average, written statement of purpose Application deadline — rolling
FINANCIAL AID Scholarships, work/study programs, student loans Application deadline — rolling
CURRICULAR EMPHASIS Television study — (1) production; (2) appreciation, educational; (3) history, criticism and aesthetics, management Television production — (1) news/documentary, educational; (2) commercial; (3) experimental/personal video
SPECIAL ACTIVITIES/OFFERINGS Film series, student publications, internships in television production, independent study, teacher training

Madonna College (continued)

FACILITIES AND EQUIPMENT Television — black and white studio cameras, color studio cameras, ½-inch VTR, ¾-inch cassette VTR, portable black and white cameras, editing equipment, monitors, special effects generators, portable color cameras, ¾-inch ENG, lighting equipment, sound recording equipment, audio mixers, circular track, studio draperies, color studio, audio studio, control room

FACULTY Patricia Derry PART-TIME FACULTY Charles Derry, Melvin Wasserman

COURSE LIST

Undergraduate

Television Production I, II
Film Appreciation
Instructional Media
Practicum/Co-op

Michigan State University

State-supported coed university. Institutionally accredited by regional association. Small town location, 5000-acre campus. Total enrollment: 43,744. Undergraduate enrollment: 35,645. Total faculty: 2607 (2491 full-time, 116 part-time). Quarter calendar. Grading system: letters or numbers.

Department of Art, 218 Kresge Art Center, East Lansing, MI 48824 517-355-7619

CONTACT Joseph Kuszai

PROGRAM OFFERED Major in design with an emphasis in film (animation and special effects)

DEPARTMENTAL MAJORS Undergraduate film — 20 students Graduate film — 2 students

ADMISSION Undergraduate requirements — interview, teachers' recommendations, written statement of purpose, portfolio, professional recommendations Graduate requirements — interview, teachers' recommendations, written statement of purpose, portfolio, professional recommendations

CURRICULAR EMPHASIS Undergraduate film study — criticism and aesthetics Graduate film study — criticism and aesthetics Undergraduate filmmaking — (1) animated; (2) experimental

FACILITIES AND EQUIPMENT Film — complete 16mm equipment, 8mm cameras, projectors, Super-8 to video (¾-inch), screening room, editing room, sound mixing room, animation board, permanent film library of student films Television — ¾-inch cassette VTR, editing equipment, monitors

FACULTY Joseph Kuszai

COURSE LIST

Undergraduate

Film Art I, II

Undergraduate and Graduate

Film Workshop

Michigan

Michigan Technological University

State-supported coed university. Institutionally accredited by regional association. Small town location, 205-acre campus. Total enrollment: 6902. Undergraduate enrollment: 6657. Total faculty: 367 (346 full-time, 21 part-time). Quarter calendar. Grading system: letters or numbers.

Humanities Department, Houghton, MI 49931 906-482-5521

CONTACT Film — J B Kirkish Television — Barry Pegg

ADMISSION Application deadline — 8/1

CURRICULAR EMPHASIS Film study — (1) appreciation; (2) history; (3) criticism and aesthetics Filmmaking — (1) educational; (2) documentary; (3) narrative Television study — (1) production; (2) educational; (3) criticism and aesthetics Television production — (1) educational; (2) news/documentary; (3) experimental/personal video

SPECIAL ACTIVITIES/OFFERINGS Film series, film societies, program material produced for on-campus closed-circuit television, independent study

FACILITIES AND EQUIPMENT Film — complete 8mm equipment, screening room, editing room, sound mixing room, animation board Television — complete black and white studio and exterior production equipment, complete color studio and exterior production equipment, black and white studio, color studio, audio studio, control room

Monroe County Community College

County-supported 2-year coed college. Institutionally accredited by regional association. Rural location, 150-acre campus. Undergraduate enrollment: 2026. Total faculty: 80 (45 full-time, 35 part-time). 4-1-4 calendar. Grading system: letters or numbers.

Humanities Department, 1555 South Raisinville Road, Monroe, MI 48161 313-242-7300

CONTACT John Holladay

ADMISSION Application deadline — 9/1, rolling

FINANCIAL AID Scholarships, student loans, work/study programs Application deadline — 4/15

CURRICULAR EMPHASIS Film study — (1) appreciation; (2) production; (3) history, criticism and aesthetics Filmmaking — (1) narrative; (2) documentary Television study — educational Television production — educational

SPECIAL ACTIVITIES/OFFERINGS Film series, film societies, student publications, independent study

FACILITIES AND EQUIPMENT Film — complete 8mm equipment, screening room, editing room Television — complete black and white studio production equipment, black and white studio

FACULTY John Holladay

COURSE LIST

Undergraduate

Introduction to Film
Audio Visual Instruction Workshop

Muskegon Community College

County-supported 2-year coed college. Institutionally accredited by regional association. Urban location. Undergraduate enrollment: 2926. Total faculty: 198 (123 full-time, 75 part-time). Semester calendar. Grading system: letters or numbers.

English/Communications Department, 221 Quarterline, Muskegon, MI 49442 616-773-9131

CONTACT Kent DeYoung
DEGREE OFFERED AA in communications media
FINANCIAL AID Scholarships, work/study programs, student loans
CURRICULAR EMPHASIS Film study — history, criticism and aesthetics, appreciation treated equally Filmmaking — documentary, narrative treated equally Television study — history, educational, production treated equally Television production — news/documentary, educational treated equally
SPECIAL ACTIVITIES/OFFERINGS Film series, student publications, program material produced for on-campus closed-circuit television and cable television, internships in film production, internships in television production, independent study
FACILITIES AND EQUIPMENT Film — complete 8mm production equipment, animation board, permanent film library of commercial or professional films Television — black and white studio cameras, color studio cameras, ¾-inch cassette VTR, portable black and white cameras, editing equipment, monitors, special effects generators, slide chain, portable color cameras, ½-inch portapak recorders, ¾-inch ENG, lighting equipment, sound recording equipment, audio mixers, film chain, color studio, audio studio, control room
FACULTY Kent DeYoung, Bruce McCrea, John Walson PART-TIME FACULTY John Estrabrook, David Mooney

COURSE LIST

Undergraduate

Introduction to Broadcasting
Radio Production
TV Production
Film Production Workshop
Mass Media
Broadcast Journalism
Introduction to Film

Northern Michigan University

State-supported comprehensive coed institution. Institutionally accredited by regional association, programs recognized by NASM. Urban location, 300-acre campus. Total enrollment: 8727. Undergraduate enrollment: 7603. Total faculty: 396 (355 full-time, 41 part-time). Semester calendar. Grading system: letters or numbers.

Art and Design Department, Marquette, MI 49855 906-227-3703

CONTACT Michael Cinelli
DEGREES OFFERED BA, BFA, MA in art education with emphasis in film
DEPARTMENTAL MAJORS 15 students
ADMISSION Undergraduate requirement — ACT scores Undergraduate application deadline — rolling
FINANCIAL AID Scholarships, work/study programs Undergraduate application deadline — 4/1
CURRICULAR EMPHASIS Film study — (1) production; (2) criticism and theory; (3) history Filmmaking — (1) narrative; (2) experimental; (3) documentary
SPECIAL ACTIVITIES/OFFERINGS Film series, independent study
FACILITIES AND EQUIPMENT Film — complete 16mm equipment, screening room, editing room, sound mixing room, animation board, permanent film library
FACULTY Michael Cinelli

COURSE LIST

Undergraduate

Guided Studies in Film
Practice of Film
Junior Seminar in Film
Senior Seminar in Film
BFA Seminar in Film

Oakland Community College, Orchard Ridge Campus

State and locally supported 2-year coed college. Institutionally accredited by regional association. Urban location, 572-acre campus. Undergraduate enrollment: 20,032. Total faculty: 550 (250 full-time, 300 part-time). Semester calendar. Grading system: letters or numbers.

Communication Arts Department, 27055 Orchard Lake Road, Farmington Hills, MI 48018 313-476-9400

CONTACT Dan Greenberg
ADMISSION Application deadline — rolling
SPECIAL ACTIVITIES/OFFERINGS Film series, film festivals, program material produced for classroom use
FACILITIES AND EQUIPMENT Film — complete 16mm equipment, 8mm cameras, editing equipment, editing room Television — black and white studio cameras, ½-inch VTR, ¾-inch cassette VTR, portable black and white cameras, slide chain, ½-inch portapak recorder, lighting equipment, sound recording equipment, audio mixers, film chain, black and white studio, audio studio, control room
FACULTY Dan Greenberg, Ted Rancont, Wallace Smith PART-TIME FACULTY Vic Hurwitz, Dave Kelley

COURSE LIST

Undergraduate

Introduction to Film
Introduction to Broadcasting
Broadcast Journalism
Broadcast Laboratory I, II
Fundamentals of Cinematography
Advanced Cinematography
Linguistics for Communicators
Communications and the Law
Radio Station Production I, II
Radio and Television Station Management
Scriptwriting I, II

Oakland University

State-supported coed university. Institutionally accredited by regional association. Suburban location. Total enrollment: 11,220. Undergraduate enrollment: 8992. Total faculty: 345 (289 full-time, 56 part-time). Semester calendar. Grading system: letters or numbers.

Department of English, Rochester, MI 48063 313-377-2250

CONTACT Robert Eberwein
PROGRAM OFFERED Liberal arts major with concentration in film
CURRICULAR EMPHASIS Undergraduate film study — (1) history; criticism and aesthetics; (2) appreciation Graduate film study — (1) criticism and aesthetics; (2) appreciation
SPECIAL ACTIVITIES/OFFERINGS Film series, film societies
FACILITIES AND EQUIPMENT Film — 8mm editing equipment, projectors, 16mm projectors, sound stage Television — black and white studio cameras, ½-inch VTR, ¾-inch cassette VTR, portable black and white cameras, editing equipment, monitors, special effects generators, portable color cameras, ½-inch portapak recorders, ¾-inch ENG, lighting equipment, sound recording equipment, audio mixers, black and white studio, audio studio, control room
FACULTY Herbert Appleman, Peter Bertocci, Dolores Burdick, Alfred DuBruck, Robert Eberwein, Brian Murphy, Charlotte Stokes

COURSE LIST

Undergraduate
Introduction to Film
Film: A Literary Approach
Studies in the Foreign Film
Topics in Film
Cultural Anthropology and the Ethnographic Film
Film and the Visual Arts

Graduate
Modes or Special Forms

Undergraduate and Graduate
History and Theory of Film Criticism
Silent Film
Sound Film to 1958
The New Wave and Beyond

Communication Arts Department 313-377-2155

CONTACT Donald Hildum, Chairman
PROGRAM OFFERED Major in communication arts with emphasis in film or television
ADMISSION Application deadline — rolling
CURRICULAR EMPHASIS Film study — criticism and aesthetics

COURSE LIST

Undergraduate
Introduction to Television Production
Media Hardware
Introduction to Cinematography
Directing for Stage, Film, and Television

Saint Mary's College

Independent Roman Catholic 4-year coed college. Institutionally accredited by regional association. Suburban location, 120-acre campus. Undergraduate enrollment: 191. Total faculty: 40 (15 full-time, 25 part-time). Semester calendar. Grading system: letters or numbers.

Communication Arts Department, Orchard Lake, MI 48033 313-682-1885

CONTACT Reverend Clifford F Ruskowski
DEGREE OFFERED BA with a major in communications
DEPARTMENTAL MAJORS Film — 40 students Television — 30 students
ADMISSION Requirements — 2.0 minimum grade point average, ACT or SAT scores, interview, teachers' recommendations, written statement of purpose Application deadline — 8/15
FINANCIAL AID Scholarships, work/study programs, student loans Application deadline — 8/1
CURRICULAR EMPHASIS Film study — history, criticism and aesthetics, appreciation, educational media/instructional technology treated equally Filmmaking — documentary, narrative, theory of filmmaking treated equally Television study — history, criticism and aesthetics, appreciation, educational, production treated equally Television production — commercial, news/documentary, experimental/personal video, educational treated equally
SPECIAL ACTIVITIES/OFFERINGS Filmmaking clubs, student publications, program material produced for on-campus closed-circuit television, vocational placement service
FACILITIES AND EQUIPMENT Film — 16mm cameras, editing equipment, sound recording equipment, lighting, black and white film stock, projectors, editing room, sound mixing room, permanent film library of commercial or professional films Television — black and white studio cameras, ½-inch VTR, ¾-inch cassette VTR, editing equipment, monitors, ½-inch portapak recorders, ¾-inch ENG, lighting equipment, sound recording equipment, audio mixers
FACULTY Reverend Clifford Ruskowski PART-TIME FACULTY Jay Roberts, Rhonda Tanton

COURSE LIST

Undergraduate
Introduction to Communication Arts
Film Study
Photography and Cinematography
Television Production and Practicum

University of Michigan

State-supported coed university. Part of University of Michigan System. Institutionally accredited by regional association. Small town location, 2,580-acre campus. Total enrollment: 35,824. Undergraduate enrollment: 22,076. Total faculty: 2828 (2220 full-time, 608 part-time). Semester calendar. Grading system: letters or numbers.

Program in Film and Video Studies, 131 Old A&D Building, Ann Arbor, MI 48109 313-764-0147

CONTACT Hubert Cohen, Director
DEGREE OFFERED BA in film/video
PROGRAM MAJORS Film — 50 students
ADMISSION Requirements — interview, written statement of purpose Application deadline — 2/1
FINANCIAL AID Work/study programs, student loans Application deadline — 2/1
CURRICULAR EMPHASIS Film study — history, criticism and aesthetics, appreciation, production treated equally Filmmaking — documentary, narrative, experimental, animated treated equally Television study — history, criticism and aesthetics, appreciation, production treated equally Television production — news/documentary, experimental/personal video treated equally
SPECIAL ACTIVITIES/OFFERINGS Film series, film festivals, film societies, student showings, internships in film production, internships in television production, independent study
FACILITIES AND EQUIPMENT Film — 8mm and 16mm cameras, editing equipment, sound recording equipment, lighting, projectors, screening room, editing room, sound mixing room, animation board, permanent film library of commercial or professional films Television — black and white studio cameras, color studio cameras, ½-inch VTR, ¾-inch cassette VTR, portable black and white cameras, editing equipment, monitors, special effects generators, slide chain, ½-inch portapak recorders, lighting equipment, sound recording equipment, audio mixers, film chain, time base corrector, black and white studio, color studio, audio studio, control room
FACULTY Buzz Alexander, Frank Beaver, Hubert Cohen, Herb Eagle, Diane Kirkpatrick, Stuart McDougal, Al Montalvo, Barbara Morris, Ron Rollet

Michigan

COURSE LIST

Undergraduate

The Art of the Film
Introduction to the Film
Introduction to Film Techniques
Introduction to Video Art
History of the American Film
Studies in Film Genre
Le Cinéma Français
German Cinema
Japanese Cinema
Soviet and East European Cinema
Women and Film
Art of the Film
Problems in Film Criticism
Cinematic Experience
Philosophy of Film
Critical Approaches to European Cinema
Cinematography I, II
Video: Autobiography and Documentary
Video Production Seminar

Undergraduate and Graduate

History of the Motion Picture
Film Theory
Mass Media and the Visual Arts
Perception and Expressionism
Aesthetics of Film
Telecommunication Arts Workshop
Intensive Study of Problems in Film and Video

Wayne State University

State-supported coed university. Institutionally accredited by regional association, programs recognized by NASM, AACSB, ACPE. Urban location. Total enrollment: 33,514. Undergraduate enrollment: 23,549. Total faculty: 2200. Quarter calendar. Grading system: letters or numbers.

Department of Speech Communication, Theatre & Journalism: Mass Communications, 585 Manoogian Hall, Detroit, MI 48202 313-577-4163 or 577-2943

CONTACT Film — George Cozyris Television — Patrick Welch
DEGREES OFFERED BA, MA, PhD in mass communications with a major in film or radio-television
DEPARTMENTAL MAJORS Undergraduate film — 65 students Undergraduate television — 138 students Graduate film — 18 students Graduate television — 41 students
ADMISSION Undergraduate requirement — 2.0 minimum grade point average Graduate requirements — 3.0 minimum grade point average for MA, 3.3 minimum grade point average for PhD, interview, teachers' recommendations, written statement of purpose, professional recommendations, academic credentials in chosen discipline
FINANCIAL AID Scholarships, work/study programs, student loans, fellowships, teaching assistantships, research assistantships, grants: BEOG, BOG, SEOG, FAF, LEEP, GI-Bill, BIA, VA-Education, Vocational Rehabilitation Undergraduate application deadline — 3/15
CURRICULAR EMPHASIS Undergraduate film study — (1) appreciation; (2) criticism and aesthetics; (3) history Graduate film study — (1) criticism and aesthetics; (2) appreciation; (3) history Undergraduate filmmaking — (1) documentary; (2) narrative; (3) experimental Graduate filmmaking — (1) documentary; (2) narrative; (3) experimental Undergraduate television study — (1) production; (2) appreciation; (3) management Graduate television study — (1) management; (2) production; (3) appreciation Undergraduate television production — (1) commercial; (2) news/documentary; (3) experimental/personal video Graduate television production — (1) commercial; (2) news/documentary; (3) experimental/personal video
SPECIAL ACTIVITIES/OFFERINGS Film series, program material produced for classroom, internships in film production, internships in television production, independent study
FACILITIES AND EQUIPMENT Film — complete 16mm equipment, 8mm cameras, editing equipment, lighting, projectors, editing room, permanent film library of student films Television — color studio cameras, 1-inch VTR, portable black and white cameras, monitors, special effects generators, slide chain, lighting equipment, sound recording equipment, audio mixers, film chain, color studio, audio studio, control room
FACULTY George Cozyris, J Daniel Logan, Lawrence Silverman, John Spalding, James Tintera, Jack Warfield PART-TIME FACULTY John Buckstaff, Tony Ferri, Andrea Gomez, James Limbacher, Hal Youngblood

COURSE LIST

Undergraduate

Introduction to Film
History of Film
Survey of Mass Communications
Radio and Television Announcing
Writing for Radio-Television-Film
Radio-Television-Film Laboratory
Mass Media Appreciation and Criticism
Television Performance
Mass Media and the Black Community

Wayne State University (continued)

Graduate
Seminar in Film
Seminar in Mass Communications
Seminar in Mass Media Research
Seminar in Broadcast Programming and Management
Seminar in Media Production
Seminar in Educational Utilization of Instructional Media and Mass Communications
Content Analysis of Mass Communications
Criticism of Mass Media
Mass Media and Political Communication
Seminar in Computer-Assisted Instruction

Undergraduate and Graduate
Documentary and Non-Fiction Film
Studies in Film History
Screenwriting
Film Production I, II
Motion Picture Animation Techniques
Advanced Radio-Television-Film Writing
Radio Production
Television Production I, II
Mass Communications and Society
Audience Measurement and Survey Techniques in Mass Media
Broadcast Management
International Communications
Individual Projects and Internships in Radio-Television-Film

English Department, State Hall — Cass, Detroit, MI 48202 313-577-2450

ADMISSION Application deadline — 8/15, rolling
FACULTY Joseph A Gomez

COURSE LIST

Undergraduate
Film and Literature
Introduction to Film

Undergraduate and Graduate
Literature into Film
Styles and Genres in Film
Topics in Film

Western Michigan University

State-supported coed university. Institutionally accredited by regional association, programs recognized by NASM, AACSB, NASA. Suburban location, 375-acre campus. Total enrollment: 20,617. Undergraduate enrollment: 16,868. Total faculty: 1034 (873 full-time, 161 part-time). Trimester calendar. Grading system: letters or numbers.

Communication Arts and Sciences Department, Kalamazoo, MI 49008 616-383-4071

CONTACT George Custen, Jules Rossman
DEGREE OFFERED BA in mass communication (radio/TV), minor in film
DEPARTMENTAL MAJORS Film — 25 students Television — 256 students
ADMISSION Undergraduate requirements — 2.5 minimum grade point average, ACT or SAT scores Graduate requirement — 3.0 minimum grade point average
FINANCIAL AID Scholarships, work/study programs, student loans, fellowships, teaching assistantships Undergraduate application deadline — rolling
CURRICULAR EMPHASIS Undergraduate film study — (1) criticism and aesthetics; (2) history; (3) appreciation Undergraduate filmmaking — (1) experimental; (2) documentary; (3) narrative Undergraduate television study — (1) related theory and applications of TV; (2) management; (3) criticism and aesthetics Undergraduate television production — (1) commercial; (2) experimental/personal video; (3) news/documentary
SPECIAL ACTIVITIES/OFFERINGS Filmmaking clubs, film series, film festivals, program material produced for on-campus closed-circuit television and cable television, internships in television production, independent study, vocational placement service
FACILITIES AND EQUIPMENT Film — complete 8mm equipment, 16mm cameras, editing equipment, sound recording equipment, lighting, projectors, screening room, editing room, sound mixing room, permanent film library of commercial or professional films Television — black and white studio cameras, ½-inch VTR, ¾-inch cassette VTR, portable black and white cameras, editing equipment, monitors, special effects generators, slide chain, portable color cameras, ½-inch portapak recorders, ¾-inch ENG, lighting equipment, sound recording equipment, audio mixers, film chain, character generator, black and white studio, audio studio, control room, small-format VTR editing room and equipment
FACULTY George Custen, Tom Pagel, George Robeck, Jules Rossman, Barry Sherman PART-TIME FACULTY Roy Beck

COURSE LIST

Undergraduate
The Individual and the Mass Media
Broadcast Communication
Film Communication
The Film Industry
Broadcast Operations
Radio Programming and Production
Special Topics in Communication
Small Format Video Production
Film Production
TV Studio Production
TV and Film Scripting
Broadcast Journalism
Independent Study
Advanced TV Studio Production
Television Performance
Documentary in Film and Television

Undergraduate and Graduate
Special Topics in Communication
Studies in Mass Communication: Variable Topics
Mass Communication Law
Mass Media and the Child
Mass Communication and Social Change
Mass Communication, News and Public Affairs
Television Criticism
Mass Entertainment
Organizational Uses of Radio and Television
Broadcast Management
Public Relations and Organization
Methods of Film Analysis
Independent Study

MINNESOTA

Augsburg College

Independent Lutheran 4-year coed college. Institutionally accredited by regional association. Urban location. Undergraduate enrollment: 1625. Total faculty: 140 (90 full-time, 50 part-time). 4-1-4 calendar. Grading system: letters or numbers.

Art Department, Film Studio, 731 21st Avenue S, Minneapolis, MN 55454 612-330-1065

CONTACT Film — Paul Rusten Television — Ray Anderson
ADMISSION Requirements — minimum grade point average, SAT scores Application deadline — 8/1, rolling
FINANCIAL AID Scholarships, student loans, work/study programs Application deadline — 8/1, rolling
CURRICULAR EMPHASIS Film study — (1) production; (2) criticism and aesthetics; (3) appreciation Filmmaking — (1) documentary; (2) educational; (3) experimental Television study — (1) production; (2) educational; (3) appreciation Television production — (1) experimental/personal video; (2) news/documentary; (3) educational
SPECIAL ACTIVITIES/OFFERINGS Film series, program material produced for on-campus closed-circuit television, internships in film and television production, independent study
FACILITIES AND EQUIPMENT Film — complete 16mm equipment, screening room, editing room, sound mixing room, permanent film library Television — complete black and white studio and exterior production equipment, black and white studio, audio studio, control room
FACULTY John Mitchell PART-TIME FACULTY Paul Rusten

COURSE LIST
Undergraduate
Filmmaking I, II
Television Production
Introduction to Cinema Art

Bemidji State University

State-supported comprehensive coed institution. Part of Minnesota State University System. Institutionally accredited by regional association, programs recognized by AACSB. Rural location, 83-acre campus. Total enrollment: 4250. Undergraduate enrollment: 4032. Total faculty: 210 (198 full-time, 12 part-time). Quarter calendar. Grading system: letters or numbers.

Speech, Theater, Mass Communication Department, Bemidji, MN 56601 218-755-2000

CONTACT Robert K Smith, Chairman
PROGRAM OFFERED Major in communication with emphasis in film or television
DEPARTMENTAL MAJORS 80 students
ADMISSION Application deadline — 8/15
CURRICULAR EMPHASIS Film study — history, criticism and aesthetics, production treated equally Filmmaking — documentary, narrative, experimental, animated, educational treated equally Television study — (1) production; (2) history, educational; (3) criticism and aesthetics Television production — (1) news/documentary; (2) educational; (3) experimental/personal video
SPECIAL ACTIVITIES/OFFERINGS Program material produced for cable television and local commercial television station, internships in film and television production, independent study, vocational placement service
FACILITIES AND EQUIPMENT Film — complete 8mm and 16mm equipment, sound stage, screening room, editing room, sound mixing room Television — complete black and white studio and exterior production facilities, complete color studio and exterior production facilities.
FACULTY Allen Bowes, Sandy Fellman, Chris Geisen, Allen Mussehl, Pete Nordgren, Roger Paskuan, Rick Robinson, Robert K Smith

COURSE LIST
Undergraduate
Radio-Television-Film
Graphics of the Media
Radio-Television Internship

Brainerd Community College

State-supported 2-year coed college. Part of Minnesota State Community College System. Institutionally accredited by regional association. Small town location, 125-acre campus. Undergraduate enrollment: 608. Total faculty: 37 (26 full-time, 11 part-time). Quarter calendar. Grading system: letters or numbers.

Humanities Department, College Drive, Brainerd, MN 56401 218-828-2525

CONTACT Joseph Plut
ADMISSION Application deadline — rolling
FACULTY Joseph Plut

COURSE LIST
Undergraduate
Introduction to Film

Carleton College

Independent 4-year coed college. Institutionally accredited by regional association, programs recognized by NASA. Small town location. Undergraduate enrollment: 1850. Total faculty: 168 (132 full-time, 36 part-time). 3-3 calendar. Grading system: letters or numbers.

Carleton College (continued)

Film Arts Department, Northfield, MN 55057 507-645-4431

CONTACT John Schott
DEGREE OFFERED BA in film arts
ADMISSION Requirement — interviews Application deadline — 3/1
FINANCIAL AID Scholarships, student loans Application deadline — 3/1
CURRICULAR EMPHASIS Film study — (1) script; (2) production; (3) criticism and aesthetics; (4) history; (5) educational media/instructional technology; (6) appreciation Filmmaking — (1) narrative; (2) documentary; (3) educational; (4) animated; (5) experimental
SPECIAL ACTIVITIES/OFFERINGS Film series, film societies, program material produced for on-campus closed-circuit television, internships in film and television production, independent study, vocational placement service
FACILITIES AND EQUIPMENT Film — complete 8mm and 16mm equipment, screening room, editing room, sound mixing room, animation board Television — complete black and white studio and exterior production equipment, complete color studio and exterior production equipment, black and white studio, color studio, audio studio, control room
FACULTY Peter Bundy, John Schott

COURSE LIST
Undergraduate
Language of Cinema
Screenwriting I–III
Bergman Seminar
Film and Television, Genres and Styles
Expressionism: Film and Theatre
Renoir Seminar
Anthropology and Film
Film as Art
Film and Television Workshops I–III
Documentary Film History and Theory

Colleges of St Catherine/St Thomas

St Catherine: Independent Roman Catholic 4-year women's college. Institutionally accredited by regional association. Urban location, 110-acre campus. Undergraduate enrollment: 2100. Total faculty: 150. 4-1-4 calendar. Grading system: letters or numbers.

St Thomas: Independent Roman Catholic comprehensive institution, coed as of 1977. Institutionally accredited by regional association. Suburban location, 65-acre campus. Total enrollment: 4482. Undergraduate enrollment: 2862. Total faculty: 245 (145 full-time, 100 part-time). 4-1-4 calendar. Grading system: letters or numbers.

Communication/Theatre Department, 2004 Randolph Avenue, St Paul, MN 55105 612-690-6680

CONTACT Film — George Poletes Television — James Townsend
DEGREES OFFERED BA with majors offered in communication — television/radio, film/television, etc
ADMISSION Requirements — ACT or SAT scores, interview, teachers' recommendations, written statement of purpose Application deadline — by end of sophomore year
FINANCIAL AID Work/study programs, student loans, paraprofessional assistantships
CURRICULAR EMPHASIS Film study — history, criticism and aesthetics, appreciation treated equally Filmmaking — documentary, narrative, experimental treated equally Television study — history, criticism and aesthetics, appreciation, educational, production, management treated equally Television production — news/documentary, experimental/personal video, educational treated equally
SPECIAL ACTIVITIES/OFFERINGS Film series; film festivals; film societies; program material produced for on-campus closed-circuit television, cable television, local public television station, local commercial television station; apprenticeships; internships in film production; internships in television production; independent study; teacher training; vocational placement service
FACILITIES AND EQUIPMENT Film — complete 8mm equipment, editing room, sound mixing room, permanent film library of student films, permanent film library of commercial or professional films Television — complete black and white and color studio production equipment, complete black and white exterior production equipment, black and white studio, color studio, audio studio, control room, portapak
FACULTY George Poletes, James Townsend, Gene Vonmosch PART-TIME FACULTY John Mitchell

COURSE LIST
Undergraduate
Introduction to Film
Filmmaking
Introduction to Broadcasting
Introduction to Audio Production
Current Issues in Broadcasting
Video Production

College of St Scholastica

Independent Roman Catholic comprehensive coed institution. Institutionally accredited by regional association. Urban location, 160-acre campus. Total enrollment: 1162. Undergraduate enrollment: 1083. Total faculty: 126 (73 full-time, 53 part-time). Quarter calendar. Grading system: letters or numbers.

Media Arts Department, 1200 Kenwood Avenue, Duluth, MN 55811 218-723-6144

CONTACT Steve Erickson
DEGREE OFFERED BA in media arts with an emphasis in film, TV, advertising, and photography
DEPARTMENTAL MAJORS Film — 3 students Television — 5 students
ADMISSION Requirements — ACT or SAT scores, interview
FINANCIAL AID Scholarships, work/study programs, student loans, grants
CURRICULAR EMPHASIS Film study — (1) appreciation; (2) criticism and aesthetics; (3) history Filmmaking — (1) narrative; (2) educational; (3) experimental Television study — (1) production; (2) appreciation; (3) criticism and aesthetics Television production — (1) commercial; (2) news/documentary; (3) experimental/personal video
SPECIAL ACTIVITIES/OFFERINGS Film series; film societies; student publications; program material produced for on-campus closed-circuit television, local public television station, local commercial television station; internships in film production; internships in television production; independent study

FACILITIES AND EQUIPMENT Film — complete 8mm and 16mm production equipment, editing room Television — ½-inch VTR, ¾-inch cassette VTR, portable black and white cameras, monitors, portable color cameras, ¾-inch ENG, lighting equipment, sound recording equipment, audio mixers, black and white studio
FACULTY Geoff Bowen, Steve Erickson PART-TIME FACULTY Marlene Nordstrom, Steve Stark, Sister Noemi Weygant

COURSE LIST
Undergraduate
Film and Television Appreciation
Beginning Filmmaking/Super-8
Advanced Filmmaking/Super-8
Studies in Motion Picture History
Introduction to Broadcasting
Writing for the Media
16mm Film Production
Television Production I, II
Studies in Contemporary Film
Television Criticism
Alternative Video
Media Ethics/Law
Broadcast Management

Film in the Cities

State and locally run 2-year nonprofit coed organization. All college courses are accredited by Inver Hills Community College. Urban location. Total enrollment: 350. Total faculty: 20. Quarter calendar. Grading system: pass/fail, and letters or numbers.

2388 University Avenue, St Paul, MN 55114 612-646-6104

CONTACT Sheryl Mousley
DEGREE OFFERED AA in filmmaking (offered in conjunction with Inver Hills Community College)
PROGRAM MAJORS 25 students
ADMISSION Requirements — interviews, portfolio Application deadline — 7/1
FINANCIAL AID Student loans, work/study programs Application deadline — 7/1
CURRICULAR EMPHASIS Film study — (1) production; (2) history, criticism and aesthetics, educational media/instructional technology Filmmaking — (1) experimental; (2) documentary, narrative, animated
SPECIAL ACTIVITIES/OFFERINGS Film series, film festivals, program material produced for local public television station, internships in film production, independent study, teacher training, vocational placement service
FACILITIES AND EQUIPMENT Film — complete 8mm and 16mm equipment, screening room, 35mm screening facilities, editing room, sound mixing room, animation board, permanent film library
PART-TIME FACULTY Phil Anderson, Peter Bundy, Rod Eaton, Jim Gambone, Roger Jacoby, Stuart Klipper, Kathleen Laughlin, Richard Weise, Greg Winter

COURSE LIST
Undergraduate
Synchronous Sound
16mm Film Production
Editing
Finance for Filmmakers
Silent Filmmaking
Sound: Recording and Composition
Sound Filmmaking
Advanced Filmmaking I & II
Internship
Technical Survival
Documentary Film
Silent Film History
History of Sound Cinema
History of New American Film
Elements of Film Art
Film Theory I, II
Scriptwriting I, II
Education or Commercial Internships
Animation I, II
Investigative Research for Film
Optical Printing
Special Effects

Undergraduate and Graduate
Teaching Media in the Schools

Hamline University

Independent 4-year and professional coed institution affiliated with United Methodist Church. Institutionally accredited by regional association. Urban location, 30-acre campus. Undergraduate enrollment: 1189. Total faculty: 170 (125 full-time, 45 part-time). 4-1-4 calendar. Grading system: letters or numbers.

Instructional Services/Theatre/Communication Arts Department, 1536 Hewitt Avenue, St Paul, MN 55104 612-641-2380

CONTACT Bob Bauman
ADMISSION Requirements — interviews, written statement of purpose
FINANCIAL AID Scholarships, student loans, work/study programs, fellowships
CURRICULAR EMPHASIS Film study — (1) appreciation; (2) history; (3) criticism and aesthetics Filmmaking — (1) experimental; (2) documentary; (3) narrative; (4) educational; (5) animated Television study — (1) appreciation; (2) production; (3) criticism and aesthetics; (4) management; (5) history; (6) educational Television production — (1) commercial; (2) news/documentary; (3) experimental/personal video; (4) educational
SPECIAL ACTIVITIES/OFFERINGS Film series; film festivals; film societies; program material produced for on-campus closed-circuit television, cable television, local public television station; apprenticeships; internships in television production; independent study; practicum; teacher training
FACILITIES AND EQUIPMENT Film — complete 8mm, 16mm, and 35mm equipment, sound stage, screening room, editing room, sound mixing room, permanent film library Television — complete black and white studio and exterior production equipment, black and white studio, audio studio, control room
FACULTY Bob Bauman, Carol Brown, William Kimes

COURSE LIST
Graduate
Film History
Film as Art
Television Production I, II
Filmmaking: 8mm
Independent Study: 16mm
Independent Study: Television Programming
Independent Study: Motion Photography

Minneapolis College of Art and Design

Independent 4-year coed college. Institutionally accredited by regional association. Urban location. Semester calendar. Grading system: letters or numbers.

Design Division, 133 East 25th Street, Minneapolis, MN 55404 612-870-3346

CONTACT Film — Tom DeBiaso Television — Ken Feingold
DEGREE OFFERED BFA
PROGRAM MAJORS Film — 25 students Television — 15 students
ADMISSION Requirements — teachers' recommendations, written statement of purpose, portfolio Application deadline — 5/1, rolling
FINANCIAL AID Scholarships, work/study programs, student loans Application deadline — 3/1
CURRICULAR EMPHASIS Film study — history, criticism and aesthetics treated equally Filmmaking — documentary, narrative, experimental, animated treated equally Television study — criticism and aesthetics, video art treated equally Television production — commercial, news/documentary, experimental/personal video treated equally
SPECIAL ACTIVITIES/OFFERINGS Film series, film festivals, student publications, program material produced for local public television station, independent study
FACILITIES AND EQUIPMENT Film — complete 8mm and 16mm equipment, sound stage, screening room, editing room, sound mixing room, animation board, permanent film library of student films Television — black and white studio cameras, color studio cameras, ½-inch VTR, ¾-inch cassette VTR, portable black and white cameras, editing equipment, monitors, special effects generators, slide chain, portable color cameras (limited access), ½-inch portapak recorders, lighting equipment, sound recording equipment, audio mixers, Beta Max recorders, black and white studio, color studio, audio studio, control room
FACULTY Tom DeBiaso, Ken Feingold, Sandy Maliza PART-TIME FACULTY Phil Anderson, David Higgins, John Maliga

COURSE LIST
Undergraduate
Film I: Introduction
Film II: Intermediate
Film III: Advanced
Advanced Intermedia
Introduction to Video
Intermediate Video
Film History
Topics in Film Study
Critical Studies
Visual Communications

Moorhead State University

State-supported comprehensive coed institution. Part of Minnesota State University System. Institutionally accredited by regional association. Suburban location. Total enrollment: 7033. Undergraduate enrollment: 6358. Total faculty: 336 (287 full-time, 49 part-time). Quarter calendar. Grading system: letters or numbers.

Department of Speech Communication, Moorhead, MN 56560 218-236-2126

CONTACT Film — Ted M Larson Television — Douglas Hamilton
DEGREE OFFERED BA in speech communication with a concentration in radio-TV-film, individualized major in film
DEPARTMENTAL MAJORS Film — 25 students Television — 15 students
ADMISSION Requirements — 2.0 minimum grade point average, ACT or SAT scores Application deadline — 8/15
FINANCIAL AID Scholarships, work/study programs, student loans
CURRICULAR EMPHASIS Film study — history, criticism and aesthetics, appreciation treated equally Filmmaking — documentary, narrative, experimental, animated treated equally Television study — (1) production; (2) criticism and aesthetics; (3) appreciation Television production — (1) news/documentary; (2) commercial; (3) experimental/personal video
SPECIAL ACTIVITIES/OFFERINGS Filmmaking clubs, film series, film festivals, film societies, program material produced for on-campus closed-circuit television and cable television, apprenticeships, internships in film production, internships in television production, independent study, vocational placement service
FACILITIES AND EQUIPMENT Film — complete 8mm equipment, screening room, editing room, sound mixing room, permanent film library of commercial or professional films Television — black and white studio cameras, color studio cameras, ½-inch VTR, 1-inch VTR, ¾-inch cassette VTR, portable black and white cameras, editing equipment, monitors, special effects generators, slide chain, portable color cameras, ½-inch portapak recorders, ¾-inch ENG, lighting equipment, sound recording equipment, audio mixers, film chain, time base corrector, black and white studio, color studio, control room
FACULTY Douglas Hamilton, Ted M Larson

COURSE LIST
Undergraduate
History of Film
Survey of Film Styles
Film Form and Criticism
Experimental Filmmaking
Radio-TV Performance I, II
TV Production I, II
TV and Film Directing
Undergraduate and Graduate
The Animated Film
Critical Film Genre Studies
Critical Film Personality Studies

St Cloud State University

State-supported comprehensive coed institution. Part of Minnesota State University System. Institutionally accredited by regional association, programs recognized by NASM, AACSB. Urban location, 82-acre campus. Total enrollment: 10,487. Undergraduate enrollment: 9429. Total faculty: 539 (515 full-time, 24 part-time). Quarter calendar. Grading system: letters or numbers.

Theatre Department, St Cloud, MN 56301 612-255-3229

CONTACT Dale L Swanson

DEGREES OFFERED BA, BS, BES in theatre with an emphasis in film
ADMISSION Requirements — ACT or SAT scores
FINANCIAL AID Scholarships, work/study programs, student loans
CURRICULAR EMPHASIS Film study — history, criticism and aesthetics, appreciation treated equally
SPECIAL ACTIVITIES/OFFERINGS Film series, film festivals
FACILITIES AND EQUIPMENT Film — screening room, permanent film library of commercial or professional films
FACULTY Ronald G Perrier, Dale L Swanson

COURSE LIST
Undergraduate
Introduction to Theatre and Film
Art of the Cinema
Development of the American Cinema
Development of the Non-American Cinema
Studies in Cinema: Topics Course

Mass Communications Department 612-255-3294

CONTACT E Scott Bryce or Francis Voelker
DEGREES OFFERED BS, BES in mass communications–cinematography; BS, BES in mass communications–television
DEPARTMENTAL MAJORS Television — 25 students
ADMISSION Application deadline — 8/15
FINANCIAL AID Scholarships, student loans, work/study programs Application deadline — rolling
CURRICULAR EMPHASIS Film study — (1) production; (2) educational media/instructional technology; (3) criticism and aesthetics Filmmaking — (1) documentary; (2) narrative; (3) educational Television study — (1) production; (2) educational; (3) management Television production — (1) news/documentary; (2) commercial; (3) educational; (4) experimental/personal video
SPECIAL ACTIVITIES/OFFERINGS Film series, internships in film and television production, independent study, vocational placement service
FACILITIES AND EQUIPMENT Film — complete 8mm and 16mm equipment, sound stage, screening room, editing room, sound mixing room, animation board, permanent film library Television — complete black and white studio and exterior production equipment, complete color studio and exterior production equipment, black and white studio, color studio, audio studio, control room
FACULTY E Scott Bryce, Francis Voelker

COURSE LIST
Undergraduate
Introduction to Mass Communications
History of Mass Media
Visual Communications
Communication Activities
Cinematography I, II
Radio-Television News Writing and Editing
Introduction to Television Production and Direction
Advanced Television Activities
Sportswriting and Broadcasting
Management of Broadcasting
Mass Media and Social Institutions
Public Relations
Film Documentary
Advanced Television Production
Advanced Television Direction
Broadcast Law
Commercial Writing for Radio-TV

Undergraduate and Graduate
Mass Communications Law

Philosophy Department 612-255-4151

CONTACT Ted Sherarts
ADMISSION Application deadline — 8/15
CURRICULAR EMPHASIS Film study — (1) criticism and aesthetics; (2) history; (3) appreciation
SPECIAL ACTIVITIES/OFFERINGS Film series, film societies
FACILITIES AND EQUIPMENT Film — 8mm cameras, editing equipment, lighting equipment, black and white film stock, color film stock, projectors
FACULTY Ruel Fischmann (on leave)

COURSE LIST
Undergraduate and Graduate
Film Aesthetics

St Olaf College

Independent Lutheran 4-year coed college. Institutionally accredited by regional association, programs recognized by NASM. Small town location, 350-acre campus. Undergraduate enrollment: 2971. Total faculty: 294 (216 full-time, 78 part-time). 4-1-4 calendar. Grading system: letters or numbers.

Art Department, Northfield, MN 55057 507-663-3248

CONTACT Arch Leean
DEGREE OFFERED BA in art
ADMISSION Requirements — ACT or SAT scores, teachers' recommendations, written statement of purpose, portfolio Application deadline — 3/31
FINANCIAL AID Scholarships, work/study programs, student loans
CURRICULAR EMPHASIS Film study — drawing and design Filmmaking — experimental, animated treated equally
SPECIAL ACTIVITIES/OFFERINGS Film series, film festivals, film societies, student publications, apprenticeships, internships in film production, independent study, teacher training, vocational placement service
FACILITIES AND EQUIPMENT Film — 8mm cameras, editing equipment, projectors, 16mm cameras, editing equipment, sound recording equipment, projectors, film printer, optical printer, animation stands, roto scope, screening room, editing room, sound mixing room, animation board, permanent film library of student films, permanent film library of commercial or professional films
FACULTY Arch Leean

St Olaf College (continued)

COURSE LIST

Undergraduate

Graphic Film Production I, II
Independent Study
Senior Studies
Apprenticeships

University of Minnesota, Duluth

State-supported comprehensive coed institution. Part of University of Minnesota System. Institutionally accredited by regional association, programs recognized by NASM. Urban location. Total enrollment: 6809. Undergraduate enrollment: 6450. Total faculty: 425 (300 full-time, 125 part-time). Quarter calendar. Grading system: letters or numbers.

Department of Communication, Duluth, MN 55812 218-726-8576

CONTACT Jon Crane, Jerry K Frye, or Greg Swanson
PROGRAM OFFERED Major in communication with emphasis in film or television
ADMISSION Requirement — 2.0 minimum grade point average Application deadline — 7/15, rolling
CURRICULAR EMPHASIS Film study — (1) history; (2) criticism and aesthetics; (3) production Filmmaking — (1) documentary; (2) narrative; (3) experimental Television study — (1) production; (2) criticism and aesthetics; (3) history Television production — (1) news/documentary; (2) educational; (3) commercial
SPECIAL ACTIVITIES/OFFERINGS Film series; film festivals; film societies; program material produced for on-campus closed-circuit television, cable television, on-campus public television station, 3 local commercial television stations; internships in television production; independent study
FACILITIES AND EQUIPMENT Film — complete 16mm equipment, screening room, editing room, sound mixing room, permanent film library Television — complete color studio and exterior production equipment, color studio, audio studio, control room
FACULTY Jon Crane, Jerry K Frye, Greg Swanson

Minnesota

COURSE LIST

Undergraduate

Writing for Radio and Television
Television Production I, II
History of Broadcasting
Mass Communication and Society
Cinema Workshop
Film Production
Cinema and Society
Documentary Film and Television
Broadcasting and Government
Mass Communication Theory
Seminar: Film Theory to Criticism
Seminar: Public Television
Seminar: Broadcast Journalism

University of Minnesota, Minneapolis—St Paul

State-supported coed university. Part of University of Minnesota System. Institutionally accredited by regional association. Urban location. Total enrollment: 45,062. Undergraduate enrollment: 33,803. Total faculty: 5286 (4350 full-time, 936 part-time). Quarter calendar. Grading system: letters or numbers.

General College, 106 Nicholson Hall, 216 Pillsbury Drive SE, Minneapolis, MN 55455 612-373-4104

CONTACT Robert Yahnke
CURRICULAR EMPHASIS Undergraduate film study — (1) appreciation; (2) criticism and aesthetics; (3) history Undergraduate filmmaking — narrative, experimental, educational treated equally Undergraduate television study — history, criticism and aesthetics, appreciation treated equally
SPECIAL ACTIVITIES/OFFERINGS Independent study
FACILITIES AND EQUIPMENT Film — 8mm cameras, sound recording equipment, lighting Television — ½-inch VTR, ¾-inch cassette VTR, portable black and white cameras, editing equipment, portable color cameras, ½-inch portapak recorders
FACULTY William Adamsen, J MacInnes, Robert Yahnke PART-TIME FACULTY Danny Grossnickle

COURSE LIST

Undergraduate

Literature of the Theater: Film and Drama
Film and Society
Film and the Experience of Aging
Radio, Television

Speech-Communication Department, 317 Folwell Hall, 9 Pleasant Street SE, Minneapolis, MN 55455 612-373-2617

CONTACT Donald Browne
DEGREES OFFERED MA, PhD in communications with an emphasis in television
DEPARTMENTAL MAJORS Undergraduate television — 250 students Graduate television — 15 students
ADMISSION Requirements — 3.0 minimum grade point average, teachers' recommendations, written statement of purpose, Miller Analogies Test score
FINANCIAL AID Scholarships, work/study programs, student loans, fellowships, teaching assistantships
CURRICULAR EMPHASIS Undergraduate television study — (1) production; (2) regulation and economics; (3) criticism and aesthetics; (4) history; (5) management Graduate television study — (1) regulation and economics; (2) management; (3) history; (4) criticism and aesthetics; (5) educational; (6) production Undergraduate television production — commercial, news/documentary, experimental/personal video treated equally Graduate television production — commercial, news/documentary, experimental/personal video treated equally
SPECIAL ACTIVITIES/OFFERINGS Program material produced for on-campus closed-circuit television, cable television, local public television station; internships in television production; independent study
FACILITIES AND EQUIPMENT Film — 8mm cameras, editing equipment, projectors, screening room, editing room Television — black and white studio cameras, color studio cameras, ½-inch VTR, ¾-inch cassette VTR, portable black and white cameras, editing equipment, monitors, special effects generators, slide chain, portable color cameras, ½-inch portapak recorders, lighting equipment, sound recording equipment, audio mixers, film chain, time base corrector, color studio, audio studio, control room
FACULTY Leonard Bart, Charles Bartz, Donald Browne, David Rarick

COURSE LIST

Undergraduate

Fundamentals of Speech-Communication: The Creative Process and the Mass Media
Introduction to Broadcasting Production
Broadcast Practicum
Radio Production
Television Production
Determinants of Broadcast Programming

Graduate

Seminar: Current Issues in Broadcasting
Seminar: Broadcast Organizations and Decision Making
Seminar: International and Comparative Broadcasting

Undergraduate and Graduate

Advanced Television Production
Writing Radio and Television Drama
Contemporary Problems in American Broadcasting
Educational Television Production
Educational Television Programming and Administration
Comparative Broadcast Systems
International Broadcasting
Broadcasting and National Development
The Communicative Processes of Television

Winona State University

State-supported comprehensive coed institution. Part of Minnesota State University System. Institutionally accredited by regional association. Small town location, 40-acre campus. Total enrollment: 4300. Undergraduate enrollment: 4000. Total faculty: 240 (210 full-time, 30 part-time). Quarter calendar. Grading system: letters or numbers.

English Department, Winona, MN 55987 507-457-2942

CONTACT Emilio DeGrazia
SPECIAL ACTIVITIES/OFFERINGS Film series, film societies
FACILITIES AND EQUIPMENT Film — film library
FACULTY Emilio DeGrazia, David Robinson

COURSE LIST

Undergraduate

Approaches to Film
Film Comedy

Photo, Film and Television Department, Phelps Hall, Winona, MN 55987 507-457-2016

CONTACT Film — John Fisk Television — Dennis Pack
DEGREE OFFERED BA with major in mass communications and emphasis in photography, telecommunications
DEPARTMENTAL MAJORS Television — 39 students
ADMISSION Requirement — 2.0 minimum grade point average Application deadline — 8/26, rolling
FINANCIAL AID Work/study programs, student loans
CURRICULAR EMPHASIS Filmmaking — documentary, narrative, educational treated equally Television study — (1) production; (2) history; (3) criticism and aesthetics Television production — commercial, news/documentary, educational treated equally
SPECIAL ACTIVITIES/OFFERINGS Film series, film festivals, program material produced for on-campus closed-circuit television and cable television, internships in television production, independent study, teacher training
FACILITIES AND EQUIPMENT Film — complete 8mm equipment, 16mm cameras, editing equipment, lighting, black and white film stock, color film stock, projectors, screening room, editing room, sound mixing room Television — black and white studio cameras, color studio cameras, ½-inch VTR, 1-inch VTR, ¾-inch cassette VTR, portable black and white cameras, editing equipment, monitors, special effects generators, slide chain, portable color cameras, ¾-inch ENG, lighting equipment, sound recording equipment, audio mixers, film chain, time base corrector, character generator, black and white studio, color studio, audio studio, control room
FACULTY John Fisk, Dennis Pack

COURSE LIST

Undergraduate

Production Planning and Scripting
Introduction to Broadcasting
Preparation of Visual Materials
Filmmaking I, II
Video Workshop
Basic TV Production
Broadcast Journalism

Undergraduate and Graduate

Intermediate TV Production
Advanced TV Production
Television Workshop
Special Problems

MISSISSIPPI

Jackson State University

State-supported comprehensive coed institution. Institutionally accredited by regional association, programs recognized by NASM, NASA. Urban location, 113-acre campus. Total enrollment: 7646. Undergraduate enrollment: 6013. Total faculty: 375. Semester calendar. Grading system: letters or numbers.

Mass Communications Department, PO Box 17112, Jackson, MS 39217 601-948-2151

CONTACT Film — Robert List Television — Elayne Hayes or Omega Wilson
DEGREE OFFERED BS in mass communications (film)

Jackson State University (continued)

ADMISSION Requirements — minimum grade point average, ACT scores
FINANCIAL AID Scholarships, student loans, work/study programs
CURRICULAR EMPHASIS Film study — (1) production; (2) history; (3) criticism and aesthetics; (4) appreciation Filmmaking — (1) documentary; (2) educational; (3) narrative
SPECIAL ACTIVITIES/OFFERINGS Film series; film societies; program material produced for on-campus closed-circuit television, local public television station, local commercial television station; internships in film and television production; independent study; vocational placement service
FACILITIES AND EQUIPMENT Film — 16mm sound recording equipment, sound stage, screening room, editing room, permanent film library Television — complete black and white studio and exterior production equipment, complete color studio and exterior production equipment, black and white studio, color studio, audio studio, control room
FACULTY Elayne Hayes, Robert List, Omega Wilson

Mississippi State University

State-supported coed university. Institutionally accredited by regional association, programs recognized by AACSB. Small town location. Total enrollment: 11,265. Undergraduate enrollment: 9588. Total faculty: 813 (813 full-time, 0 part-time). Semester calendar. Grading system: letters or numbers.

Communication Department, PO Drawer NJ, Mississippi State, MS 39762 601-325-4908

CONTACT Robert G Anderson
DEGREE OFFERED BA in communication with a major in television
DEPARTMENTAL MAJORS 300 students
ADMISSION Application deadline — 8/9, rolling
FINANCIAL AID Student loans, work/study programs Application deadline — 3/1, rolling
CURRICULAR EMPHASIS Television — (1) production; (2) management; (3) social aspects
SPECIAL ACTIVITIES/OFFERINGS Program material produced for on-campus closed-circuit television and cable television, internships in television production, independent study, vocational placement service
FACILITIES AND EQUIPMENT Film — 8mm cameras, editing equipment, lighting equipment, projectors, screening room, editing room Television — complete black and white studio and exterior production equipment, black and white studio, audio studio, control room
FACULTY Robert G Anderson

COURSE LIST

Undergraduate

Introduction to Broadcast Programming and Advertising
Introduction to Mass Media
History of the Mass Media
Introduction to News Writing and Reporting
Writing for Radio-Television-Film
Broadcast Announcing
Motion Picture Production
Radio-Television-Film Survey
Introduction to Cinema
Television Production

Undergraduate and Graduate

Broadcast Management
Mass Media and Law
Mass Media and Society
Social Control of Mass Media

University of Mississippi

State-supported coed university. Institutionally accredited by regional association, programs recognized by NASM, AACSB, ACPE. Small town location. Total enrollment: 9655. Undergraduate enrollment: 7865. Total faculty: 590 (437 full-time, 153 part-time). Semester calendar. Grading system: letters or numbers.

Journalism Department, University, MS 38655 601-232-7146

CONTACT S Kittrell Rushing
DEGREES OFFERED BA in journalism with an emphasis in broadcasting, MA in journalism with an emphasis in mass communication
DEPARTMENTAL MAJORS Undergraduate television — 245 students
ADMISSION Undergraduate requirements — ACT or SAT scores, completion of 15 high school units (3 English, 2 math, 2 in social science) Graduate requirements — 3.0 minimum grade point average, GRE scores, teachers' recommendations, professional work experience, professional recommendations Undergraduate application deadline — 20 days before scheduled registration
FINANCIAL AID Scholarships, work/study programs, student loans, fellowships, teaching assistantships, research assistantships
CURRICULAR EMPHASIS Undergraduate filmmaking — television news and documentary Undergraduate television study — production, management treated equally Undergraduate television production — commercial, news/documentary treated equally
SPECIAL ACTIVITIES/OFFERINGS Film series, student publications, program material produced for cable television, internships in television production, independent study
FACILITIES AND EQUIPMENT Film — 8mm cameras, editing equipment, lighting, projectors, 16mm cameras, editing equipment, sound recording equipment, lighting, black and white film stock, projectors, editing room, sound mixing room, permanent film library of commercial or professional films Television — color studio cameras, ¾-inch cassette VTR, editing equipment, monitors, special effects generators, slide chain, portable color cameras, ¾-inch ENG, lighting equipment, sound recording equipment, audio mixers, film chain, time base corrector, color studio, mobile van/unit, audio studio, control room
FACULTY Daniel Gardner, S Kittrell Rushing PART-TIME FACULTY Ronald Douthet, Robert Lewis, Jimmy Mitchell, Edward Welch

COURSE LIST

Undergraduate

Fundamentals of Broadcast
Writing for Radio-TV
Introduction to Television Production
Advanced Television Production
Advanced Audio Production
Fundamentals of Motion Pictures
Motion Picture Production Techniques
Broadcast Journalism
Broadcast Management
Broadcast Programming
Broadcast Advertising and Sales
Introduction to Television Graphics
Public Relations

Graduate

Research in Mass Communication
Seminar in Mass Communication
Problems in Public Opinion
Seminar in Communication Law
Seminar in History of Mass Media
Seminar in Human Communication Theory
Thesis—Project

Undergraduate and Graduate

Public Relations Technique
Communications Law
History of Journalism
Mass Communication and Society
Public Opinion
The Press and Contemporary Thought
Public Relations Case Problems
Media Problems

MISSOURI

Avila College

Independent Roman Catholic comprehensive coed institution. Institutionally accredited by regional association. Suburban location, 50-acre campus. Total enrollment: 1917. Undergraduate enrollment: 1853. Total faculty: 199 (69 full-time, 130 part-time). Semester calendar. Grading system: letters or numbers.

Department of Performing and Visual Arts, Communication Division, 11901 Wornall Road, Kansas City, MO 64145 816-942-8400, ext 289 or 290

CONTACT William J Louis
DEGREE OFFERED BA in communication with minor in TV/radio
DEPARTMENTAL MAJORS 30 students
ADMISSION Requirements — ACT or SAT scores, maintain B average for one year
FINANCIAL AID Scholarships, work/study programs, student loans
CURRICULAR EMPHASIS Film study — (1) appreciation; (2) criticism and aesthetics; (3) history Television study — (1) appreciation; (2) production; (3) educational Television production — experimental/personal video, educational treated equally
SPECIAL ACTIVITIES/OFFERINGS Film series, film festivals, program material produced for class projects, internships in television production, independent study
FACILITIES AND EQUIPMENT Television — black and white studio cameras, ¾-inch cassette VTR, portable black and white cameras, monitors, special effects generators, ½-inch portapak recorders, lighting equipment, sound recording equipment, audio mixers, black and white studio
FACULTY Michael Burks PART-TIME FACULTY Jay Cooper, Pete Modica, John Tibbetts

COURSE LIST

Undergraduate

Introduction to Radio/TV
Producing/Directing for TV
Radio Broadcasting/Programming
Advanced Radio Performance
Script Writing Radio/TV
Directed Studies Radio/TV
Introduction to Mass Communication Media
Aspects of the Horror Film
History of the Motion Picture: US
Aspects of the Comedy Film
The Genre Film
Film Seminar: Selected Director
History of Film, Europe
American Film Series
Shakespeare Film Festival
Film: Topical Selection

Central Missouri State University

State-supported comprehensive coed institution. Institutionally accredited by regional association, programs recognized by NASM. Small town location, 1000-acre campus. Total faculty: 477 (449 full-time, 28 part-time). Quarter calendar. Grading system: letters or numbers.

Department of Mass Communication, Warrensburg, MO 64093 816-429-4841

CONTACT David Eshelman
DEGREES OFFERED BS, MA in broadcasting and film
DEPARTMENTAL MAJORS Undergraduate — 365 students Graduate — 35 students
ADMISSION Undergraduate requirement — 2.0 minimum grade point average Graduate requirement — 2.5 minimum grade point average Undergraduate application deadline — rolling
FINANCIAL AID Student loans, work/study programs, laboratory assistantships, teaching assistantships
SPECIAL ACTIVITIES/OFFERINGS Program material produced for on-campus PBS television, internships in film and television production, independent study, practicum, teacher training, vocational placement service
FACILITIES AND EQUIPMENT Television — complete black and white studio and exterior production equipment, black and white studio, audio studio, control room
FACULTY Robert Clark, Ferrell Ervin, David Eshelman, Peggy Meinders, Kuldip Rampal, John Smead, Linda Smogor, Rik Whitaker

Central Missouri State University (continued)

COURSE LIST

Undergraduate

Fundamentals of Production
Foundations of Broadcasting
Television Techniques
Film Techniques
Broadcast Performance
Broadcast Programming
Education and Public Affairs Programs
Media Economics
Media Management

Graduate

Seminar: Law
Seminar: Film
Seminar: Television

Undergraduate and Graduate

Advanced Television
Advanced Film
Writing for Broadcast and Film
Instructional Television

Drury College

Independent comprehensive coed institution. Institutionally accredited by regional association. Urban location, 40-acre campus. Total enrollment: 1124. Undergraduate enrollment: 973. Total faculty: 104 (64 full-time, 40 part-time). 4-1-4 calendar. Grading system: letters or numbers.

Department of Speech and Dramatic Arts, Springfield, MO 65802 417-865-8731

CONTACT Ben Andrews
DEGREE OFFERED BA in speech with emphasis in film or television; concentration in broadcast communications
DEPARTMENTAL MAJORS Film — 3 students Television — 8 students
ADMISSION Requirements — ACT or SAT scores, interviews Application deadline — rolling
FINANCIAL AID Scholarships, student loans, work/study programs, activity grants Application deadline — rolling
CURRICULAR EMPHASIS Film study — (1) production; (2) educational media/instructional technology Filmmaking — (1) narrative; (2) documentary; (3) educational; (4) animated; (5) experimental Television study — (1) production; (2) educational; (3) history; (4) criticism and aesthetics; (5) appreciation; (6) management Television production — (1) educational; (2) commercial; (3) experimental/personal video; (4) news/documentary
SPECIAL ACTIVITIES/OFFERINGS Program material produced for local public television station, internships in television production, independent study, practicum
FACILITIES AND EQUIPMENT Film — complete 16mm equipment, editing room, permanent student film library Television — complete color studio production equipment, color studio
FACULTY Ben Andrews

COURSE LIST

Undergraduate

Introduction to Film Art
Special Problems in Film
Radio and Television as Communication
Mass Communication
Laboratory in Television Production
Special Problems in Television
Senior Internship in Television

Jefferson College

County-supported 2-year coed college. Institutionally accredited by regional association. Rural location. Undergraduate enrollment: 1886. Total faculty: 85 (50 full-time, 35 part-time). Semester calendar. Grading system: letters or numbers.

English Department, Hillsboro, MO 63050 314-789-3951

CONTACT John White or Trish Loomis
ADMISSION Application deadline — rolling

COURSE LIST

Undergraduate

Film Appreciation

Missouri Valley College

Independent Presbyterian 4-year coed college. Institutionally accredited by regional association. Small town location, 40-acre campus. Undergraduate enrollment: 376. Total faculty: 38. Semester plus 2 summer sessions calendar. Grading system: letters or numbers and pass/fail.

Mass Communications Department, College Street, Marshall, MO 65340 816-886-6924

CONTACT John McCallum
DEGREE OFFERED BS in mass communications
DEPARTMENTAL MAJORS Television — 20 students
ADMISSION Requirements — 2.0 minimum grade point average, ACT or SAT scores, interview
FINANCIAL AID Scholarships, work/study programs, student loans
CURRICULAR EMPHASIS Television study — (1) production; (2) educational; (3) management Television production — (1) commercial; (2) news/documentary; (3) educational
SPECIAL ACTIVITIES/OFFERINGS Film series, program material produced for cable television, internships in television production
FACILITIES AND EQUIPMENT Television — complete color studio production equipment, color studio, audio studio, control room
FACULTY Larry Koch, Denise Mackey, John McCallum

COURSE LIST

Undergraduate

TV Workshop I, II
Mass Communications
Special Problems

Northwest Missouri State University

State-supported comprehensive coed institution. Institutionally accredited by regional association, programs recognized by NASM. Small town location, 170-acre campus. Total enrollment: 4100. Undergraduate enrollment: 3740. Total faculty: 245 (220 full-time, 25 part-time). Semester calendar. Grading system: letters or numbers.

Mass Media Program, Speech Department, Maryville, MO 64468

CONTACT Film — Leo Kivijarv Television — William Christ
DEGREES OFFERED BS in broadcasting, BA in mass media
PROGRAM MAJORS Television — 29 students
ADMISSION Requirement — Act or SAT scores Application deadline — 4/30
FINANCIAL AID Scholarships, work/study programs, student loans Application deadline — 4/30
CURRICULAR EMPHASIS Film study — criticism and aesthetics, appreciation, educational media/instructional technology treated equally Filmmaking — documentary, narrative treated equally Television study — history, criticism and aesthetics, educational, production, management treated equally Television production — news/documentary, educational treated equally
SPECIAL ACTIVITIES/OFFERINGS Film festivals, program material produced for cable television, internships in television production, independent study, teacher training
FACILITIES AND EQUIPMENT Film — 8mm cameras, editing equipment, sound recording equipment, lighting, projectors, screening room, editing room, sound mixing room Television — black and white studio cameras, color studio cameras, 1-inch VTR, ¾-inch cassette VTR, portable black and white cameras, editing equipment, monitors, slide chain, portable color cameras, ¾-inch ENG, lighting equipment, sound recording equipment, audio mixers, film chain, time base corrector, black and white studio, color studio, audio studio, control room
FACULTY Robert Bohlken, Bill Christ, Carrol Fry, Leo Kivijarv, Jeff McCall

COURSE LIST

Undergraduate

Introduction to Mass Media
Introduction to Broadcast Operations
Broadcast Announcing
Radio Production
Broadcast Newswriting
Television Production
Cinematography
Broadcast Advertising and Continuity Writing
Phonetics
Media Scriptwriting
Communication Law
Practicum in Radio
Practicum in Television
Practicum in Cinematography
Introduction to Communication Disorders
Introduction to Theatre
Fundamentals of Interpretation
Stagecraft
Development of Broadcast Programming
Principles of Advertising
Introduction to Film Study
Broadcasting Practicum
Commercial Broadcasting Internship
Broadcast Station Management

St Louis Community College at Florissant Valley

District-supported 2-year coed college. Part of St. Louis Community College District System. Institutionally accredited by regional association. Suburban location. Undergraduate enrollment: 9347. Total faculty: 241. Semester calendar. Grading system: letters or numbers.

Mass Communications Department, 3400 Pershall Road, St Louis, MO 63135 314-595-4434

CONTACT Roger W Carlson
DEGREE OFFERED AA in communications arts (film)
DEPARTMENTAL MAJORS Film — 15 students Television — 30 students
ADMISSION Requirement — ACT or SAT scores Application deadline — 8/25
FINANCIAL AID Scholarships, work/study programs, student loans
CURRICULAR EMPHASIS Film study — (1) appreciation; (2) history Filmmaking — (1) documentary; (2) animated Television study — (1) production; (2) history; (3) educational Television production — (1) educational; (2) news/documentary
SPECIAL ACTIVITIES/OFFERINGS Film series, film festivals, student publications, program material produced for on-campus closed-circuit television and cable television, internships in television production, independent study
FACILITIES AND EQUIPMENT Film — 8mm cameras, editing equipment, sound recording equipment, lighting, black and white film stock, projectors, sound stage, screening room, editing room, sound mixing room, animation board, permanent film library of student films Television — black and white studio cameras, color studio cameras, ½-inch VTR, 1-inch VTR, ¾-inch cassette VTR, portable black and white cameras, editing equipment, monitors, slide chain, portable color cameras, ½-inch portapak recorders, lighting equipment, sound recording equipment, audio mixers, film chain, time base corrector, color studio, audio studio, control room
FACULTY Edward Donnelly PART-TIME FACULTY David Hunt, Arthur Meyer, Herb Niemeyer, Charles Rock, Roger Schnell

COURSE LIST

Undergraduate

Filmmaking
Film Appreciation
History of Film
Major Themes in Film
Television Production
Introduction to Broadcasting

St Louis Community College at Forest Park

District-supported 2-year coed college. Institutionally accredited by regional association. Urban location. Undergraduate enrollment: 6761. Total faculty: 464 (164 full-time, 300 part-time). Semester calendar. Grading system: letters or numbers.

Mass Communications Department, 5600 Oakland Avenue, St Louis, MO 63110 314-644-3300

CONTACT Film — James C Hoelscher Television — Lynn Wilbur
DEGREES OFFERED AA, AS in mass communications with emphasis in film or broadcasting
FINANCIAL AID Scholarships, student loans, work/study programs Application deadline — 5/1
CURRICULAR EMPHASIS Film study — (1) appreciation; (2) history; (3) production Television study — (1) production; (2) history; (3) criticism and aesthetics, appreciation Television production — (1) commercial; (2) news/documentary; (3) experimental/personal video
SPECIAL ACTIVITIES/OFFERINGS Film series, program material produced for on-campus closed-circuit television, internships in television production, independent study, vocational placement service
FACILITIES AND EQUIPMENT Film — complete 8mm equipment, 16mm cameras, lighting equipment, projectors, sound stage, screening room, sound mixing room, permanent film library Television — complete black and white studio production equipment, black and white studio, audio studio, control room, portable ¾-inch equipment
FACULTY Kathe Dunlop, James C Hoelscher PART-TIME FACULTY Harold Petty, Lynn Wilbur

COURSE LIST

Undergraduate

Introduction to Broadcasting
Applied Broadcasting
Television Production
Film Appreciation
History of Film
Major Themes in Film
Major Directors
Communicating with Film
Advanced Super-8 Filmmaking

Saint Mary's College of O'Fallon

Independent Roman Catholic 2-year coed college. Institutionally accredited by regional association. Small town location, 30-acre campus. Undergraduate enrollment: 494. Total faculty: 42 (25 full-time, 17 part-time). Semester calendar. Grading system: letters or numbers.

English Department, 200 North Main Street, O'Fallon, MO 63366 314-272-3420

CONTACT Sister Bernice Moellering
ADMISSION Requirement — ACT scores Application deadline — 8/17, rolling
CURRICULAR EMPHASIS Film study — (1) criticism and aesthetics; (2) appreciation; (3) educational media/instructional technology; (4) history; (5) production
PART-TIME FACULTY Sister Bernice Moellering

COURSE LIST

Undergraduate

Film Study and Techniques

Southwest Missouri State University

State-supported comprehensive coed institution. Institutionally accredited by regional association. Suburban location, 125-acre campus. Total enrollment: 13,315. Undergraduate enrollment: 12,067. Total faculty: 716 (538 full-time, 178 part-time). Semester calendar. Grading system: letters or numbers.

Speech-Theater Department, Springfield, MO 65802 417-836-5000

CONTACT Robert H Bradley, Head
ADMISSION Application deadline — 8/1, rolling
CURRICULAR EMPHASIS Film study — criticism and aesthetics Television study — production
SPECIAL ACTIVITIES/OFFERINGS Program material produced for local public television station, internships in television production
FACILITIES AND EQUIPMENT Television — complete black and white studio and exterior production facilities, complete color studio production facilities
FACULTY David Daly, Minrose Quinn, Robert Rouse

COURSE LIST

Undergraduate

History of Film I, II
Seminar in Film Communication
Understanding Film
Television Production
Directing for Television
Broadcast Program Planning
Instructional Television

Stephens College

Independent 4-year women's college. Institutionally accredited by regional association. Small town location, 325-acre campus. Undergraduate enrollment: 1630. Total faculty: 148 (124 full-time, 24 part-time). Modified modular calendar. Grading system: letters or numbers.

Communications Department, Columbia, MO 65215 314-442-2211

CONTACT Faye Elizabeth Smith
DEGREE OFFERED BA in communications
DEPARTMENTAL MAJORS Film — 10 students Television — 35 students
ADMISSION Requirements — interviews, teachers' recommendations Application deadline — 8/15, rolling
FINANCIAL AID Production assistantships Application deadline — 4/15

CURRICULAR EMPHASIS Film study — (1) criticism and aesthetics; (2) production Television study — (1) criticism and aesthetics; (2) production; (3) history; (4) management; (5) appreciation; (6) educational Television production — (1) experimental/personal video; (2) news/documentary; (3) educational
SPECIAL ACTIVITIES/OFFERINGS Film series, film festivals, film workshop, program material produced for on-campus closed-circuit television and cable television, internships in film and television production, independent study, practicum
FACILITIES AND EQUIPMENT Film — projectors, screening room, permanent film library Television — complete black and white studio and exterior production equipment, complete color studio and exterior production equipment, black and white studio, color studio, audio studio, control room
FACULTY Elizabeth Barnes, Richard Carlson, Eugene Ferraro, Dave Irwin, Phyllis Pearson, Lyndon Preston, Faye Elizabeth Smith

COURSE LIST

Undergraduate

Mass Communications: Introduction
Mass Communications: Television
Mass Communications: Film
Language of the Cinema
Television Producing/Directing
Writing I, II
Cinematography Techniques
Film Criticism
Presentational Performance I, II
Communication Photography
Advanced Television Producing/Directing
Film Directors
Film Genres
Broadcast Programming
Broadcast Management
Instructional Television
Public Broadcasting
Communications Studies
Guided Group Study

University of Missouri—Columbia

State-supported coed university. Part of University of Missouri System. Institutionally accredited by regional association, programs recognized by NASM, AACSB. Small town location. Total enrollment: 23,064. Total faculty: 1610 (1535 full-time, 75 part-time). Semester calendar. Grading system: letters or numbers.

Area of Radio-Television-Film, Speech and Dramatic Art Department, 200 Swallow Hall, Columbia, MO 65201 314-882-3046

CONTACT Film — Edward S Small Television — G Joseph Wolfe
DEGREES OFFERED BA, MA, PhD in radio-television-film
PROGRAM MAJORS Undergraduate film and television — 150 students Graduate film and television — 15 students
ADMISSION Undergraduate requirement — 2.0 minimum grade point average Graduate requirements — 3.0 minimum grade point average, teachers' recommendations Undergraduate application deadline — 5/1, rolling
FINANCIAL AID Scholarships, work/study programs, student loans, teaching assistantships Undergraduate application deadline — 4/30, rolling
CURRICULAR EMPHASIS Undergraduate film study — history, appreciation, theory treated equally Graduate film study — history, criticism and aesthetics, theory treated equally Undergraduate filmmaking — narrative, experimental, animated treated equally Graduate filmmaking — documentary, experimental, educational treated equally Undergraduate television study — criticism and aesthetics, appreciation, production treated equally Graduate television study — history, criticism and aesthetics, management treated equally Undergraduate television production — commercial, experimental/personal video, dramatic treated equally Graduate television production — news/documentary, experimental/personal video, educational treated equally
SPECIAL ACTIVITIES/OFFERINGS Film series; interdepartmental film studies program; program material produced for on-campus closed-circuit television, cable television, and local commercial television station; internships in film production; internships in television production
FACILITIES AND EQUIPMENT Film — complete 16mm production equipment, screening room, editing room, animation board Television — complete color studio and exterior production equipment, color studio, audio studio, control room
FACULTY Michael J Porter, Edward S Small, G Joseph Wolfe PART-TIME FACULTY Theodore Eldredge, Barton Griffith

COURSE LIST

Undergraduate

Television and Radio in Modern Society
Principles of Radio and Television
Elementary Radio and Television Production

Graduate

History and Criticism of Broadcasting
Seminar in Film Theory
Research in Broadcasting
Educational Television
International Broadcasting
Non-Broadcast Media Management
EFP Production
Broadcasting and Mass Culture
Seminar in Animation
Political Broadcasting

Undergraduate and Graduate

Radio and Television Programming
Basic Television Techniques
Advanced Television Direction
Broadcast Regulation and Responsibility
Writing for Radio-Television-Film
Film Production
Advanced Film Production
Experimental Film
Documentary Film

University of Missouri—Kansas City

State-supported coed university. Institutionally accredited by regional association. Urban location. Total enrollment: 10,746. Undergraduate enrollment: 6528. Total faculty: 1500. Semester calendar. Grading system: letters or numbers.

Department of Communication Studies, College of Arts & Sciences, 5100 Rockhill Road, Kansas City, MO 64110 816-276-1185

CONTACT Robert Musburger, Chairman; Robin League, Undergraduate Advisor; Douglas Moore, Graduate Advisor
DEGREES OFFERED BA, MA in communication studies; emphasis areas: film or television — production, performance, writing, history, theory

University of Missouri—Kansas City (continued)

DEPARTMENTAL MAJORS Undergraduate film — 15 students Undergraduate television — 150 students Graduate film — 2 students Graduate television — 25 students

ADMISSION Undergraduate requirements — professional recommendations, teachers' recommendation, written statement of purpose Graduate requirements — 2.5 minimum grade point average, GRE scores, professional recommendations, teachers' recommendations, written statement of purpose Undergraduate application deadline — 5/1, rolling

FINANCIAL AID Scholarships, student loans, work/study programs, teaching assistantships, fellowships Undergraduate application deadline — 2/1, rolling

CURRICULAR EMPHASIS Film study — (1) production; (2) writing; (3) performance Filmmaking — (1) broadcast; (2) documentary; (3) animation Television study — (1) production; (2) history; (3) writing; (4) performance Television production — (1) news/documentary; (2) educational; (3) experimental/personal video

SPECIAL ACTIVITIES/OFFERINGS Film series, film festivals, film production for nonprofit clients, program material produced for local commercial television station, internships in film and television production, independent study, teacher training, vocational placement service

FACILITIES AND EQUIPMENT Film — complete 8mm and 16mm equipment, sound stage, screening room, editing room, sound mixing room, animation and titling stand, permanent film library Television — complete color and black and white studios and exterior production equipment, both mobile van and portable hand-held color video equipment, audio studio and control room, color telecine facilities, ¾-inch, 1-inch, and 2-inch VTR equipment

FACULTY James Bray, Larry Ehrlich, Faye Kircher, Robin League, Gaylord Marr, Doug Moore, Walter Murrish, Robert Musburger, Sam Scott PART-TIME FACULTY Joyce Bessmer, Walt Bodine, Mary Loy Brown, Richard Brown, Mark Morelli, Buddy Turner, Charles Welborn

COURSE LIST

Undergraduate

Fundamentals of Broadcast Peformance
Introduction: Modern Communications Media
Press in America
Film Form: USA
Film Form: Europe & Asia
Fundamentals of Audio
Fundamentals of Video
Media Photography

Graduate

Advanced Media Performance
Modern Communication Theory
Advanced Media Writing
Advanced Media Production
Methods and Techniques of Communication Research
Seminar in Production Techniques
Contemporary Issues in Mass Media
Directed Studies & Thesis

Undergraduate and Graduate

Radio Performance
TV/Film Performance
Mass Media in America I, II, III
Politics, Protest, Propaganda
Communications in the Classroom
Fundamentals of Writing for the Media
Radio-TV Programming
Radio Production
Media Graphics
Video Production
Industrial Video Production
EFP/ENG Production
Fundamentals of Cinematography
Electronic Journalism Performance
Advertising
Public Relations
Continuity Writing
Dramatic Media Writing
Electronic Journalism Writing
Multi-channel Sound Production
Public Broadcasting
Media Rules and Regulations
Television Directing
Documentary Cinematography
Dramatic Cinematography
Audio/Video Archives

English Department 816-276-1305

CONTACT Ralph Berets
ADMISSION Application deadline — 5/1, rolling
FACULTY Ralph Berets

COURSE LIST

Undergraduate

Film as Art

Washington University

Independent coed university. Institutionally accredited by regional association, programs recognized by NASM, AACSB, NASA. Suburban location, 176-acre campus. Total enrollment: 8429. Undergraduate enrollment: 4431. Total faculty: 2277 (1249 full-time, 1028 part-time). Semester calendar. Grading system: letters or numbers.

Performing Arts Department, PO Box 1108, St Louis, MO 63130 314-889-5885

CONTACT Gene Boomer
ADMISSION Application deadline — rolling
PART-TIME FACULTY Gene Boomer, Van McElwee, Shannon Scheafly

COURSE LIST

Undergraduate

Filmmaking
History of the Cinema
Contemporary Cinema
Topics in Film
Video Production

Westminster College

Independent 4-year men's college coordinate with William Woods College (will become coed in 1979-80). Institutionally accredited by regional association. Small town location, 252-acre campus. Undergraduate enrollment: 664. Total faculty: 57 (53 full-time, 4 part-time). 5-4-1 calendar. Grading system: letters or numbers.

Division of Fine Arts, Fulton, MO 65251 314-642-3361

CONTACT William Bleifuss
ADMISSION Application deadline — rolling
FINANCIAL AID Scholarships, student loans, work/study programs Application deadline — rolling

CURRICULAR EMPHASIS Film study — (1) criticism and aesthetics; (2) appreciation and history Filmmaking — (1) experimental; (2) documentary; (3) narrative; (4) animated; (5) educational
SPECIAL ACTIVITIES/OFFERINGS Film series, film festivals
FACILITIES AND EQUIPMENT Film — complete 8mm equipment, 16mm editing equipment, sound recording equipment, projectors, screening room, editing room
FACULTY William B Bleifuss, Henry Ottinger

COURSE LIST

Undergraduate

History of Film
Great Film Genres
Film and Other Arts
Film and Society

MONTANA

Montana State University

State-supported coed university. Institutionally accredited by regional association, programs recognized by NASA. Small town location, 1170-acre campus. Total enrollment: 9920. Undergraduate enrollment: 9156. Total faculty: 743 (529 full-time, 214 part-time). Quarter calendar. Grading system: letters or numbers.

Department of Film and Television Production, Bozeman, MT 59717 406-994-2484

CONTACT Fred L Gerber
DEGREE OFFERED BS in film and television production with options in motion picture, television, or photography
DEPARTMENTAL MAJORS Undergraduate film — 66 students Undergraduate television — 79 students
ADMISSION Undergraduate requirements — 2.0 minimum grade point average, ACT or SAT scores
FINANCIAL AID Work/study programs, student loans
CURRICULAR EMPHASIS Film study — (1) history; (2) criticism and aesthetics; (3) appreciation Filmmaking — (1) narrative; (2) documentary; (3) educational Television study — (1) production; (2) criticism and aesthetics; (3) appreciation Television production — (1) commercial; (2) news/documentary; (3) educational
SPECIAL ACTIVITIES/OFFERINGS Film series; student festival (film, video, and still photography); program material produced for on-campus closed-circuit television, cable television, and local commercial television station; internships in television production; independent study
FACILITIES AND EQUIPMENT Film — 8mm and 16mm editing equipment, sound recording equipment, lighting, projectors, video record and playback, 35mm cameras, sound stage, screening room, editing room, sound mixing room, animation board, permanent film library of student films, permanent film library of commercial or professional films Television — black and white studio cameras, color studio cameras, ½-inch VTR, 1-inch VTR, ¾-inch cassette VTR, portable black and white cameras, editing equipment, monitors, special effects generators, slide chain, portable color cameras, ¾-inch ENG, lighting equipment, sound recording equipment, audio mixers, film chain, black and white studio, color studio, audio studio, control room, editing room
FACULTY E Phil Eftychiadis, Fred L Gerber, Jack A Hyyppa, William A Neff, Salah Sayed-Ahmed, John M Stonnell

COURSE LIST

Undergraduate

Introduction to Communication
Fundamental Cinematography
Fundamental Film Editing
Fundamental Television Production
History of the Silent Motion Picture
History of the Sound Motion Picture
History of Broadcasting
Fundamental Scriptwriting
Intermediate Television Production
Fundamental Sound for Film and Television
Cinema Production I
Special Topics
Announcing and Narration
Creative Scriptwriting
Advanced Television Production
Studio Set Design and Construction
Technical Operations
Television Programming, Sales and Management
Advanced Cinematography
Advanced Film Editing
Theory of Motion Picture Direction
Theory of Television Direction
Advanced Sound Recording
Television Dramatic Production Techniques
Cinema Production II
Seminar
Motion Picture Criticism
Special Effects
FCC Regulations and Policies
Motion Picture Production Management
Public Television
Nonfiction Film
Individual Problems
Motion Picture Senior Production Workshop
Television Senior Production Workshop
Special Topics

Graduate

Individual Problems
Special Topics

University of Montana

State-supported coed university. Part of Montana University System. Institutionally accredited by regional association, programs recognized by NASM, AACSB. Small town location. Total enrollment: 8363. Undergraduate enrollment: 7106. Total faculty: 400 part-time. Quarter calendar. Grading system: letters or numbers.

Radio-Television Department, School of Journalism, Missoula, MT 59812 406-243-4931

CONTACT Gregory MacDonald
DEGREE OFFERED BA in radio-TV
DEPARTMENTAL MAJORS Undergraduate television — 80 students Graduate television — 2 students
ADMISSION Requirements — ACT or SAT scores, high school or college transcripts Undergraduate application deadline — 7/15

University of Montana (continued)

FINANCIAL AID Scholarships, work/study programs, student loans Undergraduate application deadline — 3/1
CURRICULAR EMPHASIS Undergraduate film study — (1) history; (2) criticism and aesthetics; (3) appreciation Undergraduate filmmaking — (1) news film; (2) documentary; (3) narrative Undergraduate television study — (1) production; (2) law; (3) history Undergraduate television production — (1) commercial; (2) news/documentary; (3) educational
SPECIAL ACTIVITIES/OFFERINGS Film series; film festivals; program material produced for on-campus closed-circuit television, cable television, local commercial television station, out-of-state public TV; apprenticeships; internships in television production; independent study; vocational placement service
FACILITIES AND EQUIPMENT Film — complete 8mm and 16mm equipment, screening room, editing room, sound mixing room, permanent film library of commercial or professional films Television — black and white studio cameras, 2-inch VTR, ¾-inch cassette VTR, editing equipment, monitors, special effects generators, slide chain, portable color cameras, ¾-inch ENG, lighting equipment, sound recording equipment, audio mixers, film chain, time base corrector, character generator, black and white studio, audio studio, control room
FACULTY Nathaniel Blumberg, Warren J Brier, Kenneth Brusic, Andrew C Cogswell, Edward B Dugan, Philip Hess, Jerry Holloron, Charles E Hood, Gregory MacDonald, Robert C McGiffert

COURSE LIST

Undergraduate

Introduction to Radio and Television
Special Topics
Radio-Television Writing
Basic Radio Production
Radio News
Radio Station Operation
Radio-Television Public Affairs
Radio-Television Advertising and Management

Undergraduate and Graduate

Television News
Basic Television Techniques
Advanced Radio-Television Problems
Cinematography
Television Production and Direction
Radio-Television Seminar

NEBRASKA

Creighton University

Independent Roman Catholic coed university. Accredited by regional association and AICS, programs recognized by AACSB. Urban location, 65-acre campus. Total enrollment: 5027. Undergraduate enrollment: 3171. Total faculty: 881 (423 full-time, 458 part-time). 4-1-4 calendar. Grading system: letters or numbers.

Journalism/Mass Communication Department, 2500 California, Omaha, NE 68178 402-449-2825

CONTACT Film — Daniel R Vnuk or Timothy R Roesler Television — Bruce Hough
PROGRAM OFFERED Major in mass communication with emphasis in film or television
ADMISSION Application deadline — rolling
CURRICULAR EMPHASIS Film study — (1) history, production; (2) criticism and aesthetics, appreciation Filmmaking — (1) narrative; (2) documentary Television study — (1) production; (2) criticism and aesthetics; (3) history Television production — (1) news/documentary; (2) commercial; (3) experimental/personal video
SPECIAL ACTIVITIES/OFFERINGS Film series, program material produced for on-campus closed-circuit television, internships in film and television production, independent study, teacher training, vocational placement service
FACILITIES AND EQUIPMENT Film — 8mm and 16mm cameras, editing equipment, lighting equipment, color film stock, projectors, 8mm black and white film stock, screening room, editing room Television — complete black and white studio and exterior production equipment, portable color cameras, ½-inch portapak recorder, black and white studio, audio studio, control room
FACULTY David Haberman, Bruce Hough, Daniel R Vnuk PART-TIME FACULTY Timothy R Roesler

COURSE LIST

Undergraduate

Projects in Communication
The Broadcast Documentary
Senior Seminar in Mass Communication
Directed Independent Readings
Broadcast News Production
Introduction to Filmmaking
Basic Communication Design for Radio-Television
Broadcast Continuity Writing and Announcing
Broadcast News Writing and Editing
Broadcast News Programming
Broadcast Station Programming
History and Criticism of Cinema
The Television Audience
Advanced Broadcast Program Design

Kearney State College

State-supported comprehensive coed institution. Institutionally accredited by regional association, programs recognized by NASM. Small town location, 195-acre campus. Total enrollment: 6165. Undergraduate enrollment: 5865. Total faculty: 300. Semester calendar. Grading system: letters or numbers.

Radio-Television Department, 25th Street and Ninth Avenue, Kearney, NE 68847 308-236-4078

CONTACT Maurine Eckloff
DEGREE OFFERED BS in television
DEPARTMENTAL MAJORS 60 students
ADMISSION Requirements — 2.0 minimum grade point average, ACT or SAT scores, teachers' recommendations Application deadline — rolling

CURRICULAR EMPHASIS Television study — (1) production; (2) management; (3) educational Television production — (1) news/documentary; (2) commercial; (3) educational
SPECIAL ACTIVITIES/OFFERINGS Program material produced for on-campus closed-circuit television and cable television, internships in television production, independent study, practicum, vocational placement service
FACILITIES AND EQUIPMENT Film — 8mm cameras, 8mm and 16mm editing equipment, lighting equipment, projectors, editing room Television — complete black and white studio and exterior production equipment, black and white studio, audio studio, control room
FACULTY Bruce Elving, David Whillock PART-TIME FACULTY Jeff Scheiman

COURSE LIST

Undergraduate

Introduction to Mass Communication
Broadcast Announcing
Television Lighting
Television Writing
Television Production
Television Direction
Public Broadcasting

University of Nebraska at Omaha

State-supported comprehensive coed institution. Part of University of Nebraska System. Institutionally accredited by regional association, programs recognized by AACSB. Urban location. Total enrollment: 15,058. Undergraduate enrollment: 12,906. Total enrollment: 560 (425 full-time, 135 part-time). Semester calendar. Grading system: letters or numbers.

Communication Department, Omaha, NE 68182 402-554-2600

CONTACT Film — Bernard Timberg Television — Mary Williamson
PROGRAM OFFERED Major in communication with emphasis in television
ADMISSION Requirements — interviews, teachers' recommendations, portfolio Undergraduate application deadline — rolling
FINANCIAL AID Teaching assistantships Undergraduate application deadline — rolling
CURRICULAR EMPHASIS Film study — (1) production; (2) educational media/instructional technology; (3) appreciation Filmmaking — (1) newsfilm; (2) documentary; (3) narrative Television study — (1) production; (2) educational; (3) appreciation Television production — (1) news/documentary; (2) educational; (3) commercial
SPECIAL ACTIVITIES/OFFERINGS Film series, program material produced for local public television station, internships in film and television production, independent study, practicum
FACILITIES AND EQUIPMENT Film — complete 16mm equipment, screening room, editing room Television — complete color studio and exterior production equipment, mobile van/unit, remote truck, audio studio, control room
FACULTY Julianne Crane, Bernard Timberg, Mary Williamson

COURSE LIST

Undergraduate

Basic Television Production
Broadcast Practicum
Film History Appreciation
Film Theory and Criticism

Undergraduate and Graduate

Newsfilm and Documentary
Advanced Television Production
Seminar in Mass Communication

University of Nebraska—Lincoln

State-supported coed university. Part of University of Nebraska System. Institutionally accredited by regional association, programs recognized by NASM, AACSB, ACPE. Urban location, 552-acre campus. Total enrollment: 21,458. Undergraduate enrollment: 17,222. Total faculty: 1259. Semester calendar. Grading system: letters or numbers.

Department of Art, Woods Building, Lincoln, NE 68588 402-472-2631

CONTACT Edward Azlant
ADMISSION Undergraduate application deadline — 8/15, rolling
FINANCIAL AID Scholarships, work/study programs, student loans Undergraduate application deadline — 2/15
CURRICULAR EMPHASIS Undergraduate filmmaking — documentary, narrative, experimental treated equally
SPECIAL ACTIVITIES/OFFERINGS Filmmaking clubs, film series, film festivals, film societies, independent study
FACILITIES AND EQUIPMENT Film — 8mm and 16mm cameras, editing equipment, lighting, projectors, 16mm sound recording equipment, screening room, editing room, sound mixing room, permanent film library of commercial or professional films
FACULTY Edward Azlant

COURSE LIST

Undergraduate

Beginning Filmmaking
Projects in Filmmaking

Wayne State College

State-supported comprehensive coed institution. Institutionally accredited by regional association. Small town location, 127-acre campus. Total enrollment: 2589. Undergraduate enrollment: 2143. Total faculty: 119 (89 full-time, 30 part-time). Semester calendar. Grading system: letters or numbers.

Broadcasting Department, Wayne, NE 68787 402-375-2200

CONTACT Film — Robert Zahniser Television — Herbert Meinert
DEGREES OFFERED BA, BS in broadcasting
DEPARTMENTAL MAJORS Television — 40 students
ADMISSION Requirement — ACT or SAT scores

Wayne State College (continued)

FINANCIAL AID Scholarships, work/study programs, student loans
CURRICULAR EMPHASIS Film study — history, educational media/instructional technology treated equally Filmmaking — educational Television study — production, management treated equally Television production — commercial, news/documentary, educational treated equally
SPECIAL ACTIVITIES/OFFERINGS Program material produced for cable television, apprenticeships, internships in television production, independent study, teacher training, vocational placement service
FACILITIES AND EQUIPMENT Film — complete 8mm and 16mm equipment Television — black and white studio cameras, color studio cameras, ¾-inch cassette VTR, portable black and white cameras, editing equipment, monitors, slide chain, lighting equipment, sound recording equipment, audio mixers, film chain, color studio, control room
FACULTY Harold Drake, Herb Meinert, Robert Zahniser

COURSE LIST

Undergraduate

Broadcast Operations
Radio Production-Direction
Radio Workshop
Elements of Broadcasting
Television Workshop
Television Production-Direction
Radio-TV News
Radio-TV Continuity
Advanced TV Production-Direction
Advanced Radio Production-Direction
Introduction to Cinematography
Senior Project/Recital/Thesis
Advanced Radio Workshop
Mass Media in Society
Supervised Creation Production
Seminar in Communication Arts
Radio and TV in Education
Cinema in Education
Advanced Broadcast News
Communication Law
Advanced TV Workshop

NEVADA

University of Nevada, Las Vegas

State-supported comprehensive coed institution. Part of University of Nevada System. Institutionally accredited by regional association. Urban location, 335-acre campus. Total enrollment: 6431. Undergraduate enrollment: 5824. Total faculty: 380. 4-1-4 calendar. Grading system: letters or numbers.

Department of Communication Studies, 4505 Maryland Parkway, Las Vegas, NV 89154 702-739-3325

CONTACT Allan B Padderud
DEGREES OFFERED BA in communications with an emphasis in broadcasting, MA in communications with an emphasis in mass communications
DEPARTMENTAL MAJORS Undergraduate television — 75 students Graduate television — 5 students
ADMISSION Undergraduate requirements — 2.3 minimum grade point average, ACT or SAT scores Graduate requirements — 3.0 minimum grade point average, teachers' recommendations, written statement of purpose, professional recommendations
FINANCIAL AID Scholarships, work/study programs, student loans, teaching assistantships
CURRICULAR EMPHASIS Undergraduate television study — (1) production; (2) history Graduate television study — (1) criticism and aesthetics; (2) regulation; (3) research Undergraduate television production — (1) experimental/personal video; (2) news/documentary; (3) commercial
SPECIAL ACTIVITIES/OFFERINGS Program material produced for on-campus closed-circuit television and local public television station, internships in film production, internships in television production, internships in TV news
FACILITIES AND EQUIPMENT Television — black and white studio cameras, ½-inch VTR, ¾-inch cassette VTR, portable black and white cameras, monitors, special effects generators, slide chain, ½-inch portapak recorders, ¾-inch ENG, lighting equipment, sound recording equipment, audio mixers, film chain, black and white studio, audio studio, control room
FACULTY Allan B Padderud PART-TIME FACULTY Betty Ellis

COURSE LIST

Undergraduate

Introduction to Broadcasting
Television Production
Writing for TV & Radio
Advanced TV Production
Broadcasting and the Public Interest
Internship in Broadcasting
Broadcast Practicum

Graduate

Effects of Mass Communication
Broadcast Regulation

Undergraduate and Graduate

Broadcast Audience Analysis

Film Studies 702-739-3431

CONTACT Hart Wegner, Chairman
CURRICULAR EMPHASIS Film study — (1) appreciation; (2) history Filmmaking — (1) narrative; (2) documentary; (3) experimental
FACULTY Paul Burns, Jean Decock, Chris Hudgins, Allan Padderud, Hart Wegner

COURSE LIST

Undergraduate

Introduction to Film
Language of Film

Undergraduate and Graduate
History of the American Film
Continental Film
Drama and Film of German Expressionism
History of the French Film
History of the Russian Film
Film and Literature
The American Hero in Film and Literature
Genre Studies in Film
From French Literature to Film
Politics and Film
Art Filmmaking

University of Nevada, Reno

State-supported coed university. Part of University of Nevada System. Institutionally accredited by regional association, programs recognized by AACSB. Urban location, 200-acre campus. Total enrollment: 7474. Undergraduate enrollment: 5890. Total faculty: 398 (331 full-time, 67 part-time). Semester calendar. Grading system: letters or numbers.

Department of Art, Reno, NV 89507 702-784-6682

CONTACT Howard Rosenberg
ADMISSION Application deadline — 7/15, rolling
CURRICULAR EMPHASIS Film study — history, appreciation treated equally Filmmaking — (1) popular; (2) narrative; (3) documentary; (4) experimental; (5) animated
FACILITIES AND EQUIPMENT Film — complete 8mm and 16mm equipment, permanent film library, revolving rentals
FACULTY Howard Rosenberg

COURSE LIST
Undergraduate
Cinema I: The Silent Era
Cinema II, III: The Sound Era

NEW HAMPSHIRE

Dartmouth College

Independent coed university. Founded 1769. Institutionally accredited by regional association. Small town location. Total enrollment: 3900. Undergraduate enrollment: 3200. Total faculty: 671 (486 full-time, 185 part-time). Quarter calendar. Grading system: letters or numbers.

Film Studies, Drama Department, Hanover, NH 03755 603-646-3402

CONTACT Film — David Thomson Television — John F Mills
PROGRAM OFFERED Major in drama with emphasis in film
ADMISSION Application deadline — 1/1
CURRICULAR EMPHASIS Film study — (1) history; (2) appreciation; (3) criticism and aesthetics Filmmaking — (1) narrative; (2) documentary; (3) experimental Television study — (1) appreciation; (2) criticism and aesthetics; (3) production Television production — (1) experimental/personal video; (2) news/documentary; (3) educational
SPECIAL ACTIVITIES/OFFERINGS Film societies, program material produced for on-campus closed-circuit television
FACILITIES AND EQUIPMENT Film — complete 8mm and 16mm equipment, 35mm projectors, screening room, 35mm screening facilities, editing room, sound mixing room, animation board, permanent film library Television — complete black and white studio and exterior production equipment, color studio camera, black and white studio, audio studio, control room
FACULTY Maurice H Rapf, David Thomson, John Blair Watson Jr PART-TIME FACULTY Ron Boehm, Alan T Gaylord, Errol G HIll, Arthur L Mayer, Neal Oxenhandler, David Parry, Barry Scherr

COURSE LIST
Undergraduate
Film: Practical Criticism
History of Film
Basic Elements of Film
Films of Information and Persuasion
Cinematic Style and Structure
Writing for the Screen
The American Independent Cinema
Film and History
Movie-going: A Critical Approach
The Soviet Film
TV: A Critical Approach
Film Style and Structure: Age of Movies
The Creative Process: Videotape
The Black Experience in Drama and Films
Film Style and Structure: Age of Film Culture
The Film Director: Jean Renoir

Keene State College

State-related comprehensive coed institution. Part of University System of New Hampshire. Institutionally accredited by regional association. Small town location, 70-acre campus. Total enrollment: 2900. Undergraduate enrollment: 2700. Total faculty: 232 (197 full-time, 35 part-time). Semester calendar. Grading system: letters or numbers.

English Department, Keene, NH 03431 603-352-1909

CONTACT William Sullivan

Keene State College (continued)

ADMISSION Application deadline — 3/15, rolling
FACULTY Larry Benaquist, William Sullivan

COURSE LIST

Undergraduate

Introduction to Film
Film Genres and Directors
Film Criticism: From Theory to Practice
Seminar in Specialized Studies

New England College

Independent 4-year coed college. Institutionally accredited by regional association. Small town location, 212-acre campus. Undergraduate enrollment: 1683. Total faculty: 141 (79 full-time, 62 part-time). 4-1-4 calendar. Grading system: letters or numbers.

Communications Program, Administration Building, Henniker, NH 03242 603-428-2334

CONTACT V Fossel
DEGREE OFFERED BA in communications (television)
PROGRAM MAJORS Television — 30 students
ADMISSION Requirements — 2.0 minimum grade point average, ACT or SAT scores, interview, teachers' recommendations, production credits, successful completion of core course
FINANCIAL AID Scholarships, work/study programs, student loans
CURRICULAR EMPHASIS Film study — (1) criticism and aesthetics; (2) appreciation Television study — (1) production; (2) educational; (3) criticism and aesthetics Television production — commercial, news/documentary, experimental/personal video treated equally
SPECIAL ACTIVITIES/OFFERINGS Filmmaking clubs, film series, program material produced for cable television and local public television station, internships in television production, independent study, vocational placement service
FACILITIES AND EQUIPMENT Film — complete 8mm equipment, videotaping equipment, screening room, 35mm screening facilities, editing room, sound mixing room, animation board Television — black and white studio cameras, ½-inch VTR, portable black and white cameras, editing equipment, monitors, special effects generators, slide chain, portable color cameras, ½-inch portapak recorders, lighting equipment, sound recording equipment, audio mixers, black and white studio
FACULTY Bill L Beard, Hunter Corday, Dennis D'Andrea, Virginia Fossel, Thomas Mickey, Gregory Morell, Clapham W Murray PART-TIME FACULTY Thomas H Joslin

COURSE LIST

Undergraduate

Mass Media
Law and Ethics of the Media
Beginning Television Workshop
Art of Film
History of Cinema
Advanced Television Workshop
Directing I
Lighting Fundamentals
Lighting Design
Stagecraft
Acting for Television

University of New Hampshire

State-supported coed university. Part of University System of New Hampshire. Institutionally accredited by regional association. Small town location, 188-acre campus. Total enrollment: 10,500. Undergraduate enrollment: 8887. Total faculty: 625 (570 full-time, 55 part-time). Semester calendar. Grading system: letters or numbers.

Theater and Communication Department, Paul Arts Center, Durham, NH 03824 603-862-2291

CONTACT David Magidson, Chairman
PROGRAM OFFERED Major in theater or communication with emphasis in film or television
CURRICULAR EMPHASIS Film study — (1) criticism and aesthetics; (2) production; (3) appreciation; (4) history Filmmaking — (1) experimental; (2) narrative; (3) documentary Television study — (1) criticism and aesthetics; (2) production Television production — commercial, news/documentary, experimental/video, educational treated equally
SPECIAL ACTIVITIES/OFFERINGS Film series, film societies, program material produced for cable television, internships in television production, independent study
FACILITIES AND EQUIPMENT Film — complete 8mm equipment, screening room, editing room, permanent film library Television — complete color studio production equipment, portable black and white cameras, ½-inch portapak recorder, color studio, audio studio, control room
FACULTY David Magidson, Joshua Meyerowitz PART-TIME FACULTY Gene Franceware, Jeffrey Martin

COURSE LIST

Undergraduate

Introduction to Film
Introduction to Mass Communication
Introduction to Television Production
Media Aesthetics/Theory
Media Criticism
History & Law of Mass Communication
Writing Broadcast News
Filmmaking

Undergraduate and Graduate

Writing for Television and Film

NEW JERSEY

Atlantic Community College

County-supported 2-year coed college. Institutionally accredited by regional association. Rural location, 546-acre campus. Undergraduate enrollment: 4016. Total faculty: 229 (119 full-time, 110 part-time). Semester calendar. Grading system: letters or numbers.

English Department, Mays Landing, NJ 08330 609-646-4950

CONTACT Richard Kirchoffer
ADMISSION Application deadline — 9/15
FACULTY Richard Kirchoffer

COURSE LIST

Undergraduate
Film and Fiction

Bergen Community

County-supported 2-year coed college. State accredited. Urban location. Undergraduate enrollment: 6136. Total faculty: 509 (197 full-time, 312 part-time). Semester calendar. Grading system: letters or numbers.

Department of Speech, Theatre, and Related Arts, 400 Paramus Road, Paramus, NJ 07652 201-447-1500

CONTACT Film — Michael Esposito Television — Emanuel Levy
DEGREES OFFERED AA in communications, AA in broadcasting
ADMISSION Application deadline — rolling
FINANCIAL AID Student loans
CURRICULAR EMPHASIS Film study — appreciation Television study — criticism and aesthetics, production treated equally
SPECIAL ACTIVITIES/OFFERINGS Filmmaking clubs, program material produced for on-campus closed-circuit television and cable television, internships in film production, internships in television production, independent study
FACILITIES AND EQUIPMENT Film — complete 8mm equipment, editing room, sound mixing room, permanent film library of commercial or professional films Television — black and white studio cameras, color studio cameras, ½-inch VTR, ¾-inch cassette VTR, portable black and white cameras, editing equipment, monitors, special effects generators, slide chain, portable color cameras, ½-inch portapak recorders, ¾-inch ENG, lighting equipment, sound recording equipment, audio mixers, film chain, time base corrector, black and white studio, color studio, audio studio, control room
FACULTY Michael Esposito, Emanuel Levy

COURSE LIST

Undergraduate
TV Production
Radio Production
Media Internship
Film Production
Introduction to Broadcasting
Media Production
Introduction to Cinema
Mass Media of Communication
The Classic Cinema

Brookdale Community College

County-supported 2-year coed college. Institutionally accredited by regional association. Suburban location. Undergraduate enrollment: 6731. Total faculty: 362 (172 full-time, 190 part-time). 6-15-15-6 calendar. Grading system: letters or numbers.

Mass and Visual Communication Department, Newman Springs Road, Lincroft, NJ 07738 201-842-1900

CONTACT Louis Pullano
PROGRAM OFFERED Major in mass and visual communication with emphasis in film and television
ADMISSION Application deadline — rolling
FINANCIAL AID Student loans, work/study programs Application deadline — 4/15
CURRICULAR EMPHASIS Film study — (1) appreciation; (2) production; (3) educational media/instructional technology Filmmaking — (1) narrative; (2) documentary; (3) educational Television study — (1) production; (2) history Television production — (1) news/documentary; (2) educational
SPECIAL ACTIVITIES/OFFERINGS Filmmaking clubs, film series, program material produced for on-campus closed-circuit television, internships in film and television production, independent study
FACILITIES AND EQUIPMENT Film — 8mm cameras, editing equipment, sound recording equipment, lighting equipment, projectors, sound stage, screening room, editing room, sound mixing room, animation board Television — complete black and white studio and exterior production equipment, complete color studio production equipment, black and white studio, color studio, audio studio, control room
FACULTY Stewart Beach, Carolyn Coudert, Patricia Endress, Paul Keating, Tim Nesterak, Louis Pullano

COURSE LIST

Undergraduate
Motion Picture as an Art Form
Motion Picture Production I, II
The Mass Media
Television Production I, II
TV: The Popular Art

Brookdale Community College (continued)

Undergraduate and Graduate
Special Projects: Film/Television
Internship: Film/Television

Burlington County College

County-supported 2-year coed college. Institutionally accredited by regional association. Suburban location, 225-acre campus. Undergraduate enrollment: 6151. Total faculty: 287 (87 full-time, 200 part-time). Semester plus two 7-week term calendar. Grading system: letters or numbers.

Learning Resources Department, Presentation Services, Pemberton, NJ 08068 609-894-9311

CONTACT Michael Gallagher
ADMISSION Application deadline — 9/1
DEGREE OFFERED AA in communication arts with an emphasis in production
ADMISSION Rolling
CURRICULAR EMPHASIS Television study — production
SPECIAL ACTIVITIES/OFFERINGS Head end for cable feed for state
FACILITIES AND EQUIPMENT Complete color studio and exterior production equipment, editing, sound mixing room, screening room
FACULTY Michael Gallagher, Michael Intintolli, Charles Savanna

COURSE LIST
Undergraduate
TV Production
Advanced TV Production
Cable Production
Mini Cam
Communications and Society
Writing for TV
Audio Production

Centenary College

Independent 4-year college primarily for women. Institutionally accredited by regional association. Small town location. 46-acre campus. Undergraduate enrollment: 703. Total faculty: 67 (42 full-time, 25 part-time). Semester calendar. Grading system: letters or numbers.

Radio and Television Department, 400 Jefferson Street, Hackettstown, NJ 07840 201-852-1400

CONTACT Michael Fisher
DEGREE OFFERED BS, AS in radio/television
ADMISSION Requirement — interviews Application deadline — 9/1, rolling
CURRICULAR EMPHASIS Television study — production Television production — news/documentary
FACILITIES AND EQUIPMENT Film — Super-8mm and 16mm film production and editing equipment Television — black and white studio and exterior production facilities, ½-inch, ¾-inch, and 1-inch VTR, editing equipment, monitors, lighting equipment, sound recording equipment, audio mixers, audio studio, control room
FACULTY Michael Fisher, Philip Lazguerre, Steve White

COURSE LIST
Undergraduate
Introduction to Film Production
Introduction to Cinema
Advanced Film Production
Animation
Introduction to TV Production
Advanced TV Production

Drew University

Independent coed university. Institutionally accredited by regional association. Suburban location, 186-acre campus. Total enrollment: 2205. Undergraduate enrollment: 1558. Total faculty: 189 (117 full-time, 72 part-time). 4-1-4 calendar. Grading system: letters or numbers.

Route 24, Madison, NJ 07940 201-377-300 (NJ toll-free 800-452-9191; CT, DC, Middle Atlantic States toll-free 800-631-8101)

CONTACT Film — Robert McLaughlin, Director, Performing Arts Television — Kurt W Remmers
ADMISSION Application deadline — 3/1
FINANCIAL AID Scholarships, work/study programs, student loans
CURRICULAR EMPHASIS Film study — (1) appreciation; (2) history; (3) scriptwriting Filmmaking — (1) narrative; (2) documentary; (3) educational Television production — (1) commercial; (2) experimental/personal video; (3) educational
SPECIAL ACTIVITIES/OFFERINGS Program material produced for on-campus closed-circuit television, cable television, admissions recruiting; internships in television production at local cable TV station; independent study; teacher training
FACILITIES AND EQUIPMENT Film — complete 8mm equipment, sound recording equipment, lighting equipment, black and white film stock, projectors Television — black and white studio cameras, ½-inch VTR, 1-inch VTR, ¾-inch cassette VTR, VHS, portable black and white cameras, editing equipment, color ENG equipment, monitors, special effects generators, ½-inch ENG recorder, lighting equipment, sound recording equipment, audio mixers, black and white studio, control room
FACULTY Robert McLaughlin, Kurt W Remmers

COURSE LIST
Undergraduate
The Art of Film
The History of Film to Citizen Kane
The History of Film since Citizen Kane
Writing for Video Production
Advanced Studies in Film

Essex County College

County-supported 2-year coed college. Institutionally accredited by regional association. Urban location. Undergraduate enrollment: 6305. Total faculty: 226. Semester calendar. Grading system: letters or numbers.

Media Production and Technology (TV), Fine and Performing Arts (Film), 303 University Avenue, Newark, NJ 07102 201-877-3274 or 201-877-3082

CONTACT Film — Donald Nemeyer Television — Spencer A Freund
DEGREE OFFERED AAS in broadcast operations and engineering
DEPARTMENTAL MAJORS Film — 20 students Television — 40 students
ADMISSION Requirements — ACT or SAT scores, teachers' recommendations, written statement of purpose Application deadline — 4/30, 11/30
FINANCIAL AID Scholarships, work/study programs, student loans, part-time employment
CURRICULAR EMPHASIS Film study — history, criticism and aesthetics, appreciation treated equally Television study — history, criticism and aesthetics, appreciation, educational, production, management, engineering and operations, cable TV treated equally Television production — commercial, news/documentary, experimental/personal video, educational, industrial treated equally
SPECIAL ACTIVITIES/OFFERINGS Film series; film festivals; program material produced for on-campus closed-circuit television, cable television, local public television station, local commercial television station; internships in film production; internships in television production; independent study
FACILITIES AND EQUIPMENT Television — complete color studio production and exterior production equipment, color studio, audio studio, control room, electronic field production facilities
FACULTY Spencer A Freund, Donald Nemeyer

COURSE LIST

Undergraduate

Art of Film I, II
Beginning TV Production
Advanced TV Production
Introduction Broadcasting and Electronics Telecommunication
Mass Communications
Broadcast Systems and Equipment
Cable TV Systems and Equipment
Career and Cooperative Education Internship

New Jersey

Fairleigh Dickinson University, Madison

Independent comprehensive coed institution. Institutionally accredited by regional association. Suburban location. Total enrollment: 5121. Undergraduate enrollment: 3576. Total faculty: 303 (118 full-time, 185 part-time). Semester calendar. Grading system: letters or numbers.

English Department, 285 Madison Avenue, Madison, NJ 07940 201-377-4700

CONTACT Film — T J Ross Television — V B Holpert
PROGRAM OFFERED Minor in television
ADMISSION Requirement — minimum grade point average Application deadline — rolling
FINANCIAL AID Scholarships, student loans, work/study programs Application deadline — 4/15
CURRICULAR EMPHASIS Film study — history, criticism and aesthetics, appreciation treated equally Filmmaking — (1) narrative; (2) documentary; (3) educational Television study — (1) educational; (2) management; (3) criticism and aesthetics Television production — (1) commercial; (2) educational; (3) experimental/personal video
SPECIAL ACTIVITIES/OFFERINGS Film series, film societies, independent study
FACILITIES AND EQUIPMENT Film — complete 8mm, 16mm, and 35mm equipment, sound stage, screening room, 35mm screening facilities, editing room, sound mixing room, permanent film library Television — complete black and white exterior production equipment, black and white studio, color studio, mobile van/unit, remote truck
FACULTY V Holpert, T J Ross

COURSE LIST

Undergraduate

Literature and Film
Film and Society
Film and the Self
Drama and Film
Media Criticism: Film and TV
Film Genres
Shakespeare on Film
The Film Experience

Fairleigh Dickinson University, Teaneck

Independent comprehensive coed institution. Institutionally accredited by regional association. Suburban location, 138-acre campus. Total enrollment: 8845. Undergraduate enrollment: 5649. Total faculty: 788 (269 full-time, 519 part-time). Semester calendar. Grading system: letters or numbers.

Department of Communications, Speech, and Theatre, 1000 River Road, Teaneck, NJ 07666 201-836-6300, ext 239

CONTACT Film — Russ Ratsch Television — Jack Colldeweih
DEGREE OFFERED BA in communications
ADMISSION Requirements — 2.0 minimum grade point average for transfers, SAT scores Undergraduate application deadline — rolling
FINANCIAL AID Scholarships, work/study programs, student loans
CURRICULAR EMPHASIS Film study — (1) history; (2) appreciation; (3) criticism and aesthetics Filmmaking — (1) narrative; (2) animated; (3) documentary; (4) experimental Television study — (1) criticism and aesthetics; (2) appreciation; (3) production; (4) management; (5) history Television production — (1) news/documentary; (2) commercial; (3) experimental/personal video
SPECIAL ACTIVITIES/OFFERINGS Program material produced for on-campus closed-circuit television and cable television, internships in film production, internships in television production, independent study

Fairleigh Dickinson University, Teaneck (continued)

FACILITIES AND EQUIPMENT Film — 8mm cameras, editing equipment, sound recording equipment, lighting, projectors, animation board, permanent film library of student films, permanent film library of commercial or professional films, Super-8 facilities Television — complete black and white and color studio and exterior production equipment, color studio, control room, portable color and black and white equipment

FACULTY Theodore Chesler, Jack Colldeweih, Jane Dale, Joel Justesen, Paul Levinson, Russ Ratsch PART-TIME FACULTY Cliff Bedford, Charles Christensen, Arnold Snyder

COURSE LIST

Undergraduate

Introduction to Telecommunications
Telecommunications Seminar
History of Film I–III
The Art of Film
Film Going and Analysis
Film Production I, II
Animation
Contemporary Television: Content and Techniques
Development of Contemporary Television
Television Around the World
Television: Special Programming
Television News: The Big Issues
Basic Television Production
Portable Television and Videotape Editing
Advanced Television Production
Media Center Internship
Television Equipment Maintenance
Television Studio Operations
Script Writing for TV, Film, and AV
Television Acting and Performance
Speech for Actors and Announcers

Glassboro State College

State-supported comprehensive coed institution. Part of New Jersey State College System. Institutionally accredited by regional association. Small town location, 180-acre campus. Total enrollment: 10,950. Undergraduate enrollment: 9800. Total faculty: 685 (385 full-time, 300 part-time). Semester calendar. Grading system: letters or numbers.

Communications Department, Bunce Hall, Glassboro, NJ 08028 609-445-7187

CONTACT Film — E Michael Desilets Television — Edgar Eckhardt
DEGREE OFFERED BA in communications with specialization in radio/television/film
DEPARTMENTAL MAJORS Film and television — 220 students.
ADMISSION Requirement — ACT or SAT scores
FINANCIAL AID Scholarships, work/study programs, student loans
CURRICULAR EMPHASIS Film study — history, criticism and aesthetics, appreciation treated equally Filmmaking — documentary, narrative, educational treated equally Television study — criticism and aesthetics, production, management treated equally Television production — commercial, news/documentary, educational treated equally
SPECIAL ACTIVITIES/OFFERINGS Filmmaking clubs; film festivals; student publications; program material produced for on-campus closed-circuit television, cable television, local public television station, and local commercial television station; internships in film production; internships in television production; independent study; teacher training
FACILITIES AND EQUIPMENT Film — complete 8mm equipment, 16mm cameras, editing equipment, lighting, projectors, screening room, editing room, permanent film library of commercial or professional films Television — complete black and white and color studio production equipment, black and white studio, color studio, audio studio, control room
FACULTY Richard J Ambacher, E Michael Desilets, R Michael Donovan, Edgar Eckhardt, Richard Grupenhoff, Linda Mather

COURSE LIST

Undergraduate

Introduction to Broadcasting
Film History I, II
Film Theory and Technique I, II
Television Production I, II
Television Scenario Writing
Techniques of Documentary Films
Advanced Filmmaking
Communications Techniques in Film
Images of Women in Film
American Film Directors
Media Ecology
Mass Media and Their Influences
Communications Projects I, II
Internship in Communications
Film Scenario Writing

Jersey City State College

State-supported comprehensive coed institution. Institutionally accredited by regional association. Urban location. Total enrollment: 8700. Undergraduate enrollment: 7700. Total faculty: 469 (305 full-time, 164 part-time). Semester calendar. Grading system: letters or numbers.

Media Arts Department, 2039 Kennedy Boulevard, Jersey City, NJ 07305 201-547-3207

CONTACT John F Egan
DEGREES OFFERED BS, MA, MFA in film and television
DEPARTMENTAL MAJORS Film — 175 students Television — 250 students
ADMISSION Undergraduate requirements — 2.5 minimum grade point average, SAT scores, interviews, teachers' recommendations, portfolio Graduate requirements — 2.5 minimum grade point average, interviews, teachers' recommendations, portfolio Undergraduate application deadline — rolling
FINANCIAL AID Scholarships, student loans, work/study programs Undergraduate application deadline — 4/15
CURRICULAR EMPHASIS Film study — (1) production; (2) criticism and aesthetics; (3) history; (4) educational media/instructional technology Filmmaking — (1) documentary; (2) narrative; (3) animated; (4) experimental; (5) educational; (6) public service Television study — (1) production; (2) management; (3) history; (4) criticism and aesthetics; (5) appreciation; (6) educational Television production — (1) experimental/personal video; (2) news/documentary; (3) commercial
SPECIAL ACTIVITIES/OFFERINGS Filmmaking clubs, program material produced for on-campus closed-circuit television and cable television, internships in film and television production, independent study, cooperative education program, Eastern terminus for KTVU-TV, East Coast/West Coast Weekly News Commentary

FACILITIES AND EQUIPMENT Film — complete 8mm, 16mm, and Super-16mm equipment, screening room, editing room, sound mixing room, animation board, permanent film library, complete processing laboratory Television — complete black and white exterior production facilities, complete color studio production equipment, color studio, mobile van/unit, remote truck, audio studio, control room, television editing rooms
FACULTY Richard Allaire, Walter Bojsza, Leonardo Dachille, Maria De Luca, John F Egan, Andrea Eisenstein, Mark Eisenstein, Herbert Leder, Frank Miceli, Chuck Saaf, Joseph Sauder, Louis Tiscornia, Michael Wodynski PART-TIME FACULTY Judith Lipja, Anthony Magarelle, Thomas O'Leary, Gail Pellett, Lynn Sharp

COURSE LIST
Undergraduate
Media as Radical Education
Exploration in Communication
Propaganda in Media Systems
Media in American Society
Media Ecology
Mass Media and Society
History of Communications
Symbols, Thoughts, and Behavior
Introduction to Semantic Analysis
Television Production I, II
Creating a Television Production
Critical Development of Television
Film Production I, II
Practicum in Film Production
Analysis in Cinema
Media and the Graphic Arts
Black America in the Media
Media Patterns
Music in Media
Women's Media Today
Media and Technology in Education
Development of Cinema I, II
Films of Famous Directors
Experimental Film
The Documentary Film
Radio/Television Writing
Speech for Broadcasting
Media Graphics
The Relationship of Broadcasting to Ethnic Groups
Social Responsibility in Broadcasting
Radio and Television Announcing
Broadcasting in the Public Interest
Television and Radio Advertising
Radio-Television News
Radio-Television Management
Broadcast Sales Management
Advertising and the Economics of Media
Public Affairs Broadcasting
Trends in Radio and Television Programming
Screenwriting
Film Criticism
Non-Theatrical Film
Production of Television Commercials
Television Film News
Television Directing
Educational Television
Documentary Cinematography
Animated Filming
Post-Production Techniques
Film-Television Lighting
Film Directing
Film Production Management
Senior Seminar
Jobs in Media

Kean College of New Jersey

State-supported comprehensive coed institution. Part of New Jersey State College System. Institutionally accredited by regional association, programs recognized by NASM. Suburban location, 120-acre campus. Total enrollment: 10,576. Undergraduate enrollment: 9094. Total faculty: 716 (364 full-time, 352 part-time). 4-1-4 calendar. Grading system: letters or numbers.

Fine Arts Department, Morris Avenue, Union, NJ 07083 201-527-2000

CONTACT David Troy
ADMISSION Application deadline — 4/1
FACULTY Samuel Hefney, David Troy

COURSE LIST
Undergraduate
Filmmaking I, II
Television Production

Mercer County Community College

County-supported 2-year coed college. Institutionally accredited by regional association. Suburban location. Undergraduate enrollment: 4472. Total faculty: 275 (132 full-time, 143 part-time). 4-1-4 calendar. Grading system: letters or numbers.

Telecommunications Department, 1200 Old Trenton Road, Trenton, NJ 08690 609-586-4800

CONTACT George Schwartz, Director of Telecommunications
DEGREES OFFERED AAS in telecommunications with emphasis in television or radio, AA in liberal arts with emphasis in telecommunications
DEPARTMENTAL MAJORS Television — 140 students
ADMISSION Requirement — high school diploma or equivalent Application deadline — rolling
FINANCIAL AID Scholarships, work/study programs, student loans Application deadline — rolling
CURRICULAR EMPHASIS Television production — commercial, experimental/personal video, educational, cable television, industrial television treated equally
SPECIAL ACTIVITIES/OFFERINGS Program material produced for cable television, internships in television production, independent study, vocational placement service
FACILITIES AND EQUIPMENT Television — color studio cameras, ½-inch VTR, 1-inch VTR, ¾-inch cassette VTR, editing equipment, monitors, special effects generators, slide chain, portable color cameras, ½-inch portapak color recorders, ¾-inch ENG, lighting equipment, sound recording equipment, audio mixers, film chain, time base corrector, color studio, audio studio, control room, cable television and distribution master control center

COURSE LIST
Undergraduate
Introduction to TV Production
Advanced TV Production
Industrial and Educational TV Production
Experimental TV Production
Mass Media
Radio-TV Management
Broadcast Sales
Audio-Visual Production
Internship
Writing for Radio-TV
Cinema

Montclair State College

State-supported comprehensive coed institution. Institutionally accredited by regional association, programs recognized by NASM. Suburban location, 120-acre campus. Total enrollment: 15,246. Undergraduate enrollment: 11,695. Total faculty: 779 (489 full-time, 290 part-time). 4-1-4 calendar. Grading system: letters or numbers.

Speech and Theater Department, Valley Road and Normal Avenue, Upper Montclair, NJ 07043 201-893-4217

CONTACT Wayne Bond
DEGREES OFFERED BA in broadcasting, MA in public media arts with a major in television
DEPARTMENTAL MAJORS Undergraduate television — 100 students Graduate television — 25 students
ADMISSION Undergraduate requirements — 2.0 minimum grade point average, SAT scores, interviews Graduate requirements — 3.0 minimum grade point average, GRE scores, interviews Undergraduate application deadline — 2/1, rolling
FINANCIAL AID Work/study programs, teaching assistantships Undergraduate application deadline — rolling
CURRICULAR EMPHASIS Undergraduate television study — (1) production; (2) management; (3) history, appreciation, educational; (4) criticism and aesthetics Graduate television study — (1) management; (2) criticism and aesthetics; (3) history, appreciation, production, educational Undergraduate television production — (1) dramatic/entertainment; (2) news/documentary; (3) educational; (4) commercial Graduate television production — (1) educational; (2) news/documentary; (3) commercial
SPECIAL ACTIVITIES/OFFERINGS Program material produced for on-campus closed-circuit television and cable television, internships in television production, independent study
FACILITIES AND EQUIPMENT Television — black and white studio cameras, ½-inch VTR, 1-inch VTR, ¾-inch cassette VTR, portable black and white cameras, editing equipment, monitors, special effects generators, slide chain, ½-inch portapak recorders, lighting equipment, sound recording equipment, audio mixers, film chain, time base corrector, character generator, black and white studio, audio studio, control room
FACULTY Christopher Stasheff, Howard Travis PART-TIME FACULTY Shirley Laird, Cliff Love, Jack Lupack, David Ochoa, Harry Olsson Jr, Michael Silver

COURSE LIST
Undergraduate
Introduction to Broadcasting
Television Practicum
Writing for Broadcast Media
Television Production
Elements of Public Media
Political Television and Radio
International Broadcasting

Graduate
Techniques in Broadcasting Communication
Broadcast Media and Mass Culture
Proseminar in Broadcasting

Undergraduate and Graduate
Radio and Television Production I, II
Internship in Broadcasting
Station Management
Public Relations
Broadcast Engineering
Broadcast Law
Broadcasting and Community Affairs
Electronic Journalism

English Department, School of Humanities 201-893-4249

CONTACT David Meranze
PROGRAM OFFERED The film courses listed below may be taken by anyone in the college as electives or in partial fulfillment of certain requirements such as the one in General Humanities
CURRICULAR EMPHASIS All of the courses are concerned with film literature and include the viewing of films in class. The introductory course is given every term; the other undergraduate courses are all offered within a two-year cycle.
FACULTY Janet Cutler, David Meranze, Theodore Price

COURSE LIST
Undergraduate
Introduction to the Film
Film Comedy
Film and Society
Film of the Hollywood Studio Years
The American Film
Major Film Figures
World Film
Major Film Genres
The Silent Film
Drama on Film
The Contemporary Film

Graduate
Film Studies

New Jersey Institute of Technology

State-related coed university. Institutionally accredited by regional association. Urban location, 23-acre campus. Total enrollment: 5110. Undergraduate enrollment: 4194. Total faculty: 387 (267 full-time, 120 part-time). Semester calendar. Grading system: letters or numbers.

Humanities Department, Newark, NJ 07102 201-645-5321

CONTACT James Camp
ADMISSION Application deadline — 5/1, rolling
FACULTY James Camp, John O'Connor

COURSE LIST
Undergraduate
History and Criticism of Film
Historical Problems of the Twentieth Century through Film

Princeton University

Independent coed university. Institutionally accredited by regional association. Suburban location. Total enrollment: 5844. Undergraduate enrollment: 4422. Total faculty: 777 (652 full-time, 125 part-time). Semester calendar. Grading system: letters or numbers.

Visual Arts Program, 185 Nassau Street, Princeton, NJ 08544 609-452-5457

ADMISSION Undergraduate requirement — interview
FINANCIAL AID Student loans
CURRICULAR EMPHASIS Film study — (1) history; (2) criticism and aesthetics
SPECIAL ACTIVITIES/OFFERINGS Filmmaking clubs, film societies
FACULTY P Adams Sitney

COURSE LIST
Undergraduate
Introduction to Film
Silent Cinema
Special Topics in Film History
Contemporary Cinema
Major Filmmakers

Ramapo College of New Jersey

State-supported 4-year coed college. Part of New Jersey State College System. Institutionally accredited by regional association. Suburban location, 300-acre campus. Undergraduate enrollment: 4022. Total faculty: 185 (163 full-time, 22 part-time). Semester calendar. Grading system: letters or numbers.

School of Contemporary Arts, 505 Ramapo Valley Road, Mahwah, NJ 07430 201-825-2800

CONTACT James B Hollenbach
PROGRAM OFFERED Major in art with emphasis in film
ADMISSION Application deadline — 4/1, rolling
FINANCIAL AID Scholarships, student loans, work/study programs Application deadline — 4/1
CURRICULAR EMPHASIS Film study — (1) production; (2) criticism and aesthetics; (3) history Filmmaking — (1) experimental; (2) documentary; (3) narrative Television study — (1) criticism and aesthetics; (2) production Television production — (1) experimental/personal video; (2) news/documentary
SPECIAL ACTIVITIES/OFFERINGS Film series, film festivals, program material produced for cable television, internships in film and television production, independent study
FACILITIES AND EQUIPMENT Film — complete 8mm and 16mm equipment, editing room, sound mixing room, animation board, permanent film library Television — ½-inch VTR, portable black and white cameras, editing equipment, monitors, portable color cameras, ½-inch portapak recorder, lighting equipment, sound recording equipment, audio mixers, audio studio, control room
FACULTY Robert Fresco, Eileen Popiel PART-TIME FACULTY C Gazit, Jay Kaufman

COURSE LIST
Undergraduate
Film — Structure and Process
Films and Filmmaking
Documentary Film
Film History
Performing for the Electronic Media
Writing for the Media

Rutgers University, Newark

State-supported 4-year coed college. Part of Rutgers, The State University of New Jersey. Institutionally accredited by regional association. Urban location. Undergraduate enrollment: 4887. Total faculty: 313 (289 full-time, 24 part-time). Semester calendar. Grading system: letters or numbers.

Theatre Arts (Stage, Film, Television) and Speech Department, The Newark College of Arts and Sciences, Warren and High Streets, Newark, NJ 07102 201-648-5248

CONTACT Film — Lester L Moore Television — Nathan Shoehalter
DEGREE OFFERED BA in theatre arts with an emphasis in stage, film, or television
PROGRAM MAJORS 80 students
ADMISSION Application deadline — rolling
FINANCIAL AID Work/study programs, student loans
CURRICULAR EMPHASIS Film study — history, criticism and aesthetics, intensive analysis treated equally Filmmaking — (1) narrative; (2) documentary; (3) experimental Television study — appreciation, production treated equally Television production — news/documentary, experimental/personal video treated equally
SPECIAL ACTIVITIES/OFFERINGS Film series, internships in film production, internships in television production, independent study
FACILITIES AND EQUIPMENT Film — 8mm cameras, editing equipment, sound recording equipment, lighting, projectors, 16mm projectors, screening room, editing room, sound mixing room, permanent film library of commercial or professional films Television — complete black and white equipment, black and white studio, audio studio, control room
FACULTY Donald A Borchardt, Lester L Moore, Nathan Shoehalter PART-TIME FACULTY Eliot Frankel, Ray Weiss

COURSE LIST
Undergraduate
Art and History of the Film I, II
American Film I, II
Modern Film I, II
Principles of Dramatic Film Production I, II
Television and Broadcasting I, II
Media and Method I, II
Principles of Television Production I, II
Practicum in Theater Arts–Film I, II
Practicum in Broadcasting I, II
Seminar in Theater Arts–Film I, II
Seminar in Broadcasting I, II

Saint Peter's College

Independent Roman Catholic 4-year coed college. Institutionally accredited by regional association. Urban location. Undergraduate enrollment: 2790. Total faculty: 315 (129 full-time, 186 part-time). Semester calendar. Grading system: letters or numbers.

Fine Arts Department, 2641 Kennedy Boulevard, Jersey City, NJ 07306 201-333-4400

CONTACT Oscar Magnan, S J, Chairman
PART-TIME FACULTY Barbara Lund, William Thomaier

COURSE LIST

Undergraduate
Comedy Film
Motion Picture Study
Contemporary Film

Seton Hall University

Independent Roman Catholic coed university. Institutionally accredited by regional association, programs recognized by AACSB. Suburban location, 56-acre campus. Total enrollment: 9966. Undergraduate enrollment: 6261. Total faculty: 602 (387 full-time, 215 part-time). Semester calendar. Grading system: letters or numbers.

Communication Department, South Orange, NJ 07079 201-762-9000

CONTACT Al Paul Klose, Chairman
DEGREE OFFERED BA in communication with concentration in television and/or film
DEPARTMENTAL MAJORS Film — 50 students Television — 350 students
ADMISSION Requirements — ACT or SAT scores, interview, better than average high school record Application deadline — 5/1, rolling
FINANCIAL AID Work/study programs, student loans Application deadline — 5/1
CURRICULAR EMPHASIS Film study — (1) criticism and aesthetics; (2) history Filmmaking — (1) documentary; (2) narrative; (3) animated; (4) experimental Television study — (1) criticism and aesthetics; (2) history Television production — (1) news/documentary; (2) narrative
SPECIAL ACTIVITIES/OFFERINGS Filmmaking clubs, film series, film societies, program material produced for on-campus closed-circuit television and cable television, internships in film production, internships in television production, independent study
FACILITIES AND EQUIPMENT Film — complete 8mm and 16mm equipment, screening room, editing room, sound mixing room, animation board Television — black and white studio cameras, ½-inch VTR, ¾-inch cassette VTR, portable black and white cameras, editing equipment, monitors, special effects generators, slide chain, ½-inch portapak recorders, lighting equipment, sound recording equipment, audio mixers, film chain, VHF/UHF tuner, color monitors, black and white studio, control room
FACULTY Robert J Allen, Kevin W Hislop, E Kenneth Hoffman, Al Paul Klose, William H Rockett, Priscilla Travis PART-TIME FACULTY Howard Travis

COURSE LIST

Undergraduate
Mass Communication in Modern America
Evolution of the Film Art
Electronic Age in America
Television/Film Writing
Broadcast News
Broadcast Advertising
Ethics and Laws of Broadcasting
Development and Significance of Cable Television
Film Criticism
Basic Film Theory and Technique
Film Production
Documentary Film
Creative Film Marketing I, II
Contemporary Cinema
Film Editing
Introduction to Studio Television
Television Forms and Techniques
Television Directing
Television Production
Lighting for Television, Film, and Theatre
Still Photography
Photojournalism

Graduate
Film-Visual Communication

Trenton State College

State-supported comprehensive coed institution. Part of New Jersey State College System. Institutionally accredited by regional association. Suburban location, 210-acre campus. Total enrollment: 10,000. Undergraduate enrollment: 7500. Total faculty: 500 (380 full-time, 120 part-time). Semester calendar. Grading system: letters or numbers.

English Department/Media Communication Science Department, Pennington Road, Trenton, NJ 08625 609-771-2318 or 609-771-2297

CONTACT Film — Barry H Novick Television — Kenneth Kaplowitz
PROGRAM OFFERED Major in English or media communication science with emphasis in film and television
ADMISSION Application deadline — 3/1, rolling
CURRICULAR EMPHASIS Film study — (1) criticism and aesthetics; (2) history; (3) production Filmmaking — (1) narrative; (2) experimental; (3) documentary Television study — (1) production; (2) criticism and aesthetics; (3) appreciation Television production — (1) experimental/personal video; (2) commercial; (3) educational
SPECIAL ACTIVITIES/OFFERINGS Film series, film festivals, film societies, program material produced for on-campus closed-circuit television and local public television station, independent study, vocational placement service
FACILITIES AND EQUIPMENT Film — complete 8mm equipment, 16mm projectors, editing room, permanent film library Television — complete black and white studio and exterior production equipment, black and white studio, control room

FACULTY Kenneth Kaplowitz, Milton Levin, Robert Mehlman, Barry H Novick, Peter Panos, Dave Rogosky, Arthur Tiffany, Richard Warner, Gary Woodward

COURSE LIST

Undergraduate

The Film
Studies in Film
Motion Picture Production I, II
Expanded Multimedia Workshop
Television as an Art Form
Television Production I, II
Television Programming Workshop
Introduction to Television (Technical)
The History of Media
Directing and Acting for Film and Television
Broadcasting in America
Film and Society

William Paterson College of New Jersey

State-supported comprehensive coed institution. Institutionally accredited by regional association. Suburban location, 320-acre campus. Total enrollment: 12,000. Undergraduate enrollment: 9862. Total faculty: 601 (404 full-time, 197 part-time). Semester calendar. Grading system: letters.

Communication Department, 300 Pompton Road, Wayne, NJ 07470 201-595-2167

CONTACT Film — U Bonsignoiri Television — Anthony Maltese
DEGREES OFFERED BA in communication with emphasis in radio, television, film, or journalism; MA in communication arts with emphasis in television
DEPARTMENTAL MAJORS Undergraduate film — 47 students Undergraduate television — 275 students Graduate television — 27 students
ADMISSION Undergraduate requirements — ACT or SAT scores, interview, teachers' recommendations Graduate requirements — GRE scores, interview Undergraduate application deadline — 3/1
FINANCIAL AID Scholarships, work/study programs, student loans, teaching assistantships Undergraduate application deadline — 3/1
CURRICULAR EMPHASIS Graduate film study — (1) educational media/instructional technology; (2) criticism and aesthetics; (3) history Undergraduate filmmaking — (1) documentary; (2) animated; (3) educational Graduate filmmaking — (1) experimental; (2) documentary; (3) educational Undergraduate television study — (1) production; (2) educational; (3) history Graduate television study — (1) production; (2) criticism and aesthetics; (3) history Undergraduate television production — (1) commercial; (2) news/documentary; (3) experimental/personal video Graduate television production — (1) experimental/personal video; (2) commercial; (3) educational
SPECIAL ACTIVITIES/OFFERINGS Filmmaking clubs; film festivals; student publications; program material produced for on-campus closed-circuit television, cable television, and local public television station; apprenticeships; internships in film production; internships in television production; independent study; teacher training
FACILITIES AND EQUIPMENT Film — complete 8mm equipment, 16mm cameras, screening room, editing room, sound mixing room, animation board Television — complete color studio and exterior production equipment, color studios, mobile unit, audio studio, control room
FACULTY Umberto Bonsignoiri, Jerry Chamberlain, Paul Dell Colle, James Kearney, Thornton Kloss, Anthony Maltese, Mike Rhea PART-TIME FACULTY Jay Campbell, Mary Federico, Jim Hunt

COURSE LIST

Undergraduate

Filmmaking I, II
Documentary Film Production
Dramatic Film Production
Screenwriting
Editing for Film
Film as Medium
Current Cinema
Animation I, II
History of Film
Cable TV Workshop
Corporate Video
Television News

Graduate

Directing for Television
Instructional Television

Undergraduate and Graduate

Television Production I, II
Television Workshop
Writing for Radio and TV
Audio Production

NEW MEXICO

Anthropology Film Center

Independent 2-year coed institution. Accredited by state agency. Small town location. Total enrollment: 12. Total faculty: 3. Semester calendar. Grading system: reports written by faculty members.

PO Box 493, 1626 Canyon Road, Santa Fe, NM 87501 505-983-4127

CONTACT Carroll Warner Williams, Director
DEGREE OFFERED MA in visual anthropology (offered in conjunction with Temple University) or certificate (from AFC)
ADMISSION Requirement — written statement of purpose, personal interview if possible
CURRICULAR EMPHASIS Film study — (1) production; (2) educational media/instructional technology; (3) research Filmmaking — (1) documentary; (2) research; (3) educational
FACILITIES AND EQUIPMENT Film — complete 16mm equipment, screening room, editing rooms, animation stand and camera, research analysis projector, sound analysis playback
FACULTY Ernest Shinagawa, Carroll Warner Williams

Anthropology Film Center (continued)

COURSE LIST

Undergraduate and Graduate

Social Science Film Part One: Production Lab
Social Science Film Part Two: Advanced Theory, Production Technique, Volunteer Internships, Independent Study, Directed Reading

University of New Mexico

State-supported coed university. Institutionally accredited by regional association, programs recognized by NASM, AACSB, ACPE. Urban location, 600-acre campus. Total enrollment: 21,547. Undergraduate enrollment: 17,527. Total faculty: 1271 (1000 full-time, 271 part-time). Semester calendar. Grading system: letters or numbers.

Theatre Arts Department, Albuquerque, NM 87131 505-277-3540

CONTACT Ira S Jaffe
PROGRAM OFFERED Major in theatre arts with emphasis in film
ADMISSION Undergraduate application deadline — rolling
FINANCIAL AID Scholarships, student loans, teaching assistantships Undergraduate application deadline — 4/1
CURRICULAR EMPHASIS Film study — (1) criticism and aesthetics; (2) history; (3) production Filmmaking — (1) experimental; (2) narrative; (3) documentary
SPECIAL ACTIVITIES/OFFERINGS Film series, film festivals, film societies, independent study
FACILITIES AND EQUIPMENT Film — 8mm and 16mm cameras, editing equipment, sound recording equipment, projectors, editing room
FACULTY Ira S Jaffe

COURSE LIST

Undergraduate

Introduction to Film
History of Silent Era
Film Comedy
Elements of Filmmaking
History of Sound Era
American Avant-Garde Cinema
Individual Directors
Film Theory

Graduate

Advanced Problems in Film History, Criticism, and Theory

NEW YORK

Adelphi University

Independent coed university. Accredited by regional association and AICS. Suburban location, 75-acre campus. Total enrollment: 11,653. Undergraduate enrollment: 6927. Total faculty: 800. 4-1-4 calendar. Grading system: letters or numbers.

Department of Communications, South Avenue, Garden City, NY 11530 516-294-8700

CONTACT Film — Paul Pitcoff, Chairman Television — Len Price
DEGREE OFFERED BA in film, TV, radio, or theory
DEPARTMENTAL MAJORS Film — 45 students Television — 55 students
ADMISSION Requirements — interviews, portfolio, written statement of purpose Application deadline — rolling
FINANCIAL AID Filmmaking grants Application deadline — 2/1
CURRICULAR EMPHASIS Film study — (1) production; (2) criticism and aesthetics; (3) history Filmmaking — (1) documentary; (2) narrative; (3) experimental; (4) animated Television study — (1) production; (2) criticism and aesthetics; (3) history Television production — (1) news/documentary; (2) experimental/personal video; (3) educational
SPECIAL ACTIVITIES/OFFERINGS Film festivals; professional film company; program material produced for on-campus closed-circuit television, cable television, local public television station, medical and service institutions; apprenticeships; internships in film and television production; independent study; practicum
FACILITIES AND EQUIPMENT Film — complete 16mm equipment, sound stage, screening room, editing room, sound mixing room, animation board, permanent film library Television — complete black and white studio and exterior production equipment, black and white studio, audio studio, editing rooms, control room, portable color facilities
FACULTY Leslie Austin, Peter Costello, Marge Hudson, Lynne McVeigh, Paul Pitcoff, Len Price, Helen Stritzler

COURSE LIST

Undergraduate

Art of the Film
History of Cinema I, II
Impact of Modern Cinema
Fiction and Film
Explorations in Documentary Film
American Independent Cinema
Special Topics in Cinema Studies
Elementary Film Production: 16mm
Newsreel Journalism
Film Editing
Advanced Filmmaking I, II
Animation
Light and Sound for Film and Television
Summer Film Trip Workshop
Television Environments
½-Inch Video Production
Advanced Video Production
Television Workshop
Television Program Development
Special Studies in Film and Video Production
Television Commercial Workshop
Advanced Film Workshop
Advanced Video Workshop
Screenwriting
Documentary Filmmaking
Directing for Film and Television
Communications Law
Advertising
Music and Media
Professional Internships

Adirondack Community College

State and locally supported 2-year coed college. Part of State University of New York System, automatic transfer to main campus for baccalaureate. Institutionally accredited by regional association. Rural location, 141-acre campus. Undergraduate enrollment: 2014. Total faculty: 101 (66 full-time, 35 part-time). Semester calendar. Grading system: letters or numbers.

English Department, Bay Road, Glens Falls, NY 12801 518-793-4491

CONTACT Chairman
ADMISSION Application deadline — 8/10, rolling

Alfred University

Independent coed university. Institutionally accredited by regional association. Rural location, 232-acre campus. Total enrollment: 1825. Undergraduate enrollment: 1758. Total faculty: 176 (155 full-time, 21 part-time). Semester calendar. Grading system: letters or numbers.

Humanities Division, PO Box 806, Alfred, NY 14802 607-871-2256

CONTACT David Ohara
ADMISSION Application deadline — 2/1
CURRICULAR EMPHASIS Film study — criticism and aesthetics
FACULTY David Ohara

COURSE LIST
Undergraduate
Film Criticism

Bard College

Independent 4-year coed college. Institutionally accredited by regional association. Rural location, 1000-acre campus. Undergraduate enrollment: 700. Total faculty: 90 (55 full-time, 35 part-time). 4-1-4 calendar. Grading system: letters or numbers.

Film Department, Annandale-on-Hudson, NY 12504 914-758-6822

CONTACT Adolfas Mekas, Chairman
DEGREE OFFERED BA in film
DEPARTMENTAL MAJORS 35 students
ADMISSION Requirements — minimum grade point average, interviews Application deadline — rolling
FINANCIAL AID Student loans, work/study programs Application deadline — 3/1, rolling
CURRICULAR EMPHASIS Film study — (1) production; (2) criticism and aesthetics; (3) history Filmmaking — (1) narrative; (2) experimental; (3) documentary
SPECIAL ACTIVITIES/OFFERINGS Film series, film societies, student publications, independent study, vocational placement service
FACILITIES AND EQUIPMENT Film — complete 8mm and 16mm equipment, screening room, editing room, animation board, permanent film library
FACULTY Adolfas Mekas PART-TIME FACULTY Tom Brener, Raymond Foery

COURSE LIST
Undergraduate
Introduction to Filmmaking
Film History
Seminar: History
Screenwriting
Pre-Production
Post-Production
Cinema Analysis
Color Seminar
Sound
Editing
8mm Editing
Avant-Garde Workshop
Narrative Workshop
Documentary Workshop
Anthropological Film
16mm Workshop

Canisius College

Independent comprehensive coed institution. Institutionally accredited by regional association, programs recognized by AACSB. Urban location. Total enrollment: 4089. Undergraduate enrollment: 2200. Total faculty: 217 (173 full-time, 44 part-time). Semester calendar. Grading system: letters or numbers.

Communication Department, 2001 Main Street, Buffalo, NY 14208 716-883-7000, ext 781

CONTACT Film — B Hammond Television — J Howell
PROGRAM OFFERED Major in communication with emphasis in film or television
ADMISSION Requirements — 2.0 minimum grade point average, interviews Application deadline — rolling
FINANCIAL AID Scholarships, student loans, work/study program Application deadline — 3/1
CURRICULAR EMPHASIS Film study — (1) criticism and aesthetics; (2) history; (3) limited production Television study — (1) production; (2) criticism and aesthetics; (3) management Television production — (1) news/documentary; (2) experimental/personal video; (3) commercial
SPECIAL ACTIVITIES/OFFERINGS Program material produced for on-campus closed-circuit television and cable television, internships in film and television production, independent study, practicum
FACILITIES AND EQUIPMENT Film — complete 8mm equipment, audio studio, editing room, animation board Television — complete black and white and color studio and exterior production facilities
FACULTY B Berlin, B Hammond, J Howell, Marilyn Watt

Canisius College (continued)

COURSE LIST

Undergraduate

History of Cinema
Film Theory and Criticism
Contemporary Cinema
Films of World War II
Introduction to Cinematography
Television Production
Audio Production
Women in Television
Media Criticism
History of Broadcasting
Practicum in Film
Practicum in Video Production
Broadcast Journalism
Still Photography

Cayuga County Community College

State and locally supported 2-year coed college. Part of State University of New York System. Institutionally accredited by regional association. Suburban location, 10-acre campus. Undergraduate enrollment: 2871. Total faculty: 114 (86 full-time, 28 part-time). Semester calendar. Grading system: letters or numbers.

Theatre Arts—Telecommunications Department, Franklin Street, Auburn, NY 13021 315-255-1743

CONTACT Dan LaBeille
DEGREES OFFERED AA in radio and TV broadcasting, AA in radio and TV technology
DEPARTMENTAL MAJORS 50 students
FINANCIAL AID Work/study programs
CURRICULAR EMPHASIS Film study — (1) production; (2) educational media/instructional technology Filmmaking — (1) news; (2) educational; (3) experimental Television study — (1) production; (2) educational; (3) electronics Television production — (1) educational; (2) news/documentary; (3) commercial
SPECIAL ACTIVITIES/OFFERINGS Film series, program material produced for on-campus closed-circuit television and cable television, independent study, head end for cable system
FACILITIES AND EQUIPMENT Film — complete 16mm equipment, sound stage, screening room, editing room, permanent film library Television — complete color studio and exterior production equipment, black and white studio, audio studio, control room, ENG capacity
FACULTY Dan LaBeille, Frank Messere PART-TIME FACULTY Norm Cohen

COURSE LIST

Undergraduate

Introduction to Broadcasting
Broadcasting Techniques
Radio and Television Announcing
Television Production I, II
Film Production and Technique
Film History and Appreciation

City University of New York, Baruch College

State and locally supported comprehensive coed institution. Part of City University of New York System. Institutionally accredited by regional association. Urban location. Total enrollment: 14,151. Undergraduate enrollment: 11,813. Total faculty: 780 (465 full-time, 315 part-time). Semester calendar. Grading system: letters or numbers.

English Department, 17 Lexington Avenue, New York, NY 10010 212-725-7110

CONTACT Roslyn Mass
ADMISSION Application deadline — rolling
CURRICULAR EMPHASIS Film study — history, appreciation treated equally
FACULTY Roslyn Mass

COURSE LIST

Undergraduate

Art of Film
Film and Literature
Selected Themes in American Film

City University of New York, Brooklyn College

State and locally supported comprehensive coed institution. Part of City University of New York System. Institutionally accredited by regional association. Urban location. Total enrollment: 17,990. Undergraduate enrollment: 16,149. Total faculty: 1549. Semester calendar. Grading system: letters or numbers.

Film Department, Bedford Avenue and Avenue H, Brooklyn, NY 11210 212-780-5665

CONTACT Cynthia Contreras
DEGREE OFFERED BA in film
DEPARTMENTAL MAJORS 125 students
FINANCIAL AID Scholarships, work/study programs, student loans
CURRICULAR EMPHASIS Film study — history, criticism and aesthetics, appreciation treated equally Filmmaking — (1) documentary; (2) narrative; (3) experimental; (4) animated
SPECIAL ACTIVITIES/OFFERINGS Filmmaking clubs, film series, film societies, internships in film production, independent study
FACILITIES AND EQUIPMENT Film — complete 8mm and 16mm equipment, screening room, editing room, sound mixing room, animation board, permanent film library of commercial or professional films
FACULTY Cynthia Contreras, Lindley Hanlon, Foster Hirsch, Lawrence Kellerman, Dennis Lanson, Igal Mashiah, Alister Sanderson, Leo Seltzer, Elisabeth Weis PART-TIME FACULTY Jonathan Baumbach, Eduardo Darino, Sybil DelGaudio, William Hornsby, Steven Stockage, Lucy Winer

COURSE LIST

Undergraduate

Language of Film
Literature and Film
History of Film I, II
The Nonfiction Film
French Literature and French Cinema
Italian Literature and Italian Cinema
Women in Film
American Film Comedy
Experimental, Underground, and Avant-garde Films
The Director's Cinema
Film Theory, Aesthetics, and Criticism
Special Topics in Film
Film Research Methods
Independent Research
Seminars in Genres
Seminars in Directors
Film Production I–III
Documentary Production: Television Format
Film Sound Techniques
Advanced Cinematography I, II
Film Editing I, II
Animation I, II
Screenwriting
Music For Film
Film Directing Workshop
Intensive Film Workshop I–IV

Television/Radio Department 212-780-5555

CONTACT Robert C Williams
DEGREES OFFERED BA, MA, MS in television/radio
DEPARTMENTAL MAJORS Undergraduate — 350 students Graduate — 80 students
ADMISSION Undergraduate requirements — 2.0 minimum grade point average, teachers' recommendations, written statement of purpose Graduate requirements — 2.5 minimum grade point average, GRE scores, teachers' recommendations, written statement of purpose
FINANCIAL AID Teaching assistantships
CURRICULAR EMPHASIS Television study — (1) production; (2) history; (3) criticism and aesthetics Undergraduate television production — (1) news/documentary; (2) educational; (3) experimental/personal video Graduate television production — (1) news/documentary; (2) educational; (3) commercial
SPECIAL ACTIVITIES/OFFERINGS Program material produced for on-campus closed-circuit television, cable television, local public television station; apprenticeships; internships in television production; independent study; practicum
FACILITIES AND EQUIPMENT Film — complete 16mm equipment, 8mm cameras, projectors, editing equipment, editing room, sound mixing room Television — complete black and white studio and exterior production equipment, complete color studio production equipment, black and white studio, color studio, audio studio, control room
FACULTY Camille D'Arienzo, James Day, Christopher Dodrill, Eugene S Foster, R Dale Franzwa, Reginald Gamar, Dimitrius Gemeos, Donald W MacLennan, George Rodman, Brian Rose, Clarence Schimmel, William Sheppard, Lillian Trzesinski, George Wallace, Robert C Williams PART-TIME FACULTY Alan Bernstein, Lori Breslow, Eva Bronstein, William Chase, Stuart Gray, Harry Kovsky, Warren Russell, Ronald Weaver

COURSE LIST

Undergraduate

Mass Media: Content, Structure, and Control
Broadcast Speech and Writing
Introduction to Broadcasting
Photography for Television
Sight/Sound/Motion
Elements of Television Production
Television Production and Direction
Alternate Television
Broadcast Advertising
Educational Television
Broadcast Journalism
Broadcast News Performance
Broadcast News Production
Television Program Planning and Building
Television Criticism
Television and Radio Laboratory
Production Management

Graduate

Television Production for Non-Majors
Broadcasting and Education
Rhetoric of Broadcasting
Problems in Television Program Production
Foundations of Broadcasting
The Broadcast Documentary
Problems in Film Production for Television
Advanced Cinema for Television
Instructional Television Production
Television Program Directing
Design for Television
Broadcasting and Society
Seminar in Public Broadcasting
Seminar in Broadcast Management
Broadcast Journalism
International Broadcasting
Seminar in Television Program Development

City University of New York, City College

State and locally supported comprehensive coed institution. Part of City University of New York System. Institutionally accredited by regional association. Urban location, 35-acre campus. Total enrollment: 14,360. Undergraduate enrollment: 12,325. Total faculty: 800 (600 full-time, 200 part-time). Semester calendar. Grading system: letters or numbers.

Leonard Davis Center for the Performing Arts, 138th Street and Convent Avenue, New York, NY 10033 212-690-8173

CONTACT Chairperson
DEGREES OFFERED BA in film studies, BFA in film production
ADMISSION Requirement — interviews Undergraduate application deadline — rolling
FINANCIAL AID Scholarships, student loans, work/study programs Undergraduate application deadline — rolling
CURRICULAR EMPHASIS Film study — (1) production; (2) criticism and aesthetics; (3) history Filmmaking — (1) documentary; (2) narrative; (3) experimental
SPECIAL ACTIVITIES/OFFERINGS Film series, film festivals, student publications, program material produced for cable television, independent study, Picker Film Institute
FACILITIES AND EQUIPMENT Film — complete 16mm equipment, 8mm cameras, editing equipment, black and white film stock, color film stock, projectors, sound stage, screening room, editing room, sound transfer equipment, permanent film library Television — portable black and white cameras, monitors, ½-inch portapak recorder, lighting equipment

City University of New York, College of Staten Island

City-supported 4-year coed college. Accredited by state agency. Urban location. Undergraduate enrollment: 10,500. Total faculty: 400. Semester calendar. Grading system: letters.

City University of New York, College of Staten Island (continued)

Cinema Studies Program, 130 Stuyvesant Place, Staten Island, NY 10301 212-390-7992

CONTACT Richard Barsam
DEGREES OFFERED BA, MA in cinema studies
PROGRAM MAJORS Undergraduate film — 50 students Graduate film — 20 students
ADMISSION Undergraduate requirements — 2.0 minimum grade point average, high school diploma Graduate requirements — 3.0 minimum grade point average, GRE scores, teachers' recommendations, portfolio Undergraduate application deadline — 3/15, rolling
FINANCIAL AID Work/study programs, student loans, fellowships
CURRICULAR EMPHASIS Undergraduate film study — history, criticism and aesthetics, appreciation treated equally Graduate film study — history, criticism and aesthetics, appreciation treated equally Undergraduate filmmaking — documentary, narrative, experimental treated equally
SPECIAL ACTIVITIES/OFFERINGS Filmmaking clubs, film series, film festivals, student publications, independent study, vocational placement service
FACILITIES AND EQUIPMENT Film — complete 8mm and 16mm equipment, screening room, editing room, sound mixing room, animation board, permanent film library of student films, permanent film library of commercial or professional films Television — ½-inch VTR, portable black and white cameras, monitors
FACULTY Mirella Affron, Richard Barsam, Phill Niblock, Leonard Quart, Elliot Rubinstein, Jiri Weiss PART-TIME FACULTY Richard Pena

COURSE LIST

Undergraduate

Introduction to Film
Filmmaking I, II
Film History
Contemporary European Filmmakers
Politics and Film
Film Theory
Literature into Film
American Film and Myth
Screen Comedy
Nonfiction Film
Cinema Workshop
Major American Directors I, II
Major French Directors I, II
Postwar Italian Cinema
Advanced Cinema Workshop
Experimental Film and Multi-Media Production
Selected Topics Courses
Independent Study

Graduate

Perception of Film
Cinema Research Methods
Analysis of the Individual Film
Seminar in Major Directors
Film Criticism and Theory
Studies in National Cinemas
Experimental Film
Studies in American Genres
Contemporary Nonfiction Film
Selected Topics Courses
Independent Study

City University of New York, Hunter College

State and locally supported comprehensive coed institution. Part of City University of New York System. Institutionally accredited by regional association. Urban location. Total enrollment: 18,000. Undergraduate enrollment: 14,872. Total faculty: 1234 (651 full-time, 583 part-time). Semester calendar. Grading system: letters or numbers.

Department of Theatre and Film, 695 Park Avenue, New York, NY 10021 212-570-5747

CONTACT Kenneth Roberts
DEGREES OFFERED BA in film production, BA in cinema studies
DEPARTMENTAL MAJORS 90 students
ADMISSION Requirement — minimum grade point average Application deadline — rolling
CURRICULAR EMPHASIS Film study — (1) criticism and aesthetics, production; (2) history, appreciation Filmmaking — (1) narrative; (2) experimental; (3) documentary; (4) animated; (5) educational
SPECIAL ACTIVITIES/OFFERINGS Filmmaking clubs, film series, film festivals, film societies, student publications, internships in film production, independent study
FACILITIES AND EQUIPMENT Film — complete 16mm equipment, 8mm cameras, editing equipment, lighting equipment, projectors, screening room, editing room, optical printer, permanent film library
FACULTY Dalton Alexander, Barbara Leaming, Kenneth Roberts, Richard Tomkins, Joel Zuker PART-TIME FACULTY Jerome Coopersmith, Henry Markosfeld, Ron Mottram, David Packman

COURSE LIST

Undergraduate

Problems in Film Research
Narrative: Authorship and Subject
Film Technology and Aesthetic Theory
Soviet Cinema
Theories of Film Acting
Introduction to Cinema
Introduction to Film Production
Fundamentals of Filmmaking
Film Writing I, II
Acting for Film
Editing
Cinematography
Sound for Film
Directing for Film
Film Production
Film Production Seminar
History of the Cinema
Theories of Genre
Film Theory I, II
Studies of Selected Directors
Avant-Garde Cinema

City University of New York, LaGuardia Community College

City-supported 2-year coed college. Part of City University of New York System, automatic transfer to main campus for baccalaureate. Institutionally accredited by regional association. Urban location. Undergraduate enrollment: 6117. Total faculty: 368 (129 full-time, 239 part-time). Quarter calendar. Grading system: letters or numbers.

Communication Arts Department, 31-10 Thomson Avenue, Long Island City, NY 11101 212-626-5572 or 212-626-5573

CONTACT Film — Joyce Rheuban Television — Barbara Lass
DEGREES OFFERED AA in cinema studies, AA in film/TV production
DEPARTMENTAL MAJORS Film — 10 students Television — 12 students
ADMISSION Requirement — 3.0 minimum grade point average Application deadline — 3/31
FINANCIAL AID Scholarships, work/study programs, student loans, BEOG, TAP, NDSL Application deadline — 3/31

CURRICULAR EMPHASIS Film study — history, criticism and aesthetics, appreciation treated equally Filmmaking — documentary, narrative, experimental, animated treated equally Television study — history, criticism and aesthetics, appreciation treated equally Television production — commercial, news/documentary, educational treated equally
SPECIAL ACTIVITIES/OFFERINGS Filmmaking clubs, film series, film festivals, program material produced for on-campus closed-circuit television, internships in film production, internships in television production, vocational placement service
FACILITIES AND EQUIPMENT Film — 8mm cameras, editing equipment, sound recording equipment, projectors, screening room, editing room, permanent film library of commercial or professional films Television — black and white studio cameras, ½-inch VTR, ¾-inch cassette VTR, portable black and white cameras, editing equipment, monitors, special effects generators, slide chain, portable color cameras, ½-inch portapak recorders, ¾-inch ENG, lighting equipment, sound recording equipment, audio mixers, film chain, black and white studio, color studio, control room
FACULTY Mary Pat Kelly, Barbara Lass, Joyce Rheuban PART-TIME FACULTY John Knecht

COURSE LIST

Undergraduate

The Art of Film
American Film
Film and the Supernatural
Media Production Workshop: Video
Media Production Workshop: Film
Mass Media and Their Evolution
Mass Media and Society
Literature and Film

City University of New York, Queens College

State and locally supported comprehensive coed institution. Part of City University of New York System. Institutionally accredited by regional association. Urban location, 76-acre campus. Total enrollment: 19,000. Undergraduate enrollment: 13,000. Total faculty: 1000 full-time. Semester calendar. Grading system: letters or numbers.

Department of Communication Arts and Sciences, Flushing, NY 11367 212-520-7355

CONTACT Gary Gumpert
DEGREES OFFERED Major in media studies with emphasis in film or television, MA in communication sciences, MA in communication studies
ADMISSION Undergraduate application deadline — 1/15, rolling
CURRICULAR EMPHASIS Film study — (1) criticism and aesthetics, appreciation; (2) history; (3) production Filmmaking — (1) narrative; (2) experimental; (3) documentary Television study — (1) criticism and aesthetics; (2) production; (3) history
SPECIAL ACTIVITIES/OFFERINGS Film series
FACILITIES AND EQUIPMENT Film — complete 8mm and 16mm equipment, screening room, editing room, sound mixing room, permanent film library Television — complete black and white exterior production facilities, complete color studio production facilities
FACULTY Jonathan Buchsbaum, Peter Dahlgren, Manuel Grossman, Gary Gumpert, John Haney, Stuart Liebman, John Pollock, Ann Shaw PART-TIME FACULTY Royce Froehlich, Lisa Johnson, Leon Volskis

COURSE LIST

Undergraduate

Telecommunications: Sound
Telecommunications: Television
History of the Cinema I: 1880 to 1930
History of the Cinema II: 1960 to the Present
The Script and the Medium I, II
Cinematic and Video Forms: An Interdisciplinary Approach
Advanced Film Production
Media Performance
Communication Fellows Program
Theory of Film
Studies in Film
Styles of Cinema
Documentary in Film and Broadcasting
Italian Cinema from Neo-Realism to the Present
Freedom of Speech
Media Analysis and Criticism
Informational Broadcasting
Television Direction
Comparative Broadcasting Systems
Management in Communications Media
Research in Media Production

Graduate

Studies in Communication
Special Problems

College of Mount Saint Vincent

Independent 4-year college primarily for women. Institutionally accredited by regional association. Suburban location. Undergraduate enrollment: 1228. Total faculty: 99 (72 full-time, 27 part-time). Semester calendar. Grading system: letters or numbers.

Communication Arts Department, Riverdale Avenue, Riverdale, NY 10471 212-549-8000

CONTACT Film — Michael Sevastakis Television — Frances Broderick
DEGREE OFFERED BA in communication arts with a concentration in film, broadcasting, speech, and journalism
DEPARTMENTAL MAJORS Film — 52 students Television — 70 students
ADMISSION Requirements — ACT or SAT scores, interview, teachers' recommendations, written statement of purpose Undergraduate application deadline — rolling
FINANCIAL AID Scholarships, work/study programs, student loans Undergraduate application deadline — 12/1
CURRICULAR EMPHASIS Film study — (1) criticism and aesthetics; (2) history; (3) appreciation Filmmaking — (1) experimental; (2) narrative; (3) documentary Television study — (1) criticism and aesthetics; (2) production; (3) history Television production — (1) experimental/personal video; (2) news/documentary; (3) commercial
SPECIAL ACTIVITIES/OFFERINGS Filmmaking clubs, film series, film festivals, film societies, student publications, internships in film production, internships in television production, independent study, teacher training, vocational placement service

College of Mount Saint Vincent (continued)

FACILITIES AND EQUIPMENT Film — complete 8mm equipment, screening room, editing room, sound mixing room, animation board, permanent film library of student films, permanent film library of commercial or professional films Television — black and white studio cameras, ½-inch VTR, ¾-inch cassette VTR, portable black and white cameras, editing equipment, monitors, special effects generators, portable color cameras, ½-inch portapak recorders, lighting equipment, sound recording equipment, audio mixers, black and white studio

COURSE LIST

Undergraduate

Speech for Radio and Television
Film Production I, II
Film as Art
Advanced Film Production
Scriptwriting
Major Filmmakers
American Silent Film
American Sound Film
Documentary Film
Experimental Film
Film Criticism
Films of Western Europe
Films of Eastern Europe
Video Production
Introduction to Broadcasting
Radio
Non-Commercial Broadcasting
Television Production
Advanced Video
Mass News
Producing
Advanced Production Techniques
Television Programming
Introduction to Communication Arts
Internship for Juniors
Advertising
International Communication
Communications and the Law
Seminar in Communication
Internship for Seniors
Topics in Advertising
Topics in Communication

College of New Rochelle

Independent comprehensive institution primarily for women. Institutionally accredited by regional association. Suburban location, 50-acre campus. Total enrollment: 4066. Undergraduate enrollment: 3248. Total faculty: 398 (76 full-time, 322 part-time). Semester calendar. Grading system: letters or numbers.

Communication Arts Department, Castle Place, New Rochelle, NY 10801 914-632-5300, ext 544

CONTACT Joel Persky
DEGREE OFFERED BA in communication arts with specializations in either film or television
DEPARTMENTAL MAJORS Film — 20 students Television — 40 students
ADMISSION Requirements — SAT scores, teachers' recommendations, written statement of purpose Application deadline — rolling
FINANCIAL AID Scholarships, work/study programs, student loans Undergraduate application deadline — 4/1
CURRICULAR EMPHASIS Film study — (1) history; (2) criticism and aesthetics; (3) appreciation; (4) educational media/instructional technology Filmmaking — (1) narrative; (2) documentary Television study — (1) history; (2) criticism and aesthetics; (3) production Television production — (1) experimental/personal video; (2) educational; (3) commercial
SPECIAL ACTIVITIES/OFFERINGS Filmmaking clubs, film series, film festivals, film societies, program material produced for cable television, internships in film production, internships in television production, independent study
FACILITIES AND EQUIPMENT Film — 8mm cameras, editing equipment, black and white film stock, projectors, screening room, editing room, permanent film library of student films, permanent film library of commercial or professional films Television — complete black and white studio production equipment, black and white studio, audio studio, control room
FACULTY James O'Brien, Joel Persky

COURSE LIST

Undergraduate

Introduction to Television
Introduction to Film
Film History I and II
Major Filmmakers
Film Genres
American Film Culture
Film and Literature
The European Film
Television Programming
The Art of the Documentary
Educational Television
Television Studio Production Workshop
Small Format Television Workshop
Seminar in Communications

Columbia—Greene Community College

State and locally supported 2-year coed college. Part of State University of New York System, automatic transfer to main campus for baccalaureate. Institutionally accredited by regional association. Rural location. Undergraduate enrollment: 1214. Total faculty: 59 (40 full-time, 19 part-time). 4-1-4 calendar. Grading system: letters or numbers.

AV Library/Media Laboratory, PO Box 1000, Hudson, NY 12534 518-828-4181, ext 62, 58

CONTACT Susan K Simovich
SPECIAL ACTIVITIES/OFFERINGS Program material produced for on-campus closed-circuit television, cable television, local public television station
FACILITIES AND EQUIPMENT Film — complete 8mm, 16mm, and 35mm equipment, sound mixing room, permanent videotape collection Television — black and white studio cameras, color studio cameras, audio studio
FACULTY James Reily, Susan K Simovich

Columbia University

Independent coed university. Institutionally accredited by regional association. Urban location, 30-acre campus. Total enrollment: 17,500. Total faculty: 4000. Semester calendar. Grading system: letters.

Film Division, School of the Arts, 513 Dodge Hall, 116th Street and Broadway, New York, NY 10027 212-280-2815

CONTACT David Werner

DEGREES OFFERED MFA through School of the Arts, BA/MFA through Columbia College, undergraduate major through School of General Studies, PhD through General School of Arts and Sciences; three areas of concentration: screenwriting, directing, and scholarship
DEPARTMENTAL MAJORS Undergraduate film — 13 students Graduate film — 90 students
ADMISSION Undergraduate requirement — ACT or SAT scores Graduate requirements — interview, teachers' recommendations, written statement of purpose Undergraduate application deadline — 3/10
FINANCIAL AID Work/study programs, student loans, fellowships, teaching assistantships
CURRICULAR EMPHASIS Undergraduate film study — (1) history; (2) criticism and aesthetics Graduate film study — history, criticism and aesthetics treated equally Undergraduate filmmaking — (1) narrative; (2) documentary; (3) animated; (4) experimental Graduate filmmaking — (1) narrative; (2) documentary
SPECIAL ACTIVITIES/OFFERINGS Film series, guest lecture series, internships in film production, independent study
FACILITIES AND EQUIPMENT Film — 8mm cameras and editing equipment, 16mm cameras, editing equipment, sound recording equipment, lighting, projectors, 35mm projectors, screening room, 35mm screening facilities, editing room, animation board, permanent film library of student films Television — editing equipment, monitors, portable color cameras, ½-inch portapak recorders
FACULTY John Belton, Frantisek Daniel, Lawrence Engel, Milos Forman, John MacGruer, Nick Proferes, Andrew Sarris, Stefan Sharff PART-TIME FACULTY Geof Bartz, James Blue, Sybil Del Gaudio, Francois de Menil, Mark Dichter, Michael Hausman, Ken Kobland, Vasilis Koronakes, Nancy Littlefield, Terence McAteer, Jose Quintero, Samson Raphaelson, Paul Shrader, Matthew Weisman

COURSE LIST

Undergraduate
Film Aesthetics
Introduction to Filmmaking
Sound Filmmaking
Filmmaking I, II
Cinema and the Arts

Graduate
The Documentary Film
Documentary Filmmaking
Genre Study
Animation Techniques
Film Research Methods
Film Producing
Screenwriting I–III
Film Production I–III
Acting-Directing
History of the American Cinema
Film Theory and Criticism I, II
Post-production Methods
Film Sound Techniques
Advanced Cinematography

Undergraduate and Graduate
Script Analysis
Film and Ideology
Cinematic Design
History of the Motion Picture I, II
Analysis of Film Language I, II
Seminar in International Film History
The Screenplay
Auteur Study

Cooper Union for the Advancement of Science and Art

Independent comprehensive coed institution. Institutionally accredited by regional association, programs recognized by NASA. Urban location. Total enrollment: 890. Undergraduate enrollment: 881. Total faculty: 132 (50 full-time, 82 part-time). Semester calendar. Grading system: letters or numbers.

Communications Department, School of Art, 7 East Seventh Street, New York, NY 10003 212-254-6300

PROGRAM OFFERED Major in communications with emphasis in film or television
ADMISSION Requirements — competitive examination, interviews, portfolio Application deadline — 1/1
CURRICULAR EMPHASIS Film study — history, criticism and aesthetics, appreciation, production, educational media/instructional technology treated equally Filmmaking — (1) animated; (2) experimental; (3) documentary Television study — history, criticism and aesthetics, appreciation, production, educational, management treated equally Television production — (1) experimental/personal video; (2) news/documentary
SPECIAL ACTIVITIES/OFFERINGS Film societies, program material produced for cable television and local public television station, internships in television production, independent study
FACILITIES AND EQUIPMENT Film — complete 8mm and 16mm equipment, screening room, editing room, sound mixing room, animation board Television — complete black and white exterior production equipment, black and white studio, audio studio, ¾-inch color equipment
PART-TIME FACULTY Robert Breer, Del Hillgartner, Jeffrey Lukowsky, D A Pennebaker, Curt Roseman

COURSE LIST

Undergraduate
Time and Motion
Animation Workshop
Beginning Film
Advanced Film
Beginning Video
Advanced Video

Cornell University

Independent coed university. Institutionally accredited by regional association. Small town location, 740-acre campus. Total enrollment: 17,098. Undergraduate enrollment: 11,978. Total faculty: 1620. Semester calendar. Grading system: letters or numbers.

Theatre Arts Department, College of Arts and Sciences, Lincoln Hall, Ithaca, NY 14853 607-256-3533

CONTACT Don Fredericksen
DEGREE OFFERED BA in film studies (Independent major program, College of Arts and Sciences)
DEPARTMENTAL MAJORS 4 students
ADMISSION Requirements — 2.5 minimum grade point average, SAT scores, teachers' recommendations, written statement of purpose
FINANCIAL AID Scholarships, student loans, work/study programs Application deadline — 1/1

Cornell University (continued)

CURRICULAR EMPHASIS Film study — (1) criticism and aesthetics; (2) history; (3) production Filmmaking — (1) experimental; (2) documentary; (3) narrative
SPECIAL ACTIVITIES/OFFERINGS Filmmaking clubs, film series, film societies, independent study, academic year abroad program offered through affiliation with the Inter-University Center for Film Studies in Paris
FACILITIES AND EQUIPMENT Film — 16mm cameras, editing equipment, sound recording equipment, black and white film stock, projectors, screening room, editing room, permanent film library
FACULTY Don Fredericksen PART-TIME FACULTY Marilyn Rivchin

COURSE LIST

Undergraduate
History and Theory of the Commercial Narrative Cinema
History and Theory of Russian Film of the 1920s and French Film of the 1960s
History and Theory of Documentary and Experimental Film
History and Theory of the Contemporary Documentary Film
Introduction to Film Analysis: Meaning and Value
Fundamentals of 16mm Filmmaking
Intermediate Filmmaking Projects

Undergraduate and Graduate
Seminar in the Cinema I
Seminar in the Cinema II

D'Youville College

Independent 4-year coed college. Institutionally accredited by regional association. Urban location. Undergraduate enrollment: 1440. Total faculty: 119 (82 full-time, 37 part-time). Semester calendar. Grading system: letters or numbers.

Continuing Education Department, Buffalo, NY 14201 716-886-8100

CONTACT Charles Stein
ADMISSION Application deadline — 6/30, rolling
FACULTY Charles Stein

COURSE LIST

Undergraduate
Art of the Film
Survey of American Film Comedy from Silents to the Present

Eisenhower College

Independent 4-year coed college. Administratively affiliated with Rochester Institute of Technology. Institutionally accredited by regional association. Small town location, 286-acre campus. Undergraduate enrollment: 475. Total faculty: 61 (55 full-time, 6 part-time). 4-1-4 calendar. Grading system: letters or numbers.

Division of Humanities, Seneca Falls, NY 13148 315-568-7173

CONTACT Sandra Saari
ADMISSION Application deadline — 2/15, rolling
CURRICULAR EMPHASIS Film study — (1) criticism and aesthetics; (2) appreciation; (3) history; (4) production Filmmaking — (1) narrative; (2) experimental; (3) documentary; (4) animated
SPECIAL ACTIVITIES/OFFERINGS Film series, film festivals
FACILITIES AND EQUIPMENT Film — complete 8mm equipment, screening room, editing room, animation board, permanent film library
FACULTY Sandra Saari

COURSE LIST

Undergraduate
The Art of the Cinema

Elizabeth Seton College

Independent 2-year coed college. Accredited by state agency. Rural location. Total enrollment: 1100. Total faculty: 35 full-time. Semester calendar. Grading system: letters or numbers.

Radio-Television Department, 1061 North Broadway, Yonkers, NY 10701 914-969-4000, ext 236

CONTACT Brad Gromelski, Chairman
DEGREES OFFERED AOS in radio and television, AAS in radio, AAS in television
DEPARTMENTAL MAJORS Television — 75 students
ADMISSION Requirements — ACT or SAT scores, interview, teachers' recommendations
FINANCIAL AID Scholarships, work/study programs, student loans Application deadline — 6/30
CURRICULAR EMPHASIS Television study — (1) production; (2) management; (3) educational Television production — (1) educational; (2) experimental/personal video; (3) news/documentary
SPECIAL ACTIVITIES/OFFERINGS Apprenticeships, internships in television production, vocational placement service
FACILITIES AND EQUIPMENT Television — black and white studio cameras, color studio cameras, ½-inch VTR, ¾-inch cassette VTR, portable black and white cameras, editing equipment, monitors, special effects generators, slide chain, lighting equipment, sound recording equipment, audio mixers, film chain, black and white studio, audio studio
FACULTY Don Bayley, Brad Gromelski PART-TIME FACULTY Bob Davis, Gerald Delaney, Rich Grebow, Robin Landa, Maryellen McGovern, Arch Robb, Rob Ross

COURSE LIST

Undergraduate

Television Production Workshop I, II
Lighting for Television
Radio and Television Management
Seminar in Television
Videotape Workshop
Internship
Graphics
Radio and TV Writing

Elmira College

Independent comprehensive coed institution. Institutionally accredited by regional association. Urban location, 40-acre campus. Total enrollment: 2629. Undergraduate enrollment: 2134. Total faculty: 179 (74 full-time, 105 part-time). 4-1-4 calendar. Grading system: letters or numbers.

Theatre and Communication Department, Elmira, NY 14901 607-734-3911, ext 270

CONTACT R L Held
DEGREE OFFERED BA in communication with emphasis in mass media
ADMISSION Requirements — ACT or SAT scores, interview, teachers' recommendations Undergraduate application deadline — 7/1
FINANCIAL AID Work/study programs, student loans
CURRICULAR EMPHASIS Film study — educational media/instructional technology Filmmaking — (1) narrative; (2) educational Television study — (1) criticism and aesthetics; (2) management Television production — industrial business
SPECIAL ACTIVITIES/OFFERINGS Film series, program material produced for local commercial television station, independent study, teacher training, vocational placement service
FACILITIES AND EQUIPMENT Film — 8mm cameras, editing equipment, sound recording equipment, lighting, projectors, 16mm cameras, editing equipment, projectors, screening room, editing room, permanent film library of commercial or professional films Television — complete black and white and color exterior production facilities, black and white studio, color studio

COURSE LIST

Undergraduate

Radio Production
Television Production
Techniques and Applications of Audio
Film Techniques
Graphics
Mass Media and Society
Communication Law

New York

Fordham University

Independent Roman Catholic coed university. Institutionally accredited by regional association, programs recognized by AACSB. Urban location, 84-acre campus. Total enrollment: 14,865. Undergraduate enrollment: 8312. Total faculty: 930 (476 full-time, 454 part-time). Semester calendar. Grading system: letters or numbers.

Communications Department, Bronx, NY 10458 212-933-2233

CONTACT Film — Trisha Curran Television — Daniel Mack
DEGREES OFFERED BA, BS in communications with emphasis in film or broadcasting
ADMISSION Application deadline — rolling
FINANCIAL AID Scholarships Application deadline — 2/15
CURRICULAR EMPHASIS Film study — (1) criticism and aesthetics; (2) history; (3) appreciation Television study — (1) criticism and aesthetics; (2) history; (3) appreciation Television production — (1) news/documentary; (2) experimental/personal video; (3) educational
SPECIAL ACTIVITIES/OFFERINGS Film series, apprenticeships, internships in television production, independent study
FACILITIES AND EQUIPMENT Film — complete 8mm and 16mm equipment, screening room, editing room Television — complete black and white studio and exterior production equipment, black and white studio, audio studio, control room
FACULTY Trisha Curran, Ralph Dengler, Daniel Mack PART-TIME FACULTY M Irene Fugazy, Henry Herx

COURSE LIST

Undergraduate

American Film Industry
Television News
Writing for Television and Film
Grammar of Film
Fundamentals of Film Art and History
Film Genres
Basics of Documentary and News Film
Contemporary Film Criticism
Introduction to Film Production

Genesee Community College

State and locally supported 2-year coed college. Part of State University of New York System. Institutionally accredited by regional association. Rural location, 256-acre campus. Undergraduate enrollment: 1882. Total faculty: 99 (68 full-time, 31 part-time). Semester calendar. Grading system: letters or numbers.

Communication and Media Arts Program, Humanities Department, College Road, Batavia, NY 14020 716-343-0055

CONTACT Chairperson
DEGREE OFFERED AS in communication and media arts
ADMISSION Application deadline — rolling
FINANCIAL AID Scholarships, student loans, work/study programs Application deadline — 7/1, rolling
CURRICULAR EMPHASIS Film study — (1) appreciation; (2) criticism and aesthetics; (3) history

Genesee Community College (continued)

FACILITIES AND EQUIPMENT Film — sound stage, sound mixing room, animation board Television — black and white studio, control room

Hamilton College

Independent 4-year college, coed as of 1978. Institutionally accredited by regional association. Rural location. Undergraduate enrollment: 1600. Total faculty: 147 (138 full-time, 9 part-time). 4-1-4 calendar. Grading system: letters or numbers.

Art Department, Clinton, NY 13323

CONTACT Robert Nickson
DEGREE OFFERED BA in art
DEPARTMENTAL MAJORS Film — 10 students
ADMISSION Requirements — minimum grade point average, ACT or SAT scores, interview Undergraduate application deadline — 3/15
FINANCIAL AID Scholarships, work/study programs Undergraduate application deadline — 3/15
CURRICULAR EMPHASIS Film study — (1) history; (2) criticism and aesthetics Filmmaking — (1) narrative; (2) animated; (3) documentary
SPECIAL ACTIVITIES/OFFERINGS Film series, film festivals, film societies
FACILITIES AND EQUIPMENT Film — 16mm cameras, editing equipment, sound recording equipment, lighting, projectors, sound stage, screening room, editing room, animation stand, permanent film library of commercial or professional films Television — black and white studio cameras, 1-inch VTR, ¾-inch cassette VTR, portable black and white cameras, editing equipment, monitors, special effects generators, ½-inch portapak recorders, black and white studio
FACULTY Robert Nickson

COURSE LIST

Undergraduate

Language of Film—Historical
Animation—Production
Seminar in Selected Film Topics (Aesthetic)
Introductory 16mm Production
Advanced 16mm Production
Senior Projects

New York

Hartwick College

Independent 4-year and professional coed institution. Institutionally accredited by regional association. Small town location, 175-acre campus. Undergraduate enrollment: 1422. Total faculty: 124 (110 full-time, 14 part-time). Trimester calendar. Grading system: letters or numbers.

Art Department, Oneonta, NY 13820 607-432-4200

CONTACT Bruce Kurtz
ADMISSION Application deadline — 3/1, rolling

COURSE LIST One course in video is offered

Hobart and William Smith Colleges

Independent 4-year men's and 4-year women's colleges, coordinate. Institutionally accredited by regional association. Small town location, 170-acre campus. Total enrollment: 1050. Total faculty: 121 (121 full-time, 0 part-time). Trimester calendar. Grading system: letters or numbers.

English Department, Geneva, NY 14456 315-789-5500

CONTACT B P Atkinson, Chair
PROGRAM OFFERED Major in English with emphasis in film
ADMISSION Application deadline — 2/15
FINANCIAL AID Scholarships, student loans Application deadline — 2/15
CURRICULAR EMPHASIS Film study — (1) history; (2) production; (3) criticism and aesthetics; (4) appreciation Filmmaking — (1) narrative; (2) documentary; (3) experimental
SPECIAL ACTIVITIES/OFFERINGS Film series, film societies, student publications, independent study
FACILITIES AND EQUIPMENT Film — complete Super-8mm equipment, screening room, editing room, sound mixing room
FACULTY Roger Farrand

COURSE LIST

Undergraduate

History and Development of Film
Screenplay Writing
Filmmaking Workshop
Myth of the Western
American Film as Artifact
Film Theory

Hofstra University

Independent coed university. Institutionally accredited by regional association, programs recognized by AACSB. Suburban location, 238-acre campus. Total enrollment: 10,083. Undergraduate enrollment: 6683. Total faculty: 660 (375 full-time, 285 part-time). 4-1-4 calendar. Grading system: letters or numbers.

Communication Arts Department, Hempstead, NY 11550 516-560-3676

CONTACT Film — Jerry Delamater Television — William Renn
DEGREE OFFERED BA in communication arts with an emphasis in broadcasting/film
DEPARTMENTAL MAJORS Film — 75 students Television — 300 students
ADMISSION Requirements — 2.5 minimum grade point average, ACT or SAT scores

FINANCIAL AID Scholarships, work/study programs, student loans
CURRICULAR EMPHASIS Film study — (1) criticism and aesthetics; (2) history; (3) appreciation Filmmaking — documentary, narrative, experimental treated equally Television study — (1) production; (2) history; (3) criticism and aesthetics Television production — (1) commercial; (2) news/documentary; (3) educational
SPECIAL ACTIVITIES/OFFERINGS Filmmaking clubs; film series; film festivals; film societies; student publications; program material produced for on-campus closed-circuit television, cable television, local public television station; internships in film production; internships in television production; independent study
FACILITIES AND EQUIPMENT Film — complete 8mm and 16mm equipment, screening room, editing room Television — black and white studio cameras, color studio cameras, ¾-inch cassette VTR, editing equipment, monitors, special effects generators, slide chain, portable color cameras, ¾-inch ENG, lighting equipment, sound recording equipment, audio mixers, film chain, black and white studio, color studio, audio studio, control room
FACULTY Jerry Delamater, William Renn PART-TIME FACULTY Gregg Burton, Bette Gordon, Shalom Gorewitz, Nancy Kaplan, David Levy, Ruth Prigozy

COURSE LIST
Undergraduate
Basic Television Production
Intermediate Television Production
Production Workshop: Television
Intermediate Production Workshop: Television
Television Performing
Television Lighting Workshop
Television Production Workshop: Audio and SEG
Television Directing and Producing
Advanced Television Production
Workshop: Video Production Techniques
Workshop: Electronic Field Production Techniques
Workshop: Color Television Production
Introduction to Film Study
Film Theory and Technique I, II
Cinema-TV Writing: Theory and Application
Cinema Adaptation of Plays and Novels
Film Genres
Film Comedy: Silent and Sound
Advanced Film Production
Film Directing
History of the Motion Picture
The Documentary Film
Theories of Cinema
Auteur-Director Series
Workshop: Experimental Film Production

Houghton College

Independent Wesleyan 4-year coed college. Institutionally accredited by regional association, programs recognized by NASM. Rural location. Undergraduate enrollment: 1229. Total faculty: 80 (72 full-time, 8 part-time). Semester calendar. Grading system: letters or numbers.

Communication Department, Houghton, NY 14744 716-567-2211

DEGREES OFFERED BA, BS in communication
ADMISSION Requirements — ACT or SAT scores, written statement of purpose Application deadline — rolling
FINANCIAL AID Scholarships, work/study programs, student loans
CURRICULAR EMPHASIS Television study — (1) appreciation; (2) criticism and aesthetics; (3) production Television production — (1) news/documentary; (2) commercial; (3) experimental/personal video
SPECIAL ACTIVITIES/OFFERINGS Program material produced for on-campus closed-circuit television, independent study
FACILITIES AND EQUIPMENT Television — complete black and white and color studio production equipment, black and white studio, color studio, audio studio, control room
FACULTY Roger J Rozendal

COURSE LIST
Undergraduate
Mass Communication
Radio and TV Announcing
Television Production
Advanced Television Production
Broadcast Law and Engineering
Broadcasting Internship

Iona College

Independent comprehensive coed institution. Institutionally accredited by regional association. Suburban location, 55-acre campus. Total enrollment: 5293. Undergraduate enrollment: 3500. Total faculty: 246 (157 full-time, 89 part-time). 4-1-4 calendar. Grading system: letters or numbers.

Communication Arts Department, 715 North Avenue, New Rochelle, NY 10801 914-636-2100, ext 229 or 230

CONTACT Joel Persky, Chairman
DEGREE OFFERED BA in communication arts with emphasis in film or television
ADMISSION Requirements — SAT scores, interviews, teachers' recommendations, written statement of purpose Application deadline — rolling
FINANCIAL AID Student loans, work/study programs Application deadline — 4/1
CURRICULAR EMPHASIS Undergraduate film study — (1) criticism and aesthetics; (2) history; (3) appreciation; (4) educational media/instructional technology Graduate film study — (1) educational media/instructional technology; (2) appreciation; (3) criticism and aesthetics Filmmaking — (1) narrative; (2) documentary; (3) experimental Television study — (1) production; (2) criticism and aesthetics; (3) history Television production — (1) commercial; (2) news/documentary; (3) educational
SPECIAL ACTIVITIES/OFFERINGS Film series, film festivals, film societies, internships in film and television production, independent study
FACILITIES AND EQUIPMENT Film — 8mm cameras, editing equipment, sound recording equipment, black and white film stock, projectors, screening room, editing room, sound mixing room, permanent film library Television — complete black and white studio and exterior production equipment, complete color studio production facilities, black and white studio, audio studio
FACULTY John Darretta, Paul Del Colle, Gary Kriss, Joel Persky, Stanley Solomon, George Thottam

Iona College (continued)

COURSE LIST

Undergraduate

Introduction to Television
Masterpieces of World Cinema
Film History I, II
Major Filmmakers
American Film Culture
Film Criticism
European Film I, II
Filmmaking
Television Programming
Television Documentary
Educational Television
Television Production Workshop
Television Studio Production
Seminar: Television or Film

Undergraduate and Graduate

Introduction to the Film
Film and Literature

Ithaca College

Independent comprehensive coed institution. Institutionally accredited by regional association, programs recognized by NASM, AACSB. Small town location, 400-acre campus. Total enrollment: 4738. Undergraduate enrollment: 4550. Total faculty: 409 (287 full-time, 122 part-time). Semester calendar. Grading system: letters or numbers.

Department of Cinema Studies and Photography, School of Communications, Danby Road, Ithaca, NY 14850 607-274-3242

CONTACT Skip Landen, Chairman
DEGREE OFFERED BS in cinema studies and photography
DEPARTMENTAL MAJORS 100 students
ADMISSION Requirements — 3.0 minimum grade point average, SAT scores, interviews, professional recommendations, teachers' recommendations, portfolio, written statement of purpose Application deadline — 3/1, rolling
CURRICULAR EMPHASIS Film study — (1) production; (2) criticism and aesthetics; (3) educational media/instructional technology Filmmaking (1) industrial; (2) documentary; (3) educational
SPECIAL ACTIVITIES/OFFERINGS Internships in film and television production, independent study
FACILITIES AND EQUIPMENT Film — complete 16mm equipment, editing equipment, lighting equipment, black and white film stock, projectors, 16mm black and white laboratory, sound stage, screening room, editing rooms, sound mixing room, animation board, permanent film library
FACULTY Doug Clapp, Monte Gerlach, Dan Guthrie, John Keshishoglou, Peter Klinge, Sheila Laffey, Skip Landen PART-TIME FACULTY Richard Steinhaus

COURSE LIST

Undergraduate

Introduction to Film Aesthetics
American Film
Screen Writing
Film Production
Advanced Film Production
Film Directing
Nonfiction Film
Advanced Analysis
Motion Picture Theatre Management
Production Budgets
Film Makeup
Motion Picture Rating
Survey of European Film
Film and Photo Workshop
Film as Art
Censorship and Obscenity Legislation
Film Industries
The Industrial Film
Motion Picture Advertising and Publicity

Department of Television-Radio

CONTACT Don Woodman, Chairman
DEGREE OFFERED BS in television-radio
DEPARTMENTAL MAJORS 250 students
ADMISSION Requirements — 3.0 minimum grade point average, SAT scores, interviews, professional recommendations, teachers' recommendations, portfolio, written statement of purpose Application deadline — 3/1, rolling
CURRICULAR EMPHASIS Television study — (1) production; (2) management; (3) educational Television production — (1) news/documentary; (2) commercial; (3) educational
SPECIAL ACTIVITIES/OFFERINGS Program material produced for on-campus closed-circuit television and cable television, internships in film and television production, independent study
FACILITIES AND EQUIPMENT Television — complete black and white studio and exterior production equipment, complete color studio and exterior production equipment, black and white studio, color studio, mobile van/unit, remote truck, audio studio, control room
FACULTY Joanne Gula, Barbara Moore, Steve Ryan, Paul Smith, James Treble, Tom Wickenden, Donald Woodman PART-TIME FACULTY Charles Bachrach, Mitch Davis, Graham Hovey, Ted Nathanson, Rudy Paolangeli, Jessica Savitch, Robert Smith, Ed Tobias

COURSE LIST

Undergraduate

Research in Communications
Broadcast Operations
Television Production and Direction
Dynamics of Communications
Media Writing
Broadcast Fundamentals
Mass Media (National)
Mass Media (International)
Broadcast Journalism
Television Directing
Broadcast Regulations
Television News Production
Public Opinion and Propaganda
Station Management
Advanced Writing for Television
Social Responsibility in Communications
Instructional Television Design
Instructional Television Production
Television News
Television Workshop
Comparative Mass Media
Broadcast Sales

Jamestown Community College

State and locally supported 2-year coed college. Part of State University of New York System, automatic transfer to main campus for baccalaureate. Institutionally accredited by regional association. Urban location, 107-acre campus. Undergraduate enrollment: 3472. Total faculty: 196 (122 full-time, 74 part-time). Semester calendar. Grading system: letters or numbers.

Fine Arts Department/Language and Literature Department, Jamestown, NY 14701 716-665-5220

CONTACT Film — Gerald Molenda Television — Alfred Broska
ADMISSION Application deadline — 8/15, rolling
FACILITIES AND EQUIPMENT Film — complete 8mm equipment, editing room Television — complete black and white studio and exterior production facilities
FACULTY Alfred Broska, Gerald Molenda

COURSE LIST
Undergraduate
Film Appreciation
Television Production
Introduction to Filmmaking I, II

LeMoyne College

Independent Roman Catholic 4-year coed college. Institutionally accredited by regional association. Suburban location, 140-acre campus. Undergraduate enrollment: 1941. Total faculty: 160 (105 full-time, 55 part-time). Semester calendar. Grading system: letters or numbers.

Communications/Drama Department, Salt Springs Road, Syracuse, NY 13214 315-446-2882

CONTACT Thomas R Hogan
DEGREES OFFERED BA in English/communications with emphasis on television or journalism, minor in communications for non-English/communications majors
DEPARTMENTAL MAJORS Television — 35 students
ADMISSION Requirements — 2.5 minimum grade point average, ACT or SAT scores, interview, teachers' recommendations, written statement of purpose, production credits, professional recommendations Application deadline — 4/1, rolling
FINANCIAL AID Scholarships, work/study programs, student loans Application deadline — 3/1, rolling
CURRICULAR EMPHASIS Film study — criticism and aesthetics, appreciation, educational media/instructional technology treated equally Filmmaking — documentary, experimental, educational treated equally Television study — history, criticism and aesthetics, educational, production treated equally Television production — news/documentary, experimental/personal video, educational treated equally
SPECIAL ACTIVITIES/OFFERINGS Film series, program material produced for on-campus closed-circuit television and cable television, internships in film production, internships in television production, independent study, teacher training
FACILITIES AND EQUIPMENT Film — 8mm cameras, editing equipment, lighting, color film stock, projectors, 16mm cameras, editing equipment, lighting, black and white film stock, projectors, screening room, editing room, animation board, permanent film library of student films, permanent film library of commercial or professional films Television — black and white studio cameras, color studio cameras (through local cable operator), ½-inch VTR, ¾-inch cassette VTR, portable black and white cameras, editing equipment, monitors, special effects generators, portable color cameras (through local cable operator), ½-inch portapak recorders, lighting equipment, sound recording equipment, audio mixers, black and white studio, color studio (through local cable operator), audio studio, control room
FACULTY John Cooke, Thomas R Hogan, Alma Ilacqua PART-TIME FACULTY Caroline Fitzgerald, John Miller

COURSE LIST
Undergraduate
Basic Studio Operations
The Art and Forms of Advertising
Advanced Studio Operations
Survey of Broadcasting
Training the Speaking Voice
Communications Theory and Practice
Film as Literature
Speech for TV and Radio
TV Criticism
TV News Production

Medaille College

Independent 4-year coed college. Institutionally accredited by regional association. Urban location, 13-acre campus. Undergraduate enrollment: 1058. Total faculty: 64 (22 full-time, 42 part-time). Semester calendar. Grading system: letters or numbers.

Media Communications Department, 18 Agassiz Circle, Buffalo, NY 14214 716-884-3281
DEGREE OFFERED BS in media communications
ADMISSION Requirements — 2.75 minimum grade point average, ACT or SAT scores, interview
FINANCIAL AID Work/study programs, student loans
CURRICULAR EMPHASIS Film study — appreciation Filmmaking — commercial Television study — production, management treated equally Television production — commercial, news/documentary, public access, sports treated equally
SPECIAL ACTIVITIES/OFFERINGS Student publications, program material produced for cable television, apprenticeships, internships in film production, internships in television production, independent study, vocational placement service
FACILITIES AND EQUIPMENT Television — color studio cameras, ¾-inch cassette VTR, editing equipment, monitors, special effects generators, slide chain, portable color cameras, ¾-inch ENG, lighting equipment, sound recording equipment, audio mixers, film chain, time base corrector, color studio, audio studio, control room
FACULTY David Brugnone, Lawrence H Sherlick PART-TIME FACULTY Fran Cheslik

COURSE LIST
Undergraduate
Field Experience Seminar I–III
Television Production Techniques
Advanced Television Techniques
Scriptwriting for Media
Broadcast Management
Special Topics in Broadcasting
Media Practicum/Seminar in Professional Practices
Media Independent Study

Mohawk Valley Community College

State-supported 2-year coed college. Part of State University of New York System, automatic transfer to main campus for baccalaureate. Institutionally accredited by regional association. Suburban location. Undergraduate enrollment: 6000. Total faculty: 427 (155 full-time, 272 part-time). Trimester calendar. Grading system: letters or numbers.

Humanities/Communication Department, 1101 Sherman Drive, Utica, NY 13501 315-792-5500

CONTACT James Gifford
ADMISSION Application deadline — rolling
FINANCIAL AID Scholarships, student loans, work/study programs Application deadline — 5/1
CURRICULAR EMPHASIS Film study — (1) appreciation; (2) criticism and aesthetics; (3) history Filmmaking — (1) narrative; (2) documentary; (3) experimental
SPECIAL ACTIVITIES/OFFERINGS Film series, film festivals
FACILITIES AND EQUIPMENT Film — complete 8mm equipment, screening room, editing room, permanent film library
FACULTY James Gifford, Steven Mocko

COURSE LIST
Undergraduate
Film
Filmmaking I–III

Nassau Community College

State and locally supported 2-year coed college. Part of State University of New York System. Institutionally accredited by regional association, programs recognized by NASM. Suburban location, 225-acre campus. Undergraduate enrollment: 14,600. Total faculty: 1196 (449 full-time, 747 part-time). Semester calendar. Grading system: letters or numbers.

Communications Department, Garden City, NY 11530 516-222-7170

CONTACT Film — Steven B Samuels Television — Edward Deroo
DEGREE OFFERED AA in communications with an emphasis in media
FINANCIAL AID Scholarships, work/study programs, student loans
CURRICULAR EMPHASIS Film study — history, criticism and aesthetics, appreciation treated equally Filmmaking — narrative, animated treated equally Television study — appreciation, production treated equally Television production — commercial, news/documentary, experimental/personal video treated equally
SPECIAL ACTIVITIES/OFFERINGS Filmmaking clubs, film festivals, program material produced for on-campus closed-circuit television, internships in television production, work-study positions
FACILITIES AND EQUIPMENT Film — 8mm cameras, editing equipment, sound recording equipment, lighting, color film stock, projectors, complete 16mm equipment, screening room, editing room, animation board, permanent film library of student films, permanent film library of commercial or professional films Television — black and white studio cameras, ½-inch VTR, 1-inch VTR, 2-inch VTR, portable black and white cameras, editing equipment, monitors, special effects generators, slide chain, ½-inch portapak recorders, lighting equipment, sound recording equipment, audio mixers, film chain, black and white studio, mobile van/unit, control room

COURSE LIST
Undergraduate
Film Production I, II
Radio-TV Production I, II
Film Appreciation
Film History
Television Journalism
Documentary Media
Mass Media

Nazareth College of Rochester

Independent comprehensive coed institution. Institutionally accredited by regional association, programs recognized by NASM. Suburban location, 200-acre campus. Total enrollment: 2456. Undergraduate enrollment: 1408. Total faculty: 142 (99 full-time, 43 part-time). Semester calendar. Grading system: letters or numbers.

Theater Arts Program, 4245 East Avenue, Rochester, NY 14610 716-586-2525

CONTACT James J Kolb
ADMISSION Application deadline — rolling
FACULTY James J Kolb

COURSE LIST
Undergraduate
Language of Film

New School for Social Research

Independent coed university. Institutionally accredited by regional association. Urban location. Total enrollment: 3000. Undergraduate enrollment: 325. Total faculty: 125. Semester calendar. Grading system: letters or numbers.

Department of Cinematic Arts and Television, 66 West 12th Street, New York, NY 10011 212-741-5625

CONTACT Peter L Haratonik, Chairman
DEGREE OFFERED BA with concentration in film or television
ADMISSION Requirements — interviews, professional work experience, 30 credits for BA candidates
FINANCIAL AID student loans, work/study programs, technical assistantships
CURRICULAR EMPHASIS Film study — (1) criticism, history and aesthetics; (2) appreciation; (3) production Filmmaking — (1) narrative; (2) animated; (3) experimental Television study — (1) industry training; (2) management; (3) production Television production — (1) news/documentary; (2) educational; (3) experimental/personal video
SPECIAL ACTIVITIES/OFFERINGS Film series, film festivals, material produced for cable television, internships in film and television production, cooperative program with the National Academy of Television Arts and Sciences
FACILITIES AND EQUIPMENT Film — complete 8mm and 16mm equipment, screening room, editing room, sound mixing room, animation board Television — complete black and white studio and exterior production equipment, complete color studio production equipment, portable color cameras, black and white studio, color studio, control room
PART-TIME FACULTY Robert Ahrens, Robbin Ahrold, John Belton, Mervin Block, Andrew Bonime, Joseph Cates, Dan Chaykin, Harvey Chertok, Jim Chladek, Sona Robbins Cohen, Stephan Cohen, Hal Cranton, Robert F Davis, Sybil Del Gaudio, Barry Downes, Arnold Eagle, William K Everson, Steve Glauber, Samuel Goldrich, David Gordon, Jessica Scott Gray, Arthur Greenfield, Gene Gurlitz, Julie Gustafson, Stephen Harvey, Sanford Alan Haver, Murray Horowitz, Philip Jostrom, Sandra Klewan, Stuart Krane, Doe Lang, Ann Loring, David Lowe, Leonard Maltin, Michael F Mayer, Joe Michaels, Bruce Minnix, Lee Minoff, Hardie Mintzer, Laura Morgan, George Morris, Ellen Muir, George Orick, James D Pasternak, George Perno, Martin Phillips, Lee Polk, John Reilly, Dan Robinson, Keith Robinson, Ralph Rosenbloom, Steve Rutt, Nathan J Sambul, John Sanfratello, George Scheck, Marvin Shabsis, John Shike, Jody Silver, Mort Slakoff, Donald Spoto, Manya Starr, Elhanan C Stone, Helen Taub, Claude Underwood, Robert Warner, Henry White, Susan Zeig

COURSE LIST
Undergraduate
The Geometry of the Wide Screen
The Art of Alfred Hitchcock
Design, Structure and Style in the American Genre Film
John Ford and the Cinema of Memory
Introduction to Cinema Studies
Major Filmmakers and Major Directors in Contemporary Film
Film Semiotics and Film Narrative
The Editor's Point of View: The Aesthetics, Components, and Realities of Feature Film Editing
The Documentary Today: Its Art, History, and Social Utility
Film Comedy: Rebellion and Attack
The Art Director for Film
Acting for Film
Film Production and Workshop
Beginning 16mm Film: Intensive Workshop
Advanced Film Production: Intensive Workshop
Film Directing
Introduction to 16mm Film Production
Basic Film Editing Workshop: Theory and Technique
Sound Technique for Film
Music and Sound Direction for Film
The Filmmaker and the Film Laboratory
Writing Movies I, II
Super-8 Filmmaking as a Personal Medium
Synchronous Sound Super-8 Production Workshop
Introduction to 16mm Film Animation
Film Animation II
Motion Picture Accounting: Financial Analysis of Production and Distribution
Film and the Entertainment Industries: Business Problems in Production, Distribution and Exhibition
Making Money with the Sponsored Film
Intensive Video Workshop
Video Workshop in Electronic Editing
Advanced Video Workshop
Producing for Television
Directing for Television
Writing for Television
Advanced Writing for Television
Auditioning and Performing for Television Commercials
Actors' Workshop in Television Skills and Techniques
Interview Techniques and the Talk Show
Color Studio Production, Operations and Administration
Videotape Post-Production: Editing, Mixing, Special Effects
Advanced Television Production Workshop
Television Time Sales
Television Time Buying and Selling
The Business of Television: The People Who Make It Work
Development and Packaging of Television Program Ideas
Television Ratings: Understanding and Using Them
Television Programming
Television News Techniques
Local News Production
Investigative Reporting
Newswriting
Documentary Film Production for Television
Advertising Agency Commercial Production
Public Relations: The Vital Force
Television Advertising, Promotion and Publicity for Programming
Broadcast Business Affairs

Graduate Media Studies Program, 66 Fifth Avenue, New York, NY 10011 212-741-8903

CONTACT Peter L Haratonik, Director
DEGREES OFFERED MA in media studies, BA/MA in media studies
ADMISSION Requirements —professional recommendation, academic recommendation, BA for MA program, 60 undergraduate credits for BA/MA program, professional experience, essay, interview
FINANCIAL AID Research assistantships, technical assistantships, teaching assistantships, student loans, work/study program
CURRICULAR EMPHASIS Film study — (1) criticism and aesthetics; (2) history; (3) educational media/instructional technology Filmmaking — (1) animated; (2) documentary; (3) narrative Television study — (1) criticism and aesthetics; (2) production; (3) management Television production — (1) corporate/organizational; (2) news/documentary; (3) experimental/personal video
SPECIAL ACTIVITIES/OFFERINGS Film series, film festivals, student publications, internships in film and television production, independent study and production in film and television, practica, Summer Media Education Institute, courses offered in conjunction with New School Adult Division (see above)
FACILITIES AND EQUIPMENT Film — complete 8mm equipment, 16mm cameras, editing equipment, sound recording equipment, lighting equipment, projectors, screening room, editing room, sound mixing room, animation board Television — ½-inch VTR, ¾-inch cassette VTR, portable black and white cameras, editing equipment, monitors, special effects generator, portable color cameras, ½-inch portapak recorders, lighting equipment, sound recording equipment, audio mixers, ¾-inch electronic editing, titler

New School for Social Research (continued)

FACULTY Louis Giansante, Peter L Haratonik PART-TIME FACULTY George Back, Jeanne Betancourt, Alice Bissell, Mary Carney Blake, Deirdre Boyle, Jeffrey Bush, Milo Dalbey, Bruce Eckman, Reesom Haile, Alan Hertzberg, Larry Josephson, Richard Kotuk, Kit Laybourne, Sherry Liebowitz, Lise Liepmann, Daniel Mack, Theresa Mack, Ann Mandelbaum, Tony Marks, Michael Mayer, Richard Maynard, Tim Nesterak, George Orick, Ben Park, Minrose Quinn, Robert Sarlin, Maria Simpson, Donald Spoto, Janet Sternburg, Jane Weiner, Skip Winitsky

COURSE LIST

Graduate

Foundations of Media Theory
Colloquium on Media Theory
Culture and Communication
Culture and Technology
Legal and Ethical Problems in Media
Media, Technology and International Communication
Telecommunications: Principles and Practices
Planning and Designing Telecommunication Systems
Research Methods in Media Studies
Empirical Research Methods
Research Seminar in Film as US Political and Social History
Communication and Message Analysis
Seminar in Soundscape Study
Seminar in Media Education
Media Criticism
Practicum in Media Criticism
Developing and Evaluating Media Presentations
Short Subjects
Corporate Communications
Media and the Creative Process
Seminar in Creative Writing for Media
Seminar in Inter-Media Writing
Film as Social and Political History
Television Documentary and Broadcast Journalism
Seminar in Broadcast Journalism
Television: Theory and Practice
Film: The Anatomy of a Popular Art
Acoustic Environments
Radio, Contemporay Music and Popular Culture
Photography and Art
Photography and Social Change
Media and Children
Practicum in Educational Media
Seminar in Critical Viewing Skills
Independent Study
Internships
Supervised Research
Foundations of Media Design
Seminar in Media Design
Workshop in Video
Projects in Video: Documentary
Projects in Video: Corporate Communications
Projects in Video: Electronic Editing and Postproduction
Workshop in Sound
Projects in Sound: Forms in Audio Production
Projects in Sound: Art and Environment
Workshop in Photography
Projects in Photography: Interpretive
Projects in Photography: Documentary
Projects in Photography: The Portrait
Seminar in Advanced Photography
Workshop in Animation
Projects in Animation
Independent Production
Practicum in Media Production

New York Institute of Technology, Old Westbury

Independent comprehensive coed institution. Institutionally accredited by regional association. Suburban location. Undergraduate enrollment: 10,443. Semester calendar. Grading system: letters or numbers.

Media and Arts Center, Wheatly Road, Old Westbury, NY 11568 516-686-7567

CONTACT Adrienne O'Brien, Director of Media and Arts Center
DEGREES OFFERED BA in communication arts with an emphasis in television or film, MA in communication arts with an emphasis in television or film
PROGRAM MAJORS Undergraduate film — 15 students Undergraduate television — 80 students Graduate film — 10 students Graduate television — 50 students
ADMISSION Undergraduate requirements — 2.5 minimum grade point average, ACT or SAT scores, interview, written statement of purpose Graduate requirements — 2.75 minimum grade point average, interview, written statement of purpose Undergraduate application deadline — rolling
FINANCIAL AID Scholarships, student loans, fellowships, teaching assistantships, research assistantships Undergraduate application deadline — rolling
CURRICULAR EMPHASIS Undergraduate film study — (1) producing/directing; (2) criticism and aesthetics; (3) history Graduate film study — (1) producing/directing; (2) criticism and aesthetics; (3) history Undergraduate filmmaking — (1) documentary; (2) fiction; (3) educational Graduate filmmaking — (1) documentary; (2) fiction; (3) educational Undergraduate television study — (1) production; (2) criticism and aesthetics; (3) history Graduate television study — (1) production; (2) criticism and aesthetics; (3) history Undergraduate television production — (1) drama; (2) news/documentary; (3) educational Graduate television production — (1) drama; (2) news/documentary; (3) educational
SPECIAL ACTIVITIES/OFFERINGS Filmmaking clubs, film series, film festivals, film societies, program material produced for on-campus closed-circuit television, cable television, local public television station, internships in film production, internships in television production, independent study
FACILITIES AND EQUIPMENT Film — 8mm cameras, editing equipment, sound recording equipment, lighting, black and white film stock, projectors, 16mm cameras, editing equipment, sound recording equipment, lighting, black and white film stock, projectors, sound stage, screening room, editing room, sound mixing room, animation board, permanent film library of student films, permanent film library of commercial or professional films Television — black and white studio cameras, color studio cameras, 1-inch VTR, ¾-inch cassette VTR, portable black and white cameras, editing equipment, monitors, special effects generators, slide chain, portable color cameras, lighting equipment, sound recording equipment, audio mixers, film chain, time base corrector, character generator, black and white studio, color studies, audio studio, control room, editing rooms, audio lab, scenery shop
FACULTY Efim Brook, Boris Frumin, Roy Liemer, Geri Miller, Lee Morrison, Saul Scher, Irving Weingarten PART-TIME FACULTY Stephen Churchill, Warren Johnson, Anthony Piazza

COURSE LIST

Undergraduate

Introduction to Mass Media
Fundamentals of TV Production
Television History & Criticism
TV Production Workshop I
Advanced TV Project: Preproduction Development
Set Design for TV & Film
Advanced TV Production Workshop
Communication Law
Special Studies in Television Arts
Special TV Projects
Motion Pictures, History & Criticism
Fundamentals of Filmmaking
Special Studies in Film Art
Externships
Special Film Projects

Graduate
Workshop in Fundamentals of TV Production
Advanced TV Workshop I
Advanced TV Projects, Preproduction Development
Advanced TV Production Workshop
Portable TV Technique Workshop
Workshop in Fundamentals of Filmmaking
Advanced Filmmaking Workshop I–III
Basic Animation
Advanced Animation
Writing for the Media: Advanced Workshop I–III
Guided Projects
Creative Projects
Communication Law

Undergraduate and Graduate
Film History & Criticism
Acting/Directing for TV
Fundamentals of Film Production
Film Production Workshop I, II
The Art of Writing Documentaries
The Art of Dramatic Writing

New York University

Independent coed university. Institutionally accredited by regional association, programs recognized by AACSB. Urban location. Total enrollment: 31,597. Undergraduate enrollment: 11,313. Total faculty: 6250. Semester calendar. Grading system: letters or numbers.

The Dramatic Writing Program, Institute of Film and Television, School of the Arts, 74 South Building, Washington Square, New York, NY 10003 212-598-7845

CONTACT Jacqueline Park, Chairman
DEGREES OFFERED BFA, MFA
PROGRAM MAJORS Undergraduate — 80 students Graduate — 30 students
ADMISSION Undergraduate requirements — 3.0 minimum grade point average, combined SAT scores of 1100 Graduate requirements — writing sample, letters of recommendation, statement of purpose
FINANCIAL AID Scholarships, work/study programs, student loans, teaching assistantships
CURRICULAR EMPHASIS Screenwriting, playwriting, television and radio writing, dramatic literature, production and/or acting minor, foreign language requirement
SPECIAL ACTIVITIES/OFFERINGS Seminars, readings, screenings, lectures
FACULTY Patricia Cooper, Jacqueline Park PART-TIME FACULTY Tony Barsha, Ed Bullins, Lonnie Carter, Mark Dickerman, Arnaud D'Usseau, David Epstein, Kenneth Fishman, Venable Herndon, Ian Hunter, Len Jenkins, Daniel Kleinman, Jesse Kornbluth, Marilyn Miller, Honor Moore, Tad Mosel, Ezra Sacks, Lamar Sanders, Thomas Schachtman, Louis Solomon, Brian Winston, Thomas Zafian

COURSE LIST
Undergraduate
Artists' Seminar
Craft of Visual and Dramatic Writing

Graduate
Criticism Seminar
Actors/Directors/Writers Workshop
Graduate Seminar
Internship
Graduate Script Workshop

Undergraduate and Graduate
Free Writing Workshop
Performance (Acting)
Performance (Movement)
Using Video as Tool and Art
Text Analysis—Plays, Film Scripts, Broadcast
Apprenticeship—Video, Script, Script Clinic
Developing the Screenplay
Adapting from Fact and Fiction
Workshop in Research and Writing Documentary for Film and Television
Comedy Workshop
Writing the Short Screenplay
From Script to Performance in the Theater
From the Word to the Image
Independent Study
Advanced Screenwriting

Department of Cinema Studies, School of the Arts, 51 West Fourth Street, New York, NY 10003 212-598-7777

CONTACT Robert Sklar, Chairman
DEGREES OFFERED BFA, MA, PhD in cinema studies
DEPARTMENTAL MAJORS Undergraduate — 50 students Graduate — 200 students
ADMISSION Undergraduate requirements — 3.0 minimum grade point average, SAT scores, professional recommendations, teachers' recommendations, written statement of purpose Graduate requirements — 3.0 minimum grade point average, professional recommendations, teachers' recommendations, written statement of purpose
FINANCIAL AID Scholarships, student loans, work/study programs, teaching assistantships, research assistantships, fellowships
CURRICULAR EMPHASIS Film study — (1) criticism and aesthetics; (2) history; (3) theory
SPECIAL ACTIVITIES/OFFERINGS Film series, film festivals, independent study, practicum, teacher training, part-time study is facilitated
FACILITIES AND EQUIPMENT Film — George Amberg Film Study Center, screening rooms, permanent film library
FACULTY Noel Carroll, William K Everson, Jay Leyda, Annette Michelson, William G Simon, Robert Sklar, Robert Stam

COURSE LIST
Undergraduate
Film History
Contemporary Cinema
Aesthetic Principles of Film
Documentary Tradition
Politics and Film
Advanced Film Criticism
Third World Cinema
Revolutionary Cinema
Seminar in Current Cinema
History of American Film

Graduate and Advanced Undergraduate
The American "B" Film
American Film Industry from World War II to 1960
East Coast Production
The American Narrative Film
Four American Directors: Borzage, von Sternberg, Hawks, Sirk
D W Griffith: The Years at Biograph
Film/Television: Structures and Issues
The Myth of the "Last" Western

New York University (continued)

The New American Cinema: Independents and the Avant-Garde
Film Theory
Seminar in Contemporary Film Theory
Psychoanalysis and Film Theory
Semiotics and Film Theory
Soviet Film Theory
Soviet Cinema: Aesthetics and Stylistics
Problems in Soviet Film History
The French Film from 1920 to the Death of Vigo
French Films of the 30's and 40's
The New Wave
History of British Film
British Comedy
Italian Cinema
German Expressionist Film
New German Cinema
Japanese Cinema
Brazilian Cinema
Scandinavian Cinema
The Western
War and Film
Film Noir
The Gangster Film
Film Comedy
The Horror Film
Film Melodrama
Science Fiction Film
The Films of Michelangelo Antonioni
The Films of Stan Brakhage
The Films of Luis Buñuel
The Films of Frank Capra
The Films of Michael Curtiz
The Films of Carl Dreyer
The Films of Dreyer/Bresson
The Films and Theory of Sergei Eisenstein
The Films of John Ford
The Films of Jean-Luc Godard
The Films of D W Griffith
The Films of Howard Hawks
The Films of Alfred Hitchcock
The Films of Stanley Kubrick
The Films of Jean Renoir
The Films of Michael Snow
The Films of Dziga Vertov
The Films of Josef von Sternberg
The Films of Raoul Walsh
The Films of Orson Welles
The Films of James Whale
The Moving Camera
Film Acting
Theater, Film, Narrative: Transformations of Style
Cinema: The Language of Sight and Sound
Dada/Pop/Surrealism and the Cinema
Films and Twentieth-Century Literature
Studies in the Analysis of Movement
Photography and Film
Cinema and Language
Art Direction
Introduction to Graduate Study
The Transition to Sound
Narrative Structures of Film
Film Criticism
Authorship and Manufacture of Film
The "Classical Cinema": Hitchcock, Hawks, Renoir
The Birth of the Cinema 1896-1915
Problems and Topics in the Narrative Film

Undergraduate Institute of Film and Television, 65 South Building, Washington Square, New York, NY 10003 212-598-3702

CONTACT Haig Manoogian
DEGREES OFFERED BFA in film, BFA in television
PROGRAM MAJORS 725 students
ADMISSION Requirements — 3.0 minimum grade point average, combined SAT score of 1100
CURRICULAR EMPHASIS Filmmaking — documentary, narrative, experimental, animated, educational treated equally Television study — production, management treated equally Television production — commercial, news/documentary, experimental/personal video, educational treated equally
SPECIAL ACTIVITIES/OFFERINGS Film series; film festivals; career seminars; program material produced for cable television, local public television station, local commercial television station; apprenticeships; internships in television production; independent study
FACILITIES AND EQUIPMENT Film — complete 8mm and 16mm equipment, sound stage, screening rooms, editing rooms, sound mixing rooms, animation board Television — complete black and white studio and exterior production equipment, complete color studio production facilities available, black and white studios
FACULTY Mark Chernichaw, Patricia Cooper, Thomas Drysdale, Irving Falk, Richard Goggin, Marketa Kimbrell, Haig Manoogian, Charles Milne, Paul Owen, Jacqueline Park, Bruce Rasmussen, David Sirota, George Stoney, Nicholas Tanis, Brian Winston PART-TIME FACULTY Paul Barnes, Tony Barsha, Lee Bobker, Ronald Brindle, Neal Brodsky, Meryl Bronstein, Jacqueline Brookes, Lonnie Carter, Abigail Child, A D Coleman, Gardner Compton, Theodore Conant, Mark Dickerman, Arnaud D'Usseau, David Epstein, Bob Fair, Shelley Farkas, C Robert Fine, Ken Fishman, John Giancola, Murray Gross, Sheldon Gunsberg, Lora Hays, Venable Herndon, Jeff Hodges, Tom Hurwitz, Paul Jaeger, Larry Josephson, Jesse Kornbluth, J J Linsalata, Barbara London, Tom Mangravite, James Manilla, Marilyn Miller, Philip Miller, Richard Neer, Robert Nickson, Irving Oshman, Leon Perer, Richard Protovin, Ezra Sacks, Lamar Sanders, Lou Solomon, Susan Sussman, Neil Walden, Orin Wechsberg, Elihu Winer

COURSE LIST

Undergraduate

History of Broadcasting: Medium and Message
Film History
Broadcasting, CATV and the New Technology
Programs and Program Building: Broadcasting and CATV
Experimentalists in Video
Mass Media in Contemporary Civilization
Aesthetics of Film
Contemporary Cinema
Advertising, Audiences, Marketing: Broadcasting and CATV
Broadcast and CATV Programming
Aesthetic Principles and Problems in Broadcasting
Producing for Television
Station Management: Radio, Television and CATV
Advanced Elements of Film
Producing for Film
Future Technologies: Image and Sound
The Documentary Tradition
Introduction to ½-Inch Video
Nonverbal Communication
Motion, Matter and Meaning
Language of Sight and Sound
Beginning Television: Basic Techniques and Production-Direction
Community Video and Public Access
The Actor's Craft
Camera Technology
Editing Technology
Electronics Technology
Intermediate Photography
Still Photography and Its Processes: Pre-Visualization and the Zone System
Still Photography and Its Processes: Experimental Photography
Still Photography and Its Processes: The Studio and Large Format Photography
Still Photography and Its Processes: Introduction to Color Photography
Image and Idea: A Seminar in Contemporary Photography
Advanced Still Photography and Its Processes II
Portable Videotape Workshop
Media Internship
The Documentary Workshop I
Animation Workshop
The Narrative Workshop
The Experimental Workshop
Lighting: Motion Picture and Television
Advanced Lighting-Cinematography
Senior Production Workshop and Seminar
The Production Company Workshop
Sound: Function and Editing
Sound: Recording Methods and Techniques
Music for Film and Television
Motion Picture Editing
Cinematography
Creative Sound Workshop

Directing: Working with Actors
Directing: Working with Visuals
Radio Workshop: Contemporary Methods and Techniques
Radio Workshop: Contemporary Documentary and Drama I
Radio Workshop: Contemporary Music Programming
Radio Workshop: Contemporary Station Management
Radio: Programming Perspectives
Media Internship: Contemporary Radio
Television Drama Laboratory
Television News, Features and Documentary Laboratory
University Broadcast Lab
Children's Television Laboratory
Industrial, Educational, and Instructional Television Laboratory—A Studio Course
Introduction to Dramatic and Visual Writing I, II
Writing the Short Screenplay
Script Clinic I
Seminar in Work in Progress
The Writing Experience
Developing the Screenplay
Comedy Workshop
Workshop in Research and Writing Documentary for Film and Television
Advanced Independent Study

Niagara University

Independent comprehensive coed institution affiliated with Roman Catholic Church. Institutionally accredited by regional association. Suburban location, 160-acre campus. Total enrollment: 4403. Undergraduate enrollment: 3267. Total faculty: 244 (184 full-time, 60 part-time). Semester calendar. Grading system: letters or numbers.

Communication Studies Program/English Department, Lewiston, NY 14109 716-285-1212, ext 524

CONTACT Bruce R Powers
DEGREE OFFERED BA in English/communication studies with an emphasis in broadcast journalism and film
PROGRAM MAJORS Undergraduate film and television — 84 students
ADMISSION Undergraduate requirements — 2.5 minimum grade point average, ACT or SAT scores, interview Undergraduate application deadline — rolling
FINANCIAL AID Scholarships, work/study programs, student loans Undergraduate application deadline — 3/1, rolling
CURRICULAR EMPHASIS Film study — (1) production techniques related to visual story-telling; (2) criticism and aesthetics; (3) history Filmmaking — (1) documentary; (2) narrative; (3) experimental Television study — (1) production; (2) criticism and aesthetics; (3) history Television production — (1) news/documentary; (2) commercial; (3) educational
SPECIAL ACTIVITIES/OFFERINGS Filmmaking clubs; film series; film festivals; film societies; film archive; program material produced for on-campus closed-circuit television and cable television, instructional television tapes for circulation by College of Nursing; internships in film production; internships in television production; independent study; teacher training
FACILITIES AND EQUIPMENT Film — complete 16mm production equipment, sound stage, screening room, editing room, permanent film library of student films Television — complete black and white studio production equipment, complete color studio production equipment, black and white studio, color studio, audio studio, control room, graphics workroom, specially constructed master multimedia console for taped programming and electronic scoring
FACULTY Bruce R Powers PART-TIME FACULTY Robert Crawford, Daniel Kane, John Kreiger, Paul Maze, Robert Rogers, Michael Whalen, Thomas Zarbo

COURSE LIST

Undergraduate
Understanding Media
Power of Mass Media
Television News
Film/TV Writing
Basic Photography
Basic Filmmaking
Television Production I, II
Radio Station Operations
Advertising Fundamentals
Basic Journalism
Editing and Page Design
Graphics for Communication
Media Independent Study
Media Theory/Criticism

Graduate
Television/Film Workshop

Undergraduate and Graduate
Cinema—The Art and History of the Film I, II
Classics of the Silent Screen
Cinema—The Advent of Sound
History/Management of Broadcasting
Politics and Media

Onondaga Community College

State and locally supported 2-year coed college. Part of State University of New York System. Institutionally accredited by regional association. Suburban location. Undergraduate enrollment: 6185. Total faculty: 300 (200 full-time, 100 part-time). Semester calendar. Grading system: letters or numbers.

Radio-Television Department, Route 173, Syracuse, NY 13215 315-469-7741

CONTACT Catherine Hawkins, Chairperson
DEGREE OFFERED AAS in radio/television
DEPARTMENTAL MAJORS Television — 150 students
ADMISSION Requirements — C minimum grade point average, ACT or SAT scores, interview
FINANCIAL AID Work/study programs, student loans, federal grants
CURRICULAR EMPHASIS Television study — (1) production; (2) management; (3) educational; (4) history; (5) criticism and aesthetics; (6) appreciation Television production — (1) educational; (2) commercial; (3) news/documentary; (4) experimental/personal video
SPECIAL ACTIVITIES/OFFERINGS Program material produced for on-campus closed-circuit television, cable television, local public television station, and local commercial television station; internships in television production, vocational placement service

Onondaga Community College (continued)

FACILITIES AND EQUIPMENT Television — color studio cameras, ¾-inch cassette VTR, editing equipment, monitors, special effects generators, slide chain, portable color cameras, ½-inch portapak recorders, lighting equipment, sound recording equipment, audio mixers, film chain, color studio, mobile van/unit, audio studio, control room
FACULTY Robert Gaurnier, Catherine Hawkins, David Hawkins, Vincent Spadafora PART-TIME FACULTY Jerry Barsha

COURSE LIST

Undergraduate

Introduction to Broadcasting
Radio-TV Announcing
News and Public Affairs
Television Production
Educational Broadcasting
Broadcast Station Operations
Audio Control
Radio Production

Pace University, College of White Plains

Independent 4-year coed college. Administratively affiliated with Pace University. Institutionally accredited by regional association. Suburban location. Undergraduate enrollment: 1004. Total faculty: 79 (36 full-time, 43 part-time). 4-1-4 calendar. Grading system: letters or numbers.

Journalism Department, 78 North Broadway, White Plains, NY 10603 914-682-7130

New York

CONTACT Bruce Underwood
DEGREE OFFERED BA in journalism (We have a very limited number of courses in film and TV)
ADMISSION Requirements — 2.0 minimum grade point average, ACT or SAT scores, teachers' recommendations, written statement of purpose Application deadline — rolling
FINANCIAL AID Scholarships, work/study programs, student loans
CURRICULAR EMPHASIS Film study — history, criticism and aesthetics, appreciation treated equally Filmmaking — documentary, narrative, experimental treated equally Television study — history, criticism and aesthetics, appreciation, production, management treated equally Television production — commercial, news/documentary treated equally
SPECIAL ACTIVITIES/OFFERINGS Film series, student publications, program material produced for cable television, internships in film production, internships in television production, independent study, vocational placement service, weekly news/feature radio and TV broadcasts
FACILITIES AND EQUIPMENT Film — complete 16mm equipment, editing room Television — black and white studio cameras, ½-inch VTR, ¾-inch cassette VTR, portable black and white cameras, editing equipment, monitors, special effects generators, ½-inch portapak recorders, lighting equipment, sound recording equipment, audio mixers, black and white studio, audio studio, control room
FACULTY Robert Klaeger, Donald Ryan, Bob Wolff

Division of Arts and Letters 914-834-1946

CONTACT Bruce Underwood, Head, Journalism Program
ADMISSION Application deadline — rolling
CURRICULAR EMPHASIS Film study — (1) appreciation; (2) criticism and aesthetics; (3) history Television study — broadcasting
FACILITIES AND EQUIPMENT Television — ½-inch VTR
FACULTY Bob Wolff PART-TIME FACULTY Susan Katz

COURSE LIST

Undergraduate

The Film as a Medium
Broadcasting

Parsons School of Design

Independent professional coed institution. Institutionally accredited by regional association, programs recognized by NASA. Urban location, 2-acre campus. Total enrollment: 1100. Undergraduate enrollment: 1340. Total faculty: 140. Semester calendar. Grading system: letters or numbers. The Parsons School of Design has a cooperative arrangement with the New School for Social Research.

Office of Continuing Education, 66 Fifth Avenue, New York, NY 10011 212-741-8933

Media Arts Program 212-741-8903

CONTACT Peter L Haratonik
PART-TIME FACULTY Janice Ball, Mary Carney Blake, Louis Giansante, Laura Morgan, Tim Nesterak

COURSE LIST

Undergraduate

Introduction to Film and Video Techniques
Art Direction for Film and Video
Art Direction for Multi-Image Production

Pratt Institute

Independent comprehensive coed institution. Institutionally accredited by regional association, programs recognized by NASA. Urban location, 18-acre campus. Total enrollment: 4249. Undergraduate enrollment: 3133. Total faculty: 490 (140 full-time, 350 part-time). 4-1-4 calendar. Grading system: letters or numbers.

Film Department, 215 Ryerson Street, Brooklyn, NY 11205 212-636-3766

CONTACT Nick Manning
DEGREES OFFERED BFA in film, BFA in animation

DEPARTMENTAL MAJORS 30 students
ADMISSION Requirements — interviews, portfolio Application deadline — 4/1, rolling
FINANCIAL AID Scholarships, student loans, work/study programs, fellowships Application deadline — 2/1, rolling
CURRICULAR EMPHASIS Film study — (1) production; (2) criticism and aesthetics; (3) appreciation; (4) history Filmmaking — (1) narrative; (2) animated; (3) experimental; (4) documentary Television study — production Television production — experimental/personal video
SPECIAL ACTIVITIES/OFFERINGS Film series, film festivals, apprenticeships, internships in film production, independent study
FACILITIES AND EQUIPMENT Film — complete 8mm and 16mm equipment, screening room, editing room, sound mixing room, animation board, permanent film library Television — complete black and white studio and exterior production equipment, complete color exterior production equipment, audio studio, control room
FACULTY Bob Fiala, Robert Knight, Nick Manning, Darryl Neube PART-TIME FACULTY Boris Bode, Regina Cornwell, Howard Danelowitz, Dan Haskett, Lewis Jacobs, Joyce Jesionowski, Paul Killian, Jim Pasternak, John Snyder, Lucy Winer

COURSE LIST

Undergraduate

Production I–III
Animation I–III
History
Criticism
Special Topics
Cinematography
Lighting
Sound
Puppet Animation
Kinetics
Video Art
Video Production
Multi-Media

Rensselaer Polytechnic Institute

Independent coed university. Founded 1824. Institutionally accredited by regional association. Suburban location, 260-acre campus. Total enrollment: 5708. Undergraduate enrollment: 4155. Total faculty: 345 full-time. Semester calendar. Grading system: letters or numbers.

Communication Department, Troy, NY 12181 518-270-6470

ADMISSION Application deadline — 1/1
FACULTY B F Hammett, Merritt Abrash

COURSE LIST

Undergraduate

Art of the Film
Nonfiction Film
Film: Social and Political Themes
Sociology in/of Film

Rochester Institute of Technology

Independent comprehensive coed institution. Institutionally accredited by regional association, programs recognized by NASA. Suburban location, 1300-acre campus. Total enrollment: 8969. Undergraduate enrollment: 7766. Total faculty: 1247 (872 full-time, 375 part-time). Quarter calendar. Grading system: letters or numbers.

Department of Film/Television, School of Photographic Arts and Sciences, College of Graphic Arts and Photography, One Lomb Memorial Drive, Rochester, NY 14623 716-464-2716

CONTACT Chairperson
DEGREES OFFERED BA in illustration or BS in photography with emphasis in film
ADMISSION Application deadline — rolling
CURRICULAR EMPHASIS Film study — (1) production; (2) history Filmmaking — (1) visual interpretation; (2) documentary, narrative, animated treated equally
SPECIAL ACTIVITIES/OFFERINGS Program material produced for on-campus closed-circuit television, cable television, local public television station, local commercial television station; consortium arrangement with Nazareth College of Rochester
FACILITIES AND EQUIPMENT Film — 8mm, 16mm, and 35mm cameras and projectors, 16mm editing equipment, sound recording equipment, lighting equipment, sound stage, screening room, 35mm screening facilities, permanent film library Television — complete black and white studio and exterior production equipment, black and white studio, control room

St Bonaventure University

Independent Roman Catholic coed university. Institutionally accredited by regional association. Rural location, 500-acre campus. Total enrollment: 2600. Undergraduate enrollment: 2140. Total faculty: 140 full-time. Semester calendar. Grading system: letters or numbers.

Mass Communication Department, St Bonaventure, NY 14778 716-375-2520

CONTACT Russell J Jandoli
PROGRAM OFFERED Major in mass communication with emphasis in broadcasting
ADMISSION Undergraduate requirements — interview, teachers' recommendations Undergraduate application deadline — rolling
FINANCIAL AID Scholarships, work/study programs, student loans
CURRICULAR EMPHASIS Undergraduate television study — production, management, writing treated equally Undergraduate television production — news/documentary
SPECIAL ACTIVITIES/OFFERINGS Program material produced for cable television and local public television station, internships in television production
FACILITIES AND EQUIPMENT Television — black and white studio cameras, ½-inch VTR, monitors, black and white studio, color studio, mobile van/unit, remote truck, control room

St Bonaventure University (continued)

COURSE LIST

Undergraduate

Introduction to Broadcasting
Advanced Broadcasting
Video Tape Production

St John Fisher College

Independent 4-year coed college. Institutionally accredited by regional association. Suburban location. Undergraduate enrollment: 3007. Total faculty: 139 (88 full-time, 51 part-time). Semester calendar. Grading system: letters or numbers.

Communication/Journalism Department, 3690 East Avenue, Rochester, NY 14618 716-586-4140, ext 253

CONTACT Thomas P Proietti
DEGREE OFFERED BA in communication/journalism
DEPARTMENTAL MAJORS Film — 10 students Television — 60 students
ADMISSION Requirements — ACT or SAT scores, interview, teachers' recommendations, written statement of purpose Application deadline — rolling
FINANCIAL AID Scholarships, work/study programs, student loans Application deadline — rolling
CURRICULAR EMPHASIS Film study — (1) criticism and aesthetics; (2) appreciation; (3) history Filmmaking — (1) experimental; (2) documentary; (3) animated Television study — (1) management; (2) criticism and aesthetics; (3) production Television production — (1) news/documentary; (2) commercial; (3) experimental/personal video
SPECIAL ACTIVITIES/OFFERINGS Film series; film festivals; program material produced for on-campus closed-circuit television, cable television, local public television station, local commercial television station; internships in film production; internships in television production; independent study; teacher training; vocational placement service
FACILITIES AND EQUIPMENT Film — complete 8mm and 16mm equipment, sound stage, screening room, editing room, sound mixing room, animation board, permanent film library of student films, permanent film library of commercial or professional films Television — black and white studio cameras, ½-inch VTR, ¾-inch cassette VTR, portable black and white cameras, editing equipment, monitors, special effects generators, portable color cameras, ½-inch portapak recorders, ¾-inch ENG, lighting equipment, sound recording equipment, audio mixers, time base corrector, black and white studio, audio studio, control room
FACULTY Sally Buckley, Mary Lopocaro, John McGinnis, Thomas Proietti PART-TIME FACULTY Carl Battaglia, Nancy Bragg, Gary Cuminale, Frank DiProsia, Frank McNellis, Dennis O'Brien, John Palvino

COURSE LIST

Undergraduate

Introduction to Mass Communication
Media Coverage
Media Production I, II
Broadcasting: History, Development and Issues
Broadcast Operations and Management
Cable Television: Operations and Management
Broadcast Performance
Broadcast Journalism
Film Experience
Filmmaking
Communication Internships

Sarah Lawrence College

Independent comprehensive coed institution. Institutionally accredited by regional association. Suburban location, 35-acre campus. Total enrollment: 992. Undergraduate enrollment: 774. Total faculty: 126. Semester calendar. Grading system: letters or numbers and faculty reports.

Film Department, Bronxville, NY 10708 914-337-0700

CONTACT Ron Mottram
DEGREE OFFERED BA in film
DEPARTMENTAL MAJORS Undergraduate — 15 students Graduate — 1 student
ADMISSION Requirement — interviews Application deadline — 2/1
FINANCIAL AID Scholarships Application deadline — 2/1
CURRICULAR EMPHASIS Undergraduate film study — (1) criticism and aesthetics; (2) production; (3) history Graduate film study — (1) history; (2) criticism and aesthetics; (3) production Undergraduate filmmaking — (1) narrative; (2) experimental; (3) documentary Graduate filmmaking — (1) narrative; (2) documentary; (3) experimental
SPECIAL ACTIVITIES/OFFERINGS Film series, film festivals, film societies, student publications, independent study
FACILITIES AND EQUIPMENT Film — complete 8mm and 16mm equipment, screening room, editing room, sound mixing room, animation board, permanent film library Television — black and white studio cameras, color studio camera, ¾-inch cassette VTR, portable black and white cameras, editing equipment, monitors, special effects generators, portable color cameras, lighting equipment, sound recording equipment, audio mixers
FACULTY Wilford Leach, Ron Mottram PART-TIME FACULTY Bill Brand

COURSE LIST

Undergraduate and Graduate

The Movies
French Cinema
Three Directors
Film Workshop
Advanced Filmmaking

School of Visual Arts

Independent 4-year coed college. Candidate for regional accreditation. Urban location. Undergraduate enrollment: 2500. Semester calendar. Grading system: letters or numbers.

Film Department, 209 East 23rd Street, New York, NY 10010 212-679-7350

CONTACT Charles S Hirsch
DEGREE OFFERED BFA in film

DEPARTMENTAL MAJORS 200 students
ADMISSION Requirements — 2.5 minimum grade point average, interview, teachers' recommendations, portfolio, film essay Application deadline — rolling
FINANCIAL AID Scholarships, work/study programs, student loans, BEOG, SEOG, TAP, OVR, VA Application deadline — 3/15
CURRICULAR EMPHASIS Film study — (1) criticism and aesthetics; (2) history; (3) appreciation Filmmaking — (1) narrative; (2) animated; (3) experimental Television study — (1) production; (2) educational; (3) criticism and aesthetics Television production — (1) commercial; (2) experimental/personal video; (3) news/documentary
SPECIAL ACTIVITIES/OFFERINGS Filmmaking clubs; film series; film festivals; film societies; student publications; program material produced for on-campus closed-circuit television, cable television, local public television station; internships in film production; internships in television production; independent study; vocational placement service
FACILITIES AND EQUIPMENT Film — complete 8mm and 16mm equipment, sound stage, screening room, editing room, animation board, permanent film library of student films, permanent film library of commercial or professional films, sound transfer room Television — complete black and white studio production equipment, complete black and white and color exterior production equipment, black and white studio, color studio, control room, ½-inch and ¾-inch editing equipment
FACULTY Joan Braderman, Arnaud d'Usseau, Roy Frumkes, Janet Kealy, Manfred Kirchheimer, Gil Miret, Richard Pepperman PART-TIME FACULTY Martin Abrahams, Steve Bassin, Howard Beckerman, Ed Bowes, Robert Brady, Barbara Buckner, Louis Bunin, Joanne Burke, Christopher Coughlan, Dena Crane, Bill Daughton, Storm De Hirsch, William Everson, Ellen Feldman, Mark Fischer, Hermine Freed, Ed Gleason, Jim Hubbard, Charles Jarvis, John Keeler, Cora Kennedy, Sardi Klein, Beryl Korot, Richard Koszarski, Joan Kuehl, Jeff Lieberman, Bob Naud, Jerry Ozment, Domonic Paris, Victor Petrashevich, Sanford Rackow, Martin Rosenthal, Paul Schulman, Leo Seltzer, Rose Sommershield, Jake Stern, Amy Taubin, Jo Taverner, Kelly Van Horn, Frank Vitale, Leonard D. Wong

COURSE LIST
Undergraduate
8mm Production, First Year
Writing for Film
Film History
Film Theory and Criticism
Still Photography for Film
Introduction to Videotape
Introduction to Animation
Literature and Film
Film Production, 16mm, Second Year
Film Editing
The Sound Track for Film
Music for Film
Film Production Workshop, Third Year
Advanced Editing
Thesis Film Workshop
Animation Drawing
Acting
Directing
Theory of Experimental Film
Super 8mm Cinematography
Producing a Commercial Spot
Intermediate Animation, Second Year
Advanced Cinematography
Advanced Lighting
Post-Production Sound
Advanced Directing Seminar
Producing Seminar
Animation in Three-Dimensional Form
Advanced Screenwriting
The Film Documentary
Animation Workshop, Third Year
Intermediate Videotape
Commercial TV
Video Art
Advanced Videotape Workshop
Video Art Workshop
Advanced Video Art Workshop

Skidmore College

Independent 4-year coed college. Institutionally accredited by regional association, programs recognized by NASA. Small town location, 650-acre campus. Undergraduate enrollment: 2066. Total faculty: 169 full-time. 4-1-4 calendar. Grading system: letters or numbers.

English Department, Saratoga Springs, NY 12866 518-584-5000, ext 321

CONTACT James Kiehl
CURRICULAR EMPHASIS Undergraduate film study — criticism and aesthetics
SPECIAL ACTIVITIES/OFFERINGS Film series

COURSE LIST
Undergraduate
Film

State University of New York Agricultural and Technical College at Cobleskill

State-supported 2-year coed college. Part of State University of New York System. Institutionally accredited by regional association. Rural location, 500-acre campus. Undergraduate enrollment: 2693. Total faculty: 139 (134 full-time, 5 part-time). Semester calendar. Grading system: letters or numbers.

Humanities Department, Cobleskill, NY 12043 518-234-5140

CONTACT Michael Vandow
ADMISSION Application deadline — 1/15, rolling
FINANCIAL AID Student loans, work/study programs Application deadline — 3/1
CURRICULAR EMPHASIS Film study — (1) appreciation; (2) criticism and aesthetics; (3) production; (4) history Filmmaking — (1) narrative; (2) documentary; (3) educational
SPECIAL ACTIVITIES/OFFERINGS Film series
FACILITIES AND EQUIPMENT Film — 8mm cameras, lighting equipment, 8mm and 16mm projectors, permanent film library Television — black and white studio cameras, ½-inch VTR, ¾-inch cassette VTR, editing equipment, monitors, ½-inch portapak recorder, lighting equipment, sound recording equipment, audio mixer, black and white studio, audio studio
FACULTY Michael Vandow

COURSE LIST
Undergraduate
Introduction to Cinema

State University of New York at Albany

State-supported coed university. Part of State University of New York System. Institutionally accredited by regional association, programs recognized by AACSB. Suburban location. Total enrollment: 15,216. Undergraduate enrollment: 10,540. Total faculty: 810 (664 full-time, 146 part-time). Semester calendar. Grading system: letters or numbers.

Department of Anthropology, 1400 Washington Avenue, Albany, NY 12222 518-457-8404 or 518-457-8405

CONTACT George Klima
DEGREES OFFERED BA, MA in cultural anthropology with emphasis in film or television
ADMISSION Undergraduate requirements — minimum grade point average, SAT scores Graduate requirement — minimum grade point average Undergraduate application deadline — 4/1, rolling
FINANCIAL AID Work/study programs, teaching assistantships Undergraduate application deadline — rolling
CURRICULAR EMPHASIS Film study — criticism and aesthetics, production, educational media/instructional technology treated equally Filmmaking — (1) experimental; (2) documentary; (3) educational
SPECIAL ACTIVITIES/OFFERINGS Film series, film festivals, film societies, apprenticeships, independent study
FACILITIES AND EQUIPMENT Film — complete 8mm and 16mm equipment, sound stage, screening room, editing room, sound mixing room, animation board, permanent film library
FACULTY George Ghelch, George Klima, Walter Zenner

COURSE LIST
Undergraduate and Graduate
Anthropology Through Film
Ethnology of Film

English Department 518-457-8434

CONTACT Fred Silva
DEGREE OFFERED BA in English with emphasis in film
ADMISSION Application deadline — 4/1, rolling
CURRICULAR EMPHASIS Film study — (1) criticism and aesthetics; (2) history; (3) appreciation
FACULTY Fred Silva

COURSE LIST
Undergraduate
Film Theory and Criticism
American Film and Fiction of The Fifties
Crime in American Film and Fiction
The West in American Film and Fiction

Undergraduate and Graduate
Literature as Cinema
American Film Genre

State University of New York at Binghamton

State-supported coed university. Part of State University of New York System. Institutionally accredited by regional association. Suburban location, 606-acre campus. Total enrollment: 10,231. Undergraduate enrollment: 7809. Total faculty: 556 (411 full-time, 145 part-time). Semester calendar. Grading system: letters or numbers.

Cinema Department, Vestal Parkway, Binghamton, NY 13901 607-798-4998

CONTACT Francis X Newman, Chairman
DEGREES OFFERED BA in cinema, BA in video
DEPARTMENTAL MAJORS Film — 20 students Television — 3 students
ADMISSION Requirements — 3.0 minimum grade point average, SAT scores Application deadline — 1/15, rolling
FINANCIAL AID Scholarships, work/study programs, student loans
CURRICULAR EMPHASIS Film study — (1) criticism and aesthetics; (2) appreciation; (3) history Filmmaking — (1) experimental; (2) personal; (3) narrative Television study — criticism and aesthetics Television production — experimental/personal video
SPECIAL ACTIVITIES/OFFERINGS Film series, film societies, internships in television production, independent study
FACILITIES AND EQUIPMENT Film — complete 8mm and 16mm equipment, analytic projectors, screening room, editing room, sound mixing room, animation board, permanent film library of commercial or professional films Television — black and white studio cameras, color studio cameras, ½-inch VTR, ¾-inch cassette VTR, portable black and white cameras, editing equipment, monitors, special effects generators, slide chain, ½-inch portapak recorders, lighting equipment, sound recording equipment, audio mixers, film chain, video synthesizer, black and white studio, color studio
FACULTY Larry Gottheim, Ralph Hocking, Ken Jacobs, Maureen Turim

COURSE LIST
Undergraduate
The Movies
Introduction to Cinema
Film Analysis
Intermediate Film Analysis
Topics in Cinema Aesthetics
Basic Video
Advanced Film Analysis
Para Cinema
Introductory Filmmaking
Intermediate Filmmaking
Seminar in Cinema
Seminar in Video

State University of New York at Buffalo

State-supported coed university. Part of State University of New York System. Institutionally accredited by regional association, programs recognized by NASM, AACSB, NASA, ACPE. Urban location. Total enrollment: 24,579. Undergraduate enrollment: 17,060. Total faculty: 1850. Semester calendar. Grading system: letters or numbers.

Center for Media Study, 310 Hochstetter, Buffalo, NY 17222 716-831-2426

CONTACT Christine Nygren
DEGREES OFFERED BA, MAH in film or video
PROGRAM MAJORS Undergraduate — 80 students Graduate 50 students
ADMISSION Requirements — minimum grade point average, teachers' recommendations, written statement of purpose Undergraduate application deadline — 1/5
FINANCIAL AID Scholarships, work/study programs, teaching assistantships, fellowships Undergraduate application deadline — 2/1
CURRICULAR EMPHASIS Film study — history, production treated equally Filmmaking — documentary, narrative, experimental, animated treated equally Television study — criticism and aesthetics, production treated equally Television production — experimental/personal video
SPECIAL ACTIVITIES/OFFERINGS Filmmaking clubs, film series, program material produced for cable television and local public television station, independent study, academic year abroad program offered through affiliation with the Inter-University Center for Film Studies in Paris.
FACILITIES AND EQUIPMENT Film — complete 8mm and 16mm equipment, optical printer, screening room, editing room, sound mixing room, animation stand, permanent film library Television — complete black and white studio and exterior production equipment, complete color studio production equipment, black and white studio, color studio
FACULTY James Blue, Tony Conrad, Hollis Frampton, Brian Henderson, Paul Sharits, Woody Vasulka PART-TIME FACULTY Gerald O'Grady

COURSE LIST

Undergraduate

Beginning Filmmaking
Film Workshop I, II
Film Theory
Special Topics: Theory
Experimental Video
Electronic Image Analysis
Documentary Film Production
Special Topics: Japanese Film

Undergraduate and Graduate

Advanced Film Production
Problems in the Documentary
Advanced Video Production
Special Topics: Soviet Film
Nonfiction Film

State University of New York at Stony Brook

State-supported coed university. Part of State University of New York System. Institutionally accredited by regional association. Suburban location, 1100-acre campus. Total enrollment: 16,000. Undergraduate enrollment: 11,000. Total faculty: 1000. Semester calendar. Grading system: letters or numbers.

Theater Arts Department, Stony Brook, NY 11794 516-246-5670

CONTACT Chairperson
ADMISSION Application deadline — 1/5, rolling
CURRICULAR EMPHASIS Film study — (1) production; (2) criticism and aesthetics
SPECIAL ACTIVITIES/OFFERINGS Internships in film production, independent study, teacher training
FACILITIES AND EQUIPMENT Film — complete 8mm and 16mm equipment, sound stage, editing room, sound mixing room

State University of New York College at Fredonia

State-supported comprehensive coed institution. Part of State University of New York System. Institutionally accredited by regional association. Small town location, 235-acre campus. Total enrollment: 5090. Undergraduate enrollment: 4543. Total faculty: 297 (268 full-time, 29 part-time). Semester calendar. Grading system: letters or numbers.

Special Studies, Fredonia, NY 14063 716-673-3336

CONTACT Film — Robert Deming Television — William Jungels
DEGREE OFFERED BA in special studies with emphases in television and film
PROGRAM MAJORS Film — 20 students Television — 150 students
ADMISSION Requirements — ACT or SAT scores, teachers' recommendations, written statement of purpose, professional recommendations Undergraduate application deadline — 8/15
FINANCIAL AID Scholarships, work/study programs, student loans, teaching assistantships (grad only)
CURRICULAR EMPHASIS Film study — (1) criticism and aesthetics; (2) appreciation; (3) educational media/instructional technology FIlmmaking — (1) documentary; (2) narrative; (3) experimental Television study — (1) production; (2) management; (3) educational Television production — (1) news/documentary; (2) commercial; (3) experimental/personal video
SPECIAL ACTIVITIES/OFFERINGS Film series; film festivals; program material produced for on-campus closed-circuit television, cable television, local public television station; internships in film production; internships in television production; independent study; teacher training
FACILITIES AND EQUIPMENT Film — complete 8mm and 16mm equipment, sound stage, screening room, 35mm screening facilities, editing room, sound mixing room, permanent film library of student films, permanent film library of commercial or professional films Television — complete black and white and color studio production equipment, complete black and white and color exterior production equipment, black and white studio, color studio, mobile van/unit, audio studio, control room
FACULTY Bob Deming, Bill Jungels, Ted Schwalbe, Jim Shokoff PART-TIME FACULTY Jay Boylan, Don Burdick, John Malcolm, Ron Warren

COURSE LIST

Undergraduate

Introduction to Broadcast Media
Television Production I, II
Television Graphics
Television News Production
Television Documentaries
Community TV Production
Instructional TV Production
Advanced Color Television
Special Applications of Television
Basic Filmmaking
Intermediate Filmmaking
Advanced Filmmaking
Documentary Filmmaking
Rhetoric of Film
Film History I, II
Film Aesthetics
Film Criticism
Film and Literature
Nonfiction Film

State University of New York College at Geneseo

State-supported comprehensive coed institution. Part of State University of New York System. Institutionally accredited by regional association. Small town location, 225-acre campus. Total enrollment: 5342. Undergraduate enrollment: 4708. Total faculty: 311 (275 full-time, 36 part-time). Semester calendar. Grading system: letters of numbers.

Speech Communication Department, Blake Hall B117, Geneseo, NY 14454 716-245-5228

CONTACT Film — Joe Bulsys Television — William R Berry
DEGREE OFFERED BA in communication with emphasis in TV
DEPARTMENTAL MAJORS Television — 125 students
ADMISSION Requirements — ACT or SAT scores, interview, teachers' recommendations, written statement of purpose, successful high school record Application deadline — 1/30
FINANCIAL AID Scholarships, work/study programs, student loans
CURRICULAR EMPHASIS Film study — history, criticism and aesthetics, educational media/instructional technology treated equally Filmmaking — documentary, educational treated equally Television study — history, criticism and aesthetics, appreciation, educational, production, management, international television, Canadian studies treated equally Television production — commercial, news/documentary, experimental/personal video, educational treated equally
SPECIAL ACTIVITIES/OFFERINGS Film series; film festivals; student publications; program material produced for on-campus closed-circuit television, cable television, local public television station, local commercial television station, college promotion and recruitment; internships in film production; internships in television production; independent study; vocational placement service
FACILITIES AND EQUIPMENT Film — 8mm cameras, editing equipment, sound recording equipment, lighting, projectors, screening room, editing room, sound mixing room, permanent film library of commercial or professional films Television — color studio cameras, portable black and white cameras, editing equipment, monitors, special effects generators, slide chain, ½-inch portapak recorders, lighting equipment, sound recording equipment, audio mixers, film chain, black and white studio, mobile van/unit, audio studio, control room
FACULTY William Berry, Joseph Bulsys, Robert Greene, Myron Shaw

COURSE LIST

Undergraduate

Introduction to Radio and Television
Radio and Television Writing
Radio and Television Announcing
Broadcast Media Arts
Radio and Television Programming
Radio Production
Television Production
History of Broadcasting
International Broadcasting
Seminar: Issues and Problems in Broadcasting
Broadcasting and Government
Radio and Television Station Management
Television and Film
Impact of Television Communication
Internship in Broadcasting
Independent Study (in Broadcasting)
Workshop in Educational Radio and Television
Speech in the Mass Media
Uses of Closed-Circuit Television in Education
Montreal Seminar in Canadian Broadcasting
Toronto Seminar in Canadian Communication

State University of New York College at New Paltz

State-supported comprehensive coed institution. Part of State University of New York System. Institutionally accredited by regional association. Rural location, 100-acre campus. Total enrollment: 6750. Undergraduate enrollment: 4980. Total faculty: 350. Semester calendar. Grading system: letters or numbers.

English Department, New Paltz, NY 12561 914-257-2598

CONTACT Irving Weiss
PROGRAM OFFERED Major in film
DEPARTMENTAL MAJORS 30 students
ADMISSION Application deadline — rolling
FINANCIAL AID Scholarships, student loans, work/study programs Application deadline — 3/1
CURRICULAR EMPHASIS Film study — (1) criticism and aesthetics; (2) history; (3) production Filmmaking — (1) documentary; (2) narrative; (3) experimental
SPECIAL ACTIVITIES/OFFERINGS Film series, film festivals, independent study
FACILITIES AND EQUIPMENT Film — 8mm cameras, editing equipment, sound recording equipment, 8mm and 16mm projectors, sound stage, screening room, editing room, permanent film library
FACULTY Barry Bort, John Frank, David Goldknopf, Henry Raleigh, Irving Weiss

COURSE LIST

Undergraduate

History of Film I, II
Film Aesthetics I, II
Filmmaking I, II
American Genre Film
American Films of a Decade
Fiction into Film
American Film Directors
Topics in Mass Culture
Contemporary Film

Speech Communication Department 914-257-2600

CONTACT James Roever, Chairman
DEGREES OFFERED BA, BS in speech communication
DEPARTMENTAL MAJORS 130 students
ADMISSION Application deadline — rolling
FINANCIAL AID Scholarships, student loans, work/study programs Application deadline — 3/1
CURRICULAR EMPHASIS Television study — (1) appreciation; (2) production; (3) history; (4) criticism and aesthetics; (5) management; (6) educational Television production — (1) commercial; (2) news/documentary; (3) experimental/personal video; (4) educational

SPECIAL ACTIVITIES/OFFERINGS Program material produced for on-campus closed-circuit television and cable television, internships in television production, independent study
FACILITIES AND EQUIPMENT Television — complete black and white studio production equipment, complete color studio production equipment, black and white studio, color studio, audio studio, control room
FACULTY Michael Banks, James Roever, James Smith

COURSE LIST
Undergraduate
Communication and Media
History and Development of Radio and Television in American Society
Radio-Television News
Radio-Television Writing
Introduction to Advertising
Children and Television
Aesthetics and Criticism of Television
Radio-Television Performance
Radio Production
Television Production I, II
Broadcast Advertising

State University of New York College at Oswego

State-supported comprehensive coed institution. Part of State University of New York System. Institutionally accredited by regional association. Small town location, 690-acre campus. Total enrollment: 7600. Undergraduate enrollment: 6800. Total faculty: 390. Semester calendar. Grading system: letters or numbers.

Communication Studies, Sheldon Hall, Oswego, NY 13126 315-341-2357

CONTACT Lewis B O'Donnell, Chairperson, or Frank J Messere, Area Coordinator
DEGREE OFFERED BA in communication studies/broadcasting
PROGRAM MAJORS Television — 200 students
ADMISSION Requirements — 2.5 minimum grade point average, interview Application deadline — 3/15
FINANCIAL AID Work/study programs, New York TAP
CURRICULAR EMPHASIS Television study — history, production, management treated equally Television production — commercial, news/documentary, experimental/personal video, educational, EFP treated equally
SPECIAL ACTIVITIES/OFFERINGS Program material produced for on-campus closed-circuit television and cable television, apprenticeships, internships in television production, independent study, semester study in London, practicum
FACILITIES AND EQUIPMENT Film — 16mm cameras, editing equipment, lighting, black and white film stock, projectors Television — black and white studio cameras, ½-inch VTR, 1-inch VTR, ¾-inch cassette VTR, editing equipment, monitors, special effects generators, slide chain, portable color cameras, ¾-inch ENG, lighting equipment, sound recording equipment, audio mixers, film chain, time base corrector, microwave, black and white studio, color studio, audio studio, control room, graphics and television film laboratory
FACULTY William Lyon, Frank Messere, Lewis B O'Donnell, Cristina Pieraccini PART-TIME FACULTY Vincent Doody, David Nellis, Lewis C Popham, Margaret Rockefeller, William Shigley

COURSE LIST
Undergraduate
Introduction to Mass Media
Introduction to Broadcasting
Social History of American Radio and TV
Broadcast Performance
Radio Production
Broadcast Journalism
Television Production
Broadcast Regulation and Control
Programs, Programming, and Effects
Broadcast Newswriting
Comparative Studies in World Broadcasting
Broadcasting in the United Kingdom
Overseas Program in International Broadcasting: Director's Seminar
Seminar in Cable Television
Broadcast Sales
Seminar in Broadcast Management
Advanced Television Production
Seminar in Broadcasting
Advanced Television Directing
Practicum in Broadcast Journalism
Broadcasting Internship
Radio Internship
Independent Study

State University of New York College at Plattsburgh

State-supported comprehensive coed institution. Part of State University of New York System. Institutionally accredited by regional association. Small town location, 150-acre campus. Total enrollment: 6022. Undergraduate enrollment: 5595. Total faculty: 332 (290 full-time, 42 part-time). Semester calendar. Grading system: letters or numbers.

Communication Department, Plattsburgh, NY 12901 518-564-2285

CONTACT A R Montanaro Jr or Phillip Reines
DEGREE OFFERED BA in communication with a study option in mass media
DEPARTMENTAL MAJORS Television — 100 students
ADMISSION Requirements — 85% minimum grade average, ACT or SAT scores Application deadline — 5/1
FINANCIAL AID Scholarships, work/study programs, student loans Application deadline — 1/15
CURRICULAR EMPHASIS Film study — criticism and aesthetics, appreciation treated equally Television study — criticism and aesthetics, appreciation, educational, production treated equally Television production — news/documentary
SPECIAL ACTIVITIES/OFFERINGS Film series; program material produced for on-campus closed-circuit television, cable television, local public television station, local commercial television station; internships in television production; independent study
FACILITIES AND EQUIPMENT Film — 8mm and 16mm cameras, editing equipment, sound recording equipment, lighting, projectors, sound stage, screening room, editing room, sound mixing room, permanent film library of commercial or professional films Television — complete color studio and exterior production equipment, color studios, audio studio, control room
FACULTY Ralph Donald, Herbert McCoy, Phillip Reines, Frank Sorrell

State University of New York College at Plattsburgh (continued)

COURSE LIST

Undergraduate

Introduction to Film Art
American Cinema
Advanced Filmmaking
TV Production I, II
Nonstudio TV
Experimental TV
Internship: TV Production and Engineering
Internship: Industrial TV
Directing/Producing TV News

State University of New York College at Purchase

State-supported 4-year coed college. Part of State University of New York System. Institutionally accredited by regional association. Suburban location. Undergraduate enrollment: 1950. Total faculty: 189 (150 full-time, 39 part-time). Semester calendar. Grading system: pass/fail.

Film Program, Lincoln Avenue, Purchase, NY 10577

CONTACT Richard P Rogers
DEGREE OFFERED BFA in film production
PROGRAM MAJORS — 60 students
ADMISSION Requirements — interviews, teachers' recommendations, portfolio, written statement of purpose
FINANCIAL AID Scholarships, student loans, work/study programs Application deadline — 3/15, rolling
CURRICULAR EMPHASIS Film study — (1) production; (2) criticism and aesthetics; (3) history Filmmaking — documentary, narrative, experimental treated equally
SPECIAL ACTIVITIES/OFFERINGS Film series, film societies, independent study
FACILITIES AND EQUIPMENT Film — complete 8mm and 16mm equipment, screening room, editing room, sound mixing room, animation board, permanent film library
FACULTY Miriam Arsham, Tom Gunning, Guy Jaconelli, Richard Rogers, Joseph Stockdale PART-TIME FACULTY Howard Enders, Wheaton Galentine, Dezo Magyar, Joan Potter, Jon Rubin, Willard Van Dyke

COURSE LIST

Undergraduate

Film Workshop
Photography for Filmmakers
Introduction to Film Study
History of the Nonfiction Film
Introduction to Documentary Filmmaking
Film Editing
Technical Studio
Sound on Film
Directors' Scene Workshop
Japanese Cinema
The Film Noir
The American Avant-Garde Film
The French New Wave
The Films of Alfred Hitchcock
Cinematic Expression
Film Directors' Workshop
Documentary Workshop
Experimental Workshop
The Narrative Film
The Western: From Stage Coach to Clint Eastwood
Writing for Film
Senior Production: Filmmaking
Readings in Film Theory
Problems in Film Theory

Syracuse University

Independent coed university. Institutionally accredited by regional association, programs recognized by NASM, NASA. Urban location. Total enrollment: 15,314. Undergraduate enrollment: 11,044. Total faculty: 1233 (819 full-time, 414 part-time). Semester calendar. Grading system: letters or numbers.

College of Visual and Performing Arts, Syracuse, NY 13210 315-423-2214

CONTACT Chairperson
DEGREES OFFERED BFA, MFA in film drama; BFA, MFA in film art
ADMISSION Requirements — interviews, professional recommendations, teachers' recommendations, portfolio Undergraduate application deadline — 2/1
FINANCIAL AID Scholarships, student loans, work/study programs, teaching assistantships, research assistantships, fellowships Undergraduate application deadline — 3/1
CURRICULAR EMPHASIS Film study — history, criticism and aesthetics, production treated equally Filmmaking — (1) narrative, experimental; (2) animated; (3) documentary
SPECIAL ACTIVITIES/OFFERINGS Filmmaking clubs, film series, film festivals, internships in film production, independent study, practicum, summer program in Europe
FACILITIES AND EQUIPMENT Film — complete 8mm and 16mm equipment, sound stage, screening room, editing room, sound mixing room, animation board, permanent film library

Television-Radio-Film Department, School of Public Communications, 215 University Place 315-423-4004

CONTACT Chairperson
DEGREES OFFERED BS in film, BS in television-radio, BS in broadcast journalism, MS in television
ADMISSION Undergraduate requirements — teachers' recommendations, written statement of purpose Graduate requirements — GRE scores, teachers' recommendations, written statement of purpose Undergraduate application deadline — 2/1
FINANCIAL AID Scholarships, teaching assistantships, research assistantships, fellowships Undergraduate application deadline — 3/1
CURRICULAR EMPHASIS Film study — (1) production; (2) history; (3) criticism and aesthetics Undergraduate filmmaking — (1) experimental; (2) narrative; (3) animated Graduate filmmaking — (1) experimental; (2) documentary; (3) animated Television study — (1) production; (2) history; (3) management Television production — (1) commercial; (2) news/documentary; (3) experimental/personal video
SPECIAL ACTIVITIES/OFFERINGS Independent study, vocational placement service
FACILITIES AND EQUIPMENT Film — complete 16mm equipment, screening room, editing room, sound mixing room, animation board, permanent film library Television — complete color studio and exterior production equipment, color studio, remote truck, audio studio, control room

Tompkins-Cortland Community College

State-supported 2-year coed college. Part of State University of New York System, automatic transfer to main campus for baccalaureate. Institutionally accredited by regional association. Rural location. Undergraduate enrollment: 3200. Total faculty: 48 full-time. Semester calendar. Grading system: letters or numbers.

Department of LRC Radio and Television, North Street, Dryden, NY 13053 607-844-8211

CONTACT Brooks Sanders
DEGREE OFFERED AAS in radio-TV broadcasting
DEPARTMENTAL MAJORS Television — 60 students
FINANCIAL AID Work/study programs, TAP, BEOG
CURRICULAR EMPHASIS Film study — (1) criticism and aesthetics; (2) appreciation; (3) history Television study — (1) production; (2) management; (3) history Television production — (1) commercial; (2) news/documentary; (3) experimental/personal video
SPECIAL ACTIVITIES/OFFERINGS Film festivals, program material produced for on-campus closed-circuit television and cable television, independent study
FACILITIES AND EQUIPMENT Film — 8mm cameras, editing equipment, lighting, black and white film stock, color film stock, projectors Television — black and white studio cameras, color studio cameras, ½-inch VTR, ¾-inch cassette VTR, portable black and white cameras, editing equipment, monitors, special effects generators, slide chain, ½-inch portapak recorders, lighting equipment, sound recording equipment, audio mixers, film chain, color studio, audio studio, control room
FACULTY Al Grunwell, Henry Linhart, Brooks Sanders

COURSE LIST
Undergraduate
Broadcast Rules and Regulations
TV Production and Direction
Radio Production
Broadcast Journalism
Announcing
Special Topics in Television and Radio
Fieldwork in Television and Radio
Independent Studies in Broadcasting
Mass Media
History and Appreciation of Film

Ulster County Community College

State and locally supported 2-year coed college. Part of State University of New York System. Institutionally accredited by regional association. Rural location, 185-acre campus. Undergraduate enrollment: 2003. Total faculty: 149 (86 full-time, 63 part-time). 4-1-4 calendar. Grading system: letters or numbers.

Communications Media/Speech and Theatre Department, Vanderlyn Hall, Stone Ridge, NY 12484 914-687-7621

CONTACT Film — Jack Lawson Television — Lawrence Borzumato
DEGREE OFFERED AS in communications and media arts/broadcasting and journalism
ADMISSION Application deadline — rolling
FINANCIAL AID Scholarships, student loans, work/study programs Application deadline — 6/15
CURRICULAR EMPHASIS Film study — (1) criticism and aesthetics; (2) appreciation; (3) educational media/instructional technology Television study — (1) performance; (2) management; (3) educational Television production — (1) news/documentary; (2) educational; (3) commercial
SPECIAL ACTIVITIES/OFFERINGS Program material produced for on-campus closed-circuit television, independent study
FACILITIES AND EQUIPMENT Television — black and white studio cameras, ½-inch VTR, 1-inch VTR, 2-inch VTR, ¾-inch cassette VTR, portable color cameras, lighting equipment, sound recording equipment, film chain, color studio, audio studio, control room
FACULTY Jack Lawson PART-TIME FACULTY Lawrence Borzumato

COURSE LIST
Undergraduate
Introduction to Broadcasting
Broadcast Media Arts
Art of the Film

University of Rochester

Independent coed university. Institutionally accredited by regional association, programs recognized by NASM, AACSB. Suburban location, 500-acre campus. Total enrollment: 6780. Undergraduate enrollment: 4380. Total faculty: 1957 (1698 full-time, 259 part-time). 4-4 calendar. Grading system: letters or numbers.

Film Studies Program, Rush Rhees Library, River Station, Rochester, NY 14627

CONTACT Richard M Gollin
DEGREES OFFERED BA in film, PhD in English or other departments with a dissertation in film
PROGRAM MAJORS Undergraduate — 20 students Graduate — 3 students
ADMISSION Undergraduate requirements — 2.0 minimum grade point average, SAT scores, interviews, teachers' recommendations, written statement of purpose Graduate requirements — 2.0 minimum grade point average, interviews, teachers' recommendations, written statement of purpose Undergraduate application deadline — 1/15
FINANCIAL AID Work/study programs, fellowships Undergraduate application deadline — 1/15
CURRICULAR EMPHASIS Film study — (1) criticism and aesthetics; (2) history; (3) appreciation Filmmaking — (1) experimental; (2) documentary
SPECIAL ACTIVITIES/OFFERINGS Filmmaking clubs, film series, film societies, apprenticeships in archival preservation, independent study, film archive study at nearby George Eastman House

University of Rochester (continued)

FACILITIES AND EQUIPMENT Film — complete 8mm equipment, film studies center, screening room, editing room, permanent film library, 16mm facilities available through Rochester Institute of Technology Television — facilities available through Rochester Institute of Technology

FACULTY Philip Berk, Richard M Gollin, George Grella, William Hauser, John Mueller, John Waters PART-TIME FACULTY Carl Battaglia, James Card, Marshall Deutelbaum, John Kuiper

COURSE LIST

Undergraduate

History, Aesthetics of Silent Film
History, Aesthetics of Sound Film
Film Narrative
French Film
Film Comedy
Introduction to Filmmaking
Dance on Film
International Relations: Film
Film as Propaganda

Undergraduate and Graduate

Master Film Artists
Japanese Film
Film Criticism
Russian Film
Special Topics in Film
Avant-Garde Film
Popular Film Genres
Religion in Film

Utica College of Syracuse University

Independent 4-year coed college. Administratively affiliated with Syracuse University. Institutionally accredited by regional association. Suburban location. Undergraduate enrollment: 1360. Total faculty: 93 (93 full-time). Semester calendar. Grading system: letters or numbers.

Division of Humanities, Burrstone Road, Utica, NY 13502 315-792-3156

CONTACT Scott MacDonald
PROGRAM OFFERED Minor in film
CURRICULAR EMPHASIS Undergraduate film study — (1) appreciation; (2) history; (3) criticism and aesthetics
SPECIAL ACTIVITIES/OFFERINGS Film series, independent study
FACILITIES AND EQUIPMENT Film — 8mm cameras Television — ½-inch VTR, ¾-inch cassette VTR, portable black and white cameras
FACULTY Scott MacDonald

COURSE LIST

Undergraduate

Introduction to Film Appreciation
Film as a Subversive Art
History of Film Comedy
History of the Horror Film
Great Directors
Images of Blacks and Whites in Film and Literature
History of Independent Film

Vassar College

Independent comprehensive coed institution. Institutionally accredited by regional association. Suburban location, 1000-acre campus. Total enrollment: 2279. Undergraduate enrollment: 2276. Total faculty: 228 (186 full-time, 42 part-time). Semester calendar. Grading system: letters or numbers.

Drama Department, Poughkeepsie, NY 12601 914-452-7000

CONTACT James B Steerman
DEGREE OFFERED BA in film/drama
ADMISSION Requirements — SAT scores, interviews, teachers' recommendations, written statement of purpose Application deadline — 2/1
FINANCIAL AID Scholarships, student loans, work/study programs Application deadline — 2/1
CURRICULAR EMPHASIS Film study — (1) production; (2) criticism and aesthetics; (3) history Filmmaking — (1) experimental; (2) narrative; (3) documentary
SPECIAL ACTIVITIES/OFFERINGS Film series, film societies, independent study
FACILITIES AND EQUIPMENT Film — complete 8mm and 16mm equipment, screening room, editing room, sound mixing room, permanent film library
FACULTY James B Steerman PART-TIME FACULTY Ken Ross

COURSE LIST

Undergraduate

Film History/Theory I, II
Filmmaking I, II
Advanced Film Production
Advanced Film Theory
New American Cinema
Playwriting/Screenwriting
Independent Film Study
Problems in Directing

Yeshiva College

Independent 4-year men's college coordinate with Stern College for Women. Administratively affiliated with Yeshiva University. Institutionally accredited by regional association. Urban location. Undergraduate enrollment: 859. Total faculty: 347 (193 full-time, 154 part-time). Semester calendar. Grading system: letters or numbers.

Speech and Drama Department, 500 West 185th Street, New York, NY 10033 212-568-8400

CONTACT Laurel Keating
PROGRAM OFFERED Major in speech with emphasis in film
ADMISSION Requirement — minimum grade point average Application deadline — 4/15, rolling
FINANCIAL AID Work/study programs Application deadline — 4/15, rolling
CURRICULAR EMPHASIS Film study — (1) appreciation; (2) production; (3) criticism and aesthetics; (4) history Filmmaking — (1) narrative; (2) documentary; (3) animated; (4) experimental Television — (1) legal aspects; (2) history

SPECIAL ACTIVITIES/OFFERINGS Independent study
FACILITIES AND EQUIPMENT Film — complete 8mm equipment
FACULTY Laurel Keating

COURSE LIST

Undergraduate
Techniques of Film Production I, II
Film Criticism
Broadcasting

NORTH CAROLINA

Appalachian State University

State-supported comprehensive coed institution. Part of The University of North Carolina System. Institutionally accredited by regional association, programs recognized by NASM, AACSB. Small town location, 255-acre campus. Total enrollment: 8966. Undergraduate enrollment: 8026. Semester calendar. Grading system: letters or numbers.

Communication Arts Department, Boone, NC 28608 704-262-2221

CONTACT Jon Currie
DEGREE OFFERED BS in broadcasting with a major in television
DEPARTMENTAL MAJORS 80 students
ADMISSION Requirements — 2.3 minimum grade point average, interviews Application deadline — rolling
FINANCIAL AID Scholarships, student loans, work/study programs Application deadline — 3/15
CURRICULAR EMPHASIS Television study — (1) production; (2) history; (3) educational Television production — (1) educational; (2) news/documentary; (3) experimental/personal video
SPECIAL ACTIVITIES/OFFERINGS Program material produced for cable television, internships in television production, independent study, teacher training, vocational placement service
FACILITIES AND EQUIPMENT Television — complete black and white studio and exterior production equipment, complete color studio production equipment, black and white studio, color studio, audio studio, control room
FACULTY Jon Currie

COURSE LIST

Undergraduate
History and Development of Broadcasting
Broadcasting in Public Interest
Television Production
Writing for Radio and Television
Broadcast Mangement
Selected Topics

Bennett College

Independent United Methodist 4-year women's college. Institutionally accredited by regional association. Urban location, 125-acre campus. Undergraduate enrollment: 637. Semester calendar. Grading system: letters or numbers.

Interdisciplinary Studies Program, Greensboro, NC 27420 919-273-4431

CONTACT Anthony Fragola or Denise Troutman
DEGREE OFFERED BAS in interdisciplinary studies with emphasis in communications media and public relations
ADMISSION Requirement — minimum grade point average
FINANCIAL AID Scholarships, student loans, work/study programs, Basic Educational Opportunity grants, teaching assistantships, research assistantships, fellowships
CURRICULAR EMPHASIS Film study — (1) production; (2) criticism and aesthetics; (3) appreciation Filmmaking — (1) experimental; (2) documentary; (3) narrative Television study — (1) production; (2) management; (3) criticism and aesthetics Television production — (1) experimental/personal video; (2) educational
SPECIAL ACTIVITIES/OFFERINGS Student publications, apprenticeships, internships in film and television production, independent study, practicum
FACILITIES AND EQUIPMENT Film — complete 8mm equipment, editing room, permanent film library Television — complete black and white studio facilities available through North Carolina Agricultural and Technical State University
FACULTY LeAnder Canady, Elliott Moffitt

COURSE LIST

Undergraduate
Filmmaking
Radio/Television Production

Davidson College

Independent Presbyterian 4-year coed college. Institutionally accredited by regional association. Small town location, 464-acre campus. Undergraduate enrollment: 1352. Total faculty: 102 (95 full-time, 7 part-time). 3 equal term calendar. Grading system: letters or numbers.

Theatre Department, Davidson, NC 28036 704-892-2000

CONTACT J T Gardner
CURRICULAR EMPHASIS Film study — appreciation
SPECIAL ACTIVITIES/OFFERINGS Film series
FACULTY Joseph Gardner

Davidson College (continued)

COURSE LIST

Undergraduate

History and Art of the American Film

Duke University

Independent coed university affiliated with United Methodist Church. Institutionally accredited by regional association. Suburban location. Total enrollment: 9100. Undergraduate enrollment: 5700. Total faculty: 1256. Semester calendar. Grading system: letters or numbers.

Comparative Literature Program, Romance Languages Department, 301 Languages Building, Durham, NC 27706 919-684-3706

CONTACT Inez Hedges
ADMISSION Application deadline — 2/1
FACULTY Inez Hedges

COURSE LIST

Undergraduate

The French Film
Film and the French Novel
Urban Myths: Literature and Film
Psychoanalysis, Literature and Film

Durham Technical Institute

State-supported 2-year coed college. Part of North Carolina Community College System. Institutionally accredited by regional association, programs recognized by AOA. Urban location. Undergraduate enrollment: 2800. Total faculty: 120 (80 full-time, 40 part-time). Quarter calendar. Grading system: letters or numbers.

Communications Technology Department, 1637 Lawson Street, Durham, NC 27703 919-596-9311

CONTACT Mark Weinkle
DEGREE OFFERED AAS in general media
DEPARTMENTAL MAJORS Film — 15 students Television — 15 students
ADMISSION Requirement — high school diploma or equivalent
FINANCIAL AID Work/study programs, student loans, BEOG
CURRICULAR EMPHASIS Film study — history, criticism and aesthetics, appreciation, educational media/instructional technology treated equally Filmmaking — documentary, educational treated equally Television study — educational Television production — news/documentary, educational treated equally
SPECIAL ACTIVITIES/OFFERINGS Program material produced for on-campus closed-circuit television and cable television, internships in television production, special project
FACILITIES AND EQUIPMENT Film — 8mm cameras, lighting, black and white film stock, projectors, 16mm cameras, editing equipment, sound recording equipment, lighting, black and white film stock, projectors, screening room, editing room, sound mixing room, permanent film library of commercial or professional films Television — black and white studio cameras, color studio cameras, ½-inch VTR, ¾-inch cassette VTR, portable black and white cameras, editing equipment, monitors, special effects generators, slide chain, portable color cameras, ½-inch portapak recorders, ¾-inch ENG, lighting equipment, sound recording equipment, audio mixers, film chain, time base corrector, black and white studio, color studio, mobile van/unit, remote truck, control room
PART-TIME FACULTY John Freeman, Douglas Herbert, James Roberts, Mark Weinkle

COURSE LIST

Undergraduate

Filmmaking
Introduction to TV Production
AV Production I–IV
Visual Communications

Fayetteville State University

State-supported 4-year coed college. Part of University of North Carolina System. Institutionally accredited by regional association. Urban location, 145-acre campus. Undergraduate enrollment: 2125. Total faculty: 154 (141 full-time, 13 part-time). Semester calendar. Grading system: letters or numbers.

English and Communications Department, 1200 Murchison Road, Fayetteville, NC 28301 919-486-1381

FINANCIAL AID Work/study programs, student loans
CURRICULAR EMPHASIS Undergraduate television study — production Undergraduate television production — educational
SPECIAL ACTIVITIES/OFFERINGS Program material produced for on-campus closed-circuit television, internships in television production, teacher training
FACILITIES AND EQUIPMENT Television — complete black and white and color studio production equipment, black and white studio, color studio, control room

Louisburg College

Independent United Methodist 2-year coed college. Institutionally accredited by regional association. Small town location, 75-acre campus. Undergraduate enrollment: 672. Total faculty: 45 (31 full-time, 14 part-time). Semester calendar. Grading system: letters or numbers.

English Department, Louisburg, NC 27549 919-496-2521

CONTACT Umphrey Lee, Chairman
ADMISSION Application deadline — rolling

North Carolina Agricultural and Technical State University

State-supported comprehensive coed institution. Part of University of North Carolina System. Institutionally accredited by regional association. Small town location, 181-acre campus. Total enrollment: 5385. Undergraduate enrollment: 4632. Total faculty: 362 (347 full-time, 15 part-time). Semester calendar. Grading system: letters or numbers.

Speech Communication and Theatre Arts Department, 312 North Dudley Street, Greensboro, NC 27411 919-379-7900

CONTACT Richard Edwards
DEGREE OFFERED BA in speech communication and theatre arts with a concentration in television
DEPARTMENTAL MAJORS Undergraduate television — 105 students
ADMISSION Undergraduate requirements — interview, teachers' recommendations, written statement of purpose
FINANCIAL AID Scholarships, work/study programs, student loans
CURRICULAR EMPHASIS Undergraduate television study — production, management treated equally Undergraduate television production — commercial, news/documentary, educational treated equally
SPECIAL ACTIVITIES/OFFERINGS Program material produced for on-campus closed-circuit television, internships in television production
FACILITIES AND EQUIPMENT Film — 35mm cameras Television — color studio production facilities, color studio cameras, ½-inch VTR, ¾-inch cassette VTR, portable black and white cameras, monitors, special effects generators, slide chain, lighting equipment, sound recording equipment, audio mixers, film chain, color studio, audio studio, control room
FACULTY Richard Edwards, Gary Flanigan, Ernest Parhboo

COURSE LIST

Undergraduate
Television Production I, II
Writing and Announcing for Radio and Television
Minorities in Mass Media
Media Internship
History and Law of Mass Communication
Broadcast Management
Cable Television Seminar
Current Issues in Mass Communication
Introduction to Communication Theory
Newswriting
Advanced Newswriting

North Carolina Central University

State-related comprehensive coed institution. Part of University of North Carolina system. Institutionally accredited by regional association. Urban location, 109-acre campus. Total enrollment: 4810. Undergraduate enrollment: 3922. Total faculty: 423 (327 full-time, 96 part-time). Semester calendar. Grading system: letters or numbers.

Educational Technology Department, Fayetteville Street, Durham, NC 27707 919-683-6218

CONTACT Marvin E Duncan
DEGREE OFFERED MA in Educational Technology
FINANCIAL AID Work/study programs, teaching assistantships
SPECIAL ACTIVITIES/OFFERINGS Program material produced for on-campus closed-circuit television, independent study
FACILITIES AND EQUIPMENT Film — complete 8mm and 16mm equipment, screening room, editing room, sound mixing room, permanent film library of commercial or professional films Television — complete black and white and color studio production equipment, black and white studio, control room
FACULTY Marvin E Duncan, James E Parker

COURSE LIST

Undergraduate and Graduate
Introduction to Filming
Radio and Television in Education

North Carolina State University at Raleigh

State-supported coed university. Part of University of North Carolina System. Institutionally accredited by regional association. Suburban location, 600-acre campus. Total enrollment: 18,476. Undergraduate enrollment: 14,637. Total faculty: 1352 (1235 full-time, 117 part-time). Semester calendar. Grading system: letters or numbers.

Department of Speech-Communication, Box 5110, Raleigh, NC 27650 919-737-2450

CONTACT Film — James Alchediak Television — Edward Funkhouser, Robert Schrag
DEGREE OFFERED BA in speech-communication with an emphasis in television and film
DEPARTMENTAL MAJORS Television — 150 students
ADMISSION Requirement — ACT or SAT scores Application deadline — rolling
FINANCIAL AID Scholarships, work/study programs, student loans
CURRICULAR EMPHASIS Film study — (1) history; (2) criticism and aesthetics Filmmaking — (1) narrative; (2) experimental; (3) documentary Television study — history, educational, production, management, social effects, regulation treated equally Television production — commercial, experimental/personal video, narrative treated equally
SPECIAL ACTIVITIES/OFFERINGS Film series; student publications; program material produced for cable television, local public television station, local commercial television station; internships in television production; independent study; vocational placement service; co-op programs with TV stations

North Carolina State University at Raleigh (continued)

FACILITIES AND EQUIPMENT 8mm cameras, editing equipment, sound recording equipment, lighting, projectors, editing room Television — black and white studio cameras, color studio cameras, ¾-inch cassette VTR, editing equipment, monitors, special effects generators, slide chain, portable color cameras, ¾-inch ENG, lighting equipment, sound recording equipment, audio mixers, film chain, time base corrector, black and white studio, color studio, mobile van/unit, audio studio, control room

FACULTY James Alchediak, Edward Funkhouser, Robert Schrag

COURSE LIST

Undergraduate

Introduction to Radio Production
Introduction to TV Production
Survey of Broadcasting
Introduction to Film Production
Portable Video Production
Advanced Radio Production
Advanced TV Production
Writing for the Electronic Media
Advanced Studies in Telecommunications
A Short History of the Cinema

St Andrews Presbyterian College

Independent Presbyterian 4-year coed college. Institutionally accredited by regional association. Small town location. Undergraduate enrollment: 601. Total faculty: 60 (52 full-time, 8 part-time). 4-1-4 calendar. Grading system: letters or numbers.

Theatre Department, Laurinburg, NC 28352 919-276-3652

CONTACT Arthur McDonald
DEGREE OFFERED BA with major in theater
ADMISSION Requirements — 2.0 minimum grade point average, ACT or SAT scores, teachers' recommendations, written statement of purpose
FINANCIAL AID Scholarships, work/study programs, student loans
CURRICULAR EMPHASIS Film study — history, criticism and aesthetics, appreciation treated equally Filmmaking — narrative, experimental, animated treated equally
SPECIAL ACTIVITIES/OFFERINGS Film series, film festivals, independent study
FACILITIES AND EQUIPMENT Film — 8mm cameras, editing equipment, sound recording equipment, lighting, projectors, 16mm editing equipment, lighting, projectors Television — ½-inch VTR, ¾-inch cassette VTR, portable black and white cameras, monitors, ½-inch portapak recorders, lighting equipment, sound recording equipment, black and white studio

COURSE LIST

Undergraduate

Filmmaking
History of the Motion Picture

University of North Carolina at Chapel Hill

State-supported coed university. Part of University of North Carolina System. Institutionally accredited by regional association, programs recognized by NASM, AACSB, NASA. Small town location, 474-acre campus. Total enrollment: 20,294. Undergraduate enrollment: 14,025. Total faculty: 1745 (1745 full-time). Semester calendar. Grading system: letters or numbers.

Department of Radio, Television, and Motion Pictures, College of Arts and Sciences, Swain Hall 044A, Chapel Hill, NC 27514 919-933-2313

CONTACT Chairperson
DEGREES OFFERED BA in radio, television, and motion pictures; MA in communications
ADMISSION Requirement — admission to the University Undergraduate application deadline — 2/1, rolling
FINANCIAL AID Student loans, work/study programs, graduate assistantships, research assistantships, fellowships Undergraduate application deadline — 2/1
CURRICULAR EMPHASIS Film study — (1) history; (2) criticism and aesthetics; (3) production Filmmaking — (1) narrative; (2) documentary; (3) experimental Television study — (1) production; (2) management; (3) criticism and aesthetics; (4) history; (5) educational Television production — (1) commercial; (2) news/documentary; (3) educational
SPECIAL ACTIVITIES/OFFERINGS Film series, film festivals, program material produced for local public television station
FACILITIES AND EQUIPMENT Film — complete 16mm equipment, sound stage, screening room, editing room, sound mixing room, permanent film library, scene shop, graphics shop Television — complete black and white studio production equipment, black and white studio, audio studio, control room

University of North Carolina at Charlotte

State-supported comprehensive coed institution. Part of University of North Carolina System. Institutionally accredited by regional association, programs recognized by ECPD. Urban location, 1000-acre campus. Total enrollment: 8705. Undergraduate enrollment: 7437. Total faculty: 606 (413 full-time, 193 part-time). Semester calendar. Grading system: letters or numbers.

English Department, Charlotte, NC 28223 704-597-2296

CONTACT Byron Petrakis
ADMISSION Application deadline — 7/1, rolling
FACULTY Byron Petrakis

COURSE LIST

Undergraduate

Film Criticism

University of North Carolina at Greensboro

State-supported coed university. Part of University of North Carolina System. Institutionally accredited by regional association, programs recognized by NASM. Urban location, 141-acre campus. Total enrollment: 9684. Undergraduate enrollment: 7082. Total faculty: 637 (551 full-time, 86 part-time). Semester calendar. Grading system: letters or numbers.

Broadcasting/Cinema Division, 201 Taylor Building, UNC-G, Greensboro, NC 27412 919-379-5576

CONTACT John Lee Jellicorse
DEGREES OFFERED BA, MA in communications and theatre with emphasis in broadcasting/cinema
PROGRAM MAJORS Undergraduate film — 80 students Undergraduate television — 120 students Graduate film — 5 students Graduate television — 10 students
ADMISSION Undergraduate requirement — ACT or SAT scores Graduate requirement — GRE scores, teachers' recommendations, written statement of purpose, professional work experience, production credits, professional recommendations Undergraduate application deadline — rolling
FINANCIAL AID Scholarships, work/study programs, student loans, teaching assistantships, research assistantships Undergraduate application deadline — rolling
CURRICULAR EMPHASIS Emphasizes history, theory, and production work in both broadcasting and cinema; students who desire may also integrate some work in acting, directing, design, speech communication, or organizational communication
SPECIAL ACTIVITIES/OFFERINGS Film series, film festivals, film societies, student publications, program material produced for on-campus closed-circuit television and local public television station, apprenticeships, internships in film production, internships in television production, independent study, teacher training
FACILITIES AND EQUIPMENT Film — 8mm and 16mm cameras, editing equipment, sound recording equipment, lighting, projectors, sound stage, screening room, 35mm screening facilities, editing room, sound mixing room, animation board, permanent film library of commercial or professional films Television — black and white studio cameras, ½-inch VTR, 1-inch VTR, ¾-inch cassette VTR, portable black and white cameras, editing equipment, monitors, slide chain, portable color cameras, ½-inch portapak recorders, lighting equipment, sound recording equipment, audio mixers, film chain, time base corrector, black and white studio, audio studio, control room
FACULTY David Batcheller, Tony Fragola, Ethel Glenn, John Lee Jellicorse, Robert Mandigo, Elliott Pood, Tom Tedford PART-TIME FACULTY Emil W Young Jr

COURSE LIST

Undergraduate
Communication in Society
Speech Performance: Broadcasting
Radio-TV-Cinema Laboratory
The Development of the Cinema
The Development of Broadcasting
Writing for Cinema
Basic Broadcast Electronics
Special Problems: Broadcasting
Special Problems: Cinema
Communication Theory
Film Music
News and Documentary in Broadcasting and Cinema
Science Fiction in Broadcasting and Cinema
Television Production
Radio-Television News Production
Motion Picture Production
Radio-TV-Film Production Workshop
Internship in Broadcasting
Internship in Cinema
Internship in Public Relations

Graduate
Introduction to Graduate Studies
Seminar in Broadcasting
Seminar in Film
Advanced Communication Theory
Independent Study: Broadcasting
Independent Study: Film
Advanced Experimentation: Broadcasting
Advanced Experimentation: Film
Thesis

Undergraduate and Graduate
Advanced Motion Picture Production
TV and Film Lighting
The Auteur Director
Studies in Film Genre
Film Animation
Freedom of Speech and Censorship
Directing for Television
Advanced Broadcast Production
Experimentation: Broadcasting
Experimentation: Cinema

Wake Forest University

Independent Baptist coed university. Institutionally accredited by regional association. Suburban location, 320-acre campus. Total enrollment: 4500. Undergraduate enrollment: 3055. Total faculty: 237 (208 full-time, 29 part-time). Semester calendar. Grading system: letters or numbers.

Speech, Communication and Theatre Arts Department, PO Box 7347, Winston-Salem, NC 27109 919-761-5406

CONTACT Julian C Burroughs Jr
DEGREE OFFERED BA in radio-TV-film
DEPARTMENTAL MAJORS Film — 10 students Television — 10 students
ADMISSION Requirements — ACT or SAT scores, admission to Wake Forest University Undergraduate application deadline — late fall
FINANCIAL AID Scholarships, work/study programs, student loans, student assistantships Undergraduate application deadline — late fall
CURRICULAR EMPHASIS Film study — (1) criticism and aesthetics; (2) history; (3) TV-film production Filmmaking — (1) narrative; (2) documentary; (3) educational; (4) animated; (5) experimental Television study — (1) criticism and aesthetics; (2) history; (3) educational, production treated equally Television production — (1) news/documentary; (2) commercial; (3) educational
SPECIAL ACTIVITIES/OFFERINGS Film series, student publications, program material produced for on-campus closed-circuit television and local commercial television station, internships in film production, internships in television production, independent study, vocational placement service

Wake Forest University (continued)

FACILITIES AND EQUIPMENT Film — complete 16mm equipment, 8mm cameras, editing equipment, sound recording equipment, lighting, color film stock, projectors, complete single system and double system in Super 8, screening room, editing room, sound mixing room, animation board, permanent film library of student films, permanent film library of commercial or professional films Television — black and white studio cameras, color studio cameras (through local TV station), 2-inch VTR, ¾-inch cassette VTR, monitors, special effects generators, lighting equipment, sound recording equipment, audio mixers, black and white studio, color studio (local TV station), audio studio, control room

FACULTY Julian C Burroughs Jr

COURSE LIST

Undergraduate

Film Practicum I, II
TV Practicum I, II
Film Production
TV Production
Introduction to Film
Film Criticism
Introduction to Broadcasting
Seminar in Radio-TV
Special Seminar and Honors

Warren Wilson College

Independent 4-year coed college. Institutionally accredited by regional association. Rural location, 1070-acre campus. Undergraduate enrollment: 527. Total faculty: 75 (45 full-time, 30 part-time). Modular calendar. Grading system: letters or numbers.

English Department, Swannanoa, NC 28778 704-298-3325

CONTACT Jack Boozer

ADMISSION Application deadline — 5/1, rolling

CURRICULAR EMPHASIS Film study — history/criticism, production treated equally Filmmaking — depends upon current student interest

SPECIAL ACTIVITIES/OFFERINGS Film series, film festivals, independent study

FACILITIES AND EQUIPMENT Film — complete Super-8mm equipment, screening room, animation board Television — black and white studio cameras, ½-inch VTR, ¾-inch cassette VTR, portable black and white cameras, ½-inch portapak recorder

FACULTY Jack Boozer

COURSE LIST

Undergraduate

Super-8 Filmmaking Workshop
Film Appreciation: History and Criticism

Western Carolina University

State-supported comprehensive coed institution. Part of University of North Carolina System. Institutionally accredited by regional association. Rural location, 600-acre campus. Total enrollment: 6205. Undergraduate enrollment: 5368. Total faculty: 349 (311 full-time, 38 part-time). Semester calendar. Grading system: letters or numbers.

Speech and Theatre Arts Department, Cullowhee, NC 28723 704-227-7491

CONTACT Donald L Loeffler

DEGREES OFFERED BA, BS in radio/TV

DEPARTMENTAL MAJORS Television — 50 students

ADMISSION Requirements — 2.0 minimum grade point average, ACT or SAT scores, teachers' recommendations

FINANCIAL AID Work/study programs, student loans, internships, cooperative education

CURRICULAR EMPHASIS Film study — history, appreciation, educational media/instructional technology treated equally Filmmaking — educational Television study — (1) production; (2) history; (3) educational Television production — (1) educational; (2) experimental/personal video; (3) news/documentary

SPECIAL ACTIVITIES/OFFERINGS Program material produced for on-campus closed-circuit television, internships in film production, internships in television production, teacher training

FACILITIES AND EQUIPMENT 8mm cameras, editing equipment, color film stock, projectors, editing room Television — complete color studio production equipment, color studio, control room

FACULTY John A Davlin, Jay Mesbahee

COURSE LIST

Undergraduate

Introduction to Radio-Television-Film
Motion Pictures
Writing for Radio-TV-Film
Radio-Television Programming
Broadcast Operations (Management)
Television Production
Mass Media and Society
Advanced Studies in Mass Media
Voice and Articulation
Film Production
Radio Production
Broadcasting Rules and Regulations

NORTH DAKOTA

University of North Dakota

State-supported coed university. Institutionally accredited by regional association. Rural location, 20-acre campus. Total enrollment: 9505. Undergraduate enrollment: 7729. Semester calendar. Grading system: letters or numbers.

Speech Department, Grand Forks, ND 58202 701-777-2192

CONTACT Neil McCutchan or Hazel Heiman
DEGREES OFFERED BA, MA in speech with emphasis in radio-television and film
DEPARTMENTAL MAJORS Undergraduate television — 50 students Graduate television — 2 students
ADMISSION Undergraduate requirement — 2.0 minimum grade point average, ACT or SAT scores Graduate requirements — 3.0 minimum grade point average, GRE scores, teachers' recommendations, written statement of purpose Undergraduate application deadline — 8/1
FINANCIAL AID Scholarships, work/study programs, student loans, fellowships, teaching assistantships, research assistantships Undergraduate application deadline — 4/1
CURRICULAR EMPHASIS Undergraduate film study — criticism and aesthetics, educational media/instructional technology treated equally Undergraduate filmmaking — documentary, narrative, experimental, educational, treated equally Graduate filmmaking — documentary, narrative, experimental, educational, treated equally Undergraduate television study — history, criticism and aesthetics, educational, production, management treated equally Graduate television study — history, criticism and aesthetics, educational, production, management treated equally Undergraduate television production — commercial, news/documentary, experimental/personal video, educational treated equally Graduate television production — commercial, news/documentary, experimental/personal video, educational treated equally
SPECIAL ACTIVITIES/OFFERINGS Film series; program material produced for on-campus closed-circuit television, cable television, local public television station, apprenticeships; internships in television production; independent study; teacher training; vocational placement service
FACILITIES AND EQUIPMENT Film — complete 8mm equipment, 35mm cameras, lighting, black and white film stock, color film stock, projectors, editing room, sound mixing room Television — complete black and white and color studio production equipment, black and white studio, color studio, mobile van/unit, audio studio, control room, recorders and monitors in classrooms
FACULTY Myron Curry, Neil McCutchan PART-TIME FACULTY David Beach, Raymond Fischer, Lee Gangelhoff, Bill Lesko

COURSE LIST

Undergraduate

Introduction to Broadcasting
Equipment Orientation, Audio
Equipment Orientation, Video
Equipment Orientation, Film
Radio TV News Writing
Voice, Articulation, Diction and Phonetics
Radio-TV Advertising
TV Practicum
Internships and Projects
Criticism of TV

Graduate

Special Topics Seminars in TV
Readings and Study — TV
Research in TV

Undergraduate and Graduate

Radio TV Writing
Audio Production and Announcing
TV Production
Advertising Media Techniques
Radio-TV Programming
TV Direction
Cinematography
Using Radio and TV in Education

OHIO

Antioch College

Independent 4-year coed college. Administratively affiliated with Antioch University. Institutionally accredited by regional association. Small town location, 100-acre campus. Undergraduate enrollment: 1050. Total faculty: 80 (70 full-time, 10 part-time). Quarter calendar. Grading system: pass/fail.

Communication-Video Department, Yellow Springs, OH 45387 513-767-7331

CONTACT Robert Devine
DEGREES OFFERED BA, BS in communication with a major in video; interdisciplinary majors with emphasis in video
DEPARTMENTAL MAJORS 40 students
ADMISSION Requirement — admission to the college Application deadline — 3/1, rolling
FINANCIAL AID Application deadline — 3/1, rolling
CURRICULAR EMPHASIS Television study — (1) structure of tools; (2) community and cable; (3) production Television production — (1) communication process; (2) experimental/personal video; (3) news/documentary
SPECIAL ACTIVITIES/OFFERINGS Program material produced for cable television and other institutions through a free-dub library, apprenticeships, internships in video production, independent study, practicum, teacher training, project work as practicing professionals
FACILITIES AND EQUIPMENT Television — complete black and white studio and exterior production facilities
FACULTY Robert Devine

COURSE LIST

Undergraduate

Video
Video Sketchwork (Aesthetics)
Video Sketchwork (Documentary Skills)
Video Production
Dance/Video Workshop
Documentary American Lifestyles
TV News
Community Media
Images of Women
Public Access Cable
Senior Project in Video

Film Section, Art Department 513-767-7331 ext 239 or 464

CONTACT Janis Crystal Lipzin
DEGREES OFFERED BA, BFA in art with a concentration in film
ADMISSION Requirement — interview Application deadline — 3/1, rolling
FINANCIAL AID Work/study programs Application deadline — 3/1, rolling

Antioch College (continued)

CURRICULAR EMPHASIS Film study — (1) production; (2) criticism and aesthetics; (3) history Filmmaking — experimental
SPECIAL ACTIVITIES/OFFERINGS Film series, apprenticeships, internships in film production, independent study, practicum
FACILITIES AND EQUIPMENT Film — complete 8mm and 16mm equipment, screening room, 35mm screening facilities, editing room, animation board, permanent film library, processing facility, sound mix facility
FACULTY Janis Crystal Lipzin

COURSE LIST

Undergraduate

Introduction to Cinema Expression I
Workshop in Cinema Expression II
History of Cinema Art to 1940
History of Cinema Art from 1940 to Present
Women Artists as Filmmakers
Aesthetic Bases of Cinema Art
Further Work in Filmmaking I–III
Aesthetic Bases for Cinematic Art

Ashland College

Independent comprehensive coed institution. Institutionally accredited by regional association, programs recognized by NASM, AACSB. Small town location, 30-acre campus. Total enrollment: 2078. Undergraduate enrollment: 1629. Total faculty: 137 (106 full-time, 31 part-time). Semester calendar. Grading system: letters or numbers.

Speech Department, College Avenue, Ashland, OH 44805 419-289-4142

CONTACT Richard Leidy, Director of Radio-Television
DEGREES OFFERED BA in radio-television, BS in broadcast production and technology
DEPARTMENTAL MAJORS 100 students
ADMISSION Requirements — SAT scores, interviews Application deadline — rolling
FINANCIAL AID Scholarships, student loans, work/study programs Application deadline — rolling
CURRICULAR EMPHASIS Television study — (1) production; (2) criticism and aesthetics; (3) management; (4) appreciation; (5) educational; (6) history Television production — (1) commercial; (2) news/documentary; (3) educational; (4) experimental/personal video; (5) broadcast engineering
SPECIAL ACTIVITIES/OFFERINGS Program material produced for cable television, apprenticeships, internships in television production, independent study
FACILITIES AND EQUIPMENT Film — 8mm and 16mm equipment, editing room, sound mixing room Television — complete black and white exterior production facilities, complete color studio production equipment, color studio, mobile van/unit, audio studio, control room
FACULTY Elizabeth Boardman, Lawrence Hiner, Robert Lewis, Jay Pappas

COURSE LIST

Undergraduate

Mass Media
Introduction to Radio-Television
Program Management
Television Production
Broadcast Law
Sales and Station Management
News Writing
Commercial Copy Writing
Radio/Television Announcing
Professional Seminar in Radio/Television

Bowling Green State University, Bowling Green

State-supported coed university. Institutionally accredited by regional association, programs recognized by NASM, AACSB. Small town location, 1247-acre campus. Total enrollment: 15,886. Undergraduate enrollment: 13,951. Total faculty: 791 (723 full-time, 68 part-time). Quarter calendar. Grading system: letters or numbers.

Radio/Television/Film Area, School of Speech Communication, 413 South Hall, Bowling Green, OH 43403 419-372-2138

CONTACT Film — R K Clark Television — Denise Trauth
DEGREES OFFERED BA, MA, PhD in radio/television/film
PROGRAM MAJORS Undergraduate television — 380 students Graduate film — 4 students Graduate television — 21 students
ADMISSION Undergraduate requirements — ACT or SAT scores, teachers' recommendations, written statement of purpose Graduate requirements — 3.0 minimum grade point average, GRE scores, teachers' recommendations, written statement of purpose, professional work experience Undergraduate application deadline — 2/1
FINANCIAL AID Scholarships limited, student loans, fellowships, teaching assistantships, research assistantships
CURRICULAR EMPHASIS Undergraduate film study — (1) appreciation; (2) history; (3) criticism and aesthetics Graduate film study — (1) history; (2) criticism and aesthetics; (3) appreciation Undergraduate filmmaking — (1) narrative; (2) documentary; (3) experimental Graduate filmmaking — (1) narrative; (2) documentary; (3) experimental Undergraduate television study — history, criticism and aesthetics, production treated equally Graduate television study — history, criticism and aesthetics, production treated equally Undergraduate television production — commercial, news/documentary, experimental/personal video treated equally Graduate television production — commercial, news/documentary, experimental/personal video treated equally
SPECIAL ACTIVITIES/OFFERINGS Film series, film festivals, program material produced for on-campus closed-circuit television and local public television station, internships in television production, independent study, vocational placement service
FACILITIES AND EQUIPMENT Film — 8mm editing equipment, lighting, projectors, 16mm cameras, editing equipment, sound recording equipment, lighting, projectors, screening room, editing room, sound mixing room, permanent film library of student films Television — color studio cameras, 1-inch VTR, ¾-inch cassette VTR, portable black and white cameras, editing equipment, monitors, slide chain, portable color cameras, ¾-inch ENG, lighting equipment, sound recording equipment, audio mixers, film chain, color studio, audio studio, control room
FACULTY R K Clark, Gary Edgerton, David Ostroff, Karin Sandell, Malachi Topping, Denise Trauth PART-TIME FACULTY Patrick Fitzgerald, Ronald Gargasz, David Kennedy, Duane Tucker

COURSE LIST

Undergraduate

Radio and Television Broadcasting
Introduction to Broadcast Announcing
Introduction to Television Program Production
8mm Filmmaking
Procedures of Audience Measurement
Understanding Movies
Producing and Directing for Television
Freedom and Responsibility in Broadcasting
16mm Filmmaking
Patterns of Programming in Radio and Television
History and Criticism of Film
Television Workshop
Broadcast History
Seminar: Contemporary Aspects of Broadcasting and Film
Internship in Broadcasting and Film
Problems in Radio-Television-Film
Broadcast Economics and Promotion
Process and Effects of Mass Communication

Graduate

History of American Broadcasting
Regulation of American Broadcasting
Educational Broadcasting
History and Criticism of Film
Producing and Directing for Television
Producing and Directing for Film
Writing for Television and Film
Comparative Systems of Broadcasting
International Broadcasting
Programming in Radio and Television
Seminar: Research Studies in Broadcasting
Advanced Film Production
Practicum in Television
Practicum in Film
Critical Analysis of Broadcast Programs
Teaching Radio-Television-Film
Seminar: Broadcast Station Management and Operations
Topics in Radio and Television Programming
Current Issues in American Broadcasting
Seminar: Instructional Television
Seminar: Research Designs in Broadcasting
Topics in Radio and Television Producing and Directing
Seminar: Radio, Television, Film, and Mass Society

Bowling Green State University, Firelands Campus

State-supported 2-year coed college. Part of Bowling Green State University System. Institutionally accredited by regional association. Rural location, 216-acre campus. Total enrollment: 991. Undergraduate enrollment: 894. Total faculty: 51 (32 full-time, 19 part-time). Quarter calendar. Grading system: letters or numbers.

Humanities Department, 901 Rye Beach Road, Huron, OH 44839 419-433-5560

ADMISSION Application deadline — 8/31, rolling

Case Western Reserve University

Independent coed university. Institutionally accredited by regional association, programs recognized by NASM, AACSB. Urban location, 130-acre campus. Total enrollment: 8185. Undergraduate enrollment: 3395. Total faculty: 1100. Semester calendar. Grading system: letters or numbers.

English Department, Euclid Avenue, Cleveland, OH 44105 216-368-2000

CONTACT Louis D Giannetti
PROGRAM OFFERED Major in English with emphasis in film or television
ADMISSION Application deadline — 3/15, rolling
CURRICULAR EMPHASIS Film study — (1) criticism and aesthetics; (2) appreciation; (3) history; (4) interdisciplinary
SPECIAL ACTIVITIES/OFFERINGS Film series, film festivals, film societies, student publications, program material produced for on-campus closed-circuit television, internships in television production, independent study
FACULTY Louis D Giannetti

COURSE LIST

Undergraduate and Graduate

Introduction to Film
Italian Cinema
Film and Literature
Film and Drama
American Film

Cleveland Institute of Art

Independent professional 4-year coed college. Institutionally accredited by regional association, programs recognized by NASA. Urban location. Undergraduate enrollment: 520. Total faculty: 71. Semester calendar.

Photography Department, 11141 East Boulevard, Cleveland, OH 44106 216-421-4322

CONTACT Patricia Rambasek
DEGREE OFFERED BFA in film production (five-year program)
DEPARTMENTAL MAJORS 3 students
SPECIAL ACTIVITIES/OFFERINGS Independent study
FACILITIES AND EQUIPMENT Film — complete 8mm and 16mm equipment, editing room, sound mixing room, animation board, permanent film library
FACULTY Joseph Horning

COURSE LIST

Undergraduate

Beginning Film Production
Advanced Film Production

Cleveland State University

State-supported coed university. Institutionally accredited by regional association, programs recognized by AACSB. Urban location, 38-acre campus. Total enrollment: 17,340. Undergraduate enrollment: 14,323. Total faculty: 1028 (525 full-time, 503 part-time). Quarter calendar. Grading system: letters or numbers.

Communication Department, 1983 East 24th Street, Cleveland, OH 44115 216-687-4630

CONTACT Sidney Kraus, Chairperson
ADMISSION Application deadline — rolling
CURRICULAR EMPHASIS Film study — (1) appreciation; (2) criticism and aesthetics; (3) history Television study — (1) management; (2) production; (3) criticism and aesthetics Television production — (1) commercial; (2) news/documentary; (3) educational
SPECIAL ACTIVITIES/OFFERINGS Film series, film societies, independent study
FACILITIES AND EQUIPMENT Film — 16mm cameras, editing equipment, lighting equipment, projectors, editing room Television — complete black and white studio and exterior production equipment, complete color studio production equipment, black and white studio, color studio, audio studio, control room
FACULTY Dennis Davis, Leo Jeffres, Sidney Kraus, Jae Won Lee, Dennis Lynch, Becky Quarles, John Robinson, Haluk Sahin

COURSE LIST
Undergraduate
Film Appreciation
Principles of Filmmaking
Introduction to Broadcasting
Film/TV Documentary
Film Theory and Criticism
Fundamentals of Radio-TV Production
Process of TV Production
Communications and Public Relations
Problems in Mass Media
TV Directing

College of Mount St Joseph-on-the-Ohio

Independent Roman Catholic comprehensive institution primarily for women. Institutionally accredited by regional association. Suburban location. Undergraduate enrollment: 1355. Total faculty: 100 (65 full-time, 35 part-time). Semester calendar. Grading system: letters or numbers.

Communication Arts Department, Mount St Joseph, OH 45051 513-244-4856

CONTACT W C Schutzius
DEGREE OFFERED BA with a concentration in visual media
ADMISSION Requirement — ACT or SAT scores Application deadline — beginning of term
FINANCIAL AID Scholarships, work/study programs, student loans Application deadline — 4/15
CURRICULAR EMPHASIS Film study — history, appreciation, educational media/instructional technology treated equally Filmmaking — documentary, narrative, educational treated equally Television study — history, criticism and aesthetics, educational, production treated equally Television production — news/documentary, educational treated equally
SPECIAL ACTIVITIES/OFFERINGS Internships in film production, internships in television production, independent study, teacher training
FACILITIES AND EQUIPMENT Film — complete 8mm and 16mm equipment, screening room, editing room, permanent film library of student films Television — black and white studio cameras, ½-inch VTR, ¾-inch cassette VTR, portable black and white cameras, monitors, special effects generators, ½-inch portapak recorders, lighting equipment, audio mixers, black and white studio

COURSE LIST
Undergraduate
Mass Media
Film and Society
Cinematography I, II
Cinematography Seminar
Video Production I, II
Educational Media
Special Studies

Denison University

Independent 4-year coed college. Institutionally accredited by regional association, programs recognized by NASM. Small town location, 1000-acre campus. Undergraduate enrollment: 2058. Total faculty: 176 (148 full-time, 28 part-time). 4-1-4 calendar. Grading system: letters or numbers.

Department of Theatre and Cinema, Granville, OH 43023 614-587-0810

CONTACT Film — R Elliott Stout Television — Charles M Feldman
DEGREES OFFERED BA in film, BA in speech communication with emphasis in television
DEPARTMENTAL MAJORS 23 students
ADMISSION Requirement — admission to the college Application deadline — 2/15
FINANCIAL AID Scholarships, student loans, work/study programs, film production assistantships Application deadline — 3/1
CURRICULAR EMPHASIS Film study — history, criticism and aesthetics, production treated equally Filmmaking — narrative, documentary, experimental treated equally Television study — (1) history; (2) criticism and aesthetics; (3) appreciation Television production — (1) educational; (2) experimental/personal video; (3) news/documentary
SPECIAL ACTIVITIES/OFFERINGS Filmmaking clubs, film series, film festivals, film societies, apprenticeships, internships in film and television production, independent study, practicum
FACILITIES AND EQUIPMENT Film — complete 8mm and 16mm equipment, sound stage, screening room, editing room, sound mixing room, animation board, permanent film library, 16mm motion picture processing laboratory, animation stand Television — black and white studio camera, ½-inch VTR, ¾-inch cassette VTR, ½-inch portapak recorder
FACULTY Michael N Allen, Charles M Feldman, R Elliott Stout

COURSE LIST

Undergraduate

World Cinema
Basic Cinema Production
Cinema Seminar
History of Cinema
The Documentary Mode
Performance for the Screen
Advanced Cinema Production
Theory of Cinema
Cinema Workshop
Directed Studies
Radio and TV in Society
Social Impact of Mass Media
Mass Media and Government
Communication, Man, and Society

Franklin University

Independent 4-year coed college. Institutionally accredited by regional association. Urban location, 10-acre campus. Undergraduate enrollment: 4444. Total faculty: 170. Trimester calendar. Grading system: letters or numbers.

Division of Humanities, 201 South Grant Avenue, Columbus, OH 43215 614-224-6237

CONTACT Film — Sue Foley Television — R Darby Williams
FINANCIAL AID Scholarships, work/study programs, student loans
CURRICULAR EMPHASIS Undergraduate film study — (1) appreciation; (2) criticism and aesthetics; (3) history Undergraduate television study — (1) management; (2) history; (3) educational
SPECIAL ACTIVITIES/OFFERINGS Film series, program material produced for on-campus closed-circuit television and cable television, independent study
FACILITIES AND EQUIPMENT Television — complete color studio production equipment, color studio, control room
FACULTY Sue Foley, Tim Scheurer, R Darby Williams

COURSE LIST

Undergraduate

Film
Mass Media
Popular Culture

John Carroll University

Independent religious comprehensive coed institution. Institutionally accredited by regional association. Suburban location. Total enrollment: 3800. Undergraduate enrollment: 2500. Total faculty: 175. Semester calendar. Grading system: letters.

Communications Department, Cleveland, OH 44118 216-491-4378

CONTACT Joseph Miller, Chairman
DEGREE OFFERED BA in communications with emphasis in television
DEPARTMENTAL MAJORS 120 students
ADMISSION Application deadline — 8/1, rolling
CURRICULAR EMPHASIS Television study — history, criticism and aesthetics, appreciation, production, educational treated equally
SPECIAL ACTIVITIES/OFFERINGS Program material produced for on-campus closed-circuit television, internships in television production, independent study
FACILITIES AND EQUIPMENT Television — complete black and white and color studio production facilities
FACULTY James Breslin, Mary Miller, Jacqueline Schmidt

COURSE LIST

Undergraduate

Introduction to Broadcasting
TV Writing and Directing
Broadcast Journalism
Interpersonal Communication
Advanced TV Production
Radio Station Management
Interviewing
Organizational Communications
Special Topics in TV
Educational TV
Public Relations

Kent State University, Kent

State-supported coed university. Part of Kent State University System. Institutionally accredited by regional association. Small town location, 1200-acre campus. Total enrollment: 20,163. Undergraduate enrollment: 16,193. Total faculty: 825 full-time. Semester calendar. Grading system: letters or numbers.

School of Art, Kent, OH 44242 216-672-2192

CONTACT Richard Myers
ADMISSION Undergraduate requirements — ACT or SAT scores, teachers' recommendations, portfolio, professional recommendations Graduate requirements — teachers' recommendations, portfolio, professional recommendations
FINANCIAL AID Teaching assistantships
CURRICULAR EMPHASIS Undergraduate film study — appreciation Graduate film study — appreciation Undergraduate filmmaking — experimental Graduate filmmaking — experimental
SPECIAL ACTIVITIES/OFFERINGS Film series, film festivals, independent study
FACILITIES AND EQUIPMENT Film — 8mm and 16mm cameras, editing equipment, sound recording equipment, lighting, projectors, screening room, editing room, sound mixing room, animation board
FACULTY Richard Myers

COURSE LIST

Undergraduate

Filmmaking I (Super-8)
Filmmaking II (16mm)
Independent Study

Graduate

Independent Study

Kent State University, Kent (continued)

Sociology Department, Lowry Hall, Kent, OH 44242 216-672-2562

CONTACT Jerry M Lewis
ADMISSION Application deadline — 9/1, rolling
FACULTY Barbara Harkness, Jerry M Lewis

COURSE LIST
Undergraduate
Sociology of Film

Telecommunications Department, School of Speech, 511 Wright Hall, Kent, OH 44242 216-672-2468

CONTACT John C Weiser
DEGREES OFFERED BA, MA in television management, production, and performance; production, performance, theory, and research
DEPARTMENTAL MAJORS Undergraduate — 600 students Graduate — 50 students
ADMISSION Undergraduate requirements — 2.5 minimum grade point average, teachers' recommendations Graduate requirements — 3.0 minimum grade point average, GRE scores, teachers' recommendations Undergraduate application deadline — 9/1, rolling
FINANCIAL AID Student loans, work/study programs, teaching assistantships Undergraduate application deadline — 3/15, rolling
CURRICULAR EMPHASIS Undergraduate television study — history, appreciation, production, management, performance treated equally Graduate television study — criticism and aesthetics, production, educational, management, research treated equally Undergraduate television production — commercial, news/documentary, experimental/personal video treated equally Graduate television production — news/documentary, experimental/personal video, educational treated equally
SPECIAL ACTIVITIES/OFFERINGS Program material produced for on-campus closed-circuit television and local public television station, internships in television production, independent study, practicum
FACILITIES AND EQUIPMENT Television — complete black and white studio and exterior production equipment, complete color studio production equipment, black and white studio, color studio, remote truck, audio studio, control room
FACULTY Thomas Olson, James Poluzzi, Mary Ross, Gene Stebbins, John C Weiser, Robert West

COURSE LIST
Undergraduate
Survey of Radio/Television
Techniques of Media Utilization
Introduction to Broadcasting
Broadcast Speaking
Broadcast Programming
Broadcast Copywriting
Broadcast History
Broadcast Staff
Broadcast Operations I, II
Television Production I, II
Broadcast Internship
Senior Colloquium in Telecommunications
Production Broadcast News
Television Directing

Graduate
Producing Broadcast News
Television Directing
Television Electrography
Broadcast Documentary
Broadcast Scriptwriting
Performance Problems in Television
Broadcast Communication Law
Broadcast Station Management
Special Topics in Telecommunications
Research Materials and Methods in Speech: Telecommunications
Research Methods in Mass Communications
Research Problems in Telecommunications
Administrative Problems in Telecommunications
Production Problems in Telecommunications
Programming Telecommunications Media
Broadcast Criticism
Broadcast Communication Theory
Seminar in Telecommunications
Individual Investigators: Telecommunications
Research: Telecommunications

Ohio

Kent State University, Salem

State-supported 2-year coed college. Part of Kent State University System, automatic transfer to main campus for baccalaureate. Institutionally accredited by regional association. Rural location, 98-acre campus. Undergraduate enrollment: 536. Total faculty: 40 (20 full-time, 20 part-time). Semester calendar. Grading system: letters or numbers.

Telecommunications Department, PO Box 91, Salem, OH 44460 216-332-0361

CONTACT Roderic Farkas, Chairman
DEPARTMENTAL MAJORS 20 students
CURRICULAR EMPHASIS Television study — technical, production treated equally Television production — (1) experimental/personal video; (2) educational
SPECIAL ACTIVITIES/OFFERINGS Program material produced for on-campus closed-circuit television, cable television, local public television station; independent study; practicum
FACILITIES AND EQUIPMENT Television — complete black and white studio facilities, complete color ENG production facilities
FACULTY Roderic Farkas, Glen Jackson PART-TIME FACULTY Evert Dennison

COURSE LIST
Undergraduate
Video Systems
Audio Systems and Techniques
Introduction to Electronic Communication I, II
Federal Communication Commission Examination Preparation
Radio and Television Practicum

Lake Erie College

Independent 4-year women's college. Institutionally accredited by regional association. Suburban location. Quarter calendar. Grading system: letters or numbers.

History Department, Painesville, OH 44077 216-352-3361

CONTACT Barton Bean
ADMISSION Application deadline — rolling
FACULTY Barton Bean

COURSE LIST
Undergraduate
The Classic Film

Lorain County Community College

County-supported 2-year coed college. Institutionally accredited by regional association. Suburban location. Undergraduate enrollment: 5634. Total faculty: 269 (99 full-time, 170-part-time). Quarter calendar. Grading system: letters or numbers.

Language and Humanities Department, 1005 North Abbe Road, Elyria, OH 44035 216-365-4191

CONTACT Robert Dudash or Roy Berko
ADMISSION Application deadline — rolling
CURRICULAR EMPHASIS Film study — (1) appreciation; (2) history; (3) criticism and aesthetics Television study — (1) appreciation; (2) production; (3) criticism and aesthetics Television production — (1) experimental/personal video; (2) educational; (3) news/documentary
SPECIAL ACTIVITIES/OFFERINGS Film series, film festivals, independent study
FACILITIES AND EQUIPMENT Television — complete black and white studio and exterior production equipment, complete color studio and exterior production equipment, black and white studio, color studio, mobile van/unit
FACULTY Roy Berko, Robert Dudash

COURSE LIST
Undergraduate
Film Appreciation
Introduction to American Cinema
Television Production I, II
Introduction to Radio and Television (Appreciation)

Marietta College

Independent comprehensive coed institution. Institutionally accredited by regional association. Small town location, 60-acre campus. Undergraduate enrollment: 1578. Total faculty: 117 (102 full-time, 15 part-time). Semester calendar. Grading system: letters or numbers.

Mass Media Department, Marietta, OH 45750 614-373-0200

CONTACT Bernard Russi Jr
DEGREE OFFERED BA in mass media with an emphasis in radio-television, advertising, journalism, media-management, media-psychology, or political journalism
DEPARTMENTAL MAJORS Television — 50-60 students
ADMISSION Requirements — 2.0 minimum grade point average, ACT or SAT scores, teachers' recommendations
FINANCIAL AID Scholarships, work/study programs, student loans
CURRICULAR EMPHASIS Television study — criticism and aesthetics, production, management treated equally Television production — (1) commercial; (2) news/documentary
SPECIAL ACTIVITIES/OFFERINGS Program material produced for cable television, internships in television production, independent study
FACILITIES AND EQUIPMENT Television — black and white studio cameras, ½-inch VTR, ¾-inch cassette VTR, editing equipment, monitors, special effects generators, slide chain, portable color cameras, ½-inch portapak recorders, ¾-inch ENG, lighting equipment, sound recording equipment, audio mixers, film chain, black and white studio, mobile van/unit, audio studio, control room
FACULTY Ralph E Matheny, Robert McCartney, Bernard Russi Jr

COURSE LIST
Undergraduate
Introduction to Broadcasting
Radio Production
Television Production
Broadcast Journalism
Mass Communication and Society
Radio-TV Writing
Comparative Media
Freshman Seminar
Senior Seminar

Notre Dame College of Ohio

Independent Roman Catholic 4-year coed college. Institutionally accredited by regional association. Suburban location. Total enrollment: 620. Total faculty: 56. Semester calendar. Grading system: letters or numbers.

English Communications Department, 4545 College Road, South Euclid, OH 44121 216-381-1680

CONTACT Sister Mary Laboure
PROGRAM OFFERED Major in communications with emphasis in film
ADMISSION Application deadline — 7/15, rolling
FINANCIAL AID Scholarships, student loans, work/study programs Application deadline — 3/15
CURRICULAR EMPHASIS Film study — (1) criticism and aesthetics; (2) appreciation; (3) history; (4) production Filmmaking — (1) documentary; (2) narrative Television study — (1) educational; (2) criticism and aesthetics; (3) appreciation; (4) production Television production — (1) commercial; (2) news/documentary
SPECIAL ACTIVITIES/OFFERINGS Film series, independent study, vocational placement service

Notre Dame College of Ohio (continued)

FACILITIES AND EQUIPMENT Film — complete 8mm and 16mm equipment, screening room Television — black and white studio camera, color studio camera, ½-inch VTR, ¾-inch cassette VTR, portable black and white cameras, monitors, portable color cameras

FACULTY Maureen Kramanak, Sister Mary Laboure

COURSE LIST

Undergraduate

Film Literacy
Filmmaking
Communications
Cooperative Education in Radio-TV-Film
Writing for the Media

Oberlin College

Independent comprehensive coed institution. Institutionally accredited by regional association. Small town location. Total enrollment: 2770. Undergraduate enrollment: 2750. Total faculty: 226 full-time. 4-1-4 calendar. Grading system: letters or numbers.

Department of Communication Studies, Oberlin, OH 44074 216-775-8121

CONTACT Film — Christian Koch Television — Daniel J Goulding

ADMISSION Application deadline — 2/15

CURRICULAR EMPHASIS Film study — (1) film theory; (2) criticism and aesthetics; (3) appreciation Television study — (1) social effects; (2) criticism and aesthetics; (3) appreciation Television production — (1) experimental/personal video; (2) news/documentary

SPECIAL ACTIVITIES/OFFERINGS Film series, internships in film and television production, independent study, practicum

FACILITIES AND EQUIPMENT Film — complete 8mm and 16mm equipment, permanent film library Television — black and white studio cameras, ½-inch VTR, ¾-inch cassette VTR, editing equipment, monitors, ½-inch portapak recorder, lighting equipment, sound recording equipment, audio mixers, black and white studio, control room

FACULTY Daniel J Goulding, Christian Koch

COURSE LIST

Undergraduate

Mass Communication
Film, Video, Radio Workshop I, II
Semiotics and the Cinema
European Cinema
Cinema, Culture, and Society
Broadcast Journalism
Theories of the Image
Photography, Film, and Video for the Arts
An Introduction to Film Aesthetic

Ohio Northern University

Independent Methodist 4-year and professional coed institution. Institutionally accredited by regional association, programs recognized by NASM, ACPE. Small town location, 120-acre campus. Total enrollment: 2661. Undergraduate enrollment: 2126. Total faculty: 177 (160 full-time, 17 part-time). Quarter calendar. Grading system: letters or numbers.

Division of Teacher Education, Ada, OH 45810 419-634-9921

CONTACT Donald Traxler

ADMISSION Application deadline — 8/15, rolling

FACULTY Donald Traxler

COURSE LIST

Undergraduate

Instructional Media in Education
Instructional Media in Education: Laboratory

Ohio State University

State-supported coed university. Part of Ohio State University System. Institutionally accredited by regional association, programs recognized by NASM, AACSB, AOA, ACPE. Urban location, 3251-acre campus. Total enrollment: 51,343. Undergraduate enrollment: 39,118. Total faculty: 3091. Quarter calendar. Grading system: letters or numbers.

Department of Art Education, 340 Hopkins Hall, Columbus, OH 43221 614-422-7183

CONTACT Film — Janet DiLauro or Kenneth Marantz Television — Tom Linehan

CURRICULAR EMPHASIS Undergraduate film study — criticism and aesthetics, appreciation, educational media/instructional technology treated equally Graduate film study — criticism and aesthetics, appreciation, educational media/instructional technology treated equally Undergraduate television study — criticism and aesthetics, appreciation, educational treated equally Graduate television study — criticism and aesthetics, appreciation, educational, production treated equally Graduate television production — experimental/personal video, educational treated equally

SPECIAL ACTIVITIES/OFFERINGS Film series, film festivals, independent study, teacher training

FACILITIES AND EQUIPMENT Film — complete 8mm equipment Television — ¾-inch cassette VTR, portable color cameras, sound recording equipment, media lab

COURSE LIST

Undergraduate and Graduate

Film Art and Education
Production of Educational Media

Biomedical Communications Division, School of Allied Medical Professions, Medical AV/TV Center, Columbus, OH 43210 614-422-1044

CONTACT John E Burke, Director
ADMISSION Application deadline — 8/15, rolling
CURRICULAR EMPHASIS Film study — (1) production; (2) educational media/instructional technology Television study — (1) educational; (2) production; (3) management
SPECIAL ACTIVITIES/OFFERINGS Program material produced for on-campus closed-circuit television, local public television station, local commercial television station, medical and patient education; internships; practicum
FACILITIES AND EQUIPMENT Film — complete 8mm equipment, sound stage, screening room, editing room, sound mixing room, animation board, permanent film library Television — complete black and white studio and exterior production equipment, complete color studio and exterior production equipment, black and white studio, color studio, audio studio, control room
FACULTY Robert E Potts, Lilless Shilling, David Stein

COURSE LIST

Undergraduate
Medical Communications

School of Journalism, Columbus, OH 43210 614-422-6491

CONTACT Walter K Bunge, Director
DEGREE OFFERED BA in broadcast journalism
ADMISSION Requirement — minimum grade point average Application deadline — 8/15, rolling
FINANCIAL AID Scholarships, student loans, work/study programs, teaching assistantships, research assistantships, fellowships Application deadline — 3/1
CURRICULAR EMPHASIS Film study — (1) production; (2) criticism and aesthetics; (3) educational media/instructional technology; (4) history; (5) appreciation
SPECIAL ACTIVITIES/OFFERINGS Program material produced for television station, internships in broadcast journalism
FACILITIES AND EQUIPMENT Television — complete black and white studio production equipment, black and white studio, audio studio, control room
FACULTY William Drenten, James Harless PART-TIME FACULTY Hugh De Moss, William Patterson, Thomas Sawyer

COURSE LIST

Undergraduate
Producing Television News
Advanced Television News Production
Documentaries

Undergraduate and Graduate
Television News Reporting
Television News Editing
Seminar in Problems of Television News

Department of Photography and Cinema, Columbus, OH 43210 614-422-1766

CONTACT J Ronald Green
DEGREES OFFERED BA, BFA, MA in photography and cinema (thesis and production); interdisciplinary PhD
DEPARTMENTAL MAJORS Undergraduate — 238 students Graduate — 31 students
ADMISSION Undergraduate requirements — 2.5 minimum grade point average, SAT and/or ACT scores; BFA — 2.8 minimum grade point average, written statement of purpose, committee screening, portfolio, recommendations optional. Graduate requirements — 2.7 minimum grade point average or GRE scores, application form, written statement of purpose, transcripts, résumé, teachers' recommendations, written supportive materials for Plan A and portfolio materials for Plan B Undergraduate application deadline — 8/15, quarterly Graduate application deadlines — April 1 (summer and autumn), October 1 (winter), February 1 (spring)
FINANCIAL AID Scholarships, grants, awards, employment, loans, work/study programs, teaching associateships, research associateships, administrative associateships Undergraduate application deadline — 3/1
CURRICULAR EMPHASIS Undergraduate photography and cinema study — (1) history, theory and criticism; (2) studio production Graduate photography and cinema study — (1) theory and criticism; (2) history; (3) advanced production
SPECIAL ACTIVITIES/OFFERINGS Public film series, visiting artist presentations, associateships, internships in still, film and television production, planned teaching, independent study, practicum, professional film unit, departmental and university film study collection, film script collection, photographic history collection and research room
FACILITIES AND EQUIPMENT Complete 16mm equipment, 16mm projectors, 16mm rewinds, 16mm viewers, 8mm editing equipment, 8mm projectors, 8mm viewers, underwater camera equipment, high-speed cameras, reel-to-reel tape decks, cassette recorders, carousel slide projectors, computer-controlled animation stand, animation stands, lighting equipment, sound stage, screening rooms, editing rooms, sound mixing room, in house VNF processing, work printing
FACULTY Thom Andersen, Harry Binau, Noel Burch, Carl Clausen, Clyde Dilley, Mojmir Drvota, Ali Elgabri, James Friedman, Jonathan Green, J Ronald Green, Willie Longshore, Clayton Lowe, Ardine Nelson, Dana Vibberts, Robert Wagner

COURSE LIST

Undergraduate
Photography
Photography for Industrial Design Majors
Color Slide Photography

Graduate
Graduate Internship in Photography and Cinema
Practicum in Photography and Cinema
Photographic Image and Society
Design of Educational Films
Individual Studies
Group Studies in Photography and Cinema
Preparation of Master's Project—Plan B
Research in Photography and Cinema

Ohio State University (continued)

Undergraduate and Graduate

History and Systems of Film Theory
History of Photography
History of Cinema
Film Theory I, II
Photographic Communications
Photographic Process
Intermediate Photography
Zone System
Lighting for Photography
Large Format Photography
Color Photography I, II
Cinema Production I–III
Scriptwriting for Film
Editorial Process
Elements of Sound
Animation
Cinematography
Photography for Humanities and Science Students
BFA Exhibit Presentation
Studio Practices I, II
Photography: The Early Years
20th Century Photography to 1940
History of Photography 1940–Present
Reality Image I, II
Silent Cinema
Sound Film: 1928–1948
Cinema: 1948–Present
American Film Genres
Film Auteurs, Authors, and Collaborators
Film Criticism
Photographic Criticism
Cinema Production Management
High Contrast Materials
Imagemakers' Workshop
Individual Studies in Photography
Group Studies in Photography and Cinema
Comparative Study in Film and Theatre Directing
Methods and Purposes of Research
Symposium in Photography and Cinema

Ohio University, Athens

State-supported coed university. Institutionally accredited by regional association. Small town location, 600-acre campus. Total enrollment: 13,656. Undergraduate enrollment: 10,034. Total faculty: 817 (701 full-time, 116 part-time). Quarter calendar. Grading system: letters or numbers.

Film Department, Lindley Hall 378, Athens, OH 45701 614-594-5138

CONTACT David Prince, Chairman

DEGREES OFFERED MA in film with an emphasis in film theory, criticism, and history; MFA in film with an emphasis in film production and film theory and criticism

DEPARTMENTAL MAJORS Undergraduate film — students Graduate film — 28 students

ADMISSION Graduate requirements — 2.5 minimum grade point average, interview, teachers' recommendations, written statement of purpose, portfolio

FINANCIAL AID Scholarships, work/study programs, student loans, teaching assistantships, research assistantships, internships

CURRICULAR EMPHASIS Graduate film study — (1) criticism and aesthetics; (2) history; (3) appreciation Graduate filmmaking — documentary, narrative, experimental, animated, educational treated equally

SPECIAL ACTIVITIES/OFFERINGS Film series, film festivals, film societies, student publications, annual video festival, film lab, wide-angle film journal, traveling road show, internships in film production, independent study

FACILITIES AND EQUIPMENT Film — complete 8mm and 16mm equipment, screening room, 35mm screening facilities, editing room, sound mixing room, animation board, permanent film library of student films, production completion center Television — ½-inch VTR, ¾-inch cassette VTR, portable black and white cameras, monitors, lighting equipment, audio mixers, access to television facilities through Radio-Television Department and/or public access channel

FACULTY Don Daso, Peter Lehman, Karen Nulf, David Prince, George Semsel

COURSE LIST

Undergraduate

Introduction to Film I–III

Undergraduate and Graduate

Film Techniques (Super-8 and 8mm)
Advanced Super-8 Production
Motion Picture Production I–III (16mm)
Survey of Film Animation
Theory and Criticism I–III
Film Topics Seminar I–III
Film History
Study in Documentary Film
Study in Experimental Film
Festival Practicum
Wide-Angle Practicum
Film Society Practicum
Film Production Center Practicum
Advanced Motion Picture Production I–III
Film Style and Structure
Writing—Film Publications
Individual Production Problems
Individual Readings
Independent Study
Introduction to Graduate Study
Film Studio Thesis
Film Written Thesis

Radio-Television Department, College of Fine Arts, Athens, OH 45701 614-594-5503

CONTACT Drew McDaniel

DEGREES OFFERED BS in communications with a major in broadcasting, MA in radio-television, PhD in mass communication with a major in broadcasting

DEPARTMENTAL MAJORS 700 students

ADMISSION Undergraduate application deadline — 4/1, rolling

CURRICULAR EMPHASIS Television study — generalist orientation

SPECIAL ACTIVITIES/OFFERINGS Program material produced for local public television station, internships in television broadcasting, independent study, vocational placement service

FACILITIES AND EQUIPMENT Television — complete color exterior production facilities, complete color studio production facilities

FACULTY Joseph Berman, Charles Clift, Archie Greer, George Korn, Drew McDaniel, William Miller, Roderick Rightmire, Arthur Savage, Glenna Turner, James Webster

COURSE LIST

Undergraduate and Graduate

Introduction to Radio-Television
Technical Bases of Radio-Television
Electronic Media Management I, II
Introduction to Production and Writing
Broadcasting and the Public
Introduction to Television Production
Television Production-Direction
Advanced Television Production-Direction
Dramatic and Documentary Writing
Instructional Methods in Radio-Television
Broadcast Management
Television Newsfilm Production and Editing
Broadcast Law and Regulations
Broadcast Programming
Comparative Systems of Broadcasting
History of Broadcasting

Mass Communications Theory
Research Methods in Mass Communications
International Broadcasting
Colloquium in Broadcasting
Statistical Analysis in Mass Communications Research
Seminar in Mass Communications Research
Seminar in Pedagogy
Seminar in Criticism

Ohio University, Zanesville

State-supported 2-year coed college. Part of Ohio University System, automatic transfer to main campus for baccalaureate. Institutionally accredited by regional association. Rural location. Total enrollment: 1002. Undergraduate enrollment: 922. Total faculty: 65 (30 full-time, 35 part-time). Quarter calendar. Grading system: letters or numbers.

Radio-Television Department, 1425 Newark Road, Zanesville, OH 43701 614-453-0762

CONTACT Reed Smith
DEGREE OFFERED AAS in radio-television with emphasis in production-performance or technology
DEPARTMENTAL MAJORS Television — 40 students
ADMISSION Requirements — ACT or SAT scores, interview Application deadline — open
FINANCIAL AID Scholarships, work/study programs, student loans Undergraduate application deadline — March 15
CURRICULAR EMPHASIS Film study — educational media/instructional technology Television study — history, appreciation, production treated equally Television production — commercial, news/documentary, experimental/personal video, educational treated equally
SPECIAL ACTIVITIES/OFFERINGS Program material produced for on-campus closed-circuit television, cable television, local commercial television station; internships in television production; independent study; vocational placement service
FACILITIES AND EQUIPMENT Television — black and white studio cameras, color studio cameras, ¾-inch cassette VTR, editing equipment, monitors, special effects generators, portable color cameras, ¾-inch ENG, lighting equipment, sound recording equipment, audio mixers, color studio, audio studio, control room
FACULTY Tim Frye, Reed Smith PART-TIME FACULTY Joseph Berman, Wayne Ely, Roderick Rightmire, Arthur Savage

COURSE LIST

Undergraduate
Continuity Writing
Introduction to TV Production
Advanced TV Production

Otterbein College

Independent United Methodist 4-year and professional coed institution. Institutionally accredited by regional association, programs recognized by NASM. Suburban location, 54-acre campus. Undergraduate enrollment: 1585. Total faculty: 110 (88 full-time, 22 part-time). 3-3 calendar. Grading system: letters or numbers.

Department of Speech and Theatre, Westerville, OH 43081 614-890-3000

CONTACT Film — C Dedrill Television — J Grissinger
ADMISSION Application deadline — 8/15, rolling
FINANCIAL AID Student loans, work/study programs Application deadline — rolling
SPECIAL ACTIVITIES/OFFERINGS Internships in television production, independent study, vocational placement service
FACILITIES AND EQUIPMENT Television — complete black and white studio production equipment, portable black and white cameras, ½-inch portapak recorder, black and white studio, audio studio, control room
FACULTY C Dedrill, J Grissinger

COURSE LIST

Undergraduate
Broadcasting and the Media
Film Production

University of Akron

State-supported coed university. Institutionally accredited by regional association, programs recognized by AACSB. Urban location. Total enrollment: 22,608. Undergraduate enrollment: 19,360. Total faculty: 1045 (635 full-time, 410 part-time). Semester calendar. Grading system: letters or numbers.

Mass Media Communication Department, Akron, OH 44325 216-375-7954

CONTACT David Jamison
PROGRAM OFFERED Major in mass media communication with emphasis in film and television
ADMISSION Requirement — minimum grade point average
FINANCIAL AID Student loans, work/study programs, teaching assistantships
CURRICULAR EMPHASIS Film study — (1) history; (2) criticism and aesthetics; (3) production Undergraduate television study — (1) management; (2) production; (3) criticism and aesthetics; (4) history; (5) appreciation; (6) educational Graduate television study — (1) criticism and aesthetics; (2) appreciation; (3) production; (4) history; (5) management; (6) educational
SPECIAL ACTIVITIES/OFFERINGS Program material produced for on-campus closed-circuit televison and local public television station, apprenticeships, internships in film and television production, independent study, practicum
FACILITIES AND EQUIPMENT Film — complete 8mm equipment, film library Television — complete color studio and exterior production equipment, audio studio, control room
FACULTY Terry Book, Ruth Lewis

University of Akron (continued)

COURSE LIST

Undergraduate

Introduction to Radio-Television
Communication Media — Television
Communication Media — Film
Television Production
American Film History

Graduate

Studies in Communication Media — Television
Studies in Communication Media — Television
Studies in Communication Media — Film

Undergraduate and Graduate

Cinematography Workshop

University of Cincinnati

State-supported coed university. Institutionally accredited by regional association, programs recognized by NASM, AACSB, NASA, ACPE. Urban location. Total enrollment: 37,736. Undergraduate enrollment: 31,663. Total faculty: 3237 (3237 full-time, 0 part-time). Quarter calendar. Grading system: letters or numbers.

Film and Media Program, Mail Location 184, Cincinnati, OH 45221 513-475-2551

CONTACT Film — Louis Rockwood Television — Carl Dahlgren
DEGREES OFFERED BA, BS, MA, PhD
PROGRAM MAJORS Undergraduate film — 25 students Undergraduate television — 180 students
ADMISSION Undergraduate requirements — 2.0 minimum grade point average, top half of graduating class in high school Graduate requirement — 3.0 minimum grade point average Undergraduate application deadline — 12/15
FINANCIAL AID Scholarships, work/study programs, student loans, fellowships, teaching assistantships, research assistantships, intern program Undergraduate application deadline — 12/15
CURRICULAR EMPHASIS Undergraduate film study — (1) criticism and aesthetics, appreciation; (2) history, educational media/instructional technology Undergraduate filmmaking — (1) animated; (2) documentary, narrative, experimental, educational Undergraduate television study — (1) production, management, writing; (2) criticism and aesthetics, appreciation, educational; (3) history Television production — (1) commercial, news/documentary; (2) experimental/personal video, educational
SPECIAL ACTIVITIES/OFFERINGS Film series; film societies, student publications; program material produced for on-campus closed-circuit television, cable television, local public television station, local commercial television station; apprenticeships; internships in film production; internships in television production; independent study; teacher training; vocational placement service
FACILITIES AND EQUIPMENT Film — 8mm and 16mm cameras, editing equipment, sound recording equipment, lighting, black and white film stock, 16mm projectors, sound stage, screening room, editing room, sound mixing room, animation board, permanent film library of commercial or professional films Television — complete black and white and color studio production equipment, complete black and white and color exterior production equipment, black and white studio, color studio, audio studio, control room

COURSE LIST

Undergraduate

Introduction to Film and Media Studies
Film as Art and Communication
Mass Communication and the Popular Arts
Film and the History of World War II
Media Research Techniques
Survey of Mass Media
Survey of Radio and Television
Survey of Film
Introduction to Broadcast Equipment
Basic Film
Introduction to Broadcast Writing
Introduction to Broadcast Performance
Television Production Techniques I
Intermediate Film Production
Advanced Film Production
Film Criticism
Radio Production
Critical Film Study
Radio-Television Advertising and Sales I–III
Radio-Television Public Relations
Broadcast Law
Broadcast Journalism: Introduction
Broadcast Journalism: Advanced
The Business of Broadcasting
Cable TV/Alternative Media
Broadcast News Writing
Ethics of Mass Communication
Broadcast News Production
History of Documentaries
Advanced Recording Techniques
Broadcasting Criticism
Broadcast Station Management

Graduate

Communication Theory
Communication in Organizations
Persuasion
Seminar in Analysis of Media
Telecommunication
Selection and Utilization of Media
Instructional Television
Designing Curriculum Integration of the Media
Production of Instructional Materials
Advanced Seminar in Media
Recording Performance Techniques
Broadcast Advertising/Sales
Survey of Commercial Music
Radio-TV Public Relations
Cinematography
Noncommercial Broadcasting
Broadcast Law
Broadcast Journalism
Independent Study
Business of Broadcasting
Cable TV/Alternative Media
Broadcast News Writing
Television Directing
Ethics of Mass Communication
Research Methods in Mass Communication
Broadcast News Production
Industrial TV Production
Advanced Film/Video Editing
Broadcast Station Management
Scriptwriting for Film
International Broadcasting
Broadcast Performance: Free-Lance Commercial Techniques
Graduate Advertising Writing
Graduate Writing Advertising for Broadcast Media: Intermediate
Graduate Writing Advertisement for Broadcast Media: Advanced
Graduate Critical Film Study
Graduate Survey of Theatrical Form
Graduate Survey of Radio-TV
Graduate Survey of Film
Graduate Introduction to Broadcasting Equipment
Graduate Audio Review
Graduate TV Review
Graduate Film Review
Children's TV Programming
Seminar: The Producer
Graduate Film Production Techniques
Graduate TV Production Techniques I, II

Undergraduate and Graduate

Seminar: Film Structure I: Graphic Persuasion
Seminar: Film Structure II: Film Noir
Seminar: Film Structure III: Multivalenced Film
Film as Art: Silent Comedy
Film as Art: Sound Comedy
Film as Art: Musicals
Media and Technology
Film as History (Europe)
Introductory Film I–II

Department of History, Clifton Avenue, Cincinnati, OH 45221 513-475-2144

CONTACT Thomas L Sakmyster
ADMISSION Application deadline — 12/15
FINANCIAL AID Scholarships, student loans, work/study programs, teaching assistantships, research assistantships, fellowships Application deadline — 2/1
CURRICULAR EMPHASIS Film study — (1) history; (2) educational media
SPECIAL ACTIVITIES/OFFERINGS Film societies
FACILITIES AND EQUIPMENT Film — screening room
FACULTY Thomas L Sakmyster

COURSE LIST

Undergraduate and Graduate

Film as History: Modern Europe
History and Films of World War II

University of Toledo

State-supported coed university. Institutionally accredited by regional association, programs recognized by NASM, AACSB, ACPE. Suburban location, 400-acre campus. Total enrollment: 17,257. Undergraduate enrollment: 14,171. Total faculty: 708. Quarter calendar. Grading system: letters or numbers.

Department of Educational Technology, 2801 West Bancroft Street, Toledo, OH 43606 419-537-2835

CONTACT L Elsie
DEGREES OFFERED Undergraduate minor with emphasis in film and/or television, M Ed in educational technology with emphasis in film and/or television
ADMISSION Graduate requirements — 2.7 minimum grade point average, GRE scores, interview, teachers' recommendations, written statement of purpose Undergraduate application deadline — rolling
FINANCIAL AID Teaching assistantships Undergraduate application deadline — rolling
CURRICULAR EMPHASIS Undergraduate film study — educational media/instructional technology Graduate film study — educational media/instructional technology Undergraduate filmmaking — educational Graduate filmmaking — educational Undergraduate television study — educational, production, management treated equally Graduate television study — educational, production, management treated equally Undergraduate television production — educational Graduate televison production — educational
SPECIAL ACTIVITIES/OFFERINGS Filmmaking clubs, film festivals, student publications, independent study, teacher training
FACILITIES AND EQUIPMENT Film — complete 8mm equipment, editing room, sound mixing room, animation board, permanent film library of commercial or professional films Television — black and white and color studio production equipment, black and white studio, color studio, audio studio, control room
FACULTY Keith Bernhard, Andy DiPaolo, Les Elsie, Dennis Myers, Amos Patterson PART-TIME FACULTY Dennis Sherk

COURSE LIST

Undergraduate and Graduate

Educational Television
Instructional Television Production
Portable Television Workshop
Filmmaking in Schools
Film Study
Media Studies for Schools

Film/Video, Department of Theatre 419-537-4350 or 419-537-2375

CONTACT Scott Nygren
DEGREES OFFERED BA, BFA in theatre with an emphasis in film/video
PROGRAM MAJORS Undergraduate film/video — 15 students
ADMISSION Application deadline — rolling
FINANCIAL AID Scholarships, work/study programs, student loans Application deadline — 3/1
CURRICULAR EMPHASIS Film study — history, criticism and aesthetics, appreciation, theory treated equally Filmmaking — documentary, narrative, experimental, animated treated equally Television study — history, criticism and aesthetics, appreciation, theory treated equally Television production — documentary, experimental/personal video treated equally
SPECIAL ACTIVITIES/OFFERINGS Film — Film series, film societies, visiting film and video makers, independent study
FACILITIES AND EQUIPMENT Film — 8mm and 16mm equipment, sound stage, screening room, editing room, sound mixing room, animation board, permanent film library of student films, permanent film library of commercial and professional films, new theatre/music/film complex Television — black and white studio cameras, ½-inch VTR, portable black and white cameras, editing equipment, monitors, special effects generators, portable color cameras, ½-inch portapak recorders, lighting equipment, sound recording equipment, audio mixers, black and white studio, color studio, editing room
FACULTY Bernard A Coyne, Scott Nygren, Raymond J Pentzell, Jimmie Robinson, Charles Vicinus PART-TIME FACULTY Chris Nygren

COURSE LIST

Undergraduate

The Silent Film
The Sound Film
The Film Image
Documentary Film
Major Filmmaker
Expanded Cinema
Beginning Filmmaking
Super-8mm Workshop
16mm Workshop
The Electronic Image
Directing for Film and TV

University of Toledo (continued)

Professional Projects in 16mm Film and Television
Production Lighting
Production Sound
Makeup for Film and TV
Playwriting for Film and Television
Special Projects in Film and Television
Student-initiated Productions in Film and Television

Ursuline College

Independent Catholic 4-year college primarily for women. Institutionally accredited by regional association. Suburban location, 115-acre campus. Undergraduate enrollment: 840. Total faculty: 70 (50 full-time, 20 part-time). Semester calendar. Grading system: letters or numbers.

Media Department, 2600 Lander Road, Cleveland, OH 44124 216-449-4200

CONTACT Walter Hanclosky
ADMISSION Application deadline — rolling
CURRICULAR EMPHASIS Film study — (1) production; (2) educational media/instructional technology; (3) appreciation; (4) criticism and aesthetics; (5) history Filmmaking — (1) educational; (2) animated;(3) narrative; (4) experimental; (5) documentary Television study — (1) production; (2) criticism; (3) appreciation; (4) educational; (5) history; (6) management Television production — (1) educational; (2) news/documentary; (3) commercial; (4) experimental/personal video
FACILITIES AND EQUIPMENT Film — complete 8mm and 35mm equipment, sound stage, 35mm screening facilities, sound mixing room Television — black and white studio camera, ½-inch VTR, portable black and white cameras, monitors, audio studio
FACULTY Mary Pat Daley PART-TIME FACULTY Walter Hanclosky

COURSE LIST

Undergraduate

Film Appreciation
Introduction to Photography
Multimedia Presentations

Ohio

Wright State University

State-supported coed university. Institutionally accredited by regional association, programs recognized by NASM, AACSB. Suburban location. Total enrollment: 14,291. Undergraduate enrollment: 10,916. Total faculty: 800 (600 full-time, 200 part-time). Quarter calendar. Grading system: letters or numbers.

Department of Theatre Arts, Dayton, OH 45435 513-873-3072

CONTACT Abe J Bassett
DEGREES OFFERED BA in film studies, BFA in film production
DEPARTMENTAL MAJORS 30 students
ADMISSION Application deadline — rolling
FINANCIAL AID Scholarships, work/study programs, student loans
CURRICULAR EMPHASIS Film study — (1) criticism and aesthetics; (2) history; (3) appreciation Filmmaking — (1) narrative; (2) documentary; (3) experimental
SPECIAL ACTIVITIES/OFFERINGS Filmmaking clubs, film series, film festivals
FACILITIES AND EQUIPMENT Film — 8mm and 16mm cameras, editing equipment, sound recording equipment, lighting, projectors, sound stage, screening room, editing room, sound mixing room
FACULTY Charles Derry, Joseph Hill PART-TIME FACULTY Jack Kern, William Lewis

COURSE LIST

Undergraduate

Film Appreciation
History of Motion Pictures I–III
Film Genre (variable title)
Film Authorship (variable title)
Film Criticism (variable title)
Film Production I, II
Elementary Film Projects
Intermediate Film Projects
Advanced Film Projects

Xavier University

Independent Roman Catholic comprehensive coed institution. Institutionally accredited by regional association. Suburban location, 65-acre campus. Total enrollment: 6382. Undergraduate enrollment: 2871. Total faculty: 280 (163 full-time, 117 part-time). Semester calendar. Grading system: letters or numbers.

Communication Arts Department, Cincinnati, OH 45207 513-745-3737

CONTACT Reverend William J Hagerty SJ
DEGREE OFFERED BS in communication arts with a minor in radio-TV-film
DEPARTMENTAL MAJORS Film — 18 students Television — 58 students
ADMISSION Requirements — 2.0 minimum grade point average, ACT or SAT scores, interview
FINANCIAL AID Scholarships, work/study programs, student loans
CURRICULAR EMPHASIS Film study — history, criticism and aesthetics, appreciation treated equally Filmmaking — (1) experimental; (2) documentary; (3) educational Television study — (1) production; (2) management; (3) criticism and aesthetics Television production — (1) experimental/personal video; (2) educational; (3) news/documentary
SPECIAL ACTIVITIES/OFFERINGS Filmmaking clubs; film series; film societies; program material produced for on-campus closed-circuit television, cable television, local public television station; apprenticeships
FACILITIES AND EQUIPMENT Film — 8mm and 16mm cameras, editing equipment, lighting, black and white film stock, color film stock, projectors, sound stage, screening room, 35mm screening facilities, editing room, permanent film library of student films Television — complete black and white and color studio production equipment, black and white studio, color studio, mobile van/unit, audio room, control room
FACULTY Reverend Lawrence Flynn SJ, Reverend William J Hagerty SJ, James C King, Paul Potter PART-TIME FACULTY Doug Anthony, Tom Baggs, Greg Picciano

COURSE LIST

Undergraduate

Photography I, II
Art of the Film
Film History and Directors
Media Aesthetics
Film Criticism
Nonfiction Film
Filmmaking
Short Story/Short Film
Special Study
Fundamentals: Radio-TV
Audio—Production and Technology
Broadcast Announcing
Video—Production and Technology
Broadcast Management
TV Directing
Advanced TV Production
Cable TV
Continuity Writing for TV
Public Broadcasting
Audiovisual Techniques

OKLAHOMA

Bethany Nazarene College

Independent Nazarene comprehensive coed institution. Institutionally accredited by regional association. Suburban location, 40-acre campus. Total enrollment: 1311. Undergraduate enrollment: 1228. Total faculty: 85 (70 full-time, 15 part-time). Semester calendar. Grading system: letters or numbers.

Speech Communication/Mass Communication Department, Bethany, OK 73008
405-789-6400

CONTACT Wayne Murrow
DEGREES OFFERED BA in mass communication, BA in speech communication with emphasis in television
DEPARTMENTAL MAJORS Television — 10 students
ADMISSION Application deadline — 8/1
FINANCIAL AID Scholarships, work/study programs, student loans
CURRICULAR EMPHASIS Television study — (1) criticism and aesthetics; (2) educational; (3) production Television production — experimental/personal video
SPECIAL ACTIVITIES/OFFERINGS Program material produced for on-campus closed-circuit television, internships in film production, internships in television production, independent study, teacher training, vocational placement service
FACILITIES AND EQUIPMENT Film — 8mm lighting, black and white film stock, color film stock, projectors, 16mm cameras, lighting, black and white film stock, color film stock, projectors, 35mm cameras, lighting, black and white film stock, color film stock, projectors, screening room, 35mm screening facilities, editing room, sound mixing room Television — black and white studio cameras, color studio cameras, ½-inch VTR, portable black and white cameras, monitors, portable color cameras, ½-inch portapak recorders, lighting equipment, sound recording equipment, audio mixers, black and white studio
FACULTY Pam Human, Jim Wilcox PART-TIME FACULTY Gene Hortsell, Ron Marchant

COURSE LIST

Undergraduate

Graphics of Communication
Basic Newswriting
Introduction to Mass Communication
Photo Journalism
Introduction to Advertising
Mass Communication Theory
Film Production
Scriptwriting
Broadcast News
Special Studies

Central State University

State-supported comprehensive coed institution. Institutionally accredited by regional association. Suburban location, 200-acre campus. Undergraduate enrollment: 12,000. Total faculty: 430 (336 full-time, 94 part-time). Semester calendar. Grading system: letters or numbers.

Creative Studies Department, 100 University Drive, Edmond, OK 73034 405-341-2980

CONTACT Clif Warren
DEGREE OFFERED MA in English with emphasis in creative writing for film or television
SPECIAL ACTIVITIES/OFFERINGS Television or motion picture scenario thesis requirement, one-to-one relationship with practicing, professional writers-in-residence
FACILITIES AND EQUIPMENT Special film screenings in cooperation with local commercial theater
FACULTY Wanda Duncan, Marilyn Harris, John Pickard, Lawana Trout, Clif Warren

COURSE LIST

Undergraduate and Graduate

Literature and the Short Film
Genres of Film
Contemporary American Film
Classic American Films
Classic Foreign Films
Literature and Films of Mysticism

Northeastern Oklahoma State University

State-supported comprehensive coed institution. Institutionally accredited by regional association. Small town location, 160-acre campus. Total enrollment: 5281. Undergraduate enrollment: 4323. Total faculty: 220 (200 full-time, 20 part-time). Semester calendar. Grading system: letters or numbers.

Audio Visual Department, Tahlequah, OK 74464 918-456-5511

CONTACT Tom W Johnson
ADMISSION Application deadline — rolling

Northeastern Oklahoma State University (continued)

CURRICULAR EMPHASIS Film study — educational media/instructional technology Filmmaking — educational Television study — educational Television production — educational
SPECIAL ACTIVITIES/OFFERINGS Program material produced for on-campus closed-circuit television
FACILITIES AND EQUIPMENT Television — complete black and white studio and exterior production equipment, complete color studio and exterior production facilities, black and white studio, control room

COURSE LIST

Undergraduate and Graduate
Educational Television and Radio Production

Oklahoma Baptist University

Independent Baptist 4-year and professional coed institution. Accredited by regional association and AICS, programs recognized by NASM. Small town location, 180-acre campus. Undergraduate enrollment: 1555. Total faculty: 113 (93 full-time, 20 part-time). Semester calendar. Grading system: letters or numbers.

English Department, Shawnee, OK 74801 405-275-4717, ext 2203

CONTACT Film — W M Hagen Television — John Lovelace
FINANCIAL AID Scholarships, student loans
CURRICULAR EMPHASIS Undergraduate film study — history, appreciation, film genres treated equally Undergraduate television study — criticism and aesthetics, appreciation treated equally
SPECIAL ACTIVITIES/OFFERINGS Film series, program material produced for cable television, teacher training
FACULTY Douglas Clark, W M Hagen

COURSE LIST

Undergraduate
American Drama and Film
Popular Culture

Oklahoma State University

State-supported coed university. Part of Oklahoma State System of Higher Education. Institutionally accredited by regional association. Small town location, 415-acre campus. Total enrollment: 22,276. Undergraduate enrollment: 19,040. Total faculty: 1618 (854 full-time, 764 part-time). Semester calendar. Grading system: letters or numbers.

English Department, Stillwater, OK 74078 405-624-6142

CONTACT Peter C Rollins
DEGREES OFFERED BA, MA, PhD in film and literature
DEPARTMENTAL MAJORS Undergraduate film — 10 students Graduate film — 4 students
ADMISSION Undergraduate requirements — B in high school English, ACT or SAT scores, Graduate requirements — teachers' recommendations, professional recommendations Undergraduate application deadline — rolling
FINANCIAL AID Scholarships, work/study programs, student loans, fellowships, teaching assistantships Undergraduate application deadline — rolling
CURRICULAR EMPHASIS Undergraduate film study — appreciation, film and literature treated equally Graduate film study — criticism and aesthetics, appreciation, film and literature treated equally Undergraduate television study — criticism and aesthetics, appreciation treated equally Graduate television study — criticism and aesthetics, appreciation treated equally
SPECIAL ACTIVITIES/OFFERINGS Filmmaking clubs, film series, film festivals
FACILITIES AND EQUIPMENT Television — black and white studio cameras, ½-inch VTR, ¾-inch cassette VTR, portable black and white cameras, editing equipment, monitors
FACULTY Leonard J Leff, Peter C Rollins

COURSE LIST

Undergraduate
Freshman Composition: Film Emphasis
Introduction to New Media: Film Genres
Film and American Society
Intermediate Creative Writing: Script
Film as Literature
Television as Literature

Graduate
Seminar in Creative Writing: Film
Studies in New Media: Theory and Criticism of Film

Undergraduate and Graduate
Advanced Creative Writing: Script
Aesthetics of Film
OSU Filmathon

Radio-Television-Film Department 405-624-6354

CONTACT Ed Paulin, Chairman
DEGREES OFFERED BA, BS in radio-television-film; MS, Ed D in mass communications with emphasis in radio-television-film
DEPARTMENTAL MAJORS Undergraduate — 275 students Graduate — 10 students
ADMISSION Undergraduate application deadline — rolling
FINANCIAL AID Assistantships Undergraduate application deadline — 6/1

CURRICULAR EMPHASIS Film study — (1) production; (2) history, criticism and aesthetics; (3) educational media/instructional technology Filmmaking — (1) documentary; (2) narrative, experimental; (3) animated Television study — (1) production; (2) educational; (3) history, criticism and aesthetics Television production — (1) studio; (2) educational; (3) experimental/personal video
FACILITIES AND EQUIPMENT Film — 8mm and 16mm cameras, double-system sound recording equipment Television — helical VTR, editing room, switcher with special effects, mixing room, film chain, black and white studio, color studio, ENG
FACULTY Bill Jackson PART-TIME FACULTY Marshall Allen, Paul Couey, William Crane, Riley Maynard

COURSE LIST

Undergraduate
Broadcast Communication
History and Significance of Film and Broadcasting
Radio-Television-Film Lab

Graduate
Process and Effects of Mass Communication
Responsibility in Mass Communication
Studies in Communication Media

Undergraduate and Graduate
Television Production
Programs and Audiences
Writing for Radio-Television-Film
Basic Motion Picture Technique
Television Directing
Broadcast Documentary
Problems in Radio-Television-Film
Broadcast Sales

Oral Roberts University

Independent nondenominational comprehensive coed institution. Institutionally accredited by regional association. Suburban location. Total enrollment: 4001. Undergraduate enrollment: 2503. Total faculty: 300 full-time. Semester calendar. Grading system: letters or numbers.

Communication Arts Department, 7777 South Lewis, Tulsa, OK 74171 918-492-6161

CONTACT Film — Robert Primrose Television — Thomas Durfey
DEGREE OFFERED BS in telecommunication
DEPARTMENTAL MAJORS 250 students
ADMISSION Application deadline — rolling
CURRICULAR EMPHASIS Film study — (1) production; (2) history Filmmaking — (1) documentary; (2) narrative; (3) educational Television study — (1) production; (2) history; (3) educational; (4) management; (5) criticism and aesthetics Television production — (1) commercial; (2) news/documentary; (3) educational
SPECIAL ACTIVITIES/OFFERINGS Program material produced for on-campus closed-circuit television and cable television, internships in film and television production, independent study
FACILITIES AND EQUIPMENT Film — complete 8mm and 16mm equipment, sound stage, screening room, editing room, sound mixing room, permanent film library Television — exterior production equipment, complete color studio production equipment, color studio, audio studio, control room
FACULTY Thomas Durfey, Paul McClendon, Harlan Stensaas, Charles Zwick PART-TIME FACULTY Even Culp, Ken Johnson, Mark Labash, Mike Mitchell

COURSE LIST

Undergraduate
Basic Broadcast Electronics
Mass Communication Workshop
Broadcast Newswriting
Introduction to Mass Media Writing
Introduction to Mass Communication
Introduction to Television Production
Technical Problems in TV/Film
Advanced Television Production
Advertisement and Marketing in Telecommunication
Fundamentals of Motion Pictures
Motion Picture Production Techniques
Editing for Film
Research Methods in the Mass Media
Administration and Management in Broadcasting
Mass Communication Strategies and Design
Television-Film Direction
Advertisement Writing

Southwestern Oklahoma State University

State-supported comprehensive coed institution. Institutionally accredited by regional association. Small town location, 73-acre campus. Total enrollment: 4800. Undergraduate enrollment: 4143. Total faculty: 226 (218 full-time, 8 part-time). Semester calendar. Grading system: letters or numbers.

English Department, Weatherford, OK 73096 405-772-6611

CONTACT Jerry G. Nye

COURSE LIST

Undergraduate
Introduction to Film
History of Film

General Education Department

CONTACT Bernice Delaney

COURSE LIST

Undergraduate
Introduction to Film
History of Film

University of Oklahoma

State-supported coed university. Part of Oklahoma State System of Higher Education. Institutionally accredited by regional association, programs recognized by NASM, AACSB, NASA, ACPE. Small town location, 1000-acre campus. Total enrollment: 20,357. Undergraduate enrollment: 15,158. Total faculty: 752 (712 full-time, 40 part-time). Semester calendar. Grading system: letters or numbers.

Video-Film Program, 520 Parrington Oval, Norman, OK 73019 405-325-2691

CONTACT Film — Debbie Mehan Television — John Alberty
DEGREES OFFERED BFA in film-video, MFA in film-video
PROGRAM MAJORS Undergraduate film — 28 students Undergraduate television — 12 students Graduate film — 4 students Graduate television — 3 students
ADMISSION Undergraduate requirements — 2.0 minimum grade point average, portfolio Graduate requirements — 2.8 minimum grade point average, teachers' recommendations, portfolio, professional recommendations
FINANCIAL AID Scholarships, work/study programs, student loans, fellowships, teaching assistantships
CURRICULAR EMPHASIS Undergraduate film study — (1) criticism and aesthetics; (2) history; (3) appreciation Graduate film study — (1) criticism and aesthetics; (2) history; (3) appreciation Undergraduate filmmaking — (1) experimental; (2) animated; (3) documentary Graduate filmmaking — (1) experimental; (2) animated; (3) documentary Undergraduate television study — (1) criticism and aesthetics; (2) production; (3) history Graduate television study — (1) criticism and aesthetics; (2) production; (3) history Undergraduate television production — (1) experimental/personal video; (2) news/documentary Graduate television production — (1) experimental/personal video; (2) news/documentary
SPECIAL ACTIVITIES/OFFERINGS Filmmaking clubs; film series; film societies; program material produced for cable television, local public television station, museums and galleries; independent study
FACILITIES AND EQUIPMENT Film — complete 8mm and 16mm equipment, screening room, editing room, sound mixing room, animation board, permanent film library of student films, permanent film library of commercial or professional films Television — black and white studio cameras, color studio cameras, ½-inch VTR, ¾-inch cassette VTR, portable black and white cameras, editing equipment, monitors, special effects generators, slide chain, portable color cameras, ½-inch portapak recorders, ¾-inch ENG, lighting equipment, sound recording equipment, audio mixers, film chain, black and white studio, color studio, audio studio, control room
FACULTY John Alberty, Debbie Mehan

COURSE LIST

Undergraduate
Video for the Artist I
Filmmaking I, II
Film Animation I, II

Undergraduate and Graduate
Video for the Artist II, III
Filmmaking III
Film Animation III
Special Problems and Film Analysis

University of Science and Arts of Oklahoma

State-supported 4-year coed college. Institutionally accredited by regional association. Small town location, 75-acre campus. Undergraduate enrollment: 1355. Total faculty: 80 (60 full-time, 20 part-time). Trimester calendar. Grading system: letters or numbers.

English Department, Box 3226, Chickasha, OK 73018 405-224-3140

CONTACT Jerry Holt
ADMISSION Undergraduate requirements — ACT or SAT scores, interview, teachers' recommendations
FINANCIAL AID Scholarships, work/study programs, student loans
CURRICULAR EMPHASIS Undergraduate film study — history, criticism and aesthetics, appreciation, educational media/instructional technology treated equally Undergraduate television study — history, criticism and aesthetics, appreciation treated equally
SPECIAL ACTIVITIES/OFFERINGS Film series, independent study, teacher training, vocational placement service
FACILITIES AND EQUIPMENT Film — 8mm cameras, editing equipment, 16mm editing equipment, projectors, screening room, editing room Television — black and white studio cameras, ½-inch VTR, ¾-inch cassette VTR, portable black and white cameras, monitors, special effects generators, lighting equipment, sound recording equipment, audio mixers, black and white studio, audio studio

COURSE LIST

Undergraduate
A Study of the Film
Literature into Film
Film Concentration Workshop
Tutorials

University of Tulsa

Independent coed university. Institutionally accredited by regional association. Urban location. Total enrollment: 6300. Undergraduate enrollment: 4709. Total faculty: 362 (275 full-time, 87 part-time). Semester calendar. Grading system: letters or numbers.

Faculty of Communication, 600 South College, Tulsa, OK 74104 918-592-6000, ext 541

CONTACT Thomas W Bohn
DEGREES OFFERED BA, BS in telecommunications; BA, BS in print/broadcast journalism
PROGRAM MAJORS Television — 125 students
ADMISSION Requirements — 2.0 minimum grade point average, ACT or SAT scores Application deadline — rolling
FINANCIAL AID Scholarships, work/study programs, student loans Application deadline — 3/1

CURRICULAR EMPHASIS Film study — history, criticism and aesthetics, appreciation treated equally Television study — (1) production; (2) criticism and aesthetics; (3) history Television production — (1) commercial; (2) news/documentary; (3) educational
SPECIAL ACTIVITIES/OFFERINGS Student publications, program material produced for cable television, apprenticeships, internships in television production, independent study, vocational placement service
FACILITIES AND EQUIPMENT Film — screening room, permanent film library of commercial or professional films Television — color studio cameras, ½-inch VTR, ¾-inch cassette VTR, portable black and white cameras, editing equipment, monitors, special effects generators, slide chain, portable color cameras, ½-inch portapak recorders, ¾-inch ENG, lighting equipment, sound recording equipment, audio mixers, film chain, time base corrector, color studio, audio studio, control room
FACULTY Maryjo Adams, Thomas W Bohn, Edward Dumit, Ken Greenwood PART-TIME FACULTY Dave Anderson, Willis Kieninger, Jim Lenertz

COURSE LIST
Undergraduate
Film Form and Analysis
Broadcast Production and Performance
Writing for Broadcasting
Broadcast Announcing
Video Production
Advanced Video Production
Broadcast Sales
Broadcast Management
Telecommunication Law
Advanced Writing for Broadcasting

Literature Department
CURRICULAR EMPHASIS Film study — history, criticism and aesthetics, appreciation treated equally
SPECIAL ACTIVITIES/OFFERINGS Film series
FACILITIES AND EQUIPMENT Film — permanent film library
FACULTY Joseph R Millichap

COURSE LIST
Undergraduate
Film and Literature
Film and Fiction
The Silent Film
The Talkies (1928–1941)
Documentary in Film Literature
Modern Film
American Film

OREGON

Chemeketa Community College

State and locally supported 2-year coed college. Part of Oregon State System of Higher Education, automatic transfer to main campus for baccalaureate. Institutionally accredited by regional association. Suburban location, 100-acre campus. Undergraduate enrollment: 5217. Total faculty: 668 (188 full-time, 480 part-time). Quarter calendar. Grading system: letters or numbers.

Humanities Department, 4000 Lancaster Drive NE, PO Box 14007, Salem, OR 97309 503-399-5184
CONTACT Robert Bibler
PROGRAM OFFERED AA (no degree specialization)
FINANCIAL AID Work/study programs, student loans Application deadline — 3/1
CURRICULAR EMPHASIS Film study — (1) appreciation; (2) criticism and aesthetics; (3) history Filmmaking — (1) documentary; (2) narrative; (3) experimental
SPECIAL ACTIVITIES/OFFERINGS Film series
FACILITIES AND EQUIPMENT Film — 8mm cameras, editing equipment, lighting, projectors, 16mm cameras, lighting, projectors, sound stage, screening room
FACULTY Robert Bibler, Leonard Held PART-TIME FACULTY Michael Markee

COURSE LIST
Undergraduate
Film and Video Arts
Film Production
Film: Styles
Film: Directors
Film: Genres

Clackamas Community College

County-supported 2-year coed college. Institutionally accredited by regional association. Small town location, 150-acre campus. Undergraduate enrollment: 3406. Total faculty: 147 (47 full-time, 100 part-time). Trimester calendar. Grading system: letters or numbers.

Video Department, 19600 Molalla, Oregon City, OR 97045 503-656-2631
DEGREE OFFERED AS in video technology
DEPARTMENTAL MAJORS 22 students
ADMISSION Requirements — interviews, professional recommendations, teachers' recommendations Application deadline — 9/1, rolling
FINANCIAL AID Scholarships, student loans, work/study programs Application deadline — rolling
CURRICULAR EMPHASIS Film study — history, criticism and aesthetics, appreciation, production, educational media/instructional technology treated equally Filmmaking — (1) documentary; (2) narrative; (3) experimental Television study — (1) technical; (2) production; (3) management; (4) criticism and aesthetics Television production — (1) news/documentary; (2) educational; (3) experimental/personal video

Clackamas Community College (continued)

SPECIAL ACTIVITIES/OFFERINGS Student publications, program material produced for on-campus closed-circuit television and classroom use, internships in film and television production, independent study, practicum, teacher training, vocational placement service

FACILITIES AND EQUIPMENT Film — complete 8mm equipment, sound stage, screening room, editing room, sound mixing room, permanent film library Television — complete black and white studio and exterior production equipment, complete color studio production equipment, black and white studio, color studio, audio studio, control rooms

FACULTY Norm Herman

COURSE LIST

Undergraduate

Audiovisual/Television Special Equipment
Closed-Circuit Television Equipment Operation
Video Production
Closed-Circuit Television Systems and Maintenance
Color Television and Audiovisual Equipment Maintenance
Color Television Systems Maintenance
Advanced Color Television Projects

Clatsop Community College

County-supported 2-year coed college. Institutionally accredited by regional association. Small town location, 150-acre campus. Undergraduate enrollment: 3406. Total faculty: 147 (47 full-time, 100 part-time). Trimester calendar. Grading system: letters or numbers.

Television Department, 16th and Jerome, Astoria, OR 97103 503-325-0910, ext 285

CONTACT Joe Flickinger

DEGREES OFFERED Associate's degree in general studies with an emphasis in broadcasting (radio or TV), Associate's degree in general studies with an emphasis in film

PROGRAM MAJORS Film — 2 students Television — 2 students

ADMISSION Application deadline — rolling

FINANCIAL AID Work/study programs, student loans

CURRICULAR EMPHASIS Film study — (1) criticism and aesthetics; (2) appreciation; (3) history Filmmaking — (1) narrative; (2) documentary; (3) experimental Television study — (1) production; (2) management; (3) educational Television production — news/documentary, educational treated equally

SPECIAL ACTIVITIES/OFFERINGS Film series, program material produced for on-campus closed-circuit television and cable television, independent study, teacher training

FACILITIES AND EQUIPMENT Film — 8mm and 16mm cameras, editing equipment, lighting, color film stock, projectors, nonsync sound equipment, 16mm black and white film stock, sound stage, screening room, editing room, sound mixing room Television — black and white studio cameras, color studio cameras, ¾-inch cassette VTR, portable black and white cameras, editing equipment, monitors, special effects generators, ½-inch portapak recorders, lighting equipment, sound recording equipment, audio mixers, film chain, black and white studio, color studio, audio studio, control room

FACULTY Joe Flickinger PART-TIME FACULTY Karin Temple

COURSE LIST

Undergraduate

Introduction to Motion Pictures
Introduction to Cinematography
Radio, TV, Film Speaking
Play Production — Set and Lighting Design
Makeup
Fundamentals of Broadcasting (Radio Production)
Basic Television (TV Production)
Advanced Radio/TV Equipment Operation (Individualized Study)
Understanding Film

Linfield College

Independent American Baptist comprehensive coed institution. Institutionally accredited by regional association, programs recognized by NASM. Small town location, 90-acre campus. Total enrollment: 1101. Undergraduate enrollment: 922. Total faculty: 104 (80 full-time, 24 part-time). 4-1-4 calendar. Grading system: letters or numbers.

Communications Department, McMinnville, OR 97128 503-472-4121

CONTACT Craig Singletary

ADMISSION Application deadline — 8/15

CURRICULAR EMPHASIS Television study — (1) production; (2) educational Television production — educational

FACILITIES AND EQUIPMENT Television — black and white studio cameras, 1-inch VTR, ¾-inch cassette VTR, monitors, special effects generators, lighting equipment, sound recording equipment, audio mixers, black and white studio, audio studio, control room

PART-TIME FACULTY Craig Singletary

COURSE LIST

Undergraduate

Broadcast Production

Mt Hood Community College

State and locally supported 2-year coed college. Institutionally accredited by regional association. Suburban location. Undergraduate enrollment: 9009. Total faculty: 473 (165 full-time, 308 part-time). Quarter calendar. Grading system: letters or numbers.

Communications Department (Television Production Technology), 26000 Southeast Stark Street, Gresham, OR 97030 503-667-7414

CONTACT Ralph E Ahseln

DEGREE OFFERED AA in television production
DEPARTMENTAL MAJORS Television — 80 students
ADMISSION Application deadline — 9/1
FINANCIAL AID Scholarships, work/study programs, student loans
CURRICULAR EMPHASIS Film study — criticism and aesthetics, appreciation treated equally Filmmaking — narrative, experimental, animated treated equally Television study — criticism and aesthetics, appreciation, educational, production treated equally Television production — commercial, news/documentary, experimental/personal video, educational treated equally
SPECIAL ACTIVITIES/OFFERINGS Program material produced for on-campus closed-circuit television, apprenticeships, internships in television production, independent study, vocational placement service
FACILITIES AND EQUIPMENT Film — 8mm cameras, editing equipment, lighting, projectors, 16mm cameras, lighting, projectors Television — complete black and white and color studio production, equipment, complete black and white and color exterior production equipment, black and white studio, color studio, control room, ½-inch video editing, ¾-inch control editing
FACULTY Ralph E Ahseln

COURSE LIST

Undergraduate

Introduction to Mass Communications
Introduction to Television
Television Production
Television Production Laboratory
Television and Society
Television and Society Laboratory
Introduction to Television Scripwriting
Television News Reporting
Colorcasting
Colorcasting Laboratory
TV Directing
TV Directing Laboratory
Advanced Telecasting
Advanced Telecasting Laboratory
Closed-Circuit Systems
Telecasting Maintenance

Northwest Film Study Center

Federally supported 4-year and professional coed institution. Urban location. Total enrollment: 125. Total faculty: 8. Quarter calendar. Grading system: letters or numbers.

1219 Southwest Park Avenue, Portland, OR 97205 503-221-1156

CONTACT Bill Foster, Associate Director
CURRICULAR EMPHASIS Film study — (1) production; (2) history; (3) criticism and aesthetics; (4) educational media/instructional technology Filmmaking — (1) experimental; (2) narrative; (3) documentary; (4) animated; (5) educational Television study — production Television production — (1) experimental/personal video; (2) news/documentary
SPECIAL ACTIVITIES/OFFERINGS Film series; film festivals; student publications; program material produced for cable television, local public television station; independent study; teacher training
FACILITIES AND EQUIPMENT Film — 8mm equipment, 16mm cameras, editing equipment, lighting equipment, projectors, screening room, editing room, animation board, permanent film library Television — black and white studio cameras, color studio cameras, ½-inch VTR, ¾-inch cassette VTR, portable black and white cameras, editing equipment, monitors, special effects generators, portable color cameras, ½-inch portapak recorder, lighting equipment, sound recording equipment, time base corrector, black and white studio, color studio, audio studio, control room available through Portland Public Schools and Video Access Project
PART-TIME FACULTY Bob Flug, Roger Kukes, Chris Ley, Ted Mahar, Roger Margolis, John Rausch, Katina Simmons, John Stewart

COURSE LIST

Undergraduate

Film History — American and European
Introduction to Filmmaking
Intermediate Filmmaking
Film Criticism
Film Theory
Animation
Video Production
Screenwriting
Film and Society
Film in the Classroom

Pacific University

Independent coed university. Institutionally accredited by regional association, programs recognized by NASM, AOA. Small town location, 55-acre campus. Total enrollment: 1053. Undergraduate enrollment: 851. Total faculty: 106 (76 full-time, 30 part-time). 7-7-3-7-7 calendar. Grading system: letters or numbers.

Speech/Communication Department, Forest Grove, OR 97116 503-357-6151

CONTACT Fred Scheller
DEGREE OFFERED BA in communications with emphasis in television
DEPARTMENTAL MAJORS 25 students
ADMISSION Requirements — minimum grade point average, teacher's recommendations, written statement of purpose Application deadline — 8/15, rolling
FINANCIAL AID Scholarships, student loans, work/study programs Application deadline — 3/15
CURRICULAR EMPHASIS Television study — (1) production; (2) educational; (3) criticism and aesthetics Television production — (1) experimental/personal video; (2) educational; (3) news/documentary
SPECIAL ACTIVITIES/OFFERINGS Film series, program material produced for on-campus closed-circuit television, internships in television production, independent study, teacher training
FACILITIES AND EQUIPMENT Film — complete 8mm equipment, 16mm cameras, editing equipment, lighting equipment, projectors, screening room Television — complete black and white studio production equipment, black and white studio, audio studio, control room
FACULTY Gary Mueller, Fred Scheller, Ward Scwarzman, Mike Steele PART-TIME FACULTY Mike Brinkman

Pacific University (continued)

COURSE LIST

Undergraduate

Television Production
Television Workshop
Television Internship
Broadcast Journalism
Photography I–III
Photojournalism
Creative Television
Special Topics in Television

Portland State University

State-supported coed university. Part of Oregon State System of Higher Education. Institutionally accredited by regional association. Urban location, 35-acre campus. Total enrollment: 15,924. Undergraduate enrollment: 9552. Total faculty: 492 full-time, 292 part-time. Quarter calendar. Grading system: letters or numbers.

Center for the Moving Image, PO Box 751, Portland, OR 97207 503-229-3539

CONTACT Film — Thomas T Taylor III Television — Robert Walker
DEGREES OFFERED BS, BA in general studies with a concentration of courses in film
FINANCIAL AID Work/study programs, student loans
CURRICULAR EMPHASIS Film study — history, criticism and aesthetics, film and society treated equally Filmmaking — (1) documentary; (2) sponsored; (3) personal Television production — (1) commercial; (2) studio; (3) experimental/personal video
SPECIAL ACTIVITIES/OFFERINGS Film series, film societies, apprenticeships, internships in film production, internships in television production, independent study, teacher training, film production for local organizations
FACILITIES AND EQUIPMENT Film — complete 8mm and 16mm equipment, screening room, editing room, sound mixing room (Super-8), permanent film library of student films, permanent film library of commercial or professional films Television — black and white studio cameras, color studio camera, ½-inch VTR, 1-inch VTR, 2-inch VTR (helical), ¾-inch cassette VTR, portable black and white cameras, ½-inch editing equipment, monitors, special effects generators, slide chain, ½-inch portapak recorders, lighting equipment, sound recording equipment, audio mixers, film chain, time base corrector, black and white studio, control room
FACULTY Andries Deinum, Thomas T Taylor III PART-TIME FACULTY Edward Geis, Susan Shadburn, Robert Walker

COURSE LIST

Undergraduate

Introduction to Filmmaking
Television Production
Filmmaking I–III
Art of the Film
Film and Society
Films and Their Directors
Scripting
Film Committee
Advanced Filmmaking
Special Projects in Film
Advanced Television Production
Special Seminars in Film Study

Undergraduate and Graduate

Community Filmmaking
Media and Community
Public Access Cable Seminar

Oregon

Southern Oregon State College

State-supported comprehensive coed institution. Part of Oregon State System of Higher Education. Institutionally accredited by regional association. Small town location, 143-acre campus. Total enrollment: 4505. Undergraduate enrollment: 4177. Total faculty: 240 (210 full-time, 30 part-time). Quarter calendar. Grading system: letters or numbers.

Speech Communications Department, 1250 Siskiyou Boulevard, Ashland, OR 97520 503-482-6300

CONTACT Ronald Kramer
PROGRAM OFFERED Major in speech communications with emphasis in television
ADMISSION Application deadline — rolling
CURRICULAR EMPHASIS Television study — (1) history; (2) production; (3) management; (4) criticism and aesthetics; (5) educational; (6) appreciation Television production — (1) commercial; (2) news/documentary; (3) experimental/personal video; (4) educational
SPECIAL ACTIVITIES/OFFERINGS Program material produced for cable television, internships in television production, independent study, practicum
FACILITIES AND EQUIPMENT Television — complete black and white studio and exterior production equipment, complete color studio production equipment, black and white studio, color studio, audio studio, control room
FACULTY John Baxter, Ronald Kramer, Howard LaMere, David Sours

COURSE LIST

Undergraduate

Survey of Television
Radio/Television Workshop
Broadcast Writing
Broadcast Announcing
Broadcast Opportunity Laboratory
Communications Media
Television Production/Directing
Public Service Advertising
Public Arts

English Department 503-482-6181

CONTACT Arlen Briggs
ADMISSION Application deadline — rolling
CURRICULAR EMPHASIS Film study — (1) criticism and aesthetics; (2) appreciation; (3) history Filmmaking — (1) narrative; (2) documentary; (3) experimental Television study — (1) criticism and aesthetics; (2) appreciation; (3) history Television production — (1) commercial; (2) news/documentary; (3) experimental/personal video
SPECIAL ACTIVITIES/OFFERINGS Filmmaking clubs, film series, film societies, independent study
FACILITIES AND EQUIPMENT Film — complete 8mm equipment, sound stage, screening room, permanent film library Television — black and white studio cameras, color studio cameras, ½-inch VTR, editing equipment, monitors, ½-inch portapak recorder, lighting equipment, sound recording equipment, black and white studio, color studio
PART-TIME FACULTY Arlen Briggs

COURSE LIST
Undergraduate
Special Studies: Film
Undergraduate and Graduate
Film as Literature
Filmmaking

University of Oregon

State-supported coed university. Part of Oregon State System of Higher Education. Institutionally accredited by regional association, programs recognized by NASM, AACSB. Small town location, 250-acre campus. Total enrollment: 16,463. Undergraduate enrollment: 11,895. Total faculty: 1287 (1049 full-time, 238 part-time). Quarter calendar. Grading system: letters or numbers.

Film Studies Area, Department of Speech, Villard Hall, Eugene, OR 97403 503-686-4228

CONTACT Jean Cutler, Director
DEGREES OFFERED BA, BS, MA, MS, PhD in film
PROGRAMS MAJORS Undergraduate — 30 students Graduate — 12 students
ADMISSION Requirements — teachers' recommendations, written statement of purpose, transcripts Undergraduate application deadline — 8/15, rolling
FINANCIAL AID Scholarships, student loans, work/study programs, teaching assistantships, research assistantships, fellowships Undergraduate application deadline — 4/1, rolling
CURRICULAR EMPHASIS Film study — (1) criticism and aesthetics; (2) history Filmmaking — (1) narrative, experimental; (2) documentary
SPECIAL ACTIVITIES/OFFERINGS Film series, film festivals, film societies, independent study, practicum, vocational placement service
FACILITIES AND EQUIPMENT Film — complete 8mm and 16mm equipment, screening room, editing room, animation board, permanent film library
FACULTY William Cadbury, Jean Cutler PART-TIME FACULTY Matt Barrows, Michelle Piso, Dennis Toney, William Willingham

COURSE LIST
Undergraduate
Basic Concepts of Visualization
Basic Film Production
History of the Motion Picture (Silent, Sound, Contemporary)
Great Filmmakers

Graduate
Introduction to Film Study
Seminar: Great Filmmakers
Seminar in Film History

Undergraduate and Graduate
Film Criticism: Formative Tradition
Film Criticism: Auteurism and Bazin
Film Criticism: Structuralism and Semiology
Acting for the Camera
Motion Picture Editing
Motion Picture Planning
Motion Picture Production
Film Directors and Genres
Experimental Film Workshop
Experimental Course
Documentary Film

Telecommunication Area 503-686-4241

CONTACT William R Elliott, Director
DEGREES OFFERED BA, BS, MA, MS, PhD in telecommunication
PROGRAM MAJORS Undergraduate — 250 students Graduate — 24 students
ADMISSION Undergraduate requirements — 2.0 minimum grade point average, teachers' recommendations, written statement of purpose Graduate requirements —3.0 minimum grade point average, GRE scores, teachers' recommendations, written statement of purpose Undergraduate application deadline — 8/15, rolling
FINANCIAL AID Student loans, work/study programs, teaching assistantships Undergraduate application deadline — 4/1, rolling
CURRICULAR EMPHASIS Undergraduate television study — (1) production; (2) communication theory and effects; (3) history Undergraduate television production — (1) news/documentary; (2) commercial; (3) educational Graduate television production — (1) news/documentary; (2) educational; (3) television drama
SPECIAL ACTIVITIES/OFFERINGS Program material produced for on-campus closed-circuit television, cable television, local public television station, local commerical television station; independent study; practicum
FACILITIES AND EQUIPMENT Television — complete black and white studio and exterior production equipment, complete color studio and exterior production equipment, black and white studio, color studio, audio studio, control room
FACULTY William R Elliott, E A Kretsinger, Deanna Robinson, John R Shephard, Ronald E Sherriffs PART-TIME FACULTY Janet Renney, D Glenn Starlin

COURSE LIST
Undergraduate
Fundamentals of Broadcasting
Television Workshop I
Radio-Television Writing
Theory of Mass Communication
Radio-Television and the Public
Government Regulation of Broadcasting
Radio Workshop
Current Topics in Mass Media Research
Communication and Social Change
Mass Media and Politics
Concepts in Visual Production
Television Directing
Radio-Television Programming
Problems of Public Broadcasting
Alternate Broadcast Systems

Graduate
Theory of Mass Communication
Visual Concepts
Research Methods
Radio-Television and the Public
Theory and Criticism of Broadcasting

University of Oregon (continued)

Fine and Applied Arts Department, School of Architecture and Allied Arts, Eugene, OR 97403 503-686-3609

CONTACT David G Foster
DEGREES OFFERED BFA, BS, MFA in graphic design with emphasis in film and video, visual research
DEPARTMENTAL MAJORS Graduate — 3 students
ADMISSION Requirements — interviews, portfolio Undergraduate application deadline — 8/15, rolling
FINANCIAL AID Work/study programs, teaching assistantships Graduate application deadline — 4/1, rolling
CURRICULAR EMPHASIS Film study — (1) motion graphics and visual thinking; (2) educational media/instructional technology Undergraduate filmmaking — experimental, animated treated equally Graduate filmmaking — (1) experimental; (2) animated; (3) documentary; (4) visual models Television study — video graphics Television production — experimental/personal video
SPECIAL ACTIVITIES/OFFERINGS Film societies, program material produced for intercurricular use, visiting artists
FACILITIES AND EQUIPMENT Film — 16mm and 35mm cameras, editing equipment, animation board Television — ½-inch VTR, editing equipment, monitors, ½-inch portapak recorder, colorizer
FACULTY David G Foster, Ken R O'Connell

COURSE LIST

Undergraduate and Graduate
Visual Continuity
Motion Graphics
Videographics
Audiographics

Instructional Technology Studies, UO College of Education, Eugene, OR 97403 503-686-3468

CONTACT Gary Ferrington, Coordinator
DEGREES OFFERED MS, MA, MEd in curriculum and instruction with an emphasis in instructional technology
PROGRAM MAJORS 26 students
ADMISSION Requirements — 2.75 minimum grade point average, interview, written statement of purpose, professional recommendations
FINANCIAL AID Scholarships, work/study programs, student loans, fellowships, teaching assistantships
CURRICULAR EMPHASIS Film study — educational media/instructional technology Filmmaking — educational Television study — educational Television production — educational
SPECIAL ACTIVITIES/OFFERINGS Independent study, teacher training, vocational placement service, internships in instructional technology in which experiences in video, film, and other media are available
FACILITIES AND EQUIPMENT Film — 8mm cameras, editing equipment, sound recording equipment, lighting, projectors, 16mm editing equipment, sound recording equipment, lighting, projectors, editing room, sound mixing room Television — ¾-inch cassette VTR, portable black and white cameras, editing equipment, monitors, portable color cameras, lighting equipment, sound recording equipment, audio mixers, color studio, audio studio
FACULTY Gary W Ferrington

COURSE LIST

Graduate
Practicum: Instructional Development Projects
Internship: Instructional Technology
Audio Design Lab

Undergraduate and Graduate
Instructional Film

PENNSYLVANIA

Albright College

Independent 4-year coed college affiliated with United Methodist Church. Institutionally accredited by regional association. Suburban location, 75-acre campus. Undergraduate enrollment: 1275. Total faculty: 125 (90 full-time, 35 part-time). 4-1-5 calendar. Grading system: letters or numbers.

English Department, 13th and Exeter Streets, Reading, PA 19604 215-921-2381

CONTACT Gary Adlestein
PROGRAM OFFERED Major in English with independent emphasis in film or art
ADMISSION Application deadline — 3/1, rolling
CURRICULAR EMPHASIS Film study — (1) appreciation; (2) production; (3) criticism and aesthetics Filmmaking — (1) experimental; (2) narrative; (3) documentary
SPECIAL ACTIVITIES/OFFERINGS Independent study; cooperative relationship with Berks Filmmakers, Incorporated
FACILITIES AND EQUIPMENT Film — complete 8mm and 16mm equipment
FACULTY Gary Adlestein

COURSE LIST

Undergraduate
Introduction to Film
Filmmaking
The Avant-Garde

Allegheny College

Independent United Methodist comprehensive coed institution. Institutionally accredited by regional association. Small town location, 165-acre campus. Undergraduate enrollment: 1850. Total faculty: 152 (130 full-time, 22 part-time). 3-3 calendar. Grading system: letters or numbers.

English Department, Meadville, PA 16335 814-724-2351

CONTACT Lloyd Michaels
ADMISSION Application deadline — 3/1
CURRICULAR EMPHASIS Film study — (1) criticism and aesthetics; (2) appreciation; (3) history
FACULTY Lloyd Michaels

COURSE LIST
Undergraduate
Film as Narrative Art
Literature Into Film

Alvernia College

Independent Roman Catholic 4-year coed college. Institutionally accredited by regional association. Suburban location, 80-acre campus. Undergraduate enrollment: 750. Total faculty: 80 (50 full-time, 30 part-time). Semester calendar. Grading system: letters or numbers.

English-Communications Department, Reading, PA 19607 215-777-5411

CONTACT Sister M Pacelli
ADMISSION Application deadline — rolling
FINANCIAL AID Scholarships, student loans, work/study programs Application deadline — 5/1
CURRICULAR EMPHASIS Film study — (1) appreciation; (2) criticism and aesthetics; (3) history Filmmaking — (1) narrative; (2) documentary; (3) educational Television study — (1) appreciation; (2) criticism and aesthetics; (3) history
SPECIAL ACTIVITIES/OFFERINGS Program material produced for on-campus closed-circuit television and cable television
FACILITIES AND EQUIPMENT Television — black and white studio camera, ½-inch VTR, monitors, black and white studio
PART-TIME FACULTY Sister M Pacelli

COURSE LIST
Undergraduate
Interpretation of Film
Mass Media in America

Bucknell University

Independent comprehensive coed institution. Institutionally accredited by regional association. Small town location, 300-acre campus. Total enrollment: 3210. Undergraduate enrollment: 3084. Total faculty: 252 (240 full-time, 12 part-time). 4-1-4 calendar. Grading system: letters or numbers.

English Department, Lewisburg, PA 17837 717-524-1553

CONTACT Louis Casimir or Karl Patten
ADMISSION Application deadline — 1/1
CURRICULAR EMPHASIS Film study — (1) criticism and aesthetics; (2) history; (3) appreciation; (4) production Filmmaking — (1) narrative; (2) documentary; (3) experimental; (4) animated
SPECIAL ACTIVITIES/OFFERINGS Filmmaking clubs, film series, independent study
FACILITIES AND EQUIPMENT Film — 8mm and 16mm cameras, editing equipment, sound recording equipment, lighting equipment, projectors, screening room, editing room
FACULTY Louis Casimir, Karl Patten

COURSE LIST
Undergraduate
Film and the Liberal Arts
The Art of Film
Seminar in Film

Bucks County Community College

County-supported 2-year coed college. Institutionally accredited by regional association. Suburban location. Undergraduate enrollment: 8146. Total faculty: 337 (190 full-time, 147 part-time). 4-1-4 calendar. Grading system: letters or numbers.

Department of Media and Performing Arts, Swamp Road, Newtown, PA 18940 215-968-5861, ext 551

CONTACT William F Brenner, Chairperson
DEGREES OFFERED AA in cinema, AA in broadcasting
DEPARTMENTAL MAJORS Film — 40 students Television — 80 students
ADMISSION Requirement — high school diploma Application deadline — rolling
FINANCIAL AID Scholarships, work/study programs, student loans Application deadline — 7/1 fall, 11/1 spring
CURRICULAR EMPHASIS Film study — (1) history; (2) appreciation; (3) criticism and aesthetics Filmmaking — documentary, narrative, experimental treated equally Television study — (1) history; (2) appreciation; (3) criticism and aesthetics Television production — commercial, news/documentary, experimental/personal video treated equally
SPECIAL ACTIVITIES/OFFERINGS Film series, film festivals, program material produced for on-campus closed-circuit television and instructional television distribution, independent study, practicum
FACILITIES AND EQUIPMENT Film — complete 16mm equipment, screening room, editing room, sound mixing room, permanent film library Television — complete black and white studio equipment, ½-inch VTR, portable black and white cameras, editing equipment, monitors, ½-inch portapak recorder, lighting equipment, sound recording equipment, audio mixers, black and white studio, color studio, audio studio, control room

Bucks County Community College (continued)

FACULTY Norman Cary, Tom Cunningham, Art Landy, John Rosenbaum, William H Wheeler PART-TIME FACULTY Dan Hauser, Leo Matson, Charles Monteleone, Stephen O'Neill

COURSE LIST

Undergraduate

Mass Media and Society
Film Production I–IV
The Art of Independent Cinema
The Art of Theatrical Cinema
Television Production I–IV
The Broadcasting System
Alternative Broadcasting Systems
Broadcast Performance
Mass Media Workshop I, II

Cabrini College

Independent Roman Catholic 4-year coed college. Institutionally accredited by regional association. Suburban location, 110-acre campus. Undergraduate enrollment: 429. Total faculty: 59 (29 full-time, 30 part-time). Semester calendar. Grading system: letters or numbers.

English and Communications Department, Radnor, PA 19087 215-687-2100

CONTACT Jerome Zurek
DEGREE OFFERED BA in English/communications with emphasis in film or television
ADMISSION Requirement — 2.0 minimum grade point average Application deadline — rolling
FINANCIAL AID Scholarships, student loans, work/study programs Application deadline — rolling
CURRICULAR EMPHASIS Film study — (1) production; (2) criticism and aesthetics; (3) history Filmmaking — introductory Television study — (1) production; (2) criticism and aesthetics Television production — news/documentary
SPECIAL ACTIVITIES/OFFERINGS Program material produced for local television station, internships in film and television production, teacher training
FACILITIES AND EQUIPMENT Film — complete 8mm equipment, screening room, editing room Television — black and white studio cameras, ½-inch VTR, 1-inch VTR, portable black and white cameras, monitors, ½-inch portapak recorders
FACULTY Marilyn Johnson, Frank Saul, Jerome Zurek

COURSE LIST

Undergraduate

Role of Mass Media
Filmmaking: An Introduction
Broadcast Reporting
Contemporary Theater and Film Criticism
Current Issues in Mass Communications
Broadcast Internship
Filmmaking Internship

California State College

State-supported comprehensive coed institution. Part of Pennsylvania State Colleges and University System. Institutionally accredited by regional association. Small town location. Total enrollment: 4453. Total faculty: 305 full-time. Semester calendar. Grading system: letters or numbers.

Speech Communication Department, California, PA 15419 412-938-4170

CONTACT Film — John Robson Television — William A Graf
DEGREE OFFERED BA in radio and television
DEPARTMENTAL MAJORS 115 students
ADMISSION Application deadline — rolling
FINANCIAL AID Scholarships, student loans, work/study programs Application deadline — 3/1
CURRICULAR EMPHASIS Television study — (1) production; (2) writing; (3) management Television production — (1) news/documentary; (2) experimental/personal video; (3) educational
SPECIAL ACTIVITIES/OFFERINGS Program material produced for on-campus closed-circuit television, cable television, local commercial television station; independent study; practicum; teacher training
FACILITIES AND EQUIPMENT Film — 8mm cameras and projectors, sound recording equipment, black and white film stock, color film stock, 16mm cameras and projectors, editing equipment, screening room, editing room Television — complete black and white studio and exterior production equipment, complete color studio production equipment, black and white studio, color studio, audio studio, control room
FACULTY Clarence Brammer, William A Graf, Richard L May, John Robson, Robert Rockinson

COURSE LIST

Undergraduate

Survey of Radio, Television, and Film
Film Appreciation
Television Appreciation
Radio Production
Television Production
Advanced Television Production
Broadcast Management
Radio-Television Announcing
Radio and Television in Free Society
Radio-Television Writing — Drama
Radio-Television News and Communication
Radio and Television Workshop I–III
Special Problems

Cedar Crest College

Independent 4-year women's college affiliated with United Church of Christ. Institutionally accredited by regional association. Suburban location, 100-acre campus. Undergraduate enrollment: 931. Total faculty: 78 (58 full-time, 20 part-time). Semester calendar. Grading system: letters or numbers.

Educational Ventures Inc, Allentown, PA 18104 215-435-6779

CONTACT George N Gordon
DEGREE OFFERED BA in liberal arts studies with a major or minor in communication studies (consortial program offered with Muhlenberg College)

PROGRAM MAJORS Film — 15 students Television — 50 students
ADMISSION Requirements — ACT or SAT scores, interview, teachers' recommendations, written statement of purpose
FINANCIAL AID Scholarships, work/study programs, student loans
CURRICULAR EMPHASIS Film study — (1) history; (2) appreciation; (3) criticism and aesthetics Filmmaking — experimental Television study — (1) criticism and aesthetics; (2) history; (3) production; (4) management; (5) appreciation Television production — (1) experimental/personal video; (2) news/documentary; (3) commercial; (4) educational
SPECIAL ACTIVITIES/OFFERINGS Film series, film festivals, apprenticeships, internships in film production, internships in television production, independent study, vocational placement service
FACILITIES AND EQUIPMENT Film — screening room Television — black and white studio cameras, ¾-inch cassette VTR, portable black and white cameras, monitors, lighting equipment, sound recording equipment, black and white studio, audio studio
FACULTY Kent Kjellegren

COURSE LIST
Undergraduate
Radio and TV Broadcasting
Television Production
Broadcast Journalism
Art of the Film
Film Criticism and Appreciation

College Misericordia

Independent Roman Catholic 4-year college, primarily women. Institutionally accredited by regional association. Suburban location. Total enrollment: 772. Total faculty: 104 (77 full-time, 27 part-time). Semester calendar. Grading system: letters or numbers.

Language, Literature and Communication Department, Lake Street, Dallas, PA 18612 717-675-2181, ext 214

CONTACT Walter C J Andersen
ADMISSION Application deadline — rolling
FINANCIAL AID Student loans, work/study programs Application deadline — 2/1
CURRICULAR EMPHASIS Film study — (1) appreciation; (2) criticism and aesthetics; (3) history; (4) educational media/instructional technology
SPECIAL ACTIVITIES/OFFERINGS Film series, independent study, teacher training
FACILITIES AND EQUIPMENT Film — 16mm projectors Television — 1-inch VTR, closed-circuit television system
FACULTY Walter C J Andersen

COURSE LIST
Undergraduate
Art of Film
Introduction to Media

Community College of Philadelphia

City-supported 2-year coed college. Institutionally accredited by regional association. Urban location. Undergraduate enrollment: 9570. Total faculty: 733 (365 full-time, 368 part-time). Semester calendar. Grading system: letters or numbers.

Photography Department, 34 South 11th Street, Philadelphia, PA 19107 215-972-7227

CONTACT Loring F Hill
CURRICULAR EMPHASIS Film study — history, criticism and aesthetics, appreciation, production, educational media/instructional technology treated equally Filmmaking — (1) documentary; (2) educational; (3) experimental Television study — production Television production — (1) commercial; (2) educational; (3) news/documentary
SPECIAL ACTIVITIES/OFFERINGS Film series
FACILITIES AND EQUIPMENT Film — complete 8mm and 16mm equipment, screening room, editing room, sound mixing room, permanent film library Television — complete color studio and exterior production equipment, color studio, control room
FACULTY Loring F Hill, Jon Spielberg

COURSE LIST
Undergraduate
Introduction to Television Production
Introduction to Film Production
A&B Roll Cutting
Special Projects in Television
Special Projects in Film

English Department 215-972-7362

CONTACT Linda R Burnett
FINANCIAL AID Scholarships, student loans, work/study programs
CURRICULAR EMPHASIS Film study — criticism and aesthetics, appreciation, production treated equally Filmmaking — (1) documentary; (2) narrative
SPECIAL ACTIVITIES/OFFERINGS Film series, film festivals, independent study
FACULTY George Beers, Peter Bergmann, Linda R Burnett, David Katz, Jalond Levin, Gerald McDade, Carol Rosenbaum

COURSE LIST
Undergraduate
The Language of Film
The Medium and the Message

Drexel University

Independent coed university. Institutionally accredited by regional association, programs recognized by AACSB. Urban location, 60-acre campus. Total enrollment: 10,346. Undergraduate enrollment: 8362. Total faculty: 292. Quarter calendar. Grading system: letters or numbers.

Humanities-Communications Department, 33rd and Chestnut Streets, Philadelphia, PA 19104 215-895-2430

ADMISSION Undergraduate requirement — ACT or SAT scores
FINANCIAL AID Scholarships, work/study programs, student loans
CURRICULAR EMPHASIS Undergraduate film study — practical applications Undergraduate filmmaking — documentary, narrative, experimental, animated, educational treated equally Undergraduate television study — production, management treated equally Undergraduate television production — commercial, news/documentary, experimental/personal video, educational treated equally
SPECIAL ACTIVITIES/OFFERINGS Film series, program material produced for local public television station and local commercial television station, apprenticeships, internships in film production, internships in television production, independent study, vocational placement service
FACILITIES AND EQUIPMENT Film — 8mm and 16mm cameras, editing equipment, sound recording equipment, lighting, projectors, screening room, editing room, animation board, permanent film library of commercial or professional films Television — complete black and white and color studio production equipment, black and white studio, color studio, audio studio, control room
FACULTY D B Jones, Walter M Merrill, Ralph Moore, Al Tedesco, Bill Wine

COURSE LIST

Undergraduate

Technique of Filmmaking
TV Production
Documentary

Duquesne University

Independent Roman Catholic coed university. Institutionally accredited by regional association, programs recognized by NASM, AACSB, ACPE. Urban location, 38-acre campus. Total enrollment: 7188. Undergraduate enrollment: 4763. Total faculty: 438 (277 full-time, 161 part-time). Semester calendar. Grading system: letters or numbers.

Journalism Department, 403 College Hall, Pittsburgh, PA 15219 412-434-6446

CONTACT Television — Nancy C Jones, Chairperson
DEGREE OFFERED BA in journalism with an emphasis in broadcasting
DEPARTMENTAL MAJORS Television — 40 students
ADMISSION Requirements — 2.0 minimum grade point average, ACT or SAT scores
FINANCIAL AID Work/study programs
CURRICULAR EMPHASIS Television study — (1) newswriting; (2) production Television production — (1) news/documentary; (2) commercial; (3) educational
SPECIAL ACTIVITIES/OFFERINGS Program material produced for on-campus closed-circuit television, internships in radio or TV newsrooms, some observation in other areas of stations
FACILITIES AND EQUIPMENT Television — color studio cameras, ¾-inch cassette VTR, editing equipment, monitors, slide chain, lighting equipment, sound recording equipment, film chain, color studio, control room
FACULTY Paul Krakowski

COURSE LIST

Undergraduate

Radio-TV: Principles and Writing
Developing the Broadcast Program
Advanced Writing for Radio-TV
Professional Internship: Broadcasting

Edinboro State College

State-supported comprehensive coed institution. Part of Pennsylvania State Colleges and University System. Institutionally accredited by regional association. Small town location. Total enrollment: 5400. Undergraduate enrollment: 4800. Total faculty: 448 (439 full-time, 9 part-time). Semester calendar. Grading system: letters or numbers.

Art Department, School of Arts and Humanities, Edinboro, PA 16412 814-732-2799

CONTACT George Shoemaker, Chairman
DEGREE OFFERED BFA in art with a major in film
DEPARTMENTAL MAJORS 10 students
ADMISSION Application deadline — rolling
FINANCIAL AID Student loans, work/study programs, payment of all production costs
CURRICULAR EMPHASIS Film study — (1) production; (2) criticism and aesthetics; (3) appreciation Filmmaking — (1) animated; (2) experimental; (3) documentary
SPECIAL ACTIVITIES/OFFERINGS Film series, film festivals, internships in film, independent study
FACILITIES AND EQUIPMENT Film — complete 16mm equipment, 8mm cameras, editing equipment, lighting equipment, black and white film stock, projectors, sound stage, screening room, 35mm screening facilities, editing room, sound mixing room, animation board, permanent film library, processing and printing of film
FACULTY David S Weinkauf PART-TIME FACULTY William Cox, James Goldsworthy

COURSE LIST

Undergraduate

Beginning Animation
Intermediate Animation
Beginning 8mm Production
Intermediate 8mm Production
Intermediate 16mm Production
Advanced 16mm Production
Experimental Film
Documentary Film

Undergraduate and Graduate
Introduction to Film

History Department, Edinboro, PA 16412 814-732-2575

CONTACT T Gay or R Reinig
ADMISSION Application deadline — rolling
CURRICULAR EMPHASIS Film study — (1) history; (2) appreciation; (3) educational media/instructional technology Filmmaking — (1) narrative; (2) documentary; (3) experimental
SPECIAL ACTIVITIES/OFFERINGS Film series, film festivals, independent study
FACULTY T Gay, R Reinig

COURSE LIST
Undergraduate
American Dream on Film
Recent US History through Film

Franklin and Marshall College

Independent 4-year coed college. Accredited by regional association and AICS. Small town location, 105-acre campus. Undergraduate enrollment: 2083. Total faculty: 137 (124 full-time, 13 part-time). 4-1-4 calendar. Grading system: letters or numbers.

Government Department, Lancaster, PA 17604 717-291-3961

CONTACT Sidney Wise
ADMISSION Application deadline — 2/10
SPECIAL ACTIVITIES/OFFERINGS Filmmaking clubs, film series, film societies
FACILITIES AND EQUIPMENT Film — screening room, 35mm screening facilities, editing room
FACULTY H Fernandez, Sidney Wise

COURSE LIST
Undergraduate
History and Art of the Film
Major European Directors

Gannon University

Independent Roman Catholic comprehensive coed institution. Institutionally accredited by regional association. Urban location, 18-acre campus. Total enrollment: 3635. Undergraduate enrollment: 3005. Total faculty: 231 (130 full-time, 101 part-time). 4-1-4 calendar. Grading system: letters or numbers.

English/Communications Department, Erie, PA 16541 814-871-7333

CONTACT Film — Reverend Paul De Sante Television — A J Miceli
DEGREE OFFERED BA in communications/English with emphasis in nonprint media
ADMISSION Requirements — ACT or SAT scores, teachers' recommendations
FINANCIAL AID Scholarships, work/study programs, student loans
CURRICULAR EMPHASIS Film study — (1) appreciation; (2) educational media/instructional technology; (3) writing Television study — (1) production; (2) educational; (3) appreciation Television production — (1) news/documentary; (2) educational; (3) commercial
SPECIAL ACTIVITIES/OFFERINGS Film series, student publications, program material produced for on-campus closed-circuit television and local commercial television station, apprenticeships, internships in television production, independent study, teacher training, vocational placement service
FACILITIES AND EQUIPMENT Television — black and white studio cameras, color studio cameras, ½-inch VTR, portable black and white cameras, editing equipment, monitors, special effects generators, slide chain, ½-inch portapak recorders, lighting equipment, black and white studio, color studio, control room
FACULTY Reverend Paul De Sante, Reverend Thomas McSweeney, A J Miceli, Robert L Vales PART-TIME FACULTY John Kupetz, Ned McGrath

COURSE LIST
Undergraduate
Art of the Film
History of Radio and TV Broadcasting
TV and Radio Performance and Broadcasting
Writing for TV and Radio
TV Directing
Criticism in TV, Radio and Film
Instructional TV and Radio
Radio-TV Engineering
Advertising for Electronic Media

Graduate
Film: The Reel Thing

Department of Theatre and Communication Arts, Perry Square, Erie, PA 16541 814-871-7325

CONTACT Anthony J Miceli
DEGREES OFFERED BA in communication arts, BA in theater and communication arts
DEPARTMENTAL/PROGRAM MAJORS Television — 110 students
ADMISSION Requirement — ACT or SAT scores
FINANCIAL AID Scholarships, work/study programs, student loans
CURRICULAR EMPHASIS Television study — (1) production; (2) management Television production — commercial
SPECIAL ACTIVITIES/OFFERINGS Program material produced for on-campus closed-circuit television, internships in television production, teacher training

Gannon University (continued)

FACILITIES AND EQUIPMENT Television — black and white studio cameras, ½-inch VTR, 1-inch VTR, ¾-inch cassette VTR, portable black and white cameras, monitors, special effects generators, slide chain, ½-inch portapak recorders, lighting equipment, sound recording equipment, audio mixers, film chain, black and white studio, audio studio, control room

FACULTY John Duda, Robert Falkewitz, Thomas McSweeney, Anthony Miceli

COURSE LIST

Undergraduate

Television Announcing
Television Directing
Broadcast Copywriting
Broadcast Newswriting
Broadcast Management
Broadcast History
Instructional Television
Introduction to Broadcast Engineering
Broadcast Sales
Internship in Television

Gettysburg College

Independent 4-year coed college affiliated with Lutheran Church of America. Institutionally accredited by regional association. Small town location, 200-acre campus. Undergraduate enrollment: 1900. Total faculty: 138 full-time. 4-1-4 calendar. Grading system: letters or numbers.

English Department, Gettysburg, PA 17353 717-334-4201

CONTACT Robert S Fredrickson
ADMISSION Application deadline — 2/15
CURRICULAR EMPHASIS Film study — (1) criticism and aesthetics; (2) history
SPECIAL ACTIVITIES/OFFERINGS Participates in Central Pennsylvania Consortium, special course with New York filmmakers and critics
FACULTY Robert S Fredrickson

COURSE LIST

Undergraduate

Film Aesthetics
The New York Film Critic

Holy Family College

Independent Roman Catholic 4-year college primarily for women. Institutionally accredited by regional association. Suburban location, 47-acre campus. Total faculty: 120 (49 full-time, 71 part-time). Semester calendar. Grading system: letters or numbers.

Education Department, Frankford Avenue at Grant, Philadelphia, PA 19114 215-637-7700

CONTACT Paul Kraft
PROGRAM OFFERED Major in education with emphasis in film and TV
PROGRAM MAJORS Undergraduate film — 16 students Undergraduate television — 11 students
ADMISSION Undergraduate requirements — ACT or SAT scores, teachers' recommendations Undergraduate application deadline — rolling
FINANCIAL AID Scholarships, work/study programs, student loans
CURRICULAR EMPHASIS Undergraduate film study — (1) educational media/instructional technology; (2) appreciation; (3) criticism and aesthetics Graduate film study — (1) criticism and aesthetics; (2) history; (3) appreciation Undergraduate filmmaking — (1) educational; (2) narrative; (3) animated Graduate filmmaking — (1) experimental; (2) narrative; (3) animated Undergraduate television study — (1) educational; (2) criticism and aesthetics; (3) production Graduate television study — (1) production; (2) appreciation; (3) criticism and aesthetics Undergraduate television production — news/documentary, experimental/personal video, educational treated equally Graduate television production — (1) educational; (2) experimental/personal video; (3) news/documentary
SPECIAL ACTIVITIES/OFFERINGS Film series, film societies, program material produced for on-campus closed-circuit television, independent study, teacher training, vocational placement service
FACILITIES AND EQUIPMENT Film — complete 8mm equipment, screening room, 35mm screening facilities, editing room, sound mixing room, permanent film library of commercial or professional films Television — complete black and white studio production equipment, black and white studio, audio studio, control room
FACULTY Paul Kraft

COURSE LIST

Graduate

Educational Film and TV Production

Undergraduate and Graduate

Film Study
Film Production
Educational Media

Indiana University of Pennsylvania

State-supported coed university. Part of Pennsylvania State Colleges and University System. Institutionally accredited by regional association, programs recognized by NASM. Small town location, 106-acre campus. Total enrollment: 12,019. Undergraduate enrollment: 10,866. Total faculty: 664 (616 full-time, 48 part-time). Semester calendar. Grading system: letters or numbers.

English Department, Indiana, PA 15701

CONTACT T Kenneth Wilson
ADMISSION Application deadline — 1/15

COURSE LIST

Undergraduate

The Art of the Film

Graduate

Literature and the Film

Kutztown State College

State-supported comprehensive coed institution. Part of Pennsylvania State Colleges and University System. Institutionally accredited by regional association. Small town location, 325-acre campus. Total enrollment: 5169. Undergraduate enrollment: 4567. Total faculty: 277 (257 full-time, 20 part-time). Semester calendar. Grading system: letters or numbers.

Television and Radio Department, Kutztown, PA 19530 215-683-4492

CONTACT Robert P Fina
DEGREE OFFERED BS in television
DEPARTMENTAL MAJORS Television — 200 students
ADMISSION Requirement — ACT or SAT scores
FINANCIAL AID Work/study programs, student loans Application deadline — 3/1, rolling
CURRICULAR EMPHASIS Film study — (1) hands-on experience; (2) criticism and aesthetics Filmmaking — hands-on experience Television study — (1) hands-on experience; (2) production; (3) management Television production — (1) hands-on experience; (2) experimental/personal video; (3) news/documentary; (4) commercial
SPECIAL ACTIVITIES/OFFERINGS Program material produced for on-campus closed-circuit television and cable television, internships in television production, independent study
FACILITIES AND EQUIPMENT Film — complete 8mm equipment, screening room, editing room, sound mixing room, animation board, permanent film library of student films Television — complete black and white and color studio production equipment, complete black and white and color exterior production equipment, black and white studio, color studio, mobile van/unit, remote truck, audio studio, control room
FACULTY John Beabout, Darrell Duhlman, Robert P Fina, David Kintsfather

COURSE LIST

Undergraduate

Introduction to Telecommunications
Fundamentals of Television Production
Writing for Television
Advanced Television Production Techniques I, II
Communications Law
On-Campus Television Internship
Independent Television Production
Audio Production
Telecommunications Systems Management
Senior Seminar Television Internship
Research with ½-Inch Video Technology

Graduate

Television Production Workshop

La Salle College

Independent Roman Catholic comprehensive coed institution. Institutionally accredited by regional association. Urban location, 45-acre campus. Total enrollment: 6934. Undergraduate enrollment: 6227. Total faculty: 289 (178 full-time, 111 part-time). Semester calendar. Grading system: letters or numbers.

English Department, 20th and Olney Avenue, Philadelphia, PA 19141 215-951-1000

CONTACT Gerard Molyneaux
DEGREE OFFERED BA in communications with emphasis in film and television
DEPARTMENTAL MAJORS Film — 20 students Television — 20 students
ADMISSION Requirement — SAT scores Application deadline — 6/1, rolling
FINANCIAL AID Scholarships, student loans, work/study programs Application deadline — 2/15
CURRICULAR EMPHASIS Film study — (1) criticism and aesthetics; (2) history; (3) appreciation; (4) production; (5) educational media/instructional technology Filmmaking — (1) narrative; (2) documentary; (3) animated; (4) experimental; (5) educational Television study — (1) production; (2) history; (3) criticism and aesthetics; (4) appreciation; (5) educational; (6) management Television production — (1) news/documentary; (2) commercial; (3) educational; (4) experimental/personal video
SPECIAL ACTIVITIES/OFFERINGS Film series, student publications
FACILITIES AND EQUIPMENT Film — complete 8mm equipment, screening room, editing room, animation board, permanent film library Television — complete black and white studio and exterior production equipment, black and white studio
FACULTY Sidney MacLeod, Gerard Molyneaux

COURSE LIST

Undergraduate

Introduction to Mass Media
Communication Theory
Journalism
Writing for the Media
Broadcasting in America
Broadcast Seminar
Film as Art
Film Seminar
Visual Literacy
Television Production

Lehigh University

Independent coed university. Institutionally accredited by regional association, programs recognized by AACSB. Suburban location, 900-acre campus. Total enrollment: 6202. Undergraduate enrollment: 4389. Total faculty: 346 (319 full-time, 27 part-time). Semester calendar. Grading system: letters or numbers.

English Department, Maginnes 9, Bethlehem, PA 18015 215-861-3310

Lehigh University (continued)

CONTACT Michael Pressler
CURRICULAR EMPHASIS Undergraduate film study — history, criticism and aesthetics, appreciation treated equally Undergraduate filmmaking — Super-8 filmmaking workshop
SPECIAL ACTIVITIES/OFFERINGS Film series
FACILITIES AND EQUIPMENT Film — 8mm cameras, editing equipment, sound recording equipment, projectors, 16mm projectors, screening room, animation board, permanent film library of commercial or professional films Television — black and white studio cameras, ¾-inch cassette VTR, portable black and white cameras, monitors, ½-inch portapak recorders, sound recording equipment, black and white studio
FACULTY Michael Pressler

COURSE LIST

Undergraduate

Writing About Films—Freshman Composition
Narrative Cinema—History and Criticism
Special Topics in Film—Directors, Genres, Periods
Aesthetics of Film—Film Theory and Criticism

Lincoln University

State-related comprehensive coed institution. Institutionally accredited by regional association. Small town location, 300-acre campus. Total enrollment: 1300. Undergraduate enrollment: 1200. Total faculty: 88 (70 full-time, 18 part-time). Trimester calendar. Grading system: letters or numbers.

English Department, Lincoln University, PA 19352 215-932-8300

CONTACT Julius Bellone
ADMISSION Application deadline — rolling
FACILITIES AND EQUIPMENT Film — 8mm cameras, editing equipment, lighting equipment, color film stock, projectors
FACULTY Julius Bellone

COURSE LIST

Undergraduate

Introduction to Cinema

Lock Haven State College

State-supported 4-year coed college. Part of Pennsylvania State Colleges and University System. Institutionally accredited by regional association. Small town location, 135-acre campus. Undergraduate enrollment: 2231. Total faculty: 168 (165 full-time, 3 part-time). Semester calendar. Grading system: letters or numbers.

Foundation Studies Department, Lock Haven, PA 17745 717-893-2011

CONTACT Ralph Dessenberger
ADMISSION Application deadline — 6/1, rolling
CURRICULAR EMPHASIS Film study — (1) production; (2) educational media/instructional technology; (3) criticism and aesthetics Filmmaking — (1) educational; (2) experimental; (3) documentary; (4) narrative; (5) animated Television study — (1) production; (2) educational; (3) appreciation Television production — (1) educational; (2) commercial; (3) news/documentary
SPECIAL ACTIVITIES/OFFERINGS Film series, program material produced for on-campus closed-circuit television and local public television station, independent study, practicum
FACILITIES AND EQUIPMENT Film — complete 8mm and 16mm equipment, screening room, editing room, animation board, permanent film library Television — complete black and white studio and exterior production equipment, black and white studio, control room
FACULTY Ralph Dessenberger

COURSE LIST

Undergraduate

Film Appreciation
Motion Picture Production
Television Production

Mercyhurst College

Independent comprehensive coed institution. Institutionally accredited by regional association. Suburban location, 75-acre campus. Total enrollment: 1406. Undergraduate enrollment: 1300. Total faculty: 127 (88 full-time, 39 part-time). 3-1-3-3 calendar. Grading system: letters or numbers.

Communications Department, Erie, PA 16501 814-864-0681

CONTACT Andrew Roth, Director
DEGREE OFFERED BA in communication arts with emphases in cable, radio, and TV
ADMISSION Application deadline — rolling
FACULTY David Palmer, Andrew Roth, William Shelly, Detmar Straub

COURSE LIST

Undergraduate

Film Appreciation
TV Production
Mass Media and Popular Culture
Radio Production
Broadcasting in America
History of Film
Film Criticism
Communications Seminar: Special Topics
Communications Internship
Documentary Video

Muhlenberg College

Independent Lutheran 4-year coed college. Institutionally accredited by regional association. Suburban location, 75-acre campus. Undergraduate enrollment: 1530. Total faculty: 117 (110 full-time, 7 part-time). Semester calendar. Grading system: letters or numbers.

Educational Ventures Inc, Allentown, PA 18104 215-435-6779

CONTACT George N Gordon
DEGREE OFFERED BA in liberal arts studies with a major in communication studies (consortial program offered with Cedar Crest College)
PROGRAM MAJORS Film — 15 students Television — 50 students
ADMISSION Requirements — ACT or SAT scores, interview, teachers' recommendations, written statement of purpose
FINANCIAL AID Scholarships, work/study programs, student loans
CURRICULAR EMPHASIS Film study — (1) history; (2) appreciation; (3) criticism and aesthetics Filmmaking — experimental Television study — (1) criticism and aesthetics; (2) history; (3) production; (4) management; (5) appreciation Television production — (1) experimental/personal video; (2) news/documentary; (3) commercial; (4) educational
SPECIAL ACTIVITIES/OFFERINGS Film series, film festivals, apprenticeships, internships in film production, internships in television production, independent study, vocational placement service
FACILITIES AND EQUIPMENT Film — screening room Television — black and white studio cameras, ¾-inch cassette VTR, portable black and white cameras, monitors, lighting equipment, sound recording equipment, black and white studio, audio studio
FACULTY Kent Kjellegren

COURSE LIST

Undergraduate
Radio and TV Broadcasting
Television Production
Broadcast Journalism
Art of the Film
Film Criticism and Appreciation

Northampton County Area Community College

County-supported 2-year coed college. Accredited by state agency. Suburban location. Total enrollment: 3895. Total faculty: 95. Semester calendar. Grading system: letters or numbers.

Telecommunication Program, 3835 Green Pond Road, Bethlehem, PA 18017 215-865-5351

CONTACT Robert Mundhenk
DEGREE OFFERED AS in broadcasting
PROGRAM MAJORS Television — 30 students
ADMISSION Undergraduate application deadline — rolling
FINANCIAL AID Scholarships, work/study programs
CURRICULAR EMPHASIS Television study — (1) production; (2) criticism and aesthetics; (3) history Television production — (1) commercial; (2) educational; (3) news/documentary
SPECIAL ACTIVITIES/OFFERINGS Film series, film festivals, internships in television production
FACILITIES AND EQUIPMENT Film — 8mm cameras, sound recording equipment Television — complete color studio and exterior production equipment, color studio, audio studio, control room
FACULTY Robert Mundhenk PART-TIME FACULTY Mark O'Brien

COURSE LIST

Undergraduate
Radio Production
Fundamentals of Broadcasting
Radio Workshop
Introduction to Film
Television Production
Advanced Television Production
Radio-TV Internship

Our Lady of Angels College

Independent Roman Catholic 4-year college primarily for women. Institutionally accredited by regional association. Suburban location. Undergraduate enrollment: 674. Total faculty: 71 (30 full-time, 41 part-time). Semester calendar. Grading system: letters or numbers.

Humanities Department, Aston, PA 19014 215-GL9-0905

CONTACT Film — William F Lynch Television — Sister Christa Marie Thompson
ADMISSION Requirement — 2.0 minimum grade point average Application deadline — 8/15
FINANCIAL AID Scholarships, work/study programs, student loans Application deadline — 7/15
CURRICULAR EMPHASIS Undergraduate film study — (1) appreciation; (2) history; (3) criticism and aesthetics
SPECIAL ACTIVITIES/OFFERINGS Film series
FACILITIES AND EQUIPMENT Film — 8mm projectors, 16mm projectors, screening room, permanent film library of commercial or professional films Television — black and white studio cameras, ¾-inch cassette VTR, portable black and white cameras, black and white studio, control room
FACULTY William F Lynch, Sister Christa Marie Thompson

COURSE LIST

Undergraduate
Introduction to Film
Film and Literature
Film: Recording a World or Creating a World?

Pennsylvania State University–University Park Campus

State-related coed university. Part of Pennsylvania State University System. Institutionally accredited by regional association, programs recognized by AACSB. Small town location, 540-acre campus. Total enrollment: 31,881. Undergraduate enrollment: 27,027. Total faculty: 1660 (1483 full-time, 177 part-time). Three 10-week term calendar. Grading system: letters or numbers.

Division of Curriculum and Instruction, 166 Chambers Building, University Park, PA 16802 814-865-1500

CONTACT Paul W Welliver
DEGREES OFFERED M Ed or MS in Instructional Systems with emphasis in television
ADMISSION Requirements — GRE scores, written statement of purpose, professional recommendations
FINANCIAL AID Student loans, fellowships, teaching assistantships, research assistantships
CURRICULAR EMPHASIS Film study — educational media/instructional technology Filmmaking — educational Television study — educational Television production — educational
SPECIAL ACTIVITIES/OFFERINGS Independent study, teacher training
FACILITIES AND EQUIPMENT Film — 8mm cameras, editing equipment, lighting, black and white film stock, color film stocks, projectors, editing room, permanent film library of commercial or professional films Television — black and white studio cameras, color studio cameras, ½-inch VTR, 1-inch VTR, ¾-inch cassette VTR, editing equipment, monitors, special effects generators, slide chain, lighting equipment, sound recording equipment, audio mixers, film chain, time base corrector, black and white studio, color studio, control room
FACULTY Paul W Welliver PART-TIME FACULTY Victor Rossi

COURSE LIST

Undergraduate and Graduate
Production of Educational Motion Pictures
Television in Education

Department of Theater and Film, University Park, PA 16802 814-865-7586

CONTACT Film Coordinator
DEGREES OFFERED BA in film with emphasis in production, BA in film with emphasis in history/criticism
DEPARTMENTAL MAJORS Undergraduate film — 50 students Graduate film — 5 students
ADMISSION Undergraduate requirements — ACT or SAT scores, teachers' recommendations, written statement of purpose Graduate requirements — GRE scores, interview, teachers' recommendations, written statement of purpose, portfolio
FINANCIAL AID Scholarships, work/study programs, student loans, teaching assistantships, research assistantships
CURRICULAR EMPHASIS Undergraduate film study — history, criticism and aesthetics treated equally Graduate film study — history, criticism and aesthetics treated equally Undergraduate filmmaking — (1) narrative; (2) documentary Graduate filmmaking — documentary, narrative treated equally
SPECIAL ACTIVITIES/OFFERINGS Filmmaking clubs, film series, film festivals, film societies, program material produced for cable television and local public television station, internships in film production, internships in television production, independent study
FACILITIES AND EQUIPMENT Film — complete 8mm and 16mm equipment, screening room, editing room, sound mixing room, animation board, permanent film library of student films, permanent film library of commercial or professional films
FACULTY Steven Fenwick, Dorn Hetzel, Jerome Holway, William Uricchio

COURSE LIST

Undergraduate
Processes of Acting
The Dramatic Arts in the Mass Media
The Art of Cinema
Basic Film Production
Introduction to Television Broadcasting Techniques
Film Production Practicum
Introduction to Screenwriting
Introduction to Motion Picture Techniques
Intermediate Film Production
Expanded Cinema
Advanced Film Projects

Undergraduate and Graduate
Advanced Lighting Techniques for Black and White Film Production
Location Lighting and Cinematography
Sound for Film
Performance for the Camera
Directing for Film and Television
Advanced Screenwriting
Advanced Film Production
American Film
Foreign Film
Documentary Film and Television
Advanced Film Production Practicum
Independent Studies
Special Topics

Pennsylvania State University–Wilkes-Barre Campus

State-related 2-year coed college. Part of Pennsylvania State University System, automatic transfer to main campus for baccalaureate. Institutionally accredited by regional association. Suburban location, 58-acre campus. Undergraduate enrollment: 553. Total faculty: 41 (27 full-time, 14 part-time). Three 10-week term calendar. Grading system: letters or numbers.

Mass Communications-Broadcasting Program, PO Box 1830, Wilkes-Barre, PA 18708 717-675-2171

CONTACT Ralph E Carmode
DEGREE OFFERED Associate's degree in broadcasting
PROGRAM MAJORS Television — 35 students
ADMISSION Requirements — 2.0 minimum grade point average, ACT or SAT scores Application deadline — rolling
FINANCIAL AID Scholarships, work/study programs, student loans
CURRICULAR EMPHASIS Television study — (1) production; (2) management; (3) criticism and aesthetics Television production — commercial, educational treated equally

SPECIAL ACTIVITIES/OFFERINGS Student publications, program material produced for on-campus closed-circuit television and cable television, internships in television production, independent study, curricular and extracurricular training with University's FM radio station
FACILITIES AND EQUIPMENT Film — 8mm cameras, editing equipment, lighting, projectors, 16mm cameras, projectors Television — color studio cameras, ¾-inch cassette VTR, editing equipment, monitors, special effects generators, slide chain, portable color cameras, lighting equipment, sound recording equipment, audio mixers, film chain, color studio, audio studio, control room
FACULTY Ralph E Carmode, Brent Spencer PART-TIME FACULTY Roy Morgan

COURSE LIST
Undergraduate
Mass Media and Society
Survey of Broadcasting
Broadcast Announcing
Basic Writing for Broadcast Media
Broadcast Programming, Production and Performance
Dramatic Arts in the Mass Media
Oral Interpretation
Internships
Directed Studies

Philadelphia College of Art

Independent professional comprehensive coed institution. Institutionally accredited by regional association, programs recognized by NASA. Urban location. Total enrollment: 1154. Undergraduate enrollment: 1131. Total faculty: 170 (70 full-time, 100 part-time). Semester calendar. Grading system: letters or numbers.

Photo/Film Department, Broad and Spruce Streets, Philadelphia, PA 19102 215-893-3140

CONTACT Ron Walker
DEGREE OFFERED BFA in filmmaking, animation, or film studies
DEPARTMENTAL MAJORS Film — 20 students
ADMISSION Requirements — interview, portfolio Application deadline — 5/1
FINANCIAL AID Work/study programs, student loans
CURRICULAR EMPHASIS Film study — history, criticism and aesthetics, appreciation treated equally Filmmaking — experimental, animated treated equally
SPECIAL ACTIVITIES/OFFERINGS Film series
FACILITIES AND EQUIPMENT Film — 8mm cameras, editing equipment, 16mm cameras, editing equipment, sound recording equipment, lighting, projectors, screening room, editing room, sound mixing room, animation board, permanent film library of student films, permanent film library of commercial or professional films, optical printer, ARP synthesizer
FACULTY Tom Porett, Peter Rose PART-TIME FACULTY Wanda Bershen, Paul Buck, Howard Danelowitz, Eric Durst, Ron Kanter

COURSE LIST
Undergraduate
Kinetics
Introduction to Animation
Introduction to Live Action
Sound
Film Technology
History of Film
Film Form
Criticism
Intermediate Cinematography
Intermediate Animation

Pittsburgh Film-Makers, Inc

Cinema, PO Box 7467, Pittsburgh, PA 15213 412-681-5449

CONTACT Marilyn J Levin, Executive Director
DEGREES OFFERED BA in film through Point Park College, two-year certificate in film studies through the University of Pittsburgh
PROGRAM MAJORS Film — 75 students
CURRICULAR EMPHASIS Film study — (1) production; (2) criticism and aesthetics; (3) history Filmmaking — (1) experimental; (2) documentary; (3) animated
SPECIAL ACTIVITIES/OFFERINGS Film series, student seminars with visiting independent film artists and scholars, independent study
FACILITIES AND EQUIPMENT Film — complete 8mm and 16mm equipment, screening room, editing room, sound mixing room, animation board, optical printer, flat-bed editor
FACULTY Charles Glassmire, Victor Grauer, Marilyn Levin PART-TIME FACULTY Brady Lewis

COURSE LIST
Undergraduate
Filmmaking I–IV
Film History I, II
Varieties of Cinematic Experience
Film Criticism
Personal Experimental Film
Animation I, II
Cinematography
Sound for Film
Film Theory
Laboratory Techniques in Cinema
Films of a Director
National Cinemas

Point Park College

Independent 4-year coed college. Institutionally accredited by regional association. Urban location. Undergraduate enrollment: 1951. Total faculty: 144 (81 full-time, 63 part-time). Semester calendar. Grading system: letters or numbers.

Cinema Department, Wood Street and Boulevard of Allies, Pittsburgh, PA 15222 412-391-4100

CONTACT Mark Lewis
DEGREE OFFERED BA in film
DEPARTMENTAL MAJORS 15 students

Point Park College (continued)

ADMISSION Requirement — interviews Application deadline — rolling
FINANCIAL AID Student loans Application deadline — rolling
SPECIAL ACTIVITIES/OFFERINGS Independent study

Robert Morris College

Independent comprehensive coed institution. Institutionally accredited by regional association. Suburban location, 240-acre campus. Total enrollment: 4640. Undergraduate enrollment: 4200. Total faculty: 179 (99 full-time, 80 part-time). Semester calendar. Grading system: letters or numbers.

Industrial Communications Department, Narrows Run Road, Coraopolis, PA 15108 412-264-9300 ext 253

CONTACT W A Holmgren
DEGREE OFFERED Bachelor of Science in Business Administration with emphasis in television and photographic communication
DEPARTMENTAL MAJORS 114 students
ADMISSION Requirement — teachers' recommendations Application deadline — rolling
FINANCIAL AID Scholarships, work/study programs, student loans Application deadline — rolling
CURRICULAR EMPHASIS Film study — educational media/instructional technology, industrial communications, broadcasting, cablecasting treated equally Filmmaking — experimental, educational, industrial-business-medical treated equally Television study — production, management, industrial communications, broadcasting, cablecasting treated equally Television production — news/documentary, educational, industrial communications, broadcasting, cablecasting treated equally
SPECIAL ACTIVITIES/OFFERINGS Student publications; program material produced for on-campus closed-circuit television, cable television, local commercial television station, industrial communications for corporations, banks, educational institutions, television production houses, advertising agencies, hospitals, local businesses; apprenticeships; internships in film production; internships in television production; independent study; teacher training; vocational placement service; television club; weekly community-college television news program
FACILITIES AND EQUIPMENT Film — 8mm and 16mm cameras, editing equipment, sound recording equipment, lighting, projectors, sound stage, screening room, 35mm screening facilities, editing room, sound mixing room, permanent film library of commercial or professional films Television — black and white studio cameras, color studio cameras, ½-inch VTR, ¾-inch cassette VTR, portable black and white cameras, editing equipment, monitors, special effects generators, slide chain, portable color cameras, ½-inch portapak recorders, ¾-inch ENG, lighting equipment, sound recording equipment, audio mixers, film chain, time base corrector, character generator, black and white studio, color studio, mobile van/unit, audio studio, control room, set shop, photographic labs (for graphics), videotape program, storage room, engineering supplies and repair room
FACULTY W A Holmgren PART-TIME FACULTY Gary Grant, David Nohling

COURSE LIST

Undergraduate

Survey of Mass Communications
Introduction to Media
Principles of Photography
Radio-Television Production
Media Management
Research/Directed Studies in Communications
Internships in Communications
Introduction to Media for Teachers

Rosemont College

Independent Roman Catholic 4-year women's college. Institutionally accredited by regional association. Suburban location, 56-acre campus. Undergraduate enrollment: 602. Total faculty: 84 (40 full-time, 44 part-time). Semester calendar. Grading system: letters or numbers.

Educational Resources Center, Montgomery Avenue, Rosemont, PA 19010 215-527-0200

ADMISSION Application deadline — rolling
FINANCIAL AID Scholarships, student loans, work/study programs Application deadline — rolling
SPECIAL ACTIVITIES/OFFERINGS Program material produced for on-campus closed-circuit television, teacher training
FACILITIES AND EQUIPMENT Film — 35mm camera, 16mm projectors Television — black and white studio camera, monitors, ½-inch portapak recorder, portable black and white camera, ¾-inch cassette VTR with color TV set

COURSE LIST

Undergraduate

Practicum for Student Teachers

Slippery Rock State College

State-supported comprehensive coed institution. Part of Pennsylvania State Colleges and University System. Institutionally accredited by regional association. Rural location, 600-acre campus. Total enrollment: 5845. Undergraduate enrollment: 5185. Total faculty: 350 (350 full-time, 0 part-time). Semester calendar. Grading system: letters or numbers.

Communication Department, Slippery Rock, PA 16057 412-794-7268

CONTACT Film — Richard C Vincent Television — Robert V Miller
DEGREE OFFERED BA in mass communication with emphasis in film and television
DEPARTMENTAL MAJORS Film — 40 students Television — 125 students
ADMISSION Requirements — ACT or SAT scores, teachers' recommendations Application deadline — rolling
FINANCIAL AID Scholarships, work/study programs, student loans Undergraduate application deadline — 4/1
CURRICULAR EMPHASIS Film study — (1) history; (2) criticism and aesthetics; (3) film business Filmmaking — (1) documentary; (2) experimental; (3) narrative Television study — (1) criticism and aesthetics; (2) production; (3) history Television production — (1) commercial; (2) educational; (3) experimental/personal video

SPECIAL ACTIVITIES/OFFERINGS Film series; program material produced for on-campus closed-circuit television, cable television, local public television station, local commercial television station; internships in film production; internships in television production; independent study; teacher training; vocational placement service
FACILITIES AND EQUIPMENT Film — complete 8mm and 16mm equipment, screening room, editing room, sound mixing room, animation board, permanent film library of commercial or professional films Television — black and white studio cameras, color studio cameras, ½-inch VTR, 1-inch VTR, ¾-inch cassette VTR, portable black and white cameras, editing equipment, monitors, special effects generators, slide chain, portable color cameras, ½-inch portapak recorders, ¾-inch ENG, lighting equipment, sound recording equipment, audio mixers, film chain, time base corrector, black and white studio, color studio, audio studio, control room
FACULTY Robert V Miller, Joe Normand, Richard C Vincent, Ed Walsh, Joan Williams

COURSE LIST

Undergraduate
Mass Communication
Broadcast History
Film History
The Documentary Film
Broadcast Management and Sales
The American Film Industry
Film Theory and Criticism
Film Production
Advanced Film Production
Television Production
Advanced Television Production
Radio Production
Advanced Radio Production
Broadcast Practicum
Media Internship
Organizational Communication
Basic Concepts in Communication
Communication Theory
Fundamentals of Directing
Applied Directing
Costuming
Makeup
Scene Design
Stage Lighting
Stagecraft
Fundamentals of Acting
Advanced Acting
Writing for the Electronic Media

English Department 412-794-7265

CONTACT William H Smith
PROGRAM OFFERED Major in English with emphasis in film
ADMISSION Requirements — 2.0 minimum grade point average, ACT or SAT scores, teachers' recommendations Application deadline — rolling
CURRICULAR EMPHASIS Film study — (1) criticism and aesthetics; (2) appreciation; (3) production Filmmaking — (1) narrative; (2) experimental
SPECIAL ACTIVITIES/OFFERINGS Film series, film festivals, film societies, internships in film production, independent study, liaison with professional filmmaker
FACILITIES AND EQUIPMENT Film — complete 8mm, 16mm, and 35mm equipment, screening room, editing room, sound mixing room, animation board, permanent film library
FACULTY William H Smith

COURSE LIST

Undergraduate
Cinematic Review
Film Analysis

Graduate
Film and the Novel

Swarthmore College

Independent 4-year coed college. Institutionally accredited by regional association. Suburban location. Undergraduate enrollment: 1280. Total faculty: 145. Semester calendar. Grading system: letters or numbers.

Department of Art, Swarthmore, PA 19081 215-544-7900

CONTACT T Kaori Kitao, Chairperson
ADMISSION Application deadline — 2/1
CURRICULAR EMPHASIS Film study — (1) criticism and aesthetics; (2) history
FACULTY T Kaori Kitao

COURSE LIST

Undergraduate
The Cinema: History
The Cinema: Critical Theories
The Cinema: Hollywood

Temple University

State-related coed university. Institutionally accredited by regional association. Urban location, 76-acre campus. Total enrollment: 24,377. Undergraduate enrollment: 17,444. Total faculty: 2527 (1791 full-time, 736 part-time). Semester calendar. Grading system: letters or numbers.

Department of Radio-Television-Film, Philadelphia, PA 19122 215-787-8423

CONTACT Gordon L Gray, Ben Levin
DEGREES OFFERED BA in radio-television-film; MFA in radio-television-film; MA, PhD in communications (joint degrees in association with journalism)
DEPARTMENTAL MAJORS Undergraduate — 1100 students Graduate — 114 students
ADMISSION Undergraduate requirements — 2.0 minimum grade point average, ACT or SAT scores, written statement of purpose Graduate requirements — 2.8 overall grade point average or 3.0 in major or last two years, GRE scores, teachers' recommendations, written statement of purpose, exhibits, professional recommendations, professional work experience desirable Undergraduate application deadline — 6/15
FINANCIAL AID Scholarships, work/study programs, student loans, fellowships, teaching assistantships, research assistantships Undergraduate application deadline — 5/1

Temple University (continued)

CURRICULAR EMPHASIS Undergraduate film study — history, criticism and aesthetics, appreciation treated equally Graduate film study — history, criticism and aesthetics, appreciation treated equally Undergraduate filmmaking — documentary, narrative, experimental treated equally Graduate filmmaking — (1) documentary; (2) narrative; (3) experimental Undergraduate television study — history, management, public policy treated equally Graduate television study — history, management, public policy treated equally Undergraduate television production — commercial, news/documentary, educational treated equally Graduate television production — commercial, news/documentary, educational treated equally

SPECIAL ACTIVITIES/OFFERINGS Film festivals, internships in film production, internships in television production, independent study

FACILITIES AND EQUIPMENT Film — complete 8mm and 16mm equipment, sound stage, screening room, 35mm screening facilities, editing room, sound mixing room, permanent film library of student films, permanent film library of commercial or professional films Television — complete black and white and color studio production equipment, complete black and white and color portapak exterior production equipment, black and white studio, color studio, audio studio, control room, portapak, VTR editing

FACULTY Jim Ambandos, Warren Bass, Laurence Blenheim, Alan Bloom, Delwin Dusenbury, Susan Eastman, Norman Felsenthal, Thomas Gordon, Gordon L Gray, Sydney Head, John M Kittross, Ben Levin, Paul Mareth, Lee McConkey, Edward McCoy, Nikos Metallinos, Calvin Pryluck, John Roberts, Daniel Schiller, Robert R Smith, Christopher H Sterling, Sari Thomas, Alexander F Toogood, Janet Wasko PART-TIME FACULTY Robert Bradley, Lewis Klein, Robert McGredy, Barry Nemcoff, Howard Rice, Franklin Tooke

COURSE LIST

Undergraduate

The Communications Arts
Communication Theory
Mass Media and Society
Honors Reading I–III
Applied Communication
Recording and Structuring Video
Recording and Structuring Film
Film and Illusion
Film and Reality
The Broadcasting System
Film Institutions
Broadcast Performance
Television-Radio Continuity Writing
Television Performance I, II
Television Studio Production
Documentary Writing
Editing Film and Video
Audio Production
Broadcast Advertising
The Bibliography of Mass Communications
Honors Independent Research
Honors Creative Project
Television and Film Dramatic Writing
Broadcast News Gathering
Broadcast Newswriting
News Broadcasting
Film Production Workshop
Television Program Design I, II
Topics in Film Study
Topics in Production
Topics in Broadcast Study
Topics in Communication
Cinematography and Film Sound
Documentary Film Workshop
British Documentary Film
Radio Production Workshop
Independent Film and Video
Television Production Workshop
Experimental Video
Broadcast Sales
Projects in Television Production
Television Aesthetics
Advanced Film/Video Workshop
Media Anthropology
Public Broadcasting
Film Theory and Aesthetics
Economics of Film and Video Production
Mass Media Research
History of Broadcasting
Broadcasting Public Policy and Regulation
Comparative Broadcasting
Theories of Communication
Broadcast Programming and Management
Instructional/Industrial TV Practicum
Internship
Broadcast Workshop
Honors Teaching
Senior Seminar

Graduate

Introduction to Communication Concepts
Introduction to Graduate Research
Communication Research I, II
Communications and Society
Ethical Standards and Responsibilities of Mass Communications
Interpreting Popular Culture
Seminar: Advanced Studies in Communication Theory
Seminar: Evaluation Research
Seminars: Communications Abroad (taught overseas)
Seminar: International Communications
Seminar: Media and Government
Special Problems in Communications
PhD Colloquium
MFA Colloquium
Directed Readings in Communications
Directed Projects in Communications
Advanced Studies
Applied Communication Workshop
Cinematography Workshop
Bibliography of Mass Communications
Communication Aesthetics
Mass Media and Children: Socialization Effects
Political Economy of Mass Communications
History of Theatrical Film
History of Documentary
Dramatic Writing for Television and Film
Documentary Writing
Documentary Film Workshop
Advanced Documentary Workshop
Advanced Problems in Film Production I, II
Television Program Design
Experiments in Visual Dynamics
Seminar: Broadcast News and Public Affairs
Seminar: Persuasion and Mass Communication
Seminar: Communications and Public Policy
Seminar: Problems of Mass Communications
Seminar: The New Technology and the Mass Media
Seminar: Communications Education
Seminar: Foreign and International Systems of Broadcasting
Seminar: Broadcast Management
Seminar: Motion Picture Management
Seminar: History of Mass Communications
Seminar: International Film
Seminar: The American Motion Picture
Seminar: Film Analysis and Criticism
Seminar: Issues in Communication Education

Anthropology Department 215-787-7775

CONTACT Richard Chalfen

DEGREES OFFERED BA, MA in visual communication

FINANCIAL AID Scholarships, student loans, work/study programs, teaching assistantships, research assistantships, fellowships Undergraduate application deadline — 5/1

CURRICULAR EMPHASIS Undergraduate film study — (1) visual communication; (2) criticism and aesthetics; (3) history Graduate film study — (1) visual communication; (2) criticism and aesthetics; (3) history; (4) production Filmmaking — (1) anthropological; (2) documentary Television study — (1) visual communication; (2) criticism and aesthetics; (3) history; (4) appreciation Television production — (1) news/documentary; (2) research

SPECIAL ACTIVITIES/OFFERINGS Independent study; joint graduate program in visual anthropology with Anthropology Film Center, Santa Fe, New Mexico
FACILITIES AND EQUIPMENT Film — complete 8mm and 16mm equipment, editing room Television — complete black and white exterior production facilities
FACULTY Richard Chalfen, Jay Ruby

COURSE LIST

Undergraduate
Human Image
Nonverbal Communication
Mass Media

Undergraduate and Graduate
Anthropological Film
Anthropological Photography
Culture and Communication
Visual Communication

University of Pennsylvania

Independent coed university. Institutionally accredited by regional association. Urban location, 250-acre campus. Total enrollment: 8300. Undergraduate enrollment: 8000. Total faculty: 2500 (2000 full-time, 500 part-time). Semester calendar. Grading system: letters or numbers.

History Department, 34th and Spruce Streets, Philadelphia, PA 19174 215-243-8452

CONTACT Stuart Samuels
DEGREE OFFERED Degree in history with independent major in film
DEPARTMENTAL MAJORS 10 students
ADMISSION Application deadline — 1/1
CURRICULAR EMPHASIS Film study — criticism and aesthetics, history treated equally Filmmaking — (1) narrative; (2) documentary; (3) experimental
FACULTY Stuart Samuels

COURSE LIST

Undergraduate
Film as Social and Intellectual History

Annenberg School of Communications, 3620 Walnut Street, Philadelphia, PA 19104 215-243-7041

CONTACT Larry Gross
DEGREES OFFERED BA in communications, MA in communications, PhD in communications
ADMISSION Undergraduate requirements — ACT or SAT scores, interview, teachers' recommendations, written statement of purpose Graduate requirements — GRE scores, teachers' recommendations, written statement of purpose Undergraduate application deadline — 1/1
FINANCIAL AID Scholarships, work/study programs, student loans, fellowships, teaching assistantships, research assistantships Undergraduate application deadline — 1/1
CURRICULAR EMPHASIS Undergraduate film study — (1) criticism and aesthetics; (2) history; (3) appreciation Graduate film study — (1) research; (2) communication; (3) criticism and aesthetics Undergraduate filmmaking — (1) documentary; (2) experimental; (3) narrative Graduate filmmaking — (1) documentary; (2) narrative; (3) research Undergraduate television study — (1) criticism and aesthetics; (2) production; (3) history Graduate television study — (1) research; (2) criticism and aesthetics; (3) production Undergraduate television production — (1) communication theory; (2) news/documentary; (3) experimental/personal video Graduate television production — (1) communication theory; (2) news/documentary; (3) experimental/personal video
SPECIAL ACTIVITIES/OFFERINGS Filmmaking clubs, film series, film festivals, independent study
FACILITIES AND EQUIPMENT Film — complete 16mm equipment, screening room, editing room, sound mixing room, permanent film library of student films, permanent film library of commercial or professional films Television — complete black and white and color studio production equipment, complete color exterior production equipment, color studio, audio studio, control room, video disc equipment
FACULTY Steven Feld, Antonin Liehm, Paul Messaris, Mark Miller, Robert Lewis Shayon PART-TIME FACULTY Al Rose

COURSE LIST

Undergraduate
Sources of Modern Cinema
Art as Communication
Visual Communication
Mass Media and Society

Graduate
Research in Film and Television

Undergraduate and Graduate
Methods of Film Analysis
Documentary Film Laboratory
Television Laboratory
Sound Communication
Mass Media Criticism

University of Pittsburgh

State-related coed university. Part of University of Pittsburgh System. Institutionally accredited by regional association, programs recognized by NASA, ACPE. Urban location. Total enrollment: 29,743. Undergraduate enrollment: 19,109. Total faculty: 2267. Trimester calendar. Grading system: letters or numbers.

Film Studies Program, College of Arts and Sciences, 526 Cathedral of Learning, Pittsburgh, PA 15260 412-624-6551

CONTACT Lucy Fischer

University of Pittsburgh (continued)

PROGRAMS OFFERED Self-designed major in film studies, major in related field with an emphasis in film, certificate in film studies
FINANCIAL AID Scholarships, work/study programs, student loans
CURRICULAR EMPHASIS Film study — (1) criticism and aesthetics; (2) history; (3) theory Filmmaking — documentary, narrative, experimental, animated treated equally
SPECIAL ACTIVITIES/OFFERINGS Filmmaking clubs, film series, film festivals, film societies, internships in film production, internships in television production, independent study
FACILITIES AND EQUIPMENT Film — complete 8mm and 16mm equipment, screening room, 35mm screening facilities, editing room, sound mixing room, animation board, permanent film library of student films, permanent film library of commercial or professional films, optical printer
FACULTY Walter Albert, Gilette Elvgren, Lucy Fischer, Bruce Goldstein, Henry Heymann, Marcia Landy, Keiko McDonald, Dana Polan, Aaron Schoen PART-TIME FACULTY Roger Conant, William Judson

COURSE LIST

Undergraduate

Introduction to Film History
Documentary Film
Film and Literature
Film and Visual Perception
Women and Film
German Film (1919-1933)
French Film (1913-1934)
Soviet Film
Italian Film
Japanese Film
Experimental Film
Theater and Film
Film Theory
Introductory Filmmaking
Advanced Filmmaking
Black-and-White Photography
Color Photography
Photography and Art
American Film History
Politics and Film
Crime and Film
British Film History
Western and Samurai Films
Directors' Course
Film Comedy

Villanova University

Independent Roman Catholic coed university. Institutionally accredited by regional association, programs recognized by AACSB. Suburban location, 125-acre campus. Total enrollment: 9500. Undergraduate enrollment: 5874. Total faculty: 524 (411 full-time, 113 part-time). Semester calendar. Grading system: letters or numbers.

Theatre Department, Villanova, PA 19085 215-527-2100 ext 340

CONTACT Joan D Lynch
DEGREE OFFERED BS in communications
CURRICULAR EMPHASIS Film study — (1) analysis; (2) criticism and aesthetics; (3) appreciation; (4) history Filmmaking — (1) narrative; (2) experimental Television study — production Television production — (1) news/documentary; (2) experimental/personal video
SPECIAL ACTIVITIES/OFFERINGS Film series, film festivals, film societies
FACILITIES AND EQUIPMENT Film — complete 8mm equipment, screening room, editing room, permanent film library of commercial or professional films Television — complete color studio production equipment
FACULTY Joan Driscoll Lynch, Ernie Schier

COURSE LIST

Undergraduate

Film Analysis I, II
Cinematography
Television Production
Film and Theater
Genre Study — Science Fiction
Women and Film
Film Criticism

Graduate

Film Study

Waynesburg College

Independent 4-year coed college affiliated with United Presbyterian Church. Institutionally accredited by regional association. Small town location. Undergraduate enrollment: 820. Total faculty: 60 (48 full-time, 12 part-time). Semester calendar. Grading system: letters or numbers.

Communication Arts–Media Studies Program, English Department, Waynesburg, PA 15370 412-627-8191 ext 270

CONTACT Chairman, English Department
DEGREE OFFERED BA in English with communications emphasis in writing for media or in electronic media
PROGRAM MAJORS 35 students
ADMISSION Requirement — ACT or SAT scores Application deadline — rolling
FINANCIAL AID Scholarships, work/study programs, student loans Application deadline — rolling
CURRICULAR EMPHASIS Film study — history, criticism and aesthetics, appreciation, educational media/instructional technology treated equally Television study — history, criticism and aesthetics, appreciation, educational, production, management, internships treated equally Television production — commercial, news/documentary, experimental/personal video, educational, programming for local cable channel
SPECIAL ACTIVITIES/OFFERINGS Film series; film festivals; student publications; speaker series; arts festival; conferences; program material produced for on-campus closed-circuit television, cable television, campus sports events; internships in film production; internships in television production; independent study; teacher training; vocational placement service
FACILITIES AND EQUIPMENT Film — 8mm sound recording equipment, lighting, 16mm sound recording equipment, lighting, projectors, screening room, sound mixing room Television — black and white studio cameras, ½-inch VTR, ¾-inch cassette VTR, portable black and white cameras, editing equipment, monitors, slide chain, ½-inch portapak recorders, lighting equipment, sound recording equipment, audio mixers, film chain, time base corrector, black and white studio, mobile van/unit, remote truck, audio studio, control room
FACULTY Rose Majestic, William Molzon, William L Sipple

COURSE LIST

Undergraduate

Understanding Media
Audio Production Techniques
Media Presentation
Radio Production
Television Production I, II
Independent Studies
Special Topics
Internship
Film and Literature

Westminster College

Independent Presbyterian comprehensive coed institution. Institutionally accredited by regional association, programs recognized by NASM. Small town location, 300-acre campus. Total enrollment: 1800. Undergraduate enrollment: 1550. Total faculty: 140 (114 full-time, 26 part-time). 4-1-4 calendar. Grading system: letters or numbers.

English Department, New Wilmington, PA 16142 412-946-8761

CONTACT Film — William J McTaggart Television — Darwin Huey
SPECIAL ACTIVITIES/OFFERINGS Film series
FACULTY Darwin Huey, William J McTaggart, Walter E Scheid

COURSE LIST

Undergraduate

Film Art
A History of Film

RHODE ISLAND

Rhode Island College

State-supported comprehensive coed institution. Institutionally accredited by regional association, programs recognized by NASM, NASA. Suburban location, 125-acre campus. Total enrollment: 9041. Undergraduate enrollment: 5976. Total faculty: 393 (361 full-time, 32 part-time). Semester calendar. Grading system: letters or numbers.

Film Studies Program, 600 Mount Pleasant Avenue, Providence, RI 02908 401-274-4900

CONTACT Mark W Estrin, Coordinator
DEGREE OFFERED BA in film studies
PROGRAM MAJORS 20 students
ADMISSION Requirements — SAT scores, teachers' recommendations Application deadline — 6/1
CURRICULAR EMPHASIS Film study — history, criticism and aesthetics, appreciation treated equally Filmmaking — (1) narrative, experimental; (2) documentary, animated, educational
SPECIAL ACTIVITIES/OFFERINGS Filmmaking clubs, film series, film festivals, internships in film production, independent study
FACILITIES AND EQUIPMENT Film — 8mm and 16mm cameras, editing equipment, lighting equipment, projectors, animation board, permanent film library
FACULTY Lawrence Budner, Joan Dagle, Mark W Estrin, David Hysell

COURSE LIST

Undergraduate

Introduction to Cinema
History of Film I, II
Approaches to Film and Film Criticism
Literature and Film
Cinematography
Basic Filmmaking
Topics in the Aesthetics of Film
Studio Topics in Art/Film

Undergraduate and Graduate

Animation

Roger Williams College

Independent 4-year coed college. Institutionally accredited by regional association. Suburban location, 80-acre campus. Undergraduate enrollment: 1800. Total faculty: 211 (80 full-time, 131 part-time). 4-1-4 calendar. Grading system: letters or numbers.

Film Studies Department, Ferry Road, Bristol, RI 02809 401-255-2196

CONTACT Nancy R Harlow
DEGREE OFFERED BA in film studies (an interdisciplinary major)
DEPARTMENTAL MAJORS Film — 9 students
ADMISSION Application deadline — rolling
FINANCIAL AID Scholarships, work/study programs, student loans Undergraduate application deadline — 2/15
CURRICULAR EMPHASIS Film study — (1) criticism and aesthetics; (2) history; (3) appreciation Filmmaking — (1) narrative; (2) animated; (3) documentary
SPECIAL ACTIVITIES/OFFERINGS Filmmaking clubs, film series, film societies, internships in film production, independent study
FACILITIES AND EQUIPMENT Film — complete 8mm equipment, 16mm cameras, editing equipment, sound recording equipment, lighting, projectors, screening room, sound mixing room
FACULTY Joseph Alaimo, Nancy Harlow, Jody Jespersen

Roger Williams College (continued)

COURSE LIST

Undergraduate

History of Film I, II
Super-8 Filmmaking I, II
Vintage French Cinema
European Film from 1945
Hollywood in the Thirties
The Documentary Film
Film Comedy
Myth of the Western Hero
Luis Buñuel Seminar
Ingmar Bergman Seminar
Federico Fellini Seminar

University of Rhode Island

State-supported coed university. Part of Rhode Island State System of Higher Education. Institutionally accredited by regional association. Small town location, 1200-acre campus. Total enrollment: 11,268. Undergraduate enrollment: 9033. Total faculty: 830 (780 full-time, 50 part-time). Semester calendar. Grading system: letters or numbers.

History Department, Kingston, RI 02881 401-789-0469

CONTACT Sharon Strom
ADMISSION Application deadline — 3/1
CURRICULAR EMPHASIS Film study — (1) history; (2) criticism and aesthetics; (3) women's cinema
FACULTY Sharon Strom

COURSE LIST

Undergraduate

Recent America in Film

SOUTH CAROLINA

Benedict College

Independent Baptist 4-year coed college. Institutionally accredited by regional association. Urban location, 22-acre campus. Undergraduate enrollment: 1761. Total faculty: 105 (96 full-time, 9 part-time). Semester calendar. Grading system: letters or numbers.

Journalism Department, Harden Street, Columbia, SC 29204 803-256-4220

CONTACT Film — David Zimmerman Television — Harold B Hayes
DEGREE OFFERED BA in journalism with a major in television
DEPARTMENTAL MAJORS 5 students
ADMISSION Application deadline — rolling
FINANCIAL AID Scholarships, student loans, work/study programs Application deadline — 3/15
CURRICULAR EMPHASIS Television study — (1) production; (2) criticism and aesthetics; (3) history Television production — (1) commercial; (2) experimental/personal video; (3) news/documentary
SPECIAL ACTIVITIES/OFFERINGS Program material produced for on-campus closed-circuit television, internships in television production
FACILITIES AND EQUIPMENT Television — 1-inch VTR, monitors, slide chain, portable color cameras, lighting equipment, sound recording equipment, audio mixers, film chain, time base corrector, color studio, control room
PART-TIME FACULTY David Zimmerman, Peter Isquick

COURSE LIST

Undergraduate

Broadcast Production
Broadcast Writing
Broadcast Directing
Broadcast Internship

Bob Jones University

Independent Protestant 4-year coed university. Accredited by state agency. Urban location. Total enrollment: 5700. Total faculty: 350. Semester calendar. Grading system: letters or numbers.

Unusual Films, Division of Cinema, 1700 Wade Hampton Boulevard, Greenville, SC 29614 803-242-5100, ext 292

CONTACT Film — Katherine Stenholm Television — Laura Pratt
DEGREES OFFERED BS, MA in cinema; BA, BS, MA in radio-television
PROGRAM MAJORS Undergraduate film — 50 students Graduate film — 3 students
ADMISSION Undergraduate requirements — minimum grade point average, ACT or SAT scores, interview, written statement of purpose Graduate requirements — minimum grade point average, GRE scores, interview, written statement of purpose, portfolio
FINANCIAL AID Scholarships, work/study programs, student loans, teaching assistantships Undergraduate application deadline — 8/1
CURRICULAR EMPHASIS Undergraduate film study — (1) production; (2) criticism and aesthetics; (3) history Graduate film study — (1) production; (2) criticism and aesthetics; (3) history Undergraduate filmmaking — (1) dramatic; (2) documentary; (3) animated Graduate filmmaking — (1) dramatic; (2) documentary; (3) animated Undergraduate television study — (1) production; (2) management; (3) educational Graduate television study — (1) production; (2) management; (3) criticism and aesthetics Undergraduate television production — commercial, news/documentary, educational treated equally Graduate television production — commercial, news/documentary, educational treated equally

SPECIAL ACTIVITIES/OFFERINGS Film series, professional production work at all levels of the film process, program material produced for on-campus closed-circuit television and nationally released weekly program, apprenticeships, internships in film production, internships in television production, independent study, vocational placement service
FACILITIES AND EQUIPMENT Film — complete 16mm and 35mm equipment, sound stage, screening room, editing room, sound mixing room, animation board, permanent film library of student films, permanent film library of commercial or professional films, film processing, film printing, optical printer, complete animation stands, camera, related equipment, crab dolly, camera crane, front-projection system, multimedia production facilities Television — complete color studio and exterior production equipment, color studio, mobile van/unit, remote truck, audio studio, control room
FACULTY Dan Calnon, Joe Clark, Terry Davenport, Ray Gahagen, Dave Gibble, Ann Glenn, John Magnuson, Fred Pachter, Bruce Polhamus, Wade Ramsey, Tim Rogers, George Rogier, Katherine Stenholm, Laura Stevenson

COURSE LIST

Undergraduate
Fundamentals of Motion Pictures
Camera I–IV
Principles of Motion Picture Sound
Electrical Theory (Film)
Film Editing I, II
Makeup for Motion Pictures and Television
Scenic Design
Motion Picture Projection
Advanced Sound Recording
Animation and Titling
Advanced Editing III, IV
Cinema Seminar
Screen Writing
Motion Picture Production Techniques
Cinema Workshop I, II
Cinema Directing
Fundamentals of Broadcasting
Basic Announcing
Writing
Control Room Techniques
Advanced Announcing
Electrical Theory (Radio and Television)
News
Principles of Religious Broadcasting
Directing
Advanced Directing
Communication Circuits
Audio and Input Equipment Workshop
Private Instruction in Broadcast Performance
Advertising
Broadcast Systems
Design Problems

Graduate
Graduate Editing
Seminar in Creative Cinema
Advanced Screen Writing
Advanced Scenic Design for Motion Pictures
Directed Research
Production Design
Color Photography
Advanced Animation
Graduate Camera
Cinema Workshop III, IV
Professional Directing
Professional Sound Recording
Seminar in Broadcasting
Special Problems in Production Directing
History of Radio and Television
Station Management
Broadcast Law
Independent Graduate Study

Winthrop College

State-supported comprehensive institution, coed as of 1974. Institutionally accredited by regional association, programs recognized by NASM. Urban location, 85-acre campus. Total enrollment: 4640. Undergraduate enrollment: 3551. Total faculty: 254 (212 full-time, 42 part-time). Semester calendar. Grading system: letters or numbers.

English and Drama Department, 701 Oakland, Rock Hill, SC 29733 803-323-2150

CONTACT Film — Lessie M Reynolds Television — John Sargent
ADMISSION Application deadline — rolling
FINANCIAL AID Student loans, work/study programs, clerical and production assistantships, research assistantships Application deadline — 2/1
CURRICULAR EMPHASIS Film study — (1) appreciation; (2) criticism; (3) history Television study — (1) production; (2) appreciation; (3) educational
SPECIAL ACTIVITIES/OFFERINGS Film series, film festivals, program material produced for cable television
FACILITIES AND EQUIPMENT Film — 8mm and 16mm cameras, projectors, editing equipment, screening room, 35mm screening facilities Television — complete black and white studio and exterior production facilities, complete color studio and exterior production equipment, color studio, audio studio, control room
FACULTY Roy Flynn, Lessie M Reynolds, John Sargent

COURSE LIST

Undergraduate
Introduction to the Film
Introduction to Broadcasting
Principles of TV

SOUTH DAKOTA

Black Hills State College

State-supported comprehensive coed institution. Institutionally accredited by regional association. Small town location, 123-acre campus. Undergraduate enrollment: 1967. Total faculty: 98 (90 full-time, 8 part-time). Semester calendar. Grading system: letters or numbers.

Communications Department, Spearfish, SD 57783 605-642-6420

CONTACT Rick Boyd
DEGREE OFFERED AA in radio-television
DEPARTMENTAL MAJORS 10 students
CURRICULAR EMPHASIS Television study — production Television production — (1) commercial; (2) news/documentary

Black Hills State College (continued)

FACILITIES AND EQUIPMENT Television — complete black and white studio production facilities
PART-TIME FACULTY Rick Boyd

COURSE LIST

Undergraduate

Radio-Television Speaking
Broadcast Operations
Broadcast Writing and Advertising
Mass Media

Dakota Wesleyan University

Independent United Methodist 4-year coed college. Institutionally accredited by regional association. Small town location, 40-acre campus. Undergraduate enrollment: 508. Total faculty: 62. 4-1-4 calendar. Grading system: letters or numbers.

Communication/Theatre Department, Mitchell, SD 57301 605-996-6511, ext 275

CONTACT Michael Turchen
DEGREE OFFERED BA in communication/theatre
DEPARTMENTAL MAJORS Television — 2 students
ADMISSION Requirement — ACT or SAT scores
FINANCIAL AID Scholarships, work/study programs, student loans, institutional employment
CURRICULAR EMPHASIS Film study — educational media/instructional technology Television study — production Television production — commercial, experimental/personal video, educational treated equally
SPECIAL ACTIVITIES/OFFERINGS Program material produced for on-campus closed-circuit television and local commercial television station, vocational placement service
FACILITIES AND EQUIPMENT Television — black and white studio cameras, color studio cameras, ½-inch VTR, 1-inch VTR, ¾-inch cassette VTR, portable black and white cameras, monitors, special effects generators, portable color cameras, lighting equipment, sound recording equipment, black and white studio, control room
FACULTY Michael Turchen

COURSE LIST

Undergraduate

Television Production

South Dakota

South Dakota State University

State-supported coed university. Institutionally accredited by regional association, programs recognized by NASM, ACPE. Rural location, 228-acre campus. Total enrollment: 6537. Undergraduate enrollment: 6115. Total faculty: 344 (301 full-time, 43 part-time). Semester calendar. Grading system: letters or numbers.

Speech Department, Pugsley Center, Brookings, SD 57007 605-688-6131

CONTACT Film — C E Denton Television — Judith Zivanovic
DEGREES OFFERED BA, BS in speech with an emphasis in film and/or television
DEPARTMENTAL MAJORS Film — 5 students Television — 15 students
ADMISSION Requirement — 2.0 minimum grade point average Application deadline — 8/25
FINANCIAL AID Work/study programs
CURRICULAR EMPHASIS Undergraduate film study — history, appreciation, educational media/instructional technology treated equally Graduate film study — criticism and aesthetics Undergraduate filmmaking — narrative, experimental, animated treated equally Undergraduate television study — history, production treated equally Undergraduate television production — news/documentary, experimental/personal video treated equally
SPECIAL ACTIVITIES/OFFERINGS Film series; film festivals; program material produced for on-campus closed-circuit television, cable television, local public television station; internships in film production; internships in television production; independent study
FACILITIES AND EQUIPMENT Film — 16mm cameras, editing equipment, sound recording equipment, projectors, screening room, editing room, animation board, permanent film library of student films, permanent film library of commercial or professional films Television — color studio cameras, ¾-inch cassette VTR, monitors, special effects generators, slide chain, portable color cameras, ¾-inch ENG, lighting equipment, sound recording equipment, audio mixers, film chain, color studio, control room
FACULTY C E Denton, Ken Eich, Dan Johnson, Robert Lytle, Judith Zivanovic

COURSE LIST

Undergraduate

Introduction to Radio and TV
Mass Communication Activities
Radio and TV Production
Radio-TV News Reporting
Writing for Radio and TV
Radio-TV Advertising
Television Production
Broadcast Journalism
Broadcast Programming
Introduction to Cinematography
Film Production
Film Narrative
Educational Radio-TV

Graduate

Theories of Communication
Research Methods in Communication

Undergraduate and Graduate

Mass Media in Society
Film Studies
Special Problems in Radio/TV/Film

University of South Dakota

State-supported coed university. Institutionally accredited by regional association, programs recognized by NASM, AACSB. Small town location, 236-acre campus. Total enrollment: 5734. Undergraduate enrollment: 4362. Total faculty: 375 full-time. 4-1-4 calendar. Grading system: letters or numbers.

Mass Communication Department, Vermillion, SD 57069 605-677-5477

CONTACT Film — Sandy Gray Television — Clay Waite
PROGRAM OFFERED Major in mass communication with emphasis in film or television
ADMISSION Application deadline — 8/9, rolling
FINANCIAL AID Scholarships, student loans, work/study programs, teaching assistantships Application deadline — 3/1
CURRICULAR EMPHASIS Film study — (1) production; (2) criticism and aesthetics; (3) history Filmmaking — (1) narrative; (2) documentary; (3) experimental Television study — (1) production; (2) management; (3) history Television production — (1) commercial; (2) news/documentary; (3) experimental/personal video
SPECIAL ACTIVITIES/OFFERINGS Filmmaking clubs; film series; film festivals; student publications; program material produced for on-campus closed-circuit television, cable television, local public television station; internships in film and television production; independent study; practicum; teacher training; vocational placement service
FACILITIES AND EQUIPMENT Film — complete 16mm equipment, screening room, editing room, sound mixing room, animation board, permanent film library Television — complete black and white studio and exterior production equipment, complete color studio and exterior production equipment, black and white studio, color studio, mobile van/unit, remote truck, audio studio, control room
FACULTY James Albert, Rich Frey, Sandy Gray, Clay Waite PART-TIME FACULTY Martin Busch, Ross King

TENNESSEE

Chattanooga State Technical Community College

State-supported 2-year coed college. Part of State University and Community College System of Tennessee. Institutionally accredited by regional association. Suburban location. Undergraduate enrollment: 4233. Total faculty: 163 (82 full-time, 81 part-time). Quarter calendar. Grading system: letters or numbers.

Advertising Arts Department, Chattanooga, TN 37406 615-622-6262
ADMISSION Application deadline — rolling

COURSE LIST
Undergraduate
Television-Radio Production I, II

East Tennessee State University

State-supported coed university. Institutionally accredited by regional association. Urban location, 325-acre campus. Total enrollment: 9947. Undergraduate enrollment: 8487. Total faculty: 527 (470 full-time, 57 part-time). Quarter calendar. Grading system: letters or numbers.

Department of Media Services, Box 24425, University Station, Johnson City, TN 37601

CONTACT Ted C Cobun
DEGREE OFFERED MA in instructional communication
DEPARTMENTAL MAJORS Graduate television — 100 students
FINANCIAL AID Assistantships
CURRICULAR EMPHASIS Film study — educational media/instructional technology Television study — instructional design Television production — instructional design
FACILITIES AND EQUIPMENT Film — 8mm cameras, editing equipment, lighting, projectors, small studio Television — black and white studio cameras, color studio cameras, ½-inch VTR, ¾-inch cassette VTR, portable black and white cameras, portable color cameras, ½-inch portapak recorders, lighting equipment, audio mixers, black and white studio

COURSE LIST
Graduate
Channels
Message Design and Transmission
Message-Media Validation Programming
Graphic Media Design
Production: Limited Concept Motion Media
Organization and Conduction of Message: Media Design and Production Agencies

Art Department 615-929-4247

CONTACT John Schrader
ADMISSION Application deadline — rolling
FACILITIES AND EQUIPMENT Film — complete 16mm equipment
FACULTY Bob Mabry, John Schrader

COURSE LIST
Undergraduate
Introduction to Film
Advanced Documentary
Animation
Sound Production

Undergraduate and Graduate
Film Project

Johnson Bible College

Independent 4-year coed college affiliated with Christian Churches/Churches of Christ. Candidate for institutional accreditation. Rural location, 350-acre campus. Undergraduate enrollment: 396. Total faculty: 29 (12 full-time, 17 part-time). Semester calendar. Grading system: letters or numbers.

Johnson Bible College (continued)

Communications Department, Kimberlin Heights Station, Knoxville, TN 37920 615-573-4517

CONTACT Richard Phillips

Middle Tennessee State University

State-supported coed university. Institutionally accredited by regional association, programs recognized by NASM, AACSB. Small town location, 500-acre campus. Total enrollment: 10,316. Undergraduate enrollment: 8770. Total faculty: 452 (398 full-time, 54 part-time). Semester calendar. Grading system: letters or numbers.

Mass Communications Department, PO Box 51, Murfreesboro, TN 37132 615-898-2814

CONTACT Film — Anne Rist Hahn Television — Van Fox
DEGREE OFFERED BS in mass communications with an emphasis in radio, TV, and film; or broadcast journalism; or recording industry management
DEPARTMENTAL MAJORS Film — 40 students Television — 200 students
ADMISSION Requirements — minimum average grade of C, ACT or SAT scores Application deadline — 8/1
FINANCIAL AID Work/study programs, student loans
CURRICULAR EMPHASIS Film study — (1) history; (2) criticism and aesthetics Filmmaking — (1) narrative; (2) animated; (3) documentary Television study — (1) production; (2) educational; (3) management Television production — (1) commercial; (2) news/documentary; (3) educational
SPECIAL ACTIVITIES/OFFERINGS Film festivals, program material produced for on-campus closed-circuit television and cable television, internships in film production, internships in television production, independent study, vocational placement service
FACILITIES AND EQUIPMENT Film — complete 8mm and 16mm equipment, screening room, editing room, sound mixing room, animation board, permanent film library of commercial or professional films Television — black and white studio cameras, color studio cameras, ½-inch VTR, 1-inch VTR, ¾-inch cassette VTR, portable black and white cameras, editing equipment, monitors, special effects generators, slide chain, portable color cameras, ½-inch portapak recorders, ¾-inch ENG, lighting equipment, sound recording equipment, audio mixers, film chain, time base corrector, black and white studio, color studio, audio studio, control room, recording studio: 16-track recording and mixing
FACULTY Harold Baker, Larry Burriss, Van Fox, Anne Rist Hahn, Chris Haseleu, Alan Mussehl

COURSE LIST

Undergraduate
Cinema Internship
Television Internship
Broadcast Announcing-Performance
Television Station Management
Television News Production — Basic
Television News Production — Advanced
Sound Studio Production
Individual Problems in Television
Individual Problems in Film

Undergraduate and Graduate
Cinema History
Documentary Film History
Basic Film Production
Advanced Film Production
Writing for Television-Film
Basic Television Production
Advanced Television Production

Nashville State Technical Institute

State-supported 2-year coed college. Institutionally accredited by regional association, programs recognized by ECPD. Suburban location, 60-acre campus. Undergraduate enrollment: 3909. Total faculty: 213 (75 full-time, 138 part-time). Quarter calendar. Grading system: letters or numbers.

Department of Photography, 120 White Road, Nashville, TN 37209 615-741-1259

CONTACT John Chastain, Chairman
ADMISSION Application deadline — 9/30
FACULTY Duane Muir

COURSE LIST

Undergraduate
Introduction to Cinematography
CCTV Production

Southern Missionary College

Independent Seventh-day Adventist 4-year coed college. Institutionally accredited by regional association. Small town location. Semester calendar. Grading system: letters or numbers.

Communication Department, Collegedale, TN 37315 615-396-4216

CONTACT Don Dick
ADMISSION Application deadline — rolling
FINANCIAL AID Student loans, work/study programs Application deadline — rolling
CURRICULAR EMPHASIS Film study — (1) production; (2) criticism and aesthetics; (3) appreciation Filmmaking — documentary, narrative, experimental, animated, educational treated equally Television study — (1) production; (2) management; (3) criticism and aesthetics Television production — (1) experimental/personal video; (2) educational; (3) commercial

SPECIAL ACTIVITIES/OFFERINGS Film festivals, program material produced for classroom use, independent study, practicum, vocational placement service
FACILITIES AND EQUIPMENT Film — complete 8mm equipment, 16mm cameras, editing equipment, lighting equipment, sound stage, editing room, sound mixing room, permanent film library Television — black and white studio cameras, ½-inch VTR, monitors, special effects generators, lighting equipment, sound recording equipment, audio mixers, black and white studio, audio studio, control room
FACULTY Don Dick PART-TIME FACULTY Olson Perry, Don Self

COURSE LIST
Undergraduate
Film Production
Television Production
Writing for Radio-Television-Film
Audio Production
Audio-Video Systems
Survey of Mass Communication
Survey of Radio and Television
Directed Studies in Communication
Communication Theory

Southwestern at Memphis

Independent Presbyterian 4-year coed college. Institutionally accredited by regional association, programs recognized by NASM. Urban location. Undergraduate enrollment: 1021. Total faculty: 104 (80 full-time, 24 part-time). 4-1-4 calendar. Grading system: letters or numbers.

Communication Arts Department, 2000 North Parkway, Memphis, TN 38112 901-274-1800

CONTACT Ray Hill
DEGREE OFFERED BA in communication arts
FINANCIAL AID Scholarships, work/study programs, student loans
CURRICULAR EMPHASIS Film study — (1) criticism and aesthetics; (2) appreciation; (3) history Television study — (1) criticism and aesthetics; (2) appreciation; (3) history
SPECIAL ACTIVITIES/OFFERINGS Internships in film production with local filmmaker groups, internships in television production with local TV stations, independent study
FACILITIES AND EQUIPMENT Film — 8mm and 16mm cameras, editing equipment, projectors
FACULTY Ray Hill PART-TIME FACULTY Mason Granger

COURSE LIST
Undergraduate
History of Cinema
Screen and TV Writing
Cinematography
Film Criticism
Aesthetics of Mass Media

Tennessee Temple Schools

Independent 4-year and professional coed institution. Urban location. Total enrollment: 4000. Total faculty: 250. Semester calendar. Grading system: letters.

Broadcasting Department, Chattanooga, TN 37404 615-698-6021

CONTACT Chairman

University of Tennessee at Knoxville

State-supported coed university. Part of University of Tennessee System. Institutionally accredited by regional association, programs recognized by NASM, AACSB. Urban location, 397-acre campus. Total enrollment: 29,720. Undergraduate enrollment: 22,592. Total faculty: 1650 (1279 full-time, 371 part-time). Quarter calendar. Grading system: letters or numbers.

Department of Broadcasting, College of Communications, 295 Communication and University Extension Building, Knoxville, TN 37916 615-974-4291

CONTACT Darrel W Holt, Head
DEGREES OFFERED BS, MS, PhD in communications
DEPARTMENTAL MAJORS Undergraduate — 350 students Graduate — 16 students
ADMISSION Undergraduate requirements — 2.0 minimum grade point average, professional recommendations, teachers' recommendations, written statement of purpose Graduate requirements — 3.0 minimum grade point average, GRE scores, professional recommendations, teachers' recommendations, written statement of purpose Undergraduate application deadline — 8/1
FINANCIAL AID Student loans, work/study programs, teaching assistantships, research assistantships, fellowships Undergraduate application deadline — 3/1
CURRICULAR EMPHASIS Undergraduate television study — (1) news and public affairs; (2) management; (3) production Graduate television study — (1) management; (2) news and public affairs; (3) production Undergraduate television production — (1) news/documentary; (2) commercial Graduate television production — (1) commercial; (2) news/documentary
SPECIAL ACTIVITIES/OFFERINGS Film series, film societies, program material produced for on-campus closed-circuit television, independent study, practicum
FACILITIES AND EQUIPMENT Film — 16mm editing equipment Television — black and white studio cameras, color studio camera, ½-inch VTR, ¾-inch cassette VTR, monitors, special effects generators, slide chain, portable color cameras, ½-inch portapak recorder, ¾-inch ENG, lighting equipment, sound recording equipment, audio mixers, film chain, black and white studio, audio studio, control room
FACULTY John H Carr, Darrel W Holt, Herbert H Howard, M Kent Sidel, Irving G Simpson PART-TIME FACULTY Frank A Lester, Larry Perry, Raymond Shirley

COURSE LIST
Undergraduate
Introduction to Broadcasting
Television and Radio Advertising
Radio-Television News
Radio-Television Writing
Television Film News

University of Tennessee at Knoxville (continued)

Graduate
Educational Broadcasting
Public Affairs Broadcasting
Broadcast Law and Regulations
Broadcast Documentary Writing
Radio-TV Program Development

Undergraduate and Graduate
Speech for Broadcasting
Television Production
Advanced Television Production
Broadcast News Operation
Radio-Television Management
Broadcast Sales Management
Advanced Radio Production
Radio Production

Vanderbilt University

Independent coed university. Institutionally accredited by regional association. Urban location, 260-acre campus. Total enrollment: 7269. Undergraduate enrollment: 6100. Total faculty: 1865 (1215 full-time, 650 part-time). Semester calendar. Grading system: letters or numbers.

Fine Arts Department, Box 1719, Nashville, TN 37235 615-322-6135

CONTACT Robert A Baldwin
CURRICULAR EMPHASIS Undergraduate film study — history, criticism and aesthetics treated equally Undergraduate filmmaking — documentary, experimental treated equally
SPECIAL ACTIVITIES/OFFERINGS Film series
FACILITIES AND EQUIPMENT Film — 8mm cameras, editing equipment, sound recording equipment, color film stock, projectors, 16mm projectors, screening room, 35mm screening facilities, editing room, permanent film library of commercial or professional films

COURSE LIST

Undergraduate
Survey of Film History
Introduction to Film
French Cinema

Volunteer State Community College

State-supported 2-year coed college. Part of State University and Community College System of Tennessee, automatic transfer to main campus for baccalaureate. Institutionally accredited by regional association. Small town location. Undergraduate enrollment: 2682. Total faculty: 139 (78 full-time, 61 part-time). Quarter calendar. Grading system: letters or numbers.

Nashville Pike, Gallatin, TN 37066 615-452-8600

CONTACT Film — Virginia Thigpen Television — Terry Heinen
DEGREES OFFERED AS, AA in communications
FINANCIAL AID Scholarships, work/study programs, student loans
SPECIAL ACTIVITIES/OFFERINGS Film series, program material produced for on-campus videotaping
FACILITIES AND EQUIPMENT Film — 8mm cameras, sound recording equipment, lighting, projectors, 16mm projectors, screening room, sound mixing room, permanent film library of commercial or professional films Television — color studio cameras, ½-inch VTR, ¾-inch cassette VTR, portable black and white cameras, editing equipment, monitors, special effects generators (black and white), slide chain, ½-inch portapak recorders, lighting equipment, sound recording equipment, audio mixers, film chain, black and white studio, color studio
FACULTY Terry Heinen, Dan Jewell, Virginia Thigpen

COURSE LIST

Undergraduate
Survey of Mass Communications
Writing for Broadcast Media
Still Photography I, II
Cinematography
Television Production
Introduction to Film

TEXAS

Abilene Christian University

Independent comprehensive coed institution affiliated with Church of Christ. Institutionally accredited by regional association, programs recognized by NASM. Suburban location, 40-acre campus. Total enrollment: 4231. Undergraduate enrollment: 3686. Total faculty: 175 (160 full-time, 15 part-time). Semester calendar. Grading system: letters or numbers.

Mass Communication Department, PO Box 7569, Abilene, TX 79699 915-677-1911

CONTACT Film — Lewis Fulks Television — H J Warr Jr
DEGREE OFFERED BA in mass communication with emphasis in television
DEPARTMENTAL MAJORS 180 students
ADMISSION Undergraduate requirements — 2.0 minimum grade point average, ACT or SAT scores, teachers' recommendations Graduate requirements — 3.0 minimum grade point average, GRE scores, teachers' recommendations Undergraduate application deadline — 7/1 rolling
FINANCIAL AID Scholarships, student loans, work/study programs, teaching assistantships Undergraduate application deadline — 4/1, rolling
CURRICULAR EMPHASIS Film study — (1) appreciation; (2) history, criticism and aesthetics; (3) educational media/instructional technology Undergraduate television study — (1) appreciation, educational; (2) criticism and aesthetics, production; (3) theory Graduate television study — (1) educational; (2) history; (3) theory Television production — (1) experimental/personal video; (2) news/documentary; (3) educational

SPECIAL ACTIVITIES/OFFERINGS Student publications, program material produced for on-campus closed-circuit television, internships in television production, independent study, practicum, teacher training, vocational placement service
FACILITIES AND EQUIPMENT Television — complete color studio production equipment, color studio, audio studio, control room, ENG color facilities, color editing, color remote production unit
FACULTY B E Davis, Lewis Fulks, Cheryl Mann, Gary Thornton, H J Warr, Sam Wylie

COURSE LIST
Undergraduate
Television Production
Film Appreciation
Broadcasting Fundamentals
Introduction to Mass Media
Religious Radio/Television
Radio/Television Advertising
Aesthetics
News I, II
Advertising Principles
Radio/Television Announcing

Undergraduate and Graduate
History of Radio/Television
Communications Law

Amarillo College

State and locally supported 2-year coed college. Institutionally accredited by regional association. Urban location, 58-acre campus. Undergraduate enrollment: 4752. Total faculty: 302 (185 full-time, 117 part-time). Semester calendar. Grading system: letters or numbers.

Radio-Television Department, PO Box 447, Amarillo, TX 79178 806-376-5111

CONTACT Joyce Herring
DEGREE OFFERED AS in radio-television
DEPARTMENTAL MAJORS 70 students
ADMISSION Requirement — ACT or SAT scores Application deadline — rolling
CURRICULAR EMPHASIS Television study — (1) production; (2) management; (3) criticism and aesthetics Television production — (1) news/documentary; (2) commercial; (3) experimental/personal video
SPECIAL ACTIVITIES/OFFERINGS Program material produced for cable television, independent study, vocational placement service, student operation of 30,000 watt FM station
FACILITIES AND EQUIPMENT Television — complete color studio and exterior production equipment, color studio, remote truck, audio studio, control room
FACULTY Dave Coons, Don Ford, Joyce Herring, Weldon Irion, Chris Johnson, Paul Matney, Allen Shifrin

COURSE LIST
Undergraduate
Radio-Television Production
Mass Media
Station Management
Announcing
Station Operation
Broadcast Survey
Color Engineering
Workshop/Internship
Legal Problems in Broadcasting

Austin College

Independent Presbyterian comprehensive coed institution. Institutionally accredited by regional association. Suburban location, 60-acre campus. Total enrollment: 1110. Undergraduate enrollment: 1069. Total faculty: 107 (101 full-time, 6 part-time). 2-2-1-4 calendar. Grading system: letters or numbers.

Communication Arts Department, 900 North Grand, Sherman, TX 75090 214-892-9101

CONTACT Dan Setterberg
ADMISSION Application deadline — rolling
FACULTY Dan Setterberg

COURSE LIST
Undergraduate
Educational Media
Radio-Television
Practicum

Baylor University

Independent Baptist coed university. Institutionally accredited by regional association. Urban location. Total enrollment: 9386. Undergraduate enrollment: 8320. Total faculty: 467 (415 full-time, 52 part-time). Semester calendar. Grading system: letters or numbers.

Division of Radio-Television, Waco, TX 76706 817-755-1511 or 817-755-1512

CONTACT Greg Porter, Director
DEGREE OFFERED BA in radio-television-film
PROGRAM MAJORS 70 students
ADMISSION Requirements — 2.0 minimum grade point average, ACT or SAT scores Application deadline — rolling
FINANCIAL AID Work/study programs Application deadline — 3/1, rolling
CURRICULAR EMPHASIS Film study — (1) appreciation; (2) production Filmmaking — documentary Television study — production Television production — general
SPECIAL ACTIVITIES/OFFERINGS Film societies, program material produced for on-campus closed-circuit television, internships in film and television production, independent study

Baylor University (continued)

FACILITIES AND EQUIPMENT Film — complete 16mm equipment, screening room, editing room Television — complete color studio and exterior production equipment, color studio, audio studio, control room
FACULTY Maryjo Adams, Greg Porter

COURSE LIST

Undergraduate

Film Appreciation
Principles of Broadcast Announcing
Broadcast Copywriting
Broadcast Scriptwriting
Broadcast News Writing
Audio Production
Television Production
Television Directing I, II
Instructional Television
Internship in Radio/Television/Film
News and Documentary Film
Seminar in Radio/Television/Film

East Texas State University

State-supported coed university. Institutionally accredited by regional association. Small town location, 140-acre campus. Total enrollment: 9282. Undergraduate enrollment: 5636. Total faculty: 456 (371 full-time, 85 part-time). Semester calendar. Grading system: letters or numbers.

Department of Journalism and Graphic Arts, PO Box D, ET Station, Commerce, TX 75428 214-468-2235

CONTACT Film — Jim Newberry Television — Bob Sanders
DEGREES OFFERED BS in photography with major in film production, MS in television production
DEPARTMENTAL MAJORS 10 students
ADMISSION Requirement — minimum grade point average Undergraduate application deadline — 6/29
FINANCIAL AID Scholarships, student loans, teaching assistantships Undergraduate application deadline — 9/11, rolling
CURRICULAR EMPHASIS Film study — (1) production; (2) criticism and aesthetics; (3) educational media/instructional technology Filmmaking — (1) television commercial; (2) documentary; (3) educational Television study — (1) educational; (2) production Television production — (1) commercial; (2) news/documentary
SPECIAL ACTIVITIES/OFFERINGS Film series, film festivals, student publications, program material produced for on-campus closed-circuit television, independent study
FACILITIES AND EQUIPMENT Film — complete 8mm and 16mm equipment, screening room, editing room, sound mixing room, permanent film library Television — complete black and white studio and exterior production equipment, complete color studio and exterior production equipment, black and white studio, color studio, audio studio, control room
FACULTY Nolan Bailey, Nell Blakley, Bill Jack, Ron Johnson, Jim Newberry, Bob Sanders, Richard Schroeder, Earl Williams

COURSE LIST

Undergraduate

Basic Cinema
Advanced Cinema
Cinema: Special Project
History and Aesthetics of Film
Audio Recording
Educational Media Tools
Basic Television
Advanced Television
Writing for Media
Commercial Illustration
Visualization

Lamar University

State-supported coed university. Institutionally accredited by regional association, programs recognized by NASM. Urban location, 200-acre campus. Total enrollment: 12,781. Undergraduate enrollment: 12,213. Total faculty: 659 (482 full-time, 177 part-time). Semester calendar. Grading system: letters or numbers.

Communications Department, PO Box 10050, Lamar University Station, Beaumont, TX 77710 713-838-7122

CONTACT D Holland, Head
PROGRAM OFFERED Major in communications with emphasis in film and television
ADMISSION Application deadline — rolling
CURRICULAR EMPHASIS Film study — (1) production; (2) educational media/instructional technology Filmmaking — news, experimental treated equally Television study — (1) production; (2) educational; (3) management Television production — (1) commercial; (2) news/documentary; (3) educational
SPECIAL ACTIVITIES/OFFERINGS Film series, film festivals, practicum, vocational placement service
FACILITIES AND EQUIPMENT Film — 16mm cameras, editing equipment, sound recording equipment, black and white film stock, projectors, editing room Television — black and white studio cameras, ½-inch VTR, 1-inch VTR, portable black and white cameras, editing equipment, monitors, slide chain, ½-inch portapak recorder, sound recording equipment, audio mixers, film chain, black and white studio
FACULTY Edward R McIntosh

COURSE LIST

Undergraduate

Basic Cinematography
Evolution of Motion Pictures
Film Genres
Mass Media and Society
TV Production

Lee College

District-supported 2-year coed college. Institutionally accredited by regional association. Suburban location. Undergraduate enrollment: 5021. Total faculty: 218 (115 full-time, 103 part-time). Semester calendar. Grading system: letters or numbers.

English Department, PO Box 818, Baytown, TX 77520 713-427-5611

CONTACT Dale T Adams

COURSE LIST

Undergraduate
Film and Literature

North Texas State University

State-supported coed university. Institutionally accredited by regional association, programs recognized by NASM, AACSB. Small town location, 380-acre campus. Total enrollment: 17,300. Undergraduate enrollment: 12,231. Total faculty: 1420 (710 full-time, 710 part-time). Semester calendar. Grading system: letters or numbers.

Radio/Television/Film Division, Denton, TX 76203 817-788-2537

CONTACT Donald E Staples, Director
DEGREES OFFERED BA in speech communication and drama with a concentration in radio/television/film, MA in radio/television/film, MS in radio/television/film, PhD in education with a concentration in radio/television/film
DEPARTMENTAL MAJORS Undergraduate film — 130 students Undergraduate television — 150 students Graduate film — 15 students Graduate television — 15 students
ADMISSION Undergraduate requirement — ACT or SAT scores Graduate requirements — GRE scores, teachers' recommendations
FINANCIAL AID Scholarships, work/study programs, student loans, fellowships, teaching assistantships
CURRICULAR EMPHASIS Undergraduate film study — history, criticism and aesthetics, appreciation treated equally Graduate film study — history, criticism and aesthetics, appreciation treated equally Undergraduate filmmaking — documentary, narrative, experimental treated equally Graduate filmmaking — documentary, narrative, experimental treated equally Undergraduate television study — history, educational, management treated equally Graduate television study — history, educational, management treated equally Undergraduate television production — commercial, news/documentary, educational treated equally Graduate television production — commercial, news/documentary, educational treated equally
SPECIAL ACTIVITIES/OFFERINGS Filmmaking clubs, film series, film societies, program material produced for cable television, internships in film production, internships in television production, independent study, teacher training
FACILITIES AND EQUIPMENT Film — 8mm and 16mm cameras, editing equipment, sound recording equipment, lighting, projectors, 35mm projectors, sound stage, screening room, 35mm screening facilities, editing room, permanent film library of commercial or professional films Television — black and white studio cameras, ½-inch VTR, 1-inch VTR, ¾-inch cassette VTR, portable black and white cameras, editing equipment, monitors, special effects generators, slide chain, portable color cameras, ½-inch portapak recorders, ¾-inch ENG, lighting equipment, sound recording equipment, audio mixers, film chain, time base corrector, black and white studio, remote truck, audio studio, control room
FACULTY Edwin L Glick, A Clay Kistler, Richard L Kunkel, F Leslie Smith, Donald E Staples, Gerry K Veeder PART-TIME FACULTY Mac R Aipperspach, Ruth G Aipperspach, Bud Buschardt, Terry L Holcomb, Tae G Kim, Bill Mercer, Victoria O'Donnell, Douglas P Starr, Reginald C Westmoreland

COURSE LIST

Undergraduate
Perspectives on Radio, Television, and Film
Radio and Television Announcing
Introduction to Film Production
Radio and Television Writing
Audio-Television Production
Television Directing
Broadcast Sports
Intermediate Film Production
Art of the Film
History of Motion Picture
Practicum in Radio/Television/Film
Audio Production
Film Aesthetics
Design and Implementation of Media Programs
Mass Media and Modern Society

Graduate
Seminar in Radio, Television and Film (Topics Vary)
History of Electronic Media
Research Methods in Mass Communication
Theories of Mass Communication
Media in Education
International Mass Communication
Political Broadcasting
Practicum in the Teaching of Radio, Television, and Film
Graduate Production Studio (Audio, Television, or Film)
Message Design and Instructional Development
Advanced Production of Instructional Materials
Seminar in Educational Tele-Communications

Undergraduate and Graduate
Advanced Television Production
Broadcast News
The Non-Theatrical Film
Advanced Film Production
Broadcast Advertising
Film Scriptwriting
Station Administration and Programming
Internship in Radio, Television, and Film
Television for Business, Industry, and Education
Persuasion in Mass Communications
Management of Persuasion in Communication Systems
Cinema and Political Ideology
Film Criticism

Rice University

Independent coed university. Institutionally accredited by regional association. Suburban location, 300-acre campus. Total enrollment: 3830. Undergraduate enrollment: 2830. Total faculty: 476 (394 full-time, 82 part-time). Semester calendar. Grading system: letters or numbers.

Department of Art and Art History, Houston, TX 77001 713-527-8101

CONTACT Chairperson
ADMISSION Application deadline — 2/1
FACILITIES AND EQUIPMENT Film — 35mm screening facilities, permanent film library

St Mary's University of San Antonio

Independent Roman Catholic comprehensive coed institution. Institutionally accredited by regional association. Urban location, 135-acre campus. Total enrollment: 3300. Undergraduate enrollment: 2337. Total faculty: 236 (171 full-time, 65 part-time). Semester calendar. Grading system: letters or numbers.

Cinema Arts Seminars, One Camino Santa Maria, San Antonio, TX 78284 512-436-3209

CONTACT Louis Reile
DEGREE OFFERED Minor in film
ADMISSION Undergraduate requirements — ACT or SAT scores, interviews, teachers' recommendations Graduate requirements — GRE scores, interviews, teachers' recommendations Undergraduate application deadline — 8/1, rolling
CURRICULAR EMPHASIS Film study — (1) criticism and aesthetics; (2) history; (3) appreciation Filmmaking — (1) narrative; (2) documentary; (3) experimental
SPECIAL ACTIVITIES/OFFERINGS Film series, Hemisfilm International Film Festival, independent study, practicum
FACILITIES AND EQUIPMENT Film — complete 8mm, 16mm, and 35mm equipment
FACULTY Louis Reile PART-TIME FACULTY Bob Richmond

COURSE LIST

Undergraduate
Film History
Comedy
International Cinema
American Cinema

Graduate
Documentary
Western Cinema
Gangster Cinema
Genre Cinema

Undergraduate and Graduate
Film-Literature
Provocative Cinema
Western Cinema

San Antonio Community College

State and locally supported 2-year coed college. Institutionally accredited by regional association. Urban location. Undergraduate enrollment: 21,000. Total faculty: 1043 (498 full-time, 545 part-time). Semester calendar. Grading system: letters or numbers.

Radio-Television-Film Department, 1300 San Pedro Avenue, San Antonio, TX 78284 512-734-7311, ext 2793

CONTACT Jean M Longwith, Chairman
DEGREES OFFERED AA with major in radio-television-film
DEPARTMENTAL MAJORS Film — 50 students Television — 150 students
ADMISSION Requirements — ACT or SAT scores, interview Application deadline — 8/20
FINANCIAL AID Scholarships, work/study programs, student loans
CURRICULAR EMPHASIS Film study — (1) educational media/instructional technology; (2) appreciation; (3) criticism and aesthetics Filmmaking — (1) documentary; (2) narrative; (3) experimental Television study — (1) production; (2) management; (3) educational Television production — (1) news/documentary; (2) commercial; (3) experimental/personal video
SPECIAL ACTIVITIES/OFFERINGS Film festivals, program material produced for on-campus closed-circuit television and cable television, apprenticeships, internships in television production, vocational placement service
FACILITIES AND EQUIPMENT Film — 8mm and 16mm cameras, editing equipment, sound recording equipment, lighting, color film stock, projectors, sound stage, editing room, sound mixing room Television — color studio cameras, ½-inch VTR, 1-inch VTR, ¾-inch cassette VTR, editing equipment, monitors, special effects generators, slide chain, portable color cameras, ½-inch portapak recorders, ¾-inch ENG, lighting equipment, sound recording equipment, audio mixers, film chain, time base corrector, color studio, audio studio, control room
FACULTY Jean M Longwith, Peggy Mangold, Terry Tackitt, Charles E Wright PART-TIME FACULTY Don Couser, Gary de Laune

COURSE LIST

Undergraduate
Introduction to Radio-TV-Film
Station Operation and Management
Writing for Radio-TV and Film
Principles of Production: Audio
Principles of Production: Video/Film
Film Production
News Writing and Production for Radio and TV
Programming
Broadcast Management and Sales
Announcing
Practicum and Internship

Southern Methodist University

Independent coed university. Institutionally accredited by regional association. Urban location. Total enrollment: 8677. Undergraduate enrollment: 5481. Total faculty: 500 full-time. Semester calendar. Grading system: letters or numbers.

Broadcast/Film Arts Department, Binkley and Bishop Streets, Dallas, TX 75275 214-692-3090

CONTACT James B McGrath Jr, Chairman
DEGREES OFFERED BFA in broadcast/film, BFA in broadcast/journalism, MFA in mass communications with an emphasis in television production
DEPARTMENTAL MAJORS Undergraduate film — 70 students Undergraduate television — 90 students Graduate television — 15 students

ADMISSION Undergraduate requirements — 2.5 minimum grade point average, ACT or SAT scores, written statement of purpose Graduate requirements — 3.0 minimum grade point average, GRE scores, teachers' recommendations, written statement of purpose, professional work experience, professional recommendations Undergraduate application deadline — 4/1
FINANCIAL AID Scholarships, work/study programs, student loans, fellowships (grad only)
CURRICULAR EMPHASIS Undergraduate film study — (1) criticism and aesthetics; (2) history; (3) educational media/instructional technology Undergraduate filmmaking — (1) narrative; (2) documentary; (3) animated Undergraduate television study — (1) production; (2) management; (3) criticism and aesthetics Graduate television study — (1) management; (2) production; (3) criticism and aesthetics Undergraduate television production — (1) experimental/personal video; (2) news/documentary; (3) commercial
SPECIAL ACTIVITIES/OFFERINGS Film series, film festivals, film societies, newsletters, program material produced for cable television and local commercial television station, internships in film production, internships in television production, independent study
FACILITIES AND EQUIPMENT Film — complete 16mm equipment, sound stage, editing room, sound mixing room, permanent film library of student films, multi media production facility, permanent film library of old films Television — color studio cameras, ¾-inch cassette VTR, editing equipment, monitors, special effects generators, slide chain, portable color cameras, ¾-inch ENG, lighting equipment, sound recording equipment, audio mixers, film chain, time base corrector, color studio, control room
FACULTY Terry Book, Ken Burke, Ted Gardner, G William Jones, James B McGrath, Donald Pasquella, G Eric Peterson

COURSE LIST

Undergraduate
Introduction to Mass Media

Graduate
Introduction to Graduate Study
Seminar in Contemporary Media
Communication, Processes and Effects

Undergraduate and Graduate
Radio/TV/Film
History of Recorded Music
Basic Audio Techniques
Visual Communications
Photography I—IV
Film Production I—IV
TV Production
Radio/TV Announcing
Film Workshop
Basic Multimedia
Basic Business of Broadcasting
Imagination, Awareness, Ideas
The Film Image
Documentary Film
Motion Picture Exhibition and Distribution
Radio News
Station Administration
The Short Film
Advanced TV Production and Directing
Development of the Art of the Film
Basic and Advanced Screenwriting
TV Documentary
Writing TV Drama
Industrial TV
World War II on Film
The Italian Film
Producer's Seminar
History of the Animated Film
Television Criticism
Film Criticism
American Popular Film
Classics of the Cinema
Advanced Audio
Multimedia Production
Bob Banner Seminar
Practica in USA Film Festival, Radio Station, Campus Radio Station (KSMU), TV Station, Media Center, Cinematheque (film series), and Southwest Film Archives

Southwestern College

District-supported 2-year coed college. Institutionally accredited by regional association. Suburban location. Total enrollment: 12,000. Total faculty: 200. Semester calendar. Grading system: letters or numbers.

Fine Arts Division, 900 Otay Lakes Road, Chula Vista, TX 92010 714-421-6700

CONTACT Robert Schneider
ADMISSION Application deadline — 8/16
CURRICULAR EMPHASIS Film study — history, production treated equally Filmmaking — (1) documentary, narrative; (2) experimental Television study — (1) appreciation; (2) production; (3) criticism and aesthetics Television production — experimental/personal video
SPECIAL ACTIVITIES/OFFERINGS Program material produced for on-campus closed-circuit television, independent study
FACILITIES AND EQUIPMENT Film — 8mm cameras, editing equipment, sound recording equipment, projectors, 16mm cameras, screening room, editing room Television — ½-inch VTR, portable black and white cameras, editing equipment, monitors, ½-inch portapak recorder, sound recording equipment, audio mixers
FACULTY Robert Schneider, Mike Schnorr

COURSE LIST

Undergraduate
Filmmaking I, II
History of Film as Art

Southwest Texas State University

State-supported comprehensive coed institution. Institutionally accredited by regional association, programs recognized by NASM. Small town location. Total enrollment: 15,071. Undergraduate enrollment: 13,510. Total faculty: 665 (471 full-time, 194 part-time). Semester calendar. Grading system: letters or numbers.

Department of Journalism, 226 Old Main, San Marcos, TX 78666 512-245-2656

CONTACT Roger Bennett, Chairman
DEGREES OFFERED BA in journalism (broadcasting), BS in education with minor in broadcasting
DEPARTMENTAL MAJORS Television — 70 students

Southwest Texas State University (continued)

ADMISSION Requirement — ACT or SAT scores
FINANCIAL AID Scholarships, work/study programs, student loans Application deadline — 1/1
CURRICULAR EMPHASIS Television study — (1) criticism and aesthetics; (2) production; (3) management; (4) performance Television production — (1) commercial; (2) news/documentary
SPECIAL ACTIVITIES/OFFERINGS Program material produced for cable television, internships in television production, teacher training, vocational placement service
FACILITIES AND EQUIPMENT Television — complete black and white studio production equipment, black and white studio, audio studio, control room
FACULTY Robert Shrader PART-TIME FACULTY William Anderson

COURSE LIST

Undergraduate

Introduction to Broadcast Journalism
Radio Broadcasting and Newswriting
Television Broadcasting and Newswriting
Radio and Television Commercial Writing
Public Affairs Reporting (broadcast emphasis)
Practicum I, II

Department of English, San Marcos, TX 78666 512-245-2164

CONTACT Jack Gravitt
FACULTY Jack Gravitt

COURSE LIST

Undergraduate

Comparative Studies in Film and Prose Fiction

Stephen F Austin State University

State-supported coed university. Institutionally accredited by regional association, programs recognized by NASM, AACSB. Small town location. Total enrollment: 10,400. Undergraduate enrollment: 9200. Total faculty: 450 (450 full-time, 0 part-time). Semester calendar. Grading system: letters or numbers.

Communication Department, PO Box 13048, SFA Station, Nacogdoches, TX 75962 713-569-4001

CONTACT R T Ramsey
DEGREES OFFERED BA, BS in cinematography; BA, BS in broadcasting; MA in communication with emphasis in cinema or television
DEPARTMENTAL MAJORS Undergraduate film — 40 students Undergraduate television — 80 students Graduate film — 3 students Graduate television — 1 student
ADMISSION Undergraduate requirements — 2.0 minimum grade point average, ACT scores, teachers' recommendations Graduate requirements — 2.8 minimum grade point average, GRE scores, teachers' recommendations, written statement of purpose
FINANCIAL AID Student loans, work/study programs, teaching assistantships, student assistantships, research assistantships Undergraduate application deadline — 7/15
CURRICULAR EMPHASIS Film study — (1) production; (2) educational media/instructional technology; (3) history Filmmaking — (1) film for television; (2) documentary; (3) educational Television study — (1) production; (2) criticism and aesthetics; (3) educational Television production — (1) news/documentary; (2) commercial; (3) educational
SPECIAL ACTIVITIES/OFFERINGS Film series, program material produced for cable television and local commercial television station, internships in film and television production, independent study, practicum, teacher training
FACILITIES AND EQUIPMENT Film — complete 8mm and 16mm equipment, sound stage, screening room, editing room, sound mixing room, film-videotape conversion equipment Television — complete black and white studio and exterior production equipment, complete color studio and exterior production equipment, black and white studio, color studio, audio studio, control room
FACULTY Bill Arscott, John Frank, Ken Waters

COURSE LIST

Undergraduate

Introduction to Radio-Television
Communication Practicum
Basic Motion Picture Production
Television Production
Television News
Advertising Techniques
Motion Picture Editing
Television Programming
Television Performance
Communication Internship

Graduate

Advanced Studies in Communication
Thesis Research and Writing
Seminar in Persuasion
Media Management
Mass Media in Society
Politics and American Media
Topics in Mass Communication

Undergraduate and Graduate

History of Film
Writing for Television
Documentary Filmmakers
Advanced Television Production
Special Problems for Communication

Sul Ross State University

State-supported comprehensive coed institution. Institutionally accredited by regional association. Small town location, 640-acre campus. Total enrollment: 2345. Undergraduate enrollment: 1666. Total faculty: 128 (99 full-time, 29 part-time). Semester calendar. Grading system: letters or numbers.

Communications and Theatre Department, Alpine, TX 79830 915-837-8221

CONTACT George Bradley
DEGREES OFFERED BA, MEd in communication with an emphasis in TV
DEPARTMENTAL MAJORS Undergraduate television — 15 students Graduate television — 3 students
ADMISSION Undergraduate requirement — 2.0 minimum grade point average Graduate requirements — 2.0 minimum grade point average, GRE scores
FINANCIAL AID Scholarships, work/study programs, student loans
CURRICULAR EMPHASIS Undergraduate television study — (1) production; (2) educational; (3) appreciation Graduate television study — (1) production; (2) educational; (3) appreciation Undergraduate television production — (1) experimental/personal video; (2) educational; (3) news/documentary Graduate television production — (1) experimental/personal video; (2) educational; (3) news/documentary
SPECIAL ACTIVITIES/OFFERINGS Program material produced for on-campus closed-circuit television and cable television, independent study, teacher training, vocational placement service
FACILITIES AND EQUIPMENT Television — black and white studio cameras, color studio cameras, ½-inch VTR, ¾-inch cassette VTR, portable black and white cameras, editing equipment, monitors, portable color cameras, ½-inch portapak recorders, lighting equipment, sound recording equipment, audio mixers, black and white studio, color studio, control room
FACULTY George L Bradley, June Compton

COURSE LIST
Undergraduate and Graduate
Video Techniques I, II
Camera Operations
Studio Production
TV in Society
Speech and the Mass Media of Communication
TV Lighting and Sound
TV Editing Techniques

Tarrant County Junior College

County-supported 2-year coed college. Institutionally accredited by regional association. Urban location. Undergraduate enrollment: 19,084. Total faculty: 822 (393 full-time, 429 part-time). Semester calendar. Grading system: letters or numbers.

Instructional Media Technology Department, 828 Harwood Road, Hurst, TX 76053 817-281-7860

CONTACT Lawrence Baker
DEGREE OFFERED AS in instructional media with emphasis in film and television
ADMISSION Application deadline — 8/15
FINANCIAL AID Student loans, work/study programs Application deadline — 7/15
CURRICULAR EMPHASIS Film study — (1) educational media/instructional technology; (2) production; (3) appreciation Filmmaking — (1) educational; (2) documentary; (3) animated Television study — (1) production; (2) educational; (3) management Television production — (1) educational; (2) experimental/personal video; (3) commercial
SPECIAL ACTIVITIES/OFFERINGS Film festivals, student publication, internships, practicum, vocational placement service
FACILITIES AND EQUIPMENT Film — complete 8mm equipment, editing room, sound mixing room, animation board Television — complete black and white studio production equipment, complete color studio production equipment, portable black and white cameras, ½-inch portapak recorder, black and white studio, color studio, audio studio
FACULTY Lawrence Baker PART-TIME FACULTY Robert Frost

COURSE LIST
Undergraduate
Audio-Video Techniques
Super-8 Film Production
Advanced Production
Media Seminar

Texas A&I University at Kingsville

State-supported coed university. Part of University System of South Texas. Institutionally accredited by regional association, programs recognized by NASM. Small town location, 255-acre campus. Total enrollment: 6225. Undergraduate enrollment: 5151. Total faculty: 293 (245 full-time, 48 part-time). Semester calendar. Grading system: letters or numbers.

Speech Communication, Theater Arts and Journalism Department, Campus Box 178, Kingsville, TX 78363 512-595-3401

CONTACT Ruth A Rascoe
DEGREE OFFERED BA in speech with emphasis in radio/television
DEPARTMENTAL MAJORS Undergraduate television — 15 students
ADMISSION Undergraduate requirement — ACT or SAT scores
FINANCIAL AID Scholarships, work/study programs, student loans
CURRICULAR EMPHASIS Television study — (1) production; (2) educational; (3) history Television production — (1) experimental/personal video; (2) commercial, news/documentary, educational treated equally
SPECIAL ACTIVITIES/OFFERINGS Film series, film festivals, student publications, program material produced for special projects, independent study
FACILITIES AND EQUIPMENT Film — 16mm projectors, 35mm cameras, lighting, black and white film stock, projectors, darkroom facilities, screening room, film library affiliation Television — black and white studio cameras, color studio cameras, 1-inch VTR, ¾-inch cassette VTR, portable black and white cameras, monitors, special effects generators, slide chain, ¾-inch ENG, lighting equipment, sound recording equipment, audio mixers, film chain, black and white studio, color studio, audio studio, control room
FACULTY Ruth A Rascoe

Texas A&I University at Kingsville (continued)

COURSE LIST

Undergraduate

Survey of Broadcasting
Radio and Television Announcing
Radio and Television Production
Radio/Television Control Room Operations
Radio and Television Script Writing
Intermediate Television Production and Direction
Broadcasting and the Public
Independent Study in Speech (Radio/Television)

Texas Southmost College

District-supported 2-year coed college. Institutionally accredited by regional association. Urban location. Semester calendar. Grading system: letters or numbers.

English Department, 80 Fort Brown, Brownsville, TX 78520 512-541-1241

CONTACT O Henry Sears
ADMISSION Application deadline — 8/31
FINANCIAL AID Scholarships, student loans, work/study programs, Basic Educational Opportunity Grants Application deadline — 3/1
CURRICULAR EMPHASIS Television study — production Television production — (1) news/documentary; (2) experimental/personal video
FACILITIES AND EQUIPMENT Television — black and white studio cameras, ½-inch VTR, ¾-inch cassette VTR, portable black and white cameras, editing equipment, monitors, special effects generators, slide chain, lighting equipment, sound recording equipment, audio mixers, film chain, audio studio, control room, theatervision
PART-TIME FACULTY Joe Colunga

COURSE LIST

Undergraduate

Television Journalism

Texas Tech University

State-supported coed university. Institutionally accredited by regional association. Urban location, 1839-acre campus. Total enrollment: 21,637. Undergraduate enrollment: 19,444. Total faculty: 864. Semester calendar. Grading system: letters or numbers.

Department of Mass Communications, Box 4710, Lubbock, TX 79409 806-742-3385

CONTACT Film — Ashton Thornhill Television — Dennis A Harp
DEGREES OFFERED BA in telecommunications, MA in mass communications
DEPARTMENTAL MAJORS Undergraduate television — 294 students Graduate television — 8 students
ADMISSION Undergraduate requirements — 2.0 minimum grade point average, ACT or SAT scores, type 30 wpm, pass English grammar exam Graduate requirement — GRE scores Undergraduate application deadline — 8/15
FINANCIAL AID Scholarships, work/study programs, student loans, teaching assistantships Undergraduate application deadline — 3/1
CURRICULAR EMPHASIS Undergraduate film study — (1) criticism and aesthetics; (2) appreciation; (3) educational media/instructional technology Undergraduate filmmaking — (1) experimental; (2) documentary; (3) educational Undergraduate television study — (1) production; (2) educational; (3) management Graduate television study — (1) educational; (2) history; (3) production Undergraduate television production — (1) commercial; (2) educational; (3) news/documentary Graduate television production — educational
SPECIAL ACTIVITIES/OFFERINGS Student publications; program material produced for cable television, local public television station, local commercial television station; apprenticeships; internships in film production; internships in television production; independent study
FACILITIES AND EQUIPMENT Film — complete 8mm and 16mm equipment, sound stage, screening room, editing room, sound mixing room, animation board Television — complete color studio and color exterior production equipment, color studios, audio studios, control rooms, video editing rooms
FACULTY Dennis Harp, Jerry Hudson, Mark Norman, Ashton Thornhill, Hershel Womack

COURSE LIST

Undergraduate

Telecommunications Laboratory
Introduction to Telecommunications
Telecommunications Activities
Radio Production
Television Production
Radio and Television Writing
Internship in Telecommunications
Broadcast Performing and Interviewing
Radio and Television Programming
Senior Projects in Telecommunications
Problems in Broadcast Operations
Advanced Television Production and Directing
Telecommunications Practicum
Noncommercial Telecommunications
Broadcast Features and Documentaries

Graduate

Studies and Problems in Telecommunications
Educational Television
Contemporary Issues in Telecommunications
Telecommunications Problems, Advanced

University of Houston

State-supported coed university. Part of University of Houston System. Institutionally accredited by regional association. Urban location. Total enrollment: 29,666. Undergraduate enrollment: 19,691. Total faculty: 1863 (1027 full-time, 836 part-time). Semester calendar. Grading system: letters or numbers.

School of Communication, Radio-TV Faculty, Houston, TX 77004 713-749-1745

CONTACT William Hawes
DEGREE OFFERED BA in communications with emphasis in television-film
DEPARTMENTAL MAJORS 400 students
ADMISSION Application deadline — 7/21
CURRICULAR EMPHASIS Television study — (1) production; (2) management; (3) journalism; (4) nonbroadcast media
SPECIAL ACTIVITIES/OFFERINGS Program material produced for local commercial television station; internships in film and television production; independent study; vocational placement service; editorial office, *Journal of the University Film Association*; on-campus television station
FACILITIES AND EQUIPMENT Film — 16mm cameras, editing equipment, lighting equipment, projectors, sound stage, editing room, sound mixing room Television — complete color studio and exterior production facilities
FACULTY Raymond Fielding, William Hawes, Timothy Lyons, Garth Jowett, Craig Ness, Basil Wright

COURSE LIST

Undergraduate
Cinematography I, II
History of Cinema
Seminar/Special Problems
TV Studio Operations
Radio-TV Film Writing
Dramatic Writing
TV Staging and Lighting
TV Directing
TV Producing and Directing
Performance
Broadcast News
Mass Media Production
Media Management
Media Programming
Laws and Ethics
Film Appreciation
Introduction to Film Aesthetics and Criticism
Social Aspects of Film
Economic Aspects of Film

University of Houston at Clear Lake City

State-supported upper-level coed institution. Part of the University of Houston System. Institutionally accredited by regional association. Suburban location. Total enrollment: 5519. Undergraduate enrollment: 2001. Total faculty: 226 (129 full-time, 97 part-time). Semester calendar. Grading system: letters or numbers.

Programs in Humanities, 2700 Bay Area Boulevard, Houston, TX 77058 713-488-9255

CONTACT Peter A Fischer
DEGREES OFFERED BA in visual arts or humanities with an emphasis in film, MA in humanities with an emphasis in film
ADMISSION Undergraduate requirements — interview, 54 semester hours of C or better Graduate requirements — GRE scores, interview Undergraduate application deadline — rolling
FINANCIAL AID Scholarships, work/study programs, student loans, fellowships
CURRICULAR EMPHASIS Undergraduate film study — (1) history; (2) criticism and aesthetics; (3) appreciation Undergraduate filmmaking — (1) documentary; (2) narrative; (3) experimental Graduate filmmaking — (1) documentary; (2) narrative; (3) experimental Undergraduate television study — (1) history; (2) criticism and aesthetics; (3) appreciation
SPECIAL ACTIVITIES/OFFERINGS Film series, film societies, student publications, internships in film production, independent study, teacher training
FACILITIES AND EQUIPMENT Film — 8mm cameras, editing equipment, sound recording equipment, projectors, 16mm editing equipment, projectors, screening room, editing room, screening facilities with 500, 100, and 50 seating capacities Television — black and white studio cameras, color studio cameras, ¾-inch cassette VTR, portable black and white cameras, editing equipment, monitors, portable color cameras, lighting equipment, sound recording equipment, black and white studio, color studio
FACULTY Jib Fowles, Edward Hugetz, George Lipsitz, John R Snyder PART-TIME FACULTY Eric Gerber

COURSE LIST

Undergraduate
Seminar in Art of Film
Literature and Film
History of Silent Film
History of Sound Film
Reel America 1900-1945
Reel America 1945-Now
Television Culture
Mass Media and Society
Critical Review

Undergraduate and Graduate
Film and Videotape Making I, II
Advanced Film and Videotape Making
Seminar in Film and Filmmakers

University of Texas at Arlington

State-supported coed university. Part of University of Texas System. Institutionally accredited by regional association, programs recognized by AACSB. Suburban location, 300-acre campus. Total enrollment: 18,261. Undergraduate enrollment: 15,497. Total faculty: 790 (556 full-time, 234 part-time). Semester calendar. Grading system: letters or numbers.

Department of Art, Arlington, TX 76019 817-273-2891

CONTACT Andy Anderson
DEGREE OFFERED BFA in art with a concentration in film or film history
DEPARTMENTAL MAJORS Film — 40 students
ADMISSION Requirement — 2.0 minimum grade point average
FINANCIAL AID Work/study programs, student loans
CURRICULAR EMPHASIS Film study — (1) history; (2) criticism and aesthetics; (3) appreciation Filmmaking — (1) narrative, experimental, animated; (2) manual; (3) documentary, educational
SPECIAL ACTIVITIES/OFFERINGS Filmmaking clubs, film series, film festivals, film societies, internships in film production, independent study
FACILITIES AND EQUIPMENT Film — 8mm and 16mm cameras, editing equipment, sound recording equipment, lighting, projectors, 8mm sound mixing equipment, 16mm double system projection equipment, sound stage, screening room, editing room, sound mixing room, animation board, permanent film library of student films, library of historically significant films

University of Texas at Arlington (continued)

FACULTY Andy Anderson, Tom Porter, Ned Rifkin PART-TIME FACULTY Jimmy Huston

COURSE LIST

Undergraduate

Film Production I
Film Production IV
Independent Studies in Film Production
Special Studies in Film
Film as Art, History
Special Studies in Film History
Independent Studies in Film History

University of Texas at Austin

State-supported coed university. Part of University of Texas System. Institutionally accredited by regional association, programs recognized by NASM, AACSB, NASA, AOA, ACPE. Suburban location, 300-acre campus. Total enrollment: 43,095. Undergraduate enrollment: 33,699. Total faculty: 1900 full-time. Semester calendar. Grading system: letters or numbers.

Department of Spanish and Portuguese, 112 Batts Hall, Austin, TX 78712

CONTACT Merlin H Forster, Chairman
CURRICULAR EMPHASIS Film study — criticism and aesthetics, appreciation treated equally
SPECIAL ACTIVITIES/OFFERINGS Film series, film festivals, film societies
FACILITIES AND EQUIPMENT Film — screening room, 35mm screening facilities, 16mm projectors, closed-circuit television
FACULTY Virginia Higginbotham, K David Jackson

COURSE LIST

Undergraduate

Latin American Literature into Film
Hispanic Film

Department of Radio-Television-Film, School of Communication, CMA 6.118, Austin, TX 78712 512-471-4071

CONTACT Robert E Davis
DEGREES OFFERED BS in radio-television-film; MA, PhD in communication
ADMISSION Undergraduate requirements — 2.0 minimum grade point average, ACT or SAT scores, interviews, professional recommendations, teachers' recommendations, written statement of purpose, portfolio Graduate requirements — 3.0 minimum grade point average, GRE scores, interviews, professional recommendations, teachers' recommendations, written statement of purpose, portfolio
FINANCIAL AID Scholarships, work/study programs, academic assistantships, teaching assistantships, fellowships
CURRICULAR EMPHASIS Undergraduate film study — (1) production; (2) history; (3) criticism and aesthetics Graduate film study — history, criticism and aesthetics, production, theory and research treated equally Filmmaking — (1) narrative; (2) documentary; (3) educational Undergraduate television study — (1) production; (2) criticism and aesthetics; (3) management Graduate television study — (1) production; (2) criticism and aesthetics; (3) research Undergraduate television production — (1) dramatic narrative; (2) commercial; (3) educational Graduate television production — (1) dramatic narrative; (2) news/documentary; (3) commercial
SPECIAL ACTIVITIES/OFFERINGS Film series, student publications, internships in film and television production, independent study, practicum, vocational placement service, Humanities Research Center
FACILITIES AND EQUIPMENT Film — complete 16mm equipment, sound transfer equipment, sound stage, screening room, editing room, sound mixing room, animation board, permanent film library Television — complete black and white studio and exterior production equipment, complete color studio and exterior production equipment, black and white studio, color studio, mobile van/unit, audio studio, control room

Western Texas College

State and locally supported 2-year coed college. Institutionally accredited by regional association. Small town location. Undergraduate enrollment: 1190. Total faculty: 75 (50 full-time, 25 part-time). Semester calendar. Grading system: letters or numbers.

English Department, Division of Communications and Letters, Snyder, TX 79549 915-573-8413

CONTACT Janet Halbert or Richard Lancaster
ADMISSION Requirements — interviews, teachers' recommendations Application deadline — rolling
CURRICULAR EMPHASIS Film study — (1) criticism and aesthetics; (2) appreciation; (3) history; (4) production Filmmaking — (1) narrative; (2) experimental; (3) documentary, educational
SPECIAL ACTIVITIES/OFFERINGS Film series
FACILITIES AND EQUIPMENT Film — 8mm cameras, editing equipment, projectors, screening room, sound mixing room, permanent film library
FACULTY Janet Halbert, Richard Lancaster

COURSE LIST

Undergraduate

Masterpieces of Literature: The Western Film

West Texas State University

State-supported comprehensive coed institution. Institutionally accredited by regional association, programs recognized by NASM. Small town location, 120-acre campus. Total enrollment: 6600. Undergraduate enrollment: 5374. Total faculty: 363 (229 full-time, 134 part-time). Semester calendar. Grading system: letters or numbers.

Speech Communication and Theatre Department, WT Box 275, Canyon, TX 79016
806-656-3248

CONTACT Jim Pratt
DEGREES OFFERED BA, BS in speech with emphasis in mass communication
DEPARTMENTAL MAJORS 55 students
ADMISSION Requirements — 2.0 minimum grade point average, ACT or SAT scores
FINANCIAL AID Scholarships, work/study programs, student loans Application deadline — 4/1
CURRICULAR EMPHASIS Television study — (1) production; (2) criticism and aesthetics; (3) management Television production — (1) news/documentary; (2) commercial; (3) educational
SPECIAL ACTIVITIES/OFFERINGS Program material produced for cable television
FACILITIES AND EQUIPMENT Television — complete color studio production equipment, color studio, audio studio, control room
FACULTY Jim Pratt PART-TIME FACULTY RuNell Coons, Allen Shifrin

COURSE LIST

Undergraduate
Introduction to Mass Communication
Radio-TV Survey
Radio-TV Announcing
Radio-TV Production
Broadcast Management
Broadcast Reporting
Radio-TV Continuity Writing
Educational TV
Radio-TV Practicum

Undergraduate and Graduate
Interviewing

UTAH

Brigham Young University

Independent coed university affiliated with Latter-Day Saints. Institutionally accredited by regional association. Small town location, 536-acre campus. Total enrollment: 26,417. Undergraduate enrollment: 24,052. Total faculty: 1315 (1075 full-time, 240 part-time). 4-4-2-2 calendar. Grading system: letters or numbers.

Theatre and Cinematic Arts Department, D-581 HFAC, Provo, UT 84602 801-378-4574

CONTACT Tad Danielewski
DEGREES OFFERED BA with major in film and television; MA with concentration in screenwriting, acting, and directing; PhD in film history, theory, and criticism
DEPARTMENTAL MAJORS Undergraduate film — 40 students Undergraduate television — 10 students Graduate film — 10 students Graduate television — 5 students
ADMISSION Undergraduate requirements — 2.5 minimum grade point average, interviews, portfolio, written statement of purpose, auditions Graduate requirements — 3.0 minimum grade point average, interviews, portfolio, written state of purpose, auditions Undergraduate application deadline — 4/30
FINANCIAL AID Scholarships, student loans, teaching assistantships, research assistantships Undergraduate application deadline — 4/30
CURRICULAR EMPHASIS Film study — (1) criticism and aesthetics, appreciation; (2) production; (3) history Filmmaking — (1) narrative; (2) experimental; (3) documentary; (4) educational Television study — (1) production; (2) educational; (3) management Television production — (1) commercial; (2) educational; (3) experimental/personal video; (4) news/documentary
SPECIAL ACTIVITIES/OFFERINGS Film series, film festivals, film societies, program material produced for on-campus national PBS network, apprenticeships, internships in film and television production, independent study
FACILITIES AND EQUIPMENT Film — complete 8mm, 16mm, and 35mm equipment, sound stage, screening room, 35mm screening facilities, editing room, sound mixing room, Brigham Young University Motion Picture Studio Television — complete black and white studio and exterior production equipment, complete color studio and exterior production equipment, black and white studio, color studio, remote truck, audio studio, control room
FACULTY Tad Danielewski, Eric Fielding, Charles Metten

COURSE LIST

Undergraduate
Introduction to Motion Picture Art
Motion Pictures as a Mirror of Our Times

Graduate
Genres and/or Directors of Motion Picture Art
The American Motion Picture

Undergraduate and Graduate
Theory and Criticism of Film Art
Actors Professional Workshop in Motion Picture/Television
Directors Professional Workshop in Motion Picture/Television
Writers Professional Workshop in Motion Picture/Television
Advanced Theatre and Studio Sound
Motion Picture and Television Art Direction

Communications Department, E-509 HFAC, Provo, UT 84602 801-378-2077

CONTACT Film — Wallace M Barrus Television — Norman Tarbox
DEGREES OFFERED BA, BS, MA, MS in film or television
DEPARTMENTAL MAJORS Graduate film — 50 students Graduate television — 150 students

Brigham Young University (continued)

ADMISSION Undergraduate requirements — 2.5 minimum grade point average, ACT or SAT scores, interviews, portfolio, professional work experience, production credits, professional recommendations, teachers' recommendations Graduate requirements — 3.0 minimum grade point average, GRE scores, interviews, portfolio, professional work experience, production credits, professional recommendations, teachers' recommendations Undergraduate application deadline — 4/30
FINANCIAL AID Scholarships, student loans, teaching assistantships, research assistantships, fellowships Undergraduate application deadline — 4/30
CURRICULAR EMPHASIS Undergraduate film study — (1) production; (2) criticism and aesthetics; (3) appreciation; (4) history; (5) educational media/instructional technology Graduate film study — (1) criticism and aesthetics; (2) production; (3) appreciation; (4) history; (5) educational media/instructional technology Filmmaking — (1) narrative; (2) documentary; (3) experimental; (4) animated; (5) educational Television study — (1) management; (2) educational; (3) production; (4) appreciation; (5) criticism and aesthetics; (6) history Television production — (1) educational; (2) commercial; (3) news/documentary; (4) experimental/personal video
SPECIAL ACTIVITIES/OFFERINGS Film series; film festivals; film societies; student publications; program material produced for on-campus closed-circuit television, cable television, local public television station, local commercial television station; apprenticeships; internships in film and television production; independent study; practicum
FACILITIES AND EQUIPMENT Film — complete 8mm, 16mm, and 35mm equipment, sound stage, screening room, 35mm screening facilities, editing room, sound mixing room, animation board, permanent film library Television — complete black and white studio and exterior production equipment, complete color studio and exterior production equipment, black and white studio, color studio, mobile van/unit, remote truck, audio studio, control room
FACULTY Wallace M Barrus, Irwin Goodman, Gordon Mills, Owen Rich, Norman Tarbox PART-TIME FACULTY Richard Bickerton, Douglas Johnson, Reed Smooth, Robert Stum

COURSE LIST

Graduate
Introduction to the Motion Picture
Motion Picture Production

Undergraduate and Graduate
Cinematography
Film Editing
Production Management
Film Criticism
Sound Recording
Directing
Scriptwriting
Acting

Southern Utah State College

State-supported 4-year coed college. Part of Utah System of Higher Education. Institutionally accredited by regional association. Small town location. Undergraduate enrollment: 1798. Total faculty: 113 (72 full-time, 41 part-time). Quarter calendar. Grading system: letters or numbers.

Communication Department, Cedar City, UT 84720 801-586-4411

CONTACT Film — Richard M Rowley Television — Frain G Pearson
DEGREES OFFERED BA, BS in communication with emphasis in television
DEPARTMENTAL MAJORS 100 students
ADMISSION Requirements — 2.5 minimum grade point average, ACT scores, interviews
FINANCIAL AID Scholarships, student loans, work/study programs
CURRICULAR EMPHASIS Filmmaking — documentary Television study — (1) production; (2) criticism and aesthetics; (3) management Television production — (1) news/documentary; (2) commercial; (3) educational
SPECIAL ACTIVITIES/OFFERINGS Student publications, program material produced for on-campus closed-circuit television, internships in television production, practicum
FACILITIES AND EQUIPMENT Film — 8mm cameras, sound recording equipment, lighting equipment, black and white film stock, color film stock, editing room, sound mixing room Television — complete black and white studio production equipment, complete color studio production equipment, black and white studio, color studio, audio studio, control room
FACULTY Frain G Pearson, Richard M Rowley

COURSE LIST

Undergraduate
Radio and Television Announcing
History and Development of Radio and Television
Reporting
Television Labs
Television Production
Special Projects in Television
Introduction to Television
Scriptwriting
Writing for Television
Workshop in Film
History of Film

University of Utah

State-supported coed university. Institutionally accredited by regional association, programs recognized by NASM, AACSB, ACPE. Urban location. Total enrollment: 21,444. Undergraduate enrollment: 16,845. Total faculty: 1358 (978 full-time, 380 part-time). Quarter calendar. Grading system: letters or numbers.

Communication Department, Salt Lake City, UT 84112 801-581-6302

CONTACT James Anderson
DEGREES OFFERED BA, BS, MA, MS in mass communication with emphasis in film or television; PhD in communication with emphasis in film or television
ADMISSION Undergraduate requirements — 2.0 minimum grade point average, teachers' recommendations, written statement of purpose Graduate requirements — 3.0 minimum grade point average, MAT scores, teachers' recommendations, written statement of purpose Undergraduate application deadline — 8/1, rolling
FINANCIAL AID Scholarships, teaching assistantships Undergraduate application deadline — 8/1, rolling

CURRICULAR EMPHASIS Undergraduate film study — (1) production; (2) criticism and aesthetics; (3) appreciation Graduate film study — (1) criticism and aesthetics; (2) history; (3) production Filmmaking — (1) documentary; (2) narrative; (3) educational Undergraduate television study — (1) production; (2) criticism and aesthetics; (3) management Graduate television study — (1) criticism and aesthetics; (2) management; (3) history Television production — (1) news/documentary; (2) commercial; (3) experimental/personal video
SPECIAL ACTIVITIES/OFFERINGS Film festivals, student publications, program material produced for on-campus closed-circuit television and cable television, internships in film and television production, practicum
FACILITIES AND EQUIPMENT Film — complete 8mm and 16mm equipment, screening room, editing room, sound mixing room Television — complete black and white studio and exterior production equipment, complete color studio production equipment, black and white studio, color studio, mobile van/unit, audio studio, control room
FACULTY James Anderson, R K Avery, Roy Gibson, Tim Larson, Ronald Scott, R K Tiemens

COURSE LIST

Undergraduate
Elements in Broadcasting
Cinema Technology
Film Production I, II
Telecommunication Production
Advanced Telecommunication Production
Script/Continuity Writing
Television News Writing/Reporting
Current Developments in Radio-Television-Film

Graduate
Seminar: Media Effects
Seminar: Broadcast History
Seminar: Non-Commercial Telecommunication
Seminar: Film Theory and Criticism
Seminar: Visual Communication

Undergraduate and Graduate
Regulation
Management
Broadcast News Organization and Management

Utah

Film Studies Program (Departments of Art, English, and Theatre), 205 Pioneer Memorial Theatre, Salt Lake City, UT 84112 801-581-6356

CONTACT William Siska or Brian Patrick
DEGREES OFFERED BA in film studies, MFA in Theatre with film emphasis, MFA in Art with film emphasis
PROGRAM MAJORS Undergraduate film — 10 students Graduate film — 2 students
ADMISSION Undergraduate requirements — 2.0 minimum grade point average, teachers' recommendations, written statement of purpose Graduate requirements — 3.0 minimum grade point average, GRE scores, teachers' recommendations, written statement of purpose Undergraduate application deadline — 8/1, rolling
FINANCIAL AID Scholarships, work/study programs, fellowships, teaching assistantships, research assistantships Undergraduate application deadline — 8/1, rolling
CURRICULAR EMPHASIS Undergraduate film study — (1) history; (2) criticism and aesthetics; (3) appreciation Graduate film study — (1) history; (2) criticism and aesthetics Undergraduate filmmaking — (1) narrative; (2) documentary; (3) experimental; (4) animated Graduate filmmaking — (1) narrative; (2) documentary; (3) experimental; (4) animated
SPECIAL ACTIVITIES/OFFERINGS Independent study
FACILITIES AND EQUIPMENT Film — 8mm and 16mm cameras, editing equipment, sound recording equipment, lighting, projectors, screening room, editing room, sound mixing room, animation board, permanent film library of commercial or professional films
FACULTY Brian Patrick, William Siska, Thomas Sobchack PART-TIME FACULTY Barbara Bannon, Elizabeth Conley, Russell Johnson, Sheila Johnson, Vivian Sobchack

COURSE LIST

Undergraduate
Critical Introduction to Film
The American Film
Cinematic Visions of the World
Beginning Film Production (Super-8mm)

Graduate
Seminar in Film

Undergraduate and Graduate
Film Genre
Documentary Film
Experimental Film
History of Film: The Silent Period
History of Film: Sound to 1955
History of Film: The Contemporary Cinema
Screenwriting I, II
Advanced Film Production I–III (16mm)
Studies in Film Theory and Criticism
Film and TV Acting

Weber State College

State-supported comprehensive coed institution. Part of Utah System of Higher Education. Institutionally accredited by regional association. Urban location, 375-acre campus. Undergraduate enrollment: 9400. Total faculty: 500 (300 full-time, 200 part-time). Quarter calendar. Grading system: letters or numbers.

Communication Department, Harrison Boulevard., Ogden, UT 84408 801-626-6454

CONTACT Raj Kumar
DEGREE OFFERED BA with an emphasis in broadcasting
DEPARTMENTAL MAJORS Television — 40 students
ADMISSION Requirements — ACT or SAT scores, teachers' recommendations, professional work experience Application deadline — 8/20
FINANCIAL AID Scholarships, work/study programs, student loans Application deadline — 8/20
CURRICULAR EMPHASIS Television study — history, educational, production, management treated equally Television production — commercial, news/documentary treated equally
SPECIAL ACTIVITIES/OFFERINGS Program material produced for on-campus closed-circuit television, apprenticeships, internships in film production, internships in television production, independent study

Weber State College (continued)

FACILITIES AND EQUIPMENT Television — black and white studio cameras, color studio cameras, ½-inch VTR, ¾-inch cassette VTR, portable black and white cameras, editing equipment, monitors, special effects generators, slide chain, portable color cameras, lighting equipment, sound recording equipment, audio mixers, film chain, time base corrector, black and white studio, color studio, audio studio, control room
FACULTY Raj Kumar

COURSE LIST
Undergraduate
Television Production
Advanced TV Direction
Television Internship
Television Apprenticeship

Westminster College

Independent comprehensive coed institution. Institutionally accredited by regional association. Suburban location, 27-acre campus. Total enrollment: 1422. Undergraduate enrollment: 1344. Total faculty: 105 (60 full-time, 45 part-time). 4-1-4 calendar. Grading system: letters or numbers.

Humanities Department, 1840 South 13th Street East, Salt Lake City, UT 84105 801-484-7651

CONTACT Stephen Baar
DEGREE OFFERED BA in communications with an emphasis in film
ADMISSION Application deadline — rolling
FINANCIAL AID Scholarships, work/study programs, student loans
CURRICULAR EMPHASIS Film study — history, criticism and aesthetics, appreciation treated equally
SPECIAL ACTIVITIES/OFFERINGS Film festivals, internships in film production, internships in television production, independent study
FACILITIES AND EQUIPMENT Film — complete 8mm equipment Television — ¾-inch cassette VTR
FACULTY Stephen Baar

COURSE LIST
Undergraduate
Introduction to Film Theory and Criticism
The Director
Film Genre
The Movies

VERMONT

Castleton State College

State-supported comprehensive coed institution. Part of Vermont State Colleges System. Institutionally accredited by regional association. Rural location, 130-acre campus. Total enrollment: 2188. Undergraduate enrollment: 1832. Total faculty: 107 (81 full-time, 26 part-time). Semester calendar. Grading system: letters or numbers.

Communications Department, Fine Arts Center, Castleton, VT 05735 802-468-5611

CONTACT Robert Gershon
DEGREES OFFERED AB in communications, BS in communications with an emphasis in mass media
DEPARTMENTAL/PROGRAM MAJORS Television — 20 students
FINANCIAL AID Work/study programs, student loans
CURRICULAR EMPHASIS Undergraduate television production — (1) news/documentary; (2) experimental/personal video; (3) dramatic
SPECIAL ACTIVITIES/OFFERINGS Film series, film societies, program material produced for on-campus closed-circuit television and occasional public television
FACILITIES AND EQUIPMENT Television — black and white studio cameras, ½-inch VTR, 1-inch VTR, portable black and white cameras, editing equipment, monitors, special effects generators, ½-inch portapak recorders, lighting equipment, sound recording equipment, audio mixers, black and white studio

COURSE LIST
Undergraduate
TV Workshop I, II
TV Documentary Workshop
TV Drama Workshop
The Motion Picture: A Study
Acting for TV
Writing for Broadcasting
History of Broadcasting
Introduction to Mass Media
Radio Programming and Production

Marlboro College

Independent 4-year coed college. Institutionally accredited by regional association. Rural location, 300-acre campus. Undergraduate enrollment: 219. Total faculty: 35 (30 full-time, 5 part-time). 4-1-4 calendar. Grading system: letters or numbers.

Theater-Film Department, Marlboro, VT 05344 802-257-4333

CONTACT Geoffrey Brown, Chairman
DEGREE OFFERED BA in film
ADMISSION Application deadline — rolling
FACULTY Geoffrey Brown

COURSE LIST
Undergraduate
Film: Style and Content
Filmmaking

Norwich University

Independent comprehensive institution primarily for men. Institutionally accredited by regional association. Rural location, 640-acre campus. Total enrollment: 1572. Undergraduate enrollment: 1459. Total faculty: 159 (143 full-time, 16 part-time). Semester calendar. Grading sytem: letters or numbers.

English Department, Northfield, VT 05663 802-485-5011

CONTACT Richard Cutts
ADMISSION Application deadline — rolling
FACULTY Richard Cutts, Charlotte Gafford

COURSE LIST
Undergraduate and Graduate
The Art of the Motion Picture
The History of the Motion Picture
The Motion Picture Director
Writing for the Media

University of Vermont

State-supported coed university. Institutionally accredited by regional association. Suburban location, 424-acre campus. Total enrollment: 8850. Undergraduate enrollment: 7670. Total faculty: 990 (670 full-time, 320 part-time). Semester calendar. Grading system: letters or numbers.

Communication Department, Burlington, VT 05401 802-656-3214

CONTACT Dharam P Yadav
ADMISSION Application deadline — 2/1
CURRICULAR EMPHASIS Film study — history, criticism and aesthetics, production treated equally Filmmaking — documentary, narrative, experimental, animated, educational treated equally Television study — production, educational, social effects treated equally Television production — news/documentary, educational treated equally
SPECIAL ACTIVITIES/OFFERINGS Program material produced for local public television station and local commercial television station, apprenticeships, internships in television production, independent study, teacher training, vocational placement service
FACILITIES AND EQUIPMENT Film — complete 8mm and 16mm equipment, editing room, sound mixing room, animation board Television — complete black and white studio production facilities, complete color exterior production facilities
FACULTY William Lewis, Norma London, Frank Manchel, John Worden, Dharan Yadav

COURSE LIST
Undergraduate
Basic Filmmaking
Survey of Mass Communication
Development of the Motion Picture
Basic Television Production
Broadcast News
Writing for Mass Communication
Audio Production

Graduate
Advanced Cinematography
Seminar in Telecommunication

Undergraduate and Graduate
Cinematography
Seminar in Film
Black Man in Film
Contemporary Cinema
Advanced Television Production
International Mass Communication
Issues in Contemporary Mass Communication

VIRGINIA

George Mason University

State-supported comprehensive coed institution. Institutionally accredited by regional association. Suburban location, 567-acre campus. Total enrollment: 10,767. Undergraduate enrollment: 8280. Total faculty: 594 (365 full-time, 229 part-time). Semester calendar. Grading system: letters or numbers.

English Department, Fairfax, VA 22030 703-323-2220

CONTACT Film — Peter Brunette Television — Karen Walowit
ADMISSION Application deadline — 7/1
SPECIAL ACTIVITIES/OFFERINGS Film festivals
FACULTY Peter Brunette, Terry Comito, Joel Foreman, Fred Grossberg, S Eric Molin, Edward A Snow, Karen Walowit

COURSE LIST
Undergraduate
Introduction to Film
Special Topics in Film
Film History and Theory

George Mason University (continued)

Undergraduate and Graduate
Popular Culture

Hampton Institute

Independent comprehensive coed institution. Institutionally accredited by regional association, programs recognized by NASM. Urban location, 200-acre campus. Total enrollment: 2808. Undergraduate enrollment: 2588. Total faculty: 226 (205 full-time, 21 part-time). Semester calendar. Grading system: letters or numbers.

Mass Media Arts Department, Hampton, VA 23668 804-727-5400

CONTACT William Kearney, Chairman
ADMISSION Application deadline — 6/30, rolling
CURRICULAR EMPHASIS Undergraduate film study — (1) history; (2) appreciation; (3) criticism and aesthetics Undergraduate filmmaking — documentary, narrative, experimental treated equally Undergraduate television study — (1) production; (2) history; (3) management Undergraduate television production — (1) commercial; (2) news/documentary; (3) educational
SPECIAL ACTIVITIES/OFFERINGS Film series; program material produced for on-campus closed-circuit television, cable television, local commercial television station; internships in film production; internships in television production; vocational placement service
FACILITIES AND EQUIPMENT Film — 8mm and 16mm cameras, editing equipment, lighting, color film stock, projectors, 8mm sound recording equipment, sound stage, screening room, editing room Television — black and white studio cameras, color studio cameras, ¾-inch cassette VTR, portable black and white cameras, editing equipment, monitors, special effects generators, slide chain, ¾-inch ENG, lighting equipment, sound recording equipment, audio mixers, film chain, character generator, color studio, audio studio, control room, Telecine, video tape editing room
FACULTY Thomas Dolan, William Kearney, Leslie Lawton, Finis Schneider

COURSE LIST
Undergraduate
Closed-Circuit Television
Introduction to Mass Media
Film and Television Production Management
Aesthetics in Mass Communication
Reporting Public Affairs
Propaganda Analysis
Political Journalism
Ethical Standards
Law of Communications
Fundamentals of Television Broadcasting
Broadcast Journalism
Radio-Television Management
Television Production and Direction
Television Workshop
Media and Contemporary Thought
Media Photography
Filmmaking
Cooperative Internship

Virginia

Hollins College

Independent comprehensive women's institution. Institutionally accredited by regional association, programs recognized by NASM. Suburban location, 450-acre campus. Total enrollment: 1012. Undergraduate enrollment: 920. Total faculty: 91 (72 full-time, 19 part-time). 4-1-4 calendar. Grading system: letters or numbers.

Theater Arts Department, Hollins, VA 24020 703-362-6000

CONTACT Thomas Atkins, Chairman
DEGREE OFFERED BA in film, MA in film
ADMISSION Application deadline — 3/1, rolling

COURSE LIST
Undergraduate
Film History I, II
Filmmaking I, II
Film as Narrative Art I, II
Advanced Studies: Contemporary Drama Film
Advanced Studies: Contemporary Popular Culture

Liberty Baptist College

Independent 4-year coed college affiliated with Independent Baptist Church. Candidate for institutional accreditation. Suburban location, 3500-acre campus. Undergraduate enrollment: 2229. Total faculty: 130 (115 full-time, 15 part-time). Semester calendar. Grading system: letters or numbers.

Division of Television, Radio, Film, Lynchburg, VA 24506 804-237-5961

CONTACT Film — Tony Black Television — Carl Windsor
DEGREE OFFERED B.S. in television-radio-film with concentration in television, or radio, or film
DEPARTMENTAL MAJORS Film — 10 students Television — 51 students
ADMISSION Requirements — minimum grade point average, ACT or SAT scores, teachers' recommendations, written statement of purpose
FINANCIAL AID Scholarships, work/study programs, student loans
CURRICULAR EMPHASIS Film study — (1) production; (2) history; (3) criticism and aesthetics Filmmaking — (1) documentary; (2) religious; (3) educational Television study — (1) production; (2) management; (3) history Television production — (1) religious; (2) commercial; (3) news/documentary
SPECIAL ACTIVITIES/OFFERINGS Program material produced for cable television, internships in film production, internships in television production, independent study, vocational placement service
FACILITIES AND EQUIPMENT Film — complete 8mm equipment, screening room, editing room, sound mixing room, permanent film library of student films, permanent film library of commercial or professional films Television — black and white studio cameras, color studio cameras, ½-inch VTR, ¾-inch cassette VTR, editing equipment, monitors, special effects generators, portable color cameras, ¾-inch ENG, lighting equipment, sound recording equipment, audio mixers, black and white studio, color studio, audio studio, control room

FACULTY James Pickering, Al Snyder, Carl Windsor PART-TIME FACULTY Anthony Black, Philip Pantana

COURSE LIST

Undergraduate

Fundamentals of Audio Control and Radio Production
Fundamentals of Television and Film Production
Fundamentals of Television, Radio, and Film Programming
Radio Production Techniques
Television Production Techniques
History of Motion Pictures
Film Production Techniques
Film Theory and Criticism
Film Writing
Filming Sports
History of Radio and Television
Television and Radio Speaking
Television and Radio Writing
Television, Radio, and Film News
Advanced Television Production
Special Television Projects
Advanced Film Production
Advanced Film Theory and Criticism
Television and Film Documentaries
Religious Films
Special Film Projects
Advanced Television and Radio Speaking
Advanced Television and Radio Writing
Television-Radio-Film Internship
Television, Radio, and Film in Education
Television and Radio Program Management
Television and Radio Station Management

Longwood College

State-supported comprehensive institution, coed as of 1976. Institutionally accredited by regional association. Small town location, 158-acre campus. Total enrollment: 2350. Undergraduate enrollment: 2200. Total faculty: 153 (148 full-time, 5 part-time). Semester calendar. Grading system: letters or numbers.

Art Department, Farmville, VA 23901 804-392-9359

CONTACT Barbara Bishop, Chairman
DEGREE OFFERED BFA with electives in film
ADMISSION Application deadline — rolling
CURRICULAR EMPHASIS Film study — (1) appreciation; (2) history, criticism and aesthetics; (3) production Filmmaking — (1) documentary; (2) animated; (3) narrative
SPECIAL ACTIVITIES/OFFERINGS Film series, film festivals, visiting filmmakers, program material produced for on-campus closed-circuit television, independent study, practicum, teacher training, vocational placement service
FACILITIES AND EQUIPMENT Film — complete 8mm equipment, 16mm projectors, screening rooms, animation board, permanent film library Television — black and white studio, color studio, control room
FACULTY Charlotte Schrader-Hooker

COURSE LIST

Undergraduate

Film Studies I — History
Film Studies II — Genre
Film Studies III — Theory and Criticism
Filmmaking I, II

Mary Washington College

State-supported 4-year coed college. Institutionally accredited by regional association. Small town location, 275-acre campus. Undergraduate enrollment: 2292. Total faculty: 145 (125 full-time, 20 part-time). Semester calendar. Grading system: letters or numbers.

Department of English, Fredericksburg, VA 22401 703-899-4386

CONTACT William Kemp
DEGREES OFFERED BA in English, BA in drama, BA in performing arts
ADMISSION Requirement — ACT or SAT scores Application deadline — 2/1
FINANCIAL AID Scholarships, work/study programs, student loans Application deadline — 2/1
CURRICULAR EMPHASIS Film study — (1) appreciation; (2) history; (3) criticism and aesthetics Television study — production Television production — (1) news/documentary; (2) educational
SPECIAL ACTIVITIES/OFFERINGS Film series, program material produced for on-campus closed-circuit television, internships in television production, independent study, teacher training, vocational placement service
FACILITIES AND EQUIPMENT Film — 8mm cameras, editing equipment, lighting, projectors, 16mm cameras, sound recording equipment, lighting, projectors, screening room, permanent film library of commercial or professional films Television — color studio cameras, ¾-inch cassette VTR, portable black and white cameras, editing equipment, monitors, special effects generators, portable color cameras, lighting equipment, sound recording equipment, audio mixers, film chain, color studio, mobile van/unit, audio studio, control room
FACULTY William Kemp, Roger Kenvin PART-TIME FACULTY Richard Maniscalco

COURSE LIST

Undergraduate

Fiction and Film
Film to 1945
Film Since 1945
TV Production Internship

Dramatic Arts and Dance Department 703-373-7250

CONTACT Roger Kenvin
ADMISSION Application deadline — 3/1
CURRICULAR EMPHASIS Film study — (1) appreciation; (2) history; (3) criticism and aesthetics
SPECIAL ACTIVITIES/OFFERINGS Internships in film and television production, independent study

COURSE LIST

Undergraduate

History of Film I, II

Norfolk State University

State-supported comprehensive coed institution. Institutionally accredited by regional association. Urban location. Total enrollment: 7283. Undergraduate enrollment: 6989. Total faculty: 425. Semester calendar. Grading system: letters or numbers.

Mass Communications Department, 2400 Corprew Avenue, Norfolk, VA 23504 804-623-8454

CONTACT Wilbert Edgerton
DEGREES OFFERED BS, MA, major in mass communications with emphasis in film or television
ADMISSION Requirement — SAT scores Application deadline — 8/1, rolling
FINANCIAL AID Scholarships, student loans, work/study programs Application deadline — 4/1, rolling
CURRICULAR EMPHASIS Film study — (1) history; (2) appreciation; (3) criticism and aesthetics Filmmaking — educational Television study — (1) production; (2) appreciation; (3) educational Television production — (1) commercial; (2) news/documentary; (3) educational
SPECIAL ACTIVITIES/OFFERINGS Film societies, program material produced for on-campus closed-circuit television and local commercial television station, internships in television production, independent study
FACILITIES AND EQUIPMENT Film — complete 8mm equipment, editing room Television — complete black and white studio production equipment, complete color studio and exterior production facilities, black and white studio, control room
FACULTY Yih-Wen Chen, Wilbert Edgerton, Grady James, Erwin Thomas, Stanly Tickton

COURSE LIST
Undergraduate
History/Appreciation of Film
Film Criticism
Basic/Advanced Filmmaking
Writing for Broadcast and Film
Graduate
History of Film
Advanced Criticism

Northern Virginia Community College

State-supported 2-year coed college. Part of Virginia Community College System. Institutionally accredited by regional association. Suburban location. Undergraduate enrollment: 31,327. Total faculty: 970 (52 full-time, 918 part-time). Quarter calendar. Grading system: letters or numbers.

Broadcast Engineering Technology Program, 8333 Little River Turnpike, Annandale, VA 22003 703-323-3248

CONTACT Edward T Montgomery
DEGREES OFFERED AAS in broadcast engineering
PROGRAM MAJORS Television — 70 students
FINANCIAL AID Work/study programs, co-op
CURRICULAR EMPHASIS Television study — engineering
SPECIAL ACTIVITIES/OFFERINGS Program material produced for laboratory experience (television) with Humanities Divison, vocational placement service
FACILITIES AND EQUIPMENT Television — black and white studio cameras, color studio cameras, 2-inch VTR, ¾-inch cassette VTR, editing equipment, monitors, special effects generators, slide chain, portable color cameras, ¾-inch ENG, lighting equipment, sound recording equipment, audio mixers, film chain, time base corrector, color studio, mobile van/unit, audio studio, control room

COURSE LIST
Undergraduate
Fundamentals of Direct Current
Introduction to Tubes and Transistors
Fundamentals of Alternating Current
Electronics
Circuit Analysis
Amplifiers
Broadcast Equipment Operation
Pulse and Switching Circuits
Communication
Broadcast Instruments and Measurements
Audio Systems I, II
Television Systems I, II
Federal Broadcast Regulations
Seminar and Project in Broadcast Technology
Advanced Circuits and New Devices
Seminar and Project in FCC First- and Second-Class License Examinations

University of Richmond

Independent Baptist comprehensive coed institution. Institutionally accredited by regional association, programs recognized by AACSB. Suburban location, 350-acre campus. Total enrollment: 3135. Undergraduate enrollment: 2526. Total faculty: 318 (193 full-time, 125 part-time). Semester calendar. Grading system: letters or numbers.

Department of English, Richmond, VA 23173 804-285-6250

CONTACT Film — Irby B Brown Television — Edward Swain
ADMISSION Application deadline — 2/15
FINANCIAL AID Scholarships, student loans, work/study programs. Application deadline — 3/1
CURRICULAR EMPHASIS Film study — (1) history; (2) criticism and aesthetics; (3) appreciation Filmmaking — (1) narrative; (2) experimental; (3) documentary Television study — (1) appreciation; (2) production; (3) educational Television production — (1) news/documentary; (2) experimental/personal video; (3) educational
SPECIAL ACTIVITIES/OFFERINGS Film series, film festivals, film societies
FACILITIES AND EQUIPMENT Film — 8mm and 16mm editing equipment, projectors, screening room, editing room, permanent film library Television — black and white studio cameras, portable black and white cameras, editing equipment, monitors, local television studio
FACULTY Irby B Brown, Rosalie Newell, Edward Swain PART-TIME FACULTY Charles Fishburne, Al Moffat

COURSE LIST

Undergraduate

History and Aesthetics of Film
Avant-Garde Film
Television

University of Virginia

State-related coed university. Institutionally accredited by regional association. Suburban location, 1800-acre campus. Total enrollment: 15,324. Undergraduate enrollment: 10,543. Total faculty: 1570 full-time. Semester calendar. Grading system: letters or numbers.

Film Studies, Drama Department, Culbreth Road, Charlottesville, VA 22903 804-924-3326

CONTACT Walter Korte
CURRICULAR EMPHASIS Undergraduate film study — (1) criticism and aesthetics; (2) history Graduate film study — (1) criticism and aesthetics; (2) history Undergraduate filmmaking — (1) documentary; (2) experimental; (3) narrative
SPECIAL ACTIVITIES/OFFERINGS Filmmaking clubs, film series, film festivals, independent study
FACILITIES AND EQUIPMENT Film — 16mm cameras, editing equipment, projectors, editing room, permanent film library of commercial or professional films
FACULTY Walter Korte PART-TIME FACULTY Ellen McWhirter

COURSE LIST

Undergraduate

Cinema as Art Form
History of Film: (Silent and Sound) I, II
Film Criticism
American Film
Independent Study in Production
French Cinema

Graduate

Film for the Critic and Teacher

Undergraduate and Graduate

Film Aesthetics
Literature and Film

Virginia Commonwealth University

State-supported coed university. Institutionally accredited by regional association, programs recognized by NASM, AACSB, NASA, ACPE. Urban location. Total enrollment: 19,113. Undergraduate enrollment: 13,733. Total faculty: 1727 (1273 full-time, 454 part-time). Semester calendar. Grading system: letters or numbers.

English Department, 901 West Franklin Street, Richmond, VA 23284 804-257-1664

CONTACT Robert Armour
ADMISSION Undergraduate application deadline — 8/1, rolling
CURRICULAR EMPHASIS Undergraduate film study — (1) criticism and aesthetics; (2) appreciation Graduate film study — educational media/instructional technology
SPECIAL ACTIVITIES/OFFERINGS Film series, film festivals
FACILITIES AND EQUIPMENT Film — 8mm cameras, editing equipment, lighting equipment, 8mm and 16mm projectors, screening room, permanent film library
FACULTY Robert Armour, Walter R Coppedge

COURSE LIST

Undergraduate

Fiction into Film

Graduate

Mass Media and the Teaching of English

Undergraduate and Graduate

Film as a Teaching Medium

Virginia Intermont College

Independent Baptist 4-year coed college. Institutionally accredited by regional association. Urban location, 150-acre campus. Undergraduate enrollment: 594. Total faculty: 40 full-time. Semester calendar. Grading sytem: letters or numbers.

Photography and Film Department, Moore Street at Harmelin Street, Bristol, VA 24201 703-669-6101, ext 49

CONTACT Jay Phyfer
CURRICULAR EMPHASIS Undergraduate film study — history, criticism and aesthetics, appreciation treated equally Undergraduate filmmaking — documentary, narrative treated equally
SPECIAL ACTIVITIES/OFFERINGS Film series, independent study
FACILITIES AND EQUIPMENT Film — 16mm cameras, editing equipment, lighting, projectors
FACULTY Jay Phyfer

COURSE LIST

Undergraduate

Elements of Film
Contempory Film
Projects

Virginia State University

State-supported comprehensive coed institution. Institutionally accredited by regional association. Suburban location, 210-acre campus. Total enrollment: 4310. Undergraduate enrollment: 3787. Total faculty: 260 (235 full-time, 25 part-time). Semester calendar. Grading system: letters or numbers.

Library Information Science/Instructional Media Department, Box 35, Petersburg, VA 23803 804-520-6321

CONTACT David J Discenza
DEGREE OFFERED MEd in education-library/media
ADMISSION Undergraduate requirement — ACT or SAT scores Graduate requirements — 2.5 minimum grade point average, GRE scores, written statement of purpose, portfolio
FINANCIAL AID Scholarships, work/study programs, student loans
CURRICULAR EMPHASIS Graduate film study — educational media/instructional technology Graduate television study — educational Graduate television production — educational
SPECIAL ACTIVITIES/OFFERINGS Program material produced for on-campus closed-circuit television, independent study
FACILITIES AND EQUIPMENT Film — permanent film library of commercial or professional films Television — complete color studio production equipment, color studio, control room

COURSE LIST

Undergraduate and Graduate
Educational Television Production

Virginia Western Community College

State-supported 2-year coed college. Part of Virginia Community College System. Institutionally accredited by regional association. Urban location, 70-acre campus. Undergraduate enrollment: 3200. Total faculty: 230 (130 full-time, 100 part-time). Quarter calendar. Grading system: letters or numbers.

Radio/Television Production Technology Department, 3095 Colonial Avenue SW, Roanoke, VA 24015 703-982-7269

CONTACT Harry Abraham
DEGREE OFFERED AAS in radio/television production
DEPARTMENTAL MAJORS Television — 45 students
ADMISSION Undergraduate requirements — ACT or SAT scores, written statement of purpose
FINANCIAL AID Scholarships, work/study programs, student loans
CURRICULAR EMPHASIS Film study — history, criticism and aesthetics, appreciation treated equally Television study — history, criticism and aesthetics, appreciation, educational, production, management treated equally Television production — commercial, news/documentary, educational, studio production treated equally
SPECIAL ACTIVITIES/OFFERINGS Film series; program material produced for on-campus closed-circuit television, cable television, local public television station, internships in television production, independent study
FACILITIES AND EQUIPMENT Television — black and white studio cameras, color studio cameras, ½-inch VTR, ¾-inch cassette VTR, editing equipment, monitors, special effects generators, slide chain, ½-inch portapak recorders, lighting equipment, sound recording equipment, audio mixers, film chain, time base corrector, production switcher, character generator, complete cassette editing, auto editing control, black and white studio, color studio, audio studio, control room
FACULTY Harry Abraham, Douglas Carter, Wayne Michie PART-TIME FACULTY George Bassett, Steve Mills, Chris Shannon, Marty Snortum

COURSE LIST

Undergraduate
Introduction to Radio/Television
Introduction to Photography
Radio/Television Production
Speech for Radio/Television
TV Studio Art
Technical Problems of Radio/Television
Radio/Television Management and Operation
Radio/Television News
Writing for Radio/Television
Broadcast Advertising and Sales
Social Problems in Broadcasting
History and Development of Motion Pictures
Advanced Radio/Television Production
Seminar Project
Internship

WASHINGTON

Bellevue Community College

State-supported 2-year coed college. Part of Washington State Community College System. Institutionally accredited by regional association. Suburban location, 83-acre campus. Undergraduate enrollment: 5700. Total faculty: 300 (80 full-time, 220 part-time). Quarter calendar. Grading system: letters or numbers.

Media Technician Program, 3000 Landerholm Circle SE, Bellevue, WA 98007 206-641-2253

CONTACT Wayne Bitterman
DEGREE OFFERED AA in media technology
CURRICULAR EMPHASIS Television production — (1) educational; (2) industrial
SPECIAL ACTIVITIES/OFFERINGS Program material produced for on-campus closed-circuit television and cable television

FACILITIES AND EQUIPMENT Television — complete black and white and color studio production equipment, black and white studio, color studio, audio studio, control room
FACULTY Wayne Bitterman

COURSE LIST
Undergraduate
Utilization of Small Format TV Equipment
Introduction to Small Studio TV Production
Intermediate TV Production
Special Project in Media

Cinema Department, 3000 145th Place SE, Bellevue, WA 98007 206-641-2358

CONTACT Scott Williams
ADMISSION Application deadline — rolling
SPECIAL ACTIVITIES/OFFERINGS Teacher training

COURSE LIST
Undergraduate
Introduction to Film Study
Art of the Film
Basic Filmmaking I,II
Film and Society: Seminar
Advanced Cinema Workshop
Film Acting
Teaching of the Film
History of Film

Central Washington University

State-supported comprehensive coed institution. Institutionally accredited by regional association, programs recognized by NASM. Small town location, 350-acre campus. Total enrollment: 7423. Undergraduate enrollment: 5548. Total faculty: 332 (298 full-time, 34 part-time). Quarter calendar. Grading system: letters or numbers.

Mass Media Program, Ellensburg, WA 98926 509-963-3342

CONTACT Film — William Schmidt Television — Roger Reynolds
DEGREES OFFERED BA in mass communications, BA in broadcast and print journalism
PROGRAM MAJORS Undergraduate film — 2 students Undergraduate television — 25 students Graduate film — 1 student Graduate television — 1 student
ADMISSION Requirements — general university requirements
FINANCIAL AID Scholarships, work/study programs, student loans
CURRICULAR EMPHASIS Undergraduate film study — (1) production; (2) history; (3) criticism and aesthetics Graduate film study — production Undergraduate filmmaking — (1) experimental; (2) documentary; (3) animated Graduate filmmaking — (1) experimental; (2) documentary; (3) animated Undergraduate television study — (1) production; (2) criticism and aesthetics; (3) history Graduate television study — (1) production; (2) criticism and aesthetics; (3) history Undergraduate television production — (1) news/documentary; (2) educational; (3) commercial
SPECIAL ACTIVITIES/OFFERINGS Program material produced for on-campus closed-circuit television, cable television, local commercial television station; internships in television production; independent study
FACILITIES AND EQUIPMENT Film — complete 8mm and 16mm equipment Television — complete color studio production equipment
FACULTY Roger Reynolds PART-TIME FACULTY William Craig, William Schmidt

COURSE LIST
Undergraduate
Broadcast News Writing
Radio Production
TV News Production
TV and Radio Announcing
Practical TV News
Film Production
Cablecasting

Eastern Washington University

State-supported comprehensive coed institution. Institutionally accredited by regional association, programs recognized by NASM, AACSB. Small town location. Total enrollment: 7013. Undergraduate enrollment: 5601. Total faculty: 390 (340 full-time, 50 part-time). Quarter calendar. Grading system: letters or numbers.

Radio-Television Department, Radio Television Center, Cheney, WA 99004 509-359-2228

CONTACT Rey L Barnes, Chairman
DEGREE OFFERED BA in radio-television
DEPARTMENTAL MAJORS Television — 150 students
FINANCIAL AID Scholarships, work/study programs, student loans
CURRICULAR EMPHASIS Filmmaking — (1) documentary; (2) educational Television study — management Television production — commercial, news/documentary treated equally
SPECIAL ACTIVITIES/OFFERINGS Program material produced for on-campus closed-circuit television, cable television, local public television station, local commercial television station; internships in television production; independent study
FACILITIES AND EQUIPMENT Film — 16mm cameras, editing equipment, sound recording equipment, lighting, black and white film stock, projectors, sound stage, screening room, editing room, sound mixing room Television — color studio cameras, 1-inch VTR, 2-inch VTR, ¾-inch cassette VTR, editing equipment, monitors, special effects generators, slide chain, portable color cameras, ¾-inch ENG, lighting equipment, sound recording equipment, audio mixers, film chain, time base corrector, color studio, audio studio, control room
FACULTY Rey Barnes, Lew Boles, Don Carey, Howard Hopf

COURSE LIST
Undergraduate
Introduction to Radio-Television Broadcasting
Radio-Television Announcing and Performance
Problems in Station Management and Program Direction
Radio-Television Traffic Scheduling and Billing
Television Directing and Producing
Radio-Television News I, II

Eastern Washington University (continued)

Legal Responsibilities and Regulations in Communications Media
Television News Filming and Editing I—III
Programming the Modern Radio and Television Station
Special Studies
Radio-Television Communications Writing
Radio-Television News
Educational Radio-Television Teaching Techniques and Production
Communications Research and Evaluation
Radio-Television Station Internship

Evergreen State College

State-supported 4-year coed college. Institutionally accredited by regional association. Suburban location. Undergraduate enrollment: 2322. Total faculty: 155 (120 full-time, 35 part-time). Quarter calendar. Grading system: faculty reports.

Media Arts — Interdisciplinary Programs, Olympia, WA 98505 206-866-6059

CONTACT Sally J Cloninger
DEGREE OFFERED BA in interdisciplinary studies
PROGRAM MAJORS Film — 60 students Television — 30 students
ADMISSION Application deadline — rolling
FINANCIAL AID Scholarships, work/study programs, student loans
CURRICULAR EMPHASIS Film study — depends upon individual student interest but also offers considerable course work in visual anthropology and collaborative arts Filmmaking — documentary, experimental treated equally Television study — depends upon individual student interest Television production — news/documentary, experimental/personal video treated equally
SPECIAL ACTIVITIES/OFFERINGS Film series; film festivals; program material produced for on-campus closed-circuit television, cable television, local public television station, local commercial television station; apprenticeships; internships in film production; internships in television production; independent study; vocational placement service
FACILITIES AND EQUIPMENT Film — complete 8mm and 16mm cameras, editing equipment, sound recording equipment, lighting, black and white film stock, color film stock, projectors, sound stage, screening room, editing room, sound mixing room, animation board, permanent film library of student films, permanent film library of commercial or professional films Television — black and white studio cameras, color studio cameras, ½-inch VTR, 1 inch VTR, ¾-inch cassette VTR, portable black and white cameras, editing equipment, monitors, slide chain, portable color cameras, ½-inch portapak recorders, ¾-inch ENG, lighting equipment, sound recording equipment, audio mixers, film chain, time base corrector, black and white studio, color studio, audio studio (16-track, 8-track and 4-track), control room
FACULTY Gordon Beck, Sally J. Cloninger, Charles Davies, Lovern King, Lynn D Patterson, Paul Sparks

COURSE LIST

Undergraduate

Program consists of entry-level courses in nonfiction film and video production, theory, history, and aesthetics; intermediate courses in film, video, and collaborative arts, independent projects for advanced students, and a wide range of internships

Spokane Falls Community College

State-supported 2-year coed college. Institutionally accredited by regional association. Urban location. Undergraduate enrollment: 4822. Total faculty: 170 (164 full-time, 6 part-time). Quarter calendar. Grading system: letters or numbers.

Communications Department, West 3410 Ft George Washington Drive, Spokane, WA 99204 509-456-2880

CONTACT Mary Hyatt
DEGREE OFFERED AA
CURRICULAR EMPHASIS Film study — (1) criticism and aesthetics; (2) appreciation; (3) history Filmmaking — documentary, narrative, experimental, animated treated equally
SPECIAL ACTIVITIES/OFFERINGS Film series
FACILITIES AND EQUIPMENT Film — screening room
FACULTY Rose Coldsnow, Fran Ellingwood, Mary Hyatt, Stan Lauderbaugh, Terry Steiner

COURSE LIST

Undergraduate

Film Communications

Washington State University

State-supported coed university. Institutionally accredited by regional association. Rural location, 620-acre campus. Total enrollment: 16,679. Undergraduate enrollment: 13,370. Total faculty: 1064 (960 full-time, 104 part-time). Semester calendar. Grading system: letters or numbers.

Communications Department, Pullman, WA 99163 509-335-1556

CONTACT Film — Jerry L Salvaggio Television — Hugh A Rundell
DEGREE OFFERED BA in communications with emphasis in film or television, MA in film or mass communication
ADMISSION Requirement — 2.0 minimum grade point average Application deadline — 5/1, rolling
FINANCIAL AID Work/study programs, teaching assistantships Application deadline — 3/1, rolling
CURRICULAR EMPHASIS Film study — (1) history; (2) criticism and aesthetics; (3) production Filmmaking — (1) documentary; (2) narrative; (3) educational
FACILITIES AND EQUIPMENT Film — complete 8mm and 16mm equipment, sound stage, screening room, editing room, sound mixing room, animation board Television — complete black and white studio and exterior production equipment, complete color and exterior production equipment, black and white studio, color studio, mobile van/unit, remote truck, audio studio, control room

FACULTY Evan Cameron, Glenn Johnson, Val E Limburg, Hugh A Rundell, Jerry Salvaggio

COURSE LIST
Undergraduate
History of the Cinema I, II
Film Criticism
Film Scripting
The American Film
Film Seminar
Evolution of Film Design
Asian Cinema
Media Management
Photo-Communications
Fundamentals of Cinema Production
Advanced Cinema Production
History of Photography
Television Production
Advanced Television Production
Television News and Public Affairs
Color Photography

Whitman College

Independent 4-year coed college. Institutionally accredited by regional association. Small town location, 45-acre campus. Undergraduate enrollment: 1171. Total faculty: 90 (85 full-time, 5 part-time). Semester calendar. Grading system: letters or numbers.

Studies in World Literature, Walla Walla, WA 99362 509-527-5176
ADMISSION Undergraduate requirements — ACT or SAT scores, teachers' recommendations Undergraduate application deadline — 3/1
FINANCIAL AID Scholarships, work/study programs, student loans Undergraduate application deadline — 2/15
CURRICULAR EMPHASIS Undergraduate film study — history, criticism and aesthetics treated equally
SPECIAL ACTIVITIES/OFFERINGS Film series

COURSE LIST
Undergraduate
Introduction to the Art of the Cinema
The American Cinema

WEST VIRGINIA

Alderson-Broaddus College

Independent 4-year coed college affiliated with Baptist Church. Institutionally accredited by regional association. Rural location, 167-acre campus. Undergraduate enrollment: 906. Total faculty: 161 (120 full-time, 41 part-time). Quarter calendar. Grading system: letters or numbers.

Humanities Department, Philippi, WV 26416 304-457-1700

CONTACT Ashton Nickerson
PROGRAM OFFERED Major in humanities with emphasis in television
ADMISSION Application deadline — 9/1, rolling
FINANCIAL AID Scholarships, student loans, work/study programs Application deadline — rolling
CURRICULAR EMPHASIS Film study — (1) criticism and aesthetics; (2) appreciation; (3) production Filmmaking — (1) educational; (2) experimental Television study — (1) production; (2) appreciation; (3) educational Television production — (1) news/documentary; (2) educational; (3) experimental/personal video
SPECIAL ACTIVITIES/OFFERINGS Film series, film festivals, program material produced for on-campus closed-circuit television and cable television, internships in television production, independent study, practicum, teacher training, vocational placement service
FACILITIES AND EQUIPMENT Film — 8mm and 16mm cameras, editing equipment, sound recording equipment, lighting equipment, projectors, sound stage, screening room, 35mm screening facilities, editing room, sound mixing room, permanent film library Television — black and white studio cameras, ½-inch VTR, editing equipment, monitors, special effects generators, lighting equipment, sound recording equipment, audio mixers, black and white studio, audio studio, control room
FACULTY Ashton Nickerson

COURSE LIST
Undergraduate
Principles of Communication
TV Programming
TV Production
Film and TV in American Life
Guided Studies

Davis and Elkins College

Independent Presbyterian 4-year coed college. Institutionally accredited by regional association. Small town location, 170-acre campus. Undergraduate enrollment: 980. Total faculty: 86 (70 full-time, 16 part-time). 4-1-4 calendar. Grading system: letters or numbers.

Division of Integrated Studies, Elkins, WV 26241 304-636-1900

CONTACT Chairperson
ADMISSION Application deadline — rolling
SPECIAL ACTIVITIES/OFFERINGS Film series, independent study
FACILITIES AND EQUIPMENT Film — 16mm projectors, screening room, sound mixing room, permanent film library Television — black and white studio camera, color studio camera, ½-inch VTR, ¾-inch cassette VTR, portable black and white cameras, portable color cameras, black and white studio, audio studio

Salem College

Independent comprehensive coed institution. Institutionally accredited by regional association. Rural location, 140-acre campus. Total enrollment: 1493. Undergraduate enrollment: 1386. Total faculty: 92 (71 full-time, 21 part-time). Semester calendar. Grading system: letters or numbers.

Communication-Theater Arts Department, Salem, WV 26426 304-782-5263

CONTACT Alan L Greule
DEGREES OFFERED AA in broadcasting, BA in broadcasting
FACULTY Alan L Greule, Rick Terry

COURSE LIST

Undergraduate

Broadcast Management
Broadcast Journalism
Broadcast Sales
Broadcast Reporting
Sportscasting
Trends in Broadcasting
Introduction to Broadcasting
Apprenticeship
Broadcast Practicum
Radio Programming
TV Performance
Writing for Radio and TV
TV Programming
TV Production
Announcing
Advanced TV
Radio Production

University of Charleston

Independent 4-year coed college. Institutionally accredited by regional association. Urban location, 40-acre campus. Undergraduate enrollment: 1685. Total faculty: 101 (64 full-time, 37 part-time). 4-1-4 calendar. Grading system: letters or numbers.

Speech Communication Program, Department of Humanities, 2300 MacCorkle Avenue SE, Charleston, WV 25304 304-346-9471

CONTACT R L Freedman
PROGRAM OFFERED Major in speech with emphasis in film or television
ADMISSION Requirement — 2.0 minimum grade point average, ACT or SAT scores Application deadline — rolling
CURRICULAR EMPHASIS Film study — (1) production; (2) educational media/instructional technology; (3) appreciation; (4) history; (5) criticism and aesthetics Filmmaking — (1) educational; (2) narrative; (3) documentary; (4) experimental; (5) animated Television study — (1) appreciation; (2) production; (3) educational; (4) management; (5) criticism and aesthetics; (6) history Television production — (1) educational; (2) news/documentary; (3) experimental/personal video; (4) commercial
SPECIAL ACTIVITIES/OFFERINGS Teacher training, cooperative program, internships
FACILITIES AND EQUIPMENT Film — 16mm sound recording equipment, projectors, sound stage Television — ½-inch VTR, sound recording equipment
FACULTY William Plumley PART-TIME FACULTY William Cheshire

COURSE LIST

Undergraduate

Radio-Television Production
Radio-Television Techniques
Media Production
Media Internship

West Virginia State College

State-supported 4-year coed college. Institutionally accredited by regional association. Suburban location. Undergraduate enrollment: 3678. Total faculty: 195 (135 full-time, 60 part-time). Semester calendar. Grading system: letters or numbers.

Department of Communications, PO Box 8, Institute, WV 25112 304-766-3197

CONTACT D Wohl
DEGREES OFFERED AAS, BS in communications with emphasis in film or television
DEPARTMENTAL MAJORS 81 students
ADMISSION Requirements — minimum grade point average, ACT scores Application deadline — rolling
FINANCIAL AID Work/study programs
CURRICULAR EMPHASIS Film study — (1) production; (2) history; (3) appreciation; (4) criticism and aesthetics Filmmaking — (1) narrative; (2) documentary; (3) educational; (4) animated; (5) experimental Television study — (1) production; (2) criticism and aesthetics; (3) management Television production — (1) commercial; (2) news/documentary; (3) educational
SPECIAL ACTIVITIES/OFFERINGS Film societies; program material produced for on-campus closed-circuit television, cable television, local public television station, local commercial television station; apprenticeships; independent study; practicum
FACILITIES AND EQUIPMENT Film — 8mm and 16mm cameras, lighting equipment, projectors, animation stand, 8mm editing equipment, color film stock, editing room, permanent film library Television — complete black and white studio and exterior production equipment, complete color studio production equipment, black and white studio, color studio, audio studio, control room
FACULTY W Till Curry, Marc Porter, David Wohl

COURSE LIST

Undergraduate

Introduction to Communications
Broadcast Lab — Television
Film Appreciation
Television Production
Design and Lighting for Stage, Film, and Television
Film History
Field Experience — Television/Radio/Film
Motion Picture Production
Motion Picture Lab
Introduction to the Moving Image
Radio/Television Newscasting
General Studies — Overview of Television
General Studies — Popular Culture: Film/Radio/Television
Seminar: Foreign Film

WISCONSIN

Beloit College

Independent 4-year coed college affiliated with United Church of Christ. Institutionally accredited by regional association. Small town location, 40-acre campus. Undergraduate enrollment: 1005. Total faculty: 120 (80 full-time, 40 part-time). Semester calendar. Grading system: letters or numbers.

Theatre Arts Department, Beloit, WI 53511 608-365-3391

CONTACT Carl G Balson
PROGRAM OFFERED Major in theatre arts with emphasis in television
ADMISSION Application deadline — rolling
FINANCIAL AID Student loans, work/study programs Application deadline — rolling
CURRICULAR EMPHASIS Film study — (1) criticism and aesthetics; (2) production; (3) appreciation Filmmaking — (1) experimental; (2) animated Television study — (1) production; (2) history; (3) criticism and aesthetics; (4) appreciation; (5) management Television production — (1) educational; (2) experimental/personal video; (3) commercial; (4) news/documentary
SPECIAL ACTIVITIES/OFFERINGS Film series, film festivals, program material produced for on-campus closed-circuit television and cable television
FACILITIES AND EQUIPMENT Film — 8mm and 16mm cameras, editing equipment, 8mm lighting equipment, projectors, sound mixing room Television — complete black and white studio and exterior production equipment, black and white studio, audio studio, control room
FACULTY Carl G Balson, Dick Olson

COURSE LIST
Undergraduate
Broadcast Production
Film Production
Mass Media
Film as a Graphic Art
History of Film

Marquette University

Independent Roman Catholic coed university. Institutionally accredited by regional association, programs recognized by AACSB. Urban location, 74-acre campus. Total enrollment: 10,992. Undergraduate enrollment: 8715. Total faculty: 852 (525 full-time, 327 part-time). Semester calendar. Grading system: letters or numbers.

Journalism College, 1131 West Wisconsin Avenue, Milwaukee, WI 53233 414-224-7132

CONTACT Film — James W Arnold Television — A L Lorenz, Arthur L Olszyk
PROGRAMS OFFERED Major in journalism with emphasis in radio and television, minor in film
DEPARTMENTAL MAJORS Undergraduate television — 80 students
ADMISSION Undergraduate requirements — 2.0 minimum grade point average, ACT or SAT scores Undergraduate application deadline — rolling
FINANCIAL AID Scholarships, work/study programs, student loans Undergraduate application deadline — rolling
CURRICULAR EMPHASIS Undergraduate film study — (1) criticism and aesthetics; (2) appreciation; (3) production Undergraduate filmmaking — documentary Undergraduate television study — production Undergraduate television production — (1) news/documentary; (2) commercial; (3) experimental/personal video
SPECIAL ACTIVITIES/OFFERINGS Film series, program material produced for on-campus closed-circuit television, internships in film production, internships in television production, independent study, vocational placement service
FACILITIES AND EQUIPMENT Film — 8mm and 16mm cameras, editing equipment, sound recording equipment, black and white film stock, projectors, screening room, 35mm screening facilities, editing room, sound mixing room, animation board Television — complete black and white and color studio production equipment, black and white studio, color studio, remote truck, audio studio, control room
FACULTY James W Arnold, Arthur H Bleich, A L Lorenz, Arthur L Olszyk PART-TIME FACULTY Dean C Maytag, Stephen J Olszyk

COURSE LIST
Undergraduate
Radio-Television Newswriting and Editing
Television Newsfilm and Script
Radio-TV News and Public Affairs Programming
Basic Film/Video Production
Intermediate Film Production
Film as Communication
Film as Art
Film and Popular Culture
The Documentary Film Tradition
Advanced Film/Video Production

Milwaukee Area Technical College

District-supported 2-year coed college. Part of Wisconsin Vocational Technical and Adult Education System. Institutionally accredited by regional association. Urban location. Undergraduate enrollment: 11,673. Total faculty: 1997 (622 full-time, 1375 part-time). Semester calendar. Grading system: letters or numbers.

Telecasting Division, 1015 North 6th Street, Milwaukee, WI 53203 414-278-6369

CONTACT Film — Joe Gradian Television — T D Adams
DEGREES OFFERED AAS in telecasting, AAS in cinematography, AAS in photography
DEPARTMENTAL MAJORS Film — 125 students Television — 40 students
ADMISSION Requirement — ACT or SAT scores
FINANCIAL AID Work/study programs, student loans, state and federal grants

Milwaukee Area Technical College (continued)

CURRICULAR EMPHASIS Film study — (1) educational media/instructional technology; (2) criticism and aesthetics; (3) history Filmmaking — (1) educational; (2) documentary; (3) narrative Television study — (1) production; (2) educational; (3) criticism and aesthetics Television production — (1) educational; (2) commercial; (3) news/documentary
SPECIAL ACTIVITIES/OFFERINGS Filmmaking clubs, program material produced for on-campus closed-circuit television and local public television station, internships in television production, vocational placement service
FACILITIES AND EQUIPMENT Film — complete 8mm and 16mm equipment, 35mm cameras, editing equipment, lighting, black and white film stock, color film stock, projectors, screening room, editing room, sound mixing room, animation board, permanent film library of commercial or professional films Television — complete black and white and color studio production equipment, complete black and white and color exterior production equipment, black and white studio, color studio, mobile van/unit, remote truck, audio studio, control room
FACULTY David Baule, James Prabst, Gathel Weston

COURSE LIST

Undergraduate

Cinematography
Film Editing
Film Production
Cinema Workshop
Motion Picture Camera Technique
Introduction to Telecasting
Broadcast Processes
Script Writing for Television, Radio, and Film
Television Production Techniques
Television Lighting and Set Construction
Technical Problems in Television
TV Studio Operations
Engineering for Production Students I, II
Telecasting Workshop I–III
Television Problems and Special Projects
Telecasting Orientation

University of Wisconsin—Eau Claire

State-supported comprehensive coed institution. Part of University of Wisconsin System. Institutionally accredited by regional association, programs recognized by NASM. Urban location, 310-acre campus. Total enrollment: 9797. Undergraduate enrollment: 9450. Total faculty: 531 (487 full-time, 44 part-time). 4-1-4 calendar. Grading system: letters or numbers.

English Department, Eau Claire, WI 54701 715-836-2639

CONTACT Douglas Pearson
ADMISSION Application deadline — rolling
CURRICULAR EMPHASIS Film study — (1) appreciation; (2) history; (3) educational media/instructional technology; (4) production; (5) criticism and aesthetics Filmmaking — (1) narrative; (2) documentary; (3) experimental
SPECIAL ACTIVITIES/OFFERINGS Film series, film festivals, independent study
FACILITIES AND EQUIPMENT Film — 8mm and 16mm cameras, editing equipment, lighting equipment, projectors, animation stand, permanent film library
FACULTY John Buchholz, Harry Harder, Mike Hilger, Tim Hirsch, John Lawler, Henry Lippold, Douglas Pearson, Judith Stanton

COURSE LIST

Undergraduate

Introduction to Film

Graduate

Film Study: Theory and Practice

Speech — Radio, Television, Film Department

CONTACT Wayne R Wolfert
PROGRAM OFFERED Major in speech with emphasis in television
ADMISSION Requirement — 2.0 minimum grade point average Application deadling — rolling
FINANCIAL AID Student loans, work/study programs Application deadline — 3/1
CURRICULAR EMPHASIS Film study — (1) educational media/instructional technology; (2) history; (3) appreciation; (4) criticism and aesthetics Filmmaking — (1) narrative; (2) documentary; (3) experimental; (4) animated Television study — (1) production; (2) management; (3) educational; (4) criticism and aesthetics; (5) appreciation Television production — (1) news/documentary; (2) commercial; (3) educational
SPECIAL ACTIVITIES/OFFERINGS Program material produced for on-campus closed-circuit television, internships in television production, independent study, practicum, teacher training
FACILITIES AND EQUIPMENT Television — complete black and white studio and exterior production facilities, complete color studio and exterior production equipment, color studio, audio studio, control room
FACULTY Robert Bailey, Martin Grindeland, Wayne R Wolfert

University of Wisconsin—Green Bay

State-supported comprehensive coed institution. Part of University of Wisconsin System. Institutionally accredited by regional association, programs recognized by NASM. Urban location, 640-acre campus. Total enrollment: 3715. Undergraduate enrollment: 3406. Total faculty: 166 (158 full-time, 8 part-time). 4-1-4 calendar. Grading system: letters or numbers.

Communication Processes Department, Green Bay, WI 54302 414-465-2348

CONTACT Jerry Dell
PROGRAM OFFERED Major in communication with emphasis in television
ADMISSION Application deadline — 8/15, rolling
FINANCIAL AID Student loans, work/study programs Application deadline — 3/1, rolling
CURRICULAR EMPHASIS Film study — history, criticism and aesthetics treated equally Television study — (1) production; (2) criticism and aesthetics; (3) educational Television production — (1) educational; (2) experimental/personal video; (3) news/documentary
SPECIAL ACTIVITIES/OFFERINGS Film series, program material produced for on-campus closed-circuit television, internships in television production, independent study, practicum

FACILITIES AND EQUIPMENT Film — 8mm cameras, editing equipment, lighting equipment, projectors, permanent film library Television — complete black and white studio and exterior production equipment, black and white studio, audio studio, control room
FACULTY Jerry Dell

COURSE LIST

Undergraduate and Graduate
Electronic Media I, II
Radio and Television Internship
Film and Society

University of Wisconsin—La Crosse

State-supported comprehensive coed institution. Part of University of Wisconsin System. Institutionally accredited by regional association. Urban location, 100-acre campus. Total enrollment: 8431. Undergraduate enrollment: 7926. Total faculty: 777 (306 full-time, 471 part-time). Semester calendar. Grading system: letters or numbers.

Educational Media Program, College of Education, 1705 State Street, La Crosse, WI 54601 608-784-6050

CONTACT Film — Roger A Grant Television — Bonnie Burroughs
DEGREE OFFERED MS in educational media, undergraduate minor in educational media or instructional materials
FINANCIAL AID Scholarships, work/study programs, graduate assistantships
CURRICULAR EMPHASIS Undergraduate film study — production Graduate film study — criticism and aesthetics Filmmaking — (1) narrative; (2) educational; (3) animated; (4) documentary Television study — (1) production; (2) educational; (3) management Undergraduate television production — (1) news/documentary; (2) educational Graduate television production — (1) educational; (2) news/documentary
SPECIAL ACTIVITIES/OFFERINGS Film festivals, program material produced for on-campus closed-circuit television and cable television, internships in television production, independent study
FACILITIES AND EQUIPMENT Film — complete 8mm equipment, permanent film library Television — complete black and white studio and exterior production equipment, complete color studio production facilities, black and white studio
FACULTY Roger A Grant, Russell Phillips, Dwan T Wick, Gleen M Wolfe

COURSE LIST

Undergraduate
Television Production Techniques

Graduate
Cinematography
Television Production I, II

Undergraduate and Graduate
Fundamentals of Management of Motion Picture Production
Writing for Visual Media
Seminar in Professional Film Production

University of Wisconsin—Madison

State-supported coed university. Part of University of Wisconsin System. Institutionally accredited by regional association, programs recognized by NASM, AACSB, ACPE. Urban location, 900-acre campus. Total enrollment: 39,430. Undergraduate enrollment: 25,911. Total faculty: 3400 (2300 full-time, 1100 part-time). Semester calendar. Grading system: letters or numbers.

Communication Arts Department, 821 University Avenue, Madison, WI 53705 608-262-2544

CONTACT Film — Russell Merritt Television — Richard Lawson
DEGREES OFFERED BA, MA, MFA, PhD in communication arts
DEPARTMENTAL MAJORS Undergraduate film — 100 students Undergraduate television — 150 students Graduate film — 20 students Graduate television — 30 students
ADMISSION Undergraduate requirement — ACT or SAT scores Graduate requirements — 3.25 minimum grade point average, GRE scores, teachers' recommendations, written statement of purpose, professional recommendations, sample of scholarly writing
FINANCIAL AID Scholarships, work/study programs, student loans, fellowships, teaching assistantships, research assistantships
CURRICULAR EMPHASIS Undergraduate film study — history, criticism and aesthetics, appreciation treated equally Graduate film study — history, criticism and aesthetics, appreciation treated equally Undergraduate filmmaking — documentary, narrative treated equally Graduate filmmaking — documentary, narrative treated equally Undergraduate television study — history, criticism and aesthetics, appreciation, production treated equally Graduate television study — history, criticism and aesthetics, appreciation, production, social and psychological effects treated equally Undergraduate television production — news/documentary, experimental/personal video, dramatic treated equally Graduate television production — news/documentary, experimental/personal video, dramatic treated equally
SPECIAL ACTIVITIES/OFFERINGS Film series, program material produced for local public television station, independent study
FACILITIES AND EQUIPMENT Film — 8mm cameras, editing equipment, sound recording equipment, lighting, black and white film stock, projectors, 16mm cameras, editing equipment, sound recording equipment, lighting, color film stock, projectors, screening room, 35mm screening facilities, editing room, sound mixing room, animation board Television — complete black and white and color studio production equipment, complete black and white and color exterior production equipment, black and white studio, color studio, audio studio, control room
FACULTY Jeanne Allen, Tino Balio, David Bordwell, Joanne Cantor, Richard Lawson, Russell Merritt, J J Murphy
PART-TIME FACULTY Dick Hiner

University of Wisconsin—Madison (continued)

COURSE LIST

Undergraduate

Survey of Radio, Television, Film as Mass Media

Graduate

Theories of Broadcasting
Advanced Television and Film Writing
Telecommunication Regulation and Policy
Comparative and International Systems of Broadcasting
Broadcasting/Film Audiences and Effects
Radio-Television-Film
History of Broadcasting
Criticism in Broadcasting/Film
National Cinemas
Film History
Film Theory

Undergraduate and Graduate

Introduction to Film
History of the Motion Picture
Film Styles and Genres
Motion Picture Production
Film and Broadcasting Documentary
Critical Film Analysis
History of the Motion Picture Industry
History of Broadcasting
Broadcasting Regulation and Responsibility
French Film
Radio-Television-Film and Society
Comparative Systems of Broadcasting
Cable Communications and Society
Elements of Broadcasting
Public Broadcasting Policies and Programming
Special Topics in Broadcasting and Film
Introduction to Television
Television Production and Direction
Television Dramatic Production
Advanced Motion Picture Production
Writing for Television and Film
Mass Entertainment and the Law
Film Theory

University of Wisconsin—Milwaukee

State-supported coed university. Part of University of Wisconsin System. Institutionally accredited by regional association, programs recognized by NASM, AACSB. Urban location, 90-acre campus. Total enrollment: 24,818. Undergraduate enrollment: 20,556. Total faculty: 1688 (829 full-time, 859 part-time). Semester calendar. Grading system: letters or numbers.

BA/BFA in Film, Curtin Hall, 685 and Mitchell Hall B-69, PO Box 413, Milwaukee, WI 53201 414-963-5970 or 414-963-6015

CONTACT Teresa de Lauretis or Richard Blau
DEGREES OFFERED BA in film (College of Letters and Science); BFA in film (School of Fine Arts); graduate option in film
PROGRAM MAJORS Undergraduate film — 40 students Graduate film — 5 students
ADMISSION Undergraduate requirement — Minimum grade point average Undergraduate application deadline — rolling
FINANCIAL AID Work/study programs, student loans, fellowships, teaching assistantships, research assistantships
CURRICULAR EMPHASIS Undergraduate film study — (1) criticism and aesthetics; (2) theory; (3) history Graduate film study — (1) theory; (2) criticism and aesthetics; (3) history Undergraduate filmmaking — documentary, narrative, experimental treated equally
SPECIAL ACTIVITIES/OFFERINGS Filmmaking clubs, film series, film festivals, film societies, student publications, international film conference, independent study, practicum
FACILITIES AND EQUIPMENT Film — complete 8mm production facilities, complete 16mm production facilities, screening room, 35mm screening facilities, editing room, sound mixing room, animation board, free in-house black and white and color processing
FACULTY Diana Barrie, Richard Blau, Joseph Chang, Robert Danielson, Teresa de Lauretis, Douglas Gomery, Patricia Mellencamp, Tanya Modleski, Robert Nelson, Donald Skoller, Robert Yeo PART-TIME FACULTY Stephen Heath

COURSE LIST

Undergraduate

Basic Elements of Filmmaking I, II
Intermediate Filmmaking I, II
Advanced Filmmaking I, II
Film Tech Module
Module: The Non-Moving Image
Problem-Solving Module: Hardware
Film: The Image and the Word
Theory/Practice Seminar
Theory/Practice Workshop
Independent Study
Advanced Independent Study
History of Film I, II: Development of an Art
Introduction to Film
Integrated Film Exploration
Narrative Cinema
Film as Document
The Avant-Garde Film
Literature and Film
Literature and Media
Film as Mass Communication
Italian Cinema

Undergraduate and Graduate

Film Analysis I, II: Method and Theory
Film Directors
Film Styles
Orson Welles and American Cinema, 1940-1970
Film-Fiction Interaction
Film and the Novel
Film and Drama
Semiotics and Cinema
Film Criticism: Rhetorical, Political, and Societal
Film History: Social, Economic, and Cultural
Film Theory: Psychological and Sociological
Documentary Film

University of Wisconsin—Oshkosh

State-supported comprehensive coed institution. Part of University of Wisconsin System. Institutionally accredited by regional association, programs recognized by NASM, AACSB. Suburban location. Total enrollment: 10,000. Undergraduate enrollment: 8500. Total faculty: 675. Semester calendar. Grading system: letters or numbers.

Radio-Television-Film Division, Speech Department, Arts and Communication Center, Oshkosh, WI 54901 414-424-3131

CONTACT Robert L Snyder
DEGREES OFFERED BA in radio-television-film, BS in radio-television-film education
DEPARTMENTAL MAJORS 265 students
ADMISSION Application deadline — rolling

FINANCIAL AID Student loans, work/study programs Application deadline — 3/15, rolling
CURRICULAR EMPHASIS Film study — (1) production; (2) educational media/instructional technology; (3) appreciation Filmmaking — (1) narrative; (2) educational; (3) documentary Television study — (1) production; (2) criticism and aesthetics; (3) educational Television production — (1) news/documentary; (2) commercial; (3) educational
SPECIAL ACTIVITIES/OFFERINGS Film series; film festivals; professional feature production; program material produced for on-campus closed-circuit television, cable television, local public television station, local commercial television station; apprenticeships; internships in film and television production; independent study; practicum; teacher training; vocational placement service; Pare Lorentz Collection of documentaries and film books
FACILITIES AND EQUIPMENT Film — complete 16mm equipment, sound stage, screening room, editing room, animation board, permanent film library Television — complete black and white studio production equipment, complete color studio production equipment, color EFP units, black and white studio, color studio, audio studio, control room
FACULTY Bob Jacobs, Harris Liechti, Robert L Snyder PART-TIME FACULTY John Bredesen, Al Folker, Ron Hutson

COURSE LIST
Undergraduate
Introduction to Radio-Television
Cinema Techniques
Cinema Production
Appreciation of Cinema
History of Documentary
Seminar in Film Directing
Television Production
Television Workshop
Television Lighting
Television Directing
Broadcast News
Broadcast Announcing
Broadcast Management
Station Procedures
Broadcast Law
Radio-Television Continuity I, II
Professional Internship
Television Workshop
Understanding Media
Seminar: Documentary Film
Seminar: Television Criticism

Undergraduate and Graduate
Instructional Television

University of Wisconsin—Parkside

State-supported comprehensive coed institution. Part of University of Wisconsin System. Institutionally accredited by regional association. Suburban location, 700-acre campus. Undergraduate enrollment: 5250. Total faculty: 280 (190 full-time, 90 part-time). Semester calendar. Grading system: letters or numbers.

Communication Discipline, Kenosha, WI 53141 414-553-2331

CONTACT Communication Coordinator
DEGREE OFFERED BA in communication with emphasis in mass communication
ADMISSION Requirement — 2.0 minimum grade point average Application deadline — rolling
FINANCIAL AID Scholarships, work/study programs, student loans
CURRICULAR EMPHASIS Film study — (1) criticism and aesthetics; (2) appreciation; (3) history Filmmaking — (1) documentary; (2) experimental; (3) narrative Television study — (1) mass communication theory; (2) research; (3) criticism and aesthetics Television production — (1) experimental/personal video; (2) news/documentary; (3) organizational media
SPECIAL ACTIVITIES/OFFERINGS Film series, film festivals, program material produced for on-campus closed-circuit television and cable television, internships in television production, independent study
FACILITIES AND EQUIPMENT Film — 8mm cameras, editing equipment, sound recording equipment, lighting, projectors, 16mm cameras, editing equipment, sound recording equipment, lighting, projectors, editing room, sound mixing room, animation board, permanent film library of student films, permanent film library of commercial or professional films Television — color studio cameras, ½-inch VTR, 1-inch VTR, ¾-inch cassette VTR, portable black and white cameras, editing equipment, monitors, special effects generators, slide chain, portable color cameras, ¾-inch portapak recorders, lighting equipment, sound recording equipment, audio mixers, film chain, color studio, audio studio, control room
FACULTY Diana Graettinger, Alan M Rubin PART-TIME FACULTY Ursula Hardt

COURSE LIST
Undergraduate
Basic Filmmaking
Introduction to Film — American
Introduction to Film — Non-American
Studies in Film
Film Directors
Film Genres
Television Production
Writing for Television and Radio
Advanced Television Production
Law and Ethics in the Mass Media
Mass Communication Research
Communication Internship

University of Wisconsin—Platteville

State-supported comprehensive coed institution. Part of University of Wisconsin System. Institutionally accredited by regional association. Small town location, 380-acre campus. Total enrollment: 4800. Undergraduate enrollment: 4393. Total faculty: 238 (238 full-time). Semester calendar. Grading system: letters or numbers.

Department of Communication, 718 Pioneer Tower, Platteville, WI 53818 608-342-1627

CONTACT Film — Virgil Pufahl Television — Virginia Gregg
DEGREES OFFERED BA, BS in radio-television broadcasting
DEPARTMENTAL MAJORS Television — 180 students
FINANCIAL AID Scholarships, work/study programs, student loans
CURRICULAR EMPHASIS Television study — history, criticism and aesthetics, production, management treated equally Television production — commercial, news/documentary, dramatic treated equally
SPECIAL ACTIVITIES/OFFERINGS Program material produced for on-campus closed-circuit television and cable television, internships in television production, independent study
FACILITIES AND EQUIPMENT Film — 8mm cameras, editing equipment, lighting, color film stock, projectors, 16mm cameras, editing equipment, sound recording equipment, lighting, black and white film stock, projectors, editing room Television — black and white studio cameras, color studio cameras, ¾-inch cassette VTR, portable black and white

University of Wisconsin—Platteville (continued)

cameras, editing equipment, monitors, special effects generators, slide chain, portable color cameras, ¾-inch ENG, lighting equipment, sound recording equipment, audio mixers, film chain, time base corrector, color studio, audio studio, control room, editing facility

FACULTY F Gerald Bench, Virginia Gregg, George E Smith, Joseph Thomas PART-TIME FACULTY Glenn Brooks, John O'Neill, Virgil Pufahl, David Westermann

COURSE LIST

Undergraduate

TV Electronic Systems
Introduction to Broadcasting
Applied Communication I, II
Television Production
TV Camera Care and Capabilities
Motion Picture Photography
TV Directing
TV News
TV Drama
Broadcast Advertising and Sales
Practicum
Broadcast Management
Station Planning
Graphic Arts for Television
Electronic Communication Engineering
Required Internship

University of Wisconsin—Stevens Point

State-supported comprehensive coed institution. Part of University of Wisconsin System. Institutionally accredited by regional association. Rural location. Total enrollment: 8993. Undergraduate enrollment: 8404. Total faculty: 550 (450 full-time, 100 part-time). Semester calendar. Grading system: letters or numbers.

Communication Department, Stevens Point, WI 54481 715-346-3409

CONTACT Film — Toby Goldberg Television — Roger Bullis
DEGREES OFFERED BA, BS, MST, MA in communication with emphasis in film or television
ADMISSION Undergraduate application deadline — 9/1, rolling
CURRICULAR EMPHASIS Film study — history, criticism and aesthetics, appreciation, production treated equally Television study — history, criticism and aesthetics, appreciation, production treated equally
SPECIAL ACTIVITIES/OFFERINGS Program material produced for cable television
FACILITIES AND EQUIPMENT Film — complete 8mm and 16mm equipment, editing room Television — complete color studio and exterior production facilities
FACULTY Chip Baker, Roger Bullis, Dennis Corrigan, William C Davidson, Thomas Draper, Toby Goldberg, Elizabeth Kyes, James Moe

COURSE LIST

Undergraduate and Graduate

Introduction to Mass Communication
News and Public Affairs
Popular Arts
Directing High School Mass Communication Activities
Public Relations
Basic Television Production/Direction
Advanced Television Production
Basic Film Production
Advanced Film Production
Film Theory
Film History: Basic and Special
Writing for Television and Film
Public Communication Seminar
Media Law
Introduction to the Motion Picture
Art of Criticism
Television in American Society
Evolution of Mass Media in America

University of Wisconsin—Stout

State-supported comprehensive coed institution. Part of University of Wisconsin System. Institutionally accredited by regional association. Small town location, 120-acre campus. Total enrollment: 7032. Undergraduate enrollment: 6337. Total faculty: 443. Semester calendar. Grading system: letters or numbers.

Media Technology Department, Menomonie, WI 54751 715-232-1202

CONTACT James Daines
PROGRAM OFFERED Major in media technology with emphasis in film or television
ADMISSION Requirement — 2.25 minimum grade point average Application deadline — rolling
FINANCIAL AID Teaching assistantships, research assistantships Application deadline — 4/30
CURRICULAR EMPHASIS Film study — (1) educational media/instructional technology; (2) appreciation Filmmaking — (1) educational; (2) documentary Television study — (1) educational; (2) production Television production — educational
SPECIAL ACTIVITIES/OFFERINGS Film societies, program material produced for on-campus closed-circuit television and local educational television station, internships in television production
FACILITIES AND EQUIPMENT Film — complete 8mm equipment, screening room, sound mixing room, animation board, permanent film library Television — complete color studio and exterior production equipment, audio studio
FACULTY James Daines, John Lauson, Paul Stankovich, Robert Ward

COURSE LIST

Undergraduate and Graduate

Audio/Film/TV Production
Television Production
Motion Picture Production
Film: History and Appreciation
Broadcast Television Internship

University of Wisconsin—Superior

State-supported comprehensive coed institution. Part of University of Wisconsin System. Urban location, 230-acre campus. Total enrollment: 2282. Undergraduate enrollment: 1864. Total faculty: 200. Quarter calendar. Grading system: letters or numbers.

Communicating Arts Department, 1800 Grand Avenue, Superior, WI 54880 715-392-8101

CONTACT William Stock, Chairman
DEGREES OFFERED BA, BS, MA, MS in speech with emphasis in television-film
DEPARTMENTAL MAJORS 75 students
ADMISSION Undergraduate requirement — 2.5 minimum grade point average Graduate requirements — 2.5 minimum grade point average, MAT scores, written statement of purpose Undergraduate application deadline — rolling
CURRICULAR EMPHASIS Undergraduate film study — criticism and aesthetics, production treated equally Graduate film study — (1) appreciation; (2) production; (3) criticism and aesthetics Filmmaking — (1) narrative; (2) documentary; (3) experimental Undergraduate television study — (1) production; (2) criticism and aesthetics Graduate television study — (1) production; (2) management; (3) educational Television production — (1) commercial; (2) news/documentary; (3) educational
SPECIAL ACTIVITIES/OFFERINGS Film festivals; program material produced for on-campus closed-circuit television, cable television, local commercial television station; internships in television production; independent study; practicum; vocational placement service
FACILITIES AND EQUIPMENT Film — complete 8mm and 16mm equipment, screening room, editing room, sound mixing room, animation board, permanent film library Television — complete black and white studio and exterior production facilities, complete color studio production facilities, audio studio, control room
FACULTY Donald Cain, Stephen Erickson, Paul Kending, William Stock

COURSE LIST

Undergraduate
Continuity Writing for the Media
Documentary and Dramatic Writing for the Media
Principles of Television Production
Producing for the Media
World Communication Systems
Audio Production and Sound Systems
Broadcast Programming
Advanced Television Production
Cinematography and Film Techniques
Film Genres
Media, Society, and the Future
Advanced Television Direction
Broadcast Law
Broadcast Announcing
Mass Communication and Society
History of Film as an Art Form
Practicum in Broadcasting
Broadcast Journalism
Criticism of Film and Television
Television Direction
Motion Picture Production
Broadcast Audience Measurement and Analysis
Internship in Mass Communications
Broadcast Station Management

Graduate
Mass Media Seminar
Theory of Mass Communications
Criticism of Mass Communications
World Communications Systems
Design and Production of the Broadcast Commercial

Undergraduate and Graduate
Theory and Criticism of Film Production
Uses of Educational Television
Program Production

Western Wisconsin Technical Institute

District-supported 2-year coed college. Part of Wisconsin Vocational, Technical and Adult Education System. Institutionally accredited by regional association. Urban location, 17-acre campus. Undergraduate enrollment: 3643. Total faculty: 250 (225 full-time, 25 part-time). Quarter calendar. Grading system: letters or numbers.

Graphics Division, Sixth and Vine Streets, La Crosse, WI 54601 608-785-9178

CONTACT Film — Richard Knox Television — Karl Friedline
ADMISSION Application deadline — rolling
CURRICULAR EMPHASIS Film study — (1) production; (2) educational media/instructional technology; (3) criticism and aesthetics Filmmaking — (1) educational; (2) experimental; (3) animated Television study — (1) educational; (2) production; (3) management Television production — (1) educational; (2) news/documentary; (3) experimental/personal video
SPECIAL ACTIVITIES/OFFERINGS Program material produced for on-campus closed-circuit television, cable television, local public television station
FACILITIES AND EQUIPMENT Film — complete 8mm equipment Television — complete black and white studio and exterior production equipment, complete color studio and exterior production equipment, black and white studio, color studio, mobile van/unit, audio studio, control room
PART-TIME FACULTY Karl Friedline, Richard Knox, Henry Michaels

COURSE LIST

Undergraduate
Cinematography
Television Production I, II

The following is a selected list of foreign film and television schools. For complete information about these schools, including information about language requirements for foreign students, please consult Ernest D. Rose, *World Film and Television Study Resources: A Reference Guide to Major Training Centers and Archives* (1978 edition). For information about scholarships and grants for study abroad, please consult pages 297-98 of this volume.

ARGENTINA

Universidad Nacional de la Plata
Departamento de Cinematografía
Escuela Superior de Bellas Artes
Diagonal 78, No 680
La Plata
Argentina

AUSTRALIA

Australian Film and Television School
Box 126 PO
North Ryde, New South Wales 2113
Australia

Canberra College of Advanced Education
PO Box 1
Belconnen ACT 2616
Australia

Flinders University of South Australia
Drama Discipline
Bedford Park (Adelaide), South Australia 5066
Australia

Mitchell College of Advanced Education
Department of Communication
Bathurst, NSW 2795
Australia

Newcastle Technical College
NSW Department of Technical and Further Education
Maitland Road, Tighes Hill
2297 Newcastle, NSW
Australia

Salisbury College of Advanced Education
Department of Drama
Smith Road
Salisbury East, South Australia 5109
Australia

Western Australian Institute of Technology
Hayman Road
South Bentley, Western Australia 6102
Australia

AUSTRIA

Hochschule für Music und Darstellende Kunst
Film and Television Department
Metternichgasse 12
A-1030 Vienna
Austria

BELGIUM

Département de Communication Sociale
Catholic University of Louvain
Place Louis Pasteur, 1
1348 Louvain-La-Neuve
Belgium

Institut des Arts de Diffusion (IAD)
Avenue de Tervueren, 15
1040 Brussels
Belgium

Institut National Supérieur des Arts du Spectacle et Techniques de Diffusion (INSAS)
Rue Thérésienne, 8
1000 Brussels
Belgium

Royal Academy of Fine Arts — Gent
Film Animation Department
2, Academiestraat
B9000 Gent 1
Belgium

BRAZIL

Federacão das Escolas Federais Isoladas do Estado da Guanabara (FEFIEG)
Escola de Teatro
Praia do Flamengo, 132
Rio de Janeiro, 20000 Guanabara
Brazil

CANADA

Algonquin College of Applied Arts and Technology
Film Production Program
281 Echo Drive
Ottawa, Ontario K1S 1N3
Canada

British Columbia Institute of Technology
Broadcast Communications Department
3700 Willingdon Avenue
Burnaby, British Columbia
Canada

College of Jean-de-Brebeuf
Communications Section
3200 Chemin Côte St Catherine
Montreal, Quebec
Canada

Concordia University
Loyola Campus
Department of Communication Studies
7141 Sherbrooke Street W
Montreal, Quebec H4B 1R6
Canada

Concordia University
Visual Arts Division
Cinema Section
1455 de Maisonneuve Boulevard W
Montreal, Quebec H3G 1M8
Canada

Conestoga College of Applied Arts and Technology
Film Production Program
299 Doon Valley Drive
Kitchener, Ontario
Canada

Mohawk College of Applied Arts and Technology
Department of Broadcasting Programs
135 Fennell Avenue, W
Hamilton, Ontario L8N 3T2
Canada

Queen's University
Department of Film Studies
154 Stuart Street
Kingston, Ontario
Canada

Saint Paul University
Institute of Social Communications
223 Main Street
Ottawa, Ontario K1S 1C4
Canada

Sheridan College of Applied Arts and Technology
Media Arts Department
Trafalgar Road
Oakville, Ontario
Canada

Southern Alberta Institute of Technology
Television, Stage and Radio Department
1301 16th Avenue, NW
Calgary, Alberta T2M 0L4
Canada

University of British Columbia
Film and TV Studies Program
Department of Theater
Vancouver 8
British Columbia
Canada

University of Windsor
Department of Communication Studies
Windsor, Ontario N9B 3P4
Canada

York University
Department of Film
Faculty of Fine Arts
Room 226C, Administrative Studies Building
4700 Keele Street
Downsview, Ontario
Canada

CZECHOSLOVAKIA

Academy of Arts (AMU)
Film and Television Faculty (FAMU)
Smetanovo nabrezi 2
Prague 1
Czechoslovakia

DENMARK

Danish Broadcasting Service
Training Department
Personalekurses
TV-Byen, 2860 Soborg
Denmark

EGYPT

Higher Institute of Cinema
Academy of Arts
Madinet El-Fenoun, Giza
Egypt

FINLAND

Taidetfollinen Korreakoulu
Konstindustriella Hogskolan
Kaivokatu 2-4B
00100 Helsinki 10
Finland

FRANCE

Ecole Nationale de Photographie
Cinématographie et Télévision
85, rue de Vaugirard
Paris 75006
France

Institut des Hautes Etudes
Cinématographiques (IDHEC)
Voie des Pilotes
94369, Bry-sur-Marne (Paris)
France

GERMAN DEMOCRATIC REPUBLIC

Hochschule für Film und Fernsehen der
DDR
Karl-Marx-Strasse 33/34
1502 Potsdam-Babelsberg
German Democratic Republic

GERMAN FEDERAL REPUBLIC

Deutsche Film und Fernsehakademie
Pommernalle 1
1 Berlin 19
German Federal Republic

Hochschule für Fernsehen und Film
Ohmstrasse 9-11
Munich 40
German Federal Republic

GREAT BRITAIN

Bristol University
Radio, Film & TV, Drama Department
29 Park Row
Bristol BS1 S1T
Great Britain

London Film School
24 Shelton Street
London WC 2
Great Britain

The National Film School
Beaconsfield Film Studios
Station Road
Beaconsfield, Bucks H P 9 1LG
Great Britain

Newport College of Art and Design
Gwent College of Higher Education
Church Road
Newport, Gwent
Great Britain

Polytechnic of Central London
Film Section
The School of Communication
18-22 Riding House Street
London W1P 7PD
Great Britain

Royal College of Art
School of Film & Television
Queen's Gate
London SW 7
Great Britain

Slade School of Fine Art
Film Department
University College London
20 Flaxman Terrace
London WC 1
Great Britain

GREECE

Superior Professional School of
Cinematography and Television
26 Ioulianou Street
Athens T 104
Greece

HONG KONG

Hong Kong Baptist College
Communication Department
224 Waterloo Road
Kowloon
Hong Kong

HUNGARY

Academy for Dramatic and Film Art
Vas-Utca 2/c
Budapest VIII
Hungary

INDIA

Film and Television Institute of India
Law College Road
Poona 411 004
India

Institute of Film Technology
Madras 600 020
India

St Xavier's College
Xavier Institute of Communications
Mahapalika Marg
Bombay 400 001
India

IRAN

Academy of Dramatic Arts
(Daneshkade Honar-haye Dramatik)
Djaleh Avenue
Teheran
Iran

College of Mass Communication
Avenue Kourosh Kabir
Ketabi Street
PO Box 3352
Teheran
Iran

Television and Film School
National Iranian Radio and Television
Vozara Street, Avenue #1
Teheran
Iran

ISRAEL

Bezalel Academy of Arts and Design
10 Shmuel Hanagia Street
Jerusalem 94592
Israel

The Communications Institute
Hebrew University of Jerusalem
Givat Ram, Jerusalem
Israel

Department of Film and Television
Tel Aviv University
Tel Aviv
Israel

The School of Stage and Cinematic Art
Beit-Zvi
Gurei Yehuda Street
Ramat Gan
Israel

ITALY

Centro Sperimentale di Cinematografia
Via Tuscolana 1524
Rome
Italy

JAPAN

Film Department
Nihon University
College of Arts
2 — 42 Asahigaoka
Nerima-ku, Tokyo
Japan

Kyushu Institute of Design
Department of Visual Communications
Design
226 Shiobaru Minami-ku
Fukuoka 815
Japan

NHK Central Training Institute
Kinuta-Machi
Setagaya-ku
Japan

Tama Art School
(Tama-Geijutsu-Gakuen)
Cinema Department
135 Hisamoto, Takatsu-ku
Kawasaki-shi, Kanagawa-ken
Japan

KOREA

Korea University
Department of Mass Communications
1, Anam-dong
Seoul
Korea

KOREA (continued)

Sogang University
Department of Mass Communication
IPO Box 1142
Seoul
Korea

MALAYSIA

Asian Institute for Broadcasting Development
PO Box 1137, Pantai
Kuala Lumpur
Malaysia

National Broadcasting Training Center
(Pusat Latehan Penyiaran Negara)
Angkasapuri
Kuala Lumpur
Malaysia

MEXICO

Universidad Nacional Autónoma de Mexico
Departamento de Actividades Cinematográficas
Dirección General de Difusión Cultural
Torre de la Rectoría, 10 piso
Mexico City
Mexico

NETHERLANDS

Nederlandse Filmacademie
Overtoom 301
Amsterdam 13
Netherlands

NEW ZEALAND

University of Canterbury
School of Fine Arts
108 Ilam Road
Christchurch 4
New Zealand

PAKISTAN

National Academy for Film, Television, and Radio
288 Street
Ramna 6/3
Islamabad
Pakistan

PHILIPPINES

Film Institute of the Philippines
LVN Pictures Studio
36 P Tuason Street, Cubao
Quezon City
Philippines

The Philippine Women's University
Communication Arts
Taft Avenue
Manila
Philippines

POLAND

The Leon Schiller National School of Film, Television and Theater
U1 Targova 61
Lodz
Poland

ROMANIA

I L Caragiale Institute of Theater and Cinema (IATC)
Boulevard Dul Schitu Magureanu 1
Bucharest
Romania

SOUTH AFRICA

Rand Afrikaans University
Department of Communications
PO Box 524, Johannesburg
South Africa

Rhodes University
Department of Speech and Drama
PO Box 94, Grahamstown
South Africa

SOVIET UNION

All Union State Institute of Cinematography (VGIK)
Tretij Selskokhozajstvenni Proezd, No 3
Moscow
USSR

SPAIN

The Official School of Cinematography
Carretera de la Dehesa de la Villa
Madrid 20
Spain

SWEDEN

Dramatiska Institutet
Filmhuset
Box 27 090
10251 Stockholm 27
Sweden

Stockholms Universitet
Institutionen för Teater- och Filmvetenskap
Filmhuset
Box 27 062
102 51 Stockholm 27
Sweden

TAIWAN

Department of Cinema and Drama
National Taiwan Academy of Arts
Pan-Chiao Park
Tiepei-Hsian
Taiwan 220

URUGUAY

Escuela de Cinematografía
Avenida 18 de Julio 1235, 2do piso
Montevideo
Uruguay

YUGOSLAVIA

Academy of Theater, Film, Radio, and Television
Hosiminova 20
11,000 Belgrade
Yugoslavia

GRANTS AND SCHOLARSHIPS FOR STUDENTS

The following information was excerpted from *Factfile #12: Film/Television: Grants, Scholarships, Special Programs.* Please consult *Factfile #12** for information on grants for production as well as research grants.

Academy Foundation
Academy of Motion Picture Arts and Sciences
8949 Wilshire Boulevard
Beverly Hills, CA 90211
213-278-8990
Kathy D Arandjelovich, Program Administrator
Sponsors student film awards; scholarships at various institutions (Center for Advanced Film Studies, New York University), and grants and scholarships to individuals

Association for Educational Communications and Technology
1126 16th Street NW
Washington, DC 20036
202-833-4180
Memorial scholarships for graduate students; convention internships and leadership fellowships

Directors Guild Benevolent and Educational Foundation College Scholarships
7950 Sunset Boulevard
Hollywood, CA 90046
213-656-1220
Assistance available for the completion of a film project undertaken while student is enrolled in college

IFPA Film and Video Communications Scholarships
Information Film Producers of America
3518 Cahuenga Boulevard West, Suite 313
Hollywood, CA 90068
213-874-2266
Scholarships for college training and grants for completion of film/video/slide project

International Association of Independent Producers
767 National Press Building
Washington, DC 20045
202-638-5568
Scholarships for technical media personnel and talent

Julia Kiene Fellowships
Electrical Women's Round Table
162 Stanley
Columbia, MO 65201
Graduate fellowships in television, broadcast journalism, or education

National Association of Broadcasters
Broadcast Education Association
217 Flint Hall
University of Kansas
Lawrence, KS 66045
913-864-3991
Dr Bruce A Linton
Harol E Fellows Memorial Scholarships for advanced undergraduate or graduate study at BEA member university or college

The Poynter Fund
Personnel Department
Times Publishing Company
PO Box 1121
St Petersburg, FL 33731
Scholarships for training in media journalism; fellowships for graduate study or travel abroad which will further a broadcasting career

RCA Corporation
Education Aid Committee
Cherry Hill, NJ 08101
609-779-6604
T Todd Reboul
Undergraduate scholarships for broadcast journalism, telecommunications and urban affairs; graduate fellowships

The Scripps-Howard Foundation
200 Park Avenue
New York, NY 10017
212-867-5000
Scholarships for preparation for a career in journalism and broadcast media

**Factfile #12* is available from the American Film Institute, The John F Kennedy Center for the Performing Arts, Washington, DC 20566.

SMPTE Scholarships and Grants
Society of Motion Picture and Television Engineers
862 Scarsdale Avenue
Scarsdale, NY 10583
914-472-6606

Scholarships/grants for tuition, fees and/or living expenses, or as grants-in-aid for research on the graduate level; undergraduate scholarships for study of science/technology of motion pictures and television

UFA Scholarship Awards Program
University of Texas at Austin
Department of Radio-Television-Film
School of Communication, CMA 6.118
Austin, TX 78712
512-471-4071

Robert E Davis
Scholarships for study of film and video production and closely related fields

BIBLIOGRAPHY

Dowley, Jennifer. *Money Business: Grants and Awards for Creative Artists.* Boston: The Artists Foundation, Inc., 1979. (Order from: ACA, 570 Seventh Avenue, New York, NY 10018 — $7.00.)

Listings of scholarships available to artists, including film and video makers

Feingold, S. Norman and Marie. *Scholarships, Fellowships and Loans,* vols. V and VI. Arlington, MA: Bellman Publishing Co., 1977. ($45/volume.)

Lists a wide range of scholarships, fellowships, loans, grants, and awards not controlled by colleges or universities

Gadney, Allen. *Gadney's Guide to 1800 International Contests, Festivals and Grants.* Glendale, CA: Festival Publications, 1978. (PO Box 10180, Glendale, CA 91209 — $15.95.)

Includes grants and scholarships for artists; excellent listing of film festivals

Keeslar, Oreon. *Financial Aids for Higher Education 1978-79 Catalog.* 8th ed. Dubuque: William C. Brown Company, 1977. (2460 Kerper Boulevard, Dubuque, IA 52001 — $16.95.)

Lists over 3,000 programs intended specifically for college freshmen

Millsaps, Daniel. *National Directory of Grants and Aid to Individuals in the Arts, 4th ed.* Washington: Washington International Arts Letter, 1980. (PO Box 9005, Washington, DC 20003 — $15.95.)

Contains information on grants, prizes, and awards for artists in the United States and abroad; most of the directory comprises listings of scholarships and aid from colleges and universities

Penny, Steve. *How to Get Grants to Make Films.* Santa Barbara: Film Grants Research. (PO Box 1138, Santa Barbara, CA 93102 — $15.00.)

Excellent listing of foundations and other agencies which give grants to individuals; section of scholarships

Searles, Aysel Jr., and Anne Scott, eds. *Guide to Financial Aids for Students in Arts and Sciences for Graduate and Professional Study.* 2d ed. New York: Arco Press, 1974. (219 Park Avenue South, New York, NY 10003 — $3.95.)

A variety of funding sources for juniors, seniors, and graduate students is listed

STUDY ABROAD

The following organizations can supply information on study abroad for American students as well as information for foreign students who wish to study in the United States:

The Council on International Educational Exchange
777 United Nations Plaza
New York, NY 10017
Publishes pamphlets on education and funding for foreign students

Institute of International Education
809 United Nations Plaza
New York, NY 10017
Administers grants for foreign study; publishes a number of pamphlets of interest to students who wish to obtain grants or study in a foreign country.

BIBLIOGRAPHY

Entering Higher Education in the United States, and *Financial Planning for Study in the United States* are available from: College Entrance Examination Board, Publications Order Office, Box 592, Princeton, NJ 08541

Information About Study Opportunities in the United States for Students from Abroad is available from the Department of Education, Washington, DC 20202 (free)

List of Organizations That Accept Applications for Financial Support from Foreign Students Already in the United States. (Cornell University International Student Office, Ithaca NY, 14853 — $1.)

Study Abroad, vol. 23, 1979-80, 1980-81. Paris, France: UNESCO. (Order from: UNIPUB, 345 Park Avenue South, New York, NY 10010 — $9.95.)

STUDENT FILM/VIDEO FESTIVALS AND AWARDS

Film and video festivals offer an excellent opportunity for students to gain public exposure and possible recognition for their work. The following is a listing of film and video festivals which are intended for students, or which have a special student category for judging. Please consult AFI's *Factfile #3: Film and Video Festivals** for information on all the major film festivals in the United States, including many independent festivals that accept student-produced work. Specific dates, application forms, and further information should be requested by writing directly to the address indicated.

ACADEMY OF MOTION PICTURE ARTS AND SCIENCES AND ACADEMY FOUNDATION
STUDENT FILM AWARDS, AMPAS
8949 Wilshire Boulevard
Beverly Hills, CA 90211
213-278-8990
Contact: Karen Arandjelovich Month held: June Deadline: April 1 Fees: None Gauge of film/tape: 8mm (regional judging only), 16mm, 35mm; tape: (regional competition only) Length: No restriction

ACE STUDENT EDITING
American Cinema Editors Competition
422 S Western Avenue
Los Angeles, CA 90020
213-386-1946
Month held: March Deadline: October Fees: Vary Gauge of film/tape: Students edit a segment from professionally made film Length: Do not submit a film

AECT NATIONAL STUDENT FILM FESTIVAL AND MEDIA SHOWCASE
(Association for Educational Communications and Technology)
Instructional Resource Center
Central Washington University
Ellensburg, WA 98926
509-963-1842
Contact: Dr William Schmidt, Showcase Director Month held: Varies with annual convention Deadline: Varies Fees: None Gauge of film/tape: Super-8mm, 1/2-inch reel to reel, 3/4-inch cassette Length: 10 minutes maximum

ASIFA EAST ANIMATED FILM AWARDS (International Animated Film Association)
c/o The Optical House
25 West 45 Street
New York, NY 10036
212-288-4165
Month held: January Deadline: January Fees: $5-$40 Gauge of film/tape: 16mm Length: No restriction

BIG MUDDY FILM FESTIVAL
Department of Cinema and Photography
Southern Illinois University
Carbondale, IL 62901
618-453-2365
Contact: Linda Balek Month held: Varies Deadline: Varies Fees: $7/under 20 min, $12/over 20 min Gauge of film/tape: 16mm optical track Length: No restriction

CALIFORNIA STUDENT MEDIA FESTIVAL
California Media & Library Educators Associations/California
Audiovisual Education Distributors Association
Department of Education, San Diego County
6401 Linda Vista Boulevard
San Diego, CA 92111
714-292-3705
Contact: Martin Taylor Month held: June Deadline: April Fees: None Gauge of film/tape: Super-8mm, 1/2-inch reel to reel, 3/4-inch cassette Length: 10 min maximum

CINE AWARDS CEREMONY AND FILM SHOWCASE
Council on International Nontheatrical Events
1201 16th Street NW
Washington, DC 20036
202-785-1136
Contact: Shreeniwas Tamhane Month held: November Deadline: February and August Fees: $15-$60 Gauge of film/tape: 16mm, 35mm, Super-8mm, 3/4-inch—redubbed Length: No restriction

**Factfile #3* is available from the American Film Institute, The John F Kennedy Center for the Performing Arts, Washington, DC 20566.

CONNECTICUT FILM FESTIVAL
Connecticut State Library
231 Capitol Avenue
Hartford, CT 06115
203-243-4536
Contact: Connie McCarthy Month held: March Deadline: January 25 Fees: $10 Gauge of film/tape: 16mm Length: 60 min

FILMSOUTH FILM COMPETITION AND CONFERENCE
Center for the Humanities
Converse College
Spartanburg, SC 29301
803-585-6421
Contact: Alfred Schmitz Month held: Late January, early February Deadline: January (10-15) Fees: $2-$4 Gauge of film/tape: Super-8mm, 16mm Length: 30 min maximum

HUMBOLDT FILM FESTIVAL
Theatre Arts Department
Humboldt State University
Arcata, CA 95521
707-826-3566
Contact: Phil Middlemiss or Mike Elliot Month held: April Deadline: March Fees: $13 (indep); $20 (distr) Gauge of film/tape: 16mm Length: 60 min or less

ITVA STUDENT AWARD COMPETITION
International Television Association
26 South Street
New Providence, NJ 07974
201-464-6747
Contact: Bobette Kandle Month held: April (with ITVA International Conference) Deadline: March 1 Fees: None Gauge of film/tape: U-matric cassette Length: Less than 20 min

KENYON FILM FESTIVAL
Kenyon College
Box 17
Gambier, OH 43022
614-427-2244 ext 2502
Contact: Charles Worthen Month held: April Deadline: April Fees: $5 + postage Gauge of film/tape: 16mm Length: One reel

MAINE STUDENT FILM FESTIVAL
Maine Alliance of Media Arts (formerly M Film Alliance)
4320 Station A
Portland, ME 04101
207-773-1130
Contact: "Huey" James T Coleman Month held: May Deadline: May Fees: None Gauge of film/tape: 8mm, Super-8mm, 16mm Length: 30 min

MARIN COUNTY NATIONAL FILM COMPETITION
Marin Center Fairgrounds
San Rafael, CA 94903
415-472-2406
Contact: Yolanda F Sullivan Month held: June-July Deadline: May (30) Fees: $10/film Gauge of film/tape: 16mm Length: 30 min maximum

NATIONAL EDUCATIONAL FILM FESTIVAL
5555 Ascot Drive
Oakland, CA 94611
415-531-0626
Contact: R Spencer Allen and Barbara Allen Month held: May Deadline: March Fees: $40-$100 Student $1-$15 Gauge of film/tape: 8mm, 16mm, 35mm (feature) Length: No restriction

NATIONAL FILM AND VIDEO COMPETITION
National Trust for Historic Preservation
740-748 Jackson Place NW
Washington, DC 20006
202-673-4038
Contact: Nancy Melin Month held: October Deadline: August Fees: None Gauge of film/tape: 16mm, 3/4-inch cassette Length: Under 30 min preferred

NEW ENGLAND STUDENT FILM FESTIVAL
University Film Study Center
Box 275
Cambridge, MA 02138
617-253-7612
Contact: Jan Crocker Month held: April Deadline: March 24 Fees: None Gauge of film/tape: Regional Super-8mm, 8mm, 16mm, 35mm, optical/magnetic, must be transferred if in finals Length: No restriction

NEW RIVER MIXED MEDIA GATHERING
Educational Media Department
Appalachian State University
Boone, NC 28608
704-262-2243
Contact: Joseph R Murphy Month held: October (15-16) Deadline: September (30) Fees: $5 Gauge of film/tape: Super-8mm Length: Less than 60 min

NORTH CAROLINA FILM FESTIVAL
North Carolina Museum of Art
Raleigh, NC 27611
919-733-7568
Contact: Lorraine Laslett Month held: April 3-4, 1981, biennial Deadline: March Fees: $5/film Gauge of film/tape: Super-8mm, 16mm Length: None

PSA-MPD TEENAGE FILM FESTIVAL
Photographic Society of America
516 West 88th Street
Oaklawn, IL 60433
Contact: Peter B Crombie Month held: August Deadline: May Fees: $3/film Gauge of film/tape: 8mm, Super-8mm, 16mm sound/silent Length: 30 min maximum

REFOCUS INTERNATIONAL SPRING/NATIONAL FALL FESTIVAL
Refocus
University of Iowa
Iowa Memorial Union
Iowa City, IA 52242
319-353-5090
Contact: Greg Schmidt Month held: Varies, spring and fall Deadline: One month prior to festival Fees: $5/entry Gauge of film/tape: 16mm, 1/2-inch reel to reel or 3/4-inch cassette Length: No restriction

SINKING CREEK FILM CELEBRATION
Creekside Farm
Route 8
Greenville, TN 37743
615-638-6524
Contact: Mary Jane Coleman Month held: June Deadline: May (receiving dates April 3–May 3) Fees: None Gauge of film/tape: 16mm Length: 30 min maximum

SUPER-8 THING AT BAYLOR
Baylor School
PO Box 1337
Chattanooga, TN 37401
615-756-5621
Contact: Dr John R Miller Month held: March Deadline: February Fees: None Gauge of film/tape: Super-8mm Length: 20 min maximum

TWO-YEAR COLLEGE FILM FESTIVAL
Mount Wachusett Community College
Gardner, MA 01440
617-632-6600
Contact: Vincent Ialenti Month held: May Deadline: May Fees: $1 Gauge of film/tape: Super-8mm, 16mm, 1/2-inch videotape, 3/4-inch videocassette Length: No restriction

WASHINGTON STATE STUDENT MEDIA FESTIVAL
Washington Library Media Association
c/o Instructional Media Center
Central Washington University
Ellensburg, WA 98926
509-963-1812
Contact: Dr William D Schmidt Sponsor: Washington Association for Educational Communications and Technology Month held: February Deadline: January Fees: None Gauge of film/tape: Super-8mm, 1/2-inch reel to reel, 3/4-inch cassette Length: Less than 10 min

YOUNG PEOPLE'S FILM AND VIDEO FESTIVAL
Northwest Film Study Center (Oregon Educational Media Association, Oregon Educational and Public Broadcasting Service)
Portland Art Museum
1219 SW Park Avenue
Portland, OR 97205
503-226-2811
Contact: Bill Foster Month held: March Deadline: February Fees: None Gauge of film/tape: Super-8mm, 16mm, 1/2-inch videotape, 3/4-inch videocassette Length: No restriction (prefer short films)

SELECTED LIST OF FILM AND VIDEO CENTERS

The following organizations represent a selection of local and regional media centers across the United States that offer film and/or video facilities to the public.

ALABAMA

Alabama Filmmakers Co-op
4333 Chickasaw Drive
Huntsville, AL 35801
205-534-3247
Film center with open access to the public. Super-8 and 16mm production, and Super-8 postproduction facilities. Also provides workshops and screenings and runs an intern and apprentice program. Film and tape collection.

CALIFORNIA

Bay Area Video Coalition
2940 16th Street
Room 200
San Francisco, CA 94103
415-861-3282
Regional resource center serving Bay area with 3/4-inch video production and postproduction equipment. Provides newsletter of video information, resource library, and assistance programs for artists and producers; runs workshops.

Long Beach Museum of Art
2300 East Ocean Boulevard
Long Beach, CA 90803
213-439-0751
Media arts center with access to 1/2-inch and 3/4-inch video editing equipment. Video workshops in production and postproduction. Provides exhibition outlet for video artists. Production studio under construction. Publishes quarterly catalog.

Video Free America
442 Shotwell Street
San Francisco, CA 94110
415-648-9040
Screenings, workshops, production and postproduction video equipment. Exhibition program for independent artists.

COLORADO

Grassroots Television Network
PO Box 2006
Aspen, CO 81611
303-925-7784
Community cable TV center with access to video equipment for qualified independents. Intern and apprentice programs, workshops, and film/tape collection. Produces own TV news, dramatic and documentary shows.

Rocky Mountain Film Center
102 Hunter Building
University of Colorado
Boulder, CO 80309
303-492-7903
Community film resource center for mountain/plains region. Production and postproduction Super-8, 16mm equipment. Exhibition outlet, film series, and regular workshops. Film library.

Western States Film Institute
1629 York Street
Denver, CO 80206
303-320-0457
Community film resource center with 16mm production and postproduction equipment. Apprentice program, occasional workshops, and seminars.

DISTRICT OF COLUMBIA

Fondo del Sol/Visual Art & Media Center
2112 R Street NW
Washington, DC 20008
202-265-9235
Super-8 and 3/4-inch video production facility serving minority communities with access, exhibition, and workshops and lectures. Film editing facility, film/tape collection.

Washington Area Filmmakers League
PO Box 6475
Washington, DC 20009
202-678-3636
Provides access to film production and postproduction equipment and workshops for area filmmakers. Local publications.

GEORGIA

Atlanta Public Library
Department of Film or Department of Video
1 Margaret Mitchell Square
Atlanta, GA 30303
404-688-4636
One-half-inch and 3/4-inch video production and postproduction facilities. Film distribution service. Open access, with screenings and workshops. Occasional intern program. Film/tape collection.

Independent Media Artists of Georgia, Etcetera
(IMAGE)
972 Peachtree Street
Atlanta, GA 30303
404-874-4756
Film resource center, with Super-8 and 16mm postproduction facilities for independent filmmakers. Occasional workshops and lectures, regular screenings. Monthly newsletter.

ILLINOIS

Chicago Filmmakers
6 West Hubbard
Chicago, IL 60610
312-329-0854
Independent filmmakers' 16mm postproduction facility. Regular screenings and lectures. Provides grants for filmmakers. Local publications.

Community Film Workshop
441 North Clark
Chicago, IL 60610
312-527-4064
Media training center—16mm film and video production and postproduction. Regular screenings, workshops, and lectures. Intern and apprentice program. Sound stage, recording and production studios.

INDIANA

Video Action Center (VAC-7)
PO Box 146/618 Franklin Street
Columbus, IN 47201
812-376-9931
Community video production and postproduction facility with studio providing local programming for public access cable TV workshops and production programs.

KENTUCKY

Appalshop
Box 743
Whitesburg, KY 41858
606-633-5708
Media arts center for Appalachian region. Sixteen-mm production and postproduction equipment access. Regular screenings, workshops, and visiting artists series. Filmmakers-in-residence and apprentice programs. Exhibition and distribution resources. Emphasis on regional filmmaking.

MASSACHUSETTS

Boston Film/Video Foundation
39 Brighton Avenue
Allston, MA 02134
617-254-1616

Film and video access, exhibition, and training facility serving independent media artists; operates joint equipment access program with WGBH, Boston. Regular workshops and seminars. Bimonthly newsletter.

MINNESOTA

Film in the Cities
2388 University Avenue
St Paul, MN 55114
612-646-6104

Film access, training, exhibition, and resource center. Production, studio, and postproduction facilities plus animation and optical printing. Screenings and workshops, apprentice and intern programs.

University Community Video
425 Ontario SE
Minneapolis, MN 55414
612-376-3333

Video training and equipment access, production and postproduction in 1/2-inch and 3/4-inch formats. Regular screenings and workshops. Intership program, videotape library, publications, documentary production program.

MISSOURI

Double Helix
3226 Olive
St Louis, MO 63103
314-534-9117

Video access, training, and production facility, 1/2-inch and 3/4-inch formats. Regular workshops and tape screenings. Bimonthly newsletter.

NEW YORK

Experimental Television Center, Ltd
180 Front Street
Owego, NY 13827
607-687-1423

Video production and research facility; emphasis on electronic image processing. Three-quarter-inch production and postproduction facilities. Regular screenings and workshops. Intern program. Tape library.

Global Village Video Resource Center, Inc
454 Broome Street
New York, NY 10013
212-966-7526

Access, training, and production facility. One-half-inch and 3/4-inch production and postproduction equipment. Regular screenings, seminars, annual video documentary festival, scholarship program. Tape library. Newsletter.

The Kitchen Center for Video and Music
59 Wooster Street
New York, NY 10012
212-925-3615

Contemporary arts center specializing in video and music. Viewing room, tape collection, with emphasis on video as art form.

Media Study/Buffalo
207 Delaware Ave
Buffalo, NY 14202
716-847-2555

Regional film and video center. Production and postproduction facilities in Super-8, 16mm, 1/2-inch and 3/4-inch tape formats. Regular workshops, lectures, seminars, and summer school. Intern program. Screenings and exhibition outlets. Produces public TV series in conjunction with WNED. Film and tape collection, monthly newsletter.

Millennium Film Workshop, Inc
66 East 4th Street
New York, NY 10003
212-673-0090

Film resource center—production and postproduction equipment in Super-8 and 16mm, with emphasis on documentary and experimental films. Regular workshops, screenings. Triannual journal and quarterly newsletter.

Portable Channel, Inc
1255 University Avenue
Rochester, NY 14607
716-244-1259

Community video production facility, regular film and video screenings, workshops, and seminars. Film/tape collection, intern and apprentice programs. Emphasis on documentary. Produces tapes for public TV and public access cable.

Soho Media Co-op
154 Spring Street
New York, NY 10012
212-925-9629
Film and video production and postproduction equipment. Intern program. Film and tape library, occasional screenings. Emphasis on film and video art.

Young Filmmakers Foundation, Inc
Young Filmmakers/Video Arts
4 Rivington Street
New York, NY 10002
212-673-9361
Film and video production and postproduction facilities in Super-8, 16mm, 1/2-inch and 3/4-inch formats. Regular workshops in Spanish and English, on-site capability. Intern program. Regular screenings.

OHIO

Contemporary Media Study Center
Midcity Box 651 (136 South Ludlow Street)
Dayton, OH 45402
513-222-7480 or 513-461-2412
Multidisciplinary arts center—film and sound production and postproduction facilities. Regular screenings, workshops, and lectures. Newsletter.

OREGON

Northwest Film Study Center
1219 Southwest Park Avenue
Portland, OR 97205
503-221-1156
Film and video production and postproduction center. Workshops in film/tape production, education program. Quarterly publication. Regular screenings and film festival. Intern program. Exhibition and distribution outlet.

The Video Access Project
117 Northwest 5th Avenue
Room 215
Portland, OR 97209
503-223-3419
Regional video production, postproduction, and exhibition center, 1/2-inch and 3/4-inch format. Regular workshops and screenings, visiting artists' program. Intern program, tape library, with emphasis on feminist films.

PENNSYLVANIA

Ohio Valley Regional Arts Coalition
Film Section, Museum of Art
Carnegie Institute
4400 Forbes Avenue
Pittsburgh, PA 15213
412-622-3213
Regional film and video resource center with emphasis on noncommercial production, preservation, exhibition, and distribution.

Pittsburgh Film-makers, Inc
PO Box 7200
Pittsburgh, PA 15213
412-681-5449
Media arts center for film, photography, and video. Super-8 and 16mm production and postproduction equipment. Regular screenings and workshops, visiting artist series. Monthly newsletter and semiannual journal. Film library.

RHODE ISLAND

Electron Movers, Research in Electronic Arts
228 Weybosset Street
Providence, RI 02903
401-272-4305
Community video resource center, 1/2-inch and 3/4-inch production and postproduction equipment. Emphasis on video art. Regular screenings, workshops, and lectures. High school apprentice program. Tape collection.

SOUTH CAROLINA

South Carolina Arts Commission
1800 Gervais Street
Columbia, SC 29201
803-758-7942

Regional film development program, sponsors equipment access—Super-8 and 16mm production and postproduction—exhibition program. On-site workshops. Annual independent filmmakers conference. Grants program. Documentary/experimental emphasis.

TENNESSEE

Center for Southern Folklore
PO Box 40105 (1216 Peabody Avenue)
Memphis, TN 38104
901-726-4205

Multimedia resource center producing films and tapes with regional emphasis. Film and tape production and postproduction equipment—emphasis on documentary. Intern and apprentice programs. Newsletters and catalogs.

Knoxville Urban Ministry
1538 Highland Avenue
Knoxville, TN 37916
615-522-5851

Jubilee Community Video Center, sponsored by Knoxville Urban Ministry: 16mm and 1/2-inch production and postproduction equipment access. Documentary emphasis. Regular workshops. Produces own cable TV programs.

TEXAS

Austin Community Television
4107 Peck
Austin, TX 78571
512-453-8600

Community video production and postproduction facility with local programming for public access cable. Regular workshops. Intern program. Monthly publication.

Southwest Alternate Media Project
1506 1/2 Branard Street
Houston, TX 77006
713-522-8592

Community media arts center, production and postproduction film and tape equipment. Regular screenings and workshops in conjunction with Rice University Media Center. Film and tape collection. Fundraising, exhibition and distribution channels.

NATIONAL AND INTERNATIONAL ORGANIZATIONS

The following is a list of national and international organizations that should be of interest to students, faculty, and departments of film and television.

American Association of Schools of Film and Television

Membership available to schools and departments of film and television. At this writing, membership criteria have not been finally established. Biannual meetings devoted to information sharing and the development of standards for film and television education.

Inquiries should be directed to:

J Michael Miller, Robert E Davis, and E Russell McGregor, Executive Committee
American Association of Schools of Film and Television
School of the Arts
111 Second Avenue
New York, NY 10003
212-598-7678

American Culture Association

Individual, student, and institutional memberships that include subscription to *Journal of American Culture.* Annual conference that meets jointly with Popular Culture Association and includes sessions devoted to film and television. Regional meetings.

Inquiries should be directed to:

Pat Browne
American Culture Association
Center for Popular Culture
Bowling Green State University
Bowling Green, OH 43403
419-372-2981

American Studies Association

Individual memberships are offered on a sliding rate scale, as are institutional memberships. Both include subscriptions to *American Quarterly* and *ASA Newsletter.* Biennial convention that includes sessions devoted to film and television. Placement service.

Inquiries should be directed to:

American Studies Association
4025 Chestnut Street
Philadelphia, PA 19104
215-243-5408

Association for Educational Communications and Technology

Individual, student, and institutional memberships available that include subscriptions to *Instructional Innovator* and newsletter (*Ect.*). Reduced rates available to members for *Educational Communications and Technology Journal* and *Journal of Instructional Development.* Annual conference that includes sessions devoted to the use of film and television in education. Other irregular conferences. Placement service available at additional charge.

Inquiries should be directed to:

Association for Educational Communications and Technology
1126 16th Street NW
Washington, DC 20036
202-833-4180

Association for Education in Journalism, Radio-TV Division

Individual and student memberships that include *Journalism Quarterly, Journalism Monographs,* and *AEJ Newsletter.* Annual conference during which the Radio-TV Division schedules sessions. Placement service at extra charge.

Inquiries should be directed to:

Association for Education in Journalism
University of Southern California
University Park
Los Angeles, CA 90007

Broadcast Education Association

Individual and institutional memberships available that include *Journal of Broadcasting* and newsletter (*Feedback*). Student discount rate available for *Journal of Broadcasting.* Annual conference. (Students from schools that are institutional members may attend at a discount rate.) Occasional seminars.

Inquiries should be directed to:

Broadcast Education Association
1771 N Street NW
Washington, DC 20036
202-293-3510

Centre International de Liaison des Ecoles de Cinéma et de Télévision (CILECT)

An international organization with membership open to major schools of film and television. Occasional publications. Biennial conference featuring sessions devoted to the teaching of professional film and television production.

Inquiries should be directed to:

Raymond Ravar
Centre International de Liaison des Ecoles de Cinéma et de Télévision
Rue Thérésienne, 8
1000 Bruxelles, Belgium

College Art Association

Individual, student, and institutional memberships that include subscriptions to *Art Journal, Art Bulletin,* and *CAA Newsletter*. Annual conference that includes some sessions devoted to film and video. Placement service.

Inquiries should be directed to:

College Art Association
16 East 52d Street
New York, NY 10022
212-755-3532

Educational Film Library Association

Individual and institutional memberships including subscription to *Sightlines* and newsletter (*The EFLA Bulletin*). Many other publications offered to members at a discount rate. Members given preference on phone inquiries to EFLA Information Service. EFLA sponsors the American Film Festival and workshops.

Inquiries should be directed to:

Educational Film Library Association
43 West 61st Street
New York, NY 10023
212-246-4533

Historians' Film Committee, an affiliate society of the American Historical Association

Individual and institutional memberships that include subscriptions to *Film & History*. The annual conference of the American Historical Association includes sessions sponsored by the Historians' Film Committee.

Inquiries should be directed to:

Historians' Film Committee
c/o The History Faculty
New Jersey Institute of Technology
Newark, NJ 07102
201-748-9499
212-929-1495

International Communication Association, Mass Communication Division

Individual, student, and institutional memberships available that include subscriptions to *Journal of Communication, Human Communication Research,* and the *ICA Newsletter*. Annual conference that includes some sessions devoted to television. Workshops.

Inquiries should be directed to:

International Communication Association
Balcones Research Center
10100 Burnet Road
Austin, TX 78758
512-835-3061

International Visual Literacy Association

Individual and student memberships available that include *IVLA Newsletter* and discounts on "Provocative Papers" and other publications available from the Center for Visual Literacy. Annual conference that includes some sessions about aspects of film and television.

Inquiries should be directed to:

Dennis Pett, Executive Secretary
International Visual Literacy Association
Audiovisual Center
Indiana University
Bloomington, IN 47401
812-337-1362

Modern Language Association, Film Division

Individual and student memberships available that include subscription to *PMLA*, one of the three volumes of annual bibliography, and *MLA Newsletter*. Annual conference that includes sessions devoted to film and literature topics. Irregular seminars. Regional meetings. Placement service at additional charge.

Inquiries should be directed to:

Modern Language Association
62 Fifth Avenue
New York, NY 10011
212-741-7877

National Council of Teachers of English, Commission on Media

Individual, student, and institutional memberships available that include one of the following: *Language Arts, English Journal, College English*. Annual conference during which the Commission on Media sponsors sessions concerned with the teaching of film and television. NCTE constituent organizations hold additional conferences. Placement service.

Inquiries should be directed to:

National Council of Teachers of English
1111 Kenyon Road
Urbana, IL 61801
217-328-3870

Popular Culture Association

Individual, student, and institutional memberships available that include subscription to *Journal of Popular Culture* and *Popular Culture Association Newsletter*. Annual conference that includes many sessions on film and television. Regional meetings.

Inquiries should be directed to:

Pat Browne
Popular Culture Association
Center for Popular Culture
Bowling Green State University
Bowling Green, OH 43403
419-372-2981

Society for Cinema Studies

Individual and student memberships that include *Cinema Journal* and newsletter (*The Moving Image*). Annual conference devoted to cinema studies topics.

Inquiries should be directed to:

Society for Cinema Studies
Dan Leab, Secretary-Treasurer
121 East 78th Street
New York, NY 10021

Speech Communication Association, Mass Communication Division

Individual, student, and departmental memberships that include one or more of the following journals (depending upon rate paid): *Quarterly Journal of Speech, Communication Monographs*, and newsletter (*Spectra*). Annual conference during which the Mass Communication Division sponsors sessions. Other irregular conferences. Placement service at additional charge.

Inquiries should be directed to:

Speech Communication Association
5205 Leesburg Pike
Falls Church, VA 22041
703-379-1888

University Film Association

Individual, student, and institutional memberships that include *Journal of the University Film Association* and newsletter (*UFA Digest*). Annual conference devoted to film teaching, film production, and film studies topics. Irregular regional meetings. Placement service.

Inquiries should be directed to:

University Film Association
Charles H Harpole, Membership Chairperson
Department of Cinema and Photography
Southern Illinois University
Carbondale, IL 62901
618-453-2365

This section contains information on a variety of resources helpful to anyone pursuing a vocation in film or television. The guilds, craft unions, and professional organizations listed are all potential sources of valuable information.

While a phone call or letter to the Writers Guild, for instance, will not necessarily result in a list of job openings, it will lead to information on the central importance of the guild in the writing profession. Quite often, membership in a guild or union is a requirement for obtaining work in the theatrical film industry.

Training for a career in film or television is accomplished in a variety of ways. In some cases growing up within or around the industry is the path to a career. Formal education in the various areas of the motion picture arts—from acting to directing to writing to technical support—is available throughout the country at the many colleges and universities listed in this Guide.

Another area of training that bridges the gap between formal education and work experience is represented by the various apprenticeship and internship programs. Local television stations and small film companies as well as major networks and studios frequently offer internship or apprenticeship experience for individuals pursuing a career in the field. The value of such experience is that it allows the individual to gain actual work credits while still in a learning situation. The competitive nature of today's job market tends to require demonstration of actual work experience. Completed films, festival awards, and special recommendations provide additional testimony to an individual's career potential.

Perhaps it is the movies themselves that perpetuate the idea that the career goal of every film and television student rests in the feature film industry or the national television networks. It must be remembered that work in film or television can be found in many areas other than the fabled "big time."

The educational and industrial film/television production fields are continually expanding. Local broadcast television and, more recently, cable television have become important markets for qualified creative and technical personnel. Advertising and marketing also offer opportunities for film and television professionals.

It is important to remember that there is no single path to a career in motion pictures or television. No universal success formula exists. The best advice is to be willing to explore alternatives and maintain a flexible attitude toward both training and ultimate career goals.

UNIONS, GUILDS, AND PROFESSIONAL ASSOCIATIONS

While all work in the film and television industry does not require union membership (producers in the education and government fields often hire nonunion people), employment in large, commercial production companies is often dependent on union or guild membership.

Listed below are the national offices of large unions such as the International Alliance of Theatrical Stage Employees (IATSE), the National Association of Broadcast Employees and Technicians (NABET), and the International Brotherhood of Electrical Workers (IBEW) as well as a representative sampling of smaller, highly specialized unions, honorary societies, and associations. Services and publications of use to nonmembers and students have been highlighted. (See also AFI *Factfile #12 Film/Television: Grants, Scholarships, Special Programs.**) Contact the national offices for the addresses of their locals and for information on their rules and regulations. Consult the *International Motion Picture Almanac* (New York: Quigley Publishing, annual) and *On Location: National Film & Videotape Production Directory* (Hollywood, CA: On Location Publishing, annual) for complete listings of unions and guilds in the film, television, and theatrical fields.

American Cinema Editors (ACE)
422 South Western Avenue
Los Angeles, CA 90020
213-386-1946

This honorary society of film editors publishes a three-page pamphlet, *Career Information on Film Editing,* with good but limited advice on job hunting and education. Free upon request. They also publish the periodical *American Cinemeditor* (quarterly, free upon request).

American Federation of Television and Radio Artists (AFTRA)
1350 Avenue of the Americas
New York, NY 10019
212-265-7700

AFTRA, a labor union, negotiates wages and working conditions for performers and communicators in all live and videotaped television programs and commercials, as well as in radio. Information on union membership is available only by calling the AFTRA local in your area. r or a list of addresses of locals, consult *How to Break into Motion Pictures, Television, Commercials & Modeling* by Nina Blanchard (Garden City, NY: Doubleday, 1978).

**Factfile #12* is available from the American Film Institute, The John F Kennedy Center for the Performing Arts, Washington, DC 20566.

American Guild of Authors and Composers
6430 Sunset Boulevard
Hollywood, CA 90028
213-462-1108
Union for composers and lyricists working in film and television.

American Society of Cinematographers (ASC)
1782 North Orange Drive
Hollywood, CA 90028
213-876-5080
This honorary society of professional cinematographers publishes *American Cinematographer.*

Association of Talent Agents
9255 Sunset Boulevard, Suite 930
Los Angeles, CA 90069
213-274-0628
The Association is the trade association of talent agents in the Los Angeles area. Members are agents franchised by the state of California.

Directors Guild of America (DGA)
7950 Sunset Boulevard
Hollywood, CA 90046
213-656-1220
Members of the DGA may be booked for campus visits through the DGA Special Projects. The DGA also sponsors the Assistant Directors Training Program (see "Intern and Special Training Programs").

International Alliance of Theatrical Stage Employees and Moving Picture Machine Operators of the U.S. and Canada (IATSE)
1515 Broadway
New York, NY 10036
212-730-1770
IATSE comprises approximately 900 local unions that represent art directors, broadcasting studio employees, cameramen, costumers, editors, electricians, grips, laboratory technicians, makeup artists and hair stylists, projectionists, publicists, scenic and title artists, screen cartoonists, script supervisors, set designers and model makers, set painters, sound technicians, story analysts, studio cinetechnicians, studio mechanics, and other craftsmen. The national office of IATSE coordinates internship programs with IATSE locals (see "Intern and Special Training Programs").

International Brotherhood of Electrical Workers (IBEW)
1125 15th Street NW
Washington, DC 20005
202-833-7000

League of Professional Theatre Training Programs
1860 Broadway, Suite 1515
New York, NY 10023
212-265-6440
The eleven theater training institutions of the League share the goal of developing young persons for careers in the professional theater. Since all schools in the League require auditions for entrance, the League offers a regional auditions program in which students can audition for more than one school. The schools in the League are: American Conservatory Theatre, Boston University, California Institute for the Arts, Carnegie-Mellon University, The Juilliard School, New York University, North Carolina School of the Arts, Southern Methodist University, Temple University, and the University of Washington.

National Academy of Television Arts & Sciences (NATAS)
110 West 57th Street
New York, NY 10019
212-765-2450
College students with an interest in the study of television may become student affiliate members of the NATAS. Student affiliate members may attend special events twice a month to meet television professionals. The annual fee for student affiliate membership is $20.

National Association of Broadcast Employees and Technicians (NABET)
80 East Jackson Boulevard
Chicago, IL 60604
312-922-2462
The union for technical broadcasting professionals. Sponsors a scholarship program for children of active NABET members.

Producers Guild of America (PGA)
8201 Beverly Boulevard
Los Angeles, CA 90048
213-651-0084

Screen Actors Guild
7750 Sunset Boulevard
Los Angeles, CA 90046
213-876-3030
Negotiates wages and working conditions for actors and actresses in feature, industrial, and educational films and filmed television and commercials. A list of franchised agents is available for 25¢ and a self-addressed stamped envelope. Nonmembers may subscribe to *Screen Actor,* the journal of SAG, and the *SAG Newsletter* for $4 a year.

Screen Extras Guild
3629 Cahuenga Boulevard West
Los Angeles, CA 90068
213-851-4301

Screen Publicists Guild
c/o Dan Ratner
13 Astor Place
New York, NY 10003
212-673-5120, ext 245

Society of Motion Picture and Television Engineers (SMPTE)
862 Scarsdale Avenue
Scarsdale, NY 10583
914-472-6606

SMPTE is a professional organization dedicated to advancing the engineering and technical aspects of the motion picture, television, and allied arts and sciences. College students may become members if recommended by an SMPTE member or faculty member of the applicant's school. Student membership is $10 for the school year. Student members may attend monthly local chapter meetings and national conferences and receive the *SMPTE Journal* and *News & Notes.*

Theatre Communications Group
355 Lexington Avenue
New York, NY 10017
212-697-5230

Theatre Communications Group is the national service organization for the nonprofit professional theater offering programs and services to over 160 theaters as well as thousands of theater actors, technicians, and administrators. Maintains a Casting Information Service; holds national auditions and publishes a directory of regional theaters, *Theatre Profiles/4: A Resource Book of the Nonprofit Professional Theatres in the United States.*

Writers Guild of America, East (WGA)
555 West 57th Street
New York, NY 10019
212-245-6180

The Writers Guild of America, East has set up the Manuscript Registration Service to assist members and nonmembers of the Guild in establishing the completion date and the identity of their literary property. The aim of the registration is to prove priority of ownership. Another service for writers is the WGA, East publication *Professional Writer's Teleplay/Screenplay Format: A Brief but Thorough Guide to the Accepted Script Format of the TV and Motion Picture Industries.* It is available to students and WGA members for $2 and to nonmembers for $2.50. A list of agents for screenwriters is available from the WGA, East for $1.

Writers Guild of America, West
8955 Beverly Boulevard
Los Angeles, CA 90048
213-550-1000

The *Newsletter* of the WGA, West reports current information regarding jobs, residuals, awards, and other news of interest to writers. Each issue features the "TV Market List" of television series that are open to submissions, are staff written, or accept submissions through agents only. Nonmembers may subscribe to the monthly *Newsletter* for $18 a year. A list of agents for screenwriters is also available from the WGA, West for $1.

INTERN AND SPECIAL TRAINING PROGRAMS

Internships and special training programs exist within the film and television industry. A selected list of such programs is given here. Most are highly competitive. In addition, many colleges and universities with film and television study offer intern programs with local production facilities. Many regional media centers also offer informal internships. For a list of such centers, please see "Selected List of Film and Video Centers."

GENERAL

Astoria Internship Program
Astoria Motion Picture & Television Center Foundation
34-31 35th Street
Astoria, NY 11106
212-784-4520

The Program is an opportunity for emerging professionals with career interests in the media to learn by observing the various aspects of professional production, including film and video features and commercials. Applicants must be 21 years of age, U.S. citizens, and residents of the New York metropolitan area. Starting times are flexible, depending upon the production schedule. Semifinalists are selected based on review of candidates' backgrounds. Semifinalists then submit samples of their work and are then interviewed. Admission is highly competitive. Interns receive a stipend of $150 a week with a maximum of $1800. For further information, contact Roger Midgett.

Contract Services Administration Trust Fund
8480 Beverly Boulevard
Hollywood, CA 90048
213-655-4200

Training programs in various film and television related fields (with the exception of acting) are open to qualified applicants. For further information, contact Eileen Leonard.

International Alliance of Theatrical Stage Employees and Moving Picture Machine Operators (IATSE)
1515 Broadway
New York, NY 10036
212-730-1770

Many locals of IATSE offer apprenticeship programs of 2 to 4 years' duration. Individual locals design their own programs. The fields of study include art direction, cinematography, costuming, film editing, makeup, property craft, publicity. Mr. Alfred W. DiTolla at the National Office of IATSE in New York City will refer inquiries regarding a specific field to the proper local.

Zoetrope Studios Film School
916 Kearny Street
San Francisco, CA 94133
415-788-7500

A three-year performing arts high school is being planned by Francis Ford Coppola's production company, Zoetrope Studios. The school will teach the historical, theoretical, technological, and creative aspects of the film art. Instruction in high school academic subjects will be related to the communication arts. The initial program is scheduled to begin September, 1981. By sending a résumé and letter of interest, prospective applicants may be placed on a mailing list for further information. Contact August Coppola.

ACTING

Theatre Communications Group
355 Lexington Avenue
New York, NY 10017
212-697-5230

A service organization for regional theaters, TCG holds national auditions to present graduating students to directors of nonprofit theaters in the United States. The employment opportunities offered involve a small salary, a chance to act, and the possibility of eventually earning an Equity card. Once an actor has joined one dramatic union, membership in another is easier to attain. To be eligible for these auditions a student must be nominated by the head of the acting faculty of his school.

ANIMATION

Animation Training Program
Hanna-Barbera Productions
3400 Cahuenga Boulevard
Hollywood, CA 90068
213-851-5000

Applicants must have formal art training and be above average in life/anatomy drawing. Portfolio and résumé are required. Classes are held one night a week and are free to those accepted. Instruction is in animation and includes layout, character design, and storyboard. Employment is not promised. For more information, contact Harry Love, Producer.

Talent Development Program
Walt Disney Productions
Animation Department
500 South Buena Vista Street
Burbank, CA 91521
213-845-3141

Accepted applicants are classified as trainees. A trainee works on a personal project (not a picture in production) under the supervision of the leader in the applicant's area. Every thirty days, the trainee's progress is reviewed by the group that accepted the original portfolio. The trainee may be dropped at each review period. Should the trainee be retained at the end of ninety days, he must join the union and may then begin work on actual production. An example of what the studio looks for in the three most likely starting areas follows:

Animator: Realistic (not cartoon), loose, linear quick sketches from life of energetically moving figures. Submit a sketch book of athletes drawn from life or television.

Layout: Perspective and composition. Submit linear sketches and/or renderings of possible background settings with props.

Background: Color handling, light and shadow, values. Submit watercolor paintings from life: of landscapes or seascapes or of buildings (exteriors and interiors).

Samples may be sent to Edward Hansen, Manager, Animation Administration.

Yellow Ball Workshop
62 Tarbell Avenue
Lexington, MA 02173
617-862-4283

The Workshop offers training in animation to children and adults. Workshops are given on the premises and on a traveling basis. Contact Yvonne Andersen for more information.

DIRECTING

Academy Internship Program
The American Film Institute
Center for Advanced Film Studies
501 Doheny Road
Beverly Hills, CA 90210
213-278-8777

The Academy Internship Program is funded by the Academy of Motion Picture Arts and Sciences and is administered by the American Film Institute. The Program provides an opportunity for a limited number of promising new directors to learn by observing established directors at work during the production of a feature or television film. Interns are paid a weekly stipend for the duration of the filming. Applicants must be 21 years of age and a citizen or permanent resident of the United States. For more information contact Jan Haag or Rachel Koretsky.

Assistant Directors Training Program
8480 Beverly Boulevard
Hollywood, CA 90048
213-653-2200, ext 227

The Training Program is sponsored by the Directors Guild of America and the Association of Motion Picture and Television Producers. Trainees learn the administrative and managerial functions of second assistant director by working under the supervision of a second assistant director. Upon satisfactory completion of 400 actual workdays, the trainee's name is placed on the DGA Qualification List, thereby making him or her eligible for employment as a second assistant director. Applicants must be graduates of an accredited four-year college or university or have equivalent employment experience in the film industry. Admission is by examination and interview and is highly competitive. For further information, contact Jane Klein.

Directing Workshop for Women
The American Film Institute
Center for Advanced Film Studies
501 Doheny Road
Beverly Hills, CA 90210
213-278-8777

The Workshop was specifically created for women who have had considerable experience in feature or television films as writers, producers, actresses, editors, script supervisors, assistant directors, studio executives, etc., but who have not yet had the opportunity to direct. The Workshop offers practical experience in directing videotape productions. The Workshop is currently between funding. Prospective applicants who send a résumé and letter of interest will be notified when the Workshop is funded.

Directors Project
Young Filmmakers/Video Arts
4 Rivington Street
New York, NY 10002
212-673-9361

Young Filmmakers/Video Arts offers continuing workshops for film and television professional directors who have not worked in dramatic production to learn how to work with actors. Instructors are Directors Guild of America members, and actors and actresses are volunteer Screen Actors Guild members. Workshop participants are involved with all aspects of dramatic production, from script analysis, casting, first readings, and rehearsals to modest on-location productions that are videotaped. Videotaped productions are critiqued in group sessions with an emphasis on directing technique.

SCRIPTWRITING

Columbia Pictures–Television Writers Workshop
711 Fifth Avenue
New York, NY 10022
212-751-4400, ext 6728

The Workshop is designed to acquaint professional writers with the business and craft of television. Applicants must be individuals who earn a living by writing. Acceptance is determined by examination of writing samples and professional backgrounds. Approximately 65 applicants are accepted for the annual Workshop. Contact William Hart, Senior Vice-President, National Program Sales, for further information.

Script Development Workshop
GPO Box 1846
New York, NY 10001
212-245-6757 or 212-582-8847

The Script Development Workshop, formerly under the auspices of the National Academy of Television Arts & Sciences, is now an independent, nonprofit organization under the direction of Artistic Director, Trent Gough. The Workshop is designed for writers of film, television, and theater. Each 12-week workshop comprises a team of 25 writers, 12 actors and actresses, and 8 to 10 directors. Writers see their work performed, videotaped, and critiqued by the Workshop. Actors, actresses, and directors have the opportunity to practice their craft with other professionals. All applicants are interviewed before acceptance. A fee of $70 is charged for one 12-week workshop or $150 for one year (four 12-week workshops).

Writing for Animation Training Program
Hanna-Barbera Productions
3400 Cahuenga Boulevard
Hollywood, CA 90068
213-851-5000

Applicants must have studied writing at the college level. Writing samples and résumé are required. Classes are held one night a week and are free to those accepted. Instruction is in gag writing. Employment is not promised. For more information, contact Harry Love, Producer.

TELEVISION

American Association for the Advancement of Science
Mass Media Science Fellows Program
1776 Massachusetts Avenue NW
Washington, DC 20036
202-467-4475

To contribute to the quality and amount of coverage of science in the broadcast media the AAAS has established the Fellows Program to support graduate students in the natural and social sciences during the summer as reporters, researchers, or production assistants. Each Fellow will work for a specific media organization such as a television or radio station. During the 10- to 12-week Program, Fellows receive a stipend of $200 a week. Application deadline is February 15. Contact Arleen Richman for further information.

Intern Program
Grass-Roots Television Network
Box 2006
Aspen, CO 81611
303-925-7784

Grass-Roots Television Network is Aspen's community cablecasting station. The Network offers winter and summer intern programs for college students. During the program, the intern gains experience in television writing, editing, camera work, studio production, field production, and news reporting. A tuition fee is charged.

Video Training Program
Institute for New Cinema Artists
505 8th Avenue
New York, NY 10018
212-695-0826

The Institute for New Cinema Artists and the National Academy of Television Arts & Sciences sponsor a video training program for qualified minorities (applicants must meet CETA guidelines and be at least 18 years of age). Classes are held for 39 weeks, 5 days a week, 8 hours a day. Students are required to attend full time and are paid a modest stipend. A placement service is offered to graduates of the Program.

Women's and Minority Training Grants
Corporation for Public Broadcasting
1111 16th Street NW
Washington, DC 20036
202-293-6160
Awarded to CPB-licensed television and radio stations, associated production centers, and other telecommunications entities, the grants fund on-the-job training of women and minorities in professional, management, and technical positions. The station must apply and, to qualify, must agree to pay at least one half of a trainee's salary, benefits, and training costs for one to two years.

SUMMER WORKSHOPS

Summer workshops in film and video making, criticism, and theory are often held by universities and independent film and video organizations. Consult the spring and summer issues of the following for listings.

AFI Education Newsletter
National Education Services
The American Film Institute
J F Kennedy Center
Washington, DC 20566
Bimonthly during the academic year. Free.

The Animator
Northwest Film Study Center
Portland Art Museum
1219 Southwest Park
Portland, OR 97205
Quarterly. $3 a year.

Film & Video Makers Travel Sheet
Carnegie Institute—Film Section
Museum of Art
4400 Forbes Avenue
Pittsburgh, PA 15213
Monthly. $3 a year.

Filmmakers Monthly
PO Box 115
Ward Hill, MA 01830
Monthly. $12 a year.

IMAGE Newsletter
Independent Media Artists of Georgia, Inc
972 Peachtree Street, Suite 213
Atlanta, GA 30309
Monthly. $3 a year.

The Independent
Foundation for Independent Video and Film, Inc
625 Broadway, 9th Floor
New York, NY 10012
Ten times yearly. Included in Association of Independent Video and Filmmakers membership; $20 New York City residents, $15 individuals outside New York City.

CAREER SERVICES

The following is a selected list of career planning services and employment clearinghouses. Many independent film and video organizations also maintain job files. See *Factfile #6 Independent Film/Video** for more information.

CareerLine
American Women in Radio and Television
1321 Connecticut Avenue NW
Washington, DC 20036
800-424-8890
Once a week approximately ten job openings in radio and television across the nation are listed in this recorded toll-free service.

Educational Communications & Technology Referral Service
ECT Newsletter
Association for Educational Communications & Technology
1126 16th Street NW
Washington, DC 20036
202-833-4180
The EC&T Referral Service is an employment clearinghouse for AECT members and nonmembers ($25 members, $75 nonmembers) and is published in the *ECT Newsletter* (monthly, September through April). Examples of positions listed include: senior television engineer, audiovisual technician, media specialist, instructional communications center director, library/media specialist.

**Factfile #6* is available from the American Film Institute, The John F Kennedy Center for the Performing Arts, Washington, DC 20566.

Focus on Media Production
1888 Century Park East
Suite 10
Los Angeles, CA 90067
213-556-3000

FMP offers the following three seminars on the motion picture and television industries: "The Cast You Don't See on Screen," a one-day career planning seminar, is a general introduction to the different types of jobs in the industry and discusses how studios work. "Who Hires in Hollywood" is a one-day seminar on the specifics of job hunting and covers all aspects of hiring in the industry. Casting directors, studio personnel directors, nonunion producers, agents, and employment agency personnel are represented in the seminar panel. "Women Moving Up in Movies and Television," a half-day program, is a networking opportunity. The program is a breakfast with successful women in the industry. Contact Jane Klein for further information.

Good People
827 Hilldale Avenue
Los Angeles, CA 90069
213-278-8221

An employment agency listing jobs in the entertainment industry. Especially useful for entry-level jobs requiring secretarial skills: receptionist, production secretary, production coordinator. Associate producer and production assistant positions are also available but require extensive local experience.

NAB Employment Clearinghouse
National Association of Broadcasters
1771 N Street NW
Washington, DC 20036
202-293-3584

The Clearinghouse is an advisory service that assists women and minorities to enter the broadcast industry through career counseling and job referrals. Contact Wanda Townsend, Coordinator.

NAEB PACT: People and Careers in Telecommunications
Current: for people in public telecommunications
National Association of Educational Broadcasters
1346 Connecticut Avenue NW
Washington, DC 20036
202-785-1100

PACT, a job listing announcing positions available in all aspects of public television and radio, is published in the twice monthly newsletter *Current: for people in public telecommunications* ($25 a year).

State Film Commissions

A film commission can be a central source for information on productions currently filming in the state and their need for free-lancers. Consult the following publications for names, addresses, and telephone numbers: "City & State Film Commissions & Contacts" in *Back Stage Film & Tape Directory* (New York: Back Stage, annual) and "Film Commissions & State Liaisons" in *The On Location National Film & Videotape Production Directory* (Hollywood, CA: On Location Publishing, annual).

Theatre Communications Group
355 Lexington Avenue
New York, NY 10017
212-697-5230

Maintains a file of qualified actors that is made available to casting directors of regional, nonprofit professional theaters across the country. Actors living in the New York area who want to audition for the TCG casting staff must submit a picture and résumé for review.

BIBLIOGRAPHY

JOB LISTINGS

The following periodicals frequently list jobs available in film and television. The Sunday editions of major newspapers such as the *Los Angeles Times* and the *New York Times* are also rich sources of current job information.

Since many employment opportunities are not advertised, we have added a selective listing of directories of companies and organizations in the motion picture, television, and audiovisual fields.

Periodicals

The Alpha Viewfinder
Alpha Cine Laboratory
1001 Lenora Street
Seattle, WA 98121

Quarterly. Free.
(Classifieds for jobs available and jobs wanted in the motion picture and audiovisual industries.)

Back Stage
165 West 46th Street
New York, NY 10036

Weekly. $32 a year.
(Casting notices for film, tape, radio, television, and the stage. "Staff & Tech" lists openings for technical directors, costumers, set designers.)

Broadcasting
1735 DeSales Street NW
Washington, DC 20036

Weekly. $45 a year.
(Advertises positions in radio, television, and allied arts for managers, sales managers, engineers, technicians, reporters, and cameramen.)

Daily Variety
1400 North Cahuenga Boulevard
Hollywood, CA 90028
Daily except Saturdays and Sundays and holidays. $60 a year.
(Lists jobs available in the motion picture industry.)

Filmmakers Monthly (formerly *Filmmakers Newsletter*)
PO Box 115
Ward Hill, MA 08130
Monthly. $12 a year.
(A magazine for individuals involved in feature film and video, independent production, business, educational and instructional media. "Bulletin Board" section announces jobs wanted and positions available.)

The Hollywood Reporter
6715 Sunset Boulevard
Hollywood, CA 90028
Daily, except Saturdays, Sundays, and legal holidays. $55 a year.
("Help Wanted" and "Casting" columns.)

The Independent
Foundation for Independent Video and Film, Inc
625 Broadway, 9th Floor
New York, NY 10012
Ten times yearly. Included in Association of Independent Video and Filmmakers membership: $20 New York City residents, $15 individuals outside New York City.
("Opportunities/Gigs/Apprenticeships" lists positions available for independent film and video makers.)

Media & Methods
401 North Broad Street
Philadelphia, PA 19108
Published nine times during the school year. $11 a year.
("Situation Wanted" and "Help Wanted" listings in the field of instructional media.)

Ross Reports Television
Television Index
150 Fifth Avenue
New York, NY 10011
Monthly. $18.50 a year.
(Detailed information on script and casting requirements of continuing television programs including how and when to submit work and a listing of talent agents.)

Show Business
136 West 44th Street
New York, NY 10036
Weekly. $22 a year.
("Casting News" on jobs and auditions in New York City for actors in all media. Also publishes a list of franchised talent agents in New York.)

SMPTE Journal
Society of Motion Picture and Television Engineers
862 Scarsdale Avenue
Scarsdale, NY 10583
Monthly. Free to members. Nonmembers: $35 a year; students: $12 a year.
(Jobs listed include: assistant chief engineer, audiovisual technician, video engineer/operator, technical manager.)

T.G.I.F. Casting News/Entertainment Guide
PO Box 1683
Hollywood, CA 90028
Monthly. $10 a year.
(Covers New York City and Los Angeles.)

Variety
154 West 46th Street
New York, NY 10036
Weekly. $45 a year.
("Casting News" for Broadway, Off Broadway, Out of Town.)

Directories

Audiovisual Market Place: A Multimedia Guide. New York: R. R. Bowker Company. Annual.
A directory for the audiovisual industry (educational and industrial). Listings cover producers and distributors, production companies and services, equipment manufacturers and dealers, and related associations.

Back Stage TV Film/Tape and Syndication Directory. Hollywood, CA: Back Stage Publications. Annual.
Arranged by geographical regions.

Broadcasting Cable Sourcebook. Washington, DC: Broadcasting Publications. Annual.
A comprehensive resource for the cable television industry.

The Creative Black Book. New York: Friendly Publications. Annual.
Includes information on advertising and casting agencies, schools and creative services.

Directory of U.S. Government Audiovisual Personnel. Washington, DC: National Audiovisual Center, 1977.
A directory of Federal Government agencies and key media personnel.

Epler, Greg, ed. *The WAFL Book: A Guide to Film and Video in the Washington, DC Area.* Washington, DC: Washington Area Filmmakers League, 1978.

A guide to companies, services and film and video makers in the greater Washington, DC, area.

International Motion Picture Almanac. New York: Quigley Publishing Company. Annual.

A major reference book for the film industry.

International Television Almanac. New York: Quigley Publishing Company. Annual.

A major directory for the broadcasting television industry.

Madison Avenue Handbook. New York: Peter Glenn Publications, Ltd. Annual.

Covers advertising, film, television, and other fields in New York City, Boston, Los Angeles, San Francisco, Chicago, Detroit, Atlanta, Miami, Montreal, and Toronto. Useful for actors.

Nelson, Abigail, ed. *Guide to Film and Video Resources in New England.* Cambridge, MA: University Film Study Center, 1977.

Includes listings of film and video production companies and their policies on hiring free-lancers.

On Location: National Film and Videotape Production Directory. Hollywood, CA: On Location Publishing. Annual.

Directory of services and resources necessary to filmmakers on location nationwide. Arranged by state and major city.

CAREER INFORMATION

The bibliography that follows lists books that describe careers in film and television and books that explain the "how to" aspects of each career.

General

Bayer, William S. *Breaking Through, Selling Out, Dropping Dead.* New York: Macmillan, 1971.

Advice on every facet of filmmaking. Described by the author as "random, subjective, and often idiosyncratic notes."

Chase, Donald, for the American Film Institute. *Filmmaking: The Collaborative Art.* Boston: Little, Brown and Company, 1975.

Based upon transcripts of seminars held at AFI Center for Advanced Film Studies and personal interviews. Explores a variety of film careers.

London, Mel. *Getting into Film.* New York: Ballantine Books, 1977.

A comprehensive and highly practical look at film production careers.

Acting

Blanchard, Nina. *How to Break into Motion Pictures, Television, Commercials & Modeling.* Garden City, NY: Doubleday and Company, 1978.

By the director of a leading California talent and modeling agency. Has an excellent list of AFTRA locals.

Burton, Hal. *Acting in the Sixties.* New York: International Publications Service, 1970.

Based on a BBC series, this book offers comments on acting from Richard Burton, Albert Finney, Vanessa Redgrave, Maggie Smith, and others.

Career Handbook for Those Beginning Careers in the Performing Arts. New Haven, CT: Yale Drama Association, 1977.

Practical information with an emphasis on the New York City scene. Available from the Association of Yale Alumni, 901-A Yale Station, New Haven, CT 06520. $2.50.

Cohen, Robert. *Acting Professionally: Raw Facts About Careers in Acting.* New York: Barnes & Noble Books, 1977.

Covers the economics of the profession, auditioning, unions, schools, and training programs. Appendix has hard-to-find information on noncollegiate acting schools, like the Herbert Berghof Studio.

Cole, Toby, and Helen Chinoy. *Actors on Acting.* New York: Crown Publishers, 1970.

The theories, techniques, and practices of the great actors are discussed.

Easty, Edward D. *On Method Acting.* Orlando, FL: House of Collectibles, 1966.

Sense memory, affective memory, relaxation, improvisation, creating inner and outer character, and physical exercises are discussed.

Funke, Lewis, and John Booth. *Actors Talk About Acting.* New York: Avon Books, 1973.

Fourteen interviews with contemporary actors.

Hunt, Gordon. *How to Audition: A Casting Director's Guide for Actors.* Westport, CT: Dramatic Publishing Co., 1977.

A Los Angeles casting director gives advice on interviewing, preparing pictures and résumés, and performing well with cold readings. Included are interviews with producers, directors, critics, writers, teachers, and actors.

Joels, Merril E. *How to Get into Show Business.* New York: Hastings House, 1969.

Gives practical advice for aspiring actors in radio, television, theater, and film.

Lane, Yoti. *Psychology of the Actor.* Westport, CT: Greenwood Press, 1973.

The actor in relation to himself, his art, and society.

McGaw, Charles J. *Acting Is Believing.* New York: Holt, Rinehart and Winston, 1975.

Practical informative presentation of the Stanislavski acting method.

Moore, Sonia. *Training an Actor: The Stanislavski System in Class.* New York: Penguin Books, 1979.

Examples of the Stanislavski system in classroom sessions.

Pate, Michael. *The Film Actor: Acting for Motion Pictures and Television.* South Brunswick, NJ: A. S. Barnes, 1969.

Exercises and the staging of a scene from a screenplay are presented. A glossary of film terms is included.

Shipman, Nina. *How to Become an Actor in Television Commercials.* Santa Monica, CA: S & B Productions, 1975.

An actress tells of her experiences and offers advice.

Stanislavski, Constantin. *An Actor Prepares.* New York: Theatre Arts Books, 1948.

Inner training of an actor's imagination and spirit.

____. *Building a Character.* New York: Theatre Arts Books, 1949.
Sequel to *An Actor Prepares.* Discusses in detail how an actor's body, voice, and all his faculties can be trained for roles.

____. *Stanislavski's Legacy.* New York: Theatre Arts Books, 1968.
Stanislavski's thoughts on the life of the true artist, technique of the creative mood, drama criticism, the art of the actor, and the art of the director.

Cinematography

Campbell, Russell. *Practical Motion Picture Photography.* New York: A. S. Barnes, 1971.
Interviews with sixteen professional cinematographers.

Carlson, Verne, and Sylvia Carlson. *Professional 16/35mm Cameraman's Handbook.* New York: American Photographic Book Co., 1974.
An excellent reference book for the professional cinematographer and all filmmakers as well.

Clarke, Charles G., and Walter Strenge, eds. *American Cinematographer Manual.* Hollywood, CA: American Society of Cinematographers, 1973.
This is the 4th edition of the cinematographer's bible.

Higham, Charles. *Hollywood Cameramen: Sources of Light.* Bloomington, IN: Indiana University Press, 1970.
Interviews with Leon Shamroy, Lee Carmes, William Daniels, James Wong Howe, Stanley Cortez, Karl Struss, Arthur Miller.

Maltin, Leonard. *The Art of the Cinematographer: A Survey and Interviews with Five Masters.* New York: Dover, 1978. (Corrected and enlarged edition of *Behind the Camera: The Cinematographer's Art.* New York: New American Library, 1971.)
Introductory essay surveys Hollywood cinematography and evaluates contributions made by cameramen. Interviews with Arthur Miller, Hal Mohr, Hal Rossen, Lucien Ballard, and Conrad Hall. Filmographies included.

Maple, Jessie. *How to Become a Union Camerawoman: Film-Videotape.* New York: L J Film Productions, 1977.
Useful firsthand advice by the first black camerawoman.

Mascelli, Joseph V., ASC. *The Five C's of Cinematography.* Hollywood, CA: Cine/Grafic Publications, 1977.
The five C's represent camera angles, continuity, cutting, close-ups, and composition. A standard introduction to cinematography.

Souto, H. Mario. *The Technique of the Motion Picture Camera.* New York: Focal Press, 1977.
A comprehensive study of camera design, operation, maintenance, and filming technique.

Wheeler, Leslie. *Principles of Cinematography.* Hastings-On-Hudson, NY: Morgan, 1969.
A standard work.

Young, Freddie, and Paul Petzold. *The Work of the Motion Picture Cameraman.* New York: Hastings House, 1972.
Detailed description of the duties of the director of photography.

Design

Barsacq, Leon. *Caligari's Cabinet and Other Grand Illusions: A History of Film Design.* New York: New American Library, 1978.
The first comprehensive survey of the history and technology of production design from early Melies to late Antonioni. Includes filmographies of art directors and production designers.

Carrick, Edward. *Art and Design in the British Film.* New York: Arno Press, 1972. Reprint of 1948 ed.
A pictorial directory of British art directors and their work.

Chierichetti, David. *Hollywood Costume Design.* New York: Harmony Books, 1976.
Examines the costume design of the major studios.

Marner, Terence S. *Film Design.* New York: A. S. Barnes and Co., 1973.
A primer for the future art director and production designer.

Spencer, Charles. *Cecil Beaton Stage and Film Designs.* New York: St. Martin's Press, 1976.
Over 150 illustrations are included in this book.

Directing

Bare, Richard L. *The Film Director: A Practical Guide to Motion Picture and Television Techniques.* New York: Macmillan, 1973.
A director's viewpoints and experiences are presented here.

Bobker, Lee. *Elements of Film.* New York: Harcourt Brace Jovanovich, 1974.
An excellent introduction to the technique and art of film with chapters on story, script, image, sound, editing, the director, actor, contemporary filmmakers, and criticism.

____ with Louise Marinis. *Making Movies: From Script to Screen.* New York: Harcourt Brace Jovanovich, 1973.
This comprehensive logical book about filmmaking includes information on careers.

Geduld, Harry M., ed. *Film Makers on Filmmaking: Statements on Their Art by Thirty Directors.* Bloomington, IN: Indiana University Press, 1967.
"Pioneers and Prophets" and "Film Masters and Film Makers."

Gelmis, Joseph. *The Film Director as Superstar.* Garden City, NY: Doubleday, 1970.
Sixteen international film directors express their views of filmmaking, from aesthetics to finances.

Lipton, Lenny. *Independent Filmmaking.* San Francisco, CA: Straight Arrow Books, 1972.
An excellent guide for beginning and advanced filmmakers.

Pye, Michael, and Lynda Myles. *The Movie Brats: How the Film Generation Took Over Hollywood.* New York: Holt, Rinehart and Winston, 1979.
The careers of Francis Coppola, George Lucas, Brian DePalma, John Milius, Martin Scorsese, and Steven Spielberg are analyzed.

Reynertson, A.J. *The Work of the Film Director.* New York: Focal Press, 1970.

The basics of editing, screenwriting, music, sound, camera movement, and on-the-set and location techniques.

Sarris, Andrew. *Interviews with Film Directors.* New York: Avon Books, 1969.

A compilation of interviews with forty international directors.

Sherman, Eric. *Directing the Film: Film Directors on Their Art.* Boston: Little, Brown, 1976.

Based upon more than seventy interviews with directors at seminars and oral history projects of the AFI. Discusses what a director is and how those interviewed got started. Covers the script, rehearsal, shooting methods, directing actors, film editing, etc.

Editing

Burder, John. *16mm Film Cutting.* New York: Hastings House, 1975.

A practical step-by-step guide to solving cutting room problems.

Career Information on Film Editing. Los Angeles, CA: American Cinema Editors, Inc. (no date).

Produced by the honorary society of film editors in response to requests for career information, this three-page pamphlet gives good but limited advice on job hunting and education. Write ACE for a free copy.

Churchill, Hugh B. *Film Editing Handbook: Techniques of 16mm Film Cutting.* Belmont, CA: Wadsworth Publishing, 1972.

Explains the mechanics of film editing to the novice editor.

Pudovkin, Vladimir I. *Film Technique and Film Acting.* New York: Grove Press, 1970.

Originally published in 1929, this book is a classic work on early Russian film montage.

Reisz, Karel, and Gavin Millar. *The Technique of Film Editing.* New York: Focal Press, 1968.

A lucid account of the art, rather than the mechanics, of film editing.

Rosenblum, Ralph, and Robert Karen. *When the Shooting Stops . . . the Cutting Begins: A Film Editor's Story.* New York: Viking Press, 1979.

The editor of *The Producers, A Thousand Clowns,* and Woody Allen films discusses what editing can and cannot do by describing raw footage and scenes not used in final versions, how film is assembled, and why.

Walter, Ernst. *The Technique of the Film Cutting Room.* New York: Focal Press, 1969.

Revised to include the needs of television films, this book describes the functions of the editor in relation to each stage of film production.

Makeup

Buchman, Herman. *Film and Television Make-up.* New York: Watson-Guptill, 1973.

Tools and materials, basic technique, color and black and white filming, middle age, old age, and other aspects of makeup are treated.

Corson, Richard. *Stage Makeup,* 5th ed. Englewood Cliffs, NJ: Prentice-Hall, 1974.

Recommended by the makeup man of *The Exorcist,* this book on stage makeup explains basic principles.

Kehoe, Vincent J. R. *The Technique of Film and Television Makeup.* New York: Hastings House, 1969.

This thorough study covers color and black and white techniques.

Scriptwriting

One of the most useful ways to learn the act of screenwriting is to examine scripts. Published screenplays are listed in *The Subject Guide to Books in Print* and G. Howard Poteet's *Published Radio, Television and Film Scripts: A Bibliography.* (Troy, NY: The Whitson Publishing Co., 1975.) For other sources, including collections of unpublished screenplays, write Information Services, National Education Services, AFI, Kennedy Center, Washington, DC 20566.

Beveridge, James A. *Script Writing for Short Films.* New York: UNESCO, 1969.

An effective, concise summary of scripting for the short film.

Bluestone, George. *Novels into Film: The Metamorphosis of Fiction into Cinema.* Berkeley and Los Angeles: University of California Press, 1966.

Covers the adaptions of six novels: *The Informer, Wuthering Heights, Pride and Prejudice, The Grapes of Wrath, The Ox-Bow Incident,* and *Madame Bovary.*

Coopersmith, Jerome. *Professional Writer's Teleplay/Screenplay Format: A Brief but Thorough Guide to the Accepted Script Format of the TV and Motion Picture Industries.* New York: Writers Guild, East, 1977.

This excellent guide to the screenplay includes advice for beginners.

Corliss, Richard, ed. *The Hollywood Screenwriters.* New York: Avon Books, 1972.

Covers the history of screenwriting through articles and interviews with screenwriters from the early years of film to the present.

Froug, William. *The Screenwriter Looks at the Screenwriter.* New York: Dell, 1974.

Twelve leading American screenwriters tell their own stories in frank, penetrating interviews. Works of the screenwriters interviewed include: *Seconds, The Great Escape, Some Like It Hot, The Graduate, M*A*S*H*.*

Geduld, Harry M., ed. *Authors on Film.* Bloomington, IN: Indiana University Press, 1972.

Thirty-five celebrated writers comment on the nature of film, filmmaking, screenwriting, and the Hollywood scene.

Herman, Lewis. *A Practical Manual of Screen Playwriting for Theater and Television Films.* New York: New American Library, 1975.

An informed how-to-do-it guide.

Hilliard, Robert L. *Writing for Television and Radio.* New York: Hastings House, 1976.

In addition to material on the basic elements of television writing, this revised edition has sections on women's programs, ethnic and minority programs, information and education programs, and a discussion of professional opportunities in the field.

Lee, Robert, and Robert Misiorowski. *Script Models: A Handbook for the Media Writer.* New York: Hastings House, 1978.
Designed for beginning writers in radio, television, and film. Provides script examples of most of the situations the media writer is apt to encounter and a glossary of the vocabulary of screenwriting.

Parker, Norton S. *Audio Visual Script Writing.* New Brunswick, NJ: Rutgers University Press, 1974.
A down-to-earth approach to the nontheatrical film script.

Rilla, Wolf. *The Writer and the Screen: On Writing for Film and Television.* New York: William Morrow & Company, 1974.
Based on his career, the author examines and explains the disciplines involved in writing for the screen.

Swain, Dwight V. *Film Scriptwriting: A Practical Manual.* New York: Hastings House, 1976.
Contains a selection of scripts annotated by the author to indicate different techniques.

Trapnell, Coles. *Teleplay: An Introduction to Television Writing.* San Francisco: Chandler Publishing Co., 1967.
A good introduction.

Vale, Eugene. *The Technique of Screenplay Writing.* New York: Grosset and Dunlap, 1973.
A standard work.

Special Effects

Brodbeck, Emil. *Movie and Videotape Special Effects.* Garden City, NY: American Photographic Book Co., 1968.
Considers the entire range of special effects.

Brosnan, John. *Movie Magic: The Story of Special Effects in the Cinema.* New York: New American Library, 1976.
Combines a historical narrative survey along with clear nontechnical explanations. The state of the art today and predictions for the future are discussed.

Clark, Frank P. *Special Effects in Motion Pictures.* Scarsdale, NY: Society of Motion Picture and Television Engineers, 1979.
Methods for producing mechanical special effects are given with an account of their development and application.

Fielding, Raymond. *The Technique of Special Effects Cinematography.* New York: Focal Press, 1972.
This thorough and precise survey of special effects technique is the definitive work on the tricks of the cinematographic trade.

Harryhausen, Ray. *Film Fantasy Scrapbook.* New York: A. S. Barnes, 1978.
Front projection, traveling, matte, sodium backing process, perspective photography, and the Dynamation Process are described by an expert.

Wilkie, Bernard. *Creating Special Effects for Film-TV.* New York: Hastings House, 1977.
A basic guide to the design and use of special effects and props in film and television production.

Television

Berlyn, David. *Your Future in Television Careers.* New York: Richards Rosen Press, 1978.
Covers programming, news, management, engineering, sales, and promotion.

Bluem, A., and William and Roger Manvell, eds. *Television: The Creative Experience.* New York: Hastings House, 1976.
Television writers, producers, directors, performers, and technicians discuss their work.

Careers in Television. Washington, DC: National Association of Broadcasters, 1976.
Includes a description of a typical station. Free copies may be obtained by writing NAB, 1771 N Street NW, Washington, DC 20036.

Gates, Gary Paul. *Air Time: The Inside Story of CBS News.* New York: Harper & Row, 1978.
Inside, by a former CBS News writer.

Rather, Dan, with Mickey Herskowitz. *The Camera Never Blinks: Adventures of a TV Journalist.* New York: Ballantine Books, 1978.
Dan Rather talks about his beginnings in journalism in Houston, his break into network television, and his career as a reporter for CBS News.

Shanks, Bob. *The Cool Fire: How to Make It in Television.* New York: Vintage Books, 1977.
A firsthand account by a successful television producer.

Other

Bazelon, Irwin. *Knowing the Score: Notes on Film Music.* New York: Van Nostrand, Reinhold, 1976.
A film composer looks at the interaction of music and action in 200 films. Interviews with composers. Sample score pages and cue sheets also included.

Cantor, Muriel G. *The Hollywood Television Producer: His Work and His Audience.* New York: Basic Books, 1972.
Examines what a producer is and does.

Careers for You: In Motion Pictures, Television, Photo Science, Photoinstrumentation, Instructional Technology. . . as Engineers, Scientists, Creative Production Personnel. Scarsdale, NY: Society of Motion Picture & Television Engineers (no date).
Includes a list of professional journals and associations. This eight-page pamphlet is available, free of charge, by writing SMPTE (SMPTE, 862 Scarsdale Avenue, Scarsdale, NY 10583).

Kohner, Frederick. *The Magician of Sunset Boulevard: The Improbable Life of Paul Kohner, Hollywood Agent.* Palos Verdes, CA: Morgan Press, 1977.
The career of an agent who has represented Huston, Bronson Wyler, Moreau, Fellini, Ullmann, and others.

Libbett, Karen A., ed. *Encyclopedia of Exhibition.* New York: National Association of Theatre Owners. Annual.
A guide for motion picture theater owners to distributors, upcoming film releases, equipment and concession manufacturers and suppliers.

Rowlands, Avril. *Script Continuity and the Production Secretary in Film and TV.* New York: Hastings House, 1977.
By a producer's assistant for BBC Television. Explains the jobs of script continuity girl and production secretary.

Wise, Arthur, and Derak Ware. *Stunting in the Cinema.* New York: St. Martin's Press, 1973.
The authors comment on the special skills needed and how to become a stuntman. Out of print.

The following is a listing of the degrees offered by the schools included in the main entry section of this volume including all degrees offered with an emphasis in film or television. Please note that an "emphasis" at one school might include only a limited number of courses while at another might be a complete set of offerings. The term "film" here is used to include film production, film studies, or both. "Television" as used here includes video, cable television, television engineering, etc. Degrees offered in a combination of film and television were listed under both the film and television categories. "Related" degrees are programs in closely related fields that include work in film and/or television.

MA and Equivalent Master's Degrees

Film

American University
Auburn University
Bob Jones University
Boston University
Bowling Green State University, Bowling Green
California Institute of the Arts
California State University, Fullerton
California State University, Humboldt
Central Missouri State University
City University of New York, College of Staten Island
Emerson College
Hollins College
Jersey City State College
Loyola Marymount University
Massachusetts Institute of Technology
New York Institute of Technology, Old Westbury
New York University
Norfolk State University
Northern Illinois University
Northern Michigan University
North Texas State University
Northwestern University
Occidental College
Ohio State University
Ohio University, Athens
Oklahoma State University
San Diego State University
San Francisco State University
Southern Illinois University at Carbondale
Stanford University
State University of New York at Buffalo
Stephen F Austin State University
University of Alabama
University of Arkansas, Fayetteville
University of California, Los Angeles
University of Chicago
University of Colorado, Boulder
University of Florida
University of Houston at Clear Lake City
University of Iowa
University of Kansas
University of Maryland at College Park
University of Missouri—Columbia
University of Missouri—Kansas City
University of New Orleans
University of North Carolina at Greensboro
University of North Dakota
University of Oregon
University of Southern California
University of the Pacific
University of Utah
University of Wisconsin—Stevens Point
University of Wisconsin—Superior
Washington State University
Wayne State University

Television

Arkansas State University
Auburn University
Ball State University
Bob Jones University
Boston University
Bowling Green State University, Bowling Green
Butler University
California Institute of the Arts
California State University, Fullerton
Central Michigan University
Central Missouri State University
City University of New York, Brooklyn College
Colorado State University
East Texas State University
Emerson College
Indiana University, Bloomington
Jersey City State College
Kansas State University
Kent State University, Kent
Louisiana State University and A and M College
Loyola Marymount University
Massachusetts Institute of Technology
Montclair State College
New York Institute of Technology, Old Westbury
Norfolk State University
Northern Illinois University
North Texas State University
Northwestern University
Ohio State University
Ohio University, Athens
Oklahoma State University
Pepperdine University
San Diego State University
San Francisco State University
Southern Illinois University at Carbondale
Stanford University
State University of New York at Buffalo
Stephen F Austin State University
Syracuse University
University of Alabama
University of Arkansas, Fayetteville
University of California, Los Angeles
University of Colorado, Boulder
University of Iowa
University of Kansas
University of Maryland at College Park
University of Minnesota, Minneapolis/St Paul
University of Missouri—Columbia
University of Missouri—Kansas City
University of New Orleans
University of North Carolina at Greensboro
University of North Dakota
University of Oregon
University of Southern California
University of South Florida
University of Southwestern Louisiana
University of Utah
University of West Florida
University of Wisconsin—Stevens Point
University of Wisconsin—Superior
Wayne State University
William Paterson College of New Jersey

Related

Anthropology Film Center
Brigham Young University
California State University, Chico
California State University, Fresno
Central State University
City University of New York, Queens College
Drake University
East Tennessee State University
Fairfield University
Governors State University
Johns Hopkins University
New School for Social Research
North Carolina Central University
Northern Illinois University
Oklahoma State University
Pennsylvania State University—University Park Campus
Purdue University, West Lafayette
San Francisco State University
State University of New York at Albany
Temple University
Texas Tech University
University of California, Berkeley
University of Cincinnati
University of Colorado, Boulder
University of Georgia
University of Illinois, Chicago Circle
University of Illinois, Urbana—Champaign
University of Mississippi
University of Nevada, Las Vegas
University of North Carolina at Chapel Hill
University of Oregon
University of Pennsylvania
University of South Alabama
University of Tennessee, Knoxville
University of Texas at Austin
University of Toledo
University of Wisconsin—La Crosse
University of Wisconsin—Madison
Virginia State University
Washington State University

Wichita State University
Worcester State College

Terminal Master's Degrees (MFAs)

Film
Art Center College of Design
California College of Arts and Crafts
Columbia University
Jersey City State College
New York University
Northwestern University
Ohio University, Athens
San Francisco Art Institute
School of the Art Institute of Chicago
Southern Illinois University at Carbondale
Syracuse University
Temple University
University of California, Los Angeles
University of Illinois, Urbana—Champaign
University of New Orleans
University of Oklahoma
University of Oregon
University of Southern California
University of Utah

Television
California College of Arts and Crafts
Jersey City State College
New York University
Northwestern University
Southern Methodist University
Temple University
University of California, Los Angeles
University of New Orleans
University of Oklahoma

Related
University of Wisconsin—Madison

Doctorates

Film
Bowling Green State University, Bowling Green
Brigham Young University
Columbia University
New York University
Northwestern University
University of California, Los Angeles
University of Chicago
University of Colorado, Boulder
University of Florida
University of Iowa
University of Missouri—Columbia
University of Oregon
University of Southern California
University of Utah
Wayne State University

Television
Bowling Green State University, Bowling Green
Louisiana State University
Northwestern University
Ohio State University
University of California, Los Angeles
University of Iowa
University of Minnesota, Minneapolis/St Paul
University of Missouri—Columbia
University of Oregon
University of Utah
Wayne State University

Related
Indiana University, Bloomington
Johns Hopkins University
North Texas State University
Ohio State University
Ohio University, Athens
Oklahoma State University
Purdue University, West Lafayette
Temple University
University of Cincinnati
University of Illinois, Urbana—Champaign
University of Maryland at College Park
University of Pennsylvania
University of Rochester
University of Tennessee, Knoxville
University of Texas at Austin
University of Wisconsin—Madison

The following is a listing of the degrees offered by the schools included in the main entry section of this volume including all degrees offered with an emphasis in film or television. Please note that an "emphasis" at one school might include only a limited number of courses while at another might be a complete set of offerings. The term "film" here is used to include film production, film studies, or both. "Television" as used here includes video, cable television, television engineering, etc. Degrees offered in a combination of film and television were listed under both the film and television categories. "Related" degrees are programs in closely related fields that include work in film and/or television.

ALABAMA

Associate's Degrees, Television
- Troy State University

Bachelor's Degrees, Film
- Auburn University
- University of Alabama

Bachelor's Degrees, Television
- Auburn University
- Troy State University
- University of Alabama
- University of North Alabama

Bachelor's Degrees, Related
- Spring Hill College
- University of Montevallo

Master's Degrees, Film
- Auburn University
- University of Alabama

Master's Degrees, Television
- Auburn University
- University of Alabama

Master's Degrees, Related
- University of South Alabama

ALASKA

Bachelor's Degrees, Television
- University of Alaska

ARIZONA

Associate's Degrees, Television
- Mesa Community College

Bachelor's Degrees, Television
- Arizona State University
- University of Arizona

ARKANSAS

Associate's Degrees, Television
- John Brown University

Bachelor's Degrees, Film
- University of Arkansas, Fayetteville
- University of Arkansas, Little Rock

Bachelor's Degrees, Television
- Arkansas State University
- John Brown University
- University of Arkansas
- University of Arkansas, Little Rock
- University of Central Arkansas

Bachelor's Degrees, Related
- Arkansas College

Master's Degrees, Film
- University of Arkansas

Master's Degrees, Television
- Arkansas State University
- University of Arkansas

CALIFORNIA

Associate's Degrees, Film
- Allan Hancock College
- City College of San Francisco
- College of Marin
- College of San Mateo
- De Anza College
- Diablo Valley College
- Foothill Community College
- Long Beach City College
- Los Angeles City College
- Los Angeles Valley College
- Orange Coast College
- West Los Angeles College

Associate's Degrees, Television
- Butte College
- City College of San Francisco
- College of Marin
- College of the Desert
- College of the Redwoods
- Columbia College—Hollywood
- De Anza College
- Foothill Community College
- Grossmont College
- Laney College
- Los Angeles City College
- Los Angeles Valley College
- Pasadena City College
- San Bernardino Valley College
- San Jose City College
- Santa Monica College
- Solano Community College
- West Los Angeles College
- Yuba College

Associate's Degrees, Related
- Consumnes River College
- Diablo Valley College
- Los Angeles Southwest College

Bachelor's Degrees, Film
- Art Center College of Design
- Brooks Institute
- California College of Arts and Crafts
- California Institute of the Arts
- California State University, Fresno
- California State University, Fullerton
- California State University, Humboldt
- California State University, Los Angeles
- California State University, Northridge
- Columbia College—Hollywood
- Loyola Marymount University
- New College of California
- Occidental College
- Pitzer College
- San Diego State University
- San Francisco Art Institute
- San Francisco State University
- San Jose State University
- Scripps College
- Stanford University
- University of California, Irvine
- University of California, Los Angeles
- University of California, Santa Barbara
- University of California, Santa Cruz
- University of Southern California
- University of the Pacific

Bachelor's Degrees, Television
- Brooks Institute
- California College of Arts and Crafts
- California Institute of the Arts
- California State University, Fresno
- California State University, Fullerton
- California State University, Long Beach
- California State University, Los Angeles
- California State University, Northridge
- Columbia College—Hollywood
- Loyola Marymount University
- New College of California
- Pepperdine University
- San Diego State University
- San Francisco State University
- San Jose State University
- Southern California College
- Stanford University
- University of California, Los Angeles
- University of Santa Clara
- University of Southern California

Bachelor's Degrees, Related
- California Lutheran College
- California State Polytechnic University, Pomona
- California State University, Chico
- California State University, Dominguez Hills
- California State University, Northridge
- Chapman College
- Loma Linda University, La Sierra Campus
- Pitzer College
- San Francisco State University

Master's Degrees, Film
- Art Center College of Design
- California College of Arts and Crafts
- California Institute of the Arts
- California State University, Fullerton
- California State University, Humboldt
- Loyola Marymount University
- Occidental College
- San Diego State University
- San Francisco Art Institute

San Francisco State University
Stanford University
University of California, Los Angeles
University of Southern California
University of the Pacific

Master's Degrees, Television
California College of Arts and Crafts
California Institute of the Arts
California State University, Fullerton
Loyola Marymount University
Pepperdine University
San Diego State University
San Francisco State University
Stanford University
University of California, Los Angeles
University of Southern California

Master's Degrees, Related
California State University, Chico
California State University, Fresno
San Francisco State University
University of California, Berkeley

Doctorates, Film
University of California, Los Angeles
University of Southern California

Doctorates, Television
University of California, Los Angeles

COLORADO

Associate's Degrees, Related
Colorado Mountain College
Community College of Denver, Auraria Campus

Bachelor's Degrees, Film
Regis College
University of Colorado, Boulder
University of Denver

Bachelor's Degrees, Television
Colorado State University
Regis College
University of Colorado, Boulder
University of Denver

Bachelor's Degrees, Related
University of Colorado, Boulder
University of Colorado, Colorado Springs

Master's Degrees, Film
University of Colorado, Boulder

Master's Degrees, Television
Colorado State University
University of Colorado, Boulder

Master's Degrees, Related
University of Colorado, Boulder

Doctorates, Film
University of Colorado, Boulder

CONNECTICUT

Associate's Degrees, Television
Middlesex Community College

Associate's Degrees, Related
Asnuntuck Community College

Bachelor's Degrees, Film
Central Connecticut State College
Sacred Heart University
University of Bridgeport
University of New Haven
Wesleyan University
Western Connecticut State College

Bachelor's Degrees, Television
Central Connecticut State College
Sacred Heart University
Southern Connecticut State College
University of Bridgeport
University of New Haven
Western Connecticut State College

Master's Degrees, Related
Fairfield University

DELAWARE

Bachelor's Degrees, Film
University of Delaware

DISTRICT OF COLUMBIA

Bachelor's Degrees, Film
American University
George Washington University
Howard University
University of the District of Columbia, Mount Vernon Square Campus

Bachelor's Degrees, Television
American University
George Washington University
Howard University
University of the District of Columbia, Mount Vernon Square Campus

Bachelor's Degrees, Related
Mount Vernon College

Bachelor's Degrees, Film
American University

FLORIDA

Associate's Degrees, Film
Manatee Junior College

Bachelor's Degrees, Film
Florida Atlantic University
University of Florida
University of Miami
University of South Florida
University of West Florida

Bachelor's Degrees, Television
Florida Atlantic University
University of Miami
University of South Florida
University of West Florida

Bachelor's Degrees, Related
Florida State University
Nova University

Master's Degrees, Film
University of Florida

Master's Degrees, Television
University of South Florida
University of West Florida

Doctorates, Film
University of Florida

GEORGIA

Bachelor's Degrees, Film
Clark College
Emory University
Valdosta State College

Bachelor's Degrees, Television
Atlanta College of Art
Clark College
Georgia Southern College
Georgia State University
Valdosta State College

Bachelor's Degrees, Related
University of Georgia

Master's Degrees, Related
University of Georgia

IDAHO

Bachelor's Degrees, Television
University of Idaho

Bachelor's Degrees, Related
University of Idaho

ILLINOIS

Associate's Degrees, Film
City Colleges of Chicago, Richard J Daley College
College of DuPage

Associate's Degrees, Television
Black Hawk College, Quad Cities Campus
City Colleges of Chicago, Richard J Daley College
College of DuPage
Highland Community College
Wabash Valley College

Associate's Degrees, Related
College of DuPage
Wabash Valley College

Bachelor's Degrees, Film
Bradley University
Columbia College
Eastern Illinois University
Northern Illinois University
Northwestern University
Rosary College
Saint Xavier College
School of the Art Institute of Chicago
Southern Illinois University at Carbondale
University of Chicago
University of Illinois, Urbana—Champaign
Wheaton College

Bachelor's Degrees, Television
Bradley University
Columbia College
Eastern Illinois University
Eureka College
Illinois State University
Northern Illinois University
Northwestern University
Saint Xavier College
Southern Illinois University at Carbondale
University of Illinois, Chicago Circle
Wheaton College

Bachelor's Degrees, Related
Blackburn College
Bradley University
Governors State University
Loyola University of Chicago
University of Illinois, Chicago Circle

Master's Degrees, Film
Northern Illinois University
Northwestern University
School of the Art Institute of Chicago
Southern Illinois University at Carbondale
University of Chicago
University of Illinois, Urbana—Champaign

Master's Degrees, Television
Northern Illinois University
Northwestern University
Southern Illinois University at Carbondale

Master's Degrees, Related
Governors State University
Northern Illinois University
University of Illinois, Chicago Circle
University of Illinois, Urbana—Champaign

Doctorates, Film
Northwestern University
University of Chicago

Doctorates, Television
Northwestern University

Doctorates, Related
University of Illinois, Urbana—Champaign

INDIANA

Bachelor's Degrees, Film
Indiana State University, Terre Haute
Indiana University—Purdue University at Fort Wayne
Saint Mary's College
University of Evansville
University of Notre Dame
Valparaiso University

Bachelor's Degrees, Television
Ball State University
Butler University
Indiana State University, Terre Haute
Indiana University, Bloomington
Indiana University—Purdue University at Fort Wayne
Indiana University—Purdue University at Indianapolis
Purdue University—Calumet
Saint Mary's College
University of Evansville
University of Notre Dame

Bachelor's Degrees, Related
Calumet College
DePauw University
Hanover College
Huntington College
Purdue University, West Lafayette

Master's Degrees, Television
Ball State University
Butler University
Indiana University, Bloomington

Master's Degrees, Related
Purdue University, West Lafayette

Doctorates, Related
Indiana University, Bloomington
Purdue University, West Lafayette

IOWA

Bachelor's Degrees, Film
Iowa State University
University of Iowa

Bachelor's Degrees, Television
Iowa State University
University of Iowa

Master's Degrees, Film
University of Iowa

Master's Degrees, Television
University of Iowa

Master's Degrees, Related
Drake University

Doctorates, Film
University of Iowa

Doctorates, Television
University of Iowa

KANSAS

Bachelor's Degrees, Film
Fort Hays State University
Kansas State University
University of Kansas
Wichita State University

Bachelor's Degrees, Television
Fort Hays State University
Kansas State University
University of Kansas
Wichita State University

Bachelor's Degrees, Related
Benedictine College
McPherson College

Master's Degrees, Film
University of Kansas

Master's Degrees, Television
Kansas State University
University of Kansas

Master's Degrees, Related
Wichita State University

KENTUCKY

Bachelor's Degrees, Film
Northern Kentucky University

Bachelor's Degrees, Television
Eastern Kentucky University
Northern Kentucky University
Western Kentucky University

Bachelor's Degrees, Related
Western Kentucky University

LOUISIANA

Bachelor's Degrees, Film
University of New Orleans

Bachelor's Degrees, Television
Grambling State University
Louisiana State University and A and M College
Northwestern State University of Louisiana
Southeastern Louisiana University
University of New Orleans
University of Southwestern Louisiana

Master's Degrees, Film
University of New Orleans

Master's Degrees, Television
Louisiana State University and A and M College
University of New Orleans
University of Southwestern Louisiana

Doctorates, Television
Louisiana State University and A and M College

MAINE

Bachelor's Degrees, Television
University of Maine at Orono

MARYLAND

Associate's Degrees, Television
Montgomery College—Rockville Campus

Associate's Degrees, Related
Allegany Community College
Anne Arundel Community College
Dundalk Community College
Hagerstown Junior College

Bachelor's Degrees, Film
Johns Hopkins University
Loyola College
University of Maryland at College Park

Bachelor's Degrees, Television
College of Notre Dame of Maryland
Johns Hopkins University
University of Maryland at College Park

Bachelor's Degrees, Related
Bowie State College
Goucher College
Hood College
Salisbury State College
Towson State University
University of Maryland, Baltimore County

Master's Degrees, Film
University of Maryland at College Park

Master's Degrees, Television
University of Maryland at College Park

Master's Degrees, Related
Johns Hopkins University

Doctorates, Related
Johns Hopkins University
University of Maryland at College Park

MASSACHUSETTS

Associate's Degrees, Related
Greenfield Community College
Mount Wachusett Community College
North Shore Community College

Bachelor's Degrees, Film
Boston University
Clark University
Emerson College
Hampshire College
Harvard University
Massachusetts Institute of Technology
Simmons College
Suffolk University
University of Massachusetts, Amherst

Bachelor's Degrees, Television
Boston University
Clark University
Emerson College
Hampshire College
Massachusetts Institute of Technology
Simmons College
Suffolk University
University of Massachusetts, Amherst

Bachelor's Degrees, Related
Boston College
North Adams State College
Worcester State College

Master's Degrees, Film
Boston University
Emerson College
Massachusetts Institute of Technology

NEW YORK

Associate's Degrees, Film
City University of New York, LaGuardia Community College

Associate's Degrees, Television
Cayuga County Community College
City University of New York, LaGuardia Community College
Elizabeth Seton College
Onondaga Community College
Tompkins-Cortland Community College

Associate's Degrees, Related
Cayuga County Community College
Genesee Community College
Nassau Community College
Ulster County Community College

Bachelor's Degrees, Film
Adelphi University
Bard College
Canisius College
City University of New York, Brooklyn College
City University of New York, City College
City University of New York, College of Staten Island
City University of New York, Hunter College
City University of New York, Queens College
College of Mount Saint Vincent
College of New Rochelle
Columbia University
Cooper Union
Cornell University
Fordham University
Hobart and William Smith Colleges
Hofstra University
Iona College
Ithaca
New School for Social Research
New York Institute of Technology, Old Westbury
New York University
Niagara University
Pratt Institute
Rochester Institute of Technology
Sarah Lawrence College
School of Visual Arts
State University of New York at Albany
State University of New York at Binghamton
State University of New York at Buffalo
State University of New York College at Fredonia
State University of New York College at New Paltz
State University of New York College at Purchase
Syracuse University
University of Rochester
Vassar College
Yeshiva College

Bachelor's Degrees, Television
Adelphi University
Canisius College
City University of New York, Brooklyn College
City University of New York, Queens College
College of Mount Saint Vincent
College of New Rochelle
Copper Union
Fordham University
Hofstra University
Iona College
Ithaca College
Le Moyne College
New School for Social Research
New York Institute of Technology, Old Westbury
New York University
Niagara University
St Bonaventure University
State University of New York at Binghamton
State University of New York at Buffalo
State University of New York College at Fredonia
State University of New York College at Geneseo
State University of New York College at Oswego
Syracuse University

Bachelor's Degrees, Related
Elmira College
Houghton College
Medaille College
New School for Social Research
St John Fisher College
State University of New York at Albany
State University of New York College at New Paltz

Master's Degrees, Film
City University of New York, College of Staten Island
Columbia University
New York Institute of Technology, Old Westbury
New York University
State University of New York at Buffalo
Syracuse University

Master's Degrees, Television
City University of New York, Brooklyn College
New York Institute of Technology, Old Westbury
New York University
State University of New York at Buffalo
Syracuse University

Master's Degrees, Related
City University of New York, Queens College
New School for Social Research
State University of New York at Albany

Doctorates, Film
Columbia University
New York University

Doctorates, Related
University of Rochester

NORTH CAROLINA

Associate's Degrees, Related
Durham Technical Institute

Bachelor's Degrees, Film
North Carolina State University at Raleigh
University of North Carolina at Chapel Hill
University of North Carolina at Greensboro
Wake Forest University

Bachelor's Degrees, Television
Appalachian State University
North Carolina Agricultural and Technical State University
North Carolina State University at Raleigh
University of North Carolina at Chapel Hill
University of North Carolina at Greensboro
Wake Forest University
Western Carolina University

Bachelor's Degrees, Related
Bennett College

Master's Degrees, Film
University of North Carolina at Greensboro

Master's Degrees, Television
University of North Carolina at Greensboro

Master's Degrees, Related
North Carolina Central University
University of North Carolina at Chapel Hill

NORTH DAKOTA

Bachelor's Degrees, Film
University of North Dakota

Bachelor's Degrees, Television
University of North Dakota

Master's Degrees, Film
University of North Dakota

Master's Degrees, Television
University of North Dakota

OHIO

Associate's Degrees, Television
Ohio University, Zanesville

Bachelor's Degrees, Film
Antioch College
Bowling Green State University, Bowling Green
Case Western Reserve University
Cleveland Institute of Art
Denison University
Notre Dame College
Ohio State University
University of Akron
University of Toledo
Wright State University

Bachelor's Degrees, Television
Antioch College
Ashland College
Bowling Green State University, Bowling Green
Case Western Reserve University
Denison University
John Carroll University
Kent State University, Kent
Marietta College
Ohio State University
Ohio University, Athens
University of Akron
University of Toledo

Bachelor's Degrees, Related
College of Mount St Joseph on the Ohio
University of Cincinnati

Master's Degrees, Film
Bowling Green State University, Bowling Green
Ohio State University
Ohio University, Athens

Master's Degrees, Television
Bowling Green State University, Bowling Green
Kent State University, Kent
Ohio State University
Ohio University, Athens

Master's Degrees, Related
University of Cincinnati
University of Toledo

Doctorates, Film
- Bowling Green State University, Bowling Green

Doctorates, Television
- Bowling Green State University, Bowling Green
- Ohio State University

Doctorates, Related
- Ohio State University
- Ohio University, Athens
- University of Cincinnati

OKLAHOMA

Bachelor's Degrees, Film
- Oklahoma State University
- University of Oklahoma

Bachelor's Degrees, Television
- Bethany Nazarene College
- Oklahoma State University
- Oral Roberts University
- University of Oklahoma
- University of Tulsa

Bachelor's Degrees, Related
- Bethany Nazarene College
- Oklahoma State University
- University of Tulsa

Master's Degrees, Film
- Oklahoma State University
- University of Oklahoma

Master's Degrees, Television
- Oklahoma State University
- University of Oklahoma

Master's Degrees, Related
- Central State University
- Oklahoma State University

Doctorates, Related
- Oklahoma State University

OREGON

Associate's Degrees, Film
- Clatsop Community College

Associate's Degrees, Television
- Clackamas Community College
- Clatsop Community College
- Mt Hood Community College

Bachelor's Degrees, Film
- Portland State University
- University of Oregon

Bachelor's Degrees, Television
- Pacific University
- Southern Oregon State University
- University of Oregon

Master's Degrees, Film
- University of Oregon

Master's Degrees, Television
- University of Oregon

Master's Degrees, Related
- University of Oregon

Doctorates, Film
- University of Oregon

Doctorates, Television
- University of Oregon

PENNSYLVANIA

Associate's Degrees, Film
- Bucks County Community College

Associate's Degrees, Television
- Bucks County Community College
- Northampton County Area Community College
- Pennsylvania State University—Wilkes-Barre

Bachelor's Degrees, Film
- Cabrini College
- Edinboro State College
- Holy Family College
- La Salle College
- Pennsylvania State University—University Park Campus
- Philadelphia College of Art
- Pittsburgh Film-Makers, Inc
- Point Park College
- Slippery Rock State College
- Temple University

Bachelor's Degrees, Television
- Cabrini College
- California State College
- Duquesne University
- Holy Family College
- Kutztown State College
- La Salle College
- Mercyhurst College
- Slippery Rock State College
- Temple University

Bachelor's Degrees, Related
- Cedar Crest College
- Gannon University
- Robert Morris College
- Temple University
- University of Pennsylvania
- Villanova University
- Waynesburg College

Master's Degrees, Film
- Temple University

Master's Degrees, Television
- Temple University

Master's Degrees, Related
- Pennsylvania State University—University Park Campus
- Temple University
- University of Pennsylvania

Doctorates, Related
- Temple University
- University of Pennsylvania

RHODE ISLAND

Bachelor's Degrees, Film
- Rhode Island College
- Roger Williams College

SOUTH CAROLINA

Bachelor's Degrees, Film
- Bob Jones University

Bachelor's Degrees, Television
- Benedict College
- Bob Jones University

Master's Degrees, Film
- Bob Jones University

Master's Degrees, Television
- Bob Jones University

SOUTH DAKOTA

Associate's Degrees, Television
- Black Hills State College

Bachelor's Degrees, Film
- South Dakota State University
- University of South Dakota

Bachelor's Degrees, Television
- South Dakota State University
- University of South Dakota

Bachelor's Degrees, Related
- Dakota-Wesleyan University

TENNESSEE

Associate's Degrees, Related
- Volunteer State Community College

Bachelor's Degrees, Film
- Middle Tennessee State University

Bachelor's Degrees, Television
- Middle Tennessee State University

Bachelor's Degrees, Related
- Southwestern at Memphis
- University of Tennessee, Knoxville

Master's Degrees, Related
- East Tennessee State University
- University of Tennessee, Knoxville

Doctorates, Related
- University of Tennessee, Knoxville

TEXAS

Associate's Degrees, Film
- San Antonio Community College
- Tarrant County Junior College

Associate's Degrees, Television
- Amarillo College
- San Antonio Community College
- Tarrant County Junior College

Bachelor's Degrees, Film
- Baylor University
- East Texas State University
- Lamar University
- North Texas State University
- Southern Methodist University
- Stephen F Austin State University
- University of Houston
- University of Houston at Clear Lake City
- University of Texas at Arlington
- University of Texas at Austin

Bachelor's Degrees, Television
- Abilene Christian University
- Baylor University
- Lamar University
- North Texas State University
- Southern Methodist University
- Southwest Texas State University
- Stephen F Austin State University
- Sul Ross State University
- Texas A&I University of Kingsville
- Texas Tech University
- University of Houston
- University of Texas at Austin

Bachelor's Degrees, Related
- West Texas State University

Master's Degrees, Film
- North Texas State University
- Stephen F Austin State University
- University of Houston at Clear Lake City

Master's Degrees, Television
- East Texas State University
- North Texas State University
- Southern Methodist University
- Stephen F Austin State University

Master's Degrees, Related
- Texas Tech University
- University of Texas at Austin

Doctorates, Related
- North Texas State University
- University of Texas, Austin

UTAH

Bachelor's Degrees, Film
- Brigham Young University
- University of Utah
- Westminster College

Bachelor's Degrees, Television
Brigham Young University
Southern Utah State College
University of Utah
Weber State College

Master's Degrees, Film
University of Utah

Master's Degrees, Television
University of Utah

Master's Degrees, Related
Brigham Young University

Doctorates, Film
Brigham Young University
University of Utah

VERMONT

Bachelor's Degrees, Film
Marlboro College

Bachelor's Degrees, Related
Castleton State College

VIRGINIA

Associate's Degrees, Television
Northern Virginia Community College
Virginia Western Community College

Bachelor's Degrees, Film
Hollins College
Liberty Baptist College
Longwood College
Norfolk State University

Bachelor's Degrees, Television
Liberty Baptist College
Norfolk State University

Master's Degrees, Film
Hollins College
Norfolk State University

Master's Degrees, Television
Norfolk State University

Master's Degrees, Related
Virginia State University

WASHINGTON

Associate's Degrees, Related
Bellevue Community College
Spokane Falls Community College

Bachelor's Degrees, Film
Washington State University

Bachelor's Degrees, Television
Eastern Washington University
Washington State University

Bachelor's Degrees, Related
Central Washington University
Evergreen State College

Master's Degrees, Film
Washington State University

Master's Degrees, Related
Washington State University

WEST VIRGINIA

Associate's Degrees, Television
Salem College

Bachelor's Degrees, Film
University of Charleston
West Virginia State College

Bachelor's Degrees, Television
Alderson-Broaddus College
Salem College
University of Charleston
West Virginia State College

WISCONSIN

Associate's Degrees, Film
Milwaukee Area Technical College

Associate's Degrees, Television
Milwaukee Area Technical College

Bachelor's Degrees, Film
University of Wisconsin—Milwaukee
University of Wisconsin—Oshkosh
University of Wisconsin—Stevens Point
Uniersity of Wisconsin—Stout
University of Wisconsin—Superior

Bachelor's Degrees, Television
Beloit College
Marquette University
University of Wisconsin—Eau Claire
University of Wisconsin—Green Bay
University of Wisconsin—Oshkosh
University of Wisconsin—Platteville
University of Wisconsin—Stevens Point
University of Wisconsin—Stout
University of Wisconsin—Superior

Bachelor's Degrees, Related
University of Wisconsin—Madison
University of Wisconsin—Parkside

Master's Degrees, Film
University of Wisconsin—Stevens Point
University of Wisconsin—Superior

Master's Degrees, Television
University of Wisconsin—Stevens Point
University of Wisconsin—Superior

Master's Degrees, Related
University of Wisconsin—La Crosse
University of Wisconsin—Madison

Doctorates, Related
University of Wisconsin—Madison

The American Film Institute

GUIDE TO COLLEGE COURSES IN FILM AND TELEVISION

Seventh Edition

Contents

"A unique reference work, it is an indispensable tool for all concerned with film/TV studies in higher education."—George L George, *Film News*

Peterson's Guides, Princeton, NJ
The American Film Institute, Washington, DC

ISBN: 0-87866-158-1
$11.50

The American Film Institute, established in 1967 by the National Endowment for the Arts to advance the art of film and television in America, is an independent, nonprofit organization serving the public interest. The Institute's headquarters are located in the John F Kennedy Center for the Performing Arts, Washington, DC 20566 (telephone: 202-828-4000).